I0168959

St. Teresa of Avila Three Book Treasury

Interior Castle,
The Way of Perfection,

and

The Book of Her Life
(Autobiography)

By

Saint Teresa of Avila

The *Interior Castle* begins next page.
The Way of Perfection begins on page 110.
The Book of Her Life begins on page 206.

INTERIOR CASTLE

OR
THE MANSIONS

By *Saint Teresa of Avila*

Translated from the Autograph of St. Teresa of Jesus
by the Benedictines of Stanbrook

Third Edition Revised, with Notes and an Introduction,
by the Very Rev. Fr. Benedict Zimmerman, O.C.D.
1921

DEDICATED TO
The Martyred Daughters of St. Teresa,
The Blessed Martyrs of Compiegne, France,
by the Descendants of Their Fellow Prisoners.

TABLE OF CONTENTS

INTRODUCTION

SAINT TERESA began to write the *Interior Castle* on June 2, 1577, Trinity Sunday, and completed it on the eve of St. Andrew, November 29, of the same year. But there was a long interruption of five months,[1] so that the actual time spent in the composition of this work was reduced to about four weeks—a fortnight for the first, and another fortnight for the second half of the book. The rapidity with which it was written is easily explained by the fact that the Saint had conceived its plan some time previously. On January 17, 1577, she had written to her brother, Don Lorenzo de Cepeda, at Avila: 'I have asked the bishop—Don Alvaro Mendoza—for my book (the *Life*) because I shall perhaps complete it by adding those new favours our Lord has lately granted me. With these one may even compose a new work of considerable size, provided God grants me the grace of explaining myself; otherwise the loss will be of small account.'[2] She never asked for permission to write anything, but waited until she received a command from her superiors, which, in this case, came from Father Jerome Gracian, superior of the Discalced J. Carmelites of the Provinces of Andalusia and Castille, and from Don Alonso Velasquez, canon of Toledo, afterwards bishop of Osma.[3] The Saint was not in good health at the time; she repeatedly complains of noises in the head and other infirmities, but, worst of all, she was weighed down by troubles and anxieties resulting from the action of the superiors of the Order and of the Papal Nuncio against the nuns and friars of the Reform. Matters became even more serious when, in October, the nuns of the Incarnation of Avila proceeded to the election of a new prioress. Notwithstanding the prohibition of the provincial, fifty-five electors recorded their votes in favour of the Saint and were immediately declared excommunicated. The whole work of the Reform seemed on the brink of ruin, the Saint, as well as all her friends, was in disgrace, subject to obloquy and ill-treatment.

No trace of these trials is to be found in the *Interior Castle*. Saint Teresa possessed the power of concentration of thought in a marvellous degree. The early mornings and late evenings were devoted to the composition of the book, while the rest of the day was taken up by the affairs of the Order. Mother Mary of the Nativity, a member of the community of Toledo, where the book was begun, declared afterwards,[4] that she often saw her writing, generally after Holy Communion, her face resplendent, with such rapidity and so absorbed in her occupation that she seemed undisturbed by, and in fact quite unconscious of, any noise that was made. Mother Mariana of the Angels[5] reports having heard from the same witness, that entering her cell one day to deliver a message, the holy Mother was just beginning a new sheet of her book. While taking off her spectacles to listen to the message she was seized by a trance in which she remained for several hours. The nun, terrified at this, did not stir, but kept her eyes steadily on the Saint. When she came to, it was seen that the paper, previously blank, was covered with writing. Noticing that her visitor had discovered it, Saint Teresa put the paper quietly in the box. Another nun, Mary of St.

---

[1] Castle, Mansions v. ch. iv. I.

[2] Letters of St. Teresa, Vol. ii.

[3] The French Carmelite nuns in their new translation, Œuvres complètes de Sainte Thérèse, t. vi, Introduction, p. 5, quoting the Año Teresiano, t. vii ad 7 July, and Father Gracian's Dilucidario, as well as his additions to Ribera, show the exact share of Fr. Gracian and Dr. Velasquez in the preliminaries of this work.

[4] Fuente, Obras de Santa Teresa de Jesus. Edit. 1881, Vol. vi, p. 278.

[5] Ibid. p. 178. A somewhat similar incident is reported by Mother Anne of the Incarnation (Ibid. p. 213), but it appears to be wrongly brought into connection with the composition of the Castle. The nun in question had belonged to the convent of St. Joseph at Segovia at an earlier period, but there is no evidence that St. Teresa visited this place in the course of the six months during which she composed this work. The Bollandists, indeed, maintain that it was commenced at Toledo, continued at Segovia and completed at Avila (n. 1541), but their sole authority for including Segovia is the passage in question, which, however, must refer to some other work of the Saint. The sister, passing St. Teresa's door, saw her writing, her face being lit up as by a bright light. She wrote very fast without making any corrections. After an hour, it being about midnight, she ceased and the light disappeared. The Saint then knelt down and remained in prayer for three hours, after which she went to sleep.

Francis, left the following declaration: 'I know that our holy Mother wrote four books, the *Life*, the *Way of Perfection*, the *Foundations*, and the *Mansions*, which I have seen her writing. Once, while she was composing the last-named work, I entered to deliver a message, and found her so absorbed that she did not notice me; her face seemed quite illuminated and most beautiful. After having listened to me she said: "Sit down, my child, and let me write what our Lord has told me ere I forget it," and she went on writing with great rapidity and without stopping.'[6]

Mary of St. Joseph says she heard from Mary of the Nativity that Father Jerome Gracian commanded the Saint to write the *Mansions*; she, however, begged to be excused, because so many books having been written by holy and learned men, there remained nothing for a woman to write. At length she yielded under obedience. This nun (Mary of the Nativity) was frequently in the Saint's cell while she was writing and she noticed her resplendent face and the almost preternatural velocity with which her hand travelled over the paper.[7]

Writing to Mother Mary of St. Joseph, Prioress of Seville, November 8, 1581, St. Teresa gives her a message for Father Rodrigo Alvarez, S. J.: 'Our Father (Jerome Gracian, then provincial) tells me that he has handed you a book written by me, which perhaps you do not feel inclined to read yourself. Kindly read to Father Rodrigo Alvarez, at his next visit, the last Mansion, but under the seal of confession, as he asks this in his superior wisdom. This is only for you two. Tell him that the person he knows has arrived at this Mansion and enjoys the peace there described; that she is entirely at rest, and that some grave theologians have assured her that she is on a safe road. In case you could not read these pages to him do not send him the book, for it might lead to unpleasantness. Until I have his answer on this matter I will not write to him. Give him my compliments.'

At the end of the original manuscript, before the epilogue (marked with Ihs.) there is a notice in Father Alvarez' hand-writing to this effect: 'The Mother Prioress of the convent of Seville has read to me this seventh Mansion, whither a soul may arrive in the present life. Let all the saints praise the infinite goodness of God, Who communicates Himself to His creatures so that they truly seek His glory and the salvation of their neighbour. What I feel and judge of this matter is, that everything that has been read to me is conformable to Catholic truth and in accordance with Holy Scripture and the teaching of the Saints. Whosoever has read the doctrine of the Saints, such as the books of St. Gertrude, St. Catharine of Siena, or St. Bridget of Sweden, and other saints and spiritual writers, will clearly understand that the spirit of Mother Tireza (*sic*) of Jesus is true, since it leads to the same effects as are to be found in the saints; and because this is in truth my judgment and opinion, I have hereunto set my name, this, the 22nd day of February, 1582. P. Rodrigo Alvarez.'[8]

The work was copied, probably under the supervision of the Saint, who introduced many changes; when completed the original was handed to Father Jerome Gracian and to the Dominican, Fray Diego de Yanguas, for approval. Both, particularly the former, made numerous corrections, which Fuente, not without reason, calls impertinent, scratching out whole sentences and adding others. The book thus revised must have enjoyed a certain celebrity, though not to the same extent as the *Life*, to which St. Teresa herself preferred it. Scarcely a week after its completion she wrote to Father Salazar, S.J.: 'If Señor Carillo [Salazar himself] came, the person in question [the Saint] thinks he would find another jewel which in her opinion is superior to the former [the *Life*]. This one reflects nothing foreign to itself, but is resplendent in its own beauty. It is enriched with more delicate enamels than the former, the workmanship, too, is more perfect. For, as the person in question says, the jeweler was less experienced when he fashioned the previous one. Moreover, the gold of the new one is of better quality than that of the former, though the precious stones are not so well set. It has been done, as might be expected, according to the designs of the Jeweler Himself.'[9] Later on she wrote to Father Jerome Gracian: The book I have written since seems to me superior [to the *Life*]; at least I had more experience when I wrote it.'[10]

[6] Fuente, p. 223.
[7] Ibid. p. 255.
[8] Autograph, fol. cx.
[9] December 7, 1577. Letters Vol. II.
[10] Jan. 14, 1580. Letters Vol. IV.

One day, speaking with Mother Mary of Jesus on spiritual matters, she said that our Lord had communicated so much to her since she had reached what she described in the seventh Mansion,—the spiritual Marriage,—that she did not consider it possible to advance further in this life, in the way of prayer, nor even to wish to do so.[11]

The book was eagerly read by those who were able to obtain copies. At the archiepiscopal Seminary at Salamanca it was read publicly after dinner; the students, contrary to custom, sacrificing the recreation rather than miss so edifying an instruction. The result was that several entered the religious life, one becoming a Franciscan, two others, who had already taken their degrees, joining the Discalced Carmelites.[12] We also know of a lady who became a Poor Clare through reading the *Interior Castle*.[13] The process of Beatification contains the following evidence of Don Francisco de Mora, architect to Philip III: 'The same prioress (of a convent of Dominican nuns) being concerned about my salvation gave me a book in manuscript, called *The Mansions*, by Mother Teresa, hoping I should derive some benefit from it. I fear this was not the case, but it made me acquainted with Teresa of Jesus, the foundress of the Discalced Carmelite nuns, of whom I had not yet heard, but for whom I now felt devotion.'[14]

In August 1586 it was decided to print Saint Teresa's works, the Augustinian Fray Luis de Leon being selected as editor, as he was unconcerned in the quarrels raging round the Reform. Accordingly, the manuscript of the *Interior Castle* was handed to him. On the first leaf he wrote the following note:

'Many passages of this book written by the holy Mother have been scored through, other words being substituted or notes being added in the margin. Most of these corrections are badly done, the original text being much better. It will be noticed that the holy Mother's sentences are superior and agree with the context, which is not the case with the corrections. These improvements and glosses may therefore be dispensed with. Having myself read and considered everything with great care, it appears to me that the reader, too, should have before him the words of the author who knew best what to say; for this reason I have left out the additions, and have restored what has been changed, excepting only a few corrections made by the writer herself. I beg of the reader that he would in charity reverence the words and even the letters traced by so holy a hand, and strive to understand what has been written. He will then see that there was no need for corrections; should he fail to understand her, let him believe that the writer knew what she said, and that her words cannot be tampered with if they are not to lose their meaning; otherwise what was to the point will seem out of place. This is how books become corrupted, useless, and are finally lost.'[15]

When Luis de Leon undertook the editing of St. Teresa's writings he received a long letter from Don Diego de Yepes, afterwards Bishop of Tarazona, a former friend and confessor of the Saint, in which he records his personal recollections. I shall only insert here what he says about the *Interior Castle*:

'This holy Mother desired to see the beauty of a soul in the state of grace, a thing greatly to be coveted both for the sake of seeing and of possessing it. While this desire lasted, she was commanded to write a treatise on prayer, of which she had much personal experience. On the eve of the Blessed Trinity, while considering what subject to choose for this treatise, God, Who disposes everything in due season, fulfilled her wish and furnished a suitable subject. He showed her a most beautiful globe of crystal, in the shape of a castle, with seven rooms, the seventh, situated in the centre, being occupied by the King of glory, resplendent with the most exquisite brilliancy, which shone through and adorned the remaining rooms. The nearer these lay to the centre, the more did they partake of that wondrous light. It did not, however, penetrate beyond the crystal, for everything round about was a mass of darkness and impurity, full of toads and vipers and other venomous animals.

---

[11] Fuente, Obras. l.c. p. 275.

[12] l.c. p. 217.

[13] Ibid. p. 227.

[14] Fuente, Obras. p. 190.

[15] Autograph. fol. 1.

She was still admiring this beauty which, by the grace of God dwells in the soul, when, lo! the light suddenly disappeared, and the crystal, wherein the King of glory was still residing, became opaque and as dark as coal, emitting an intolerable odour; the venomous animals, formerly held in check outside, obtained admittance into the castle. The holy Mother wished that every one should behold this vision, for she thought that no one having seen the beauty and splendour of grace, which is forfeited by sin and replaced by such repulsive misery, would ever dare to offend God.

'She told me this vision on the same day, for in this as well as in other things she was so communicative that on the following morning she said to me: "How I forgot myself yesterday! I cannot think how it could have happened. Those high aspirations of mine, and the affection I have for you must have caused me to go beyond all reasonable limits. God grant I may have derived some profit therefrom." I promised her to say nothing about it during her lifetime, but since her death I should like to make it known to all men. From this vision she learnt four important matters.

'First, she came to understand this axiom, which in this form she had never heard of in her life,[16] that God is present in all things by His essence, presence, and power. As she was deeply humble and submissive and obedient to the doctrine of the Church and the teaching of the learned ministers of God, she never rested until her revelations had been approved of by her superiors and by theologians, and were shown to be conformable to Holy Scripture. She went so far as to say that if all the angels of heaven said one thing, and her superiors another, though she could not doubt that the former were true angels, yet she would hold what was told her by her superiors, because faith comes through these and there remains no room for deceit, whereas revelations coming from angels might be illusionary.

'With such regard for obedience, she asked me one day at Toledo—probably at the time when she saw the vision of the Castle—whether it was true that God was in all things by His power, presence, and essence, to which I replied in the affirmative, explaining it as best I could on the authority of St. Paul, particularly where he says "the sufferings of this time are not worthy to be compared with the glory to come that shall be revealed in us,"[17] Laying stress on these words, "shall be revealed in us," she was so overjoyed that I was quite astonished. Though in a way it seemed to me a kind of curiosity, I could not help thinking there was some mystery about it, for she said: "This is the very thing."

'Secondly, she was greatly surprised at the malice of sin, since, notwithstanding the presence of God in these various ways, it prevents the soul from partaking of that powerful light.

'Thirdly, she derived such humility and self-knowledge from this vision, that from that moment she never thought of herself in all the good she was doing; for she learnt that all the beauty of the soul emanates from that resplendent light, and that the powers of the soul and of the body are enlivened and strengthened by the Power established in the centre, whence comes all our good, so that we have but a small share in our good works. All the good she did, she from this moment referred to God as its principal author.

'Fourthly, she derived from it the subject of the book she was ordered to write on prayer, comparing the seven rooms of the Castle with as many degrees of prayer, whereby we enter within ourselves and draw nearer to God. So that, penetrating to the depths of our soul and gaining perfect self-knowledge, we reach the seventh room where God Himself dwells, with Whom we become united by as perfect a union as is possible in the present life, being made partakers of His light and love.

'I will say no more of this vision and the *Mansions*, because your Reverence must by now have seen this admirable book, and must know with what accuracy, with what majestic doctrine, with what lucid examples she describes the progress of the soul from the gate to the very centre. It is clearly seen in this treatise how she communicated with our Lord, and how His Majesty

---

[16] See Life, ch. xviii. 20. Mansions v. ch. i. 9. The ignorance of the priest who had told her that God was only present by His grace, made a lasting impression on St. Teresa. She was first undeceived by a Dominican.

[17] Rom. viii. 18.

vouchsafed to place her in the centre and to unite her with Himself, as she puts it, by the bonds of marriage and an inseparable union.'[18]

After the publication of the *Interior Castle*, in 1588 at Salamanca, it became not only more widely known, but also more and more appreciated. Francis Suarez, the great theologian of the Society of Jesus, says in his deposition in the process of Beatification that he had read some of St. Teresa's works, particularly the *Mansions*, which contain an absolutely safe doctrine and give proof of a wonderful spirit of prayer and contemplation.[19]

Thomas Hurtado, professor of theology at Seville, speaks as follows:

As often as I read the books of the holy Mother, I admire the wonderful manner in which God instructed her in mystical theology for the sake of souls giving themselves truly to familiar intercourse with His divine Majesty. But where I most regret my inability of expressing in fitting terms my sentiments towards this excellent teacher is when I look at, and refresh myself in that Castle with its seven rooms; for there is seen the effect of infused knowledge such as St. Denis received from St. Hierotheus[20] and both from St. Paul, and which has been committed to writing in the famous book of *Mystical Theology*. Hence comes, as from a fountain-head, notwithstanding the obscurity (to our manner of thinking) of its language, the doctrine of the great masters of the spiritual life such as Hugh of St. Victor, St. Bernard, Ruysbroek, Tauler, Gerson, and many others whom I pass by.

'Nevertheless, I will boldly say that no one has given us water more limpid from that Apostolical and Areopagitical well than the holy Mother Teresa, who, in her books, but chiefly in the *Mansions*, has cleared up in simple language the most difficult questions of this divine theology, and has brought forth light from darkness, as it is written: (He) commanded light to shine out of darkness.'[21] Who has ever been able to show as clearly as our Saint how God takes possession of the soul, how He unites Himself with its substance, whence comes to the intellect the light of faith, to the will the ardour of love, and to the senses the jubilation over His works? No one has ever turned theory into practice in a more convincing or more catholic manner. The most profound secrets of this supernatural wisdom are here treated with such ease, so amiably, so delightfully, they are illustrated by such nice and homely examples, that instead of awe-inspiring obscurity, we find lovely flowers and the sweetness of love, through which, as through an avenue, the soul passes onwards. When God made known His exalted doctrine to St. Dionysius and other mystical writers, He made use of their own language and pen. But St. Teresa in the *Mansions* is like the light of dawn whose rays are not intercepted by the clouds of this world; like a soft rain from above, whereby the soul grows and profits by its communications with God. Until the teaching of this great door became known it seemed as though God were inaccessible, being surrounded by darkness, through which Moses and some other persons had to pass when approaching Him;[22] but they neither explained the manner nor showed the way whereby they came to the enjoyment of the sweetness of the Spouse. Now, however, this way is clear and patent to all, having been pointed out in the *Mansions*, in language so straight and so methodical, and no longer such as could not be understood, or required further explanation. In my opinion this holy writer derived not only the substance of her teaching from infused knowledge, but even the words with which she explains it.'[23]

Likewise Don Alvaro de Villegas, canon of Toledo, expressed his opinion that the *Way of Perfection* and the *Interior Castle* contain 'heavenly doctrine.' The weight of the subject-matter, the propriety of the comparisons, the force of the expressions, the consistency of the teaching, the sweetness of her well-chosen, vivid words, the clearness of the arguments, all this proves that she was guided by her heavenly Spouse, in Whom are hidden the treasures of the wisdom of God; and that the Holy Ghost, Who more than once was seen resting on her head like a dove, was

[18] Fuente; pp. 131-133.

[19] l.c. 184.

[20] Allusion to the famous Mystical Theology attributed to Dionysius the Areopagite, and long considered the chief authority on this subject.

[21] 2 Cor. iv. 6.

[22] The example of Moses is scarcely to the point (cf. Exod. xxxiii. 11, and Num. xii. 7, 8).

[23] Fuente, pp. 330-332.

dilating these works. Villegas does not believe that any one could read them, as such books ought to be read, without becoming himself a master of the spiritual life. For they are like heavenly dew, rendering the soul fruitful in the matter of prayer.[24]

It would be a mistake to consider the *Interior Castle* a complete treatise of mystical theology. Like St. Teresa's other works, it is intensely personal: she describes the road by which she has been led, being well aware that others may be led in a different way. In the heavenly Father's house there are many mansions, not only seven, and many paths lead to them. What gives the work such high value is, that it is the result of a most searching inquiry into the various phases whereby a soul is gradually transformed into the likeness of God Himself. Here St. Teresa is always at her best. She takes nothing for granted, even her own personal experiences are admitted only after having been fully investigated and found to be consistent one with the other, and conformable to the teaching of the Church and the words of Holy Scripture.

Mystical theology is generally divided into three parts, respectively called the purgative, the illuminative, and the unitive life. In the first, man is cleansed from sin and habitual imperfection by the use of the sacraments and by voluntary mortification of the passions. The mind is purified by sedulous meditation on the last end and on the Life and Passion of Christ, which must ever be the great model of the Christian. This first portion of the way to heaven can be covered by the help of the ordinary means of grace, without any direct and extraordinary intervention of divine power. The second part differs in many ways from the first. It comprises the passive purification of the soul and the passive enlightenment of the mind. By sending it keen interior and exterior trials and sufferings, God completes the cleansing of the soul in a manner far surpassing any voluntary effort of man. By raising it to the stage of contemplation He gives it fresh light on the mysteries of our Redemption. The mind is then no longer compelled to strain the memory, the reason, and the will, in order to dwell upon the great truths of religion and to derive some personal benefit therefrom, for these truths are now more or less permanently before it and fill it with holy thoughts, sometimes giving it consolation in trouble, at other times striking a warning note against imperfection. Again, the subtraction of sensible consolation, and the interior aridity arising therefrom, leave a terrible blank in the soul, showing it that, without God's help, it is mere nothingness. This apparent estrangement from God is the keenest trial that can befall a soul, but also the most powerful means of cleansing it from the least, the most subtle imperfections.

Emerging from this state of probation, the soul enters upon the third stage, in which, though perhaps in the midst of severe suffering and sharp persecution, it knows itself to be a chosen child of God, to Whom it is united by perfect conformity of the will. Such phenomena as revelations, visions, locutions, and even more wonderful manifestations, like the wound of love, spiritual betrothal and nuptials, are incidental rather than essential to the second and third stages. Some great contemplatives have never experienced anything of the kind, while, on the other hand, some of these occurrences may sometimes have been merely the work of an exuberant imagination, or even the result of diabolical illusion. They should therefore never be wished for, or cherished, but rather shunned and ignored, in as far as that is possible. If they are real and come from God, they will do their work without the co-operation of the soul. The danger of self-deception is so great that a person labouring under such phenomena should offer every resistance, and the spiritual director should exercise the utmost vigilance. St. Teresa is very eloquent on this point, and undeceived many would-be contemplatives, while her disciple, St. John of the Cross, is even more thorough-going in the deprecation of spiritual favours. Among the numerous marks whereby the trained theologian may discriminate between real and imaginary phenomena, there is one about which Saint Teresa speaks with wonderful clearness. If they proceed from hysteria the imagination alone is active and the higher powers of the soul are torpid; if, however, they come from God, the intellect and the will are so intensely active, that the lower powers and even the body lose all strength for the time being.

It will be noticed that the first two Mansions belong to the purgative life, the third and fourth to the illuminative, and the remaining three to the unitive life. Compared with similar works, the treatment of the first stage must be called meagre. True, in her *Life* and in the *Way of Perfection* St. Teresa has dealt with this subject somewhat more fully. Indeed, the last-named work was

---

[24] l.c. p. 334. These testimonies could be easily multiplied.

designed as a treatise on Christian Ascetics, dealing with the purgation of the soul by mortification and the enlightenment of the mind by meditation. There, too, appears the first idea of the *Mansions*,[25] and Fuente remarks that the passage in question may be taken for the parting of the ways between the two works. However, this is not the only, nor, indeed, the chief reason why St. Teresa is so reticent about the preliminary stage of the contemplative life. The fact is that she herself did not pass through these experiences. By God's grace she was preserved from childhood from grievous sin and gross imperfection. Though she never grows tired of bewailing her faults and unfaithfulness, these avowals must be taken *cum grano salis*. While yet a child, she sometimes gave way to vanity in dress and wasted her time in reading romances. As a young religious, she was sought after by friends and relatives who took pleasure in her attractive conversation. This proved further loss of time and caused distractions. Owing to acute suffering, she for some years left off the practice of mental prayer, though she faithfully performed all her religious obligations, as far as her weak state of health allowed. This is all. The war of the flesh against the spirit, the insubordination of the lower parts of nature, the fickleness of the will, which so often thwart the most noble aspirations of a soul, were unknown to her. Under these circumstances, we cannot be surprised to find her entering upon the journey towards God at a point which in many cases marks but the closing stage.

As to the remaining parts of this book, it will be seen from the parallel passages that they cover much the same ground as her *Life* and the *Relations*. With her singular gift of introspection and analysis, the Saint studied her own case from every point of view, so as to make sure that her extraordinary experiences were due to no illusion, and offered no obstacle to the safety of her soul. Although the *Interior Castle* contains little that we do not already know from her other works, it is superior to them by reason of its logical order and the masterly treatment of the most recondite matters of mystical theology. While ostensibly dealing with general facts, St. Teresa in reality records her personal experiences. How definite these were, how little room there remained for the freaks of the imagination, will appear from the fact that she nearly always repeats the very words she had used in her *Life* and in the other reports of her interior progress, although she did not have these writings before her eyes, nor had she ever seen them since they first left her hands. Every one of her experiences must have produced a profound impression to be remembered so minutely after an interval of years.

There is that in the *Interior Castle* which reminds one of Dante's *Paradiso*. In the one and the other, the soul, purified from earthly dross, is gradually being invested with new and glorious qualities, and is being led through regions unknown until it arrives at the very threshold of the throne of God. Not even the boldest imagination could have designed so wonderful a picture of a soul adorned with graces at once so varied and so true. In one case we know, the poet has drawn abundantly from the treasury of the Angelical Doctor, putting in verse the conclusions of the scholastic theologian. In the other case we can follow, chapter by chapter, the influence of the teaching of St. Thomas Aquinas. St. Teresa had never studied it herself, but her directors and confessors were deeply versed in it and solved her doubts and perplexities on the lines of the greatest of the school men. The *Interior Castle* might almost be considered a practical illustration of certain parts of the *Summa theologica*,[26] as it describes the progress of the soul through every stage of perfection. When we have reached the second chapter of the seventh Mansion, there remains but one thing: the Beatific Vision, and this is reserved for the next life.

After the publication of the *Interior Castle* by Luis de Leon, the manuscript came into the possession of Father Jerome Gracian, who, after having made a copy of it which is still extant, presented the original, on the occasion of a visit to the convent of Seville, to Don Pedro Cereso Pardo, a great friend of the Saint, and a benefactor to the convent. When his only daughter took the habit there, the precious manuscript was part of her dowry. Doña Juana de Mendoza, Duchess of Beguiar, a novice in the same convent, had it bound in silver and precious stones. It is still there,[27] and the present writer had the privilege of seeing it. It comprises a hundred and thirteen leaves in folio, but originally there must have been some more leaves which at a later period were

[25] Way of Perf. ch. xx. 1
[26] S. Theol. 2da 2dæ, qq. 171-184.
[27] Bollandists, Acta, n. 1495. See also Impressions in Spain. By Lady Herbert. London, 1867, p, 171.

torn out. These, it is presumed, contained the headings of the chapters. Unlike the *Life* and the *Foundations*, the text of the *Castle* is divided only by figures, without indication of the contents of each chapter, but the arguments which have come down to us are so entirely similar to those of the two works named, that it is impossible to consider them otherwise than the genuine work of the author. In the present translation they have been inserted in their proper places.

On the occasion of the ter-centenary of Saint Teresa's death, a photo-lithographic edition of the original was published under the direction of Cardinal Lluch, Carmelite of the old observance, Archbishop of Seville:

1. El Castillo Ynterior ó Tratado de las Moradas,
2. escrito por Sta. Teresa de Jesús.
3. Litografia de Juan Moyano (Seville) 1882.

The present translation, the third in English,[28] has been made directly from this autograph edition. It has been thought advisable that, as far as the genius of the language allows it, the wording of the author should be strictly adhered to, and that not even a shade of her expression should be sacrificed. For Teresa is not only a saint whose every word is telling, but she is a classic in her own language who knows how to give expression to her deepest thoughts. Having compared word for word the translation with the original, I am in a position to affirm that this programme has been faithfully carried out. For the foot-notes—with few exceptions—as well as for the Index, I am responsible. It seemed to me important to point out all the parallel passages from the various works of the Saint. Only by this means can it be seen how consistent Saint Teresa is in all her writings.[29] It would have been easy to multiply quotations from the works of other writers on mystical theology. Thus, the influence of the *Imitation of Christ* and of the *Life of our Lord* by Ludolphus the Carthusian can be distinctly traced in the *Interior Castle*. Both these works, as well as some Spanish books, were held in such esteem by St. Teresa, that she ordered the prioress of each convent to keep them at the disposal of the nuns. As there is a limit to footnotes, I have contented myself with such references as seemed to me conducive to the elucidation of the doctrine laid down in this treatise.

In conclusion I venture to express the hope that this new translation will be found helpful by those who feel called to a higher life.

BENEDICT ZIMMERMAN,
Prior, O.C.D.
ST. LUKE'S PRIORY,
WINCANTON, SOMERSET.
July, 1, 1905, and *December* 25, 1911.

---

[28] The first translation is to be found in the *Works of the Holy Mother St. Teresa of Jesus* (third part). Printed in the year MDCLXXV, pp. 137-286. It bears the title: *The Interiour Castle: or, Mansions*. As to the authors of this translation—Abraham Woodhead and another, whose name is not known—see my book *Carmel in England*, p. 342, note. It is stated there that the third part, containing the *Way of Perfection* and the *Castle*, has no title-page. This is true with regard to the copy I had before me when writing that book. The one I have now is more complete.

The second translation, by the Rev. John Dalton, appeared in 1852 and has been repeatedly reprinted. It was dedicated to Bishop Ullathorne.

Of foreign translations it will be sufficient to mention the one by Cyprien de la Nativité, in *Œuvres de la Sainte Mère Térèse de Jésus*, Paris, 1657, and the new one in *Œuvres* already mentioned.

[29] The present translation ought to dispose of the reservations expressed by an able critic in his otherwise valuable appreciation of the works of the Saint. See *Santa Teresa*, by the late Alexander Whyte, D.D. London, 1898, p. 32.

Criticisms which have appeared in various papers, or have been privately conveyed, have been gratefully received and acted upon in the second and the present edition.

INTERIOR CASTLE
OR THE MANSIONS
BY ST. TERESA

THIS TREATISE, STYLED THE INTERIOR CASTLE, WAS WRITTEN BY TERESA OF JESUS,
NUN OF OUR LADY OF CARMEL, FOR HER SISTERS AND DAUGHTERS,
THE DISCALCED CARMELITE NUNS.

RARELY has obedience laid upon me so difficult a task as this of writing about prayer; for one reason, because I do not feel that God has given me either the power or the desire for it, besides which, during the last three months I have suffered from noises and a great weakness in my head that have made it painful for me to write even on necessary business.[1]

However, as I know the power obedience has of making things easy which seem impossible, my will submits with a good grace, although nature seems greatly distressed, for God has not given me such strength as to bear, without repugnance, the constant struggle against illness while performing many different duties. May He, Who has helped me in other more difficult matters, aid me with His grace in this, for I trust in His mercy. I think I have but little to say that has not already been put forth in my other works written under obedience; in fact, I fear this will be but repetition of them. I am like a parrot which has learnt to talk; only knowing what it has been taught or has heard, it repeats the same thing over and over again. If God wishes me to write anything new, He will teach it me, or bring back to my memory what I have said elsewhere. I should be content even with this, for as I am very forgetful, I should be glad to be able to recall some of the matters about which people say I have spoken well, lest they should be altogether lost. If our Lord will not even grant me this, still, if I weary my brains and increase my headache by striving to obey, I shall gain in merit, though my words should be useless to any one. So I begin this work on the Feast of the Blessed Trinity in the year 1577, in the Convent of St. Joseph of Carmel at Toledo, where I am living, and I submit all my writings to the judgment of those learned men by whose commands I undertake them. That it will be the fault of ignorance, not malice, if I say anything contrary to the doctrine of the Holy Roman Catholic Church, may be held as certain. By God's goodness I am, and always shall be, faithful to the Church, as I have been in the past. May He be for ever blessed and glorified. Amen.

He who bids me write this, tells me that the nuns of these convents of our Lady of Carmel need some one to solve their difficulties about prayer: he thinks that women understand one another's language best and that my sisters' affection for me would make them pay special attention to my words, therefore it is important for me to explain the subject clearly to them. Thus I am writing only to my sisters; the idea that any one else could benefit by what I say would be absurd. Our Lord will be doing me a great favour if He enables me to help but one of the nuns to praise Him a little better; His Majesty knows well that I have no other aim. If anything is to the point, they will understand that it does not originate from me and there is no reason to attribute it to me, as with my scant understanding and skill I could write nothing of the sort, unless God, in His mercy, enabled me to do so.

---

[1] 'I am always suffering from my head.' Letter of June 28, 1577. Letters. VOL. II.

THE FIRST MANSIONS

CHAPTER I.

THIS CHAPTER TREATS OF THE BEAUTY AND DIGNITY OF OUR SOULS AND MAKES A COMPARISON TO EXPLAIN THIS. THE ADVANTAGE OF KNOWING AND UNDERSTANDING THIS AND THE FAVOURS GOD GRANTS TO US IS SHOWN, AND HOW PRAYER IS THE GATE OF THE SPIRITUAL CASTLE.

1. Plan of this book. 2. The Interior Castle. 3. Our curable self ignorance. 4. God dwells in the centre of the soul. 5. Why all souls do not receive certain favours. 6. Reasons for speaking of these favours. 7. The entrance of the Castle. 8. Entering into oneself. 9. Prayer. 10. Those who dwell in the first mansion. 11. Entering. 12. Difficulties of the subject.

1. WHILE I was begging our Lord to-day to speak for me, since I knew not what to say nor how to commence this work which obedience has laid upon me, an idea occurred to me which I will explain, and which will serve as a foundation for that I am about to write.

2. I thought of the soul as resembling a castle,[1] formed of a single diamond or a very transparent crystal,[2] and containing many rooms, just as in heaven there are many mansions.[3] If we reflect, sisters, we shall see that the soul of the just man is but a paradise, in which, God tells us, He takes His delight.[4] What, do you imagine, must that dwelling be in which a King so mighty, so wise, and so pure, containing in Himself all good, can delight to rest? Nothing can be compared to the great beauty and capabilities of a soul; however keen our intellects may be, they are as unable to comprehend them as to comprehend God, for, as He has told us, He created us in His own image and likeness.[5]

3. As this is so, we need not tire ourselves by trying to realize all the beauty of this castle, although, being His creature, there is all the difference between the soul and God that there is between the creature and the Creator; the fact that it is made in God's image teaches us how great are its dignity and loveliness. It is no small misfortune and disgrace that, through our own fault, we neither understand our nature nor our origin. Would it not be gross ignorance, my daughters, if, when a man was questioned about his name, or country, or parents, he could not answer? Stupid as this would be, it is unspeakably more foolish to care to learn nothing of our nature except that we possess bodies, and only to realize vaguely that we have souls, because people say so and it is a doctrine of faith. Rarely do we reflect upon what gifts our souls may possess, Who dwells within them, or how extremely precious they are. Therefore we do little to preserve their beauty; all our care is concentrated on our bodies, which are but the coarse setting of the diamond, or the outer walls of the castle.[6]

4. Let us imagine, as I said, that there are many rooms in this castle, of which some are above, some below, others at the side; in the centre, in the very midst of them all, is the principal chamber in which God and the soul hold their most secret intercourse.[7] Think over this comparison very

---

[1] Way of Perfection, ch. xxviii, 9.

[2] In her Life St. Teresa likened God to a diamond (ch. xl, 14); and elsewhere (ch. xi, 10) the soul to a garden wherein our Lord takes His delight.

[3] St. John xiv. 2: 'In domo Patris mei mansiones multæ sunt.' St. John of the Cross uses the same comparison: 'If the soul shall overcome the devil in the first combat, it shall then pass on to the second; and if it shall be victorious there also, it shall then pass on to the third; and then through the seven mansions, the seven degrees of love, until the Bridegroom shall bring it to the "cellar of wine" of perfect charity.' (Ascent of Mount Carmel, bk. ii. ch. xi. 7.)

[4] Prov. viii. 31: 'Deliciæ meæ esse cum filiis hominum.'

[5] Gen. i. 26: 'Faciamus hominem ad imaginem et similitudinem nostram.'

[6] Way of Perf. ch. xxviii.

[7] St. John of the Cross on the words of his stanza: 'In the inner cellar of my Beloved have I drunk.' 'Here the soul speaks of that sovereign grace of God in taking it into the house of His love, which is the

carefully; God grant it may enlighten you about the different kinds of graces He is pleased to bestow upon the soul. No one can know all about them, much less a person so ignorant as I am. The knowledge that such things are possible will console you greatly should our Lord ever grant you any of these favours; people themselves deprived of them can then at least praise Him for His great goodness in bestowing them on others. The thought of heaven and the happiness of the saints does us no harm, but cheers and urges us to win this joy for ourselves, nor will it injure us to know that during this exile God can communicate Himself to us loathsome worms; it will rather make us love Him for such immense goodness and infinite mercy.

5. I feel sure that vexation at thinking that during our life on earth God can bestow these graces on the souls of others shows a want of humility and charity for one's neighbour, for why should we not feel glad at a brother's receiving divine favours which do not deprive us of our own share? Should we not rather rejoice at His Majesty's thus manifesting His greatness wherever He chooses?[8] Sometimes our Lord acts thus solely for the sake of showing His power, as He declared when the Apostles questioned whether the blind man whom He cured had been suffering for his own or his parents' sins.[9] God does not bestow these favours on certain souls because they are more holy than others who do not receive them, but to manifest His greatness, as in the case of St. Paul and St. Mary Magdalen, and that we may glorify Him in His creatures.

6. People may say such things appear impossible and it is best not to scandalize the weak in faith by speaking about them. But it is better that the latter should disbelieve us, than that we should desist from enlightening souls which receive these graces, that they may rejoice and may endeavour to love God better for His favours, seeing He is so mighty and so great. There is no danger here of shocking those for whom I write by treating of such matters, for they know and believe that God gives even greater proofs of His love. I am certain that if any one of you doubts the truth of this, God will never allow her to learn it by experience, for He desires that no limits should be set to His work: therefore, never discredit them because you are not thus led yourselves.

7. Now let us return to our beautiful and charming castle and discover how to enter it. This appears incongruous: if this castle is the soul, clearly no one can have to enter it, for it is the person himself: one might as well tell some one to go into a room he is already in! There are, however, very different ways of being in this castle; many souls live in the courtyard of the building where the sentinels stand, neither caring to enter farther, nor to know who dwells in that most delightful place, what is in it and what rooms it contains.

8. Certain books on prayer that you have read advise the soul to enter into itself,[10] and this is what I mean. I was recently told by a great theologian that souls without prayer are like bodies, palsied and lame, having hands and feet they cannot use. Just so, there are souls so infirm and accustomed to think of nothing but earthly matters, that there seems no cure for them. It appears impossible for them to retire into their own hearts; accustomed as they are to be with the reptiles and other creatures which live outside the castle, they have come at last to imitate their habits. Though these souls are by their nature so richly endowed, capable of communion even with God Himself, yet their case seems hopeless. Unless they endeavour to understand and remedy their

---

union or transformation of love in God…The cellar is the highest degree of love to which the soul can attain in this life, and is therefore said to be the inner. It follows from this that there are other cellars not so interior; that is, the degrees of love by which souls reach to this, the last. These cellars are seven in number, and the soul has entered them all when it has in perfection the seven gifts of the Holy Ghost, so far as it is possible for it… Many souls reach and enter the first cellar, each according to the perfection of its love, but the last and inmost cellar is entered by few in this world, because therein is wrought the perfect union with God, the union of the spiritual marriage.' A Spiritual Canticle, stanza xxvi. 1-3. Concept. ch. vi. (Minor Works of St. Teresa.)

[8] St. Matt. xx. 15: 'Alit non licet mihi quod volo, facere? an oculus tuus nequam est, quia ego bonus sum?'

[9] St. John ix. 2: 'Quis peccavit, hic, aut parentes ejus, ut cæcus nasceretur?'

[10] Imitation, bk. II. ch. 1: 'Regnum Dei intra vos est.' Luke. xvii. 21. The Imitation is one of the books which according to St. Teresa's Constitutions, (sec. 7) every prioress was bound to provide for her convent.

most miserable plight, their minds will become, as it were, bereft of movement, just as Lot's wife became a pillar of salt for looking backwards in disobedience to God's command.[11]

9. As far as I can understand, the gate by which to enter this castle is prayer and meditation. I do not allude more to mental than to vocal prayer, for if it is prayer at all, the mind must take part in it. If a person neither considers to Whom he is addressing himself, what he asks, nor what he is who ventures to speak to God, although his lips may utter many words, I do not call it prayer.[12] Sometimes, indeed, one may pray devoutly without making all these considerations through having practiced them at other times. The custom of speaking to God Almighty as freely as with a slave—caring nothing whether the words are suitable or not, but simply saying the first thing that comes to mind from being learnt by rote by frequent repetition—cannot be called prayer: God grant that no Christian may address Him in this manner. I trust His Majesty will prevent any of you, sisters, from doing so. Our habit in this Order of conversing about spiritual matters is a good preservative against such evil ways.

10. Let us speak no more of these crippled souls, who are in a most miserable and dangerous state, unless our Lord bid them rise, as He did the palsied man who had waited more than thirty years at the pool of Bethsaida.[13] We will now think of the others who at last enter the precincts of the castle; they are still very worldly, yet have some desire to do right, and at times, though rarely, commend themselves to God's care. They think about their souls every now and then; although very busy, they pray a few times a month, with minds generally filled with a thousand other matters, for where their treasure is, there is their heart also.[14] Still, occasionally they cast aside these cares; it is a great boon for them to realize to some extent the state of their souls, and to see that they will never reach the gate by the road they are following.

11. At length they enter the first rooms in the basement of the castle, accompanied by numerous reptiles[15] which disturb their peace, and prevent their seeing the beauty of the building; still, it is a great gain that these persons should have found their way in at all.

12. You may think, my daughters, that all this does not concern you, because, by God's grace, you are farther advanced; still, you must be patient with me, for I can explain myself on some spiritual matters concerning prayer in no other way. May our Lord enable me to speak to the point; the subject is most difficult to understand without personal experience of such graces. Any one who has received them will know how impossible it is to avoid touching on subjects which, by the mercy of God, will never apply to us.

CHAPTER II.

DESCRIBES THE HIDEOUS APPEARANCE OF A SOUL IN MORTAL SIN AS REVEALED BY GOD TO SOME ONE: OFFERS A FEW REMARKS ON SELF-KNOWLEDGE: THIS CHAPTER IS USEFUL AS IT CONTAINS SOME POINTS REQUIRING ATTENTION. AN EXPLANATION OF THE MANSIONS.

1. Effects of mortal sin. 2. It prevents the soul's gaining merit. 3. The soul compared to a tree. 4. Disorder of the soul in mortal sin. 5. Vision of a sinful soul. 6. Profit of realizing these lessons. 7. Prayer. 8. Beauty of the Castle. 9. Self-knowledge 10. Gained by meditating on the divine perfections. 11. Advantages of such meditation. 12. Christ should be our model. 13. The devil entraps beginners. 14. Our strength must come from God. 15. Sin blinds the soul. 16. Worldliness. 17. The world in the cloister. 18. Assaults of the devil. 19. Examples of the devil's arts. 20. Perfection consists in charity. 21. Indiscreet zeal. 22. Danger of detraction.

---

[11] Gen. xix. 26: 'Respiciensque uxor ejus post se, versa est in statuam salis.'

[12] Way of Perf. ch. xxi. 6; xxix. 4.

[13] St. John v. 5: 'Erat autem quidam homo ibi triginta et octo annos habens in infirmitate sua.'

[14] St. Matt. vi. 21: 'Ubi enim est thesaurus tuus ibi est et cor tuum.

[15] Many an ancient castle was provided with a bear-garden where rare animals were kept for the amusement of the inhabitants. This may have supplied the material for St. Teresa's comparison.

1. BEFORE going farther, I wish you to consider the state to which mortal sin[16] brings this magnificent and beautiful castle, this pearl of the East, this tree of life, planted beside the living waters of life[17] which symbolize God Himself. No night can be so dark, no gloom nor blackness can compare to its obscurity. Suffice it to say that the sun in the centre of the soul, which gave it such splendour and beauty, is totally eclipsed, though the spirit is as fitted to enjoy God's presence as is the crystal to reflect the sun.[18]

2. While the soul is in mortal sin nothing can profit it; none of its good works merit an eternal reward, since they do not proceed from God as their first principle, and by Him alone is our virtue real virtue. The soul separated from Him is no longer pleasing in His eyes, because by committing a mortal sin, instead of seeking to please God, it prefers to gratify the devil, the prince of darkness, and so comes to share his blackness. I knew a person to whom our Lord revealed the result of a mortal sin[19] and who said she thought no one who realized its effects could ever commit it, but would suffer unimaginable torments to avoid it. This vision made her very desirous for all to grasp this truth, therefore I beg you, my daughters, to pray fervently to God for sinners, who live in blindness and do deeds of darkness.

3. In a state of grace the soul is like a well of limpid water, from which flow only streams of clearest crystal. Its works are pleasing both to God and man, rising from the River of Life, beside which it is rooted like a tree. Otherwise it would produce neither leaves nor fruit, for the waters of grace nourish it, keep it from withering from drought, and cause it to bring forth good fruit. But the soul by sinning withdraws from this stream of life, and growing beside a black and fetid pool, can produce nothing but disgusting and unwholesome fruit.

Notice that it is not the fountain and the brilliant sun which lose their splendour and beauty, for they are placed in the very centre of the soul and cannot be deprived of their luster. The soul is like a crystal in the sunshine over which a thick black cloth has been thrown, so that however brightly the sun may shine the crystal can never reflect it.

4. O souls, redeemed by the Blood of Jesus Christ, take these things to heart; have mercy on yourselves! If you realize your pitiable condition, how can you refrain from trying to remove the darkness from the crystal of your souls? Remember, if death should take you now, you would never again enjoy the light of this Sun. O Jesus! how sad a sight must be a soul deprived of light! What a terrible state the chambers of this castle are in! How disorderly must be the senses—the inhabitants of the castle—the powers of the soul its magistrates, governors, and stewards—blind and uncontrolled as they are! In short, as the soil in which the tree is now planted is in the devil's domain, how can its fruit be anything but evil? A man of great spiritual insight once told me he was not so much surprised at such a soul's wicked deeds as astonished that it did not commit even worse sins. May God in His mercy keep us from such great evil, for nothing in this life merits the name of evil in comparison with this, which delivers us over to evil which is eternal.

5. This is what we must dread and pray God to deliver us from, for we are weakness itself, and unless He guards the city, in vain shall we labour to defend it.[20] The person of whom I spoke[21] said that she had learnt two things from the vision granted her. The first was, a great fear of offending God; seeing how terrible were the consequences, she constantly begged Him to preserve her from falling into sin. Secondly, it was a mirror to teach her humility, for she saw that nothing good in us springs from ourselves but comes from the waters of grace near which the soul remains like a tree planted beside a river, and from that Sun which gives life to our works. She realized this so vividly that on seeing any good deed performed by herself or by other people she at once turned to God as to its fountain head—without whose help she knew well we can do

---

[16] Life, ch. xxxviii. 31; ch. xl. 15.

[17] Ps. i. 3: 'Et erit tamquam lignum quod plantatum eat secus decursus aquarum.'

[18] Way of Perf. ch. xxviii. 9.

[19] In this as in most other cases when the Saint speaks of 'a person she knows,' she means herself. Life, ch. xl, 15.

[20] cxxvi. 1: 'Nisi Dominus custodierit civitatem, frustra vigilat qui custodit eam.'

[21] Life, ch. xxxviii. 33; ch. xl. 15, 16.

nothing—and broke out into songs of praise to Him. Generally she forgot all about herself and only thought of God when she did any meritorious action.

6. The time which has been spent in reading or writing on this subject will not have been lost if it has taught us these two truths; for though learned, clever men know them perfectly, women's wits are dull and need help in every way. Perhaps this is why our Lord has suggested these comparisons to me; may He give us grace to profit by them!

7. So obscure are these spiritual matters that to explain them an ignorant person like myself must say much that is superfluous, and even alien to the subject, before coming to the point. My readers must be patient with me, as I am with myself while writing what I do not understand; indeed, I often take up the paper like a dunce, not knowing what to say, nor how to begin. Doubtless there is need for me to do my best to explain these spiritual subjects to you, for we often hear how beneficial prayer is for our souls; our Constitutions oblige us to pray so many hours a day, yet tell us nothing of what part we ourselves can take in it and very little of the work God does in the soul by its means.[22] It will be helpful, in setting it before you in various ways, to consider this heavenly edifice within us, so little understood by men, near as they often come to it. Our Lord gave me grace to understand something of such matters when I wrote on them before, yet I think I have more light now, especially on the more difficult questions. Unfortunately I am too ignorant to treat of such subjects without saying much that is already well known.

8. Now let us turn at last to our castle with its many mansions. You must not think of a suite of rooms placed in succession, but fix your eyes on the keep, the court inhabited by the King.[23] Like the kernel of the palmito,[24] from which several rinds must be removed before coming to the eatable part, this principal chamber is surrounded by many others. However large, magnificent, and spacious you imagine this castle to be, you cannot exaggerate it; the capacity of the soul is beyond all our understanding, and the Sun within this palace enlightens every part of it.

9. A soul which gives itself to prayer, either much or little, should on no account be kept within narrow bounds. Since God has given it such great dignity, permit it to wander at will through the rooms of the castle, from the lowest to the highest. Let it not force itself to remain for very long in the same mansion, even that of self-knowledge. Mark well, however, that self-knowledge is indispensable, even for those whom God takes to dwell in the same mansion with Himself. Nothing else, however elevated, perfects the soul which must never seek to forget its own nothingness. Let humility be always at work, like the bee at the honeycomb, or all will be lost. But, remember, the bee leaves its hive to fly in search of flowers and the soul should sometimes cease thinking of itself to rise in meditation on the grandeur and majesty of its God. It will learn its own baseness better thus than by self-contemplation, and will be freer from the reptiles which enter the first room where self-knowledge is acquired. Although it is a great grace from God to practice self-examination, yet 'too much is as bad as too little,' as they say; believe me, by God's help, we shall advance more by contemplating the Divinity than by keeping our eyes fixed on ourselves, poor creatures of earth that we are.

10. I do not know whether I have put this clearly; self-knowledge is of such consequence that I would not have you careless of it, though you may be lifted to heaven in prayer, because while on earth nothing is more needful than humility. Therefore, I repeat, not only a *good* way, but the *best* of all ways, is to endeavour to enter first by the room where humility is practiced, which is far better than at once rushing on to the others. This is the right road;—if we know how easy and safe it is to walk by it, why ask for wings with which to fly? Let us rather try to learn how to advance quickly. I believe we shall never learn to know ourselves except by endeavouring to know God, for, beholding His greatness we are struck by our own baseness, His purity shows our foulness, and by meditating on His humility we find how very far we are from being humble.

---

[22] Life, ch. x. 2 sqq. Constitut. 2, 6.

[23] Way of Perf.. ch. xxviii. 1.

[24] The palmito here referred to is not a palm, but a shrub about four feet high and very dense with leaves, resembling palm leaves. The poorer classes and principally children dig it up by the roots, which they peel of its many layers until a sort of kernel is disclosed, which is eaten, not without relish, and is somewhat like a filbert in taste. See St. John of the Cross, Accent of Mount Carmel, bk. ii. ch, xiv, 3.

11. Two advantages are gained by this practice. First, it is clear that white looks far whiter when placed near something black, and on the contrary, black never looks so dark as when seen beside something white. Secondly, our understanding and will become more noble and capable of good in every way when we turn from ourselves to God: it is very injurious never to raise our minds above the mire of our own faults. I described how murky and fetid are the streams that spring from the source of a soul in mortal sin.[25] Thus (although the case is not really the same, God forbid! this is only a comparison), while we are continually absorbed in contemplating the weakness of our earthly nature, the springs of our actions will never flow free from the mire of timid, weak, and cowardly thoughts, such as: 'I wonder whether people are noticing me or not! If I follow this course, will harm come to me? Dare I begin this work? Would it not be presumptuous? Is it right for any one as faulty as myself to speak on sublime spiritual subjects?[26] Will not people think too well of me, if I make myself singular? Extremes are bad, even in virtue; sinful as I am I shall only fall the lower. Perhaps I shall fail and be a source of scandal to good people; such a person as I am has no need of peculiarities.'

12. Alas, my daughters, what loss the devil must have caused to many a soul by such thoughts as these! It thinks such ideas and many others of the same sort I could mention arise from humility. This comes from not understanding our own nature; self-knowledge becomes so warped that, unless we take our thoughts off ourselves, I am not surprised that these and many worse fears should threaten us. Therefore I maintain, my daughters, that we should fix our eyes on Christ our only good, and on His saints; there we shall learn true humility, and our minds will be ennobled, so that self-knowledge will not make us base and cowardly. Although only the first, this mansion contains great riches and such treasures that if the soul only manages to elude the reptiles dwelling here, it cannot fail to advance farther. Terrible are the wiles and stratagems the devil uses to hinder people from realizing their weakness and detecting his snares.

13. From personal experience I could give you much information as to what happens in these first mansions. I will only say that you must not imagine there are only a few, but a number of rooms, for souls enter them by many different ways, and always with a good intention. The devil is so angry at this that he keeps legions of evil spirits hidden in each room to stop the progress of Christians, whom, being ignorant of this, he entraps in a thousand ways. He cannot so easily deceive souls which dwell nearer to the King as he can beginners still absorbed in the world, immersed in its pleasures, and eager for its honours and distinctions. As the vassals of their souls, the senses and powers bestowed on them by God, are weak, such people are easily vanquished, although desirous not to offend God.

14. Those conscious of being in this state must as often as possible have recourse to His Majesty, taking His Blessed Mother and the saints for their advocates to do battle for them, because we creatures possess little strength for self-defense. Indeed in every state of life all our help must come from God; may He in His mercy grant it us, Amen! What a miserable life we lead! As I have spoken more fully in other writings[27] on the ill that results from ignoring the need of humility and self-knowledge, I will treat no more about it here, my daughters, although it is of the first importance. God grant that what I have said may be useful to you.

15 You must notice that the light which comes from the King's palace hardly shines at all in these first mansions; although not as gloomy and black as the soul in mortal sin, yet they are in semi-darkness, and their inhabitants see scarcely anything. I cannot explain myself; I do not mean that this is the fault of the mansions themselves, but that the number of snakes, vipers, and venomous reptiles from outside the castle prevent souls entering them from seeing the light. They resemble a person entering a chamber full of brilliant sunshine, with eyes clogged and half closed with dust. Though the room itself is light, he cannot see because of his self-imposed impediment. In the same way, these fierce and wild beasts blind the eyes of the beginner, so that he sees nothing but them.

---

[25] Supra, sec. 3.

[26] Life, ch. viii. 6, x. 4, xxiii. 3-5. Way of Perf. ch. xxxix. 1.

[27] Life ch. xiii. 23. Way of Perf. ch. x. 4. Castle, M. iii. ch. ii. 8. Concep. ch. ii. 20. Const. 21.

16. Such, it appears to me, is the soul which, though not in a state of mortal sin, is so worldly and preoccupied with earthly riches, honours, and affairs, that as I said, even if it sincerely wishes to enter into itself and enjoy the beauties of the castle, it is prevented by these distractions and seems unable to overcome so many obstacles. It is most important to withdraw from all unnecessary cares and business, as far as compatible with the duties of one's state of life, in order to enter the second mansion. This is so essential, that unless done immediately I think it impossible for any one ever to reach the principal room, or even to remain where he is without great risk of losing what is already gained; otherwise, although he is inside the castle, he will find it impossible to avoid being bitten some time or other by some of the very venomous creatures surrounding him.

17. What then would become of a religious like ourselves, my daughters, if, after having escaped from all these impediments, and having entered much farther into the more secret mansion, she should, by her own fault, return to all this turmoil? Through her sins, many other people on whom God had bestowed great graces would culpably relapse into their wretched state. In our convents we are free from these exterior evils; please God our minds may be as free from them, and may He deliver us from such ills.

18. Do not trouble yourselves, my daughters, with cares which do not concern you. You must notice that the struggle with the demons continues through nearly all the mansions of this castle. True, in some of them, the guards, which, as I explained, are the powers of the soul, have strength for the combat, but we must be keenly on the watch against the devil's arts, lest he deceive us in the form of an angel of light. He creeps in gradually, in numberless ways, and does us much harm, though we do not discover it until too late.[28]

19. As I said elsewhere,[29] he works like a file, secretly and silently wearing its way: I will give you some examples to show how he begins his wiles. For instance: a nun has such a longing for penance as to feel no peace unless she is tormenting herself in some way.[30] This is good in itself; but suppose that the Prioress has forbidden her to practice any mortifications without special leave, and the sister thinking that, in such a meritorious cause, she may venture to disobey, secretly leads such a life that she loses her health and cannot even fulfil the requirements of her rule—you see how this show of good ends. Another nun is very zealous about religious perfection; this is very right, but may cause her to think every small fault she sees in her sisters a serious crime, and to watch constantly whether they do anything wrong, that she may run to the Prioress to accuse them of it. At the same time, she never notices her own shortcomings because of her great zeal about other people's religious observance, while perhaps her sisters, not seeing her intention but only knowing of the watch she keeps on them, do not take her behaviour in good part.

20. The devil's chief aim here is to cool the charity and lessen the mutual affection of the nuns, which would injure them seriously. Be sure, my daughters, that true perfection consists in the love of God and our neighbour, and the better we keep both these commandments, the more perfect we shall be. The sole object of our Rule and Constitutions is to help us to observe these two laws.

21. Indiscreet zeal about others must not be indulged in; it may do us much harm; let each one look to herself. However, as I have spoken fully on this subject elsewhere,[31] I will not enlarge on it here, and will only beg you to remember the necessity of this mutual affection. Our souls may lose their peace and even disturb other people's if we are always criticizing trivial actions which often are not real defects at all, but we construe them wrongly through ignorance of their motives. See how much it costs to attain perfection! Sometimes the devil tempts nuns in this way about the Prioress, which is still more dangerous. Great prudence is then required, for if she disobeys the Rule or Constitutions the matter must not always be overlooked, but should be

---

[28] Life ch. xxxi. 23.

[29] No doubt the Saint often used this excellent comparison in her verbal instructions, but it occurs nowhere else in her writings.

[30] Way of Perf. ch. x. 5; xxxix. 4; Rel. iii. 12.

[31] The Saint must frequently have spoken on the subject, but she never treated it more fully than in this place. Way of Perf. ch. xii. 7. Life, ch. xiii. 11, 14 sqq. Visitation of convents.

mentioned to her;[32] if, after this, she does not amend, the Superior of the Order should be informed of it. It is true charity to speak in this case, as it would be if we saw our sisters commit a grave fault; to keep silence for fear that speech would be a temptation against charity, would be that very temptation itself.[33]

22. However, I must warn you seriously not to talk to each other about such things, lest the devil deceive you. He would gain greatly by your doing so, because it would lead to the habit of detraction; rather, as I said, state the matter to those whose duty it is to remedy it. Thank God our custom here of keeping almost perpetual silence gives little opportunity for such conversations, still, it is well to stand ever on our guard.

---

[32] Way of Perfection, ch. ii. 3. Visit. 20-22, 34, 36.

[33] 'It is terrible to think what harm a Prioress can do! For although the Sisters witness things which scandalize them (of which there are plenty here!), yet they think it would be sinning against obedience to see any harm in them.' (Letter to Father Gracian, Letters, Vol. III.)

THE SECOND MANSIONS

ONLY CHAPTER

TREATS OF THE GREAT IMPORTANCE OF PERSEVERANCE IN ORDER TO ENTER THE LAST MANSIONS, AND OF THE FIERCE WAR THE DEVIL WAGES AGAINST US. HOW ESSENTIAL IT IS TO TAKE THE RIGHT PATH FROM THE VERY COMMENCEMENT OF OUR JOURNEY. A METHOD OF ACTION WHICH HAS PROVED VERY EFFICACIOUS.

1. Souls in the second mansions. 2. Their state. 3. Their sufferings. 4. They cannot get rid of their imperfections. 5. How God calls these souls. 6. Perseverance is essential. 7. Temptations of the devil. 8. Delusion of earthly joys. 9. God alone to be loved. 10. Reasons for continuing the journey. 11. War fare of the devil. 12. Importance of choice of friends. 13. Valour required. 14. Presumption of expecting spiritual consolations at first. 15. In the Cross is strength. 16. Our falls should raise us higher. 17. Confidence and perseverance. 18. Recollection. 19. Why we must practice prayer. 20. Meditation kindles love.

1. Now let us consider which are the souls that enter the second mansions, and what they do there: I do not wish to enlarge on this subject, having already treated it very fully elsewhere,[1] for I could not avoid repeating myself, as my memory is very bad. If I could state my ideas in another form they would not weary you, for we never tire of reading books on this subject, numerous as they are.

2. In this part of the castle are found souls which have begun to practice prayer; they realize the importance of their not remaining in the first mansions, yet often lack determination to quit their present condition by avoiding occasions of sin, which is a very perilous state to be in.

3. However, it is a great grace that they should sometimes make good their escape from the vipers and poisonous creatures around them and should understand the need of avoiding them. In some way these souls suffer a great deal more than those in the first mansions, although not in such danger, as they begin to understand their peril and there are great hopes of their entering farther into the castle. I say that they suffer a great deal more, for those in an earlier stage are like deaf-mutes and are not so distressed at being unable to speak, while the others, who can hear but cannot talk, find it much harder. At the same time, it is better not to be deaf, and a decided advantage to hear what is said to us.

4. These souls hear our Lord calling them, for as they approach nearer to where His Majesty dwells He proves a loving Neighbour, though they may still be engaged in the amusements and business, the pleasures and vanities of this world. While in this state we continually fall into sin and rise again, for the creatures amongst whom we dwell are so venomous, so vicious, and so dangerous, that it is almost impossible to avoid being tripped up by them. Yet such are the pity and compassion of this Lord of ours, so desirous is He that we should seek Him and enjoy His company, that in one way or another He never ceases calling us to Him. So sweet is His voice, that the poor soul is disconsolate at being unable to follow His bidding at once, and therefore, as I said, suffers more than if it could not hear Him.

5. I do not mean that divine communications and inspirations received in this mansion are the same as those I shall describe later on; God here speaks to souls through words uttered by pious people, by sermons or good books, and in many other such ways. Sometimes He calls souls by means of sickness or troubles, or by some truth He teaches them during prayer, for tepid as they may be in seeking Him, yet God holds them very dear.

6. Do not think lightly, sisters, of this first grace, nor be downcast if you have not responded immediately to Our Lord's voice, for His Majesty is willing to wait for us many a day and even many a year, especially when He sees perseverance and good desires in our hearts. Perseverance is the first essential; with this we are sure to profit greatly. However, the devils now fiercely assault the soul in a thousand different ways: it suffers more than ever, because formerly it was mute and

---

[1] Life, ch. xi.-xiii. Way of Perf. ch. xx.-xxix.

deaf, or at least could hear very little, and offered but feeble resistance, like one who has almost lost all hope of victory.

7. Here, however, the understanding being more vigilant and the powers more on the alert, we cannot avoid hearing the fighting and cannonading around us. For now the devils set on us the reptiles, that is to say, thoughts about the world and its joys which they picture as unending; they remind us of the high esteem men held us in, of our friends and relations; they tell us how the penances which souls in this mansion always begin to wish to perform would injure our health: in fine, the evil spirits place a thousand impediments in the way.

8. O Jesus! What turmoil the devils cause in the poor soul! How unhappy it feels, not knowing whether to go forward or to return to the first mansion! On the other hand, reason shows it the delusion of overrating worldly things, while faith teaches what alone can satisfy its cravings. Memory reminds the soul how all earthly joys end, recalling the death of those who lived at ease; how some died suddenly and were soon forgotten, how others, once so prosperous, are now buried beneath the ground and men pass by the graves where they lie, the prey of worms,[2] while the mind recalls many other such incidents.

9. The will inclines to love Our Lord and longs to make some return to Him Who is so amiable, and Who has given so many proofs of His love, especially by His constant presence with the soul, which this faithful Lover never quits, ever accompanying it and giving it life and being. The understanding aids by showing that however many years life might last, no one could ever wish for a better friend than God; that the world is full of falsehood, and that the worldly pleasures pictured by the devil to the mind were but troubles and cares and annoyances in disguise.

10. Reason convinces the soul that as outside its interior castle are found neither peace nor security, it should cease to seek another home abroad, its own being full of riches that it can enjoy at will. Besides, it is not every one who, like itself, possesses all he needs within his own dwelling, and above all, such a Host, Who will give it all it can desire, unless, like the prodigal son, it chooses to go astray and feed with the swine.[3] Surely these arguments are strong enough to defeat the devil's wiles! But, O my God, how the force of worldly habits and the example of others who practice them ruin everything! Our faith is so dead that we trust less to its teaching than to what is visible, though, indeed, we see that worldly lives bring nothing but unhappiness. All this results from those venomous thoughts I described, which, unless we are very careful, will deform the soul as the sting of a viper poisons and swells the body.

11. When this happens, great care is evidently needed to cure it, and only God's signal mercy prevents its resulting in death. Indeed, the soul passes through severe trials at this time, especially when the devil perceives from a person's character and behaviour that she is likely to make very great progress, for then all hell will league together to force her to turn back. O my Lord! what need there is here that, by Thy mercy, Thou shouldst prevent the soul from being deluded into forsaking the good begun! Enlighten it to see that its welfare consists in perseverance in the right way, and in the withdrawing from bad company.

12. It is of the utmost importance for the beginner to associate with those who lead a spiritual life,[4] and not only with those in the same mansion as herself, but with others who have travelled farther into the castle, who will aid her greatly and draw her to join them. The soul should firmly resolve never to submit to defeat, for if the devil sees it staunchly determined to lose life and comfort and all that he can offer, rather than return to the first mansion, he will the sooner leave it alone.

---

[2] 'How many, thinking to live long, have been deceived and unexpectedly have been snatched away! How often hast thou heard that such a one was slain by the sword; another drowned; another, falling from on high, broke his neck; this man died at the table; that other came to his death while he was at play... Thus death is the end of all; and man's life passeth suddenly like a shadow' (Imitation, bk. 1. ch. xxiii. 7). The edition of the Imitation known to St. Teresa under the title of Contemptus Mundi was translated by Luis de Granada, printed at Seville in 1536, at Lisbon in 1542, and at Alcalá in 1548. See Life, ch. xxxix. 21, note.

[3] St. Luke xv. 16: 'Et cupiebat implere ventrem suum de siliquis quas porci manducabant.'

[4] Life, ch. vii. 33-37; xvi. 1 2; XXX. 6. Way of Perfection, ch. vi. 1; Vii. 4.

13. Let the Christian be valiant; let him not be like those who lay down to drink from the brook when they went to battle (I do not remember when).⁵ Let him resolve to go forth to combat with the host of demons, and be convinced that there is no better weapon than the cross. I have already said,⁶ yet it is of such importance that I repeat it here: let no one think on starting of the reward to be reaped: this would be a very ignoble way of commencing such a large and stately building. If built on sand it would soon fall down.⁷ Souls who acted thus would continually suffer from discouragement and temptations, for in these mansions no manna rains;⁸ farther on, the soul is pleased with all that comes, because it desires nothing but what God wills.

14. What a farce it is! Here are we, with a thousand obstacles, drawbacks, and imperfections within ourselves, our virtues so newly born that they have scarcely the strength to act (and God grant that they exist at all!) yet we are not ashamed to expect sweetness in prayer and to complain of feeling dryness.⁹

15. Do not act thus, sisters; embrace the cross your Spouse bore on His shoulders; know that your motto should be: 'Most happy she who suffers most if it be for Christ!'¹⁰ All else should be looked upon as secondary: if our Lord give it you, render Him grateful thanks. You may imagine you would be resolute in enduring external trials if God gave you interior consolations: His Majesty knows best what is good for us; it is not for us to advise Him how to treat us, for He has the right to tell us that we know not what we ask.¹¹ Remember, it is of the greatest importance— the sole aim of one beginning to practice prayer should be to endure trials, and to resolve and strive to the utmost of her power to conform her own will to the will of God.¹² Be certain that in this consists all the greatest perfection to be attained in the spiritual life, as I will explain later. She who practices this most perfectly will receive from God the highest reward and is the farthest advanced on the right road. Do not imagine that we have need of a cabalistic formula or any other occult or mysterious thing to attain it our whole welfare consists in doing the will of God. If we start with the false principle of wishing God to follow our will and to lead us in the way we think best, upon what firm foundation can this spiritual edifice rest?

16. Let us endeavour to do our best: beware of the poisonous reptiles—that is to say, the bad thoughts and aridities which are often permitted by God to assail and torment us so that we cannot repel them. Indeed, perchance we feel their sting! He allows this to teach us to be more on our guard in the future and to see whether we grieve much at offending Him. Therefore if you occasionally lapse into sin, do not lose heart and cease trying to advance, for God will draw good even out of our falls, like the merchant who sells theriac, who first takes poison, then the theriac, to prove the power of his elixir.¹³ This combat would suffice to teach us to amend our habits if we realized our failings in no other way, and would show us the injury we receive from a life of dissipation. Can any evil be greater than that we find at home? What peace can we hope to find elsewhere, if we have none within us? What friends or kindred can be so close and intimate as the powers of our soul, which, whether we will or no, must ever bear us company? These seem to wage war on us as if they knew the harm our vices had wrought them. 'Peace, peace be unto you,' my sisters, as our Lord said, and many a time proclaimed to His Apostles.¹⁴ Believe me, if we neither possess nor strive to obtain this peace at home, we shall never find it abroad.

17. By the blood which our Lord shed for us, I implore those who have not yet begun to enter into themselves, to stop this warfare: I beg those already started in the right path, not to let the

---

⁵ With Gedeon. Jud. vii. 5: 'Qui lingua lambuerint aquas, sicut solent canes lambere, separabis eos seorsum.'

⁶ Life, ch. xi 16.

⁷ St. Matt. vii. 26, 27: 'Qui ædificavit domum suam super arenam… et fuit ruina illius magna.'

⁸ Ps. lxxvii. 24: 'Pluit illis manna ad manducandum.' Way of Perf. ch. x. 4.

⁹ Life, ch. xii. 5.

¹⁰ Way of Perf. ch. xvii. 6; xxiii. 1.

¹¹ St. Matt. xx. 22: 'Nescitis quid petatis.'

¹² Way of Perf. ch. xvi. 2. Found. ch. v. 2, 3. Life, ch. iv. II; xi. 20.

¹³ A drug greatly in vogue until recent times. It was composed of all the essences supposed to contain life-giving and life-preserving qualities of animals and plants.

¹⁴ St. Luke xxiv. 36. St. John xx. 19.

combat turn them back from it. Let them reflect that a relapse is worse than a fall, and see what ruin it would bring. They should confide in God's mercy, trusting nothing in themselves; then they will see how His Majesty will lead them from one mansion to another, and will set them in a place where these wild beasts can no more touch or annoy them, but will be entirely at their mercy and merely objects of ridicule. Then, even in this life, they will enjoy a far greater happiness than they are able even to desire.

18. As I said at the beginning of this work, I have explained elsewhere[15] how you should behave when the devil thus disturbs you. I also told you that the habit of recollection is not to be gained by force of arms, but with calmness, which will enable you to practice it for a longer space of time.[16] I will say no more now, except that I think it very helpful for those of you who are beginners to consult persons experienced in such matters, lest you imagine that you are injuring yourselves by leaving your prayer to perform any necessary duties. This is not the case; our Lord will direct such things to our profit, although we may have no one to counsel us.[17] The only remedy for having given up a habit of recollection is to recommence it, otherwise the soul will continue to lose it more and more every day, and God grant it may realize its danger.

19. You may think, that if it is so very injurious to desist, it would have been better never to have begun, and to have remained outside the castle. But, as I began by saying, and as God Himself declares: 'He that loves danger shall perish by it,'[18] and the door by which we must enter this castle is prayer. Remember, we *must* get to heaven, and it would be madness to think we could do so without sometimes retiring into our souls so as to know ourselves, or thinking of our failings and of what we owe to God, or frequently imploring His mercy. Our Lord also says, 'No man cometh to the Father but by Me'[19] (I am not sure whether this quotation is correct, but I think so), and, 'He that seeth Me seeth the Father also.'[20]

20. If we never look up at Him and reflect on what we owe Him for having died for us, I do not understand how we can know Him, or perform good deeds in His service. What value is there in faith without works? and what are they worth if they are not united to the merits of Jesus Christ, our only good? What would incite us to love our Lord unless we thought of Him? May He give us grace to understand how much we cost Him; that 'the servant is not above his lord;'[21] that we must toil for Him if we would enjoy His glory; and prayer is a necessity to prevent us from constantly falling into temptation.[22]

---

[15] Life, ch. xi. and xix. 8. Way of Perfection, ch. xxiii. 3.

[16] Way of Perf. ch. xix. 3.

[17] Way of Perf. ch. xxiii. 3.

[18] Ecclus. iii. 27: 'Qui amat periculum, in illo peribit.'

[19] St. John xiv. 6: 'Nemo venit ad Patrem, nisi per Me.'

[20] St. John xiv. 9. 'Qui videt me, videt et Patrem.'

[21] St. Matt. x. 24: 'Nec servus super dominum suum.'

[22] St. Matt. xxvi. 41: 'Orate ut non intretis in tentationem.'

THE THIRD MANSIONS

CHAPTER I.

TREATS OF THE INSECURITY OF LIFE IN THIS EXILE, HOWEVER HIGH WE MAY BE RAISED, AND
OF HOW WE MUST ALWAYS WALK IN FEAR. CONTAINS SOME GOOD POINTS.

1. Souls in the Third Mansions. 2. Insecurity of this life. 3. Our danger of falling from grace. 4. The Saint bewails her past life. 5. Our Lady's patronage. 6. Fear necessary even for religious. 7. St. Teresa's contrition. 8. Characteristics of those in the Third Mansions. 9. The rich young man in the Gospel. 10. Reason of aridities in prayer. 11. Humility. 12. Tepidity. 13. We must give all to God. 14. Our debt. 15. Consolations and aridities.

1. As for those who, by the mercy of God, have vanquished in these combats and persevered until they reached the third mansions, what can we say to them but 'Blessed is the man that feareth the Lord'?[1] It is no small favour from God that I should be able to translate this verse into Spanish so as to explain its meaning, considering how dense I usually am in such matters. We may well call these souls blessed, for, as far as we can tell, unless they turn back in their course they are on the safe road to salvation. Now, my sisters, you see how important it is for them to conquer in their former struggles, for I am convinced that our Lord will henceforth never cease to keep them in security of conscience, which is no small boon.

2. I am wrong in saying 'security,' for there is no security in this life; understand that in such cases I always imply: 'If they do not cease to continue as they have begun.' What misery to live in this world! We are like men whose enemies are at the door, who must not lay aside their arms, even while sleeping or eating, and are always in dread lest the foe should enter the fortress by some breach in the walls. O my Lord and my all! How canst Thou wish us to prize such a wretched existence? We could not desist from longing and begging Thee to take us from it, were it not for the hope of losing it for Thy sake or devoting it entirely to Thy service—and above all because we know it is Thy will that we should live. Since it is so, 'Let us die with Thee!'[2] as St. Thomas said, for to be away from Thee is but to die again and again, haunted as we are by the dread of losing Thee for ever!

3. This is why I say, daughters, that we ought to ask our Lord as our boon to grant us one day to dwell in safety with the Saints, for with such fears, what pleasure can she enjoy whose only pleasure is to please God? Remember, many Saints have felt this as we do, and were even far more fervent, yet fell into grave sin, and we cannot be sure that God would stretch forth His hand to raise us from sin again to do such penance as they performed. This applies to extraordinary grace.[3] Truly, my daughters, I feel such terror as I tell you this, that I know not how to write it, nor even how to go on living, when I reflect upon it as I very often do. Beg of His Majesty, my daughters, to abide within me, for otherwise, what security could I feel, after a life so badly spent as mine has been?

4. Do not grieve at knowing this. I have often seen you troubled when I spoke about it, for you wish that my past had been a very holy one, in which you are right—indeed, I wish the same myself. But what can be done, now that I have wasted it entirely through my own fault? I have no right to complain that God withheld the aid I needed to fulfil your wishes. It is impossible for me to write this without tears and great shame, when I see that I am explaining these matters to those capable of teaching me. What a hard task has obedience laid, upon me! God grant that, as I do it for Him, it may be of some service to you; therefore beg Him to pardon me for my miserable presumption.

---

[1] Ps. cxi: 1. 'Beatus vir qui timet Dominum.'

[2] St. John xi. 16: 'Eamus et nos ut moriamur cum eo.'

[3] These last words, in the margin, but in the handwriting of the Saint, were scored through by one of the censors, but Fr. Luis de Leon wrote underneath, (as he did in other cases) 'Nothing to be crossed out.'

5. His Majesty knows that I have nothing to rely upon but His mercy; as I cannot cancel the past, I have no other remedy but to flee to Him, and to confide in the merits of His Son and of His Virgin Mother, whose habit, unworthy as I am, I wear as you do also. Praise Him, then, my daughters, for making you truly daughters of our Lady, so that you need not blush for my wickedness as you have such a good Mother. Imitate her; think how great she must be and what a blessing it is for you to have her for a patroness, since my sins and evil character have brought no tarnish on the luster of our holy Order.

6. Still I must give you one warning: be not too confident because you are nuns and the daughters of such a Mother. David was very holy, yet you know what Solomon became.[4] Therefore do not rely on your enclosure, on your penitential life, nor on your continual exercise of prayer and constant communion with God, nor trust in having left the world or in the idea that you hold its ways in horror. All this is good, but is not enough, as I have already said, to remove all fear; therefore meditate on this text and often recall it: 'Blessed is the man that feareth the Lord.'[5]

7. I do not recollect what I was saying, and have digressed very much: for when I think of myself my mind cannot soar to higher things but is like a bird with broken wings; so I will leave this subject for the present.

8. To return to what I began to explain about the souls which have entered the third mansions. God has shown them no small favour, but a very great one, in enabling them to pass through the first difficulties. Thanks to His mercy I believe there are many such people in the world: they are very desirous not to offend His Majesty even by venial sins, they love penance and spend hours in meditation, they employ their time well, exercise themselves in works of charity to their neighbours, are well-ordered in their conversation and dress, and those who own a household govern it well. This is certainly to be desired, and there appears no reason to forbid their entrance to the last mansions; nor will our Lord deny it them if they desire it, for this is the right disposition for receiving all His favours.

9. O Jesus! can any one declare that he does not desire this great blessing, especially after he has passed through the chief difficulties? No; no one can! We all say we desire it, but there is need of more than that for the Lord to possess entire dominion over the soul. It is not enough to say so, any more than it was enough for the young man when our Lord told him what he must do if he desired to be perfect.[6] Since I began to speak of these dwelling-rooms I have him constantly before my mind, for we are exactly like him; this very frequently produces the great dryness we feel in prayer, though sometimes it proceeds from other causes as well. I am not speaking of certain interior sufferings which give intolerable pain to many devout souls through no fault of their own; from these trials, however, our Lord always delivers them with much profit to themselves. I also except people who suffer from melancholy and other infirmities. But in these cases, as in all others, we must leave aside the judgments of God.

10. I hold that these effects usually result from the first cause I mentioned; such souls know that nothing would induce them to commit a sin (many of them would not even commit a venial sin advertently), and that they employ their life and riches well. They cannot, therefore, patiently endure to be excluded from the presence of our King, Whose vassals they consider themselves, as indeed they are. An earthly king may have many subjects yet all do not enter his court. Enter then, enter, my daughters, into your interior; pass beyond the thought of your own petty works, which are no more, nor even as much, as Christians are bound to perform: let it suffice that you are God's servants, do not pursue so much as to catch nothing.[7] Think of the saints, who have entered the Divine Presence, and you will see the difference between them and ourselves.

11. Do not ask for what you do not deserve, nor should we ever think, however much we may have done for God, that we merit the reward of the saints, for we have offended Him. Oh,

---

[4] St. Teresa wrote 'Solomon'; Father Gracian corrected 'Absalom,' and Fr. Luis de Leon restored the original text.

[5] Ps. cxi. 1

[6] Matt. xix. 21

[7] Proverbially, like 'having too many irons in the fire.'

humility, humility! I know not why, but I am always tempted to think that persons who complain so much of aridities must be a little wanting in this virtue. However, I am not speaking of severe interior sufferings, which are far worse than a want of devotion.

12. Let us try ourselves, my sisters, or let our Lord try us; He knows well how to do so (although we often pretend to misunderstand Him). We will now speak of these well-ordered souls. Let us consider what they do for God and we shall see at once what little right we have to murmur against His Majesty. If we turn our backs on Him and go away sorrowfully like the youth in the Gospel[8] when He tells us what to do to be perfect, what can God do? for He must proportion the reward to our love for Him. This love, my daughters, must not be the fabric of our imagination; we must prove it by our works. Yet do not suppose that our Lord has need of any works of ours; He only expels us to manifest our goodwill.[9]

13. It seems to us we have done everything by taking the religious habit of our own will, and renouncing worldly things and all our possessions for God (although they may have been but the nets of St. Peter,[10] yet they seemed much to us, for they were our all). This is an excellent disposition: if we continue in it and do not return, even in desire, to the company of the reptiles of the first rooms, doubtless, by persevering in this poverty and detachment of soul, we shall obtain all for which we strive. But, mark this—it must be on one condition—that we 'hold ourselves for unprofitable servants,'[11] as we are told either by St. Paul or by Christ, and that we do not consider that our Lord is bound to grant us any favours, but that, as we have received more from Him, we are the deeper in His debt.

14. How little is all we can do for so generous a God, Who died for us, Who created us, Who gives us being, that we should not think ourselves happy to be able to acquit ourselves of part of the debt we owe Him for having served us, without asking Him for fresh mercies and favours? I am loath to use this expression, yet so it is, for He did nothing else during the whole time He lived in this world but serve us.

15. Think well my daughters, over some of the points I have treated, although confusedly, for I do not know how to explain them better. Our Lord will make you understand them, that you may reap humility from your dryness, instead of the disquietude the devil strives to cause by it. I believe that where true humility exists, although God should never bestow consolations, yet He gives a peace and resignation which make the soul happier than are others with sensible devotion. These consolations, as you have read, are often given by the Divine Majesty to the weakest souls who, I suppose would not exchange them for the fortitude of Christians serving God in aridities: we love consolations better than the cross! Do Thou, O Lord, Who knowest all truth, so prove us that we may know ourselves.

CHAPTER II.

CONTINUES THE SAME SUBJECT AND SPEAKS OF ARIDITIES IN PRAYER AND THEIR RESULTS: OF THE NECESSITY OF TRYING OURSELVES AND HOW OUR LORD PROVES THOSE WHO ARE IN THESE MANSIONS.

1. Imperfections of dwellers in the first three mansions. 2. Our trials show us our weakness. 3. Humility learnt by our faults. 4. Love of money. 5. Liberty of spirit. 6. On bearing contempt. 7. Detachment proved by trials. 8. Virtue and humility are the essentials. 9. Perfection requires detachment. 10. We should try to make rapid progress. 11. Leave our cares in God's hands. 12. Humility more necessary than corporal penances. 13. Consolations rarely received until the fourth mansions. 14. Advantages of hearing of them. 15. Perfection consists in love, not in reward. 16. St. Teresa's joy at seeing other souls favoured. 17. These graces should be striven for. 18. Obedience and direction, 19. Misguided zeal for others.

---

8 St. Mark. x. 22. Way of Perf. ch. xvii. 5.
9 Rel. ix. 15.
10 St. Matt. iv. 20: 'Relictis retibus secuti sunt eum.'
11 St. Luke xvii. 10: 'Servi inutiles sumus: quod debuimus facere fecimus.'

1. I HAVE known some, in fact, I may say numerous souls, who have reached this state, and for many years lived, apparently, a regular and well-ordered life, both of body and mind. It would seem that they must have gained the mastery over this world, or at least be extremely detached from it, yet if His Majesty sends very moderate trials they become so disturbed and disheartened as not only to astonish but to make me anxious about them. Advice is useless; having practiced virtue for so long they think themselves capable of teaching it, and believe that they have abundant reason to feel miserable.

2. The only way to help them is to compassionate their troubles;[12] indeed, one cannot but feel sorry at seeing people in such an unhappy state. They must not be argued with, for they are convinced they suffer only for God's sake, and cannot be made to understand they are acting imperfectly, which is a further error in persons so far advanced. No wonder that they should feel these trials for a time, but I think they ought speedily to overcome their concern about such matters. God, wishing His elect to realize their own misery, often temporarily withdraws His favours: no more is needed to prove to us in a very short time what we really are.[13]

3. Souls soon learn in this way; they perceive their faults very clearly, and sometimes the discovery of how quickly they are overcome by but slight earthly trials is more painful than the subtraction of God's sensible favours. I consider that God thus shows them great mercy, for though their behaviour may be faulty, yet they gain greatly in humility. Not so with the people of whom I first spoke; they believe their conduct is saintly, and wish others to agree with them. I will give you some examples which will help us to understand and to try ourselves, without waiting for God to try us, since it would be far better to have prepared and examined ourselves beforehand.

4. A rich man, without son or heir, loses part of his property,[14] but still has more than enough to keep himself and his household. If this misfortune grieves and disquiets him as though he were left to beg his bread, how can our Lord ask him to give up all things for His sake? This man will tell you he regrets losing his money because he wished to bestow it on the poor.

5. I believe His Majesty would prefer me to conform to His will, and keep peace of soul while attending to my interests, to such charity as this. If this person cannot resign himself because God has not raised him so high in virtue, well and good: let him know that he is wanting in liberty of spirit; let him beg our Lord to grant it him, and be rightly disposed to receive it. Another person has more than sufficient means to live on, when an opportunity occurs for acquiring more property: if it is offered him, by all means let him accept it; but if he must go out of his way to obtain it and then continues working to gain more and more—however good his intention may be (and it must be good, for I am speaking of people who lead prayerful and good lives), he cannot possibly enter the mansions near the King.

6. Something of the same sort happens if such people meet with contempt or want of due respect. God often gives them grace to bear it well, as He loves to see virtue upheld in public, and will not have it condemned in those who practice it, or else because these persons have served Him faithfully, and He, our supreme Good, is exceedingly good to us all; nevertheless, these persons are disturbed, and cannot overcome or get rid of the feeling for some time.[15] Alas! have they not long meditated on the pains our Lord endured and how well it is for us to suffer, and have even longed to do so? They wish every one were as virtuous as they are; and God grant they do not consider other people to blame for their troubles and attribute merit to themselves!

7. You may think, my daughters, that I have wandered from the subject, for all this does not concern you: nothing of the sort occurs to us here, where we neither own nor wish for any property, nor endeavour to gain it, and no one does us any wrong. The instances I have mentioned do not coincide exactly, yet conclusions applicable to us may be drawn from them, which it would be neither well nor necessary to state. These will teach you whether you are really detached from

---

[12] See letter concerning Francisco de Salcedo. Nov. 1576. Vol. II.
[13] Way of Perf. ch, xxxviii. 7.
[14] Way of Perf. ch, xxxviii, 10. Concep. ch. ii. 11, 12. Life, xi. 3.
[15] Way of Perf.. ch. xxxviii. 12.

all you have left; trifling occasions often occur, although perhaps not quite of the same kind, by which you can prove to yourselves whether you have obtained the mastery over your passions.

8. Believe me, the question is not whether we wear the religious habit or not, but whether we practice the virtues and submit our will in all things to the will of God. The object of our life must be to do what He requires of us: let us not ask that *our* will may be done, but *His*. If we have not yet attained to this, let us be humble, as I said above. Humility is the ointment for our wounds; if we have it, although perhaps He may defer His coming for a time, God, Who is our Physician, will come and heal us.

9. The penances performed by the persons I spoke of are as well regulated as their life, which they value very highly because they wish to serve our Lord with it—in which there is nothing to blame—so they are very discreet in their mortifications lest they should injure their health. Never fear they will kill themselves: they are far too sensible! Their love is not strong enough to overcome their reason; I wish it were—that they might not be content to creep on their way to God: a pace that will never bring them to their journey's end!

10. We seem to ourselves to be making progress, yet we become weary, for, believe me, we are walking through a mist; it will be fortunate if we do not lose ourselves. Do you think, my daughters, if we could travel from one country to another in eight days, that it would be well to spend a year on the journey, through wind, snow, and inundations and over bad roads?[16] Would it not be better to get it over at once, for it is full of dangers and serpents? Oh, how many striking instances could I give you of this! God grant that I have passed beyond this state myself: often I think that I have not.

11. All things obstruct us while prudence rules our actions; we are afraid of everything and therefore fear to make progress—as if we could reach the inner chambers while others make the journey for us! As this is impossible, sisters, for the love of God let us exert ourselves, and leave our reason and our fears in His hands, paying no attention to the weaknesses of nature which might retard us. Let our Superiors, to whom the charge belongs, look after our bodies; let our only care be to hasten to our Lord's presence—for though there are few or no indulgences to be obtained here, yet, regard for health might mislead us and it would be none the better for our care, as I know well.

12. I know, too, that our bodies are not the chief factors in the work we have before us; they are accessory: extreme humility is the principal point. It is the want of this, I believe, that stops people's progress. It may seem that we have made but little way: we should believe that is the case, and that our sisters are advancing much more rapidly than we are. Not only should we wish others to consider us the worst of all; we should endeavour to make them think so. If we act in this manner, our soul will do well; otherwise we shall make no progress and shall always remain the prey to a thousand troubles and miseries. The way will be difficult and wearisome without self-renunciation, weighed down as we are by the burden and frailties of human nature, which are no longer felt in the more interior mansions.

13. In these third mansions the Lord never fails to repay our services, both as a just and even as a merciful God, Who always bestows on us far more than we deserve, giving us greater happiness than could be obtained from any earthly pleasures and amusements. I think He grants few consolations here, except, perhaps, occasionally to entice us to prepare ourselves to enter the last mansions by showing us their contents. There may *appear* to you to be no difference except in name between sensible devotion, and consolations and you may ask why I distinguish them. I think there *is* a very great difference, but I may be mistaken.

14. This will be best explained while writing of the fourth mansion, which comes next, when I must speak of the consolations received there from our Lord. The subject may appear futile, yet may prove useful by urging souls who know what each mansion contains to strive to enter the best. It will solace those whom God has advanced so far; others, who thought they had reached the summit, will be abashed, yet if they are humble they will be led to thank God.

---

[16] St. Teresa very probably had in her mind her journey, to make a foundation at Seville, when the boat, which was crossing the Guadalquivir, narrowly escaped being carried down the river by the current. Found. ch. xxiv, 6

15. Those who do not receive these consolations may feel a despondency that is uncalled for, since perfection does not consist in consolation but in greater love; our reward will be in proportion to this, and to the justice and sincerity of our actions. Perhaps you wonder, then, why I treat of these interior favours and their nature. I do not know; ask him who bade me write this. I must obey Superiors, not argue with them, which I have no right to do.

16. I assure you that when I had neither received these favours,[17] nor understood them by experience, or ever expected to (and rightly so, for I should have felt reassured if I had known or even conjectured that I was pleasing to God in any way), yet when I read of the mercies and consolations that our Lord grants to His servants, I was delighted and praised Him fervently. If such as myself acted thus, how much more would the humble and good glorify Him! I think it is worth while to explain these subjects and show what consolations and delights we lose through our own fault, if only for the sake of moving a single soul to praise God once.

17. When these joys are from God they come laden with love and strength, which aid the soul on its way and increase its good works and virtues. Do not imagine that it is unimportant whether you try to obtain these graces or no; if you are not to blame, the Lord is just: what He refuses in one way, His Majesty will give you in another, as He knows how; His secret ways are very mysterious, and doubtless He will do what is best for you.

18. Souls who by God's mercy are brought so far (which, as I said, is no small mercy, for they are likely to ascend still higher) will be greatly benefited by practicing prompt obedience. Even if they are not in the religious state, it would be well if they, like certain other people, were to take a director,[18] so as never to follow their own will, which is the cause of most of our ills. They should not choose one of their own turn of mind[19] (as the saying goes), who is over prudent in his actions, but should select one thoroughly detached from worldly things; it is very helpful to consult a person who has learnt and can teach this. It is encouraging to see that trials which seemed to us impossible to submit to are possible to others, and that they bear them sweetly. Their flight makes us try to soar, like nestlings taught by the elder birds, who, though they cannot fly far at first, little by little imitate their parents: I know the great benefit of this. However determined such persons may be not to offend our Lord, they must not expose themselves to temptation: they are still near the first mansions to which they might easily return. Their strength is not yet established on a solid foundation like that of souls exercised in sufferings, who know how little cause there is to fear the tempests of this world and care nothing for its pleasures: beginners might succumb before any severe trial. Some great persecution, such as the devil knows how to raise to injure us, might make beginners turn back; while zealously trying to withdraw others from sin they might succumb to the attacks made upon them.

19. Let us look at our own faults, and not at other persons'. People who are extremely correct themselves are often shocked at everything they see;[20] however, we might often learn a great deal that is essential from the very persons whom we censure. Our exterior comportment and manners may be better—this is well enough, but not of the first importance. We ought not to insist on every one following in our footsteps, nor to take upon ourselves to give instructions in spirituality when, perhaps, we do not even know what it is. Zeal for the good of souls, though given us by God, may often lead us astray, sisters; it is best to keep our rule, which bids us ever to live in silence and in hope.[21] Our Lord will care for the souls belonging to Him; and if we beg His Majesty to do so, by His grace we shall be able to aid them greatly. May He be for ever blessed!

---

[17] Life, ch. xii. 2. Rel. vii. 3.

[18] Life. ch. xiii. 29.

[19] Rel. vii. 18.

[20] Way of Perf. ch. vii. 6. Castle, M. I. ch. ii. 20, 21.

[21] Isa. xxx. 15: 'In silentio et in spe erit fortitudo vestra.' Rule Sec. 13.

THE FOURTH MANSIONS

CHAPTER I.

HOW SWEETNESS AND TENDERNESS IN PRAYER DIFFER FROM CONSOLATIONS. EXPLAINS HOW ADVANTAGEOUS IT WAS FOR ST. TERESA TO COMPREHEND THAT THE IMAGINATION AND THE UNDERSTANDING ARE NOT THE SAME THING. THIS CHAPTER IS USEFUL FOR THOSE WHOSE THOUGHTS WANDER MUCH DURING PRAYER.

1. Graces received in this mansion. 2. Mystic favours. 3. Temptations bring humility and merit. 4. Sensible devotion and natural joys. 5. Sweetness in devotion. 6. St. Teresa's experience of it. 7. Love of God, and how to foster it. 8. Distractions. 9. They do not destroy divine union. 10. St. Teresa's physical distractions. 11. How to treat distractions. 12. They should be disregarded. 13. Self-knowledge necessary.

1. Now that I commence writing about the fourth mansions, it is requisite, as I said,[1] to commend myself to the Holy Ghost and to beg Him henceforth to speak for me, that I may be enabled to treat these matters intelligibly. Henceforth they begin to be supernatural and it will be most difficult to speak clearly about them,[2] unless His Majesty undertakes it for me, as He did when I explained the subject (as far as I understood it) somewhat about fourteen years ago.[3] I believe I now possess more light about the favours God grants some souls, but that is different from being able to elucidate them.[4] May His Majesty enable me to do so if it would be useful, but not otherwise.

2. As these mansions are nearer the King's dwelling they are very beautiful, and so subtle are the things seen and heard in them, that, as those tell us who have tried to do so, the mind cannot give a lucid idea of them to those inexperienced in the matter. People who have enjoyed these favours, especially if it was to any great extent, will easily comprehend me.

3. Apparently a person must have dwelt for a long time in the former mansions before entering these; although in ordinary cases the soul must have been in the last one spoken of, yet, as you must often have heard, there is no fixed rule, for God gives when, how, and to whom He wills[5]—the goods are His own, and His choice wrongs no one.[6] The poisonous reptiles rarely come into these rooms, and, if they enter, do more good than harm. I think it is far better for them to get in and make war on the soul in this state of prayer; were it not tempted, the devil might sometimes deceive it about divine consolations, thus injuring it far more. Besides, the soul would benefit less, because all occasions of gaining merit would be withdrawn, were it left continually

---

[1] First Mansions, ch. i. 1.

[2] There are two kinds of contemplation: acquired or natural, and infused or supernatural. In their widest sense, including many remarkable phenomena of Natural religion, and, of course, the most wonderful manifestations recorded in the Old Testament, they form the system called Mysticism and are the proper object of Mystical theology. Natural or acquired contemplation is based upon an idealistic turn of mind which enables the soul to gaze upon the Godhead (simple gaze, as St. Teresa calls it) without approaching Him by the laborious process of reasoning, and in so doing embraces Him with its affective powers; like a person who, devoid of technical skill, takes in and is enamoured by, the beauty of a painting. Infused contemplation is the highest act of the Gifts of the Holy Ghost of Knowledge and Wisdom. It is often impossible, nor is it always essential, to determine where acquired contemplation ends and infused contemplation begins. But it should be borne in mind that both the one and the other are operations and not merely a passive state or mere fruition. Even the highest form of contemplation, the Beatific Vision, is a supernatural act of the soul, an operation of unending duration. A ship moved by a gentle breeze is rightly said to be actually sailing though the rowers are at rest.

[3] Life, ch. xii. 11.

[4] Life, ch. xvii. 7.

[5] Philippus a SS. Trinitate, Summa Tleologiæ Mysticæ, pars iii. tract. i. disc. iii. art. 2. Life, ch. xv. 11, xxii. 22, 23. Way of Perf. ch. xvi. 4, xli. 2. Concep. ch. v. 3.

[6] S. Matt. xx. 15: 'Aut non licet mihi quod volo facere?'

absorbed in God. I am not confident that this absorption is genuine when it always remains in the same state, nor does it appear to me possible for the Holy Ghost to dwell constantly within us, to the same extent, during our earthly exile.

4. I will now describe, as I promised, the difference between sweetness in prayer and spiritual consolations. It appears to me that what we acquire for ourselves in meditation and petitions to our Lord may be termed 'sweetness in devotion.'[7] It is natural, although ultimately aided by the grace of God. I must be understood to imply this in all I say, for we can do nothing without Him. This sweetness arises principally from the good work we perform, and appears to result from our labours: well may we feel happy at having thus spent our time. We shall find, on consideration, that many temporal matters give us the same pleasure—such as unexpectedly coming into a large fortune, suddenly meeting with a dearly-loved friend, or succeeding in any important or influential affair which makes a sensation in the world. Again, it would be felt by one who had been told her husband, brother, or son was dead, and who saw him return to her alive. I have seen people weep from such happiness, as I have done myself. I consider both these joys and those we feel in religious matters to be natural ones. Although there is nothing wrong about the former, yet those produced by devotion spring from a more noble source—in short, they begin in ourselves and end in God. Spiritual consolations, on the contrary, arise from God, and our nature feels them and rejoices as keenly in them, and indeed far more keenly, than in the others I described.

5. O Jesus! how I wish I could elucidate this point! It seems to me that I can perfectly distinguish the difference between the two joys, yet I have not the skill to make myself understood; may God give it me! I remember a verse we say at Prime at the end of the final Psalm; the last words are: 'Cum dilatasti cor meum'—'When Thou didst dilate my heart:[8] To those with much experience, this suffices to show the difference between sweetness in prayer and spiritual consolations; other people will require more explanation. The sensible devotion I mentioned does not dilate the heart, but generally appears to narrow it slightly; although joyful at seeing herself work for God, yet such a person sheds tears of sorrow which seem partly produced by the passions. I know little about the passions of the soul, or I could write of them more clearly and could better define what comes from the sensitive disposition and what is natural, having passed through this state myself, but I am very stupid. Knowledge and learning are a great advantage to every one.

6. My own experience of this delight and sweetness in meditation was that when I began to weep over the Passion I could not stop until I had a severe headache;[9] the same thing occurred when I grieved over my sins: this was a great grace from our Lord. I do not intend to inquire now which of these states of prayer is the better, but I wish I knew how to explain the difference between the two. In that of which I speak, the tears and good desires are often partly caused by the natural disposition, but although this may be the case, yet, as I said, these feelings terminate in God. Sensible devotion is very desirable if the soul is humble enough to understand that it is not more holy on account of these sentiments, which cannot always with certainty be ascribed to charity, and even then are still the gift of God.

7. These feelings of devotion are most common with souls in the first three mansions, who are nearly always using their understanding and reason in making meditations. This is good for them, for they have not been given grace for more; they should, however, try occasionally to elicit some acts such as praising God, rejoicing in His goodness and that He is what He is: let them desire that He may be honoured and glorified. They must do this as best they can, for it greatly inflames the will. Let them be very careful, when God gives these sentiments, not to set them aside in order to finish their accustomed meditation. But, having spoken fully on this subject

---

[7] Way of Perf., ch. xix. 8. Castle, M. iv. ch. ii. 4. The first three mansions of the Interior Castle correspond with the 'first water,' or the prayer of Meditation, explained in ch. xi-xiii. of the Life; the fourth mansion, or the prayer of Quiet, with the 'second water,' Life, ch. xiv. and xv.; the fifth mansion, or the prayer of Union, with the 'third water,' Life, ch. xvi. and xvii.; and the sixth mansion, ecstasy, etc., with the 'fourth water,' Life, ch. xviii.-xxi.

[8] Ps. cxviii. 32. Way of Perf. ch. xxviii. 11.

[9] Life, ch. iii. 1.

elsewhere,[10] I will say no more now. I only wish to warn you that to make rapid progress and to reach the mansions we wish to enter, it is not so essential to *think* much as to *love* much: therefore you must practice whatever most excites you to this. Perhaps we do not know what love is, nor does this greatly surprise me. Love does not consist in great sweetness of devotion, but in a fervent determination to strive to please God in all things, in avoiding, as far as possible, all that would offend Him, and in praying for the increase of the glory and honour of His Son and for the growth of the Catholic Church. These are the signs of love; do not imagine that it consists in never thinking of anything but God, and that if your thoughts wander a little all is lost.[11]

8. I, myself, have sometimes been troubled by this turmoil of thoughts. I learnt by experience, but little more than four years ago, that our thoughts, or it is clearer to call it our imagination, are not the same thing as the understanding. I questioned a theologian on the subject; he told me it was the fact, which consoled me not a little. As the understanding is one of the powers of the soul, it puzzled me to see it so sluggish at times, while, as a rule, the imagination takes flight at once, so that God alone can control it by so uniting us to Himself[12] that we seem, in a manner, detached from our bodies. It puzzled me to see that while to all appearance the powers of the soul were occupied with God and recollected in Him, the imagination was wandering elsewhere.

9. Do Thou, O Lord, take into account all that we suffer in this way through our ignorance. We err in thinking that we need only know that we must keep our thoughts fixed on Thee. We do not understand that we should consult those better instructed than ourselves, nor are we aware that there is anything for us to learn. We pass through terrible trials, on account of not understanding our own nature and take what is not merely harmless, but good, for a grave fault. This causes the sufferings felt by many people, particularly by the unlearned, who practice prayer. They complain of interior trials, become melancholy, lose their health, and even give up prayer altogether for want of recognizing that we have within ourselves as it were, an interior world. We cannot stop the revolution of the heavens as they rush with velocity upon their course, neither can we control our imagination. When this wanders we at once imagine that all the powers of the soul follow it; we think everything is lost, and that the time spent in God's presence is wasted. Meanwhile, the soul is perhaps entirely united to Him in the innermost mansions, while the imagination is in the precincts of the castle, struggling with a thousand wild and venomous creatures and gaining merit by its warfare. Therefore we need not let ourselves be disturbed, nor give up prayer, as the devil is striving to persuade us. As a rule, all our anxieties and troubles come from misunderstanding our own nature.

10. Whilst writing this I am thinking of the loud noise in my head which I mentioned in the Introduction, and which has made it almost impossible to obey the command given me to write this. It sounds as if there were a number of rushing waterfalls within my brain, while in other parts, drowned by the sound of the waters, are the voices of birds singing and whistling. This tumult is not in my ears, but in the upper part of my head, where, they say, is placed the superior part of the soul. I have long thought that this must be so because the flight of the spirit seems to take place from this part with great velocity.[13] Please God I may recollect to explain the cause when writing of the latter mansions, this not being the proper place for it. It may be that God has sent this suffering in my head to help me to understand the matter, for all this tumult in my brain does not interfere with my prayer, nor with my speaking to you, but the great calm and love and desires in my soul remain undisturbed and my mind is clear.

11. How, then, can the superior part of the soul remain undisturbed if it resides in the upper part of the brain? I cannot account for it, but am sure that I am speaking the truth. This noise disturbs my prayer when unaccompanied with ecstasy, but when it is ecstatic I do not feel any pain, however great. I should suffer keenly were I forced to cease praying on account of these infirmities. We should not be distressed by reason of our thoughts, nor allow ourselves to be worried by them: if they come from the devil, he will let us alone if we take no notice of them; and if they are, as often happens, one of the many frailties entailed by Adam's sin, let us be patient

---

[10] Life, ch. xii. 2-4..
[11] Found. ch. v. 2. Way of Perf. ch. xxxi. 6, 12. Life, ch. xv, 16, ch. XXX. 19.
[12] Life, ch. xv. 9, 10.
[13] Second Relation addressed to Fr. Rodrigo Alvarez.

and suffer them for the love of God. Likewise, since we must eat and sleep without being able to avoid it, much to our grief, let us acknowledge that we are human, and long to be where no one may despise us.[14] Sometimes I recall these words, spoken by the Spouse in the Canticle;[15] truly never in our lives have we better reason to say them, for I think no earthly scorn or suffering can try us so severely as these struggles within our souls. All uneasiness or conflict can be borne while we have peace in ourselves, as I said; but if, while seeking for rest amidst the thousand trials of the world—knowing that God has prepared this rest for us—the obstacle is found in ourselves, the trial must prove painful and almost insufferable.

12. Take us therefore, O Lord, to where these miseries can no longer cause us to be despised, for sometimes it seems as if they mocked our souls. Even in this life God delivers us from them when we reach the last mansion, as by His grace I will show you. Everybody is not so violently distressed and assaulted by these weaknesses as I have been for many years,[16] on account of my wickedness, so that it seems as if I strove to take vengeance on myself.[17] Since I suffer so much in this way, perhaps you may do the same, so I shall continue to explain the subject to you in different ways, in order to find some means of making it clear. The thing is inevitable, therefore do not let it disturb or grieve you, but let the mill clack on while we grind our wheat; that is, let us continue to work with our will and intellect.

13. These troubles annoy us more or less according to the state of our health or in different circumstances. The poor soul suffers; although not now to blame, it has sinned at other times, and must be patient. We are so ignorant that what we have read and been told has not sufficed to teach us to disregard wandering thoughts, therefore I shall not be wasting time in instructing and consoling you about these trials. However, this will help you but little until God chooses to enlighten you, and additional measures are needed: His Majesty wishes us to learn by ordinary means to understand ourselves and to recognize the share taken in these troubles by our wandering imagination, our nature, and the devil's temptations, instead of laying all the blame on our souls.

CHAPTER II.

CONTINUES THE SAME SUBJECT, EXPLAINING BY A COMPARISON IN WHAT DIVINE CONSOLATIONS CONSIST: AND HOW WE OUGHT TO TRY TO PREPARE OURSELVES TO RECEIVE THEM, WITHOUT ENDEAVOURING TO OBTAIN THEM.

1. Physical results of sensible devotion. 2. Effects of divine consolations. 3. The two fountains. 4. They symbolize two kinds of prayer. 5. Divine consolations shared by body and soul. 6. The incense within the soul. 7. Graces received in this prayer. 8. Such favours not to be sought after.

1. GOD help me! how I have wandered from my subject! I forget what I was speaking about, for my occupations and ill-health often force me to cease writing until some more suitable time. The sense will be very disconnected; as my memory is extremely bad and I have no time to read over what is written, even what I really understand is expressed very vaguely, at least so I fear. I think I said that spiritual consolations are occasionally connected with the passions. These feelings of devotion produce fits of sobbing; I have even heard that sometimes they cause a compression of the chest, and uncontrollable exterior motions violent enough to cause bleeding at the nose and other painful effects.[18]

2. I can say nothing about this, never having experienced anything of the kind myself; but there appears some cause for comfort in it, because, as I said, all ends in the desire to please God and to enjoy His presence. What I call divine consolations, or have termed elsewhere the 'prayer

---

[14] Way of Perf. ch. xxxiii. 8. Life, ch. xxi. S. Rel. ii. 12.

[15] According to Fr. Gracian the Saint here refers to Cant. viii. 1: 'Et jam me nemo despiciat.'

[16] Way of Perf. ch. xvii. 2.

[17] Way of Perf. ch. xxxi. 9.

[18] 'A clear description of an attack of hysteria with the significant remark that she herself had never experienced anything of the kind'. (Dr. Goix, quoted by P. Grégoire, La prétendue hystérie de Sainte Thérèse, Lyon, Vitte, 1895, p. 53.)

of quiet,' is a very different thing, as those will understand who, by the mercy of God, have experienced them.

3. To make the matter clearer, let us imagine we see two fountains with basins which fill with water. I can find no simile more appropriate than water by which to explain spiritual things, as I am very ignorant and have poor wits to help me.[19] Besides, I love this element so much that I have studied it more attentively than other things. God, Who is so great, so wise, has doubtless hidden secrets in all things He created, which we should greatly benefit by knowing, as those say who understand such matters. Indeed, I believe that in each smallest creature He has made, though it be but a tiny ant, there are more wonders than can be comprehended. These two basins are filled in different ways; the one with water from a distance flowing into it through many pipes and waterworks, while the other basin is built near the source of the spring itself and fills quite noiselessly. If the fountain is plentiful, like the one we speak of, after the basin is full the water overflows in a great stream which flows continually. No machinery is needed here, nor does the water run through aqueducts.

4. Such is the difference between the two kinds of prayer. The water running through the aqueducts resembles sensible devotion, which is obtained by meditation. We gain it by our thoughts, by meditating on created things, and by the labour of our minds; in short, it is the result of our endeavours, and so makes the commotion I spoke of, while profiting the soul.[20] The other fountain, like divine consolations, receives the water from the source itself, which signifies God: as usual, when His Majesty wills to bestow on us any supernatural favours, we experience the greatest peace, calm, and sweetness in the inmost depths of our being; I know neither where nor how.

5. This joy is not, like earthly happiness, at once felt by the heart; after gradually filling it to the brim, the delight overflows throughout all the mansions and faculties, until at last it reaches the body. Therefore, I say it arises from God and ends in ourselves, for whoever experiences it will find that the whole physical part of our nature shares in this delight and sweetness. While writing this I have been thinking that the verse 'Dilatasti cor meum,' 'Thou hast dilated my heart,'[21] declares that the heart is dilated. This joy does not appear to me to originate in the heart, but in some more interior part and, as it were, in the depths of our being. I think this must be the centre of the soul, as I have since learnt and will explain later on. I discover secrets within us which often fill me with astonishment: how many more must there be unknown to me! O my Lord and my God! how stupendous is Thy grandeur! We are like so many foolish peasant lads: we think we know something of Thee, yet it must be comparatively nothing, for there are profound secrets even in ourselves of which we know naught. I say 'comparatively nothing' in proportion with all the secrets hidden within Thee, yet how great are Thy mysteries that we are acquainted with and can learn even by the study of such of Thy works as we see![22]

6. To return to the verse I quoted, which may help to explain the dilation begun by the celestial waters in the depths of our being. They appear to dilate and enlarge us internally, and benefit us in an inexplicable manner, nor does even the soul itself understand what it receives. It is conscious of what may be described as a certain fragrance, as if within its inmost depths were a brazier sprinkled with sweet perfumes. Although the spirit neither sees the flame nor knows where it is, yet it is penetrated by the warmth, and scented fumes, which are even sometimes perceived by the body. Understand me, the soul does not feel any real heat or scent, but something far more subtle, which I use this metaphor to explain. Let those who have never experienced it believe that it really occurs to others: the soul is conscious of it and feels it more distinctly than can be expressed. It is not a thing we can fancy or gain by anything we can do; clearly it does not arise from the base coin of human nature, but from the most pure gold of Divine Wisdom. I believe that in this case the powers of the soul are not united to God, but are absorbed and

---

[19] Way of Perf. ch. xix. 5; also St. John of the Cross, Ascent of Mount Carmel, bk. ii, ch. xiv, 2, and xxi. 3.

[20] Life, ch. x. 2.

[21] Ps. cxviii. 32. Life, ch. xvii. 14,

[22] Life, ch. xiv. 9. Way of Perf. ch. xxviii. 11.

astounded at the marvel before them. I may possibly be contradicting what I wrote elsewhere;[23] nor would this be surprising, for it was done about fifteen years ago, and perhaps God has given me since then a clearer insight into the matter. I may be entirely mistaken on the subject, both then and now, but never do I willfully say what is untrue. No; by the mercy of God, I would rather die a thousand times than tell a falsehood: I speak of the matter as I understand it. I believe that in this case the will must in some way be united with that of God. The after effects on the soul, and the subsequent behaviour of the person, show whether this prayer was genuine or no: this is the best crucible by which to test it.

7. Our Lord bestows a signal grace on the soul if it realizes how great is this favour, and another greater still if it does not turn back on the right road. You are longing, my daughters, to enter into this state of prayer at once, and you are right, for, as I said, the soul cannot understand the value of the graces there bestowed by God upon it, nor the love which draws Him ever closer to it: we should certainly desire to learn how to obtain this favour. I will tell you what I know about it, setting aside certain cases in which God bestows these graces for no other reason than His own choice, into which we have no right to enquire.

8. Practice what I advised in the preceding mansions, then—humility, humility! for God lets Himself be vanquished by this and grants us all we ask.[24] The first proof[25] that you possess humility is that you neither think you now deserve these graces and consolations from God, nor that you ever will as long as you live. You ask me: 'How shall we receive them, if we do not try to gain them?' I answer, that there is no surer way to obtain them than the one I have told you, therefore make no efforts to acquire them, for the following reasons. The first is, that the chief means of obtaining them is to love God without self-interest. The second, that it is a slight lack of humility to think that our wretched services can win so great a reward. The third, that the real preparation for them is to desire to suffer and imitate our Lord, rather than to receive consolations, for indeed we have all offended Him. The fourth reason is, that His Majesty has not promised to give us these favours in the same way as He has bound Himself to bestow eternal glory on us if we keep His commandments. We can be saved without these special graces; He sees better than we do what is best for us and which of us love Him sincerely. I know for a certain truth, being acquainted with some who walk by the way of love (and therefore only seek to serve Jesus Christ crucified), that not only they neither ask for nor desire consolation, but they even beg Him not to give it them during this life: this is a fact. Fifthly, we should but labour in vain: this water does not flow through aqueducts, like that we first spoke of, and if the spring does not afford it, in vain shall we toil to obtain it. I mean, that though we may meditate and try our hardest, and though we shed tears to gain it, we cannot make this water flow. God alone gives it to whom He chooses, and often when the soul is least thinking of it. We are His, sisters, let Him do what He will with us, and lead us where He will. If we are really humble and annihilate ourselves, not only in our imagination (which often deceives us), but if we truly detach ourselves from all things, our Lord will not only grant us these favours but many others that we do not know even how to desire. May He be for ever praised and blessed! Amen.

---

[23] Life, ch. xiv. 3: 'The faculties are not lost, neither are they asleep; the will alone is occupied in such a way that without knowing how it has become a captive it gives a simple consent to become the prisoner of God.' Ibid. § 4: 'The other two faculties help the will that it may render itself capable of the fruition of so great a good; nevertheless, it occasionally happens even when the will is in union that they hinder it very much.' See also Way of Perf. ch. xxxi. 8.

[24] Way of Perf. ch. xvi. i. Life, ch. xxii. 16.

[25] Philippus a SS. Trinitate, l.c. art. 3.

CHAPTER III.

OF THE PRAYER OF RECOLLECTION WHICH GOD GENERALLY GIVES THE SOUL BEFORE GRANTING IT THAT LAST DESCRIBED. ITS EFFECTS: ALSO THOSE OF THE PRAYER OF DIVINE CONSOLATIONS DESCRIBED IN THE LAST CHAPTER.

1. The Prayer of recollection compared to the inhabitants of the castle. 2. The Shepherd recalls His flock into the castle. 3. This recollection supernatural. 4. It prepares us for higher favours. 5. The mind must act until God calls it to recollection by love. 6. The soul should here abandon itself into God's hands. 7. The prayer of recollection, and distractions in Prayer. 8. Liberty of spirit gained by consolations. 9. The soul must be watchful. 10. The devil specially tempts such souls. 11. False trances and raptures. 12. How to treat those deluded in this way. 13. Risks of delusion in this mansion.

1. THE effects of divine consolations are very numerous: before describing them, I will speak of another kind of prayer which usually precedes them. I need not say much on this subject, having written about it elsewhere.[26] This is a kind of recollection which, I believe, is supernatural. There is no occasion to retire nor to shut the eyes, nor does it depend on anything exterior; involuntarily the eyes suddenly close and solitude is found. Without any labour of one's own, the temple of which I spoke is reared for the soul in which to pray: the senses and exterior surroundings appear to lose their hold, while the spirit gradually regains its lost sovereignty. Some say the soul enters into itself; others, that it rises above itself.[27] I can say nothing about these terms, but had better speak of the subject as I understand it. You will probably grasp my meaning, although, perhaps, I may be the only person who understands it. Let us imagine that the senses and powers of the soul (which I compared in my allegory to the inhabitants of the castle) have fled and joined the enemy outside. After long days and years of absence, perceiving how great has been their loss, they return to the neighborhood of the castle, but cannot manage to re-enter it, for their evil habits are hard to break off; still, they are no longer traitors, and they wander about outside.

2. The King, Who holds His court within it, sees their good will, and out of His great mercy desires them to return to Him. Like a good Shepherd, He plays so sweetly on His pipe, that although scarcely hearing it they recognize His call and no longer wander, but return, like lost sheep, to the mansions. So strong is this Pastor's power over His flock, that they abandon the worldly cares which misled them and re-enter the castle.

3. I think I never put this matter so clearly before. To seek God within ourselves avails us far more than to look for Him amongst creatures; Saint Augustine tells us how he found the Almighty

---

26 Life, ch. xiv. 2. The Saint says in the second chapter of this mansion, § 5, and also in letters dated Dec. 7, 1577 (Vol. II) and Jan. 14, 1580, that when writing the Interior Castle she had more experience in spiritual things than when she composed her former works. This is fully borne out by the present chapter. In the corresponding part of her Life she practically confounded the prayer of recollection with the prayer of quiet (the second state of the soul). Likewise, in the Way of Perfection, ch. xxviii., she speaks of but one kind of prayer of recollection and then passes on to the prayer of quiet. Here, however, she mentions a second form of the prayer of recollection. See Philippus a SS. Trinitate, pars iii. tract. i, disc. iii. art. 1, 'De oratione recollectionis' (page 81 of the third vol. of the edition of 1874); 'de secundo modo recollectionis' (ibid. p. 82.); and art. 2: 'De oratione quietis' (ibid. p. 84.) Antonius a Spiritu Sancto, Direct. Mystic. tract. iv. n. 78: 'Duo sunt hujus recollectionis modi, primus quidem activus [reference to the Way of Perfection, l.c.], secundus autem passivus, [reference to this chapter of the Fourth Mansion].' The former is not supernatural, in the sense that with special grace from above it can be acquired; the second is altogether supernatural and more like gratuitous grace (ibid. no. 80 and 81). On the meaning of 'Solitude,' 'Silence,' etc., see Anton. a Sp. S. l.c., tract. i, n. 78-82.

27 The edition of Burgos (vol. iv, P. 59) refers appropriately to the following passage in the Tercer Abecedario (See Life, ch. iv, 8) by the Franciscan friar Francisco de Osuna, a work which exercised a profound influence on St. Teresa: 'Entering within oneself; and rising above oneself, are the two principal points in this exercise, those which, above all others, one ought to strive after, and which give the highest satisfaction to the soul. There is less labour in entering within oneself than in rising above oneself and therefore it appears to me that when the soul is ready and fit for either, you ought to do the former, because the other will follow without any effort, and will be all the more pure and spiritual; however, follow what course your soul prefers as this will bring you more grace and benefit,' (Tr. ix, ch, viii).

within his own soul, after having long sought for Him elsewhere.[28] This recollection helps us greatly when God bestows it upon us. But do not fancy you can gain it by thinking of God dwelling within you, or by imagining Him as present in your soul: this is a good practice and an excellent kind of meditation, for it is founded on the fact that God resides within us;[29] it is not, however, the prayer of recollection, for by the divine assistance every one can practice it, but what I mean is quite a different thing. Sometimes, before they have begun to think of God, the powers of the soul find themselves within the castle. I know not by what means they entered, nor how they heard the Shepherd's pipe; the ears perceived no sound but the soul is keenly conscious of a delicious sense of recollection experienced by those who enjoy this favour, which I cannot describe more clearly.

4. I think I read somewhere[30] that the soul is then like a tortoise or sea-urchin, which retreats into itself. Those who said this no doubt understood what they were talking about; but these creatures can withdraw into themselves at will, while here it is not in our power to retire into ourselves, unless God gives us the grace. In my opinion, His Majesty only bestows this favour on those who have renounced the world, in *desire* at least, if their state of life does not permit their doing so in *fact*. He thus specially calls them to devote themselves to spiritual things; if they allow Him power to at freely He will bestow still greater graces on those whom He thus begins calling to a higher life. Those who enjoy this recollection should thank God fervently: it is of the highest importance for them to realize the value of this favour, gratitude for which would prepare them to receive still more signal graces. Some books advise that as a preparation for hearing what our Lord may say to us we should keep our minds at rest, waiting to see what He will work in our souls.[31] But unless His Majesty has begun to suspend our faculties, I cannot understand how we are to stop thinking, without doing ourselves more harm than good. This point has been much debated by those learned in spiritual matters; I confess my want of humility in having been unable to yield to their opinion.[32]

5. Some one told me of a certain book written on the subject by the saintly Friar Peter of Alcantara (as I think I may justly call him); I should have submitted to his decision, knowing that he was competent to judge, but on reading it I found he agreed with me that the mind must act until called to recollection by love, although he stated it in other words.[33] Possibly I may be

---

[28] Some editors of the Interior Castle think that St. Teresa refers to the following passage taken from the Confessions of St. Augustine: 'Too late have I loved Thee, O Beauty, ever ancient yet ever new! too late have I loved Thee! And behold, Thou wert within me and I abroad, and there I searched for Thee, and, deformed as I was, I pursued the beauties that Thou hast made. Thou wert with me, but I was not with Thee. Those things kept me far from Thee, which, unless they were in Thee, could have had no being' (St. Augustine's Confessions, bk. x, ch. xxvii.). The Confessions of St. Augustine were first translated into Spanish by Sebastian Toscano, a Portuguese Augustinian. This edition, which was published at Salamanca in 1554, was the one used by St. Teresa. However, it is more probable that here and elsewhere (Life, ch. xli. 10; Way of Perf. ch. xxviii. 2) St. Teresa quotes a passage which occurs in a pious book entitled Soliloquia, and erroneously attributed to St. Augustine: 'I have gone about the streets and the broad ways of the city of this world seeking Thee, but have not found Thee for I was wrong in seeking without for what was within.' (ch. xxxi.) This treatise which is also quoted by St. John of the Cross, Spiritual Canticle, stanza i. 7, Ascent of Mount Carmel, bk. i. ch. v. 1, appeared in a Spanish translation at Valladolid in 1515, at Medina del Campo in 1553, and at Toledo in 1565.

[29] Life, ch. xiv. 7, 8; 20.

[30] St. Teresa read this in the Tercer Abecedario of Francisco de Osuna (tr. vi, ch, iv): 'This exercise concentrates the senses of man in the interior of the heart where dwells 'the daughter of the king'; that is, the Catholic soul; thus recollected, man may well be compared to the tortoise or sea-urchin which rolls itself up and withdraws within itself, disregarding everything outside.'

[31] Life. ch, xii. 8.

[32] Life, ch. xiv, 10.

[33] *A Golden Treatise of Mental Prayer* by St. Peter of Alcantara, translated by Rev. G. F. Bullock M.A. and edited by Rev. George Seymour Hollings S.S.J.E. London, Mowbray, 1905, p. 117.

Eighth Counsel. Let the last and chiefest counsel be that in this holy exercise we should endeavour to unite Meditation with Contemplation making of the one a ladder for attaining to the other. For this we

mistaken, but I rely on these reasons. Firstly, he who reasons less and tries to do least, does most in spiritual matters. We should make our petitions like beggars before a powerful and rich Emperor; then, with downcast eyes, humbly wait. When He secretly shows us He hears our prayers, it is well to be silent, as He has drawn us into His presence; there would then be no harm in trying to keep our minds at rest (that is to say, if we can). If, however, the King makes no sign of listening or of seeing us, there is no need to stand inert, like a dolt, which the soul would resemble if it continued inactive. In this case its dryness would greatly increase, and the imagination would be made more restless than before by its very effort to think of nothing. Our Lord wishes us at such a time to offer Him our petitions and to place ourselves in His presence; He knows what is best for us.

6. I believe that human efforts avail nothing in these matters, which His Majesty appears to reserve to Himself, setting this limit to our powers. In many other things, such as penances, good

---

must know that (p. 118) the very office of Meditation is to consider Divine things with studiousness and attention passing from one to another, to move our hearts to some affection and deep feeling for them, which is as though one should strike a flint to draw from it the spark.

For Contemplation is to have drawn forth this spark: I mean to have now found this affection and feeling which were sought for, and to be in peace and silence enjoying them; not with many discursive and intellectual speculations but with simple gaze upon the truth.

Wherefore, says a holy teacher, Meditation goes its way and brings forth fruit, with labour, but Contemplation bears fruit without labour. The one seeketh, the other findeth; the one consumeth the food, the other enjoys it; the one discourseth, and maketh reflections, the other is contented with a simple gaze upon the things, for it hath in possession their love and joy. Lastly, the one is as the means, the other as the end; the one as the road and journeying along it, the other as the end of the road and of the journeying.

From this is to be inferred a very common thing, which all masters of the spiritual life teach, although it is little (p. 119) understood of those who learn it; which is this, that, as the means cease when the end has been attained, as the voyaging is over when the port has been touched, so when, through the working out of our Meditation, we have come to the repose and sweet savour of Contemplation, we ought then to cease from that pious and laborious searching; and being satisfied with the simple gaze upon, and thought of, God—as though we had Him there present before us—we should rest in the enjoyment of that affection then given, whether it be of love, or of admiration, or joy, or other like sentiment.

The reason why this counsel is given is this, that as the aim of this devotion is love and the affections of the will rather than the speculations of the understanding, when the will has been caught and taken by this affection, we should put away all those discursive and intellectual speculations, so far as we can, in order that our soul with all its forces may be fastened upon this affection without being diverted by the action of other influences. A learned teacher, therefore, counsels us that as soon as anyone feels himself fired by the love of God, he should first put aside (p. 120.) all these considerations and thoughts—however exalted they may seem—not because they are really not good in themselves, but because they are then hindrances to what is better. and more important. For this is nothing else than that, having come to the end and purpose of our work, we should stay therein, and leave Meditation for the love of Contemplation. This may especially be done at the end of any exercise, that is, after the petition for the Divine love of which we have spoken, for one reason, because then it is supposed that the labour of the exercise we have just gone through has produced some divine devotion and feeling, since, saith the wise man, 'Better is the end of prayer than the beginning': and for another reason, that, after the work of Prayer and Meditation, it is well that one should give his mind a little rest, and allow it to repose in the arms of Contemplation. At this point, then, we should put away all other thoughts that may present themselves, and, quieting the mind and stilling the memory, fix all upon our Lord; and remembering that we are then in His presence, no longer dwell upon the details of divine things.

Ibidem p. 121. And not only at the end of the exercise but in the midst of it, and at whatever part of it, this spiritual swoon should come upon us, when the intellect is laid to sleep, we should make this pause, and enjoy the blessing bestowed; and then, when we have finished the digestion of it, turn to the matter we have in hand, as the gardener does, when he waters his garden-bed; who, after giving it (p. 122) a sufficiency of water, holds back the stream, and lets it soak and spread itself through the depths of the earth; and then when this hath somewhat dried up, he turns down upon it again the flow of water that it may receive still more, and be well irrigated.'

works, and prayers, with His aid we can help ourselves as far as human weakness will allow. The second reason is, that these interior operations being sweet and peaceful,[34] any painful effort does us more harm than good. By 'painful effort' I mean any forcible restraint we place on ourselves, such as holding our breath.[35] We should rather abandon our souls into the hands of God, leaving Him to do as He chooses with us, as far as possible forgetting all self-interest and resigning ourselves entirely to His will. The third reason is, that the very effort to think of nothing excites our imagination the more. The fourth is, because we render God the most true and acceptable service by caring only for His honour and glory and forgetting ourselves, our advantages, comfort and happiness. How can we be self-oblivious, while keeping ourselves under such strict control that we are afraid to move, or even to think, or to leave our minds enough liberty to desire God's greater glory and to rejoice in the glory which He possesses? When His Majesty wishes the mind to rest from working He employs it in another manner, giving it a light and knowledge far above any obtainable by its own efforts and absorbing it entirely into Himself. Then, though it knows not how, it is filled with wisdom such as it could never gain for itself by striving to suspend the thoughts. God gave us faculties for our use; each of them will receive its proper reward. Then do not let us try to charm them to sleep, but permit them to do their work until divinely called to something higher.[36]

7. In my opinion, when God chooses to place the soul in this mansion it is best for it to do as I advised, and then endeavour, without force or disturbance, to keep free from wandering thoughts. No effort, however, should be made to suspend the imagination entirely from arming, for it is well to remember God's presence and to consider Who He is. If transported out of itself by its feelings, well and good; but let it not try to understand what is passing within it, for this favour is bestowed on the will which should be left to enjoy it in peace, only making loving aspirations occasionally. Although, in this kind of prayer, the soul makes no effort towards it, yet often, for a very short time, the mind ceases to think at all. I explained elsewhere why this occurs during this spiritual state.[37] On first speaking of the fourth mansions, I told you I had mentioned divine consolations before the prayer of recollection. The latter should have come first, as it is far inferior to consolations, of which it is the commencement. Recollection does not require us to give up meditation, nor to cease using our intellect. In the prayer of quiet, when the water flows from the spring itself and not through conduits, the mind ceases to act; it is forced to do so, although it does not understand what is happening, and so wanders hither and thither in bewilderment, finding no place for rest. Meanwhile the will, entirely united to. God, is much disturbed by the tumult of the thoughts: no notice, however, should be taken of them, or they would cause the loss of a great part of the favour the soul is enjoying. Let the spirit ignore these distractions and abandon itself in the arms of divine love: His Majesty will teach it how best to act, which chiefly consists in its recognizing its unworthiness of so great a good and occupying itself in thanking Him for it.

8. In order to treat of the prayer of recollection, I passed over in silence the effects and symptoms to be found in souls thus favoured by God. Divine consolations evidently cause a dilation or enlargement of the soul that may be compared to water flowing from a spring into a basin which has no outlet, but is so constructed as to increase in size and proportion to the quantity poured into it. God seems to work the same effect by this prayer, besides giving many other marvellous graces, so preparing and disposing the soul to contain all He intends to give it. After

---

[34] Sap. viii. i: 'Disponit omnia suaviter.'

[35] Life, ch. xv. i.

[36] 'The whole of the time in which our Lord communicates the simple, loving general attention of which I made mention before, or when the soul, assisted by grace, is established in that state, we must contrive to keep the understanding in repose, undisturbed by the intrusion of forms, figures, or particular knowledge, unless it were slightly and for an instant, and that with sweetness of love, to enkindle our souls the more. At other times, however, in all our acts of devotion and good works, we must make use of good recollections and meditations, so that we may feel an increase of profit and devotion; most especially applying ourselves to the life, passion, and death of Jesus Christ, our Lord, that our life and conduct may be an imitation of His.' (St. John of the Cross, Ascent of Mount Carmel, bk. ii. ch. xxxii. 7.)

[37] Life, ch. xv. 2.

interior sweetness and dilation the soul is not so restrained as formerly in God's service, but possesses much more liberty of spirit. It is no longer distressed by the terror of hell, for though more anxious than ever not to offend God, it has lost servile fear and feels sure that one day it will possess its Lord. It does not dread the loss of health by austerities;[38] believing that there is nothing it could not do by His grace, it is more desirous than before of doing penance. Greater indifference is felt for sufferings because faith being stronger, it trusts that if borne for God He will give the grace to endure them patiently. Indeed, such a one at times even longs for trials, having a most ardent desire to do something for His sake. As the soul better understands the Divine Majesty, it realizes more vividly its own baseness. Divine consolation shows it how vile are earthly pleasures; by gradually withdrawing from them, it gains greater self-mastery. In short, its virtues are increased and it will not cease to advance in perfection, unless it turns back and offends God. Should it act thus, it would lose everything, however high the state it may have reached.

9. It is not to be supposed that all these effects are produced merely by God's having shown these favours once or twice. They must be received continually, for it is on their frequent reception that the whole welfare of the soul depends. I strongly urge those who have reached this state to avoid most carefully all occasions of offending God.[39] The soul is not yet fully established in virtue, but is like a new-born babe first feeding at its mother's breast:[40] if it leaves her, what can it do but die? I greatly fear that when a soul to whom God has granted this favour discontinues prayer, except under urgent necessity, it will, unless it returns to the practice at once, go from bad to worse.

10. I realize the danger of such a case, having had the grief of witnessing the fall of persons I knew through their withdrawal from Him Who sought, with so much love, to make Himself their friend, as He proved by His treatment of them. I urgently warn such persons not to run the risk of sinning, for the devil would rather gain one of these souls than many to whom our Lord does not grant such graces,[41] as the former may cause him severe loss by leading others to follow their example, and may even render great service to the Church of God. Were there no other reason except that he saw the special love His Majesty bears these people, it would suffice to make Satan frantic to destroy God's work in them, so that they might be lost eternally. Therefore they suffer grievous temptations, and if they fall, they fall lower than others.

11. You, my sisters, are free from such dangers, as far as we can tell: God keep you from pride and vainglory! The devil sometimes offers counterfeits of the graces I have mentioned: this can easily be detected—the effects being exactly contrary to those of the genuine ones.[42] Although I have spoken of it elsewhere,[43] I wish to warn you here of a special danger to which those who practice prayer are subject, particularly women, whose weakness of constitution makes them more liable to such mistakes. On account of their penances, prayers, and vigils, or even merely because of debility of health, some persons cannot receive spiritual consolation without being overcome by it. On feeling any interior joy, their bodies being languid and weak, they fall into a slumber—they call it spiritual sleep—which is a more advanced stage of what I have described; they think the soul shares in it as well as the body, and abandon themselves to a sort of intoxication. The more they lose self-control, the more do their feelings get possession of them, because the frame becomes more feeble. They fancy this is a trance and call it one, but I call it nonsense; it does nothing but waste their time and injure their health.

12. This state lasted with a certain person for eight hours, during which time she was neither insensible, nor had she any thought of God.[44] She was cured by being made to eat and sleep well and to leave off some of her penances. Her recovery was owing to some one who understood her case; hitherto she had unintentionally deceived both her confessor and other people, as well as herself. I feel quite sure the devil had been at work here to serve his own ends and he was

---

[38] Life, ch. xxiv. 2.

[39] Way of Perf. ch. xvi. 5. Castle, M. v. ch. i, 2, 3; ii. 4, 5; iii. 2, 6, 12.

[40] Way of Perf. ch. xxxi. 7. Concept. ch. iv. 6.

[41] Way of Perf. ch. xl. 3.

[42] Life, ch. xx. 31.

[43] Found. ch. vi.

[44] Found. ch. vi. 15.

beginning to gain a great deal from it. It should be known that when God bestows such favours on the soul, although there may be languor both of mind and body, it is not shared by the soul, which feels great delight at seeing itself so near God, nor does this state ever continue for more than a very short time.[45] Although the soul may become absorbed again, yet, as I said, unless already feeble, the body suffers neither exhaustion nor pain. I advise any of you who experience the latter to tell the Prioress, and to divert your thoughts as much as possible from such matters. The Superior should prevent such a nun from spending more than a very few hours in prayer, and should make her eat and sleep well until her usual strength is restored, if she has lost it in this way.[46] If the nun's constitution is so delicate that this does not suffice, let her believe me when I tell her that God only calls her to the active life. There must be such people in monasteries: employ her in the various offices and be careful that she is never left very long alone, otherwise she will entirely lose her health. This treatment will be a great mortification to her: our Lord tests her love for Him by the way in which she bears His absence. He may be pleased, after a time, to restore her strength; if not, she will make as much progress, and earn as great a reward by vocal prayer and obedience as she would have done by contemplation, and perhaps more.

13. There are people, some of whom I have known, whose minds and imaginations are so active as to fancy they see whatever they think about, which is very dangerous.[47] Perhaps I may treat of this later on, but cannot do so now. I have dwelt at length on this mansion, as I believe it to be the one most souls enter. As the natural is combined with the supernatural, the devil can do more harm here than later on, when God does not leave him so many opportunities. May God be for ever praised! Amen.

---

[45] Life ch. xviii. 16, 17.

[46] Letter of Oct. 23, 1 376. Vol. II.

[47] Found. ch. viii. 7-8.

THE FIFTH MANSIONS

CHAPTER I.

BEGINS TO TREAT OF THE UNION OF THE SOUL WITH GOD IN PRAYER. HOW TO BE SURE THAT
WE ARE NOT DECEIVED IN THIS MATTER.

1. Graces of the fifth mansions. 2. Contemplation to be striven for. 3. Physical effects of the Prayer of union. 4. Amazement of the intellect. 5. The Prayer of union and of quiet contrasted. 6. Divine and earthly union. 7. Competent directors in these matters. 8. Proof of union. 9. Assurance left in the soul. 10. Divine union beyond our Power to obtain.

1. OH, my sisters, how shall I describe the riches, treasures, and joys contained in the fifth mansions! Would it not be better to say nothing about them? They are impossible to depict, nor can the mind conceive, nor any comparisons portray them, all earthly things being too vile to serve the purpose. Send me, O my Lord, light from heaven that I may give some to these Thy servants, some of whom by Thy good will often enjoy these delights, lest the devil in the guise of an angel of light should deceive those whose only desire is to please Thee.

2. I said 'some,' but in reality there are very *few*[1] who never enter this mansion: some more and some less, but most of them may be said at least to gain admittance into these rooms. I think that certain graces I am about to describe are bestowed on only a few of the nuns, but if the rest only arrive at the portal they receive a great boon from God, for 'many are called, but few are chosen.'[2] All we who wear the holy habit of the Carmelites are called to prayer and contemplation. This was the object of our Order,[3] to this lineage we belong. Our holy Fathers of Mount Carmel sought in perfect solitude and utter contempt of the world for this treasure, this precious pearl,[4] of which we speak, and we are their descendants. How little do most of us care to prepare our souls, that our Lord may reveal this jewel to us! Outwardly we may appear to practice the requisite virtues, but we have far more to do than this before it is possible to attain to contemplation, to gain which we should neglect no means, either small or great. Rouse yourselves, my sisters, and since some foretaste of heaven may be had on earth, beg our Lord to give us grace not to miss it through our own fault. Ask Him to show us where to find it—ask Him to give us strength of soul to dig until we find this hidden treasure, which lies buried within our hearts, as I wish to show you if it please God to enable me. I said 'strength of *soul*,' that you might understand that strength of *body* is not indispensable when our Lord God chooses to withhold it. He makes it impossible for no one to gain these riches, but is content that each should do his best. Blessed be so just a God!

3. But, daughters, if you would purchase this treasure of which we are speaking, God would have you keep back nothing from Him, little or great. He will have it all;[5] in proportion to what you know you have given will your reward be great or small. There is no more certain sign whether or not we have reached the prayer of union. Do not imagine that this state of prayer is, like the one preceding it, a sort of drowsiness (I call it 'drowsiness' because the soul seems to slumber, being neither quite asleep nor wholly awake). In the prayer of union the soul is asleep, fast asleep, as regards the world and itself: in fact, during the short time this state lasts it is deprived of all feeling whatever, being unable to think on any subject, even if it wished. No effort is needed here to suspend the thoughts: if the soul can love it knows not how, nor whom it loves, nor what

---

[1] Found. ch. iv. 8.

[2] St. Matt. xx. 16: 'Multi enim sunt vocati, pauci vero electi.'

[3] Maneant singuli in cellulis suis, vel juxta eas, die ac nocte in lege Domini meditantes et in orationibus vigilantes.' (Carmelite Rule).

[4] St. Matt. xiii. 46.

[5] 'The reason why there are so few contemplatives is that there are so few persons who wholly withdraw themselves from transitory and created things' (Imitation, bk. iii. ch. xxxi. 1). See also Way of Perf. ch. xvi. 5. Life, ch. xi. 2-4; xxii. 18, 19.

it desires. In fact, it has died entirely to this world, to live more truly than ever in God. This is a delicious death, for the soul is deprived of the faculties it exercised while in the body:[6] delicious because, (although not really the case), it seems to have left its mortal covering to abide more entirely in God. So completely does this take place, that I know not whether the body retains sufficient life to continue breathing; on consideration, I believe it does not; at any rate, if it still breathes, it does so unconsciously.

4. The mind entirely concentrates itself on trying to understand what is happening, which is beyond its power; it is so astounded that, if consciousness is not completely lost, at least no movement is possible: the person may be compared to one who falls into a dead faint with dismay.[7]

5. Oh, mighty secrets of God! Never should I weary of trying to explain them if I thought it possible to succeed! I would write a thousand foolish things that one might be to the point, if only it might make us praise God more. I said this prayer produced no drowsiness in the mind; on the other hand, in the prayer (of quiet) described in the last mansion, until the soul has gained much experience it doubts what really happened to it. 'Was it nothing but fancy, or was it a sleep? Did it come from God or from the devil, disguised as an angel of light?' The mind feels a thousand misgivings, and well for it that it should, because, at I said, nature may sometimes deceive us in this case. Although there is little chance of the poisonous reptiles entering here, yet agile little lizards will try to slip in, though they can do no harm, especially if they remain unnoticed. These, as I said, are trivial fancies of the imagination, which are often very troublesome. However active these small lizards may be, they cannot enter the fifth mansion, for neither the imagination, the understanding, nor the memory has power to hinder the graces bestowed on it.

6. I dare venture to assert that, if this is genuine union with God, the devil cannot interfere nor do any harm, for His Majesty is so joined and united with the essence of the soul, that the evil one dare not approach, nor can he even understand this mystery. This is certain, for it is said that the devil does not know our thoughts, much less can he penetrate a secret so profound that God does not reveal it even to us.[8] Oh, blessed state, in which this cursed one cannot injure us! What riches we receive while God so works in us that neither we ourselves nor any one else can impede Him! What will He not bestow, Who is so eager to give, and Who can give us all He desires! You may perhaps have been puzzled at my saying 'if this is genuine union with God,' as if there might be other unions. There are indeed—not with God, but with vanities—when the devil transports the soul passionately addicted to them, but the union differs from that which is divine and the mind misses the delight and satisfaction, peace and happiness of divine union. These heavenly consolations are above all earthly joys, pleasure, and satisfaction. As great a difference exists between their origin and that of worldly pleasures as between their opposite effects, as you know by experience.

7. I said somewhere[9] that the one seems only to touch the surface of the body, while the other penetrates to the very marrow: I believe this is correct, and I cannot express myself better. I fancy that you are not yet satisfied on this question, but are afraid of deception, for spiritual matters are very hard to explain. Enough, however, has been said for those who have received this grace, as the difference between divine union and any other is very striking. However, I will give you a clear proof which cannot mislead you, nor leave any doubt whether the favour comes from God or no. His Majesty brought it back to my memory this very day; it appears to me to be an unmistakable sign. In difficult questions, although I think I understand them and am speaking the truth, I always say 'it appears to me'; for, in case my opinion is wrong, I am most willing to submit to the judgment of theologians. Although they may not have had personal experience in such matters, yet in some way I do not understand, God Who sets them to give light to His Church enables them to recognize the truth when it is put before them. If they are not thoughtless and

---

[6] Way of Perf. ch. xxv. 1. Life, ch. xvi. Rel. I. i; viii. 7.

[7] Life, ch. xvii. 2.

[8] According to St. Thomas, angels—whether good or bad—do not know the thoughts of man unless they become manifest by some exterior sign. S. Theol. I. q. lvii. art. 4. See also St. John of the Cross, Dark Night, bk. II, ch. xxiii. 2, 5.

[9] Mansion iv. ch. i, 5.

undevout, but servants of God, they are never dismayed at His mighty works, knowing perfectly well that it is in His power to perform far greater wonders. If some of the marvels told are new to them, yet they have read of others of the same kind, showing the former to be possible. I have had great experience as to this and have also met with timid, half-instructed people whose ignorance has cost me very dear.[10] I am convinced that those who refuse to believe that God can do far more than this, and that He is pleased now, as in the past, to communicate Himself to His creatures, shut fast their hearts against receiving such favours themselves. Do not imitate them, sisters: be convinced that it is possible for God to perform still greater wonders. Do not concern yourselves as to whether those who receive these graces are good or wicked; as I said, He knows best and it is no business of yours: you should serve Him with a single heart and with humility, and should praise Him for His works and wonders.[11]

8. Let us now speak of the sign which proves the prayer of union to have been genuine. As you have seen, God then deprives the soul of all its senses that He may the better imprint in it true wisdom: it neither sees, hears, nor understands anything while this state lasts, which is never more than a very brief time;[12] it appears to the soul to be much shorter than it really is. God visits the soul in a manner which prevents its doubting, on returning to itself, that it dwelt in Him and that He was within it, and so firmly is it convinced of this truth that, although years may pass before this favour recurs, the soul can never forget it nor doubt the fact,[13] setting aside the effects left by this prayer, to which I will refer later on. The conviction felt by the soul is the main point.

9. But, you may ask, how can a person who is incapable of sight and hearing see[14] or know these things? I do not say that she saw it at the time, but that she perceives it clearly afterwards, not by any vision but by a certitude which remains in the heart which God alone could give. I know of some one who was unaware of God's being in all things by presence, power and essence, yet was firmly convinced of it by a divine favour of this sort.[15] She asked an ill-instructed priest of the kind I mentioned to tell her in what way God dwelt within us: he was as ignorant on the subject as she had been before our Lord revealed to her the truth, and answered that the Almighty was only present in us by grace.[16] Yet so strong was her conviction of the truth learnt during her prayer that she did not believe him and questioned other spiritual persons on the subject, who confirmed her in the true doctrine, much to her joy. Do not mistake and imagine that this certainty

---

[10] Life, ch. viii. 15.

[11] Life, ch. xviii. 16.

[12] Life, ch. xx. 13, 24.

[13] Philippus a SS. Trinitate, l.c., pars iii. tr. i. disc. iv. art, 2, where he adds some further signs. Anton. a Sp. S., l.c., tract. i. no. 116 and 117.

[14] 'The soul does not see the good Master who teaches it, although clearly conscious of His presence.' (Concept. ch. iv. 3.)

[15] 'There are three ways in which God is present in the soul. The first is His presence in essence, not in holy souls only, but in wretched and sinful souls as well, and also in all created things; for it is by this presence that He gives life and being, and were it withdrawn at once all things would return to nothing. This presence never fails in the soul. The second is His presence by grace, whereby He dwells in the soul, pleased and satisfied with it. This presence is not in all souls; for those who fall into mortal sin lose it, and no soul can know in a natural way whether it has it or not. The third is His presence by spiritual affection. God is wont to show His presence in many devout souls in divers ways, in refreshment, joy and gladness.' (St. John of the Cross, *Spiritual Canticle*, stanza xi. 2.)

'In every soul, even that of the greatest sinner in the world, God dwells and is substantially present. This way of union or presence of God, in the order of nature, subsists between Him and all His creatures; by this He preserves them in being, and if He withdraws it they immediately perish and cease to be. And so, when I speak of the union of the soul with God, I do not mean this substantial presence which is in every creature, but that union and transformation of the soul in God by love which is only then accomplished when there subsists the likeness which love begets.' (St. John of the Cross, *Ascent*, bk. ii. ch. v. 3.)

Fr. Gracian, *Peregrinacion de Anastasio* (Burgos, 1905), p. 171.

[16] Life, ch. xviii. 20. Rel. ix. 17; xi. 8. St. Teresa was so deeply impressed by the ignorance of this priest that she very frequently referred to it.

of God's having visited the soul concerns any corporal presence such as that of our Lord Jesus Christ Who dwells in the Blessed Sacrament, although we do not see Him: it relates solely to the Divinity. If we did not see it, how can we feel so sure of it? That I do not know: it is the work of the Almighty and I am certain that what I say is the fact. I maintain that a soul which does not feel this assurance has not been united to God entirely, but only by one of its powers, or has received one of the many other favours God is accustomed to bestow on men. In all such matters we must not seek to know how things happened: our understanding could not grasp them, therefore why trouble ourselves on the subject? It is enough to know that it is He, the all-powerful God, Who has performed the work. We can do nothing on our own part to gain this favour; it comes from God alone; therefore let us not strive to understand it.

10. Concerning my words: 'We can do nothing on our own part,' I was struck by the words of the Bride in the Canticles, which you will remember to have heard: 'The King brought me into the cellar of wine,'[17] (or 'placed me' I think she says): she does not say she went of her own accord, although telling us how she wandered up and down seeking her Beloved.[18] I think the prayer of union is the 'cellar' in which our Lord places us when and how He chooses, but we cannot enter it through any effort of our own. His Majesty alone can bring us there and come into the centre of our souls. In order to declare His wondrous works more clearly, He will leave us no share in them except complete conformity of our wills to His and abandonment of all things: He does not require the faculties or senses to open the door to Him; they are all asleep. He enters the innermost depths of our souls without a door, as He entered the room where the disciples sat, saying 'Pax vobis,'[19] and as He emerged from the sepulcher without removing the stone that closed the entrance. You will see farther on, in the seventh mansion, far better than here, how God makes the soul enjoy His presence in its very centre. O daughters, what wonders shall we see, if we keep ever before our eyes our own baseness and frailty and recognize how unworthy we are to be the handmaids of so great a Lord, Whose marvels are beyond our comprehension! May He be for ever praised! Amen.

CHAPTER II.

CONTINUES THE SAME SUBJECT: EXPLAINS THE PRAYER OF UNION BY A DELICATE COMPARISON AND SPEAKS OF THE EFFECTS IT LEAVES UPON THE SOUL. THIS CHAPTER SHOULD RECEIVE GREAT ATTENTION.

1. The soul compared to a butterfly. 2. The grandeurs of creation. 3. Symbol of the soul and the silkworm. 4. Preparation of the soul for God's indwelling. 5. Mystic death of the silkworm. 6. Effects of divine union. 7. Increase of fervour and detachment. 8. Trials succeeding the prayer of union. 9. Longing for death and zeal for God's honour. 10. This zeal supernatural. 11. God alone works this grace. 12. The same zeal as that felt by our Lord on earth. 13. Christ's keenest suffering.

1. You may imagine that there is no more left to be described of the contents of this mansion, but a great deal remains to be told, for as I said, it contains favours of various degrees. I think there is nothing to add about the prayer of union, but when the soul on which God bestows this grace disposes itself for their reception, I could tell you much about the marvels our Lord works in it. I will describe some of them in my own way, also the state in which they leave the soul, and will use a suitable comparison to elucidate the matter, explaining that though we can take no active part in this work of God within us,[20] yet we may do much to prepare ourselves to receive this grace. You have heard how wonderfully silk is made—in a way such as God alone could plan—how it all comes from an egg resembling a tiny pepper-corn. Not having seen it myself, I only know of it by hearsay, so if the facts are inaccurate the fault will not be mine. When, in the warm weather, the mulberry trees come into leaf, the little egg which was lifeless before its food

[17] Cant. i. 3: 'Introduxit me rex in cellaria sua.' Castle, M. v. ch. i. Way of Perf. ch. xviii. I. Concep. ch. iv. 4-8; v. 5; vi. 7; vii. 2-5. Life, ch. xviii. 17.
[18] Cant. iii. 2: 'Per vicos et plateas quæram quem diligit anima mea.'
[19] St. John, xx. 19.
[20] Way of Perf. ch. xxv. 3.

was ready, begins to live. The caterpillar nourishes itself upon the mulberry leaves until, when it has grown large, people place near it small twigs upon which, of its own accord, it spins silk from its tiny mouth until it has made a narrow little cocoon in which it buries itself. Then this large and ugly worm leaves the cocoon as a lovely little white butterfly.

2. If we had not seen this but had only heard of it as an old legend, who could believe it? Could we persuade ourselves that insects so utterly without the use of reason as a silkworm or a bee would work with such industry and skill in our service that the poor little silkworm loses its life over the task? This would suffice for a short meditation, sisters, without my adding more, for you may learn from it the wonders and the wisdom of God. How if we knew the properties of all things? It is most profitable to ponder over the grandeurs of creation and to exult in being the brides of such a wise and mighty King.

3. Let us return to our subject. The silkworm symbolizes the soul which begins to live when, kindled by the Holy Spirit, it commences using the ordinary aids given by God to all, and applies the remedies left by Him in His Church, such as regular confession, religious hooks, and sermons; these are the cure for a soul dead in its negligence and sins and liable to fall into temptation. Then it comes to life and continues nourishing itself on this food and on devout meditation until it has attained full vigor, which is the essential point, for I attach no importance to the rest. When the silkworm is full-grown as I told you in the first part of this chapter, it begins to spin silk and to build the house wherein it must die. By this house, when speaking of the soul, I mean Christ. I think I read or heard somewhere, either that our life is hid in Christ, or in God (which means the same thing) or that Christ is our life.[21] It makes little difference to my meaning which of these quotations is correct.

4. This shows, my daughters, how much, by God's grace, we can do, by preparing this home for ourselves, towards making Him our dwelling-place as He is in the prayer of union. You will suppose that I mean we can take away from or add something to God when I say that He is our home, and that we can make this home and dwell in it by our own power. Indeed we can: though we can neither deprive God of anything nor add aught to Him, yet we can take away from and add to ourselves, like the silkworms. The little we can do will hardly have been accomplished when this insignificant work of ours, which amounts to nothing at all, will be united by God to His greatness and thus enhanced with such immense value that our Lord Himself will be the reward of our toil. Although He has had the greatest share in it, He will join our trifling pains to the bitter sufferings He endured for us and make them one.

5. Forward then, my daughters! hasten over your work and build the little cocoon. Let us renounce self-love and self-will,[22] care for nothing earthly, do penance, pray, mortify ourselves, be obedient, and perform all the other good works of which you know. Act up to your light; you have been taught your duties. Die! die as the silkworm does when it has fulfilled the office of its creation, and you will see God and be immersed in His greatness, as the little silkworm is enveloped in its cocoon. Understand that when I say 'you will see God,' I mean in the manner described, in which He manifests Himself in this kind of union.

6. Now let us see what becomes of the 'silkworm,' for all I have been saying leads to this. As soon as, by means of this prayer, the soul has become entirely dead to the world, it comes forth like a lovely little white butterfly![23] Oh, how great God is! How beautiful is the soul after having been immersed in God's grandeur and united closely to Him for but a short time! Indeed, I do not think it is ever as long as half an hour.[24] Truly, the spirit does not recognize itself, being as different from what it was as is the white butterfly from the repulsive caterpillar. It does not know how it can have merited so great a good, or rather, whence this grace came[25] which it well knows

---

21 Col. iii. 3: 'Vita vestra est abscondita cum Christo in Deo.' Gal. ii. w: 'Vivo autem, jam on ego; vivit vero in me Christus.'

22 Way of Perf. ch. xxxi. i 1.

23 St. Teresa must have been thinking of this simile when she chose 'butterflies' as the pseudonym for her nuns in her letters at the time when she was obliged to be cautious on account of the troubles of the Reform.

24 Life, ch. xviii. 16.

25 Life, ch. xviii. 5-7.

it merits not. The soul desires to praise our Lord God and longs to sacrifice itself and die a thousand deaths for Him. It feels an unconquerable desire for great crosses and would like to perform the most severe penances; it sighs for solitude and would have all men know God, while it is bitterly grieved at seeing them offend Him. These matters will be described more fully in the next mansion; there they are of the same nature, yet in a more advanced state the effects are far stronger, because, as I told you, if; after the soul has received these favours, it strives to make still farther progress, it will experience great things. Oh, to see the restlessness of this charming little butterfly, although never in its life has it been more tranquil and at peace! May God be praised! It knows not where to stay nor take its rest; everything on earth disgusts it after what it has experienced, particularly when God has often given it this wine which leaves fresh graces behind it at every draught.

7. It despises the work it did while yet a caterpillar—the slow weaving of its cocoon thread by thread—its wings have grown and it can fly; could it be content to crawl? All that it can do for God seems nothing to the soul compared with its desire. It no longer wonders at what the saints bore for Him, knowing by experience how our Lord aids and transforms the soul until it no longer seems the same in character and appearance. Formerly it feared penance, now it is strong: it wanted courage to forsake relations, friends, or possessions: neither its actions, its resolutions, nor separation from those it loved could detach the soul, but rather seemed to increase its fondness. Now it finds even their rightful claims a burden,[26] fearing contact with them lest it should offend God. It wearies of everything, realizing that no true rest can be found in creatures.

8. I seem to have enlarged on this subject, yet far more might be said about it; those who have received this favour will think I have treated it too briefly. No wonder this pretty butterfly, estranged from earthly things, seeks repose elsewhere. Where can the poor little creature go? It cannot return to whence it came, for as I told you, that is not in the soul's power, do what it will, but depends upon God's pleasure. Alas, what fresh trials begin to afflict the mind! Who would expect this after such a sublime grace?[27] In fact in one way or another we must carry the cross all our lives. If people told me that ever since attaining to the prayer of union they had enjoyed constant peace and consolation, I should reply that they could never have reached that state, but that, at the most, if they had arrived as far as the last mansion, their emotion must have been some spiritual satisfaction joined to physical debility. It might even have been a false sweetness caused by the devil, who gives peace for a time only to wage far fiercer war later on. I do not mean that those who reach this stage possess no peace; they do so in a very high degree, for their sorrows, though extremely severe, are so beneficial and proceed from so good a source as to procure both peace and happiness.

9. Discontent with this world gives such a painful longing to quit it that, if the heart finds comfort, it is solely from the thought that God wishes it to remain here in banishment. Even this is not enough to reconcile it to fate, for after all the gifts received, it is not yet so entirely surrendered to the will of God as it afterwards becomes. Here, although conformed to His will, the soul feels an unconquerable reluctance to submit, for our Lord has not given it higher grace. During prayer this grief breaks forth in floods of tears, probably from the great pain felt at seeing God offended and at thinking how many souls, both heretics and heathens, are lost eternally, and keenest grief of all, Christians also! The soul realizes the greatness of God's mercy and knows that however wicked men are, they may still repent and be saved; yet it fears that many precipitate themselves into hell.

10. Oh, infinite greatness of God! A few years ago—indeed, perhaps but a few days—this soul thought of nothing but itself. Who has made it feel such tormenting cares? If we tried for many years to obtain such sorrow by means of meditation, we could not succeed.

11. God help me! If for long days and years I considered how great a wrong it is that God should be offended, and that lost souls are His children and my brethren; if I pondered over the dangers of this world and how blessed it would be to leave this wretched life, would not that suffice? No, daughters, the pain would not be the same. For this, by the help of God, we can

[26] Rel. ix, 11.
[27] Way of Perf. ch. xviii. 1-4. Castle, M. vi ch. i. 3, sqq. M. vii. ch. iv. 7.

obtain by such meditation; but it does not seem to penetrate the very depths of our being like the other which appears to cut the soul to pieces and grind it to powder through no action—even sometimes with no wish—of its own. What is this sorrow, then? Whence does it come? I will tell you. Have you not heard (I quoted the words to you just now, but did not apply to them this meaning) how the Bride says that God 'brought her into the cellar of wine and set in order charity in her'?28 This is what happens here. The soul has so entirely yielded itself into His hands and is so subdued by love for Him that it knows or cares for nothing but that God should dispose of it according to His will. I believe that He only bestows this grace on those He takes entirely for His own. He desires that, without knowing how, the spirit should come forth stamped with His seal for indeed it does no more than does the wax when impressed with the signet. It does not mold itself but need only be in a fit condition—soft and pliable; even then it does not soften itself but must merely remain still and submit to the impression.

12. How good Thou art, O God! All is done for us by Thee, Who dost but ask us to give our wills to Thee that we may be plastic as wax in Thy hands. You see, sisters, what God does to this soul so that it may know that it is His. He gives it something of His own—that which His Son possessed when living on earth—He could bestow on greater gift on us. Who could ever have longed more eagerly to leave this life than did Christ? As He said at the Last Supper: 'With desire have I desired'29 this. O Lord! does not that bitter death Thou art to undergo present itself before Thine eyes in all its pain and horror? 'No, for My ardent love and My desire to save souls are immeasurably stronger than the torments. This deeper sorrow I have suffered and still suffer while living here on earth, makes other pain seem as nothing in comparison.'

13. I have often meditated on this and I know that the torture a friend of mine[30] has felt, and still feels, at seeing our Lord sinned against is so unbearable that she would far rather die than continue in such anguish. Then I thought that if a soul whose charity is so weak compared to that of Christ—indeed, in comparison with His this charity might be said not to exist—experiences this insufferable grief, what must have been the feelings of our Lord Jesus Christ and what must His life have been? for all things were present before His eyes and He was the constant witness of the great offences committed against His Father. I believe without doubt that this pained Him far more than His most sacred Passion. There, at least, He found the end of all His trials, while His agony was allayed by the consolation of gaining our salvation through His death and of proving how He loved His Father by suffering for Him. Thus, people who, urged by fervent love, perform great penances hardly feel them but want to do still more and count even that as little. What, then, must His Majesty have felt at thus publicly manifesting His perfect obedience to His Father and His love for His brethren? What joy to suffer in doing God's will! Yet I think the constant sight of the many sins committed against God and of the numberless souls on their way to hell must have caused Him such anguish that, had He not been more than man, one day of such torment would have destroyed not only His life but many more lives, had they been His.

CHAPTER III.

THIS CHAPTER CONTINUES THE SAME SUBJECT AND SPEAKS OF ANOTHER KIND OF UNION WHICH THE SOUL CAN OBTAIN WITH THE HELP OF GOD. THE IMPORTANCE OF LOVE OF OUR NEIGHBOUR IN THIS MATTER. THIS IS VERY USEFUL TO READ.

1. Zeal for souls left by divine union. 2. The soul may fall from such a state. 3. How divine union may always be obtained. 4. Union with the will of God the basis of all supernatural union. 5. Advantage of union gained by self-mortification. 6. Defects which hinder this union. 7. Divine union obtained by perfect love of God and our neighbour. 8. Love for God and our neighbour are proportionate. 9. Real and imaginary virtues. 10. Illusionary good resolutions. 11. Works, not feelings, procure union. 12. Fraternal charity will certainly gain this union.

---

28 Cant. ii. 4. 'Introduxit me in cellam vinariam, ordinavit in me caritatem.'

29 St. Luke xxii. 15: 'Desiderio desideravi hoc pascha manducare vobiscum, antequam patiar.'

30 This friend is, of course, St. Teresa herself. See Life, ch. xiii. 14; xxxii. 9. Way of Perf. ch. i. 3. Castle, M. vii. ch. i. 5, 6. Excl. x. 9.

1. LET us now return to our little dove and see what graces God gives it in this state. This implies that the soul endeavours to advance in the service of our Lord and in self-knowledge. If it receives the grace of union and then does no more, thinking itself safe, and so leads a careless life, wandering off the road to heaven (that is, the keeping of the commandments) it will share the fate of the butterfly that comes from the silkworm, which lays some eggs that produce more of its kind and then dies for ever. I say it leaves some eggs, for I believe God will not allow so great a favour to be lost but that if the recipient does not profit by it, others will. For while it keeps to the right path, this soul, with its ardent desires and great virtues, helps others and kindles their fervour with its own. Yet even after having lost this it may still long to benefit others and delight to make known the mercies shown by God to those who love and serve Him.[31]

2. I knew a person to whom this happened. Although greatly erring, she longed that others should profit by the favours God had bestowed on her and taught the way of prayer to people ignorant of it, thus helping them immensely. God afterwards bestowed fresh light upon her; indeed the prayer of union had not hitherto produced the above effects in her. How many people there must be to whom our Lord communicates Himself, who, like Judas, are called to the Apostleship and made kings by Him, as was Saul, yet who afterwards lose everything by their own fault! We should learn from this, sisters, that if we would merit fresh favours and avoid losing those we already possess, our only safety lies in obedience and in following the law of God. This I say, both to those who have received these graces and to those who have not.[32]

3. In spite of all I have written, there still seems some difficulty in understanding this mansion. The advantage of entering is so great, that it is well that none should despair of doing so because God does not give them the supernatural gifts described above. With the help of divine grace true union can always be attained by forcing ourselves to renounce our own will and by following the will of God in all things.[33]

4. Oh, how many of us affirm that we do this, and believe we seek nothing else—indeed we would die for the truth of what we say! If this be the case I can only declare, as I fancy I did before, and I shall again and again, that we have already obtained this grace from God. Therefore we need not wish for that other delightful union described above, for its chief value lies in the resignation of our will to that of God without which it could not be reached.[34] Oh, how desirable is this union! The happy soul which has attained it will live in this world and in the next without care of any sort. No earthly events can trouble it, unless it should see itself in danger of losing God or should witness any offence offered Him. Neither sickness, poverty, nor the loss of any one by death affect it, except that of persons useful to the Church of God, for the soul realizes thoroughly that God's disposal is wiser than its own desires.

5. You must know that there are different kinds of sorrow: there are both griefs and joys rising from an impulse of nature or from a charity which makes us pity our neighbour, like that felt by our Savior when He raised Lazarus from the dead.[35] These feelings do not destroy union with the will of God nor do they disturb the soul by a restless, turbulent, and lasting passion. They soon pass away, for as I said of sweetness in prayer,[36] they do not affect the depths of the soul but only its senses and faculties. They are found in the former mansions, but do not enter the last of all. Is it necessary, in order to attain to this kind of divine union, for the powers of the soul to be suspended? No; God has many ways of enriching the soul and bringing it to these mansions besides what might be called a 'short cut.' But, be sure of this, my daughters: in any case the silkworm must die and it will cost you more in this way. In the former manner this death is facilitated by finding ourselves introduced into a new life; here, on the contrary, we must give ourselves the death-blow. I own that the work will be much harder, but then it will be of higher

---

[31] Life, ch. vii. 18. Way of Perf. xli. 8.

[32] Life. ch, vii. 21.

[33] Found. ch. v. 10. 'These shall not attain to the true liberty of a pure heart, nor to the grace of a delightful familiarity with Me, unless they first resign themselves and offer themselves a daily sacrifice to Me: for without this, divine union neither is nor will be obtained.' (Imitation, book iii. ch. xxxvii. 4.)

[34] Philippus a SS. Trinitate, l.c., p. iii. tr. i, disc. ii. art. 4.

[35] St. John xi. 35, 36: 'Et lacrymatus est Jesus. Dixerunt ergo Judæi: Ecce quomodo amabat cum.'

[36] Fourth Mansions, ch. i. 5. Fifth Mansions, ch. i. 7.

value so that your reward will be greater if you come forth victorious;[37] yet there is no doubt it is possible for you to attain this true union with the will of God.

6. This is the union I have longed for all my life and that I beg our Lord to grant me; it is the most certain and the safest. But alas, how few of us ever obtain it! Those who are careful not to offend God, and who enter the religious state, think there is nothing more to do. How many maggots remain in hiding until, like the worm which gnawed at Jonas's ivy,[38] they have destroyed our virtues. These pests are such evils as self-love, self-esteem, rash judgment of others even in small matters, and a want of charity in not loving our neighbour quite as much as ourselves. Although perforce we satisfy our obligations sufficiently to avoid sin, yet we fall far short of what must be done in order to obtain perfect union with the will of God.

7. What do you think, daughters, is His will? That we may become quite perfect and so be made one with Him and with His Father as He prayed we might be.[39] Observe, then, what is wanting in us to obtain this. I assure you it is most painful for me to write on this subject, for I see how far I am, through my own fault, from having attained perfection. There is no need for us to receive special consolations from God in order to arrive at conformity with His will; He has done enough in giving us His Son to teach the way. This does not mean that we must so submit to the will of God as not to sorrow at such troubles as the death of a father or brother, or that we must bear crosses and sickness with joy.[40] This is well, but it sometimes comes from common sense which, as we cannot help ourselves, makes a virtue of necessity. How often the great wisdom of the heathen philosophers led them to act thus in trials of this kind! Our Lord asks but two things of us: love, for Him and for our neighbour: these are what we must strive to obtain. If we practice both these virtues perfectly we shall be doing His will and so shall be united to Him. But, as I said, we are very far from obeying and serving our great Master perfectly in these two matters: may His Majesty give us the grace to merit union with Him; it is in our power to gain it if we will.

8. I think the most certain sign that we keep these two commandments is that we have a genuine love for others. We cannot know whether we love God although there may be strong reasons for thinking so, but there can be no doubt about whether we love our neighbour or no.[41] Be sure that in proportion as you advance in fraternal charity, you are increasing in your love of God,[42] for His Majesty bears so tender an affection for us that I cannot doubt He will repay our love for others by augmenting, in a thousand different ways, that which we bear for Him. We should watch most carefully over ourselves in this matter, for if we are faultless on this point we have done all. I believe human nature is so evil that we could not feel a perfect charity for our neighbour unless it were rooted in the love of God.

9. In this most important matter, sisters, we should be most vigilant in little things, taking no notice of the great works we plan during prayer which we imagine that we would perform for other people, even perhaps for the sake of saving a single soul. If our actions afterwards belie these grand schemes, there is no reason to imagine that we should do anything of the sort. I say the same of humility and the other virtues. The devil's wiles are many; he would turn hell upside down a thousand times to make us think ourselves better than we are. He has good reason for it, for such fancies are most injurious; sham virtues springing from this root are always accompanied by a vainglory never found in those of divine origin, which are free from pride.

10. It is amusing to see souls who, while they are at prayer, fancy they are willing to be despised and publicly insulted for the love of God, yet afterwards do all they can to hide their

---

[37] Way of Perf. ch. xvii. 2.

[38] Jonas iv. 6, 7: 'And the Lord God prepared an ivy, and it came up over the head of Jonas, to be a shadow over his head, and to cover him, for he was fatigued; and Jonas was exceeding glad of the ivy. But God prepared a worm, when the morning arose on the following day: and it struck the ivy and it withered.'

[39] St. John xvii. 22, 23: 'Ut sint unum, sicut et nos unum sumus. Ego in eis, et tu in me: ut sint consummati in unum.' Way of Perf. ch. xxxii. 6.

[40] Way of Perf. ch. ix. i, 2.

[41] 1 St. John iv. 20: 'Qui enim non diligit fratrem suum quem videt, Deum quem non videt quomodo potest diligere?'

[42] Way of Perf. ch. xviii. 5.

small defects; if any one unjustly accuses them of a fault, God deliver us from their outcries! Let those who cannot bear such things take no notice of the splendid plans they made when alone, which could have been no genuine determination of the will but only some trick of the imagination, or the results would have been very different. The devil assaults and deceives people in this way, often doing great harm to women and others too ignorant to understand the difference between the powers of the soul and the imagination, and a thousand other matters of the sort. O sisters! how easy it is to know which of you have attained to a sincere love of your neighbour, and which of you are far from it. If you knew the importance of this virtue, your only care would be to gain it.

11. When I see people very anxious to know what sort of prayer they practice, covering their faces and afraid to move or think lest they should lose any slight tenderness and devotion they feel, I know how little they understand how to attain union with God since they think it consists in such things as these. No, sisters, no; our Lord expects *works* from us. If you see a sick sister whom you can relieve,[43] never fear losing your devotion; compassionate her; if she is in pain, feel for it as if it were your own and, when there is need, fast so that she may eat, not so much for her sake as because you know your Lord asks it of you. This is the true union of our will with the will of God. If some one else is well spoken of, be more pleased than if it were yourself; this is easy enough, for if you were really humble it would vex you to be praised. It is a great good to rejoice at your sister's virtues being known and to feel as sorry for the fault you see in her as if it were yours, hiding it from the sight of others.

12. I have often spoken on this subject elsewhere,[44] because, my sisters, if we fail in this I know that all is lost: please God this may never be our case. If you possess fraternal charity, I assure you that you will certainly obtain the union I have described. If you are conscious that you are wanting in this charity, although you may feel devotion and sweetness and a short absorption in the prayer of quiet (which makes you think you have attained to union with God), believe me you have not yet reached it. Beg our Lord to grant you perfect love for your neighbour, and leave the rest to Him. He will give you more than you know how to desire if you constrain yourselves and strive with all your power to gain it, forcing your will as far as possible to comply in all things with your sisters' wishes although you may sometimes forfeit your own rights by so doing. Forget your self-interests for theirs, how ever much nature may rebel; when opportunity occurs take some burden upon yourself to ease your neighbour of it. Do not fancy it will cost you nothing and that you will find it all done for you: think what the love He bore for us cost our Spouse, Who to free us from death, Himself suffered the most painful death of all—the death of the Cross.

CHAPTER IV.

FURTHER EXPLANATION OF THE SAME SUBJECT; EXPLAINS THIS PRAYER. THE IMPORTANCE OF BEING ON ONE'S GUARD, AS THE DEVIL EAGERLY DESIRES TO TURN SOULS BACK FROM THE RIGHT PATH.

1. The spiritual espousals. 2. The prayer of union resembles a betrothal. 3. Before the spiritual nuptials temptations are dangerous. 4. The great good done by souls faithful to these graces. 5. Religious subject to the devil's deceptions. 6. Satan's strata-gems. 7. Why they are permitted. 8. Prayer and watchfulness our safeguards. 9. God's watchfulness over such souls. 10. Progress in virtue. 11. Insignificance of our actions compared with their reward. 12. St. Teresa's motives for writing on prayer.

1. You appear anxious to know what has become of the little dove and where she obtains rest, since obviously she can find it neither in spiritual consolations nor in earthly pleasures but takes a higher flight. I cannot tell you until we come to the last mansion: God grant I may remember or have leisure to write it. It is nearly five months since I began this work, and as my head is too weak to read it again, no doubt it will be very disconnected and full of repetitions: however, as it is only for my sisters, that will matter little. Yet I should like to express myself

[43] Way of Perf. ch. vii. 4.
[44] Way of Perf. ch. iv. 3; vii. 4.

more fully about the prayer of union and will make use, to the best of my scanty wits, of a comparison. Later on we will speak of the little butterfly, which is never still, for it can find no true repose, yet always fertile, doing good both to itself and others.[45] You have often heard that God spiritually espouses souls: may He be praised for His mercy in thus humbling Himself so utterly. Though but a homely comparison, yet I can find nothing better to express my meaning than the Sacrament of Matrimony although the two things are very different. In divine union everything is spiritual and far removed from anything corporal, all the joys our Lord gives and the mutual delight felt in it being celestial and very unlike human marriage, which it excels a thousand times. Here all is love united to love; its operations are more pure, refined, and sweet than can be described, though our Lord knows how to make the soul sensible of them.

2. I think this union does not attain as far as the spiritual espousals but resembles the preliminaries that take place when two people are contemplating a betrothal. Their suitability and willingness for the alliance are first discussed; then they may be allowed to see one another sometimes so as to come to a decision. Thus it is in the spiritual espousals: when the preliminary agreement has been made and the soul thoroughly understands what great advantages she will gain, having resolved to fulfil the will of her Spouse in all things and to do all she can to please Him, His Majesty Who knows well whether this is so in reality, wishes in return to gratify His bride. He therefore bestows this favour upon her, visits her and draws her into His presence, as He wishes her to know Him better. We might compare the prayer of union to a visit, for it lasts but a very little while.[46] There is no longer any question of deliberation, but the soul in a secret manner sees to what a Bridegroom it is betrothed; the senses and faculties could not, in a thousand years, gain the knowledge thus imparted in a very short time. The Spouse, being Who He is, leaves the soul far more deserving of completing the espousals, as we may call them; the enamored soul in its love for Him makes every effort to prevent their being frustrated. Should it grow neglectful and set its affections on anything except our Lord, it will forfeit everything: this loss is as great as are the favours the soul has continually received, which are precious beyond description.[47]

3. O Christian souls! you whom God has brought thus far! I implore you for His dear sake not to grow careless, but to avoid all occasions of sin; you are not strong enough yet to undergo temptation, as you will be after the espousals which take place in the next mansion. Here the betrothed are, as they say, only acquainted by sight,[48] and the devil will spare no pains to oppose and prevent their nuptials. Afterwards, when he sees the Bride is wholly given to her Bridegroom, he is afraid to interfere, having learnt by experience that if he molests her, while he loses much, she will gain greatly in merit.

4. I can assure you, my daughters,[49] that I have known people far advanced in the spiritual life who had reached this state of prayer yet whom the devil reclaimed by his subtlety and wiles: as I have often said, all hell leagues together against such souls because the loss of one of them entails the perdition of many more, as Satan is well aware. If we considered how many men God draws to Himself by means of one, we should praise Him fervently. Think of the multitudes converted by the martyrs or by one young maiden like St. Ursula! Again, of how many victims the evil one was deprived by St. Dominic, St. Francis, and other founders of religious orders. How many more he loses, even now, through Father Ignatius [Loyola], who founded the Company [of Jesus]! As we read their lives, we learn that they received such graces from God. How was this great good done except by their efforts not to forfeit, through any fault of theirs, these divine espousals? Oh, my daughters, how willing our Lord is to grant us the same graces! In fact, there is even more urgent need now for persons to prepare for such favours, since there are fewer who care for His honour. We love ourselves too much and are too prudent to give up any of our rights. What a deception! May God in His mercy give us light, lest we sink into such darkness.

[45] Compare: 'habebit fructum in respectione animarum sanctarum' (Breviar. Rom. Ant. ad Laudes de Com. Virg.); 'quasi apis argumentosa Domino deservisti' (Ibid. Feast of St. Cæcilia.)

[46] Life, ch. xviii.

[47] Way of Perf. ch. xxxi. 10.

[48] Phil. a SS. Trinit. l.c. p. iii. tract. i. disc. ii. art. 2.

[49] Contrast with this paragraph what the Saint says in her Life, ch. xix. § 8.

5. You may question or be in doubt on two points. Firstly: if the soul is entirely united with the will of God, as I have stated, how can it be deceived, since it ever seeks to follow His pleasure? Secondly, how can the devil enter and work such havoc as to destroy your soul while you are so utterly withdrawn from the world and constantly frequent the Sacraments?[50] At the same time you enjoy the society of angels (as we might call them) and by the mercy of God you desire nothing but to serve and please Him in all things?[51] It is not surprising that people in the world should run such risks. I admit you have the right to say this, for God has shown us signal mercy; but, as I said above, knowing as I do that Judas was amongst the Apostles and that he held constant intercourse with God Himself, to Whose words he listened, I learn that the state of religion does not make us safe.

6. To your first question I reply that doubtless if such a soul is always faithful to the will of God, it cannot be lost; the evil one, however, comes with his keen subtlety and, under the pretext of good, leads it astray in some trivial matter and causes it to commit small defects which he makes it believe are harmless. Thus, little by little, the reason is obscured and the will is weakened while the devil fosters his victim's self-love, until, by degrees, he succeeds in withdrawing it from union with the will of God and makes it follow its own will.

7. The answer to your first inquiry will serve for the second. No enclosure can be too strict for Satan to enter nor any desert too remote for him to visit. Besides, God may permit him to tempt the soul to prove its virtue; for as He intends it to enlighten others, it is better for it to fail in the beginning than when it might do them great harm.

8. We must beg God constantly in our prayers to uphold us by His hand; we should keep ever in our minds the truth that if He leaves us, most certainly we shall fall at once into the abyss, for we must never be so foolish as to trust in ourselves. After this I think the greatest safeguard is to be very careful and to watch how we advance in virtue; we must notice whether we are making progress or falling back in it, especially as regards the love of our neighbour, the desire to be thought the least of all and how we perform our ordinary, everyday duties. If we attend to this and beg Our Lord to enlighten us, we shall at once perceive our gain or loss.

9. Do not suppose that after advancing the soul to such a state God abandons it so easily that it is light work for the devil to regain it. When His Majesty sees it leaving Him, He feels the loss so keenly that He gives it in many a way a thousand secret warnings which reveal to it the hidden danger.[52]

10. In conclusion, let us strive to make constant progress: we ought to feel great alarm if we do not find ourselves advancing, for without doubt the evil one must be planning to injure us in some way; it is impossible for a soul that has come to this state not to go still farther, for love is never idle. Therefore it is a very bad sign when one comes to a stand-still in virtue. She who aspires to become the spouse of God Himself, and has treated with His Majesty and come to such an understanding with Him, must not leave off and go to sleep.[53]

11. To show you, my daughters, how Christ treats the souls He takes for His brides, I will now speak of the sixth mansions. You will then see how little in comparison is all that we can do or suffer in His service to prepare ourselves for the reception of such immense favours. Perhaps our Lord decreed that I should write this in order that the knowledge of the great reward to come, and of His infinite mercy in seeking to give and to manifest Himself to such worms as we are, might make us forget our wretched, petty, earthly pleasures and run on our way with eyes fixed on His grandeur, inflamed with love for Him.

12. May He enable me to explain some of these difficult matters; if our Lord and the Holy Ghost do not guide my pen, I know the task will prove impossible. 1 beg Him to prevent my saying anything unless it will profit you. His Majesty knows that, as far as I can judge, I have no other wish but that His Name may be glorified and that we may strive to serve a Lord Who thus recompenses our efforts even in this world. What, then, will be our joy in heaven where it will be

---

[50] Life, ch, xxxvi. 26; xxxix. 14. Found. ch. i. 1-4.
[51] Way of Perf. ch. i, 2; xiii. 3. Found. ch. i. 3.
[52] Life, ch. xix. 9.
[53] Life, ch. xix. 7.

continuous, without the interruptions, labours, and dangers of this tempestuous sea of life? Were it not for the fear of losing or offending Him, we should wish to live until the end of the world[54] in order to work for so great a God—our Lord and our Spouse. May His Majesty enable us to render Him some service free from the many faults we always commit, even in good works! Amen.

---

[54] Rel. ix. 19.

THE SIXTH MANSIONS

CHAPTER I.

THIS CHAPTER SHOWS HOW, WHEN GOD BESTOWS GREATER FAVOURS ON THE SOUL, IT SUFFERS MORE SEVERE AFFLICTIONS. SOME OF THE LATTER ARE DESCRIBED AND DIRECTIONS HOW TO BEAR THEM GIVEN TO THE DWELLERS IN THIS MANSION. THIS CHAPTER IS USEFUL FOR THOSE SUFFERING INTERIOR TRIALS.

1. Love kindled by divine favours. 2. Our Lord excites the soul's longings. 3. Courage needed to reach the last mansions. 4. Trials accompanying divine favours. 5. Outcry raised against souls striving for perfection. 6. St. Teresa's personal experience of this. 7. Praise distasteful to an enlightened soul. 8. This changes to indifference. 9. Humility of such souls. 10. Their zeal for God's glory. 11. Perfect and final indifference to praise or blame. 12. Love of enemies. 13. Bodily sufferings. 14. St. Teresa's physical ills. 15. A timorous confessor. 16. Anxiety on account of past sins. 17. Fears and aridity. 18. Scruples and fears raised by the devil. 19. Bewilderment of the soul. 20. God alone relieves these troubles. 21. Human weakness. 22. Earthly consolations are of no avail. 23. Prayer gives no comfort at such a time. 24. Remedies for these interior trials. 25. Trials caused by the devil. 26. Other afflictions. 27. Preparatory to entering the seventh mansions.

1. BY the aid of the Holy Ghost I am now about to treat of the sixth mansions, where the soul, wounded with love for its Spouse, sighs more than ever for solitude, withdrawing as far as the duties of its state permit from all that can interrupt it. The sight it has enjoyed of Him is so deeply imprinted on the spirit that its only desire is to behold Him again. I have already said that,[1] even by the imagination, nothing is seen in this prayer that can be called sight. I speak of it as 'sight' because of the comparison I used.

2. The soul is now determined to take no other Bridegroom than our Lord, but He disregards its desires for its speedy espousals, wishing that these longings should become still more vehement and that this good, which far excels all other benefits, should be purchased at some cost to itself. And although for so great a gain all that we must endure is but a poor price to pay, I assure you, daughters, that this pledge of what is in store for us is needed to inspire us with courage to bear our crosses.

3. O My God, how many troubles both interior and exterior must one suffer before entering the seventh mansions! Sometimes, while pondering over this I fear that, were they known beforehand, human infirmity could scarcely bear the thought nor resolve to encounter them, however great might appear the gain. If, however, the soul has already reached the seventh mansions, it fears nothing: boldly undertaking to suffer all things for God,[2] it gathers strength from its almost uninterrupted union with Him.

4. I think it would be well to tell you of some of the trials certain to occur in this state. Possibly all souls may not be led in this way, but I think that those who sometimes enjoy such truly heavenly favours cannot be altogether free from some sort of earthly troubles. Therefore, although at first I did not intend to speak on this subject, yet afterwards I thought that it might greatly comfort a soul in this condition if it knew what usually happens to those on whom God bestows graces of this kind, for at the time they really seem to have lost everything.

5. I shall not enumerate these trials in their proper order, but will describe them as they come to my memory, beginning with the least severe. This is an outcry raised against such a person by those amongst whom she lives, and even from others she has nothing to do with but who fancy that at some time in her life they recollect having seen her. They say she wants to pass for a saint, that she goes to extremes in piety to deceive the world and to depreciate people who are better Christians than herself without making such a parade of it. But notice that she does nothing except endeavour to carry out the duties of her state more perfectly. Persons she thought were her friends

---

[1] Castle, M. v. ch. i. 9. Life, ch. xxviii. 5.

[2] Life, ch. xl. 28. sqq.

desert her, making the most bitter remarks of all. They take it much to heart that her soul is ruined—she is manifestly deluded—it is all the devil's work—she will share the fate of so-and-so who was lost through him, and she is leading virtue astray. They cry out that she is deceiving her confessors, and tell them so, citing examples of others who came to ruin in the same way and make a thousand scoffing remarks of the same sort.[3]

6. I know some one who feared she would be unable to find any priest who would hear her confession, to such a pass did things come; but as it is a long story, I will not stop to tell it now. The worst of it is, these troubles do not blow over but last all her life, for one person warns the other to have nothing to do with people of her kind. You will say that, on the other hand, some speak in her favour. O my daughters, how few think well of her in comparison with the many who hate her!

7. Besides this, praise pains such a soul more than blame because it recognizes clearly that any good it possesses is the gift of God and in no wise its own, seeing that but a short time ago it was weak in virtue and involved in grave sins.[4] Therefore commendation causes it intolerable suffering, at least at first, although later on, for many reasons, the soul is comparatively indifferent to either.

8. The first is that experience has shown the mind that men are as ready to speak well as ill of others, so it attaches no more importance to the one than to the other. Secondly, our Lord having granted it greater light, it perceives that no good thing in it is its own but is His gift, and becomes oblivious of self, praising God for His graces as if they were found in a third person.

9. The third reason is that, realizing the benefit reaped by others from witnessing graces given it by God, such a one thinks that it is for their profit He causes them to discover in her virtues that do not exist.

10. Fourthly, souls seeking God's honour and glory more than their own are cured of the temptation (which usually besets beginners) of thinking that human praise will cause them the injury they have seen it do to others. Nor do these souls care much for men's contempt if only, by their means, any one should praise God at least once—come what may afterwards.

11. These and other reasons to a certain extent allay the great distress formerly given by human praise which, however, still causes some discomfort unless the soul has become utterly regardless of men's tongues. It is infinitely more grieved at being undeservedly esteemed by the world than by any calumny; and when at last it becomes almost indifferent to praise, it cares still less for censure, which even pleases it and sounds like harmonious music to the ears.

12. This is perfectly true; the soul is rather strengthened than depressed by its trials, experience having taught it the great advantages derived from them. It does not think men offend God by persecuting it, but that He permits them to do so for its greater gain.[5] So strong is this belief that such a person bears a special affection for these people, holding them as truer friends and greater benefactors than those who speak well of her.[6]

13. Our Lord now usually sends severe bodily infirmity. This is a far heavier cross, especially if acute pain is felt: if this is violent, I think it is the hardest of earthly trials. I speak of exterior trials; but corporal pains of the worst kind enter the interior of our being also, affecting both spirit and body, so that the soul in its anguish knows not what to do with itself and would far rather meet death at once by some quick martyrdom than suffer thus. However, these paroxysms do not last long, for God never sends us more than we can bear and always gives us patience first.

14. Now to speak of other trials and illnesses of many kinds which generally occur to people in this state. I knew some one who, from the time when, forty years ago,[7] our Lord began to

---

[3] The Saint went through all this herself; every detail is taken from her own experience. See Life, ch. xxv. 20; xxviii. 20-24; xxx. 6; xxiii. 2. Anton. a Sp. S. l.c. tract, ii. n. 268.

[4] Life, ch. xxviii. 19.

[5] Rel. ii. 4.

[6] Anton. a Sp. S. l.c. ii. n. 272. Way of Perf. ch. xv. i; xvii. 4. Found. ch. xxvii. 19, 20. Life, ch. xix. 12; xxxi. 13-17, 25.

[7] 'Forty years ago.' The Saint seems to refer to her first experience in the mystical life, which took place during her illness in the winter of 1537-38. See Life, ch. iv. 9.

bestow on her the favour described, could not affirm with any truth that she had been a single day without pain and other kinds of suffering: I am speaking of physical infirmities besides heavy crosses sent her.[8] True, she had led a wicked life and therefore held these troubles very light in comparison with the hell she had deserved.[9] Our Lord leads those who have offended Him less by some other way, but I should always choose the way of suffering, if only for the sake of imitating our Lord Jesus Christ; though, in fact, it profits us in many other manners. Yet, oh! the rest would seem trifling in comparison could I relate the interior torments met with here, but they are impossible to describe.

15. Let us first speak of the trial of meeting with so timorous and inexperienced a confessor that nothing seems safe to him; he dreads and suspects everything but the commonplace, especially in a soul in which he deters any imperfection, for he thinks people on whom God [10]bestows such favours must be angels, which is impossible while we live in our bodies. He at once ascribes everything to the devil or melancholy. As to the latter, I am not surprised; there is so much of it in the world and the evil one works such harm in this way that confessors have the strongest reasons for anxiety and watchfulness about it.

16. The poor soul, beset by the same fears, seeks its confessor as judge, and feels a torture and dismay at his condemnation that can only be realized by those who have experienced it themselves.[11] For one of the severe trials of these souls, especially if they have lived wicked lives, is their belief that God permits them to be deceived in punishment for their sins. While actually receiving these graces they feel secure and cannot but suppose that these favours proceed from the Spirit of God; but this state lasts a very short time, while the remembrance of their misdeeds is ever before them, so that when, as is sure to happen, they discover any faults in themselves, these torturing thoughts return.[12]

17. The soul is quieted for a time when the confessor reassures it although it returns later on to its former apprehensions, but when he augments its fears they become almost unbearable. Especially is this the case when such spiritual dryness ensues that the mind feels as if it never had thought of God nor ever will be able to do so. When men speak of Him, they seem to be talking of some person heard of long ago.

18. All this is nothing without the further pain of thinking we cannot make our confessors understand the case and are deceiving them.[13] Although such a person may examine her conscience with the greatest care, and may know that she reveals even the first movement of her mind to her director, it does not help her. Her understanding being too obscure to discern the truth, she believes all that the imagination, which now has the upper hand, puts before her mind, besides crediting the falsehoods suggested to her by the devil, whom doubtless our Lord gives leave to tempt her. The evil spirit even tries to make her think God has rejected her. Many are the trials which assault this soul, causing an internal anguish so painful and so intolerable that I can compare it to nothing save that suffered by the lost in hell, for no comfort can be found in this tempest of trouble.[14]

19. If the soul seeks for consolation from its confessor, all the demons appear to help him to torment it more. A confessor who dealt with a person suffering in this manner thought that her state must be very dangerous as so many things were troubling her; therefore, after she had recovered from her trials, he bade her tell him whenever they recurred: however, he found this made matters worse than ever. She lost all control over herself: although she had learnt to read,

---

[8] Life, ch. iv. 6; v; vi; vii. 18; xi. 23; XXX. 9.

[9] Ibid. ch. iii. 6, 7.

[10] Life, ch. xiii. 21-27. Way of Perf. ch. v. 1, 2.

[11] Ibid, ch. xxx. 15.

[12] Ibid, ch. xxxviii. 21. Rel. ii. 15.

[13] Life, ch. xxviii. 20 sqq.

[14] Anton. a Sp. S. l.c. tr. ii. n. 313. On this subject which is commonly called the passive purgation of the intellect, it would be advisable to consult some good author such as Philippus a SS. Trinitate, l.c. part. i. tr. iii. disc. iii.-v., especially disc. iv. art. 5, 6.

yet she could no more understand a book in the vulgar tongue than if she had not known the alphabet, for her mind was incapable of acting.[15]

20. In short, there is no other remedy in such a tempest except to wait for the mercy of God Who, unexpectedly, by some casual word or unforeseen circumstance, suddenly dispels all these sorrows; then every cloud of trouble disappears and the mind is left full of light and far happier than before.[16] It praises our Lord God like one who has come out victorious from a dangerous battle, for it was He Who won the victory. The soul is fully conscious that the conquest was not its own as all weapons of self-defense appeared to be in the enemies' hands. Thus it realizes its weakness and how little man can help himself if God forsake him.

21. This truth now needs no demonstration, for past experience has taught the soul its utter incapacity; it realizes the nothingness of human nature and what miserable creatures we are. Although in a state of grace from which it has not fallen—for, in spite of these torments, it has not offended God, nor would it do so for any earthly thing[17] —yet so hidden is this grace, that the sufferer believes that neither now, nor in the past, has she ever possessed the faintest spark of love for God.[18] If at any time she has done good, or if His Majesty ever bestowed any favours on her, they seem to have been but a dream or a fancy, while her sins stand clearly before her.

22. O Jesus! how sad it is to see a soul thus forsaken, and how little, as I said, can any earthly comfort avail! Do not imagine, sisters, if you are ever brought to such a state, that rich and independent people have more resources than yourselves in these troubles. No, no! to offer such consolations would be like setting all the joys of the world before people condemned to death: far from mitigating, it would increase their torture. So with the souls I spoke of: their comfort must come from above—nothing earthly can help them. This great God wishes us to acknowledge His sovereignty and our own misery—an important point for those who are to advance still farther.

23. What can the poor soul do if such a trial lasts for many days? Prayer makes no difference as far as comforting the heart, which no consolation can enter, nor can the mind even grasp the meaning of the words of vocal prayer: mental prayer is out of the question at such a time, since the faculties are unequal to it. Solitude harms the soul, yet society or conversation is a fresh torment. Strive as the sufferer may to hide it, she is so wearied and out of sorts with all around that she cannot but manifest her condition.

24. How can the soul possibly tell what ails it? Its pains are indescribable; it is wrung with nameless anguish and spiritual suffering. The best remedy for these crosses (I do not mean for gaining deliverance from them, for I know of nothing that will do that, but for enabling one to bear them) is to perform external works of charity and to trust in the mercy of God, which never fails those who hope in Him.[19] May He be for ever blessed! Amen

25. The devils also bring about exterior trials which being more unusual need not be mentioned. They are far less painful, for whatever the demons may do, I believe they never succeed in paralyzing the faculties or disturbing the soul in the former manner. In fact, the reason is able to discern that the evil spirits can do no more harm than God permits; and while the mind has not lost its powers, all sufferings are comparatively insignificant.

26. I shall treat of other internal afflictions met with in this mansion when describing the different kinds of prayer and favours bestowed here by our Lord. Although some of these latter pains are harder to endure, as appears by their bodily effects, yet they do not deserve the name of crosses, nor have we the right to call them so. Indeed, they are great graces from God as the soul recognizes amidst its pangs, realizing how far it is from meriting such graces.

27. This severe torture felt by souls just at the entrance of the seventh mansion is accompanied by many other sufferings, some of which I will mention: to speak of them all would be impossible, nor could I portray them because they come from another and far higher source

[15] Life, ch. xxv. 21.
[16] Ibid. ch. xxv. 23.
[17] Ibid. ch. xxiv. 3. Way of Perf. ch. xli. 5. Castle, M. vii. ch. iv. 1.
[18] Excl. xvi. 4.
[19] Life, ch. xxxi. 27.

than the rest. If I have succeeded so ill in writing of trials of a lower kind, much less could I treat of the others. May God assist me in all things, through the merits of His Son! Amen.

CHAPTER II.

TREATS OF SEVERAL WAYS WHEREBY OUR LORD QUICKENS THE SOUL; THERE APPEARS NO CAUSE FOR ALARM IN THEM ALTHOUGH THEY ARE SIGNAL FAVOURS OF A VERY EXALTED NATURE.

1. Our Lord excites the love of His spouse. 2. The wound of love. 3. The pain it causes. 4. The call of the Bridegroom. 5. Effect on the soul. 6. A spark of the fire of love. 7. The spark dies out. 8. This grace evidently divine. 9. One such wound repays many trials. 10. First reason of immunity from deception. 11. Second and third reasons. 12. The imagination not concerned in it. 13. St. Teresa never alarmed at this prayer. 14. 'The odour of Thine ointment.' 15. No reason to fear deception here.

1. IT seems as if we had deserted the little dove for a long time, but this is not the case, for these past trials cause her to take a far higher flight. I will now describe the way in which the Spouse treats her before uniting her entirely to Himself. He increases her longing for Him by devices so delicate that the soul itself cannot discern them; nor do I think I could explain them except to people who have personally experienced them. These desires are delicate and subtle impulses springing from the inmost depths of the soul; I know of nothing to which they can be compared.

2. These graces differ entirely from anything we ourselves can gain, and even from the spiritual consolation before described.[20] In the present case, even when the mind is not recollected or even thinking of God, although no sound is heard, His Majesty arouses it suddenly as if by a swiftly flashing comet or by a clap of thunder.[21] Yet the soul thus called by God hears Him well enough—so well, indeed, that sometimes, especially at first, it trembles and even cries out, although it feels no pain. It is conscious of having received a delicious wound but cannot discover how, nor who gave it, yet recognizes it as a most precious grace and hopes the hurt will never heal.

3. The soul makes amorous complaints to its Bridegroom, even uttering them aloud; nor can it control itself, knowing that though He is present He will not manifest Himself so that it may enjoy Him. This causes a pain, keen although sweet and delicious from which the soul could not escape even if it wished; but this it never desires.[22] This favour is more delightful than the pleasing absorption of the faculties in the prayer of quiet which is unaccompanied by suffering.[23]

4. I am at my wits' end, sisters, as to how to make you understand this operation of love: I know not how to do so. It seems contradictory to say that the Beloved clearly shows He dwells in the soul and calls by so unmistakable a sign and a summons so penetrating, that the spirit cannot choose but hear it, while He appears to reside in the seventh mansion. He speaks in this manner, which is not a set form of speech, and the inhabitants of the other mansions, the senses, the imagination and the faculties, dare not stir.[24]

5. O Almighty God! how profound are Thy secrets and how different are spiritual matters from anything that can be seen or heard in this world! I can find nothing to which to liken these graces, insignificant as they are compared with many others Thou dost bestow on souls. This favour acts so strongly upon the spirit that it is consumed by desires yet knows not what to ask, for it realizes clearly that its God is with it. You may inquire, if it realizes this so clearly, what more does it desire and why is it pained? What greater good can it seek? I cannot tell: I know that

---

[20] Mansion iv. ch. i. Life, ch. xxix. 10-15. Rel. ch. viii. 15.

[21] The saint first wrote 'relampago,' flash of lightning, but afterwards altered it to 'trueno,' clap of thunder.

[22] Rel. viii. 16. St. John of the Cross, Spiritual Cant. st. i. 22 sqq. Poems 7, 8.

[23] Life, ch. xxix. 18.

[24] Life, ch. xv. 1.

this suffering seems to pierce the very heart, and when He Who wounded it draws out the dart He seems to draw the heart out too, so deep is the love it feels.[25]

6. I have been thinking that God might be likened to a burning furnace[26] from which a small spark flies into the soul that feels the heat of this great fire, which, however, is insufficient to consume it. The sensation is so delightful that the spirit lingers in the pain produced by its contact. This seems to me the best comparison I can find, for the pain is delicious and is not really pain at all, nor does it always continue in the same degree; sometimes it lasts for a long time; on other occasions it passes quickly. This is as God chooses, for no human means can obtain it; and though felt at times for a long while, yet it is intermittent.

7. In fact it is never permanent and therefore does not wholly inflame the spirit; but when the soul is ready to take fire, the little spark suddenly dies out, leaving the heart longing to suffer anew its loving pangs. No grounds exist for thinking this comes from any natural cause or from melancholy, or that it is an illusion of the devil or the imagination. Undoubtedly this movement of the heart comes from God Who is unchangeable; nor do its effects is resemble those of other devotions in which the strong absorption of delight makes us doubt their reality.

8. There is no suspension here of the senses or other faculties: they wonder at what is happening, without impeding it. Nor do I think that they can either increase or dispel this delightful pain. Any one who has received this favour from our Lord will understand my meaning on reading this: let her thank Him fervently: there is no need to fear deception but far more fear of not being sufficiently grateful for so signal a grace. Let her endeavour to serve Him and to amend her life in every respect; then she will see what will follow and how she will obtain still higher and higher gifts.

9. A person on whom this grace was bestowed passed several years without receiving any other favour, yet was perfectly satisfied, for even had she served God for very many years in the midst of severe trials, she would have felt abundantly repaid. May He be for ever blessed! Amen.

10. Perhaps you wonder why we may feel more secure against deception concerning this favour than in other cases. I think it is for these reasons. Firstly, because the devil cannot give such delicious pain: he may cause pleasure or delight which appears spiritual but is unable to add suffering, especially suffering of so keen a sort, united to peace and joy of soul. His power is limited to what is external; suffering produced by him is never accompanied with peace, but with anxieties and struggles.

11. Secondly, because this welcome storm comes from no region over which Satan has control. Thirdly, because of the great benefits left in the soul which, as a rule, is resolute to suffer for God and longs to bear many crosses. It is also far more determined than before to withdraw from worldly pleasures and intercourse and other things of the same sort.

12. It is very clear that this is no fiction: the imagination may counterfeit some favours but not this, which is too manifest to leave room for doubt. Should any one still remain uncertain, let her know that hers were not genuine impulses;[27] that is, if she is dubious as to whether or no she experienced them, for they are as certainly perceived by the soul as is a loud voice by the ears. It is impossible for these experiences to proceed from melancholy whose whims arise and exist only in the imagination, whereas this emotion comes from the interior of the soul.

13. I may be mistaken, but I shall not change my opinion until I hear reasons to the contrary from those who understand these matters. I know some one who has always greatly dreaded such deceptions, yet could never bring herself to feel any alarm about this state of prayer.[28]

14. Our Lord also uses other means of rousing the soul; for instance—when reciting vocal prayer without seeking to penetrate the sense, a person may be seized with a delightful fervour[29] as if suddenly encompassed with a fragrance powerful enough to diffuse itself through all the

[25] Ibid. ch. xxix. 17, 18.
[26] Ibid. ch. xv, 6; xviii. 4.; xxi. 9.
[27] Life, ch. xv. 15, 16.
[28] Life, ch. xxix. 6-10.
[29] Ibid. ch. xv. 12. On the matter treated by St. Teresa in this chapter, compare St. John of the Cross, Spiritual Canticle, stanza i. (circa finem), stanza ix.; The Living Flame of Love, stanza ii.

senses. I do not assert that there really is any perfume but use this comparison because it somewhat resembles the manner by which the Spouse makes His presence understood, moving the soul to a delicious desire of enjoying Him and thus disposing it to heroic acts, and causing it to render Him fervent praise.

15. This favour springs from the same source as the former, but causes no suffering here, nor are the soul's longings to enjoy God painful: this is what is more usually experienced by the soul. For the reasons already given there appears no cause here for fear, but rather for receiving it with thanksgiving.

INTRODUCTORY NOTE TO CHAPTER III.

BY THE EDITOR

THE readers, especially those not well acquainted with Scholastic philosophy, will, perhaps, be glad to find here a short explanation of the various kinds of Vision and Locution, Corporal, Imaginary, and Intellectual. The senses of Taste, Touch, and Smell are not so often affected by mystical phenomena, but what we are about to say in respect of Sight and Hearing applies, mutatis mutandis, to these also.

I. A CORPORAL VISION is when one sees a bodily object. A Corporal Locution is when one hears words uttered by a human tongue. In both cases the respective senses are exercising their normal function, and the phenomenon differs from ordinary seeing or hearing merely by the fact that in the latter the object seen is a real body, the words perceived come from a real tongue, whereas in the Vision or Locution the object is either only apparent or at any rate is not such as it seems to be. Thus, when young Tobias set out on a journey, his companion, Azarias, was not a real human being, but an archangel in human form. Tobias did really see and hear him, and felt the grip of his hand; Sara and her parents, as well as Tobias's parents, saw and heard him too, but all the time the archangel made himself visible and audible by means of an assumed body, or perhaps of an apparent body. It would be more correct to describe such a phenomenon as an APPARITION than as a Vision, and in fact the apparitions of our Risen Lord to the holy women and the apostles belong to this category. For, though His was a real body, it was glorified and therefore no longer subject to the same laws which govern purely human things. (St. Thomas, *Summa theol.* III., qu. 54, art. I-3).

St. Teresa tells us more than once that she never beheld a Corporal Vision, nor heard a Corporal Locution.

II. AN IMAGINARY VISION OR LOCUTION is one where nothing is seen or heard by the senses of seeing or hearing, but where the same impression is received that would be produced upon the imagination by the senses if some real object were perceived by them. For, according to the Scholastics, the Imagination stands half-way between the senses and the intellect, receiving impressions from the former and transmitting them to the latter. This is the reason why imaginary Visions and Locutions are so dangerous that, according to St. Teresa, St. John of the Cross, and other spiritual writers, they should not only never be sought for, but as much as possible shunned and under all circumstances discountenanced. For the Imagination is closely connected with the Memory, so that it is frequently impossible to ascertain whether a Vision, etc., is not perhaps a semi-conscious or unconscious reproduction of scenes witnessed. It is here also that deception, willful or unwilful, self-deception or deception by a higher agency, is to be feared. Hence the general rule that such Visions or Locutions should only be trusted upon the strongest grounds. According to St. Thomas Aquinas, (*Summa theol. IIa IIæ*, gu. 175, art. 3 ad q.) the visions of Isaias, St. John in the Apocalypse etc., were Imaginary.

As an example of Imaginary Visions we may mention St. Stephen, who saw 'the heavens opened, and the Son of Man standing on the right hand of God'; or St. Peter, who saw 'the heaven opened, and a certain vessel descending, as it were a great linen sheet, let down by the four corners from heaven to the earth… and there came a voice to him: Arise, Peter, kill and eat.' (Acts, vii. 55; X. 11-13).

These Visions, Locutions, etc., are not hallucinations. The latter are due to physical disorder which affects the memory and causes it to represent impressions formerly received by it, in a disorderly and often grotesque manner. The Imaginary Vision takes place independently of a morbid state, is caused by an extraneous power, good or evil, and has for its object things of which the memory neither has nor ever has had cognizance.

III. AN INTELLECTUAL VISION OR LOCUTION is one where nothing is seen or heard by the eyes and ears, and where no sensation is received by the imagination. But the impression which would be delivered by the imagination to the intellect, had it come through the senses and been handed on to the imagination, is directly imprinted upon the intellect. To understand this it is necessary to bear in mind that the impressions we receive through the senses must undergo a transformation—must be spiritualized—before they reach the intellect. This is one of the most difficult problems of psychology; none of the solutions offered by various schools of philosophy seem to render it entirely free from obscurity. According to St. Thomas Aquinas, the impression received by the eye (*Species sensibilis*) is spiritualized by a faculty called *Intellectus agens* by means of abstraction (*Species impressa*), and is treasured up in the memory, like lantern slides, available at demand. The mind, identifying itself with the Species impressa, produces the 'Word of the mind' (*Verbum mentis*), wherein consists the act of Understanding or Mental Conception. In the Intellectual Vision or Locution, God, without co-operation on the part of the senses, the imagination, or the memory, produces directly on the mind the *Species impressa*. As this is supernatural with regard to its origin, and often also with respect to its object, it stands to reason that it is too exalted for the memory to receive it, so that such Visions and Locutions are frequently only imperfectly remembered and sometimes altogether forgotten, as St. Teresa tells us. On the other hand they are far less dangerous than Corporal or Imaginary Visions and Locutions, because the senses and imagination have nothing to do with them, whilst evil spirits are unable to act directly upon the mind, and self-deception is altogether excluded for the reasons stated by St. Teresa. An instance of such a vision is mentioned by St. Paul: 'I know a man in Christ above fourteen years ago (whether in the body I know not, or out of the body I know not: God knoweth), such an one rapt even to the third heaven. And I know such a man (whether in the body or out of the body, I know not: God knoweth): that he was caught up into paradise, and heard secret words, which it is not granted to man to utter' (2 Cor. xii. 2-4).

CHAPTER III.

TREATS OF THE SAME SUBJECT AND OF THE WAY GOD IS SOMETIMES PLEASED TO SPEAK TO THE SOUL. HOW WE SHOULD BEHAVE IN SUCH A CASE, IN WHICH WE MUST NOT FOLLOW OUR OWN OPINION. GIVES SIGNS TO SHOW HOW TO DISCOVER WHETHER THIS FAVOUR IS A DECEPTION OR NOT: THIS IS VERY NOTEWORTHY.

1. Locutions. 2. Sometimes caused by melancholia. 3. Caution needed at first. 4. Locutions frequently occur during prayer. 5. Resist those containing false doctrine. 6. First sign of genuine locutions. 7. Effect of the words: 'Be not troubled.' 8. 'It is I, be not afraid.' 9. 'Be at Peace.' 10. Second sign. 11. Third sign. 12. The devil suggests doubts about true locutions. 13. Confidence of the soul rewarded. 14. Its joy at seeing God's words verified. 15. Its zeal for God's honour. 16. Locutions coining from the fancy. 17. Imaginary answers given to prayer. 18. A confessor should be consulted about locutions. 19. Interior locutions. 20. First sign of genuine interior locutions. 21. Second sign. 22. Third sign. 23. Fourth sign. 24. Fifth sign. 25. Results of true locutions. 26. They should remove alarm. 27. Answer to an objection.

1. GOD arouses the soul in another manner which, though in some ways apparently a greater favour than the above mentioned, yet may prove more dangerous, therefore I will give some particulars about it. He does this by means of words addressed to the soul in many different ways; sometimes they appear to come from without; at other times from the inner depths of the soul; or again, from its superior part; while other speeches are so exterior as to be heard by the ears like a real voice.

2. At times, indeed very often, this may be only a fancy; especially with persons of a lively imagination or who are afflicted with melancholy to any marked extent. I think that no attention

should be paid to either class of people when they say they see, hear, or learn anything supernaturally. Do not disturb them by saying that it comes from the devil,[30] but listen to them as if they were sick persons. Let the prioress or confessor to whom they tell their story bid them think no more of it as such matters are not essential in the service of God: the devil has deceived many Christians thus, although perhaps it is not so in their case; therefore they need not trouble themselves about it. Thus we must accommodate ourselves to their humour: if we tell them their fancies proceed from melancholia, there will be no end to the matter, for they will persist in maintaining they have seen and heard these things, for so it seems to them.

3. The truth is, care should be taken to keep such people from too much prayer and to persuade them, as far as possible, to take no notice of their fancies: the devil makes use of these weak souls to injure others, even if they themselves escape unhurt. There is need for caution both with feeble and strong souls at first, until it is certain from what spirit these things proceed. I maintain that, in the beginning, it is always wiser to resist these communications; if they come from God this is the best way to receive more, for they increase when discouraged. At the same time the soul should not be too strictly controlled or disquieted, for it cannot help itself in the matter.

4. To return to discuss the words addressed to the soul: any kind I mentioned may come either from God, the devil, or the imagination. By the help of God I will endeavour to describe the signs distinguishing the one from the other, and when these locutions are dangerous, for they occur to many persons who praise prayer. I do not wish you to think, sisters, that there is any harm either in believing or in disregarding them. When they only console you, or warn you of your faults, it matters not whence they come or whether they are only fancies.

5. I caution you on one point—although they may come from God, you must not esteem yourself more highly, for He often spoke to the Pharisees[31] —all the good consists in profiting by His words. Take no more notice of any speeches you hear which disagree with the Holy Scriptures than if you heard them from Satan himself. Though they may only rise from your vivid imagination, look upon them as a temptation against the faith. Always resist them; then they will leave you, and cease, for they have little strength of their own.[32]

6. Now let us return to the first point—whether these communications come from the inferior or the superior part of the soul, or from without, does not affect their originating from God.

7. In my opinion these are the most certain signs of their being divine. The first and truest is the power and authority they carry with them, for these words are operative.[33] For example: a soul is suffering all the sorrow and disquiet I have described: the mind is darkened and dry; but it is set at peace, freed from all trouble and filled with light merely by hearing the words: 'Be not troubled.' These deliver it from all its pains, although it felt as though, if the whole world and all its theologians had united in trying to persuade it there was no cause for grief, it could not, in spite of all their efforts, have been delivered from its affliction.[34]

8. Again, a person is troubled and greatly terrified at being told by her confessor and other people that her soul is under the influence of the evil one: she hears a single sentence which says, 'It is I, be not afraid,'[35] and is at once freed from all fears and filled with consolation; indeed, she believes it would be impossible for any one to disturb her confidence.[36]

9. Again, when exceedingly anxious about important business, not knowing whether or not it will be successful, on hearing words bidding her 'Be at peace; all will go well,' she feels

---

[30] Life, ch. xxiii. 114.

[31] Antonius a Sp. S. l.c. tr. iii. n. 323. St. John of the Cross, Ascent of Mount Carmel, bk. ii. ch. xxvii.

[32] Life, ch. xxv. 13, 18.

[33] Ps. cxlviii. 5: 'Ipse dixit et facta sunt.' Life, ch. xxv. 5. Anton. a Sp. S. l.c. tr. iii. n. 353. St. John of the Cross, Ascent of Mount Carmel, bk. ii. ch. xxxi. calls these 'substantial words.'

[34] Life, ch. xxvi. 6; xxx. 17. Rel. i. 26.

[35] St. Luke xxiv. 36.

[36] Life, ch. xxv. 22; xxxiii. 10. Rel. vii. 22. St. John of the Cross, Ascent of Mount Carmel, bk. ii. ch. xxxi. 1.

reassured and free from all care in the matter.[37] Many other instances of the same sort could be mentioned.

10. The second sign is a great calm and a devout and peaceful recollection which dwell in the soul together with a desire to praise God. They say that communications, at any rate in this mansion, are not uttered direly by God but are transmitted by an angel.[38] Then, O my God, if a word sent to us by Thee through Thy messenger has such force, what effects wilt Thou not leave in the soul united to Thee in a mutual bond of love?[39]

11. The third proof is that these words do not pass from the memory but remain there for a very long time; sometimes they are never forgotten. This is not the case with what *men* may utter, which, however grave and learned they may be, is not thus impressed on our memory. Neither, if they prophesy of things to come, do we believe them as we do these divine locutions which leave us so convinced of their truth that, although their fulfilment sometimes seems utterly impossible and we vacillate and doubt about them, there still remains in the soul a certainty of their verity which cannot be destroyed. Perhaps everything may seem to militate against what was heard and years pass by, yet the spirit never loses its belief that God will make use of means unknown to men for the purpose and that finally what was foretold must surely happen; as indeed it does.[40]

12. Still, as I said, the soul is troubled at seeing many obstacles in the way of the accomplishment of the prophecy. The words, their effects, and the assurance they carry with them convinced the soul at the moment that they came from God. Afterwards, however, doubts arise as to whether the locutions came from the devil or from the imagination, although while hearing them the person would have died to defend their truth.[41] But, as I said, these misgivings must be suggested by the evil one to afflict and intimidate her, especially if by carrying out a command thus given great good will result to souls and some work be done conducing notably to the honour and service of God, concerning which great difficulties have to be overcome. In such cases, where will Satan stop short? At least, he weakens faith, and it is a terrible evil to doubt that God has power to work in a way far beyond our understanding.

13. Despite all these difficulties and although the confessors consulted on these matters say the words were but fancies, while events take such an unfavorable turn as to make the realization of these predictions seem impossible, yet there remains so lively a spark of certainty in the mind (I know not whence it comes) that, although all other hopes die out, it cannot, if it would, quench this ardent spark of confidence. At last, as I said, our Lord's words are accomplished, at which the soul is so satisfied and joyful that it can do nothing but praise His Majesty—more because it sees His words prove true than on account of the thing itself, even though it may be of consequence to the person concerned.

14. I know not why the soul attaches such importance to these communications being verified. I think that if the person herself were detected in telling falsehoods, she would not be so grieved as at these locutions proving untrue—as if she could do anything in the matter beyond repeating what has been said to her! A certain person was frequently reminded in such a case of the Prophet Jonas, when he found Nineveh was not to be destroyed.[42]

15. In fact, as these words come from the Spirit of God, it is right thus to trust them and to desire that He Who is supreme truth should not be thought a deceiver. Justly, therefore, does their hearer rejoice when, after a thousand delays and enormous difficulties, they are accomplished.

---

[37] Life, ch. xxxv. 7. Rel. ix. 6. St. John of the Cross, Ascent of Mount Carmel, bk. iii. ch. ii. 7.

[38] Rel. v. 14.

[39] Life, ch. xxv. 23-25. See also Schram, Instit. theol. myst. 528 schol.; 529 schol. ii. and iii.; 5 3 1 schol. ii.; 5 32 schol. ii. Exterior locutions may proceed direct from God, but generally are due to the ministry of angels; the same holds good with regard to the imaginary ones. Intellectual locutions, in which the words are merely impressed upon the substance of the soul without intervention of the imagination, can only proceed from God, Who alone is able to act upon the substance of the soul. See also Life, ch. xxvii. 7 (end), 8, 9, and 10, and the corresponding chapters in St. John's Ascent of Mount Carmel.

[40] Life, ch. xxv. 3, 10. Rel. ii. 17.

[41] Ibid, ch. xxv. 10.

[42] Jonas iv. 1: 'Et afflictus est Jonas afflictione magna et iratus est; et oravit ad Dominum et dixit: Obsecro, Domine, numquid non hoc est verbum meum cum adhuc essem in terra mea?'

Although this success may entail great suffering on herself, she prefers it to the nonfulfillment of what she knows our Lord most certainly foretold. Possibly every one is not so weak as this, if indeed it is a weakness, though I cannot myself condemn it as an evil.

16. If these locutions proceed from the imagination[43] they show no such signs, bringing neither conviction, peace, nor interior joy with them. But in some cases I have come across, on account of a very weak constitution or vivid imagination or of other causes I do not know, persons while absorbed in the prayer of quiet and in spiritual slumber are so entirely carried out of themselves by their deep state of recollection as to be unconscious of anything external. All their senses being thus dormant, as if asleep—as indeed, at times they really are—they thus, in a sort of dream, fancy they are spoken to or see things they imagine come from God, but which leave no more effect than dreams.

17. Again, one who very lovingly asks something of our Lord may fancy that an answer comes from Him.[44] This often occurs, but I think that no one accustomed to receive divine communications could be deceived on this point by the imagination.

18. The devil's deceptions are more dangerous; but if the foregoing signs are present, we may feel fairly confident that these locutions are from God, though not so certain but that, if they refer to some weighty matter in which we are called upon to act or if they concern a third person, we should consult some confessor who is both learned and a servant of God, before attempting or thinking of acting on them, although we may have heard them repeated several times and are convinced of their truth and divine origin.[45] His Majesty wishes us to take this course; it is not disobedience to His commands, for He has bidden us hold our confessor as His representative even where there is no doubt that the communications come from Him: thus we shall gain courage if the matter is a very difficult one. Our Lord will reassure our confessor, whom, when He so chooses, He will inspire with faith that these locutions are from the Holy Ghost.[46] If not, we are freed from all further obligations in the matter. I think it would be very dangerous to act against our confessor's advice and to prefer our own opinions in such a matter. Therefore, sisters, I admonish you in the name of our Lord, never to do anything of the sort.

19. God speaks to the soul in another way by a certain intellectual vision which I think undoubtedly proceeds from Him; it will be described later on.[47] 8 It takes place far within the innermost depths of the soul which appears to hear distinctly in a most mysterious manner, with its spiritual hearing, the words spoken to it by our Lord Himself. The way in which the spirit perceives these words and the results produced by them, convince us that they cannot in any way come from the devil. Their powerful aftereffects force us to admit this and plainly show they do not spring from the imagination.[48] Careful consideration will assure us of this for the following reasons;—

20. Firstly, the clearness of the language varies in the different kinds of locutions. Those that are divine are so distinct that the hearer remembers if there were a syllable missing, and what words were made use of even though a whole sentence was spoken. But if the speech were only a freak of fancy, it would not be so audible nor would the words be so distinct but would be only half articulated.[49]

21. The second reason is that often the person was not thinking of what is heard; sometimes the locution even comes unexpectedly during conversation, though at times it refers to some thought that passed quickly through the mind or to a subject it was before engaged upon. Frequently it concerns things of whose existence the hearer knew nothing nor even imagined such events could ever come to pass; therefore it is impossible for the imagination to have framed such

---

[43] Life, ch. xxv. 4 (end) and 5 (beginning).

[44] Ibid. ch. xxv. 4 (beginning).

[45] Way of Perf. ch. xxxix. 6. Life, ch. xxvi. 4, 5. St. John of the Cross, Ascent of Mount Carmel, bk. ii. ch. xxii. 14-18.

[46] Rel. vii. 15.

[47] Infra, ch. viii.

[48] Life, ch. xxvii, 8.

[49] Life, ch. xxv. 6 and 10 (end).

speeches and deceived the mind by fancies about what it had never wished, nor sought for, nor even thought about.[50]

22. The third reason is that in a genuine case the soul seems to listen to the words, whereas when the imagination is at work, little by little it composes what the person wishes to hear.[51]

23. The fourth reason is because divine locutions differ immensely from others, a single word comprising a depth of meaning which our understanding could not thus quickly condense into one phrase.[52]

24. Fifthly because, in a manner I cannot explain, these communications, without any further explanations, frequently give us to understand far more than is implied by the words themselves. I shall speak farther on of this way of understanding hidden things which is very subtle and a favour for which we should thank God. Some people are exceedingly suspicious about these and other communications of the same kind. I speak particularly of some one[53] who experienced them herself, though there may be others who cannot understand them. I know that she has considered the subject very carefully, God having often bestowed this grace on her. Her principal difficulty was to discover whether the locutions were merely fancied. It is easier to know when they come from the devil although being so wily, he can with facility imitate the spirit of light. However, he would do this in a form of words pronounced so distinctly that there would be no more doubt as to their reality than if they came from the spirit of truth, while those coming from the imagination leave us uncertain whether we heard the words or not. But Satan could never counterfeit the effects I spoke of;[54] he leaves neither peace nor light in the soul, only anxiety and confusion. In any case, he can do little or no harm to one who is humble and who, as I advised, does not act on what is heard.

25. If the soul receives favours and caresses from our Lord, let it examine carefully whether it rates itself more highly in consequence; unless self-abasement increases with God's expressions of love, they do not come from the Holy Spirit. Inevitably, when they are divine, the greater the favours, the less the soul esteems itself and the more keenly it remembers its sins.[55] It becomes more oblivious of self-interest: the will and memory grow more fervent in seeking solely God's honour with no thought of self. It also becomes unceasingly careful not to deviate deliberately from the will of God and feels a keener conviction that instead of meriting such favours, it deserves hell.

26. When these results follow, no graces or gifts received during prayer need alarm the soul which should rather trust in the mercy of God, Who is faithful and will not allow the devil to deceive it; but it is always well to be on one's guard.

27. Those our Lord does not lead by this path may suppose that the soul can avoid listening to these locutions and that even if they are interior it is at least possible to distract the attention from them so as not to hear them and thus escape danger. This cannot be done: I am not speaking of freaks of fancy which may be prevented by ceasing to desire certain things or by paying no attention to its inventions. This is not feasible when these communications come from the Holy Ghost Who, when He speaks, stops all other thoughts and compels the mind to listen.[56] Mark this: that I believe it would be easier for a person with very keen ears to avoid hearing a loud voice, for he could occupy his thoughts and mind in other things. Not so here; the soul can do nothing, nor has it ears to stop, nor power to think of aught but what is said to it. For He Who could stay the sun on its course (at the prayer of Josue,[57] I believe) can so quiet the faculties and the interior of

---

[50] Ibid. ch. xxv. 9, 16.

[51] Ibid. ch. xxv. 4, 6.

[52] Ibid, ch. xxv. 12 (beginning).

[53] The whole of this chapter as well as chapter xxv. of the Life prove clearly that the Saint speaks about herself and that she investigated the subject with the greatest care.

[54] Life, ch. xxv. 15.

[55] Life, ch. xii. 5: 'The nearer we draw unto God the more this virtue (humility) should grow'; xv. 16; xix. 2; xx. 38. Rel. ii. 15; vii. 17; viii. 7, 9. Way of Perf. ch. xvii. 3.

[56] Life, ch. xxv. 21.

[57] Josue x. 12. 13: 'Tunc locutus est Josue: ...sol contra Gabaon ne movearis; steteruntque sol et luna.'

the spirit as to make it perceive that another and a stronger Lord than itself governs this castle; it is thus affected with profound devotion and humility, seeing that it cannot but listen. May the divine Majesty vouchsafe that, forgetting ourselves, our only aim may be to please Him, as I said. Amen. God grant I have succeeded in explaining what I wished and that it may be some guide to those who may experience such favours.

CHAPTER IV.

TREATS OF HOW GOD SUSPENDS THE SOUL IN PRAYER BY A TRANCE, ECSTASY OR RAPTURE, WHICH I BELIEVE ARE ALL THE SAME THING. GREAT COURAGE REQUIRED TO RECEIVE EXTRAORDINARY FAVOURS FROM HIS MAJESTY.

1. Courage required by the soul for the divine espousals. 2. Raptures. 3. Rapture caused by the spark of love. 4. The powers and senses absorbed. 5. Mysteries revealed during ecstasies. 6. These mysteries are unspeakable. 7. Moses and the burning bush. 8. Simile of the museum. 9. St. Teresa's visit to the Duchess of Alva. 10. Joy of the soul during raptures. 11. No imaginary vision. 12. True and false raptures. 13. Revelations of future bliss. 14. The soul's preparation. 15. The soul blinded by its faults. 16. God ready to give these graces to all. 17. Faculties lost during ecstasy. 18. Spiritual inebriation. 19. Fervour and love of suffering left in the soul. 20. Scandal caused to spectators by such favours. 21. Our Lord's predilection for such a soul. 22. Illusionary raptures.

1. WHAT rest can the poor little butterfly find, with all the trials I have told you of and many more? They serve to make her desire the Bride-groom more ardently. His Majesty, well aware of our weakness, fortifies her by these and other means in order that she may obtain courage for union with a Lord so great and may take Him for her Spouse. Perhaps you will laugh and think I am talking foolishly: there can be no call for courage here; there is no woman, however low her class, who would not dare to wed a king. So I think, were he an earthly monarch, but there is need of more fortitude than you suppose in order to espouse the King of heaven.[58] Our nature appears too timid and base for anything so high; without doubt, unless God gave us the grace it would be impossible for us, however much we might appreciate its benefits. You will learn how His Majesty ratifies these espousals; probably this is done when He ravishes the soul by ecstasies, thus depriving it of its faculties; if the use of these were retained, I think the sight of its close vicinity to so mighty a Sovereign would probably deprive the body of life. I am speaking of genuine raptures, not fancies that come from women's weakness—which so often occur nowadays—making them imagine everything to be a rapture or an ecstasy. As I think I said, some are so feebly constituted as to die of a single prayer of quiet.[59]

2. I should like to describe here several kinds of raptures of which I have learnt from spiritual persons with whom I have discussed the subject, but I am not sure whether I shall succeed in explaining them as I did elsewhere.[60] It has been decided that it will not be amiss to repeat what was said about these and other things that happen in this state, if only that I may treat of all the mansions contain in proper order.

3. In one sort of rapture the soul, although perhaps not engaged in prayer at the time, is struck by some word of God which it either remembers or hears.[61] His Majesty, touched with pity by what He has seen it suffer for so long past in its longing for Him, appears to increase the spark I described in the interior of the spirit until it entirely inflames the soul which rises with new life like a phoenix from the flames. Such a one may piously believe her sins are now forgiven,[62] supposing that she is in the disposition and has made use of the means required by the Church. The soul being thus purified, God unites it to Himself in a way known only to Him and the spirit, nor does even the latter so understand what happens as to be able to explain it to others afterwards.

---

[58] Life, ch. xxxix. 30.
[59] Castle, M. iv. ch. iii. 11.
[60] Life, ch. xx. passim.
[61] Philippus a SS. Trinitate, l.c. tr. i. disc. iii. art. 3.
[62] Rel. ix. 4. Way of Perf. ch. xix. 8.

Yet the mind had not lost the use of its faculties, for this ecstasy does not resemble a swoon or a fit in which nothing either interior or exterior is felt.

4. What I do understand is that the soul has never been more alive to spiritual things nor so full of light and of knowledge of His Majesty as it is now. This might seem impossible; if the powers and senses were so absorbed that we might call them dead, how does the soul understand this mystery? I cannot tell; perhaps no one but the Creator Himself can say what passes in these places—I mean this and the following mansions which may be treated as one, the door leading from one to the other being wide open. However, as some things in the last rooms are only shown to those who get thus far, I thought it better to treat the mansions separately.

5. While the soul is in this suspension, our Lord favours it by discovering to it secrets such as heavenly mysteries and imaginary visions, which admit of description afterwards because they remain so imprinted on the memory that it never forgets them. But when the visions are intellectual they are not thus easily related, some of those received at such a time being so sublime that it is not fitting for man, while living in this world, to understand them in a way that can be told, although when the use of the faculties returns much can be described of what was seen in intellectual vision. Possibly you do not know what a vision is, especially an intellectual one. Since I have been bidden by one who has authority, I will tell you at the proper time. Although seemingly superfluous, it may prove useful to certain people.

6. 'But,' you will ask me, 'if the very sublime favours our Lord bestows in this mansion cannot afterwards be remembered, what profit do they bring?'[63] O daughters! their value cannot be overrated; for though the recipient is incapable of describing them, they are deeply imprinted in the centre of the soul and are never forgotten. 'How can they be remembered if no image is seen and the powers of the soul do not comprehend them?' I, too, do not understand this, but I know that certain truths of the greatness of God remain so impressed on the spirit by this favour that, did not faith teach Who He is and that it is bound to believe He is God, the soul would henceforth worship Him as such, as did Jacob when he saw the ladder.[64] Doubtless the Patriarch learnt other secrets he was unable to reveal, for unless he had received more interior light he could never have discovered such sublime mysteries merely by watching angels ascending and descending the steps. I am not certain whether this quotation is correct; although I have heard the passage, I cannot feel sure of recalling it exactly.

7. Neither was Moses able to relate more than God willed of what he had seen in the burning bush;[65] but unless the Almighty had clearly revealed certain mysteries to his soul, causing it to see and know its God was present, the lawgiver could never have undertaken so many and such great labours. Such sublime revelations were shown him amidst the thorns of the bush as to give him the needful courage for his great deeds on behalf of the Children of Israel. We must not, sisters, search out reasons for understanding the hidden things of God, but, believing Him to be Almighty, we should be convinced that such worms as ourselves, with our limited power of intelligence, are unable to comprehend His wonders. Let us praise Him fervently for allowing us to understand something of them.

8. I wish I could find some simile for my subject: none seem to suit the purpose, but I will make use of the following. Imagine that you are in an apartment—I fancy it is termed *camarin* (or private museum)—belonging to a king or a great nobleman, in which are placed numberless kinds of articles of glass, porcelain, and other things, so arranged that most of them are at once seen on entering the room.

9. While on a visit to the house of the Duchess of Alva (where at her request I was bidden by obedience to stay during a journey)[66] I was taken into such a room. I stood amazed on entering it and wondered what could be the use of such a jumble of knick-knacks; then I thought that the

---

[63] Philippus a SS. Trinitate, l.c.

[64] Gen. xxviii. 2.

[65] Exod. 2.

[66] Doña Maria Enriquez, wife of Ferdinand de Toledo, Duke of Alva. This visit took place in February, 1574, and lasted two days the Saint being then on her journey from Salamanca to Alva de Tormes. (Found. ch. xxi.)

sight of so many different things should lead one to praise God. It is fortunate I saw them, for they offer me a suitable comparison in this case. Although I was in the room some time, there were so many objects in it that I forgot what I had seen and could no more remember each object, nor of what it was made, than if I had never seen it, though I recalled the sight of the whole collection.

10. Something of this sort occurs when the spirit is very closely united to God. It is introduced into this mansion of the empyrean heaven which must be in the centre of our souls for since God resides in them, He must own one of the mansions. While the soul is in ecstasy, our Lord does not appear to wish it to apprehend these mysteries and its inebriation of joy in Him suffices it. But sometimes He is pleased to withdraw it from this rapture when it at once perceives what the mansion contains. On returning to itself, the mind can recall what has been seen but is unable to describe it, nor can it, by its natural abilities, attain to see more of the supernatural than God has chosen to show it.

11. Do I seem to own that the soul really sees something and that this is an imaginary vision? I mean nothing of the sort: I am speaking of an intellectual vision, but being so ignorant and dull I can explain nothing and am well aware that if anything is rightly stated, it does not come from myself.

12. I think that if the soul learns no mysteries at any time during raptures, they are no true raptures but some natural weakness that may occur to people of delicate constitutions, such as women, when by its strenuous efforts the spirit overpowers physical nature, and produces stupor, as I think I said in connection with the prayer of quiet.[67]

13. This is not so in genuine raptures, for then I believe God ravishes the soul wholly to Himself, as being His very own and His bride, and shows her some small part of the kingdom she has thus won. However little this may be, all is great that is in this great God. He will allow of no obstacle from the powers or the senses but bids that the doors of all the mansions should be closed at once, only leaving open the one He is in, so that we may enter it. Blessed be such mercy—well may men be accursed who do not seek to profit by it, but who forfeit it!

14. O, my sisters! what nothingness is all we have given up, or that we do, or ever could do for a God who thus wills to communicate Himself to a worm! If we hope to enjoy this favour even during our mortal life, what are we doing? Why do we delay? What can repay the loss of the time of a 'Memento'[68] in searching for this Lord, like the bride through the streets and squares.[69] Oh, what a mockery is everything in this world that does not lead towards and help us to attain to this state! Even though all the earthly pleasures, riches, and happiness that can be imagined could last for eternity, they would be disappointing and base contrasted with the treasures which are to be enjoyed for ever—and yet even *these* are nothing compared with the possession for our own of the Lord of all treasures in heaven and earth.

15. Oh, human blindness! When, oh, when shall this dust be taken from our eyes? Although we think it insufficient to blind us, yet I see some little motes or grains of dust which, if left to spread, will suffice to harm us greatly. At least, for the love of God, my sisters, let these faults convince us of our misery, serving to clear our sight as did the clay the eyes of the blind man who was cured by the Spouse.[70] Then, realizing our imperfections, we shall beg Him more fervently to let us benefit by our defers so as to please Him in all things.

16. I have unconsciously wandered far from my subject: forgive me, sisters. Believe me, when I come to these wonders of God's greatness (I mean when I come to speak of them) I cannot but feel keenly grieved at seeing what we lose by our own fault. It is true that His Majesty grants such favours to whom He chooses; yet if we sought Him as He seeks us, He would give them to

---

[67] Castle, M. iv. ch. iii. 2.

[68] The Saint wrote here and elsewhere Memento, and not momenta as is commonly printed. It refers, of course, to that short interruption at Mass when the priest makes a Memento of those for whom he intends to pray. Likewise St. Teresa often speaks of the 'space of a Credo or an Ave Maria' always implying a very short duration.

[69] Cant. iii. 2: 'Per vicos et plateas quæram quem diligit anima mea.'

[70] St. John ix. 6.

us all. He only longs for souls on whom He may bestow them, for His gifts do not diminish His riches.

17. To return to what I was describing. By the commands of the Bridegroom, the doors of the mansions and even those of the keep and of the whole castle are closed; for when He intends ravishing the soul He takes away the power of speech, and although occasionally the other faculties are retained rather longer, no word can be uttered.[71] Sometimes the person is at once deprived of all the senses, the hands and body becoming as cold as if the soul had fled; occasionally no breathing can be detected.[72] This condition lasts but a short while; I mean in the same degree,[73] for when this profound suspension diminishes the body seems to come to itself and gain strength to return again to this *death* which gives more vigorous *life* to the soul.

18. This supreme state of ecstasy never lasts long, but although it ceases, it leaves the will so inebriated,[74] and the mind so transported out of itself that for a day, or sometimes for several days, such a person is incapable of attending to anything but what excites the will to the love of God; although wide awake enough to this, she seems asleep as regards all earthly matters.

19. Oh, when the soul wholly returns to itself, how abashed does it feel at having received this favour and how passionate are its desires of serving God in any way He asks of it! If the former states of prayer caused the powerful effects described, what will not such a signal grace as this do? Such a person wishes she had a thousand lives[75] to spend for God; she would have all earthly creatures changed into as many tongues to praise Him on her account. She longs to perform most severe penances,[76] nor do they cost her much, for the power of her love almost prevents their being felt. She realizes how little the martyrs suffered during their tortures, for pain is easy when our Lord thus aids us: therefore such a soul complains to His Majesty when He gives her no suffering?[77]

20. She considers it a great favour when God sends her this rapture in secret, for when others see it the shame and confusion she feels are so great as somewhat to diminish her transport. Knowing the malice of the world, she fears her ecstasy will not be attributed to its proper cause but may give rise to rash judgment instead of the praise due for it to God. Although this pain and distress are unavoidable, they seem to me to show a certain want of humility, for if she wished to be despised, what would she care?[78]

21. Our Lord once said to some one who was troubled by such thoughts: 'Do not be disturbed; people will either praise Me or condemn thee; in either case thou wilt be the gainer.'[79] I learnt afterwards that she was greatly encouraged and comforted by this speech; I speak of it in case others may suffer in the same way. Apparently our Lord would have all men know that this soul is His own and that none may molest it, for it is all His. Men are welcome to attack, if they

---

[71] Life, ch. xx. 18. 'Like a person who, having a rope around his neck and being strangled, tries to breathe.'

[72] Life, ch. xx 23, 29. Way of Perf. ch. xxxii. Rel. viii. 8, 11. 'The first effect of ecstatic prayer concerns the body, which remains as if the soul had departed; it grows cold from a deficiency of natural heat, the eyes close gently, and the other senses are suspended; and yet a weak body recovers health in this prayer.' (Anton. a Spiritu Sancto, Direct. Mystic. tr. iv. d. 2, § 4, n. 150).

[73] 'Digo para estar in un ser.'

[74] Christusque nobis sit cibus, Potusque noster sit fides; Læti bibamus sobriam Ebrietatem Spiritus. Hymn for Lauds, Feria secunda, old version. (Compare Anton. a Sp. S. *l.c.* tr. iv. n. 30.)

[75] Life, ch. xx. 30.

[76] Castle, M. vii. ch. iii. 4. Way of Perf. ch. xxxviii. 1. Excl. xiv. 3. Life, ch. xl. 27.

[77] Life, ch. xvi. 6. Rel. i. 4.

[78] Ibid. ch. xx. 5, 6.

[79] Life, ch. xxxi. 15. St. John of the Cross in stanza xiii. 8. of the Spiritual Canticle, refers to this and the following chapters. 'This,' he says, 'is an appropriate opportunity for discussing the difference between raptures, ecstasies, and other elevations and subtle flights of the spirit, to which spiritual persons are liable; but as my object is to do nothing more than explain this canticle, I leave the subject for those who are better qualified than I am. I do this the more readily because our mother, the blessed Teresa of Jesus, has written admirably on this matter, whose writings I hope to see soon published,'

will, the body, the honour, and the possessions of such a person, for glory will accrue to His Majesty from all they do; but the soul they may not assail; unless by a most culpable presumption it withdraws from the protection of its Spouse, He will defend it against the whole world and against all hell besides.

22. I do not know whether I have succeeded in teaching you what a rapture is; to explain it fully would, as I said, be impossible. Still I do not think time has been lost in describing a genuine rapture. The effects in false raptures are very different. I do not call them 'false' because people who experience them intentionally deceive others, but because they are themselves unwittingly deceived. As the signs and effects do not correspond with this great grace, the favour itself becomes so discredited that naturally, when our Lord afterwards bestows it on any soul, nobody believes in it. May He be for ever blessed and praised! Amen, Amen!

CHAPTER V.

TREATS OF THE SAME SUBJECT AS THE LAST CHAPTER AND DESCRIBES THE FLIGHT OF THE SPIRIT, WHICH IS ANOTHER WAY BY WHICH GOD ELEVATES THE SOUL: THIS REQUIRES GREAT COURAGE IN ONE EXPERIENCING IT. THIS FAVOUR, BY WHICH GOD GREATLY DELIGHTS THE SOUL IS EXPLAINED. THIS CHAPTER IS VERY PROFITABLE.

1. The flight of the spirit. 2. Self-control completely lost. 3. Symbol of the two cisterns. 4. Obligations following these favours. 5. Humility produced by them. 6. How our crucified Lord comforted such a soul. 7. A humble soul fears these favours. 8. Mysteries learnt during the flight of the spirit. 9. Imaginary visions sometimes accompany intellectual ones. 10. How the flight of the spirit takes place. 11. The soul fortified by it. 12. Three great graces left in the soul. 13. The third grace. 14. Fear caused by this favour.

1. THERE is another form of rapture, which, though essentially the same as the last, yet produces very different feelings in the soul. I call it the 'flight of the spirit,'[80] for the soul suddenly feels so rapid a sense of motion that the spirit appears to hurry it away with a speed which is very alarming, especially at first. Therefore I said that the soul on whom God bestows this favour requires strong courage, besides great faith, trust, and resignation, so that God may do what He chooses with it.

2. Do you suppose a person in perfect possession of her senses feels but little dismay at her soul's being drawn above her, while sometimes, as we read, even the body rises with it?[81] She does not know where the spirit is going, who is raising her, nor how it happens; for at the first instant of this sudden movement one does not feel sure it is caused by God. Can it possibly be resisted? No; resistance only accelerates the motion, as some one told me. God now appears to be teaching the soul, which has so often placed itself absolutely in His hands and offered itself entirely to Him, that it no longer belongs to itself; thus it is snatched away more vehemently in consequence of its opposition. Therefore this person resolved to resist no more than does a straw when attracted by amber (a thing you may have seen); she yielded herself into the hands of Him who is Almighty, seeing it is best to make a virtue of necessity. Speaking of straw, doubtless it is as easy for a stalwart, strapping fellow to lift a straw as for our mighty and powerful Giant to elevate our spirit.[82]

---

[80] Rel. viii. 10, 11. Life, ch. xviii, 8; xx. 3.

[81] Life, ch. xx. 9. St. John of the Cross, Spiritual Canticle, stanzas xiv.-xv. 23 sqq. Philippus a SS. Trinit. l.c. p. iii. tr. i. disc. iii. art. 3. 'This prayer of rapture is superior to the preceding grades of prayer, as also to the ordinary prayer of union, and leaves much more excellent effects and operations in many other ways.' St. Catherine of Siena (Dialogue, ch. lxxix. 1) says: 'Wherefore, oftentimes, through the perfect union which the soul has made with Me, she is raised from the earth almost as if the heavy body became light. But this does not mean that the heaviness of the body is taken away, but that the union of the soul with Me is more perfect than the union of the body with the soul; wherefore the strength of the spirit, united with Me, raises the body from the earth.' (Transl. by Algar Thorold.)

[82] Life, ch. xxii. 20.

3. It seems that the cistern of water of which I spoke (but I cannot quite remember where) in the fourth mansion,[83] was formerly filled gently and quietly, without any movement; but now this great God Who restrains the springs and the waters and will not permit the ocean to transgress its bounds,[84] lets loose the streams, which with a powerful rush flow into the cistern and a mighty wave rises, strong enough to uplift on high the little vessel of our soul. Neither the ship herself nor her pilot and sailors can at their choice control the fury of the sea and stop its carrying the boat where it will: far less can the interior of the soul now stay where it chooses or force its senses or faculties to act more than He Who holds them in His dominion decrees; as for the exterior powers, they are here quite useless.

4. Indeed I am amazed, sisters, while merely writing of this manifestation of the immense power of this great King and Monarch. Then what must be felt by those who actually experience it? I am convinced that if His Majesty were to reveal Himself thus to the greatest sinners on earth, they would never dare to offend Him again—if not through love at least through fear of Him. What obligations bind those taught in so sublime a manner to strive with all their might not to displease such a Master! In His Name I beg of you, sisters, who have received these or the like favours, not to rest content with merely receiving them but to remember that she who owes much has much to pay.[85]

5. This thought terrifies the soul exceedingly: unless the great courage needed was given it by our Lord, it would suffer great and constant grief; for looking first at what His Majesty has done for it and then upon itself, it sees how little good it has performed compared with what it was bound to do, and that the paltry service it has rendered was full of faults, failures and tepidity. To efface the remembrance of the many imperfections of all its good deeds (if indeed it has ever performed any) it thinks best to forget them altogether and to be ever mindful of its sins, casting itself on the mercy of God since it cannot repay its debt to Him and begging for the pity and compassion He ever shows to sinners.

6. Perhaps He will answer as He did to some one who was kneeling before a crucifix in great affliction on this account, for she felt she had never had anything to offer God nor to sacrifice for His sake. The Crucified One consoled her by saying that He gave her for herself all the pains and labours He had borne in His passion, that she might offer them as her own to His Father.[86] I learnt from her that she at once felt comforted and enriched by these words which she never forgets but recalls whenever she realizes her own wretchedness and feels encouraged and consoled. I could relate several other incidents of the same kind learnt in conversation with many holy people much given to prayer, but I will not recount them lest you might imagine they relate to myself.

7. I think this example is very instructive; it shows that we please our Lord by self-knowledge, by the constant recollection of our poverty and miseries, and by realizing that we possess nothing but what we have received from Him.[87] Therefore courage is needed, sisters, in order to receive this and many other favours which come to a soul elevated to this state by our Lord; I think that if the soul is humble it requires more valour than ever for this last mercy. May God grant us humility for His Name's sake.

8. To return to this sudden rapture of the spirit. The soul really appears to have quitted the body, which however is not lifeless, and though, on the other hand, the person is certainly not dead, yet she herself cannot, for a few seconds, tell whether her spirit remains within her body or not.[88] She feels that she has been wholly transported into another and a very different region from that in which we live, where a light so unearthly is shown[89] that, if during her whole lifetime she had been trying to picture it and the wonders seen, she could not possibly have succeeded. In an

[83] Castle, M. iv. ch. ii. 3.

[84] Prov. viii. 29.

[85] St. Luke xii. 48: 'Cui multum datum est, multum quaeretur ab eo, et cui commendaverunt multum, plus petent ab eo.'

[86] Rel. ix. 8. This happened at Seville in 1575 or 1576.

[87] 1 Cor. iv. 7: 'Quid autem habes quod non accepisti?'

[88] 2 Cor. xii. 2: 'Sive in corpore nescio, sive extra corpus nescio, Deus scit.'

[89] This is called 'lumen prophetiæ' and is a transient form of the 'lumen gloriæ.' See St. Thomas Aquinas, Sum. theol. 2a 2æ, q. 175, art. 3 ad 2.

instant her mind learns so many things at once that if the imagination and intellect spent years in striving to enumerate them, it could not recall a thousandth part of them.

9. This vision is not intellectual but imaginary and is seen by the eyes of the soul more clearly than earthly things are seen by our bodily eyes. Although no words are pronounced, the spirit is taught many truths; for instance, if it beholds any of the saints, it knows them at once as well as if intimately acquainted with them for years.[90] Occasionally, besides what the eyes of the soul perceive in intellectual vision, other things are shown it. In an imaginary vision it usually sees our Lord accompanied by a host of angels; yet neither the bodily eyes nor the eyes of the soul[91] see anything, for these visions and many other things impossible to describe, are revealed by some wonderful intuition that I cannot explain. Perhaps those who have experienced this favour and possess more ability than myself may be able to describe it, although it seems to me a most difficult task.

10. I cannot tell whether the soul dwells in the body meanwhile or not: I would neither affirm that it does nor that the body is deprived of it. I have often thought that as, though the sun does not leave his place in the heavens yet his rays have power to reach the earth instantaneously, so the soul and the spirit, which make one and the same thing (like the sun and its rays) may, while remaining in its own place, through the strength of the ardour coming to it from the true Sun of Justice, send up some higher part of it above itself. In fact I do not understand what I am talking about, but the truth is that, with the swiftness of a bullet fired from a gun, an upward flight takes place in the interior of the soul. (I know no other name for it but 'flight.') Although noiseless, it is too manifest a movement to be any illusion[92] and the soul is quite outside itself; at least that is the impression made upon it. Great mysteries are revealed to it meanwhile, and when the person returns to consciousness she is so greatly benefited that she holds all this world's goods as filth compared with what she has seen. Henceforth earthly life is grievous to her and what used to please her now remains uncared for and unnoticed.[93]

11. Those children of Israel who were sent on first to the Land of Promise brought back tokens from it;[94] so here our Lord seems to seek to show the soul something of the land to which it is travelling, to give it courage to pass through the trials of its painful journey, now that it knows where it must go to find rest. You may fancy that such profit could not thus quickly be obtained, yet only those who have experienced what signal benefits this favour leaves in the soul can realize its value.

12. This clearly shows it to be no work of the devil; neither the imagination nor the evil one could represent what leaves such peace, calm, and good fruits in the soul, and particularly the following three graces of a very high order.[95] The first of these is a perception of the greatness of God which becomes clearer to us as we witness more of it. Secondly, we gain self-knowledge and humility from seeing how creatures so base as ourselves in comparison with the Creator of such wonders have dared to offend Him in the past or venture to gaze on Him now.

---

[90] The same thing is related of some Saints while on earth, e.g. St Paul the first hermit and St. Anthony, who greeted each other by name though neither knew nor had heard of the other.

[91] These words, though necessary for the context, were only begun, but not completed by St. Teresa.

[92] Life, ch. xx. 32. Castle, M. iv. ch. i. 10.

[93] Compare §§ 8-10 with Philippus a SS. Trinitate, *l.c.* p. iii. tr. i. disc. iii. art. 3.

'Muchas veces he pensado, si como el sol estándose en el cielo, que sus rayos tienen tanta fuerza, que no mudándose él de allí, de presto llegan acá; si el alma y el espíritu (que son una misma cosa, como le es el sol y sus rayos) puede, quedándose ella en su puesto, con la fuerza de calor que le viene del verdadero Sol de justicia, alguna parte superior salir sobre si misma. En fin, yo no sé lo que digo, lo que es verdad es, que con la presteza que sale la pelota de un arcabuz, cuando le ponen el fuego, se levanta en lo interior un vuelo (que yo no sé otro nombre que le poner) que aunque no hace ruido, hace movimiento tan claro, que no puede ser antojo en ninguna manera; y muy fuera de si misma, á todo lo que puede entender, se le muestran grandes cosas.'

[94] Num. xiii. 24.

[95] Life, ch. xx. 31. The same distinctions with respect to divine and diabolical locutions may be found in Life, ch. xxv. 5.

13. The third grace is a contempt for all earthly things unless they are consecrated to the service of so great a God. With such jewels the Bridegroom begins to deck His Bride; they are too valuable for her to keep them carelessly.[96] These visions are so deeply engraved in her memory that I believe she can never forget them until she enjoys them for evermore, for to do so would be the greatest misfortune.[97] But the Spouse Who gave her these gifts has power to give her grace not to lose them.

14. I told you that courage was required by the soul, for do you think it is a trifling matter for the spirit to feel literally separated from the body, as it does when perceiving that it is losing its senses without understanding the reason? There is need that He Who gives all the rest should include fortitude. You will say this fright is well rewarded, and so say I. May He Who can bestow such graces be for ever praised and may His Majesty vouchsafe that we may be worthy to serve Him. Amen.

CHAPTER VI.

DESCRIBES AN EFFECT WHICH PROVES THE PRAYER SPOKEN OF IN THE LAST CHAPTER TO BE GENUINE AND NO DECEPTION, TREATS OF ANOTHER FAVOUR OUR LORD BESTOWS ON THE SOUL TO MAKE IT PRAISE HIM FERVENTLY.

1. The soul longs for death. 2. The soul cannot help desiring these favours. 3. St. Teresa bewails her inability to serve God. 3. Fervour resulting from ecstasies. 5. Excessive desires to see God should be restrained. 6. They endanger health. 7. Tears often come from Physical causes. 8. St. Teresa's own experience. 9. Works, not tears, are asked by God. 10. Confide entirely in God. 11. The jubilee of the soul. 12. Impossibility of concealing this joy. 13. The world's judgment of this jubilee. 14. Which is often felt by the nuns of St. Joseph's. 15. The Saint's delight in this jubilee.

1. THESE sublime favours leave the soul so desirous of fully enjoying Him Who has bestowed them that life becomes a painful though delicious torture, and death is ardently longed for. Such a one often implores God with tears to take her from this exile where everything she sees wearies her.[98] Solitude alone brings great alleviation for a time, but soon her grief returns and yet she cannot bear to be without it. In short, this poor little butterfly can find no lasting rest. So tender is her love that at the slightest provocation it flames forth and the soul takes flight. Thus in this mansion raptures occur very frequently, nor can they be resisted even in public. Persecutions and slanders ensue;[99] however she may try, she cannot keep free from the fears suggested to her by so many people, especially by her confessors.

2. Although in one way she feels great confidence within her soul, especially when alone with God, yet on the other hand, she is greatly troubled by misgivings lest she is deceived by the devil and so should offend Him Whom she deeply loves. She cares little for blame, except when her confessor finds fault with her as if she could help what happens. She asks every one to pray for her[100] since she has been told to do so, and begs His Majesty to direct her by some other way than this which is so full of danger. Nevertheless, so great are the benefits left by these favours that she cannot but see that they lead her on the way to heaven,[101] of which she has read and heard and learnt in the law of God. As, strive how she may, she cannot resist desiring to receive these graces, she resigns herself into God's hands. Yet she is grieved at finding herself forced to wish for these favours which appears to be disobedience to her confessor, for she believes that in obedience, and in avoiding any offence against God, lies her safeguard against deception. Thus

---

[96] 'Dexteram meam et collum meum cinxit lapidibus pretiosis; tradidit auribus meis inestimabiles margaritas.' From the Office of St. Agnes.

[97] This is undoubtedly the correct rendering of this difficult and obscure passage.

[98] Excl. ii. See poem 4, 'Cuan triste es, Dios mio'; and the two versions of 'Vivir sin vivir en mi.' (Poems 3 and 4. Minor Works.)

[99] Life, ch. xxv. 18.

[100] Ibid. ch. xxv. 20. Rel. vii. 7.

[101] Ibid. ch. xxvii. 1, 2.

she feels she would prefer to be cut in pieces rather than willfully commit a venial sin, yet is greatly grieved at seeing that she cannot avoid unwittingly falling into a great number. God bestows on such people so intense a desire neither ever to displease Him in however small a matter, nor to commit any avoidable imperfection, that, were there no other reason, they would try to avoid society and they greatly envy those who live in deserts.[102] On the other hand, they seek to live amidst men in the hopes of helping if but one soul to praise God better.[103] In the case of a woman, she grieves over the impediment offered by her sex[104] and envies those who are free to proclaim aloud to all Who is this mighty God of hosts.[105]

3. O poor little butterfly! chained by so many fetters that stop thee from flying where thou wouldst! Have pity on her, O my God, and so dispose her ways that she may be able to accomplish some of her desires for Thy honour and glory! Take no account of the poverty of her merits, nor of the vileness of her nature, Lord, Thou Who hast the power to compel the vast ocean to retire, and didst force the wide river Jordan to draw back so that the Children of Israel might pass through![106] Yet spare her not, for aided by Thy strength she can endure many trials. She is resolved to do so—she desires to suffer them. Stretch forth Thine arm, O Lord, to help her lest she waste her life on trifles! Let Thy greatness appear in this Thy creature, womanish and weak as she is, so that men, seeing the good in her is not her own, may praise Thee for it! Let it cost her what it may and as dear as she desires, for she longs to lose a thousand lives to lead one soul to praise Thee but a little better. If as many lives were hers to give, she would count them well spent in such a cause, knowing as a truth most certain that she is unworthy to bear the lightest cross, much less to die for Thee.

4. I cannot tell why I have said this, sisters, nor what made me do so; indeed I never intended it. You must know that these effects are bound to follow from such trances or ecstasies: they are not transient, but permanent desires; when opportunity occurs of acting on them, they prove genuine. How can I say that they are permanent, when at times the soul feels cowardly in the most trivial matters and too timorous to undertake any work for God?

5. I believe it is because our Lord, for its greater good, then leaves the soul to its natural weakness, which at once convinces it so thoroughly that any strength it possessed came from His Majesty as to destroy its self-love, enduing it with a greater knowledge of the mercy and greatness of God which He deigned to show forth in one so vile. However, the soul is usually in the former state. Beware of one thing, sisters; these ardent desires to behold our Lord are sometimes so distressing as to need rather to be checked than to be encouraged—that is, if feasible, for in another kind of prayer of which I shall speak later, it is not possible as you will see.

6. In the state I speak of these longings can sometimes be arrested, for the reason is at liberty to conform to the will of God and can quote the words of St. Martin;[107] should these desires become very oppressive, the thoughts may be turned to some other matter. As such longings are generally found in persons far advanced in perfection, the devil may excite them in order to make us think we are of their number—in any case it is well to be cautious. For my part, I do not believe he could cause the calm and peace given by this pain to the soul, but would disturb it by such uneasiness as we feel when afflicted concerning any worldly matter. A person inexperienced in both kinds of sorrow cannot understand the difference, but thinking such grief an excellent thing, will excite it as much as possible which greatly injures the health, as these longings are incessant or at least very frequent.

---

102 Rel. i. 6.

103 Life, ch. xxxii. 14; xxxv. 13. Castle, M. vii. ch. iv. 21 . Found. ch. i. 6, 7.

104 Way of Perf. ch. i.

105 III Reg. xix. 10.

106 Ps. cxiii. 3; Exod. xiv. and Jos. iii.

107 'When St. Martin was dying, his brethren said to him: 'Why, dear Father, will you leave us? Or to whom can you commit us in our desolation? We know, indeed, that you desire to be with Christ, but your reward above is safe and will not be diminished by delay; rather have pity on us whom you are leaving desolate.' Then Martin, always pitiful, moved by these lamentations, is said to have burst into tears. Turning to God, he replied to the mourners around him only by crying: 'O Lord, if I am still necessary to Thy people, I do not shrink from toil; Thy will be done.' (Sulpitius Severus, Life of St. Martin, letter 3.)

7. You must also notice that bodily weakness may cause such pain, especially with people of sensitive characters who cry over every trifling trouble.[108] Times without number do they imagine they are mourning for God's sake when they are doing no such thing. If for a considerable space of time, whenever such a person hears the least mention of God or thinks of Him at all, these fits of uncontrollable weeping occur,[109] the cause may be an accumulation of humour round the heart, which has a great deal more to do with such tears than has the love of God. Such persons seem as if they would never stop crying: believing that tears are beneficial, they do not try to check them nor to distract their minds from the subject, but encourage them as much as possible. The devil seizes this opportunity of weakening nuns so that they become unable to pray or to keep their Rule.

8. I think you must be puzzling over this and would like to ask what I would have you do, as I see danger in everything. If I am afraid of delusions in so good a thing as tears, perhaps I myself am deluded, and may be I am! But believe me, I do not say this without having witnessed it in other people although not in my own case, for there is nothing tender about me and my heart is so hard as often to grieve me.[110] However, when the fire burns fiercely within, stony as my heart may be, it distils like an alembic.[111] It is easy to know when tears come from this source, for they are soothing and gentle rather than stormy and rarely do any harm. This delusion, when it is one, has the advantage, with a humble person, of only injuring the body and not the soul. But if one is not humble, it is well to be ever on one's guard.

9. Let us not fancy that if we cry a great deal we have done all that is needed—rather we must work hard and practice the virtues: that is the essential—leaving tears to fall when God sends them, without trying to force ourselves to shed them. Then, if we do not take too much notice of them, they will leave the parched soil of our souls well watered, making it fertile in good fruit; for this is the water which falls from heaven.[112] However we may tire ourselves in digging to reach it, we shall never get any water like this; indeed, we may often work and search until we are exhausted without finding as much as a pool, much less a springing well!

10. Therefore, sisters, I think it best for us to place ourselves in the presence of God, contemplate His mercy and grandeur and our own vileness and leave Him to give us what He will, whether water or drought, for He knows best what is good for us; thus we enjoy peace and the devil will have less chance to deceive us.

11. Amongst these favours, at once painful and pleasant, Our Lord sometimes causes in the soul a certain jubilation[113] and a strange and mysterious kind of prayer. If He bestows this grace on you, praise Him fervently for it; I describe it so that you may know that it is something real. I believe that the faculties of the soul are closely united to God but that He leaves them at liberty to rejoice in their happiness together with the senses, although they do not know what they are enjoying nor how they do so. This may sound nonsense but it really happens. So excessive is its jubilee that the soul will not enjoy it alone but speaks of it to all around so that they may help it to praise God, which is its one desire.[114]

12. Oh, what rejoicings would this person utter and what demonstrations would she make, if possible, so that all might know her happiness! She seems to have found herself again and wishes, like the father of the prodigal son, to invite all her friends to feast with her[115] and to see her soul in its rightful place, because (at least for the time being) she cannot doubt its security. I believe she is right, for the devil could not possibly infuse a joy and peace into the very centre of her being which make her whole delight consist in urging others to praise God. It requires a painful effort to keep silent and to dissemble such impulsive happiness. St. Francis must have experienced this

---

[108] Way of Perf.. ch. xvii. 4; xix. 6.

[109] Life, ch. xxix. 12.

[110] Compare with this what we have said in note 1 to the second chapter of the Fourth Mansions. Rel. ii. 12.

[111] Life, ch. xix. 1-3.

[112] Way of Perf. ch. xix. 6. Life, ch. xviii. 12 sqq.

[113] Philippus a SS. Trinit. l.c. p. iii. tr. i. disc. iv. art. 5. Antonius a Sp. S. l.c. tr. iv. n.156.

[114] Rel. ii. 12.

[115] St. Luke xv. 23.

when, as the robbers met him rushing through the fields crying aloud, he told them in answer to their questions that he was the 'herald of the great King.'[116] So felt other saints who retired into the deserts so that, like St. Francis, they might proclaim the praises of their God.

13. I knew Fray Peter of Alcantara who used to do this. I believe he was a saint on account of the life he led, yet people often took him for a fool when they heard him.[117] Oh happy folly, sisters! Would that God might let us all share it! What mercy He has shown you in placing you where, if He gave you this grace and it were perceived by others, it would rather turn to your advantage than bring on you contempt as it would do in the world, where men so rarely hear God praised that it is no wonder they take scandal at it.

14. Oh miserable times and wretched life spent in the world! How blest are those whose happy lot it is to be freed from them![118] It often delights me, when in my sisters' company to see how the joy of their hearts is so great that they vie with one another in praising our Lord for placing them in this convent: it is evident that their praises come from the very depths of their souls. I should like you to do this often, sisters, for when one begins she incites the rest to imitate her. How can your tongues be better employed when you are together than in praising God, Who has given us so much cause for it?

15. May His Majesty often grant us this kind of prayer which is most safe and beneficial; we cannot acquire it for ourselves as it is quite supernatural. Sometimes it lasts for a whole day and the soul is like one inebriated, although not deprived of the senses;[119] nor like a person afflicted with melancholia,[120] in which, though the reason is not entirely lost, the imagination continually dwells on some subject which possesses it and from which it cannot be freed. These are coarse comparisons to make in connection with such a precious gift, yet nothing else occurs to my mind. In this state of prayer a person is rendered by this jubilee so forgetful of self and everything else that she can neither think nor speak of anything but praising God, to which her joy prompts her. Let us all of us join her, my daughters, for why should we wish to be wiser than she? What can make us happier? And may all creatures unite their praises with ours for ever and ever. Amen, amen, amen!

CHAPTER VII.

DESCRIBES THE GRIEF FELT ON ACCOUNT OF THEIR SINS BY SOULS ON WHOM GOD HAS BESTOWED THE BEFORE-MENTIONED FAVOURS. SHOWS THAT HOWEVER SPIRITUAL A PERSON MAY BE, IT IS A GREAT ERROR NOT TO KEEP BEFORE OUR MIND THE HUMANITY OF OUR LORD AND SAVIOUR JESUS CHRIST AND HIS SACRED PASSION AND LIFE, AS ALSO THE GLORIOUS MOTHER OF GOD AND THE SAINTS. THE BENEFITS GAINED BY SUCH A MEDITATION. THIS CHAPTER IS MOST PROFITABLE.

1. Sorrow for sin felt by souls in the Sixth Mansion. 2. How this sorrow is felt. 3. St. Teresa's grief for her past sins. 4. Such souls, centered in God, forget self-interest. 5. The remembrance of

---

[116] 'He plunged into a large forest, and there in a loud voice and in French, he made the echoes resound with the praises of God. Some robbers, attracted by his singing, rushed out upon him. But the sight of so poor a man destroyed their hopes of booty. They questioned him, and Francis gave them no answer beyond saying in allegorical language: 'I am the herald of the great King!' The robbers considered themselves insulted by these words. They threw themselves upon him, beat him severely, and went off after having thrown him into a ditch full of snow. This treatment only added fire to the zeal of Francis. He sang his holy canticles with greater love than before.' (Rev. Father Léon, Lives of the Saints of the Order of St. Francis, vol. 1, ch, i,)

[117] 'St. Peter of Alcantara, in the jubilation of his soul through the impetuosity of divine love, was occasionally unable to refrain from singing the divine praises aloud in a wonderful manner. To do this more freely, he sometimes went into the woods where the peasants who heard him sing took him for one who was beside himself.' (Rev. Alban Butler, Lives of the Saints.)

[118] Way of Perf. ch. ii. 8; iii. i; viii. 1.

[119] Compare with this what has been said in the fourth chapter of this Mansion, § 17, note 17.

[120] Melancholia here as elsewhere means hysteria.

divine benefits increases contrition. 6. Meditation on our Lord's Humanity. 7. Warning against discontinuing it. 8. Christ and the saints our models. 9. Meditation of contemplatives. 10. Meditation during aridity. 11. We must search for God when we do not feel His presence. 12. Reasoning and mental prayer. 13. A form of meditation on our Lord's Life and Passion. 14. Simplicity of contemplatives' meditation. 15. Souls in every state of prayer should think of the Passion. 16. Need of the example of Christ and the saints. 17. Faith shows us our Lord as both God and Man. 18. St. Teresa's experience of meditation on the sacred Humanity. 19. Evil of giving up such meditation.

1. IT may seem to you, sisters, that souls to whom God has communicated Himself in such a special manner may feel so sure of enjoying Him for ever as no longer to require to fear or to mourn over their past sins. Those of you will be most apt to hold this opinion who have never received the like favours; souls to whom God has granted these graces will understand what I say. This is a great mistake, for sorrow for sin increases in proportion to the divine grace received and I believe will never quit us until we come to the land where nothing can grieve us any more. Doubtless we feel this pain more at one time than at another and it is of a different kind. A soul so advanced as that we speak of does not think of the punishment threatening its offences but of its great ingratitude towards Him to Whom it owes so much[121] and Who so justly deserves that it should serve Him, for the sublime mysteries revealed have taught it much about the greatness of God.

2. This soul wonders at its former temerity and weeps over its irreverence; its foolishness in the past seems a madness which it never ceases to lament as it remembers for what vile things it forsook so great a Sovereign. The thoughts dwell on this more than on the favours received, which, like those I am about to describe, are so powerful that they seem to rush through the soul at times like a strong, swift river. Yet the sins remain like the mire in the river bed and dwell constantly in the memory, making a heavy cross to bear.

3. I know some one who, though she had ceased to wish for death in order to see God,[122] yet desired it that she might be freed from her continual regret for her past ingratitude towards Him to Whom she owed, and always would owe, so much. She thought no one's guilt could be compared to her own, for she felt there could be none with whom God had borne so patiently nor on whom He had bestowed such graces.

4. Souls that have reached the state I speak of have ceased to fear hell. At times, though very rarely, they grieve keenly over the possibility of their losing God; their sole dread is lest He should withdraw His hand, allowing them to offend Him, and so they might return to their former miserable condition. They care nothing for their own pain or glory; if they are anxious not to stay long in Purgatory, it is more on account of its keeping them from the Presence of God than because of its torments. Whatever favours God may have shown a soul, I think it is dangerous for it to forget the unhappy state it was once in; painful as the remembrance may be, it is most beneficial.

5. Perhaps I think so because I have been so wicked and that may be the reason why I never forget my sins; people who have led good lives have no cause for grief; yet we always fall at times whilst living in this mortal body. This pain is not lessened by reflecting that our Lord has already forgiven and forgotten our faults; our grief is rather increased at seeing such kindness and favours bestowed on one who deserves nothing but hell. I think St. Paul and the Magdalen must thus have suffered a cruel martyrdom;[123] their love was intense, they had received many mercies and realized the greatness and the majesty of God and so must have found it very hard to bear the remembrance of their sins, which they must have regretted with a most tender sorrow.

6. You may fancy that one who has enjoyed such high favours need not meditate on the mysteries of the most sacred Humanity of our Lord Jesus Christ but will be wholly absorbed in

---

[121] Life, ch. vi. 7.

[122] Excl. vi. 4, 5. Supra, M. v. ch. ii, 5. Poems 2, 3, 4. Minor Works.

[123] Life, ch. xxi, 9. All editions have 'Peter'. St. Teresa only wrote 'Po' but the parallel passage proves she meant Pablo, and not Pedro. See also M. i. ch. i. 5.

love. I have written fully about this elsewhere.[124] I have been contradicted and told that I was wrong and did not understand the matter; that our Lord guides souls in such a way that after having made progress it is best to exercise oneself in matters concerning the Godhead and to avoid what is corporeal; yet nothing will make me admit that this latter is a good way.

7. I may be mistaken; we may all really mean the same thing but I found the devil was trying to lead me astray in this manner. Having been warned by experience in this respect, I have decided to speak again about it here although I have very often done so elsewhere.[125] Be most cautious on the subject; attend to what I venture to say about it and do not believe any one who tells you the contrary. I will endeavour to explain myself more clearly than I did before. If the person who undertook to write on the matter had treated it more explicitly he would have done well, for it may do much harm to speak of it in general terms to us women, who have scanty wits.

8. Some souls imagine they cannot meditate even on the Passion, still less on the most blessed Virgin or on the saints, the memory of whose lives greatly benefits and strengthens us.[126] I cannot think what such persons are to meditate upon, for to withdraw the thoughts from all corporeal things like the angelic spirits who are always inflamed with love, is not possible for us while in this mortal flesh; we need to study, to meditate upon and to imitate those who, mortals like ourselves, performed such heroic deeds for God. How much less should we willfully endeavour to abstain from thinking of our only good and remedy, the most sacred Humanity of our Lord Jesus Christ? I cannot believe that any one really does this; they misunderstand their own minds and so harm both themselves and others. Of this at least I can assure them: they will never thus enter the last two mansions of the castle. If they lose their Guide, our good Jesus, they cannot find the way and it will be much if they have stayed safely in the former mansions. Our Lord Himself tells us that He is 'the Way'; He also says that He is 'the Light'; that no man cometh to the Father but by Him; and that 'He that seeth Me, seeth the Father also.'[127]

9. Such persons tell us that these words have some other meaning; I know of no other meaning but this, which my soul has ever recognized as the true one and which has always suited me right well. Some people (many of whom have spoken to me on the subject) after our Lord has once raised them to perfect contemplation, wish to enjoy it continually. This is impossible; still, the grace of this state remains in their souls in such a way that they cannot reason as before on the mysteries of the Passion and the Life of Christ. I cannot account for it but it is very usual for the mind thus to remain less apt for meditation. I think it must be because, as the one end of meditation is to seek God, after He has once been found and the soul is accustomed to seek Him again by means of the will, it no longer wearies itself by searching for Him with the intellect.

10. It also appears to me that as the will is already inflamed with love, this generous faculty would, if it could, cease to make use of the reason. This would be well, were it not impossible, especially before the soul has reached the last two mansions.[128] Time spent in prayer would thus

---

[124] Life, ch. xxii. 9-11.

[125] Ibid. ch. xxii. i; xxiii. 18; xxiv. 2.

[126] 'Deliberate forgetfulness and rejection of all knowledge and of form must never be extended to Christ and His sacred Humanity. Sometimes, indeed, in the height of contemplation and pure intuition of the Divinity the soul does not remember the Sacred Humanity, because God raises the mind to this, as it were, confused and most supernatural knowledge; but for all this, studiously to forget it is by no means right, for the contemplation of the sacred Humanity and loving meditation upon it will help us up to all good, and it is by it we shall ascend most easily to the highest state of union. It is evident at once that, while all visible and bodily things ought to be forgotten, for they are a hindrance in our way, He, Who for our salvation became man, is not to be accounted among them, for He is the truth, the door, and the way, and our guide to all good.' (St. John of the Cross Ascent of Mount Carmel, bk. iii. ch. i. 12-14.

[127] St. John viii. 12; xiv. 6, 9.

[128] Life, ch. xv. 20. St. John of the Cross treats the subject most carefully. He shows how and when meditation becomes impossible: Ascent of Mount Carmel, bk. ii. ch. xii. (circa finem) ch. xiii. (per totum). Living Flame of Love, stanza iii. 35. Obscure Night, bk. i. ch. x. 8, and bk. ii. ch. viii. That it should be procured whenever possible: Ibid. bk. i. ch. x. (in fine); that it should be resumed; Ascent of Mount Carmel; bk. ii, ch. xv.

be lost as the will often needs the use of the understanding to rekindle its love. Notice this point, sisters, which as it is important I will explain more fully. Such a soul desires to spend all its time in loving God and wishes to do nothing else; but it cannot succeed, for though the will is not dead yet the flame which kindled it is dying out and the spark needs fanning into a glow. Ought the soul to remain quiescent in this aridity, waiting like our father Elias for fire to descend from heaven[129] to consume the sacrifice which it makes of itself to God? Certainly not; it is not right to expect miracles; God will work them for this soul when He chooses. As I have told you already and shall do again, His Majesty wishes us to hold ourselves unworthy of their being wrought on our account and desires us to help ourselves to the best of our abilities.

11. In my opinion we ought during our whole life, to act in this manner, however sublime our prayer may be. True, those whom our Lord admits into the seventh mansion rarely or never need thus to help their fervour, for the reason I will tell you of; if I recollect it when I come to write of this room where, in a wonderful manner, souls are constantly in the company of Christ our Lord both in His Humanity and His Divinity.[130] Thus, when the fire in our hearts, of which I spoke does not burn in the will, nor do we feel the presence of God, we must search for Him as He would have us do, like the Bride in the Canticles,[131] and must ask all creatures 'who it was that made them;' as St. Augustine (either in his *Soliloquies* or his *Confessions*) tells us that he did.[132] Thus we shall not stand like blockheads, wasting our time in waiting for what we before enjoyed. At first, it may be that our Lord will not renew His gift again for a year or even for many years; His Majesty knows the reason which we should not try to discover since there is no need for us to understand it.

12. As most certainly the way to please God is to keep the commandments and counsels, let us do so diligently, while meditating on His life and death and all we owe Him; then let the rest be as God chooses. Some may answer that their mind refuses to dwell on these subjects; and for the above causes, this to a certain extent is true. You know that it is one thing to reason and another thing for the memory to bring certain truths before the mind. Perhaps you may not understand me; possibly I fail to express myself rightly but I will do my best. Using the understanding much in this manner is what I call meditation.

13. Let us begin by considering the mercy God showed us by giving us His only Son; let us not stop here but go on to reflect upon all the mysteries of His glorious life; or let us first turn our thoughts to His prayer in the garden, then allow them to continue the subject until they reach the crucifixion. Or we may take some part of the Passion such as Christ's apprehension and dwell on this mystery, considering in detail the points to be pondered and thought over, such as the treachery of Judas, the flight of the Apostles, and all that followed. This is an admirable and very meritorious kind of prayer.[133]

---

[129] III Reg. xviii. 30-39.

[130] Continual sense of the presence of God: Life, ch. xxvii. 6. Rel. xi. 3: 'The intellectual vision of the Three Persons and of the Sacred Humanity seems ever present.' Castle, M. vii. ch. iv. 15.

[131] Cant, iii. 3; 'Num quem diligit anima mea, vidistis?'

[132] 'I asked the earth, and it answered me: 'I am not He'; and whatsoever it contains confessed the same. I asked the sea and the depths, and the living, creeping things, and they answered: 'We are not thy God, seek above us.' I asked the heavens, I asked the moving air; and the whole air with its inhabitants answered: 'Anaximenes was deceived, I am not God.' I asked the heavens, sun, moon, stars. 'Nor,' say they, 'are we the God Whom thou seekest.' And I replied unto all things which encompass the door of my flesh: 'Ye have told me of my God, that ye are not He; tell me something of Him.' And they cried out with a loud voice: 'He made us.' By my thought of them I questioned them, and their beauty gave their answer.' (*St. Augustine's Confessions*, bk. x. ch. 6.)

St. Teresa may have read this in St. Augustine's *Confessions*, (see above, p. 78), or in the *Soliloquies*, a collection of extracts from St. Augustine, St. Bernard, St. Anselm, etc., which was printed in Latin at Venice in 1512, translated into Spanish and brought out at Valladolid in 1515, and again at Medina del Campo in 15 53, and at Toledo in 1565. The words quoted by St. Teresa occur in chapter xxxi. See *Life*, ch. xl. 10.

[133] Life, ch. xiii. 17-23.

14. Souls led by God in supernatural ways and raised to perfect contemplation are right in declaring they cannot practice this kind of meditation. As I said, I know not why, but as a rule they are unable to do so. Yet they would be wrong in saying that they cannot dwell on these mysteries nor frequently think about them, especially when these events are being celebrated by the Catholic Church. Nor is it possible for the soul which has received so much from God to forget these precious proofs of His love which are living sparks to inflame the heart with greater love for our Lord, nor can the mind fail to understand them. Such a soul comprehends these mysteries, which are brought before the mind and stamped on the memory in a more perfect way than with other people, so that the mere sight of our Lord prostrate in the garden, covered with His terrible sweat, suffices to engross the thoughts not merely for an hour but for several days. The soul looks with a simple gaze upon Who He is and how ungratefully we treat Him in return for such terrible sufferings. Then the will, although perhaps without sensible tenderness, desires to render Him some service for such sublime mercies and longs to suffer something for Him Who bore so much for us, employing itself in similar considerations in which the memory and understanding also take their part.

15. I think this is why such souls cannot reason connectedly about the Passion and fancy they are unable to mediate on it. Those who do not meditate on this subject had better begin to do so; for I know that it will not impede the most sublime prayer nor is it well to omit praising this often. If God then sees fit to enrapture them, well and good; even if they are reluctant, He will make them cease to meditate. I am certain that this way of king is most helpful to the soul and not the hindrance it would become were great efforts made to use the intellect. This, as I said, I believe cannot be done when a higher state of prayer is attained. It may be otherwise in some cases, for God leads souls in many different ways. Let not those be blamed, however, who are unable to discourse much in prayer, nor should they be judged incapable of enjoying the great graces contained in the mysteries of Jesus Christ, our only Good, which no one, however spiritual he may be, can persuade me it is well to omit contemplating.

16. There are souls who, having made a beginning, or advanced half-way, when they begin to experience the prayer of quiet and to taste the sweetness and consolations God gives, think it is a great thing to enjoy these spiritual pleasures continually. Let them, as I advised elsewhere, cease to give themselves up so much to this absorption. Life is long and full of crosses and we have need to look on Christ our pattern, to see how He bore His trials, and even to take example by His Apostles and saints if we would bear our own trials perfectly. Our good Jesus and His most blessed Mother are too good company to be left and He is well pleased if we grieve at His pains, even though sometimes at the cost of our own consolations and joys.[134] Besides, daughters, consolations are not so frequent in prayer that we have no time for this as well. If any one should tell me she continually enjoys them, and that she is one of those who can never meditate on the divine mysteries, I should feel very doubtful about her state. Be convinced of this; keep free from this deception and to the utmost of your power stop yourselves from being constantly immersed in this intoxication. If you cannot do so, tell the Prioress so that she may employ you too busily for you to think of the matter; thus you will be free from this danger which, if it does no more, when it lasts long, greatly injures the health and brain. I have said enough to prove to those who require it that, however spiritual their state, it is an error so to avoid thinking of corporeal things as to imagine that meditation on the most sacred Humanity can injure the soul.

17. People allege, in defense, that our Lord told His disciples that it was expedient for them that He should go from them.[135] This I cannot admit. He did not say so to His blessed Mother, for her faith was firm. She knew He was both God and man; and although she loved Him more dearly than did His disciples, it was in so perfect a way that His bodily presence was a help to her. The faith of the Apostles must have been weaker than it was later on, and then ours has reason to be. I assure you, daughters, that I consider this a most dangerous idea whereby the devil might end by robbing us of our devotion to the most blessed Sacrament.

---

[134] Way of Perf. ch. xxv. 7.

[135] St. John xvi. 7: 'Expedit vobis ut ego vadam; si enim non abiero, Paraclitus non veniet ad vos.' Life, ch. xxii. 1, 2 and note.

18. The mistake I formerly made[136] did not lead me as far as this, but I did not care so much about meditating on our Lord Jesus Christ, preferring to remain absorbed, awaiting spiritual consolations. I recognized clearly that I was going wrong, for as I could not always keep in this state, my thoughts wandered hither and thither and my soul seemed like a bird, ever flying about and finding no place for rest. Thus I lost much time and did not advance in virtue nor make progress in prayer.

19. I did not understand the reason, and as I believed that I was acting wisely I think I should never have learnt it but for the advice of a servant of God whom I consulted about my mode of prayer. Then I perceived plainly how mistaken I had been and I have never ceased regretting that there was a time when I did not realize how difficult it would be to gain by so great a loss. Even if I could, I would seek for nothing save by Him through Whom comes all the good we possess. May He be for ever praised! Amen.

CHAPTER VIII.

SPEAKS OF THE MANNER IN WHICH GOD COMMUNICATES WITH THE SOUL BY INTELLECTUAL VISION AND GIVES ADVICE UPON THE SUBJECT. OF THE EFFECTS PRODUCED BY THIS VISION WHEN GENUINE. SECRECY ABOUT THESE FAVOURS IS ENJOINED.

1. Our Lord's presence accompanying the soul. 2. St. Teresa's experience of this. 3. Confidence and graces resulting from this vision. 4. Its effects . 5. It Produces humility. 6. And prepares the soul for other graces. 7. Consciousness of the presence of the saints. 8. Obligations resulting from this grace. 9. Signs that this favour is genuine. 10. A confessor should be consulted. 11. Our Lord will enlighten our advisers. 12. Cautions about this vision.

1. To prove to you more clearly, sisters, the truth of what I have been saying and to show that the more the soul advances, the closer does this good Jesus bear it company, it would be well for me to tell you how, when He so chooses, it cannot withdraw from His presence. This is clearly shown by the manners and ways in which His Majesty communicates Himself to us, manifesting His love by wonderful apparitions and visions which, if He is pleased to aid me, I will describe to you so that you may not be alarmed if any of these favours are granted you. We ought, even if we do not receive them ourselves, to praise Him fervently for thus communing with creatures, seeing how sovereign are His majesty and power.

2. For example, a person who is in no way expecting such a favour nor has ever imagined herself worthy of receiving it, is conscious that Jesus Christ stands by her side although she sees Him neither with the eyes of the body nor of the soul.[137] This is called an intellectual vision; I cannot tell why. I knew a person to whom God granted both this grace and others I shall describe later on. At first it distressed her, for she could not understand it; she could see nothing, yet so convinced did she feel that Jesus Christ was thus in some way manifesting Himself that she could not doubt that it was some kind of vision, whether it came from God or no. Its powerful effects were a strong argument that it was from Him; still she was alarmed, never having heard of an intellectual vision, nor was she aware that such a thing could be. She however felt certain of our Lord's presence,[138] and He spoke to her several times in the way that I described. Before she had received this favour, she had heard words spoken but had never known who uttered them.

3. She was frightened by this vision which, unlike an imaginary one, does not pass away quickly but lasts for several days and even sometimes for more than a year. She went, in a state of great anxiety, to her confessor[139] who asked her how, if she saw nothing, she knew that our Lord was near her, and bade her describe His appearance. She said that she was unable to do so, nor could she see His face nor tell more than she had already done, but that she was sure it was

---

[136] Life, ch. xxii. 11. Although the Saint defends herself against the charge of self-contradiction, there can be no doubt from this avowal that she too was at one time mistaken on this point.

[137] Life, ch. xxvii. 3, 5. Rel. vii. 26.

[138] Life, ch. xxvii. 7.

[139] Ibid. l.c. 4. Father Juan de Pradanos was then the Saint's confessor.

the fact that it was He Who spoke to her and it was no trick of her imagination. Although people constantly cautioned her against this vision, as a rule she found it impossible to disbelieve in it, especially when she heard the words: 'It is I, be not afraid'[140]

4. The effect of this speech was so powerful that for the time being she could not doubt its truth. She felt much encouraged and rejoiced at being in such good company, seeing that this favour greatly helped her to a constant recollection of God and an extreme care not to displease in any way Him Who seemed ever by her side, watching her. Whenever she desired to speak to His Majesty in prayer, or even at other times, He seemed so close that He could not fail to hear her though He did not speak to her whenever she wished, but unexpectedly, when necessity arose. She was conscious of His being at her right hand, although not in the way we know an ordinary person to be beside us but in a more subtle manner which cannot be described. Yet this presence is quite as evident and certain, and indeed far more so, than the ordinary presence of other people about which we may be deceived; not so in this, for it brings with it graces and spiritual effects which could not come from melancholia. Nor could the devil thus fill the soul with peace, with a constant desire to please God, and such utter contempt of all that does not lead to Him. As time went on, my friend recognized that this was no work of the evil one, as our Lord showed her more and more clearly.

5. However, I know that she often felt great alarm and was at times overcome with confusion, being unable to account for so high a favour having been granted her. She and I were so very intimate[141] that I knew all that passed in her soul, hence my account is thoroughly true and reliable. This favour brings with it an overwhelming sense of self-abasement and humility; the reverse would be the case, did it come from Satan.[142] It is evidently divine; no human effort could produce such feelings nor could any one suppose that such profit came from herself, but must needs recognize it as a gift from the hand of God.

6. Although I believe some of the former favours are more sublime, yet this brings with it a special knowledge of God; a most tender love for Him results from being constantly in His company, while the desires of devoting one's whole being to His service are more fervent than any hitherto described. The conscience is greatly purified by the knowledge of His perpetual and near presence, for although we know that God sees all we do, yet nature inclines us to grow careless and forgetful of it. This is impossible here since our Lord makes the soul conscious that He is close at hand, thus preparing it to receive the other graces mentioned by constantly making acts of love to Him Whom it sees or feels at its side. In short, the benefits caused by this grace prove how great and how valuable it is. The soul thanks our Lord for bestowing it on one unworthy of it, but who would refuse to exchange it for any earthly riches or delight.

7. When our Lord chooses to withdraw His presence, the soul in its loneliness makes every possible effort to induce Him to return. This avails but little, for this grace comes at His will and not by our endeavours. At times we may enjoy the company of some saint,[143] which also brings us great profit. You will ask me, if we see no one, how can we know whether it is Christ, or His most glorious Mother, or a saint? Such a person cannot answer this question or know how she distinguishes them, but the fact remains undoubted. It seems easy to recognize our Lord when He speaks, but it is surprising how the soul can, without hearing a word from him, recognize which saint has been sent by God to be its companion and helper.

8. There are other spiritual matters which cannot be explained. Our inability to grasp them should teach us how incapable is our nature of understanding the sublime mysteries of God. Those on whom these favours are bestowed should marvel at and praise God's mercy for them. As these particular graces are not granted to everybody, any one who receives them should esteem them highly and strive to serve God more zealously, since He has given her such special aid. Therefore such a person does not rate herself more highly on this account, but rather thinks she serves Him

---

[140] Life, ch. xxv. 22; XXX. 17. Supra, M. vi. ch. iii. 5. Rel. vii. 22. St. John of the Cross, Ascent of Mount Carmel, bk. ii. ch. xxxi. 1.

[141] In fact, one and the same person.

[142] Life, ch. xix. a; xx. 38. Way of Perf. ch. xxxvi. 10.

[143] Life, ch. xxix 6.

less than any one else in the world; feeling herself to be under greater obligations to Him than others, any fault she commits pierces her to the heart, as indeed it ought under the circumstances.

9. When the effects described are felt, any of you whom our Lord leads by this way may be certain that it is neither deception nor fancy in her case. I believe it to be impossible for the devil to produce an illusion lasting so long, neither could he benefit the soul so remarkably nor cause such interior peace. It is not his custom, nor, if he would, could such an evil creature bring about so much good; the soul would soon be clouded by self-esteem and the idea that it was better than others. The mind's continual keeping in the presence of God[144] and the concentration of its thoughts on Him would so enrage the fiend that, although he might try the experiment once, he would not often repeat it. God is too faithful to permit him so much power over one whose sole endeavour is to please His Majesty and to lay down her life for His honour and glory; He would soon unmask the demon's artifices.

10. I contend, as I always shall, that if the soul reaps the effects described from these divine graces, although God may withdraw these special favours, His Majesty will turn all things to its advantage; even should He permit the devil to deceive it at any time, the evil spirit will only reap his own confusion. Therefore, as I told you, daughters, none of you who are led by this way need feel alarm. Fear is good and we should be cautious and not overconfident, for if such favours made you careless, it would prove they were not from God as they did not leave the results I described. It would be well at first to tell your case, under the seal of confession, to a thoroughly qualified theologian (for that is the source whence we must obtain light) or to some highly spiritual person. If your confessor is not very spiritual, a good theologian would be preferable;[145] best of all, one who unites both qualities.[146] Do not be disturbed if he calls it mere fancy; if it is, it can neither harm nor benefit your soul much. Recommend yourself to the divine Majesty and beg Him not to allow you to be misled.

11. It would be worse should he tell you the devil is deceiving you, although no learned man would say so if he sees in you the effects described. Even should your adviser say this, I know that the same Lord Who is beside you will comfort and reassure you and will go to your counsellor and give him light that he may impart it to you.[147] If the director, though given to prayer, has not been led by God in this way, he will at once take fright and condemn it. Therefore I advise you to choose a qualified theologian and, if possible, one who is also spiritual. The Prioress ought to allow you this, for although she may feel sure that you are safe from delusion because you lead a good life, yet she is bound to permit you to consult some one for your mutual security. When you have conferred with these persons, be at peace; trouble yourself no more about the matter, for sometimes when there is no cause for fear, the demon gives rise to such immoderate scruples that the person cannot be satisfied with consulting her confessor only once on the subject, especially if he is inexperienced and timid or if he bids her consult him again.

12. Thus that which should have been kept strictly private becomes public;[148] such a person is persecuted and tormented and finds that what she believed to be her own secret has become public property. Hence she suffers many troubles which may even devolve upon the Order in such times as these. Consequently I warn all Prioresses that great caution is required in such matters; also they must not think a nun more virtuous than the rest because such favours are shown her. Our Lord guides every one, in the way He knows to be best. This grace, if made good use of, prepares one receiving it to become a great servant of God, but sometimes our Lord bestows it on the weakest souls; therefore in itself it is neither to be esteemed nor condemned. We must look to the virtues; she who is most mortified, humble and single-minded in serving God is the most holy.

---

144 Gen. xvii, 1: 'Ambula coram me et esto perfectus.'

145 'Magni doctores scholastici, si non sint spirituales, vel omni rerum spiritualium experientia careant, non solent esse magistri spirituales idonei—nam theologia scholastica est perfectio intellectus; mystica, perfectio intellectus et voluntatis: unde bonus theologus scholasticus potest esse malus theologus mysticus. In rebus tamen difficilibus, dubiis, spiritualibus, præstat mediocriter spiritualem theologum consulere quam spiritualem idiotam.' (Schram, Theol. Myst. § 483.)

146 Life, ch. v. 6.

147 Ibid. ch. xxv. 18 sqq. Way of Perf. ch. iv. 11; v. 3.

148 Life, ch. xxiii. 14-15. Rel. vii. 17.

However, we can never feel very certain about such matters until the true Judge rewards each one according to his merits. Then we shall be surprised to find how very different is His judgment from that of this world. May He be for ever praised. Amen.

CHAPTER IX.

THIS CHAPTER SPEAKS OF THE MANNER IN WHICH GOD COMMUNICATES WITH THE SOUL BY IMAGINARY VISIONS. STRONG REASONS ARE GIVEN FOR NOT DESIRING TO BE LED IN THIS WAY; THIS IS VERY PROFITABLE READING.

1. The jewel in the locket. 2. The simile explained. 3. The apparition explained. 4. Awe produced by this vision. 5. False and genuine visions. 6. Illusive visions. 7. Effects of a genuine vision. 8. Conviction left by a genuine vision. 9. Its effects upon the after conduct. 10. A confessor should be consulted. 11. How to treat visions. 12. Effects of seeing the face of Christ. 13. Reasons why visions are not to be sought. 14. The second reason. 15. Third reason. 16. Fourth reason. 17. Fifth reason. 18. Sixth reason. 19. Additional reasons. 20. The virtues more meritorious than consolations. 21. Fervent souls desire to serve God for Himself alone.

1. Now we come to treat of imaginary visions, whereby it is held that the devil is more liable to deceive people than by the other visions I have already described. This is probably true. Yet when imaginary visions are divine, they seem, in a certain manner, more profitable for us than the others, as being more suited to our nature—with the exception of the visions sent by our Lord in the seventh mansion which far surpass all others. The presence of our Lord described in the last chapter may thus be symbolized. Let us suppose that we have in our possession a gold locket containing a precious stone of the highest value and powers, which, though we have not seen it, we are certain is in the case, and its virtues benefit us when we wear the pendant. Although we have never gazed on it we value it highly, knowing by experience that it has cured us of maladies for which it is remedial. However, we dare not look at it nor open the locket nor could we do so even if we wished, for the owner of the jewel alone knows the secret of unfastening its casket. Although he lent it us for our use, yet he kept the key for himself; he will open the trinket when he chooses to show us its contents and close it again when he sees fit to do so.

2. Our Lord treats us here in this way. Now, suppose the owner of this locket suddenly opened it at times for the benefit of the person to whom he has entrusted it; doubtless the latter would value the diamond more highly through remembering its wonderful luster. This may be compared to what happens when our Lord is pleased to caress the soul. He shows it in vision His most sacred Humanity under whatever form He chooses; either as He was during His life on earth[149] or after His resurrection.[150] The vision passes as quickly as a flash of lightning, yet this most glorious picture makes an impression on the imagination that I believe can never be effaced until the soul at last sees Christ to enjoy Him for ever. Although I call it a 'picture,' you must not imagine that it looks like a painting; Christ appears as a living Person Who sometimes speaks and reveals deep mysteries. You must understand that though the soul sees this for a certain space of time, it is no more possible to continue looking at it than to gaze for a very long time on the sun; therefore this vision passes very quickly, although its brightness does not pain the interior sight in the same way as the sun's glare injures our bodily eyes.

3. The image is seen by the interior sight alone; but of bodily apparitions I can say nothing, for the person I know so intimately never having experienced anything of the kind herself could not speak about them with certainty.[151] The splendour of Him Who is revealed in the vision resembles an infused light like that of the sun covered with a veil as transparent as a diamond, if such a texture could be woven, while His raiment looks like fine linen. The soul to whom God grants this vision almost always falls into an ecstasy, nature being too weak to bear so dread a sight. I say 'dread,' though this apparition is more lovely and delightful than anything that could be imagined even though any one should live a thousand years and spend all that time in trying

---

[149] Life, ch, vii, 11.
[150] Ibid. xxix, 4.
[151] Life, ch, vii. 11, 12.

to picture it, for it far surpasses our limited imagination and understanding; yet the presence of such surpassing majesty inspires the soul with great fear.

4. There is no need to ask how the soul knew Who He was or who declared with absolute certainty that He was the Lord of heaven and earth. This is not so with earthly kings; unless we were told their names or saw their attendant courtiers, they would attract little notice. O Lord, how little do we Christians know Thee! What will that day be in which Thou comest as our Judge, since now, when Thou comest as a Friend to Thy spouse, the sight of Thee strikes us with such awe? O daughters! what will it be when He says in wrath: 'Go, accursed of my Father?'[152] Let this impression be the result of this favour granted by God to the soul and we shall reap no little benefit from it, since St. Jerome, saint as he was, ever kept the thought of the last judgment before his eyes.[153] Thus we shall care nothing what sufferings we endure from the austerities of our Rule, for long as they may last, the time is but a moment compared to this eternity of pain. I sincerely assure you that, wicked as I am, I have never feared the torments of hell[154] for they have seemed to me as nothing when I remembered that the lost would see the beautiful, meek and pitiful eyes of our Lord turned on them in wrath.[155] I have thought all my life that this would be more than my heart could bear.

5. How much more must any one fear this to whom our Lord so revealed Himself in vision here as to overcome her feelings and produce unconsciousness! This must be the reason that the soul remains in a rapture: our Lord strengthens its weakness so as to unite it to His greatness in this sublime communion with God. When any one can contemplate this sight of our Lord for a long time, I do not believe it is a vision but rather some overmastering idea which causes the imagination to fancy it sees something; but this illusion is only like a dead image in comparison with the living reality of the other case.

6. As not only three or four, but a large number of people have spoken to me on the subject, I know by experience that there are souls which, either because they possess vivid imaginations or active minds, or for some other reason of which I am ignorant, are so absorbed in their own ideas as to feel certain they see whatever their fancy imagines. If they had ever beheld a genuine vision, they would recognize the deception unmistakably. They themselves fabricate, piece by piece, what they fancy they see: no after effects are produced on the mind, which is less moved to devotion than by the sight of a sacred picture. It is clear that no attention should be paid to such fancies, which pass more quickly than dreams from the memory.

7. In the favour of which I speak, the case is very different. A person is far from thinking of seeing anything, no idea of which has crossed the mind, when suddenly the vision is revealed in its entirety, causing within the powers and senses of the soul a fright and confusion soon changed into a blissful peace. Thus, after St. Paul was thrown to the ground, a great tempest and noise followed from heaven;[156] so, in the interior world of the soul, there is a violent tumult followed instantly, as I said, by perfect calm. Meanwhile certain sublime truths have been so impressed on the mind that it needs no other master, for with no effort of its own, Wisdom Himself has enlightened its former ignorance.

8. The soul for some time afterwards possesses such certainty that this grace comes from God that whatever people may say to the contrary it cannot fear delusion. Later on, when her confessor suggests doubts to her, God may allow such a person to waver in her belief for a time and to feel misgivings lest, in punishment for her sins, she may possibly have been left to go astray. However, she does not give way to these apprehensions, but (as I said in speaking of other

---

[152] St. Matt. xxv. 41: 'Discedite a me, maledicti, in ignem æternum.'

[153] 'Whenever I ponder on the Day of Judgment I am overwhelmed by the thought and tremble from head to foot.' (St. Jerome). The following saying is by some attributed to St. Jerome, though not to be found in his works: 'Whether I eat or drink, or whatever else I do, the dreadful trumpet of the last day seems always sounding in my ears: Arise, ye dead, and come to judgment.' (Alban Butler, Life of St. Jerome). The Life of Christ by Ludolf of Saxony gives this quotation with the word vox instead of tuba (part ii. ch. lxxxvii. 9).

[154] Life, ch. iii.

[155] Excl. xiii, 3.

[156] Acts ix. 3, 4.

matters)[157] they only affect her in the same way as the temptations of the devil against faith, which may disturb the mind but do not shake the firmness of belief. In fact, the more severe the assault,[158] the more certain is she that the evil one could never have produced the great benefits she is conscious of having received, because he exercises no such power over the interior of the soul. He may present a false apparition but it does not possess such truth, majesty, and efficacy.

9. As confessors cannot see these effects, which perhaps the person to whom God has shown the vision is unable to explain, they are afraid of deception, as indeed they have good reason to be. Therefore caution is necessary and time should be allowed to see what effects follow. Day by day, the progress of the soul in humility and in the virtues should be watched: if the devil is concerned in the matter, he will soon show signs of himself and will be detected in a thousand lies. If the confessor is experienced and has received such favours himself, he will not take long in discovering the truth. In fact, he will know immediately, on being told of the vision, whether it is divine or comes from the imagination or the demon: more especially if he has received the gift of discerning spirits—then, if he is learned, he will understand the matter at once even though he has not personally experienced the like.

10. The great point is, sisters, that you should be perfectly candid and straightforward with your confessor: I do not mean in declaring your sins that is evident enough—but in giving him an account of your prayer.[159] Unless you do this, I cannot assure you of your safety nor that you are led by God. Our Lord desires that we should be as truthful and open with those who stand in His place as we should with Himself; that we should wish them to know not only our thoughts but especially all relating to our actions, however insignificant. Then you need feel no trouble nor anxiety[160] because even if your vision were not from God, it could do you no harm if you are humble and possess a good conscience, for His Majesty knows how to glean good from evil. What the devil intended to injure you will benefit you instead: believing that God has granted you such signal favours, you will strive to please Him better and will keep His image ever before your memory.

11. A great theologian[161] once said that he should not trouble himself though the devil, who is a clever painter, should present before his eyes the living image of Christ, which would only kindle his devotion and defeat the evil one with his own weapons. However wicked an artist may be, we should reverence his picture if it represents Him Who is our only good. This great scholar held that it was very wrong to advise any one who saw a vision of our Lord to offer it signs of scorn,[162] because we are bound to show respect to the portrait of our King wherever we see it. I am sure that he was right, for even in the world any one who was on friendly terms with a person would take it as an offence were his portrait treated with contempt. How much more should we always show respect to a crucifix or a picture of our heavenly Sovereign wherever it meets our gaze! Although I have written about this elsewhere, I am glad of the opportunity of saying it now for I know some one who was deeply pained at being bidden to behave in this way. I know not who can have invented such a torture for one who felt bound to obey the counsel given by her confessor, for she would have thought her soul was at stake had she disobeyed him. My advice is, if you are given such an order, that humbly alleging the reasons I have set before you to your confessor, you should not carry it out. I am perfectly satisfied with the motives given for doing so by him who counselled me on this subject.

12. One great advantage gained by the soul from this favour shown by our Lord is that when thinking of Him or of His life and Passion, the remembrance of His most meek and beautiful face brings with it the greatest consolation. In the same way, we feel happier after having seen a benefactor than if we had never known him personally. I can assure you that the remembrance of the joy caused by this vision gives us the greatest comfort and assistance.

---

[157] Castle, M. vi. ch. iii. 12.

[158] Way of Perf ch, xl. 4.

[159] Life, ch. xxvi. 5; xxviii. 21.

[160] Way of Perf. ch. xl. 3.

[161] This was Father Dominic Bañez. Found. ch. viii. 3. Life, ch. xxix. 6, 7 and note.

[162] Letters of Blessed John of Avila (translated by the Benedictines of Stanbrook), i. 5, p. 19.

13. Many other advantages result; but as I have written elsewhere[163] at length about the effect these visions produce, and must do so again later on, I will say no more now lest I weary us both. But I most earnestly advise you, when you know or hear of God's bestowing these graces on others, never to pray nor desire to be led by this way yourself though it may appear to you to be very good; indeed, it ought to be highly esteemed and reverenced, yet no one should seek to go by it for several reasons. Firstly, as it is a want of humility to desire what you have never deserved, I do not think any one who longs for these graces can be really humble: a common laborer never dreams of wishing to be made a king—the thing seems impossible and he is unfit for it; a lowly mind has the same feeling about these divine favours. I do not believe God will ever bestow these gifts on such a person, as before doing so He always gives thorough self-knowledge. How can that soul, while filled with such lofty aspirations, realize the truth that He has shown it great mercy in not casting it into hell?

14. The second reason is that such a one is certain to be deceived or at least is in great danger of delusion, for an entrance is thus left open to the devil, who only needs to see the door left ajar to slip in at once and play us a thousand tricks.

15. Thirdly: when people strongly desire a thing, the imagination makes them fancy they see or hear it, just as when a man's mind is set upon a subject all day he dreams of it at night.

16. Fourthly: it would be very presumptuous of me to choose a way for myself without knowing what is good for me.[164] I should leave our Lord, Who knows my soul, to guide me as is best for me so that His will may be done in all things.

17. Fifthly: do you think people on whom our Lord bestows these favours have little to suffer? No, indeed! their trials are most severe and of many kinds. How can you tell whether you would be able to bear them?

18. Sixthly: perhaps what you think would be your gain might prove your loss, as happened to Saul when he was made king.[165] In short, sisters, there are other reasons besides these; believe me, it is safer to wish only what God wishes, Who knows us better than we know ourselves and Who loves us. Let us place ourselves entirely in His hands so that His will may be done in us; we can never go astray if our will is ever firmly fixed on this.

19. Know that for having received many favours of this kind, you will not merit more glory but will be the more stringently obliged to serve, since you have received more. God does not deprive us of anything by which we merit more, for this remains in our own control. There are many saints who never knew what it was to receive one such favour, while others who have received them are not saints at all. Do not imagine that these gifts are continually bestowed; indeed, for one that is granted, the soul bears many a cross, so that instead of longing to receive more favours, it only strives to use them better.

20. True, such a grace is a most powerful aid towards practicing the virtues in their highest perfection, but it is far more meritorious to gain them at the cost of one's own toil. I was acquainted with some one,[166] indeed with two people (of whom one was a man), on whom our Lord had bestowed some of these gifts. They were both so desirous of serving His Majesty at their own cost without these great consolations and so longed to suffer for His sake, that they remonstrated with Him for giving them these favours, and if it had been possible would have refused to receive them. When I say 'consolations,' I do not mean these visions which greatly benefit the soul and are highly to be esteemed, but the delights given by God during contemplation.

21. I believe that these desires are supernatural and proper to very fervent souls who wish to prove to God that they do not serve Him for pay; so as I said, such people do not urge themselves to work harder for Him by the thought of the glory they will gain, but rather labour to satisfy their love, of which the nature is to toil for the Beloved in a thousand ways. Such souls would fain find

[163] Life, ch. xxviii. 13, 4.

[164] St. Teresa, when led in this way, always asked to be delivered from favours so dangerous as visions, etc. See Life, ch. xxv. 20; xxvii. 3.

[165] I. Reg. xv. 26-28.

[166] Life, ch. xl. 27. She herself was one, and the other, no doubt, was St. John of the Cross.

a way to consume themselves in Him, and were there need that, for the sake of God's greater glory, they should be annihilated for ever, they would count it great gain. May He be for ever praised Who, in abasing Himself to hold converse with us miserable creatures, vouchsafes to manifest His greatness! Amen.

CHAPTER X.

SPEAKS OF VARIOUS OTHER GRACES GOD BESTOWS ON THE SOUL IN DIFFERENT WAYS, AND OF THE GREAT BENEFITS CONFERRED BY THEM.

1. Reasons for speaking of these supernatural favours. 2. An intellectual vision. 3. God compared to a palace in which His creatures dwell. 4. Forgive as we are forgiven. 5. The vision shows God to be Truth itself. 6. We should imitate God by truthfulness. 7. Why God reveals these truths.

1. OUR Lord communicates with the soul by means of these apparitions on many occasions—sometimes when it is afflicted, at other times when it is about to receive some heavy cross, and again for the sake of the mutual delight of Himself and His beloved. There is no need for me to specify each different case nor do I intend to do so. I only wish to teach you (as far as I am acquainted with them myself) what are the different favours God shows a soul in this state so that you may understand their characteristics and the effects they produce. Thus you will not mistake every idle fancy for a vision and if you really see one, knowing that such a thing is possible, you will not be disturbed nor unhappy. The devil, who gains greatly by it, is delighted to see a soul troubled and distressed, knowing how this hinders it from employing itself wholly in loving and serving God.

2. His Majesty has far higher ways of communicating Himself to the soul; they are less dangerous for I do not think the evil spirit can imitate them. They are more difficult to explain, being more abstruse; therefore imaginary visions are easier to describe. God is sometimes pleased, while a person is engaged in prayer and in perfect possession of her senses, to suspend them and to discover sublime mysteries to her which she appears to see within God Himself. This is no vision of the most sacred Humanity nor can I rightly say the soul 'sees,' for it sees nothing; this is no imaginary vision but a highly intellectual one, wherein is manifested how all things are beheld in God and how He contains them within Himself.[167] It is of great value, for although passing in an instant, it remains deeply engraved in the memory, producing a feeling of great shame in the mind which perceives more clearly the malice of offences against God, since these most heinous sins are committed within His very being since we dwell within Him. I will try to explain this truth to you by a comparison, for although it is obvious and has been often told us, we either never reflect upon it or do not wish to understand it. If we realized it, we could not possibly behave with such audacity.

3. Let us compare God to a very spacious and magnificent mansion or palace and remember that this edifice is God Himself. Can the sinner withdraw from it in order to carry out his crimes? No, certainly not, for within this very palace, that is, within God Himself, are perpetrated all the abominations, impurities and evil deeds that sinners commit. Oh awful thought, well worthy to be pondered over! What profit it would bring to us, who know so little and understand these truths but partially or how could we possibly be so reckless in our daring? Let us, sisters, meditate on the infinite mercy and patience of God in not casting us down to hell at once and let us render Him hearty thanks. Surely we should be ashamed of resenting anything done or said against us— *we* who are the scum of the earth—when we see what outrages are offered to *God* our *Creator* within His very being, by us His creatures; yet we are wounded whenever we hear of an unkind word having been spoken of us in our absence, although perhaps with no evil intention.

4. Oh misery of mankind! When, daughters, shall we imitate Almighty God in any way? Oh, let us not think we are doing great things if we suffer injuries *patiently*: rather let us bear them with *alacrity*; let us love our enemies, since this great God has not ceased to love us in spite of

---

[167] Life, ch. xl. 13-16.

our many sins! This is indeed the chief reason that all should forgive any harm done them. I assure you, daughters, that though this vision passes very quickly, our Lord has bestowed signal grace on her to whom He grants it, if she seeks to profit by keeping it constantly in mind.

5. Short as the time lasts, yet, in a manner impossible to describe, God also manifests that in Him there is a verity which makes all truth in creatures seem obscure. He convinces the soul that He alone is that Truth which cannot lie, thus demonstrating the meaning of David's words in the psalm: 'Every man is a liar,'[168] which could never be thus realized by any other means, however often we might hear that God is truth infallible. As I recall Pilate and how he besought our Lord in His Passion to answer his question: 'What is truth?'[169] I realize how little mortals know of that sublime veracity.

6. I wish I could explain this better but am unable to do so. Let us learn from it, sisters, that if we would bear any resemblance to our God and our Spouse, we must strive to walk ever in the truth. I do not merely mean that we should not tell falsehoods thank God, I see that in these convents you are most careful never to do so on any account—but I desire that as far as possible we should at with perfect truth before God and man and above all that we should not wish to be thought better than we are; that in all our deeds we should ascribe to God what is His and attribute what is ours to ourselves, and that we should seek for verity in all things. Thus we shall care little for this world, which is but deception and falsehood, and therefore cannot last. Once, while I was wondering why our Lord so dearly loves the virtue of humility, the thought suddenly struck me, without previous reflection, that it is because God is the supreme Truth and humility is the *truth*, for it is most true that we have nothing good of ourselves but only misery and nothingness: whoever ignores this, lives a life of falsehood. They that realize this fact most deeply are the most pleasing to God, the supreme Truth, for they walk in the truth. God grant, sisters, that we may have the grace never to lose this self-knowledge! Amen.

7. Our Lord shows the soul these favours because she is now indeed His bride, resolute to do His will in all things; therefore He wishes to give her some idea how to accomplish it and to manifest to her some of His divine attributes. I need say no more about it, but I believe the two points above mentioned will prove very useful. These favours should cause no fear but lead us to praise God for bestowing these graces. I think neither the devil nor our own imaginations can have much to do with them, therefore the soul may rest in perfect peace.

CHAPTER XI.

TREATS OF HOW GOD INSPIRES THE SOUL WITH SUCH VEHEMENT AND IMPETUOUS DESIRES OF SEEING HIM AS TO ENDANGER LIFE. THE BENEFITS RESULTING FROM THIS DIVINE GRACE.

1. Favours increase the soul's desire for God. 2. The dart of love. 3. Spiritual sufferings produced. 4. Its physical effects. S. Torture of the desire for God. 6. These sufferings are a purgatory. 7. The torments of hell. 8. St. Teresa's painful desire after God. 9. This suffering irresistible. 10. Effects of the dart of love. 11. Two spiritual dangers to life. 12. Courage needed here and given by our Lord.

1. WILL all these graces bestowed by the Spouse upon the soul suffice to content this little dove or butterfly (you see I have not forgotten her after all!) so that she may settle down and rest in the place where she is to die? No indeed: her state is far worse than ever; although she has been receiving these favours for many years past, she still sighs and weeps because each grace augments her pain. She sees herself still far away from God, yet with her increased knowledge of His attributes her longing and her love for Him grow ever stronger as she learns more fully how this great God and Sovereign deserves to be loved. As, year by year her yearning after Him gradually becomes keener, she experiences the bitter suffering I am about to describe. I speak of 'years' because relating what happened to the person I mentioned, though I know well that with God time has no limits and in a single moment He can raise a soul to the most sublime state I

---

[168] Ps. cxv. 11. 'Omnis homo mendax.'
[169] St. John xviii. 38: Quid est veritas?

have described. His Majesty has the power to do all He wishes and He wishes to do much for us. These longings, tears, sighs, and violent and impetuous desires and strong feelings, which seem to proceed from our vehement love, are yet as nothing compared with what I am about to describe and seem but a smoldering fire, the heat of which, though painful, is yet tolerable.

2. While the soul is thus inflamed with love, it often happens that, from a passing thought or spoken word of how death delays its coming, the heart receives, it knows not how or whence, a blow as from a fiery dart.[170] I do not say that this actually is a 'dart,' but, whatever it may be, decidedly it does not come from any part of our being.[171] Neither is it really a 'blow' though I call it one, but it wounds us severely—not, I think, in that part of our nature subject to physical pain but in the very depths and centre of the soul, where this, thunderbolt, in its rapid course, reduces all the earthly part of our nature to powder. At the time we cannot even remember our own existence, for in an instant, the faculties of the soul are so fettered as to be incapable of any action except the power they retain of increasing our torture. Do not think I am exaggerating; indeed I fall short of explaining what happens which cannot be described.

3. This is a trance of the senses and faculties except as regards what helps to make the agony more intense. The understanding realizes acutely what cause there is for grief in separation from God and His Majesty now augments this sorrow by a vivid manifestation of Himself. This increases the anguish to such a degree that the sufferer gives vent to loud cries which she cannot stifle, however patient and accustomed to pain she may be, because this torture is not corporal but attacks the innermost recesses of the soul. The person I speak of learnt from this how much more acutely the spirit is capable of suffering than the body; she understood that this resembled the pains of purgatory, where the absence of the flesh does not prevent the torture's being far worse than any we can feel in this world.

4. I saw some one in this condition who I really thought would have died, nor would it have been surprising, for there is great danger of death in this state. Short as is the time it lasts, it leaves the limbs all disjointed and the pulse as feeble as if the soul were on the point of departure, which is indeed the case, for the natural heat fails, while that which is supernatural so burns the frame that were it increased ever so little God would satisfy the soul's desire for death. Not that any pain is felt by the body at the moment, although, as I said, all the joints are dislocated so that for two or three days afterwards the suffering is too severe for the person to have even the strength to hold a pen;[172] indeed I believe that the health becomes permanently enfeebled in consequence. At the time this is not felt, probably because the spiritual torments are so much more keen that the bodily ones remain unnoticed; just as when there is very severe pain in one part, slighter aches elsewhere are hardly perceived, as I know by experience. During this favour there is no physical suffering either great or small, nor do I think the person would feel it were she torn to pieces.

5. Perhaps you will say this is an imperfection, and you may ask why she does not conform herself to the will of God since she has so completely surrendered herself to it. Hitherto she has been able to do so and she consecrated her life to it; but now she cannot because her reason is reduced to such a state that she is no longer mistress of herself; nor can she think of anything but what tends to increase her torment—for why should she seek to live apart from her only Good? She feels a strange loneliness, finding no companionship in any earthly creature; nor could she, I believe, among those who dwell in heaven, since they are not her Beloved: meanwhile all society is a torture to her. She is like one suspended in mid-air, who can neither touch the earth nor mount to heaven; she is unable to reach the water while parched with thirst and this is not a thirst that can be borne, but one which nothing will quench nor would she have it quenched save with that water of which our Lord spoke to the Samaritan woman, but this is not given to her.[173]

---

[170] Life, ch. xxix. 17. (Transverberation.)

[171] Ibid. ch. xxix. 13, 14. Rel. viii. 16-19.

[172] St. John of the Cross, Obscure Night, bk. ii. ch. i. (in fine); Spiritual Canticle, stanza xiii; xiv-xv. (in fine). When this happened to St. Teresa she was unable to write for twelve days. Ribera, Acta SS. p. 555 (in fine). Rel. viii. 13. Life, ch. xx. 16.

[173] St. John iv. 15. Life, ch. xxx. 24. Way of Perf. ch. xix. 4 sqq. Concept. ch. vii. 7, 8. Found. ch. xxxi. 42. See note, Life, ch. i. 6.

6. Alas, O Lord, to what a state dost Thou bring those who love Thee! Yet these sufferings are as nothing compared with the reward Thou wilt give for them. It is right that great riches should be dearly bought. Moreover, her pains purify her soul so that it may enter the seventh mansion, as purgatory cleanses spirits which are to enter heaven:[174] then indeed these trials will appear like a drop of water compared to the sea. Though this torment and grief could not, I think, be surpassed by any earthly cross (so at least this person said and she had endured much both in body and mind), yet they appeared to her as nothing in comparison with their recompense. The soul realizes that it has not merited anguish which is of such measureless value. This conviction, although bringing no relief, enables the sufferer to bear her trials willingly—for her entire lifetime, if God so wills,—although instead of dying once for all, this would be but a living death, for truly it is nothing else.

7. Let us remember, sisters, how those who are in hell lack this submission to the divine will and the resignation and consolation God gives such a soul and the solace of knowing that their pains benefit them, for the damned will continually suffer more and more; (more and more, I mean in regard to accidental pains[175]). The soul feels far more keenly than the body and the torments I have just described are incomparably less severe than those endured by the lost, who also know that their anguish will last for ever: what, then, will become of these miserable souls? What can we do or suffer during our short lives which is worth reckoning if it will free us from such terrible and endless torments? I assure you that, unless you have learned by experience, it would be impossible to make you realize how acute are spiritual pangs and how different from physical pain. Our Lord wishes us to understand this, so that we may realize what gratitude we owe Him for having called us to a state where we may hope, by His mercy, to be freed from and forgiven our sins.

8. Let us return to the soul we left in such cruel torment. This agony does not continue for long in its full violence—never, I believe, longer than three or four hours; were it prolonged, the weakness of our nature could not endure it except by a miracle. In one case, where it lasted only a quarter of an hour, the sufferer was left utterly exhausted; indeed, so violent was the attack that she completely lost consciousness. This occurred when she unexpectedly heard some verses to the effete that life seemed unending; she was engaged in conversation at the time, which was on the last day of Easter. All Eastertide she had suffered such aridity as hardly to realize what mystery was being celebrated.[176]

9. It is as impossible to resist this suffering as it would be to prevent the flame's having heat enough to burn us if we were thrown into a fire. These feelings cannot be concealed: all who are present recognize the dangerous condition of such a person although they are unable to see what is passing within her. True, she knows her friends are near, but they and all earthly things seem to her but shadows. To show you that, should you ever be in this state, it is possible for your weakness and human nature to be of help to you, I may tell you that at times, when a person seems dying from her desire for death[177] which so oppresses her soul with grief that it appears on the point of leaving her body, yet her mind, terrified at the thought, tries to still its pain so as to keep death at bay. Evidently this fear arises from human infirmity, for the soul's longings for death do not abate meanwhile nor can its sorrows be stilled or allayed until God brings it comfort.[178] This

---

174 St. John of the Cross, Obscure Night, bk. ii. ch. xii.

175

176 *Rel.* iv. 1. *Concept.* ch. vii. 2. Isabel of Jesus, in her deposition in the Acts of Canonisation (Fuente, *Obras*, vol. vi. 316) declares that she was the singer. The words were: Véante mis ojos, Dulce Jesús bueno: Véante mis ojos, Y muérame yo luégo.

Fuente, *l.c.* vol. v. 143, note 1. *Œuvres*, ii. 231. (Poem 36, English version.) There is a slight difference in the two relations of this occurrence. In *Rel.* iv. St. Teresa seems to imply that it happened on Easter Sunday evening, but here she says distinctly: 'Pascua de Resurreccion, el postrer dia,' that is, on Easter Tuesday, April 17, 1571, at Salamanca.

177 Compare the words 'Que muero porque no muero' in the Glosa of St. Teresa. Way of Perf. ch. xlii . 2. Castle, M. vii. ch. iii. 14.

178 Way of Perf. ch. xix. 10. Excl. vi.; xii. a.; xiv.

He usually does by a deep trance or by some vision whereby the true Comforter consoles and strengthens the heart, which thus becomes resigned to live as long as He wills.[179]

10. This favour entails great suffering but leaves most precious graces within the soul, which loses all fear of any crosses it may henceforth meet with, for in comparison with the acute anguish it has gone through all else seems nothing. Seeing what she has gained, the sufferer would gladly endure frequently the same pains[180] but can do nothing to help herself in the matter. There are no means of reaching that state again until God chooses to decree it, when neither resistance nor escape is possible. The mind feels far deeper contempt for the world than before, realizing that nothing earthly can succor it in its torture; it is also much more detached from creatures, having learnt that no one but its Creator can bring it consolation and strength. It is more anxious and careful not to offend God, seeing that He can torment as well as comfort.[181]

11. Two things in this spiritual state seem to me to endanger life,—one is that of which I have just spoken which is a real peril and no small one; the other an excessive gladness and a delight so extreme that the soul appears to swoon away and seems on the point of leaving the body, which indeed would bring it no small joy.

12. Now you see, sisters, whether I had not reason to tell you that courage was needed for these favours and that when any one asks for them from our Lord He may well reply, as He did to the sons of Zebedee: 'Can you drink the chalice that I shall drink?'[182] I believe, sisters, we should all answer 'Yes'—and we should be perfectly right for His Majesty gives strength when He sees it needed: He ever defends such souls and answers for them when they are persecuted and slandered as He did for the Magdalen—if not in words, at least in deeds.[183] At last, ah, at last! before they die He repays them for all they have suffered, as you shall now learn. May He be for ever blessed and may all creatures praise Him! Amen.

---

[179] See the two versions of the poems written by the Saint on her recovery from the trance into which she was thrown, beginning 'Vivir sin vivir in me' and the poem, 'Cuan triste es, Dios mio' (Poems 2, 3, and 4, English version). See also St. Teresa's poem, 'Ya toda me entregué y dí.' (Poem 7, English version). Struck by the gentle Hunter And overthrown, Within the arms of Love My soul lay prone. Raised to new life at last, This contract 'tween us passed, That the Beloved should be mine own, I His alone.

[180] Rel. viii. 17.

[181] Acta SS. p. 64, n. 229.

[182] St. Matt. xx. 22: 'Potestis bibere calicem quem ego bibiturus sum?'

[183] St. Matt. xxvi. to: St. Mark xiv. 6; St. John xii. 7. Way of Perf. ch. xvi. 7; xvii. 4. Excl. v. 2-4.

THE SEVENTH MANSIONS

CHAPTER I.

TREATS OF THE SUBLIME FAVOURS GOD BESTOWS ON SOULS WHICH HAVE ENTERED THE SEVENTH MANSIONS. THE AUTHOR SHOWS THE DIFFERENCE SHE BELIEVES TO EXIST BETWEEN SOUL AND SPIRIT ALTHOUGH THEY ARE BOTH ONE. THIS CHAPTER CONTAINS SOME NOTEWORTHY THINGS.

1. Sublime mysteries of these mansions. 2. St. Teresa abashed at treating such subjects. 3. Our Lord introduces His bride into His presence chamber. 4. Darkness of a soul in mortal sin. 5. Intercession for sinners. 6. The soul an interior world. 7. The spiritual nuptials. 8. Former favours differ from spiritual nuptials. 9. The Blessed Trinity revealed to the soul. 10. Permanence of Its presence in the soul. 11. The effects. 12. This presence is not always equally realized. 13. It is beyond the soul's control. 14. The centre of the soul remains calm. 15. The soul and the spirit distinct though united. 16. The soul and its faculties not identical.

1. You may think, sisters, that so much has been said of this spiritual journey that nothing remains to be added. That would be a great mistake: God's immensity has no limits, neither have His works; therefore, who can recount His mercies and His greatness?[1] It is impossible, so do not be amazed at what I write about them which is but a cipher of what remains untold concerning God. He has shown great mercy in communicating these mysteries to one who could recount them to us, for as we learn more of His intercourse with creatures, we ought to praise Him more fervently and to esteem more highly the soul in which He so delights. Each of us possesses a soul but we do not realize its value as made in the image of God, therefore we fail to understand the important secrets it contains. May His Majesty be pleased to guide my pen and to teach me to say somewhat of the *much* there is to tell of His revelations to the souls He leads into this mansion. I have begged Him earnestly to help me, since He sees that my object is to reveal His mercies for the praise and glory of His name. I hope He will grant this favour, if not for my own sake, at least for yours, sisters—so that you may discover how vital it is for you to put no obstacle in the way of the Spiritual Marriage of the Bridegroom with your soul which brings, as you will learn, such signal blessings with it.

2. O great God! surely such a miserable creature as myself should tremble at the thought of speaking on such a subject so far beyond anything I deserve to understand. Indeed I felt abashed and doubted whether it would not be better to finish writing about this Mansion in a few words, lest people might imagine that I am recounting my personal experience. I was overwhelmed with shame for, knowing what I am, it is a terrible undertaking. On the other hand, this fear seemed but a temptation and weakness: even if I should be misjudged, so long as God is but a little better praised and known, let all the world revile me. Besides, I may be dead before this book is seen. May He Who lives and shall live to all eternity be praised! Amen.

3. When our Lord is pleased to take pity on the sufferings, both past and present, endured through her longing for Him by this soul which He has spiritually taken for His bride, He, before consummating the celestial marriage, brings her into this His mansion or presence chamber. This is the seventh Mansion, for as He has a dwelling-place in heaven, so has He in the soul, where none but He may abide and which may be termed a second heaven.

4. It is important, sisters, that we should not fancy the soul to be in darkness. As we are accustomed to believe there is no light but that which is exterior, we imagine that the soul is wrapt in obscurity. This is indeed the case with a soul out of the state of grace,[2] not, however, through any defer in the Sun of Justice which remains within it and gives it being, but the soul itself is incapable of receiving the light, as I think I said in speaking of the first Mansion.[3] A certain person was given to understand that such unfortunate souls are, as it were, imprisoned in a gloomy dungeon, chained hand and foot and unable to perform any meritorious action: they are also both blind and dumb.

---

[1] Ps. cxliv. 3: 'Magnitudinis ejus non est finis.'

[2] See the Saint's description of a soul in the state of sin, Rel, iii. 13. (towards the end).

[3] Supra, M. i, ch. ii. 1.

Well may we pity them when we reflect that we ourselves were once in the same state and that God may show them mercy also.

5. Let us, then, sisters, be most zealous in interceding for them and never neglect it. To pray for a soul in mortal sin is a far more profitable form of almsgiving than it would be to help a Christian whom we saw with hands strongly fettered behind his back, tied to a post and dying of hunger—not for want of food, because plenty of the choicest delicacies lay near him, but because he was unable to put them into his mouth, although he was extremely exhausted and on the point of dying, and that not a temporal death, but an eternal one. Would it not be extremely cruel of us to stand looking at him, and give him nothing to eat? What if by your prayers you could loose his bonds? Now you understand.

6. For the love of God I implore you constantly to remember in your prayers souls in a like case. We are not speaking now of them but of others who, by the mercy of God, have done penance for their sins and are in a state of grace. You must not think of the soul as insignificant and petty but as an interior world containing the number of beautiful mansions you have seen; as indeed it should, since in the centre of the soul there is a mansion reserved for God Himself.

7. When His Majesty deigns to bestow on the soul the grace of these divine nuptials, He brings it into His presence chamber and does not treat it as before, when He put it into a trance. I believe He then united it to Himself, as also during the prayer of union; but then only the superior part was affected and the soul did not feel called to enter its own centre as it does in this mansion. Here it matters little whether it is in the one way or the other.

8. In the former favours our Lord unites the spirit to Himself and makes it both blind and dumb like St. Paul after his conversion,[4] thus preventing its knowing whence or how it enjoys this grace, for the supreme delight of the spirit is to realize its nearness to God. During the actual moment of divine union the soul feels nothing, all its powers being entirely lost. But now He acts differently: our pitiful God removes the scales from its eyes[5] letting it see and understand somewhat of the grace received in a strange and wonderful manner in this mansion by means of intellectual vision.

9. By some mysterious manifestation of the truth, the three Persons of the most Blessed Trinity reveal themselves, preceded by an illumination which shines on the spirit like a most dazzling cloud of light.[6] The three Persons are distinct from one another; a sublime knowledge is infused into the soul, imbuing it with a certainty of the truth that the Three are of one substance, power, and knowledge and are one God. Thus that which we hold as a doctrine of faith, the soul now, so to speak, understands by sight, though it beholds the Blessed Trinity neither by the eyes of the body nor of the soul, this being no imaginary vision. All the Three Persons here communicate Themselves to the soul, speak to it and make it understand the words of our Lord in the Gospel that He and the Father and the Holy Ghost will come and make their abode with the soul which loves Him and keeps His commandments.[7]

---

[4] Acts ix. 8: 'Surrexit autem Saulus de terra, apertisque oculis nihil videbat.' There is, however, nothing to imply that he was dumb as well as blind.

[5] Acts ix. 18: 'Et confestim ceciderunt ab oculis ejus tamquam squamæ, et visum recepit.' Way of Perf.. ch. xxviii. 11.

[6] *Rel.* iii. 6; v. 6-8; viii. 20, 21; ix. 12, 17, 19. Deposition by Fr. Giles Gonzalez, S.J., Provincial of Old Castile, afterwards Assistant—General in Rome: 'While the holy Mother lived at the convent of the Incarnation of Avila [as prioress], I often spoke with her, and once I remember she asked me: "What am I to do, Father? Whenever I recollect myself I realize that already in this life the Three Persons of the Blessed Trinity may be seen, and that They accompany me and assist me in the management of my affairs."' (Fuente, *Obras*, vol. vi. p. 280.)

'Doña Maria Enriquez, Duchess of Alva, said that St. Teresa made known to her many revelations she had received from our Lord, and that she (the duchess) held in her possession three paintings of the Blessed Trinity made according to the description of the holy Mother, who, while they were being done, effaced with her own hand those portions which the painter failed to design conformably to the vision she had had.' (Fuente, *l.c.* p. 297.)

[7] St. John xiv. 23: 'Si quis diligit me, sermonem meum servabit, et Pater meus diliget eum, et ad eum veniemus, et mansionem apud eum faciemus.'

10. O my God, how different from merely hearing and believing these words is it to realize their truth in this way! Day by day a growing astonishment takes possession of this soul, for the three Persons of the Blessed Trinity seem never to depart; it sees with certainty, in the way I have described, that They dwell far within its own centre and depths; though for want of learning it cannot describe how, it is conscious of the indwelling of these divine Companions.

11. You may fancy that such a person is beside herself and that her mind is too inebriated to care for anything else. On the contrary, she is far more active than before in all that concerns God's service, and when at leisure she enjoys this blessed companionship. Unless she first deserts God, I believe He will never cease to make her clearly sensible of His presence: she feels confident, as indeed she may, that He will never so fail her as to allow her to lose this favour after once bestowing it; at the same time, she is more careful than before to avoid offending Him in any way.

12. This presence is not always so entirely realized, that is, so distinctly manifest, as at first, or as it is at times when God renews this favour, otherwise the recipient could not possibly attend to anything else nor live in society. Although not always seen by so clear a light, yet whenever she reflects on it she feels the companionship of the Blessed Trinity. This is as if, when we were with other people in a very well lighted room, some one were to darken it by closing the shutters; we should feel certain that the others were still there, though we were unable to see them.[8]

13. You may ask: 'Could she not bring back the light and see them again?'[9] This is not in her power; when our Lord chooses, He will open the shutters of the understanding: He shows her great mercy in never quitting her and in making her realize it so clearly. His divine Majesty seems to be preparing His bride for greater things by this divine companionship which clearly helps perfection in every way and makes her lose the fear she sometimes felt when other graces were granted her.

14. A certain person so favoured found she had improved in all virtues: whatever were her trials or labours, the center of her soul seemed never moved from its resting-place. Thus in a manner her soul appeared divided: a short time after God had done her this favour, while undergoing great sufferings, she complained of her soul as Martha did of Mary,[10] reproaching it with enjoying solitary peace while leaving her so full of troubles and occupations that she could not keep it company.

15. This may seem extravagant to you, daughters, yet though the soul is known to be undivided, it is fact and no fancy and often happens. Interior effects show for certain that there is a positive difference between the soul and the spirit, although they are one with each other.[11] There is an extremely subtle distinction between them, so that sometimes they seem to at in a different manner from one another, as does the knowledge given to them by God.

16. It also appears to me that the soul and its faculties are not identical. There are so many and such transcendental mysteries within us, that it would be presumption for me to attempt to explain them. If by God's mercy we enter heaven we shall understand these secrets.

---

[8] One of the Saint's favourite comparisons. See Life, ch. xxvii. 7. Castle, M. vi. ch. viii. 3. Rel. vii. 26.

[9] 'Though the soul be always in the high estate of marriage since God has placed it there, nevertheless, actual union in all its powers is not continuous, though the substantial union is. In this substantial union the powers of the soul are most frequently in union, and drink of His cellar, the understanding by knowledge, the will by love, etc. We are not therefore to suppose that the soul, when saying it went out, has ceased from its substantial or essential union with God, but only from the union of its faculties, which is not, and cannot be, permanent in this life.' (St. John of the Cross, Spiritual Canticle, stanza xxvi. 9. On the words: 'In the inner cellar of my Beloved have I drunk, and when I went forth').

[10] St. Luke x. 40. Excl. v. 2, 3. Way of Perf. ch. xv. 4; xxxi. 4. Rel. viii. 6. Concept. ch. vii. 4.

[11] Life, ch. xviii. 4. The distinction between soul and spirit, to be found in the Epistle to the Hebrews, iv. 12, according to Cornelius a Lapide (ad loc.) consists in this, that the term soul comprises the faculties, senses, and passions, whereas the term spirit denotes the substance of the soul independently of its powers. In the inferior degrees of the Mystical life God operates through the faculties, while in the Mystical marriage He acts directly on the substance of the soul. St. Teresa is not quite consistent in the use of these terms, which is not surprising, as she owns that she does not quite understand this subtle distinction.

CHAPTER II.

TREATS OF THE SAME SUBJECT: EXPLAINS, BY SOME DELICATELY DRAWN COMPARISONS, THE DIFFERENCE BETWEEN SPIRITUAL UNION AND SPIRITUAL MARRIAGE.

1. The spiritual nuptials introduced by an imaginary vision. 2. Spiritual betrothal and marriage differ. 3. Spiritual marriage lasting. 4. Not so spiritual betrothal. 5. Spiritual marriage permanent. 6. St. Paul and spiritual marriage. 7. The soul's joy in union. 8. Its conviction of God's indwelling. 9. Its peace. 10. Christ's prayer for the divine union of the soul. 11. Its fulfilment. 12. Unalterable peace of the soul in the seventh Mansion. 13. Unless it offends God. 14. Struggles outside the seventh Mansion. 15. Comparisons explaining this.

1. WE now come to speak of divine and spiritual nuptials, although this sublime favour cannot be received in all its perfection during our present life, for by forsaking God this great good would be lost. The first time God bestows this grace, He, by an imaginary vision of His most sacred Humanity, reveals Himself to the soul so that it may understand and realize the sovereign gift it is receiving. He may manifest Himself in a different way to other people; the person I mentioned, after having received Holy Communion beheld our Lord, full of splendour, beauty, and majesty, as He was after His resurrection.[12] He told her that henceforth she was to care for His affairs as though they were her own and He would care for hers: He spoke other words which she understood better than she can repeat them. This may seem nothing new, for our Lord had thus revealed Himself to her at other times;[13] yet this was so different that it left her bewildered and amazed, both on account of the vividness of what she saw and of the words heard at the time, also because it took place in the interior of the soul where, with the exception of the one last mentioned, no other vision had been seen.

2. You must understand that between the visions seen in this and in the former mansions there is a vast difference; there is the same distinction between spiritual espousals and spiritual marriage as between people who are only betrothed and others who are united for ever in holy matrimony. I have told you[14] that though I make this comparison because there is none more suitable, yet this betrothal is no more related to our corporal condition than if the soul were a disembodied spirit. This is even more true of the spiritual marriage, for this secret union takes place in the innermost centre of the soul where God Himself must dwell: I believe that no door is required to enter it. I say, 'no door is required,' for all I have hitherto described seems to come through the senses and faculties as must the representation of our Lord's Humanity, but what passes in the union of the spiritual nuptials is very different. Here God appears in the soul's centre, not by an imaginary but by an intellectual vision far more mystic than those seen before, just as He appeared to the Apostles without having entered through the door when He said: 'Pax vobis.'[15]

3. So mysterious is the secret and so sublime the favour that God thus bestows instantaneously on the soul, that it feels a supreme delight, only to be described by saying that our Lord vouchsafes for the moment to reveal to it His own heavenly glory in a far more subtle way than by any vision or spiritual delight. As far as can be understood, the soul, I mean the spirit of this soul, is made one with God[16] Who is Himself a spirit, and Who has been pleased to show certain persons how far His love for us extends in order that we may praise His greatness. He has thus deigned to unite Himself to His creature: He has bound Himself to her as firmly as two human beings are joined in wedlock and will never separate Himself from her.

4. Spiritual betrothal is different and like the grace of union is often dissolved; for though two things are made one by union, separation is still possible and each part then remains a thing by itself. This favour generally passes quickly, and afterwards the soul, as far as it is aware, remains without His company.

5. This is not so in the spiritual marriage with our Lord, where the soul always remains in its centre with its God. Union may be symbolized by two wax candles, the tips of which touch each other so closely that there is but one light; or again, the wick, the wax, and the light become one,

---

[12] Rel. iii. 20; ix. 8 and 25.
[13] Life, ch. xxxix. 29.
[14] Castle, M. v. ch. iv. 1.
[15] St. John xx. 19.
[16] Rel. xi. 1. sqq.

but the one candle can again be separated from the other and the two candles remain distinct; or the wick may be withdrawn from the wax. But spiritual marriage is like rain falling from heaven into a river or stream, becoming one and the same liquid, so that the river and rain water cannot be divided; or it resembles a streamlet flowing into the ocean, which cannot afterwards be disunited from it. This marriage may also be likened to a room into which a bright light enters through two windows—though divided when it enters, the light becomes one and the same.

6. Perhaps when St. Paul said, 'He who is joined to the Lord is one spirit,'[17] he meant this sovereign marriage, which presupposes His Majesty's having been joined to the soul by union. The same Apostle says: 'To me, to live is Christ and to die is gain.'[18] This, I think, might here be uttered by the soul, for now the little butterfly of which I spoke dies with supreme joy, for Christ is her life.

7. This becomes more manifest by its effects as time goes on, for the soul learns that it is God Who gives it 'life,' by certain secret intuitions too strong to be misunderstood, and keenly felt, although impossible to describe. These produce such over-mastering feelings that the person experiencing them cannot refrain from amorous exclamations, such as: 'O Life of my life, and Power which doth uphold me!' with other aspirations of the same kind.[19] For from the bosom of the Divinity, where God seems ever to hold this soul fast clasped, issue streams of milk, which solace the servants of the castle. I think He wishes them to share, in some way, the riches the soul enjoys; therefore from the flowing river in which the little streamlet is swallowed up, some drops of water flow every now and then to sustain the bodily powers, the servants of the bride and Bridegroom.

8. A person who was unexpectedly plunged into water could not fail to be aware of it; here the case is the same, but even more evident. A quantity of water could not fall on us unless it came from some source—so the soul feels certain there must be some one within it who lances forth these darts and vivifies its own life, and that there is a Sun whence this brilliant light streams forth from the interior of the spirit to its faculties.

9. The soul itself, as I said, never moves from this centre, nor loses the peace He can give Who gave it to the Apostles when they were assembled together.[20] I think this salutation of our Lord contains far deeper meaning than the words convey, as also His bidding the glorious Magdalen to 'go in peace.'[21] Our Lord's words *act* within us,[22] and in these cases they must have wrought their effect in the souls already disposed to banish from within themselves all that is corporal and to retain only what is spiritual, in order to be joined in this celestial union with the uncreated Spirit. Without doubt, if we empty ourselves of all that belongs to the creature, depriving ourselves of it for the love of God, that same Lord will fill us with Himself.

10. Our Lord Jesus Christ, praying for His Apostles, (I cannot remember the reference), asked that they might be made one with the Father and with Himself; as Jesus Christ our Lord is in the Father and the Father in Him![23] I do not know how love could be greater than this! Let none draw back from entering here, for His Majesty also said: 'Not only for them do I pray, but for them also who through their word shall believe in Me';[24] and He declared: 'I am in them.'[25]

11. God help me! how true these words are, and how clearly are they understood by the soul which in this state of prayer finds them fulfilled in itself! So should we all but for our own fault, for

---

[17] 1 Cor. vi. 17: 'Qui adhæret Domino unus spiritus est.'

[18] Philip. i. 21: 'Mihi vivere Christus est, et mori lucrum.'

[19] Such exclamations, in considerable number, form the Book of Exclamations published by Fray Luis de Leon. De Fuente thinks it was written in 1569, but as St. Teresa's spiritual betrothal took place on November 18, 1572, it seems, at least in parts, of a later date. The spiritual nuptials must be placed between the aforementioned year and May 1575, but it is not possible to ascertain the exact date. (For the Exclamations, see Minor Works).

[20] St. John xx. 19.

[21] St. Luke vii. 50.

[22] Supra, M. vi. ch. iii. 6. Life, ch. xxv. 5.

[23] St. John xvii. 2 I: 'Ut omnes unum sint, sicut tu Pater in me, et ego in te, ut et ipsi in nobis unum sint.'

[24] St. John xvii. 20: 'Non pro eis autem rogo tantum, sed et pro eis, qui credituri sunt per verbum eorum in me.'

[25] St. John xvii. 2 3: 'Ego in eis.'

the words of Jesus Christ, our King and our Lord, cannot fail. It is we who fail by not disposing ourselves fitly, nor removing all that can obstruct this light, so that we do not behold ourselves in this mirror wherein our image is engraved.[26]

12. To return to what I was saying. God places the soul in His own mansion which is in the very centre of the soul itself. They say the empyreal heavens, in which our Lord dwells, do not revolve with the rest: so the accustomed movements of the faculties and imagination do not appear to take place in any way that can injure the soul or disturb its peace.

13. Do I seem to imply that after God has brought the soul thus far it is certain to be saved and cannot fall into sin again?[27] I do not mean this: whenever I say that the soul seems in security, I must be understood to imply for as long as His Majesty thus holds it in His care and it does not offend Him. At any rate I know for certain that though such a person realizes the high state she is in and has remained in it for several years, she does not consider herself safe, but is more careful than ever to avoid committing the least offence against God. As I shall explain later on, she is most anxious to serve Him and feels a constant pain and confusion at seeing how little she can do for Him compared with all she ought.' This is no light cross but a severe mortification, for the harder the penances she can perform, the better is she pleased. Her greatest penance is to be deprived by God of health and strength to perform any. I told you elsewhere what keen pain this caused her, but now it grieves her far more. This must be because she is like a tree grafted on a stock growing near a stream which makes it greener and more fruitful.[28] Why marvel at the longings of this soul whose spirit has truly become one with the celestial water I described?

14. To return to what I wrote about. It is not intended that the powers, senses and passions should continually enjoy this peace. The soul does so, indeed, but in the other mansions there are still times of struggle, suffering, and fatigue, though as a general rule, peace is not lost by them. This 'centre of the soul' or 'spirit' is so hard to describe or even to believe in, that I think, sisters, my inability to explain my meaning saves your being tempted to disbelieve me; it is difficult to understand how there can be crosses and sufferings and yet peace in the soul.

15. Let me give you one or two comparisons—God grant they may be of use; if not, I know that what I say is true. A king resides in his palace; many wars and disasters take place in his kingdom but he remains on his throne. In the same way, though tumults and wild beasts rage with great uproar in the other mansions, yet nothing of this enters the seventh mansions, nor drives the soul from it. Although the mind regrets these troubles, they do not disturb it nor rob it of its peace, for the passions are too subdued to dare to enter here where they would only suffer still further defeat. Though the whole body is in pain, yet the head, if it be sound, does not suffer with it. I smile at these comparisons—they do not please me—but I can find no others. Think what you will about it—I have told you the truth.

---

[26] This idea is expressed in St. Teresa's poem: Alma, buscarte has en Mi' (Poem 10, *Minor Works*). Such is the power of love, O soul, To paint thee in my heart No craftsman with such art Whate'er his skill might be, could there Thine image thus impart! 'Twas love that gave thee life— Then, fair one, if thou be Lost to thyself, thou'lt see Thy portrait in my bosom stamped— Soul, seek thyself in Me.

[27] In a letter dated May 1581, addressed to Don Alonso Velasquez, then bishop of Osma, St. Teresa writes as follows:

'She [herself] has received such an assurance of coming one day to the fruition of God that she almost imagines she has already come into possession of Him, without, however, the joy that will accompany it. She is in the same position as one who by legal contract has received a splendid property which will become his, and whose fruit he will enjoy at a given date. Until then he only holds the title-deeds, without being able to take possession of the property. Nevertheless my soul would not like to come immediately into the possession of God, for it does not believe that it has deserved such a grace. It only desires to continue in His service, even at the cost of terrible sufferings. It would not mind thus serving Him to the end of the world, after having received such a pledge.' St. John of the Cross, in treating of this subject (*Spir. Cant.* stanza xxii. 3) says: 'I believe that no soul ever attains to this state without being confirmed in grace in it.' See also Ribera, in the *Acta Ss.* p. 554, *circa finem*.

[28] Ps. i. 3: 'Et erit tamquam lignum quod plantatum est secus decursus aquarum, quod fructum suum dabit in tempore suo.'

CHAPTER III.

THE GREAT FRUITS PRODUCED BY THE ABOVE-MENTIONED PRAYER. THE WONDERFUL DIFFERENCE BETWEEN THESE EFFECTS AND THOSE FORMERLY DESCRIBED SHOULD BE CAREFULLY STUDIED AND REMEMBERED.

1. Effects of the graces last received. 2. The soul only cares for God's honour. 3. But still performs its duties. 4. Other fruits of these favours. 5. The soul's fervent desire to serve God. 6. Christ dwells within this soul. 7. And recalls it to fervour if negligent. 8. God's constant care of such souls. 9. Their peace and silence. 10. Few ecstasies in the Seventh Mansions. 11. Probable reasons for this. 12. Allusions in Holy Scripture to this state. 13. Watchfulness of such souls. 14. Crosses suffered in this state.

1. THE little butterfly has died with the greatest joy at having found rest at last, and now Christ lives in her.[29] Let us see the difference between her present and her former life, for the effects will prove whether what I told you was true. As far as can be ascertained they are these: first, a self-forgetfulness so complete that she really appears not to exist, as I said,[30] for such a transformation has been worked in her that she no longer recognizes herself; nor does she remember that heaven, or life, or glory are to be hers, but seems entirely occupied in seeking God's interests. Apparently the words spoken by His Majesty have done their work: 'that she was to care for His affairs, and He would care for hers.'[31]

2. Thus she wrecks nothing, whatever happens, but lives in such strange oblivion that, as I stated, she seems no longer to exist, nor does she wish to be of any account in anything—*anything*! unless she sees that she can advance, however little, the honour and glory of God, for which she would most willingly die.

3. Do not fancy I mean, daughters, that she neglects to eat and drink, though it brings no small torment to her, or to perform the duties of her state. I am speaking of her interior; as regards her exterior actions there is little to say, for her chief suffering is to see that she has hardly strength to do anything. For nothing in the world would she omit doing all she can which she knows would honour our Lord.

4. The second fruit is a strong desire for suffering, though it does not disturb her peace as before because the fervent wish of such souls for the fulfilment of God's will in them makes them acquiesce in all He does. If He would have her suffer, she is content; if not, she does not torment herself to death about it as she used to do. She feels a great interior joy when persecuted, and is far more peaceful than in the former state under such circumstances: she bears no grudge against her enemies, nor wishes them any ill. Indeed she has a special love for them, is deeply grieved at seeing them in trouble, and does all she can to relieve them,[32] earnestly interceding with God on their behalf. She would be glad to forfeit the favours His Majesty shows her, if they might be given to her enemies instead, to prevent their offending our Lord.

5. The most surprising thing to me is that the sorrow and distress which such souls felt because they could not die and enjoy our Lord's presence[33] are now exchanged for as fervent a desire of serving Him, of causing Him to be praised, and of helping others to the utmost of their power. Not only have they ceased to long for death, but they wish for a long life and most heavy crosses, if such would bring ever so little honour to our Lord. Thus, if they knew for certain that immediately on quitting their bodies their souls would enjoy God, it would make no difference to them, nor do they think of the glory enjoyed by the saints, and long to share it. Such souls hold that their glory consists in helping, in any way, Him Who was crucified, especially as they see how men offend against Him, and how few, detached from all else, care for His honour alone. True, people in this state forget this at times, and are seized with tender longings to enjoy God and to leave this land of exile, especially as they see how little they serve Him. Then, returning to themselves and reflecting how

---

[29] Gal. ii. 20.

[30] Castle, M. vii. ch. i. 11 and 15.

[31] Castle, M. vii. ch. ii. 1. Compare the references there given.

[32] Don Alvaro de Mendoza, Bishop of Avila, used to say that the best means of obtaining St. Teresa's friendship was to injure or insult her, Acta Ss. n, 1233. Rel. vii. 20.

[33] Rel. viii. 15.

they possess Him continually in their souls, they are satisfied, offering to His Majesty their willingness to live as the most costly oblation they can make.[34]

They fear death no more than they would a delicious trance.

6. The fact is, that He Who gave them these torturing desires of death has exchanged them for the others. May He be for ever blessed and praised! Amen. In fact, such persons no longer wish for consolations nor delights, since they bear God Himself within them, and it is He Who lives in them. It is evident that His life was one continual torment: so would He have ours to be, at least in desire, for as to the rest He leads us mercifully as our weakness requires, though when He sees the need He imparts to us His strength.

7. Such a soul, thoroughly detached from all things, wishes to be either always alone or occupied on what benefits the souls of others: she feels neither aridity nor any interior troubles, but a constant tender recollection of our Lord Whom she wishes to praise unceasingly. When she grows negligent, the same Lord arouses her in the way that I told you, and it is easy to see that this impulse (I know not what term to use for it) comes from the interior of the soul, like the former impetuous desires.[35] It is now felt very sweetly, but is neither produced by the intellect nor the memory, nor is there reason to believe the soul itself has any share in it. This is so usual and so frequent that whoever has been in this state must have noticed it. However large a fire may be, the flame never burns downwards, but upwards, and so this movement is seen to come from the centre of the soul whose powers it excites. Indeed, were nothing else gained by this way of prayer but the knowledge of the special care God takes to communicate Himself to us and how He entreats us to abide with Him (for indeed I can describe it in no other way) I think that for the sake of these sweet and penetrating touches of His love all our past pains would be well spent.

8. You will have learnt this by experience, sisters, for I think that when our Lord has brought us to the prayer of union, He watches over us in this way unless we neglect to keep His commandments. When these impulses are given you, remember that they come from the innermost mansion, where God dwells in our souls. Praise Him fervently, for it is He Who sends you this message, or love letter, so tenderly written, and in a cipher that only you can understand and know what He asks. By no means neglect to answer His Majesty, even though you may be occupied exteriorly and engaged in conversation. Our Lord may often be pleased to show you this secret favour in public; but it is very easy, as the reply should be entirely interior, to respond by an act of love or to ask with Saint Paul: 'Lord, what wilt Thou have me to do?'[36] Jesus will show you in many ways how to please Him. It is a propitious moment, for He seems to be listening to us and the soul is nearly always disposed by this delicate touch to respond with a generous determination.[37] As I told you, this mansion differs from the rest in that, as I said,[38] the dryness and disturbance felt in all the rest at times hardly ever enter here, where the soul is nearly always calm. It does not fear that this sublime favour can be counterfeited by the devil, but feels a settled conviction that it is of divine origin because, as above stated, nothing is here perceived by the senses or faculties but His Majesty reveals Himself to the spirit, which He takes to be with Himself in a place where I doubt not the devil dares not enter, nor would our Lord ever permit him.

---

[34] Compare with the Saint's poem on self-oblation: 'Vuestro soy, para Vos nací' (Poem i. Minor Works). Long life bestow, or straightway let me die; Let health be mine, or pain and sickness send; Honour or foul dishonour—be my path Beset by war or peaceful till the end. My strength or weakness be as Thou dost choose, Since naught Thou askest shall I e'er refuse. Say, Lord, what is it Thou dost will for me?

[35] Castle, M. vi. ch. vi. 6.

[36] Acts ix. 6: 'Domine, quid me vis facere?"

[37] The words from 'know what He asks' to 'as I told you' are not in the original manuscript, but must have been written on a separate slip, as is proved by a marginal note in the handwriting of the Saint: 'Quando dice aqui: os pide, léase luego este papel.' This paper is now lost, but the passage it contained is preserved in the early manuscript copies of Toledo, Cordova and Salamanca, as well as in the first printed edition, and, through this, in the old translations; hence both Woodhead and Dalton have it in its proper place. It is, of course, not to be found in the autograph published in 1882, nor in Fuente's Spanish editions nor in translations based upon these, The Spanish text will be found in Œuvres vi, note.

[38] Supra §§ i and 2.

9. All the graces here divinely bestowed on the soul come, as I said, through no action of its own except its total abandonment of itself to God. They are given in peace and silence, like the building of Solomon's Temple where no sound was heard.[39] It is thus with this temple of God, this mansion of His where He and the soul rejoice in each other alone in profound silence. The mind need not act nor search for anything, as the Lord Who created it wishes it to be at rest and only to watch through a little chink, what passes within. Though at times it cannot see this, yet such intervals are very short, I believe because the powers are not here lost but only cease to work, being, as it were, dazed with astonishment.

10. I, too, am astonished at seeing that when the soul arrives at this state it does not go into ecstasies except perhaps on rare occasions—even then they are not like the former trances and the flight of the spirit and seldom take place in public as they did before.[40] They are no longer produced by any special calls to devotion, such as by the sight of a religious picture, by hearing a sermon (were it only the first few words), or by sacred music; formerly, like the poor little butterfly, the soul was so anxious that anything used to alarm it and make it take flight. This may be either because the spirit has at last found repose, or that it has seen such wonders in this mansion that nothing can frighten it, or perhaps because it no longer feels solitary since it rejoices in such Company.

11. In short, sisters, I cannot tell the reason, but as soon as God shows the soul what this mansion contains, bringing it to dwell within the precincts, the infirmity formerly so troublesome to the mind and impossible to get over, disappears at once. Probably this is because our Lord has now strengthened, dilated, and developed the soul, or it may be that He wished to make public (for some end known only to Himself) what He was doing in secret within such souls, for His judgments are beyond our comprehension in this life.

12. These effects, with all the other good fruits I have mentioned of the different degrees of prayer, are given by God to the soul when it draws near Him to receive that 'kiss of His mouth' for which the bride asked,[41] and I believe her petition is now granted. Here the overflowing waters are given to the wounded hart: here she delights in the tabernacles of God[42] : here the dove sent out by Noe to see whether the flood had subsided, has plucked the olive branch, showing that she has found firm land amongst the floods and tempests of this world.[43] O Jesus! Who knows how much in Holy Scripture refers to this peace of soul? Since, O my God, Thou dost see of what grave import is this peace to us, do Thou incite Christians to strive to gain it! In Thy mercy do not deprive those of it on whom Thou hast bestowed it, for until Thou hast given them true peace and brought them to where it is unending, they must ever live in fear.

13. I do not mean that peace is unreal on earth because I say 'true peace,' but that such souls might have to begin all their struggles over again if they forsook God. What must these people feel at the thought that it is possible to lose so great a good? Their dread makes them more careful; they try to gather strength from their weakness lest, through their own fault, they should miss any opportunity of pleasing God better. The greater the favours they have received from His Majesty, the more diffident and mistrustful are they of themselves; the marvels they have witnessed having revealed more clearly to them their own miseries and the heinousness of their sins, so that often, like the publican, they dare not so much as lift up their eyes.[44]

14. Sometimes they long to die and be in safety, but then their love at once makes them wish to live in order to serve God, as I told you; therefore they commit all that concerns them to His mercy.[45] At times they are more crushed than ever by the thought of the many graces they have received lest, like an overladen ship, they sink beneath the burden. I assure you, sisters, such souls have their cross to bear, yet it does not trouble them nor rob them of their peace, but is quickly gone like a wave or a storm which is followed by a calm, for God's presence within them soon makes them forget all else. May He be for ever blessed and praised by all His creatures! Amen,

---

[39] III Reg. vi. 7.

[40] 'That is, so as to lose the senses' (marginal note in the Saints' handwriting). Rel. iii. 5.

[41] Cant. i. I.

[42] Ps. xli, 2, 5.

[43] Gen. viii. 10, 11.

[44] St. Luke. xviii. 13.

[45] Rel. ix. 19.

CHAPTER IV.

THE CONCLUSION SETS FORTH WHAT APPEARS TO BE OUR LORD'S PRINCIPAL INTENTION IN CONFERRING THESE SUBLIME FAVOURS ON SOULS, AND EXPLAINS HOW NECESSARY IT IS FOR MARY AND MARTHA TO GO TOGETHER. THIS CHAPTER IS VERY PROFITABLE.

1. Vicissitudes of the Seventh Mansion. 2. Humility produced by them. 3. Such souls free from mortal and from willful venial sins. 4. The fate of Solomon. 5. Holy fear. 6. These favours strengthen souls to suffer. 7. Crosses borne by the saints. 8. Effect of vision of our Lord on St. Peter. 9. Fruits of these favours. 10. Why the spiritual marriage takes place. 11. Love for Christ proved by our deeds. 12. True spirituality. 13. Humility and the virtues must combine with prayer. 14. Zeal of advanced souls. 15. Strengthened by the divine Presence within them. 16. Examples of the saints. 17. Both Martha and Mary must serve our Lord. 18. Christ's food. 19. Mary's mortification. 20. Her grief at the Passion. 21. Can we lead souls to God? 22. How to do so. 23. Love gives value to our deeds. 24. Conclusion.

1. You must not suppose, sisters, that the effects I mentioned always exist in the same degree in these souls, for as far as I remember, I told you that in most cases our Lord occasionally leaves such persons to the weakness of their nature. The venomous creatures from the moat round the castle and the other mansions at once unite to revenge themselves for the time when they were deprived of their power.

2. True, this lasts but a short time—a day perhaps or a little longer—but during this disturbance, which generally arises from some passing event, these persons learn what benefits they derive from the holy Company they are in. Our Lord gives them such great fortitude that they never desert His service nor the good resolutions they have made, which only seem to gather strength by trial, nor do their hearts ever turn from them, even by a slight movement of the will. This trouble rarely happens; our Lord wishes the soul to keep in mind its natural condition so that it may be humble and may better understand how much it owes Him, and how great a grace it has received, and so may praise Him.

3. Do not fancy that in spite of the strong desire and determination of these souls that they do not commit imperfections and even fall into many sins: that is, not *willfully*; for such people are given special grace from God on this point: I mean venial sins. As far as they are aware, they are free from mortal sins, although they do not feel certain they may not be guilty of some of which they are ignorant.

4. This grieves their hearts sorely, as does the sight of the souls perishing around them; although on the one hand they have strong hopes of not being themselves among the number of the lost, yet remembering what we are told in Holy Scripture of the fate of men who, like Solomon, seemed the special favourites of God[46] and conversed so familiarly with His Majesty, they cannot help fearing for themselves.

5. Let that one among you who feels most confidence on this point fear the most, for: 'Blessed is the man who feareth the Lord,' as David said.[47] May His Majesty ever protect us. Let us beg Him never to permit us to offend Him: therein lies our greatest safety. May He be for ever praised. Amen.

6. It would be well to tell you, sisters, the reason why God bestows such favours on souls in this world, although you must have learned this by the effects produced if you have considered the matter. I return to the matter in order that none of you may think it is only for the sake of the pleasure such persons feel, which would be a great mistake on your part, for His Majesty can bestow no greater favour on us than to give us a life such as was led by His beloved Son. Therefore, as I have often told you, I feel certain that these graces are sent to strengthen our weakness so that we may imitate Him by suffering much.

7. We always find that those nearest to Christ our Lord bear the heaviest cross: think of what His glorious Mother and the Apostles bore. How do you think St. Paul went through such immense labours?[48] We learn from his conduct the fruits of genuine visions and contemplation which come

---

[46] III. Reg. xi.

[47] Ps. cxi. 1. 'Beatus vir qui timet Dominum.'

[48] Though thou shouldst have been rapt up to the third heaven with Saint Paul, thou art not thereby secured that thou shalt suffer no adversity. 'I,' said Jesus, 'will shew him how great things he must suffer for My name's sake' (Acts. ix. 16). To suffer, therefore, is what waits for thee, if thou wilt love Jesus and

from our Lord and not from our own imagination, or the devil's fraud. Do you suppose that St. Paul hid himself to enjoy these spiritual consolations at leisure and did nothing else? You know that he never took a day's rest so far as we can learn, nor could he have slept much since he worked all night to get his living.[49]

8. I am delighted with St. Peter, who when fleeing from prison was met by our Lord, Who told him He was going to Rome to be crucified again. I never recite the Office in which this is commemorated without feeling a special joy.[50] What effect did this vision have on St. Peter, and what did he do? He went at once to meet his death—and our Lord did him no small favour in finding him an executioner!

9. Oh, my sisters, how forgetful of her ease, how unmindful of honours, and how far from seeking men's esteem should she be whose soul God thus chooses for His special dwelling-place! For if her mind is fixed on Him, as it ought to be, she must needs forget herself: all her thoughts are bent on how to please Him better and when and how she can show the love she bears Him.

10. *This* is the end and aim of prayer, my daughters; *this* is the reason of the spiritual marriage whose children are always good works. *Works* are the unmistakable sign which shows these favours come from God, as I told you. It will do me little good to be deeply recollected when alone, making acts of the virtues, planning and promising to do wonders in God's service, if afterwards, when occasion offers, I do just the opposite. I did wrong in saying, 'It will do me *little* good,' for all the time we spend with God does us *great* good. Though afterwards we may weakly fail to perform our good intentions, yet some time or other His Majesty will find a way for us to practice them although perhaps much to our regret. Thus when He sees a soul very cowardly, He often sends it some great affliction, much against its will, and brings it through this trial with profit to itself, When the soul has learnt this, it is less timid in offering itself to Him.

11. I ought to have said, 'will do us *little* good' in comparison with the far *greater* good we can gain when our works fulfil our aspirations and our promises. She that cannot do all this at once should do it little by little, gradually dominating her will, if she wishes to gain fruit from prayer. Even in this little nook she will find many a chance to praise this. Remember, this is of far more importance than I know how to express. Fix your eyes on the Crucified One, and all will seem easy. If His Majesty proved His love for us by such stupendous labours and sufferings, how can you seek to please Him by words alone?

12. Do you know what it is to be truly spiritual? It is for men to make themselves the *slaves* of God—branded with His mark, which is the cross. Since they have given Him their freedom, He can sell them as slaves to the whole world, as He was, which would be doing them no wrong but the greatest favour. Unless you make up your minds to this, never expect to make much progress,[51] for as I said humility is the foundation of the whole building and unless you are truly humble, our Lord, for your own sake, will never permit you to rear it very high lest it should fall to the ground.

13. Therefore, sisters, take care to lay a firm foundation by seeking to be the least of all and the slave of others, watching how you can please and help them, for it will benefit you more than them. Built on such strong rocks, your castle can never go to ruin. I insist again: your foundation must not consist of prayer and contemplation alone: unless you acquire the virtues and praise them, you will always be dwarfs; and please God no worse may befall you than making no progress, for you know that to *stop* is to go *back*—if you love, you will never be content to come to a standstill.

---

constantly serve Him For our merit and the advancement of our state consist not in having many sweetnesses and consolations, but rather in bearing great afflictions and tribulations' (Imitation, bk. ii. ch. xii. 12).

[49] i Thess. ii. 9.

[50] The Antiphon of the Magnificat at first Vespers of the Feast of Saints Peter and Paul, June 29, in the Carmelite Breviary used by St. Teresa is: 'Beatus Petrus Apostolus vidit sibi Christum occurrere. Adorans eum ait: "Domine, quo vadis?"—"Venio Romam iterum crucifigi." 'The Blessed Apostle Peter saw Christ come to meet him. Adoring Him, he asked "Lord, where art Thou going?"— "I go to Rome to be crucified anew." The saint at once returned to Rome and was taken by the soldiers and crucified. See Letter of Jan. 17. 1577, note 4. Vol. II.

[51] "If thou wilt stand upon self and wilt not offer thyself freely to My will, thine offering is not perfect, nor will there be entire union between us." (Imitation, bk. iv. ch. viii. 2.)

14. Perhaps you think I am speaking of beginners and that one may rest later on, but, as I told you, the rest such souls feel is within them: they have less outwardly nor do they wish for it. Why, do you think, does the soul send from its centre these inspirations, or rather aspirations, (the messages of which I spoke), to the dwellers in the precincts of the castle and to the surrounding mansions? To send them to sleep? No, no, no! The soul wages a fiercer war from thence to keep the powers, senses and the whole body from being idle, than ever it did when it suffered in their company. Formerly it did not understand the immense benefit its afflictions brought, though indeed they may have been the means God used to advance it to this state.

15. Besides, the company it enjoys gives it far greater strength than ever before. If, as David says: 'With the holy thou shalt be holy,'[52] doubtless by its becoming one with the Almighty, by this sovereign union of spirit with spirit, the soul must gather strength, as we know the saints did, to suffer and to die. Beyond doubt, with the force thus gained, the soul succors all within the castle and even the very body itself, which often seems to have no feeling left in it. The vigour the soul derives from 'the wine' drunk in the 'cellar'[53] (into which the Bridegroom brought her and would not let her go) overflows into the feeble body, just as the food we eat nourishes both the head and the whole frame.

16. Indeed the body suffers much while alive, for whatever work it does, the soul has energy for far greater tasks and goads it on to more, for all it can perform appears as nothing. This must be the reason of the severe penances performed by many of the saints, especially the glorious Magdalen, who had always spent her life in luxury.[54] This caused the zeal felt by our Father Elias for the honour of God,[55] and the desires of St. Dominic,[56] and St. Francis[57] to draw souls to praise the Almighty. I assure you that, forgetful of themselves, they must have passed through no small trials.

17. This, my sisters, is what I would have us strive for—to offer our petitions and to practice prayer, not for our own enjoyment but to gain strength to serve God. Let us seek no fresh path; we should lose ourselves in ways of ease. It would be a strange thing to fancy we should gain these graces by any other road than that by which Jesus and all His saints have gone before. Let us not dream of such a thing: believe me, both Martha and Mary must entertain our Lord and keep Him as their Guest, nor must they be so inhospitable as to offer Him no food. How can Mary do this while she sits at His feet, if her sister does not help her?[58]

18. His food is that in every possible way we should draw souls to Him so that they may be saved and may praise Him for ever. You may offer two objections—first, that I said that Mary had

[52] Ps. xvii. 26: 'Cum sancto sanctus eris.'

[53] Cant. ii. 4.

[54] 'St. Mary Magdalen gave herself up to penance and contemplation in a deep excavation of the rocks at La Baume, near Marseilles. In this wild spot there was neither bread, water, nor even herbage. Thus she lived for more than thirty-two years without any kind of nourishment but that which was celestial, performing meanwhile most severe penances.' (St. Vincent Ferrer.)

[55] III Reg. xix. 10.

[56] 'There was one sentiment within him to which may almost be given the name of passion: it was his ceaseless burning thirst for the salvation of souls. As his Divine Master had come into the world to save sinners and loved them even unto death, so he, too, gave up all that was most dear to him in his life to win souls to Christ. He was always giving himself: it was the very key-note of his existence. He would have sold himself as a slave, he would have been cut to pieces by the heretics, he would spare himself neither by day nor by night, if by any means he might save some.' (From the History of St. Dominic, by Augusta Theodosia Drane. London, 1891, p. 256).

[57] 'St. Francis of Assisi, at the very beginning of his Order, when he had only seven followers, said to them: "Consider, my brethren, what is our vocation. It is not only for our own salvation that the mercy of God has called us, but for the salvation of many other souls. It is that we may go forth and exhort all men rather by our example than by our words, to do penance and keep the divine commands."' (The Life of St. Francis of Assisi, by a religious of the Order of Poor Clares, London, 1861, p. 32).

[58] St. Luke x. 39, 40. Life, ch. xvii. 6. Rel. viii. 6. Way of Perf. ch. xxxi. 4. Concep. ch. vii. 4.

chosen the better part,[59] for she had already done Martha's work by waiting on our Lord, by washing His feet and by wiping them with her hair.

19. Do you think it was a small mortification for a woman of rank, as she was, to go through the street, perhaps by herself, for in her zeal she never thought of how she went? Then she entered a house where she was a stranger and had to bear the railing of the Pharisee and many other trials.[60] It was strange to see such a woman as she had been thus publicly change her life. With a wicked nation like the Jews, the sight of her love for our Lord Whom they hated so bitterly was enough to make them cast in her face her former life and taunt her with wanting to become a saint. Doubtless she must have changed her rich robes and all the rest. Considering how men talk now of people far less known than she was, what must have been said of her?

20. I assure you, sisters, she won the better part after many crosses and mortifications. Must not the mere sight of men's hatred of her Master have been an intolerable trial? Then, think of what she endured afterwards at our Lord's death! I believe, myself, that she did not suffer martyrdom because she was already a martyr by grief at witnessing the crucifixion.[61] Then what terrible pain His absence must have caused her[62] during the long years afterwards! You see, she was not always enjoying contemplation at the feet of our Savior!

21. Secondly, you may say that you have neither the power nor the means to lead souls to God; though you would willingly do so, you do not know how, as you can neither teach nor preach as did the Apostles. I have often written an answer to this objection though I cannot tell whether I have done so in connection with the Castle. However, as the difficulty probably often crosses your minds on account of the desires our Lord gives you of serving Him, I will now speak of it again.[63] I told you elsewhere how the devil frequently fills our thoughts with great schemes, so that instead of putting our hands to what work we can do to serve our Lord, we may rest satisfied with wishing to perform impossibilities.

22. You can do much by prayer; and then, do not try to help the whole world, but principally your companions; this work will be all the better because you are the more bound to it. Do you think it is a trifling matter that your humility and mortification, your readiness to serve your sisters, your fervent charity towards them, and your love of God, should be as a fire to enkindle their zeal, and that you should constantly incite them to practice the other virtues? This would be a great work and one most pleasing to our Lord: by thus doing all that is in your power, you would prove to His Majesty your willingness to do still more and He would reward you as if you had won Him many souls. Do you answer: 'This would not be converting my sisters, for they are very good already?' What business is that of yours? If they were still better, the praise they render God would please Him more and their prayers would be more helpful to their neighbours.[64]

23. In short, my sisters, I will conclude with this advice; do not build towers without a foundation, for our Lord does not care so much for the importance of our works as for the love with which they are done. When we do all we can, His Majesty will enable us to do more every day. If we do not grow weary, but during the brief time this life lasts (and perhaps it will be shorter than any of you think) we give our Lord every sacrifice we can, both interior and exterior, His Majesty will unite them with that He offered to His Father for us on the Cross so that they may be worth the value given them by our love, however mean the works themselves may be.

24. May it please His Majesty, my sisters and my daughters, that we may all meet together where we may praise Him for ever, and may He give me grace to practice something of what I have taught you, by the merits of His Son, Who liveth and reigneth for ever! Amen. I assure you that I am filled with confusion at myself and I beg you, for the sake of the same Lord, not to forget this poor sinner in your prayers.

---

[59] Ibid. x. 42: 'Maria optimam partem elegit.'

[60] Ibid. vii. 37.

[61] Marginal note in the Saint's handwriting.

[62] Life, ch. xxi. 9.

[63] Way of Perf. ch, i. 1. Found, ch. i, 6, 7. Supra, M. vi ch. vi, 2.

[64] Way of Perf. ch. vii. 7.

EPILOGUE

ALTHOUGH, as I told you, I felt reluctant to begin this work, yet now it is finished I am very glad to have written it, and I think my trouble has been well spent, though I confess it has cost me but little. Considering your strict enclosure, the little recreation you have, my sisters, and how many conveniences are wanting in some of your convents, I think it may console you to enjoy yourselves in this interior castle which you can enter, and walk about at will, at any hour you please, without asking leave of your superiors. It is true you cannot enter all the mansions by your own power, however great it may appear to you, unless the Lord of the castle Himself admits you. Therefore I advise you to use no violence if you meet with any obstacle, for that would displease Him so much that He would never give you admission to them. He dearly loves humility:65 if you think yourselves unworthy to enter the third mansion, He will grant you all the sooner the favour of entering the fifth. Then, if you serve Him well there and often repair to it, He will draw you into the mansion where He dwells Himself, whence you need never depart unless called away by the Prioress, whose commands this sovereign Master wishes you to obey as if they were His own. If by her orders, you are often absent from His presence chamber, whenever you return He will hold the door open for you. When once you have learnt how to enjoy this castle, you will always find rest, however painful your trials may be, in the hope of returning to your Lord, which no one can prevent. Although I have only mentioned seven mansions, yet each one contains many more rooms, above, below, and around it, with fair gardens, fountains, and labyrinths, besides other things so delightful that you will wish to consume yourself in praising in return the great God Who has created the soul to His own image and likeness. If you find anything in the plan of this treatise which helps you to know Him better, be certain that it is sent by His Majesty to encourage you, and that whatever you find amiss in it is my own. In return for my strong desire to aid you in serving Him, my God and my Lord, I implore you, whenever you read this, to praise His Majesty fervently in my name and to beg Him to prosper His Church, to give light to the Lutherans, to pardon my sins and to free me from purgatory, where perhaps I shall be, by the mercy of God, when you see this book (if it is given to you after having been examined by theologians). If these writings contain any error, it is through my ignorance; I submit in all things to the teachings of the holy Catholic Roman Church, of which I am now a member, as I protest and promise I will be both in life and death. May our Lord God be for ever praised and blessed! Amen, Amen.

I finished writing this book in the convent of St. Joseph of Avila, 1577, on the Vigil of St. Andrew, for the glory of God, Who liveth and reigneth for ever and ever! Amen.

HERE ENDS THE INTERIOR CASTLE OR THE MANSIONS TRANSLATED AND PRINTED BY THE BENEDICTINES OF STANBROOK A.D. MCMXXI

---

65 Way of Perf. ch. xvi. 1.

The

Way of Perfection

By

Saint Teresa of Avila

Edited and Translated by E. Allison Peers
From the critical edition of P. Silverio de Santa Teresa, C.D.

DEDICATION
To the gracious memory of P. Edmund Gurdon
Sometime prior of the Carthusian Monastery of Miraflores, a man of God.

TABLE OF CONTENTS

INTRODUCTION

We owe this book, first and foremost, to the affectionate importunities of the Carmelite nuns of the Primitive Observance at Avila, and, in the second place, to that outstanding Dominican who was also St. Teresa's confessor, Fray Domingo Baez. The nuns of St. Joseph's knew something of their Mother Foundress' autobiography, and, though in all probability none of them had actually read it, they would have been aware that it contained valuable counsels to aspirants after religious perfection, of which, had the book been accessible to them, they would have been glad to avail themselves. Such intimate details did it contain, however, about St. Teresa's spiritual life that her superiors thought it should not be put into their hands; so the only way in which she could grant their persistent requests was to write another book dealing expressly with the life of prayer. This P. Baez was very anxious that she should do.

Through the entire *Way of Perfection* there runs the author's desire to teach her daughters to love prayer, the most effective means of attaining virtue. This principle is responsible for the book's construction. St. Teresa begins by describing the reason which led her to found the first Reformed Carmelite convent – viz., the desire to minimize the ravages being wrought, in France and elsewhere, by Protestantism, and, within the limits of her capacity, to check the passion for a so-called "freedom", which at that time was exceeding all measure. Knowing how effectively such inordinate desires can be restrained by a life of humility and poverty, St. Teresa extols the virtues of poverty and exhorts her daughters to practice it in their own lives. Even the buildings in which they live should be poor: on the Day of Judgment both majestic palaces and humble cottages will fall and she has no desire that the convents of her nuns should do so with a resounding clamor.

In this preamble to her book, which comprises Chapters 1-3, the author also charges her daughters very earnestly to commend to God those who have to defend the Church of Christ – particularly theologians and preachers.

The next part of the book (Chaps. 4-15) stresses the importance of a strict observance of the Rule and Constitutions, and before going on to its main subject – prayer – treats of three essentials of the prayer-filled life – mutual love, detachment from created things and true humility, the last of these being the most important and including all the rest. With the mutual love which nuns should have for one another she deals most minutely, giving what might be termed homely prescriptions for the domestic disorders of convents with the skill which we should expect of a writer with so perfect a knowledge of the psychology of the cloister. Her counsels are the fruit, not of lofty mental speculation, but of mature practical experience. No less aptly does she speak of the relations between nuns and their confessors, so frequently a source of danger.

Since excess is possible even in mutual love, she next turns to detachment. Her nuns must be detached from relatives and friends, from the world, from worldly honor, and – the last and hardest achievement – from themselves. To a large extent their efforts in this direction will involve humility, for, so long as we have an exaggerated opinion of our own merits, detachment is impossible. Humility, to St. Teresa, is nothing more nor less than truth, which will give us the precise estimate of our own worth that we need. Fraternal love, detachment and humility: these three virtues, if they are sought in the way these chapters direct, will make the soul mistress and sovereign over all created things – a "royal soul", in the Saint's happy phrase, the slave of none save of Him Who bought it with His blood.

The next section (Chaps. 16-26) develops these ideas, and leads the reader directly to the themes of prayer and contemplation. It begins with St. Teresa's famous extended simile of the game of chess, in which the soul gives check and mate to the King of love, Jesus. Many people are greatly attracted by the life of contemplation because they have acquired imperfect and misleading notions of the ineffable mystical joys which they believe almost synonymous with contemplation. The Saint protests against such ideas as these and lays it down clearly that, as a general rule, there is no way of attaining to union with the Beloved save by the practice of the "great virtues", which can be acquired only at the cost of continual self-sacrifice and self-conquest. The favors which God grants to contemplatives are only exceptional and of a transitory kind and they are intended to incline them more closely to virtue and to inspire their lives with greater fervor.

And here the Saint propounds a difficult question which has occasioned no little debate among writers on mystical theology. Can a soul in grave sin enjoy supernatural contemplation? At first sight, and judging from what the author says in Chapter 16, the answer would seem to be that, though but rarely and for brief periods, it can. In the original (or Escorial) autograph, however, she expressly denies this, and states that contemplation is not possible for souls in mortal sin, though it may be experienced by those who are so lukewarm, or lacking in fervor, that they fall into venial sins with ease. It would seem that in this respect the Escorial manuscript reflects the Saint's ideas, as we know them, more clearly than the later one of Valladolid; if this be so, her opinions in no way differ from those of mystical theologians as a whole, who refuse to allow that souls in mortal sin can experience contemplation at all.

St. Teresa then examines a number of other questions, on which opinion has also been divided and even now is by no means unanimous. Can all souls attain to contemplation? Is it possible, without experiencing contemplation, to reach the summit of Christian perfection? Have all the servants of God who have been canonized by the Church necessarily been contemplatives? Does the Church ever grant non-contemplatives beatification? On these questions and others often discussed by the mystics much light is shed in the seventeenth and eighteenth chapters.

Then the author crosses swords once more with those who suppose that contemplatives know nothing of suffering and that their lives are one continuous series of favors. On the contrary, she asserts, they suffer more than actives: to imagine that God admits to this closest friendship people whose lives are all favors and no trials is ridiculous. Recalling the doctrine expounded in the nineteenth chapter of her *Life* she gives various counsels for the practice of prayer, using once more the figures of water which she had employed in her first description of the Mystic Way. She consoles those who cannot reason with the understanding, shows how vocal prayer may be combined with mental, and ends by advising those who suffer from aridity in prayer to picture Jesus as within their hearts and thus always beside them – one of her favorite themes.

This leads up to the subject which occupies her for the rest of the book (Chaps. 27-42) – the Lord's Prayer. These chapters, in fact, comprise a commentary on the Paternoster, taken petition by petition, touching incidentally upon the themes of Recollection, Quiet and Union. Though nowhere expounding them as fully as in the *Life* or the *Interior Castle*, she treats them with equal sublimity, profundity and fervor and in language of no less beauty. Consider, for example, the apt and striking simile of the mother and the child (Chap. 31), used to describe the state of the soul in the Prayer of Quiet, which forms one of the most beautiful and expressive expositions of this degree of contemplation to be found in any book on the interior life whatsoever.

In Chapter 38, towards the end of the commentary on the Paternoster, St. Teresa gives a striking synthetic description of the excellences of that Prayer and of its spiritual value. She enters at some length into the temptations to which spiritual people are exposed when they lack humility and discretion. Some of these are due to presumption: they believe they possess virtues which in fact they do not – or, at least, not in sufficient degree to enable them to resist the snares of the enemy. Others come from a mistaken scrupulousness and timidity inspired by a sense of the heinousness of their sins, and may lead them into doubt and despair. There are souls, too, which make overmuch account of spiritual favors: these she counsels to see to it that, however sublime their contemplation may be, they begin and end every period of prayer with self-examination. While others whose mistrust of themselves makes them restless, are exhorted to trust in the Divine mercy, which never forsakes those who possess true humility.

Finally, St. Teresa writes of the love and fear of God – two mighty castles which the fiercest of the soul's enemies will storm in vain – and begs Him, in the last words of the Prayer to preserve her daughters, and all other souls who practice the interior life, from the ills and perils which will ever surround them, until they reach the next world, where all will be peace and joy in Jesus Christ.

Such, in briefest outline, is the argument of this book. Of all St. Teresa's writings it is the most easily comprehensible and it can be read with profit by a greater number of people than any of the rest. It is also (if we use the word in its strictest and truest sense) the most ascetic of her treatises; only a few chapters and passages in it, here and there, can be called definitely mystical. It takes up numerous ideas already adumbrated in the *Life* and treats them in a practical and familiar way – objectively, too, with an eye not so much to herself as to her daughters of the Discalced Reform. This last fact necessitates her descending to details which may seem to us trivial but were not in the least so to the religious to whom they were addressed and with whose virtues and failing she was so familiar. Skillfully, then, and in a way profitable to all, she intermingles her teaching on the most rudimentary principles of the religious life, which has all the clarity of any classical treatise, with instruction on the most sublime and elusive tenets of mystical theology.

ESCORIAL AUTOGRAPH – The Way of Perfection – or *Paternoster*, as its author calls it, from the latter part of its content – was written twice. Both autographs have been preserved in excellent condition, the older of them in the monastery of San Lorenzo el Real, El Escorial, and the other in the convent of the Discalced Carmelite nuns at Valladolid. We have already seen how Philip II acquired a number of Theresan autographs for his new Escorial library, among them that of the *Way of perfection*. The Escorial manuscript bears the title "Treatise of the Way of Perfection", but this is not in St. Teresa's hand. It plunges straight into the prologue: both the title and the brief account of the contents, which are found in most of the editions, are taken from the autograph of Valladolid, and the humble protestation of faith and submission to the Holy Roman Church was dictated by the Saint for the edition of the book made in Avora by Don Teutonio de Braganza - it is found in the Toledo codex, which will be referred to again shortly.

The text, divided into seventy-three short chapters, has no chapter-divisions in the ordinary sense of the phrase, though the author has left interlinear indications showing where each chapter should begin. The chapter-headings form a table of contents at the end of the manuscript and only two of them (55 and 56) are in St. Teresa's own writing. As the remainder, however, are in a feminine hand of the sixteenth century, they may have been dictated by her to one of her nuns: they are almost identical with those which she herself wrote at a later date in the autograph of Valladolid.

There are a considerable number of emendations in this text, most of them made by the Saint herself, whose practice was to obliterate any unwanted word so completely as to make it almost illegible. None of such words or phrases was restored in the autograph of Valladolid – a sure indication that it was she who erased them, or at least that she approved of their having been erased. There are fewer annotations and additions in other hands than in the autographs of any of her remaining works, and those few are of little importance. This may be due to the fact that a later redaction of the work was made for the use of her convents and for publication: the Escorial manuscript would have circulated very little and would never have been subjected to a minute critical examination. Most of what annotations and corrections of this kind there are were made by the Saint's confessor, P. Garc'a de Toledo, whom, among others, she asked to examine the manuscript.

There is no direct indication in the manuscript of the date of its composition. We know that it was written at St. Joseph's, Avila, for the edification and instruction of the first nuns of the Reform, and the prologue tells us that only "a few days" had elapsed between the completion of the *Life* and the beginning of the *Way of perfection*. If, therefore, the Life was finished at the end of 1565 [or in the early weeks of 1566][1] we can date the commencement of the Way of perfection with some precision. [But even then there is no indication as to how long the composition took and when it was completed.]

A complication occurs in the existence, at the end of a copy of the Way of perfection which belongs to the Discalced Carmelite nuns of Salamanca, and contains corrections in St. Teresa's hand, of a note, in the writing of the copyist, which says: This book was written in the year sixty-two – I mean fifteen hundred and sixty-two." There follow some lines in the writing of St. Teresa, which make no allusion to this date; her silence might be taken as confirming it (though she displays no great interest in chronological exactness) were it not absolutely impossible to reconcile such a date with the early chapters of the book, which make it quite clear that the community of thirteen nuns was fully established when they were written (Chap. 4, below). There could not possibly have been so many nuns at St. Joseph's before late in the year 1563, in which Mar de San Jernimo and Isabel de Santo Domingo took the habit, and it is doubtful if St. Teresa could conceivably have begun the book before the end of that year. Even, therefore, if the reference in the preface to the Way of perfection were to the first draft of the Life (1562), and not to that book as we know it, there would still be the insuperable difficulty raised by this piece of internal evidence.[2] We are forced,

---

[1] Cf. Vol. I, pp. 2-5, above.

[2] See also the reference, in the "General Argument" of the Valladolid redaction, to her being Prioress of

then, to assume an error in the Salamanca copy and to assign to the beginning of the Way of perfection the date 1565-6.

VALLADOLID AUTOGRAPH. In writing for her Avila nuns, St. Teresa used language much more simple, familiar and homely than in any of her other works. But when she began to establish more foundations and her circle of readers widened, this language must have seemed to her too affectionately intimate, and some of her figures and images may have struck her as too domestic and trivial, for a more general and scattered public. So she conceived the idea of rewriting the book in a more formal style; it is the autograph of this redaction which is in the possession of the Discalced Carmelite nuns of Valladolid.

The additions, omissions and modifications in this new autograph are more considerable than is generally realized. From the preface onwards, there is no chapter without its emendations and in many there are additions of whole paragraphs. The Valladolid autograph, therefore, is in no sense a copy, or even a recast, of the first draft, but a free and bold treatment of it. As a general rule, a second draft, though often more correctly written and logically arranged than its original, is less flexible, fluent and spontaneous. It is hard to say how far this is the case here. Undoubtedly some of the charm of the author's natural simplicity vanishes, but the corresponding gain in clarity and precision is generally considered greater than the loss. Nearly every change she makes is an improvement; and this not only in stylistic matters, for one of the greatest of her improvements is the lengthening of the chapters and their reduction in number from 73 to 42, to the great advantage of the book's symmetry and unity.

It is clear that St. Teresa intended the Valladolid redaction to be the definitive form of her book since she had so large a number of copies of it made for her friends and spiritual daughters: among these were the copy which she sent for publication to Don Teutonio de Braganza and that used for the first collected edition of her works by Fray Luis de Leon. For the same reason this redaction has always been given preference over its predecessor by the Discalced Carmelites.

TRANSLATOR'S NOTE

In the text of each of the chapters, of the Valladolid autograph there are omissions – some merely verbal, often illustrating the author's aim in making the new redaction, others more fundamental. If the Valladolid manuscript represents the *Way of perfection* as St. Teresa wrote it in the period of her fullest powers, the greater freshness and individuality of the Escorial manuscript are engaging qualities, and there are many passages in it, omitted from the later version, which one would be sorry to sacrifice.

In what form, then, should the book be presented to English readers? It is not surprising if this question is difficult to answer, since varying procedures have been adopted for the presentation of it in Spain. Most of them amount briefly to a re-editing of the Valladolid manuscript. The first edition of the book, published at Avora in the year 1583, follows this manuscript, apparently using a copy (the so-called "Toledo" copy) made by Ana de San Pedro and corrected by St. Teresa; it contains a considerable number of errors, however, and omits one entire chapter – the thirty-first, which deals with the Prayer of Quiet, a subject that was arousing some controversy at the time when the edition was being prepared. In 1585, a second edition, edited by Fray Jernimo Gracien, was published at Salamanca: the text of this follows that of the Avora edition very closely, as apparently does the text of a rare edition published at Valencia in 1586. When Fray Luis de Leon used the Valladolid manuscript as the foundation of his text (1588) he inserted for the first time paragraphs and phrases from that of El Escorial, as well as admitting variants from the copies corrected by the author: he is not careful however, to indicate how and where his edition differs from the manuscript.

Since 1588, most of the Spanish editions have followed Fray Luis de León with greater or less exactness. The principal exception is the well-known "Biblioteca de Autores Españoles" edition, in which La Fuente followed a copy of the then almost forgotten Escorial manuscript, indicating in footnotes some of the variant readings in the codex of Valladolid. In the edition of 1883, the work of a Canon of Valladolid Cathedral, Francisco Herrero Bayona, the texts of the two manuscripts are

---

St. Joseph's when the book was written. Presumably the original draft is meant.

reproduced in parallel columns. P. Silverio[3] de Santa Teresa gives the place of honor to the Valladolid codex, on which he bases his text, showing only the principal variants of the Escorial manuscript but printing the Escorial text in full in an appendix as well as the text of the Toledo copy referred to above.

The first translations of this book into English, by Woodhead (1675: reprinted 1901) and Dalton (1852), were based, very naturally, on the text of Luis de León , which in less critical ages than our own enjoyed great prestige and was considered quite authoritative. The edition published in 1911 by the Benedictines of Stanbrook, described on its title-page as "including all the variants" from both the Escorial and the Valladolid manuscript, uses Herrero Bayona and gives an eclectic text based on the two originals but with no indications as to which is which. The editors' original idea of using one text only, and showing variants in footnotes, was rejected in the belief that "such an arrangement would prove bewildering for the generality of readers" and that anyone who could claim the title of "student" would be able to read the original Spanish and would have access to the Herrero Bayona edition. Father Zimmerman, in his introduction, claimed that while the divergences between the manuscripts are sometimes "so great that the [Stanbrook] translation resembles a mosaic composed of a large number of small bits, skillfully combined", "the work has been done most conscientiously, and while nothing has been added to the text of the Saint, nothing has been omitted, except, of course, what would have been mere repetition".

This first edition of the Benedictines' translation furnished the general reader with an attractive version of what many consider St. Teresa's most attractive book, but soon after it was published a much more intelligent and scholarly interest began to be taken in the Spanish mystics and that not only by students with ready access to the Spanish original and ability to read it. So, when a new edition of the Stanbrook translation was called for, the editors decided to indicate the passages from the Escorial edition which had been embodied in the text by enclosing these in square brackets. In 1911, Father Zimmerman, suspecting that the procedure then adopted by the translators would not "meet with the approval of scholars", had justified it by their desire "to benefit the souls of the faithful rather than the intellect of the student"; but now, apparently, he thought it practicable to achieve both these aims at once. This resolution would certainly have had the support of St. Teresa, who in this very book describes intelligence as a useful staff to carry on the way of perfection. The careful comparison of two separate versions of such a work of genius may benefit the soul of an intelligent reader even more than the careful reading of a version compounded of both by someone else.

When I began to consider the preparation of the present translation it seemed to me that an attempt might be made to do a little more for the reader who combined intelligence with devoutness than had been done already. I had no hesitation about basing my version on the Valladolid MS., which is far the better of the two, whether we consider the aptness of its illustrations, the clarity of its expression, the logical development of its argument or its greater suitability for general reading. At the same time, no Theresan who has studied the Escorial text can fail to have an affection for it: its greater intimacy and spontaneity and its appeal to personal experience make it one of the most characteristic of all the Saint's writings – indeed, excepting the *Letters of St. Teresa* and a few chapters of the *Foundations*, it reveals her better than any. Passages from the Escorial MS. must therefore be given: thus far I followed the reasoning of the Stanbrook nuns.

Where this translation diverges from theirs is in the method of presentation. On the one hand I desired, as St. Teresa must have desired, that it should be essentially her mature revision of the book that should be read. For this reason I have been extremely conservative as to the interpolations admitted into the text itself: I have rejected, for example, the innumerable phrases which St. Teresa seems to have cut out in making her new redaction because they were trivial or repetitive, because they weaken rather than reinforce her argument, because they say what is better said elsewhere, because they summarize needlessly[4] or because they are mere personal observations which interrupt the author's flow of thought, and sometimes, indeed, are irrelevant to it. I hope it is not impertinent to add that, in the close study which the adoption of this procedure has involved, I have acquired a

---

[3] P. Silverio – Obras de Santa Teresa de Jesus, editadas y anotadas por el P. Silverio de Santa Teresa, C.D., Durgos, 1915-24, 9 vols.

[4] E.g., at places where a chapter ends in E. but not in V.

respect and admiration for St. Teresa as a reviser, to whom, as far as I know, no one who has written upon her has done full justice. Her shrewdness, realism and complete lack of vanity make her an admirable editor of her own work, and, in debating whether or not to incorporate some phrase or passage in my text I have often asked myself: Would St. Teresa have included or omitted this if she had been making a fresh revision for a world-wide public over a period of centuries?"

At the same time, though admitting only a minimum of interpolations into my text, I have given the reader all the other important variants in footnotes. I cannot think, as Father Zimmerman apparently thought, that anyone can find the presence of a few notes at the foot of each page "bewildering". Those for whom they have no interest may ignore them; others, in studying them, may rest assured that the only variants not included (and this applies to the variants from the Toledo copy as well as from the Escorial MS.) are such as have no significance in a translation. I have been rather less meticulous here than in my edition of St. John of the Cross, where textual problems assumed greater importance. Thus, except where there has been some special reason for doing so, I have not recorded alterations in the order of clauses or words; the almost regular use by E. of the second person of the plural where V. has the first; the frequent and often apparently purposeless changes of tense; such substitutions, in the Valladolid redaction, as those of "Dios" or "Señor m'o" for "Señior"; or merely verbal paraphrases as (to take an example at random) "Todo esto que he dicho es para…" for "En todo esto que he dicho no trato…" Where I have given variants which may seem trivial (such as "hermanas" for "hijas", or the insertion of an explanatory word, like "digo") the reason is generally that there seems to me a possibility that some difference in tone is intended, or that the alternative phrase gives some slight turn to the thought which the phrase in the text does not.

The passages from the Escorial version which I have allowed into my text are printed in italics. Thus, without their being given undue prominence (and readers of the Authorized Version of the Bible will know how seldom they can recall what words are italicized even in the passages they know best) it is clear at a glance how much of the book was intended by its author to be read by a wider public than the nuns of St. Joseph's. The interpolations may be as brief as a single expressive word, or as long as a paragraph, or even a chapter: the original Chapter 17 of the Valladolid MS., for example, which contains the famous similitude of the Game of Chess, was torn out of the codex by its author (presumably with the idea that so secular an illustration was out of place) and has been restored from the Escorial MS. as part of Chapter 16 of this translation. No doubt the striking bullfight metaphor at the end of Chapter 39 was suppressed in the Valladolid codex for the same reason. With these omissions may be classed a number of minor ones – of words or phrases which to the author may have seemed too intimate or colloquial but do not seem so to us. Other words and phrases have apparently been suppressed because St. Teresa thought them redundant, whereas a later reader finds that they make a definite contribution to the sense or give explicitness and detail to what would otherwise be vague, or even obscure.[5] A few suppressions seem to have been due to pure oversight. For the omission of other passages it is difficult to find any reason, so good are they: the conclusion of Chapter 38 and the opening of Chapter 41 are cases in point.

The numbering of the chapters, it should be noted, follows neither of the two texts, but is that traditionally employed in the printed editions. The chapter headings are also drawn up on an eclectic basis, though here the Valladolid text is generally followed.

The system I have adopted not only assures the reader that he will be reading everything that St. Teresa wrote and nothing that she did not write, but that he can discern almost at a glance, what she meant to be read by her little group of nuns at St. Joseph's and also how she intended her work to appear in its more definitive form. Thus we can see her both as the companion and Mother and as the writer and Foundress. In both roles she is equally the Saint.

But it should be made clear that, while incorporating in my text all important passages from the Escorial draft omitted in that of Valladolid, I have thought it no part of my task to provide a complete translation of the Escorial draft alone, and that, therefore, in order to avoid the multiplication of footnotes, I have indicated only the principal places where some expression in the later draft is not to be found in the earlier. In other words, although, by omitting the italicized

---

[5] One special case of this class is the suppression in V. of one out of two or three almost but not quite synonymous adjectives referring to the same noun.

portions of my text, one will be able to have as exact a translation of the Valladolid version as it is possible to get, the translation of the Escorial draft will be only approximate. This is the sole concession I have made to the ordinary reader as opposed to the student, and it is hardly conceivable, I think, that any student to whom this could matter would be unable to read the original Spanish.

One final note is necessary on the important Toledo copy, the text of which P. Silverio also prints in full. This text I have collated with that of the Valladolid autograph, from which it derives. In it both St. Teresa herself and others have made corrections and additions – more, in fact, than in any of the other copies extant. No attempt has been made here either to show what the Toledo copy omits or to include those of its corrections and additions – by far the largest number of them – which are merely verbal and unimportant, and many of which, indeed, could not be embodied in a translation at all. But the few additions which are really worth noting have been incorporated in the text (in square brackets so as to distinguish them from the Escorial additions) and all corrections which have seemed to me of any significance will be found in footnotes.

BOOK CALLED WAY OF PERFECTION[1]

Composed by TERESA OF JESUS, Nun of the Order of Our Lady of Carmel, addressed to the Discalced Nuns of Or Lady of Carmel of the First Rule.[2]

GENERAL ARGUMENT OF THIS BOOK
J. H. S.[3]

This book treats of maxims and counsels which Teresa of Jesus gives to her daughters and sisters in religion, belonging to the Convents which, with the favor of Our Lord and of the glorious Virgin, Mother of God, Our Lady, she has founded according to the First Rule of Our Lady of Carmel. In particular she addresses it to the sisters of the Convent of Saint Joseph of Avila, which was the first Convent, and of which she was Prioress when she wrote it.[4]

PROTESTATIONS[5]

In all that I shall say in this Book, I submit to what is taught by Our Mother, the Holy Roman Church; if there is anything in it contrary to this, it will be without my knowledge. Therefore, for the love of Our Lord, I beg the learned men who are to revise it to look at it very carefully and to amend any faults of this nature which there may be in it and the many others which it will have of other kinds. If there is anything good in it, let this be to the glory and honor of God and in the service of His most sacred Mother, our Patroness and Lady, whose habit, though all unworthily, I wear.

PROLOGUE
J. H. S.

The sisters of this Convent of Saint Joseph, knowing that I had had leave from Father Presentado Fray Domingo Baes,[6] of the Order of the glorious Saint Dominic, who at present is my confessor, to write certain things about prayer, which it seems I may be able to succeed in doing since I have had to do with many holy and spiritual persons, have, out of their great love for me, so earnestly begged me to say something to them about this that I have resolved to obey them. I realize that the great love which they have for me may render the imperfection and the poverty of my style

---

[1] This title, in St. Teresa's hand, appears on the first page of the Valladolid autograph (V.) which, as we have said in the Introduction, is the basis of the text here used. The Escorial autograph (E.) has the words "Treatise of the Way of Perfection" in an unknown hand, followed by the Prologue, in St. Teresa's. The Toledo copy (T.) begins with the Protestation.

[2] With few exceptions, the footnotes to the *Way of Perfection* are the translators. Square brackets are therefore not used to distinguish them from those of P. Silverio, as elsewhere. Ordinary brackets, in the footnote translations, are placed round words inserted to complete the sense.

[3] Christogram of the name "Jesus", spelt "ΙΗΣΟΥΣ" in Greek capitals, has the abbreviations JHS, IHS, IHC, or IHΣ.

[4] These lines, also in St. Teresa's hand, follow the title in the Valladolid autograph. P. Baez added, in his own writing, the words: "I have seen this book and my opinion of it is written at the end and signed with my name." Cf. ch. 42, below.

[5] This Protestation, taken from T., was dictated by St. Teresa for the edition of the *Way of perfection* published at Avora in 1583 by D. Teutonio de Braganza.

[6] The words "Fray Domingo Baes" are crossed out, probably by P. Baez himself. T. has: "from the Father Master Fray Domingo Baez, Professor at Salamanca." Baez was appointed to a Chair at Salamanca University in 1577.

in what I shall say to them more acceptable than other books which are very ably written by those who[7] have known what they are writing about. I rely upon their prayers, by means of which the Lord may be pleased to enable me to say something concerning the way and method of life which it is fitting should be practiced in this house. If I do not succeed in doing this, Father Presentado, who will first read what I have written, will either put it right or burn it, so that I shall have lost nothing by obeying these servants of God, and they will see how useless I am when His Majesty does not help me.

My intent is to suggest a few remedies for a number of small temptations which come from the devil, and which, because they are so slight, are apt to pass unnoticed. I shall also write of other things, according as the Lord reveals them to me and as they come to my mind; since I do not know what I am going to say I cannot set it down in suitable order; and I think it is better for me not to do so, for it is quite unsuitable that I should be writing in this way at all. May the Lord lay His hand on all that I do so that it may be in accordance with His holy will; this is always my desire, although my actions may be as imperfect as I myself am.

I know that I am lacking neither in love nor in desire to do all I can to help the souls of my sisters to make great progress in the service of the Lord. It may be that this love, together with my years and the experience which I have of a number of convents, will make me more successful in writing about small matters than learned men can be. For these, being themselves strong and handing other and more important occupations, do not always pay such heed to things which in themselves seem of no importance but which may do great harm to persons as weak as we women are. For the snares laid by the devil for strictly cloistered nuns are numerous and he finds that he needs new weapons if he is to do them harm. I, being a wicked woman, have defended myself but ill, and so I should like my sisters to take warning by me. I shall speak of nothing of which I have no experience, either in my own life or in the observation of others, *or which the Lord has not taught me in prayer.*

A few days ago I was commanded to write an account of my life in which I also dealt with certain matters concerning prayer. It may be that my confessor will not wish you to see this, for which reason I shall set down here some of the things which I said in that book and others which may also seem to me necessary. May the Lord direct this, as I have begged Him to do, and order it for His greater glory. Amen.

CHAPTER 1
Of the reason which moved me to found this convent in such strict observance.

When this convent was originally founded, for the reasons set down in the book which, as I say, I have already written, and also because of certain wonderful revelations by which the Lord showed me how well He would be served in this house, it was not my intention that there should be so much austerity in external matters, nor that it should have no regular income: on the contrary, I should have liked there to be no possibility of want. I acted, in short, like the weak and wretched woman that I am, although I did so with good intentions and not out of consideration for my own comfort.

At about this time there came to my notice the harm and havoc that were being wrought in France by these Lutherans and the way in which their unhappy sect was increasing.[8] This troubled me very much, and, as though I could do anything, or be of any help in the matter, I wept before the Lord and entreated Him to remedy this great evil. I felt that I would have laid down a thousand

---

[7] The pronoun (*quien*) in the Spanish is singular, but in the sixteenth century it could have plural force and the context would favor this. A manuscript note in V., however (not by P. Baez, as the Paris Carmelites – *Oeuvres*, V, 30 – suggest), evidently takes the reference to be to St. Gregory, for it says: "And he wrote something on Job, and the *Morals*, importuned by servants of God, and trusting in their prayers, as he himself says."

[8] French Protestantism which had been repressed during the reigns of Francis I and Henry II, increased after the latter's death in 1559, and was still doing so at the time of the foundation of St. Joseph's.

lives to save a single one of all the souls that were being lost there. And, seeing that I was a woman, and a sinner,[9] and incapable of doing all I should like in the Lord's service, and as my whole yearning was, and still is, that, as He has so many enemies and so few friends, these last should be trusty ones, I determined to do the little that was in me – namely, to follow the evangelical counsels as perfectly as I could, and to see that these few nuns who are here should do the same, confiding in the great goodness of God, Who never fails to help those who resolve to forsake everything for His sake. As they are all that I have ever painted them as being in my desires, I hoped that their virtues would more than counteract my defects, and I should thus be able to give the Lord some pleasure, and all of us, by busying ourselves in prayer for those who are defenders of the Church, and for the preachers and learned men who defend her, should do everything we could to aid this Lord of mine Who is so much oppressed by those to whom He has shown so much good that it seems as though these traitors would send Him to the Cross again and that He would have nowhere to lay His head.

Oh, my Redeemer, my heart cannot conceive this without being sorely distressed! What has become of Christians now? Must those who owe Thee most always be those who distress Thee? Those to whom Thou doest the greatest kindnesses, whom Thou dost choose for Thy friends, among whom Thou dost move, communicating Thyself to them through the Sacraments? Do they not think, *Lord of my soul*, that they have made Thee endure more than sufficient torments?

It is certain, my Lord, that in these days withdrawal from the world means no sacrifice at all. Since worldly people have so little respect for Thee, what can we expect them to have for us? Can it be that we deserve that they should treat us any better than they have treated Thee? Have we done more for them than Thou hast done that they should be friendly to us? What then? What can we expect – we who, through the goodness of the Lord, are free from that pestilential infection, and do not, like those others, belong to the devil? They have won severe punishment at his hands and their pleasures have richly earned them eternal fire. So to eternal fire they will have to go,[10] though none the less it breaks my heart to see so many souls traveling to perdition. I would the evil were not so great and I did not see more being lost every day.

Oh, my sisters in Christ! Help me to entreat this of the Lord, Who has brought you together here for that very purpose. This is your vocation; this must be your business; these must be your desires; these your tears; these your petitions. Let us not pray for worldly things, my sisters. It makes me laugh, and yet it makes me sad, when I hear of the things which people come here to beg us to pray to God for; we are to ask His Majesty to give them money and to provide them with incomes – I wish that some of these people would entreat God to enable them to trample all such things beneath their feet. Their intentions are quite good, and I do as they ask because I see that they are really devout people, though I do not myself believe that God ever hears me when I pray for such things. The world is on fire. Men try to condemn Christ once again, as it were, for they bring a thousand false witnesses against Him. They would raze His Church to the ground – and are we to waste our time upon things which, if God were to grant them, would perhaps bring one soul less to Heaven? No, my sisters, this is no time to treat with God for things of little importance.

Were it not necessary to consider human frailty, which finds satisfaction in every kind of help – and it is always a good thing if we can be of any help to people – I should like it to be understood that it is not for things like these that God should be importuned with such anxiety.

CHAPTER 2

Treats of how the necessities of the body should be disregarded and of the good that comes from poverty.

Do not think, my sisters, that because you do not go about trying to please people in the world you will lack food. You will not, I assure you: never try to sustain yourselves by human artifices,

---

[9] *Lit.*: "and bad."

[10] *Alli se lo hayan.* "And serve them right!" would, in most contexts, be a more exact rendering of this colloquial phrase, but there is no suspicion of *Schadenfreude* here.

or you will die of hunger, and rightly so. Keep your eyes fixed upon your Spouse: it is for Him to sustain you; and, if He is pleased with you, even those who like you least will give you food, if unwillingly, as you have found by experience. If you should do as I say and yet die of hunger, then happy are the nuns of Saint Joseph's! For the love of the Lord, let us not forget this: you have forgone a regular income; forgo worry about food as well, or thou will lose everything. Let those whom the Lord wishes to live on an income do so: if that is their vocation, they are perfectly justified; but for us to do so, sisters, would be inconsistent.

Worrying about getting money from other people seems to me like thinking about what other people enjoy. However much you worry, you will not make them change their minds nor will they become desirous of giving you alms. Leave these anxieties to Him Who can move everyone, Who is the Lord of all money and of all who possess money. It is by His command that we have come here and His words are true – they cannot fail: Heaven and earth will fail first.[11] Let us not fail Him, and let us have no fear that He will fail us; if He should ever do so it will be for our greater good, just as the saints failed to keep their lives when they were slain for the Lord's sake, and their bliss was increased through their martyrdom. We should be making a good exchange if we could have done with this life quickly and enjoy everlasting satiety.

Remember, sisters, that this will be important when I am dead; and that is why I am leaving it to you in writing. For, *with God's help*, as long as I live, I will remind you of it myself, as I know by experience what a great help it will be to you. It is when I possess least that I have the fewest worries and the Lord knows that, as far as I can tell, I am more afflicted when there is excess of anything than when there is lack of it; I am not sure if that is the Lord's doing, but I have noticed that He provides for us immediately. To act otherwise would be to deceive the world by pretending to be poor when we are not poor in spirit but only outwardly. My conscience would give me a bad time. It seems to me it would be like stealing what was being given us, as one might say; for I should feel as if we were rich people asking alms: please God this may never be so. Those who worry too much about the alms that they are likely to be given will find that sooner or later this bad habit will lead them to go and ask for something which they do not need, and perhaps from someone who needs it more than they do. Such a person would gain rather than lose by giving it us but we should certainly be the worse off for having it. God forbid this should ever happen, my daughters; if it were likely to do so, I should prefer you to have a regular income.

I beg you, for the love of God, just as if I were begging alms for you, never to allow this to occupy your thoughts. If the very least of you ever hears of such a thing happening in this house, cry out about it to His Majesty and speak to your Superior. Tell her humbly that she is doing wrong; this is so serious a matter that it may cause true poverty gradually to disappear. I hope in the Lord that this will not be so and that He will not forsake His servants; and for that reason, if for no other, what you have told me to write may be useful to you as a reminder.

My daughters must believe that it is for their own good that the Lord has enabled me to realize in some small degree what blessings are to be found in holy poverty. Those of them who practice it will also realize this, though perhaps not as clearly as I do; for, although I had professed poverty, I was not only without poverty of spirit, but my spirit was devoid of all restraint. Poverty is good and contains within itself all the good things in the world. It is a great domain – I mean that he who cares nothing for the good things of the world has dominion over them all. What do kings and lords matter to me if I have no desire to possess their money, or to please them, if by so doing I should cause the least displeasure to God? And what do their honors mean to me if I have realized that the chief honor of a poor man consists in his being truly poor?

For my own part, I believe that honor and money nearly always go together, and that he who desires honor never hates money, while he who hates money cares little for honor. Understand this clearly, for I think this concern about honor always implies some *slight* regard for endowments or money: seldom *or never* is a poor man honored by the world; however worthy of honor he may be, he is apt rather to be despised by it. With true poverty there goes a different kind of honor to which nobody can take objection. I mean that, if poverty is embraced for God's sake alone, no one has to be pleased save God. It is certain that a man who has no need of anyone has many friends: in my own experience I have found this to be very true.

---

[11] An apparent reference to St. Mark xiii, 31.

A great deal has been written about this virtue which I cannot understand, still less express, and I should only be making things worse if I were to eulogize it, so I will say no more about it now. I have only spoken of what I have myself experienced and I confess that I have been so much absorbed that until now I have hardly realized what I have been writing. However, it has been said now. Our arms are holy poverty, which was so greatly esteemed and so strictly observed by our holy Fathers at the beginning of the foundation of our Order. (Someone who knows about this tells me that they never kept anything from one day to the next.) For the love of the Lord, then, [I beg you] now that the rule of poverty is less perfectly observed as regards outward things, let us strive to observe it inwardly. Our life lasts only for a couple of hours; our reward is boundless; and, if there were no reward but to follow the counsels given us by the Lord, to imitate His Majesty in any degree would bring us a great recompense.

These arms must appear on our banners and at all costs we must keep this rule – as regards our house, our clothes, our speech, and (which is much more important) our thoughts. So long as this is done, there need be no fear, with the help of God, that religious observances in this house will decline, for, as Saint Clare said, the walls of poverty are very strong. It was with these walls, she said, and with those of humility, that she wished to surround her convents; and assuredly, if the rule of poverty is truly kept, both chastity and all the other virtues are fortified much better than by the most sumptuous edifices. Have a care to this, for the love of God; and this I beg of you by His blood. If I may say what my conscience bids me, I should wish that, on the day when you build such edifices, they[12] may fall down *and kill you all.*

It seems very wrong, my daughters, that great houses should be built with the money of the poor; may God forbid that this should be done; let our houses be small and poor in every way. Let us to some extent resemble our King, Who had no house save the porch in Bethlehem where He was born and the Cross on which He died. These were houses where little comfort could be found. Those who erect large houses will no doubt have good reasons for doing so. *I do not utterly condemn them:* they are moved by various holy intentions. But any corner is sufficient for thirteen poor women. If grounds should be thought necessary on account of the strictness of the enclosure, and also as an aid to prayer and devotion, *and because our miserable nature needs such things*, well and good; and let there be a few hermitages[13] in them in which the sisters may go to pray. But as for a large ornate convent, with a lot of buildings – God preserve us from that! Always remember that these things will all fall down on the Day of Judgment, and who knows how soon that will be?

It would hardly look well if the house of thirteen poor women made a great noise when it fell, for those who are really poor must make no noise: unless they live a noiseless life people will never take pity on them. And how happy my sisters will be if they see someone freed from hell by means of the alms which he has given them; and this is quite possible, since they are strictly bound to offer continual prayer for persons who give them food. It is also God's will that, although the food comes from Him, we should thank the persons by whose means He gives it to us: let there be no neglect of this.

I do not remember what I had begun to say, for I have strayed from my subject. But I think this must have been the Lord's will, for I never intended to write what I have said here. May His Majesty always keep us in His hand so that we may never fall. Amen.

CHAPTER 3

Continues the subject begun in the first chapter and persuades the sisters to busy themselves constantly in beseeching God to help those who work for the Church. Ends with an exclamatory prayer.

Let us now return to the principal reason for which the Lord has brought us together in this house, for which reason I am most desirous that we may be able to please His Majesty. Seeing how

---

[12] In the Spanish the subject is in the singular: P. Baez inserted "the house", but crossed this out later.

[13] St. Teresa liked to have hermitages in the grounds of her convents to give the nuns opportunity for solitude.

great are the evils of the present day and how no human strength will suffice to quench the fire kindled by these heretics (though attempts have been made to organize opposition to them, as though such a great and rapidly spreading evil could be remedied by force of arms), it seems to me that it is like a war in which the enemy has overrun the whole country, and the Lord of the country, hard pressed, retires into a city, which he causes to be well fortified, and whence from time to time he is able to attack. Those who are in the city are picked men who can do more by themselves than they could do with the aid of many soldiers if they were cowards. Often this method gains the victory; or, if the garrison does not conquer, it is at least not conquered; for, as it contains no traitors, *but picked men*, it can be reduced only by hunger. In our own conflict, however, we cannot be forced to surrender by hunger; we can die but we cannot be conquered.

Now why have I said this? So that you may understand, my sisters, that what we have to ask of God is that, in this little castle of ours, inhabited as it is by good Christians, none of us may go over to the enemy. We must ask God, too, to make the captains in this castle or city – that is, the preachers and theologians – highly proficient in the way of the Lord. And as most of these are religious, we must pray that they may advance in perfection, and in the fulfillment of their vocation, for this is very needful. For, as I have already said, it is the ecclesiastical and not the secular arm which must defend us. And as we can do nothing by either of these means to help our King, let us strive to live in such a way that our prayers may be of avail to help these servants of God, who, at the cost of so much toil, have fortified themselves with learning and virtuous living and have labored to help the Lord.

You may ask why I emphasize this so much and why I say we must help people who are better than ourselves. I will tell you, for I am not sure if you properly understand as yet how much we owe to the Lord for bringing us to a place where we are so free from business matters, occasions of sin and the society of worldly people. This is a very great favor and one which is not granted to the persons of whom I have been speaking, nor is it fitting that it should be granted to them; it would be less so now, indeed, than at any other time, for it is they who must strengthen the weak and give courage to God's little ones. A fine thing it would be for soldiers if they lost their captains! These preachers and theologians have to live among men and associate with men and stay in palaces and sometimes even behave as people in palaces do in outward matters. Do you think, my daughters, that it is an easy matter to have to do business with the world, to live in the world, to engage in the affairs of the world, and, as I have said, to live as worldly men do, and yet inwardly to be strangers to the world, and enemies of the world, like persons who are in exile – to be, in short, not men but angels? Yet unless these persons act thus, they neither deserve to bear the title of captain nor to be allowed by the Lord to leave their cells, for they would do more harm than good. This is no time for imperfections in those whose duty it is to teach.

And if these teachers are not inwardly fortified by realizing the great importance of spurning everything beneath their feet and by being detached from things which come to an end on earth, and attached to things eternal, they will betray this defect in themselves, however much they may try to hide it. For with whom are they dealing but with the world? They need not fear: the world will not pardon them or fail to observe their imperfections. Of the good things they do many will pass unnoticed, or will even not be considered good at all; but they need not fear that any evil or imperfect thing they do will be overlooked. I am amazed when I wonder from whom they learned about perfection, when, instead of practicing it themselves (for they think they have no obligation to do that and have done quite enough by a reasonable observance of the Commandments), they condemn others, and at times mistake virtue for indulgence. Do not think, then, that they need but little Divine favor in this great battle upon which they have entered; on the contrary, they need a great deal.

I beg you to try to live in such a way as to be worthy to obtain two things from God. First, that there may be many of these very learned and religious men who have the qualifications for their task which I have described, and that the Lord may prepare those who are not completely prepared already *and who lack anything*, for a single one who is perfect will do more than many who are not. Secondly, that after they have entered upon this struggle, which, as I say, is not light, *but a very heavy one*, the Lord may have them in His hand so that they may be delivered from all the dangers that are in the world, and, while sailing on this perilous sea, may shut their ears to the song of the sirens. If we can prevail with God in the smallest degree about this, we shall be fighting His battle even while living a cloistered life and I shall consider as well spent all the trouble to which I have gone in founding this retreat,[14] where I have also tried to ensure that this Rule of Our Lady and Empress shall be kept in its original perfection.

Do not think that offering this petition continually is useless. Some people think it a hardship not to be praying all the time for their own souls. Yet what better prayer could there be than this? You may be worried because you think it will do nothing to lessen your pains in Purgatory, but actually praying in this way will relieve you of some of them and anything else that is left – well, let it remain. After all, what does it matter if I am in Purgatory until the Day of Judgment provided a single soul should be saved through my prayer? And how much less does it matter if many souls profit by it and the Lord is honored! Make no account of any pain which has an end if by means of it any greater service can be rendered to Him Who bore such pains for us. Always try to find out wherein lies the greatest perfection. And for the love of the Lord I beg you to beseech His Majesty to hear us in this; I, miserable creature though I am, beseech this of His Majesty, since it is for His glory and the good of His Church, which are my only wishes.

It seems over-bold of me to think that I can do anything towards obtaining this. But I have confidence, my Lord, in these servants of Thine who are here, knowing that they neither desire nor strive after anything but to please Thee. For Thy sake they have left the little they possessed, wishing they had more so that they might serve Thee with it. Since Thou, my Creator, art not ungrateful, I do not think Thou wilt fail to do what they beseech of Thee, for when Thou wert in the world, Lord, Thou didst not despise women, but didst always help them and show them great compassion.[15] *Thou didst find more faith and no less love in them than in men, and one of them was Thy most sacred Mother, from whose merits we derive merit, and whose habit we wear, though our sins make us unworthy to do so.[16] We can do nothing in public that is of any use to Thee, nor dare we speak of some of the truths over which we weep in secret lest Thou shouldst not hear this our just petition. Yet, Lord I cannot believe this of Thy goodness and righteousness, for Thou art a righteous Judge, not like judges in the world, who, being, after all, men and sons of Adam, refuse to consider any woman's virtue as above suspicion. Yes, my King, but the day will come when all will be known. I am not speaking on my own account, for the whole world is already aware of my wickedness, and I am glad that it should become known; but, when I see what the times are like, I feel it is not right to repel spirits which are virtuous and brave, even though they be the spirits of women.*

Hear us not when we ask Thee for honors, endowments, money, or anything that has to do with the world; but why shouldst Thou not hear us, Eternal Father, when we ask only for the honor of Thy Son, when we would forfeit a thousand honors and a thousand lives for Thy sake? Not for ourselves, Lord, for we do not deserve to be heard, but for the blood of Thy Son and for His merits.

Oh, Eternal Father! Surely all these scourgings and insults and grievous tortures will not be forgotten. How, then, my Creator, can a heart so [merciful and] loving as Thine endure that an act which was performed by Thy Son in order to please Thee the more (for He loved Thee most deeply and Thou didst command Him to love us) should be treated as lightly as those heretics treat the Most Holy Sacrament today, in taking it from its resting-place when they destroy the churches? Could it be that [Thy Son and our Redeemer] had failed to do something to please Thee? No: He fulfilled everything. Was it not enough, Eternal Father, that while He lived He had no place to lay His head and had always to endure so many trials? Must they now deprive Him of the places[17] to which He can invite His friends, seeing how weak we are and knowing that those who have to labor need such food to sustain them? Had He not already more than sufficiently paid for the sin of Adam? Has this most loving Lamb to pay once more whenever we relapse into sin? Permit it not, my Emperor; let Thy Majesty be appeased; look not upon our sins but upon our redemption by Thy

---

[14] *Lit.:* "making this corner." The reference is to St. Joseph's, Avila.

[15] The italicized lines which follow, and are in the nature of a digression, do not appear in V., and in E. they have been crossed out.

[16] Here follow two erased lines which are illegible but for the words "Thou didst honor the world". The exact sense of the following words ("We can… in secret") is affected by these illegible lines and must be considered uncertain.

[17] *Lit.:* "of those." P. Baez wrote in the margin "of the mansions" using the word which is thus translated in the titles of the seven main divisions of the *Interior Castle*. T. has: "of the houses."

Most Sacred Son, upon His merits and upon those of His glorious Mother and of all the saints and martyrs who have died for Thee.

Alas, Lord, who is it that has dared to make this petition in the name of all? What a poor mediator am I, my daughters, to gain a hearing for you and to present your petition! When this Sovereign Judge sees how bold I am it may well move Him to anger, as would be both right and just. But behold, Lord, Thou art a God of mercy; have mercy upon this poor sinner, this miserable worm who is so bold with Thee. Behold my desires, my God, and the tears with which I beg this of Thee; forget my deeds, for Thy name's sake, and have pity upon all these souls who are being lost, and help Thy Church. Do not permit more harm to be wrought to Christendom, Lord; give light to this darkness.

For the love of the Lord, my sisters, I beg you to commend this poor sinner[18] to His Majesty and to beseech Him to give her humility, as you are bound to do. I do not charge you to pray particularly for kings and prelates of the Church, especially for our Bishop, for I know that those of you now here are very careful about this and so I think it is needless for me to say more. Let those who are to come remember that, if they have a prelate who is holy, those under him will be holy too, and let them realize how important it is to bring him continually before the Lord. If your prayers and desires and disciplines and fasts are not performed for the intentions of which I have spoken, reflect [and believe] that you are not carrying out the work or fulfilling the object for which the Lord has brought you here.

CHAPTER 4

Exhorts the nuns to keep their Rule and names three things which are important for the spiritual life. Describes the first of these three things, which is love of one's neighbor, and speaks of the harm which can be done by individual friendships.

Now, daughters, you have looked at the great enterprise which we are trying to carry out. What kind of persons shall we have to be if we are not to be considered over-bold in the eyes of God and of the world? It is clear that we need to labor hard and it will be a great help to us if we have sublime thoughts so that we may strive to make our actions sublime also. If we endeavor to observe our Rule and Constitutions in the fullest sense, and with great care, I hope in the Lord that He will grant our requests. I am not asking anything new of you, my daughters – only that we should hold to our profession, which, as it is our vocation, we are bound to do, although there are many ways of holding to it.

Our Primitive Rules tells us to pray without ceasing. Provided we do this with all possible care (and it is the most important thing of all) we shall not fail to observe the fasts, disciplines and periods of silence which the Order commands; for, as you know, if prayer is to be genuine it must be reinforced with these things – prayer cannot be accompanied by self-indulgence.

It is about prayer that you have asked me to say something to you. As an acknowledgment of what I shall say, I beg you to read frequently and with a good will what I have said about it thus far, and to put this into practice. Before speaking of the interior life – that is, of prayer – I shall speak of certain things which those who attempt to walk along the way of prayer must of necessity practice. So necessary are these that, even though not greatly given to contemplation, people who have them can advance a long way in the Lord's service, while, unless they have them, they cannot possibly be great contemplatives, and, if they think they are, they are much mistaken. May the Lord help me in this task and teach me what I must say, so that it may be to His glory. Amen.

Do not suppose, my friends and sisters, that I am going to charge you to do a great many things; may it please the Lord that we do the things which our holy Fathers ordained and practiced and by doing which they merited that name. It would be wrong of us to look for any other way or to learn from anyone else. There are only three things which I will explain at some length and which are taken from our Constitution itself. It is essential that we should understand how very important they are to us in helping us to preserve that peace, both inward and outward, which the Lord so earnestly

---

[18] *Lit.*, "poor little one."

recommended to us. One of these is love for each other; the second, detachment from all created things; the third, true humility, which, although I put it last, is the most important of the three and embraces all the rest.

With regard to the first – namely, love for each other – this is of very great importance; for there is nothing, however annoying, that cannot easily be borne by those who love each other, and anything which causes annoyance must be quite exceptional. If this commandment were kept in the world, as it should be, I believe it would take us a long way towards the keeping of the rest; but, what with having too much love for each other or too little, we never manage to keep it perfectly. It may seem that for us to have too much love for each other cannot be wrong, but I do not think anyone who had not been an eye-witness of it would believe how much evil and how many imperfections can result from this. The devil sets many snares here which the consciences of those who aim only in a rough-and-ready way at pleasing God seldom observe – indeed, they think they are acting virtuously – but those who are aiming at perfection understand what they are very well: little by little they deprive the will of the strength which it needs if it is to employ itself wholly in the love of God.

This is even more applicable to women than to men and the harm which it does to community life is very serious. One result of it is that all the nuns do not love each other equally: some injury done to a friend is resented; a nun desires to have something to give to her friend or tries to make time for talking to her, and often her object in doing this is to tell her how fond she is of her, and other irrelevant things, rather than how much she loves God. These intimate friendships are seldom calculated[19] to make for the love of God; I am more inclined to believe that the devil initiates them so as to create factions within religious Orders. When a friendship has for its object the service of His Majesty, it at once becomes clear that the will is devoid of passion and indeed is helping to conquer other passions.

Where a convent is large I should like to see many friendships of that type; but in this house, where there are not, and can never be, more than thirteen nuns, all must be friends with each other, love each other, be fond of each other and help each other. For the love of the Lord, refrain from making individual friendships, however holy, for even among brothers and sisters such things are apt to be poisonous and I can see no advantage in them; when they are between other relatives,[20] they are much more dangerous and become a pest. Believe me, sisters, though I may seem to you extreme in this, great perfection and great peace come of doing what I say and many occasions of sin may be avoided by those who are not very strong. If our will becomes inclined more to one person than to another (this cannot be helped, because it is natural – it often leads us to love the person who has the most faults if she is the most richly endowed by nature), we must exercise a firm restraint on ourselves and not allow ourselves to be conquered by our affection. Let us love the virtues and inward goodness, and let us always apply ourselves and take care to avoid attaching importance to externals.

Let us not allow our will to be the slave of any, sisters, save of Him Who bought it with His blood. Otherwise, before we know where we are, we shall find ourselves trapped, and unable to move. God help me! The puerilities which result from this are innumerable. And, because they are so trivial that only those who see how bad they are will realize and believe it, there is no point in speaking of them here except to say that they are wrong in anyone, and, in a prioress, pestilential.

In checking these preferences we must be strictly on the alert from the moment that such a friendship begins and we must proceed diligently and lovingly rather than severely. One effective precaution against this is that the sisters should not be together except at the prescribed hours, and that they should follow our present custom in not talking with one another, or being alone together, as is laid down in the Rule: each one should be alone in her cell. There must be no workroom at Saint Joseph's; for, although it is a praiseworthy custom to have one, it is easier to keep silence if one is alone, and getting used to solitude is a great help to prayer. Since prayer must be the foundation on which this house is built, it is necessary for us to learn to like whatever gives us the greatest help in it.

---

[19] *Lit.*: "are seldom ordered in such a way as."

[20] "Other" is not in the Spanish. "When they are only between", is the reading of T., which also omits: "and become a pest."

Returning to the question of our love for one another, it seems quite unnecessary to commend this to you, for where are there people so brutish as not to love one another when they live together, are continually in one another's company, indulge in no conversation, association or recreation with any outside their house and believe that God loves us and that they themselves love God since they are leaving everything for His Majesty? More especially is this so as virtue always attracts love, and I hope in God that, with the help of His Majesty, there will always be love in the sisters of this house. It seems to me, therefore, that there is no reason for me to commend this to you any further.

With regard to the nature of this mutual love and what is meant by the virtuous love which I wish you to have here, and how we shall know when we have this virtue, which is a very great one, since Our Lord has so strongly commended it to us and so straightly enjoined it upon His Apostles – about all this I should like to say a little now as well as my lack of skill will allow me; if you find this explained in great detail in other books, take no notice of what I am saying here, for it may be that I do not understand what I am talking about.

There are two kinds of love which I am describing. The one is *purely* spiritual, and apparently has nothing to do with sensuality or the tenderness of our nature, either of which might stain its purity. The other is also spiritual, but mingled with it are our sensuality and weakness;[21] yet it is a worthy love, which, as between relatives and friends, seems lawful. Of this I have already said sufficient.

It is of the first kind of spiritual love that I would now speak. It is untainted by any sort of passion, for such a thing would completely spoil its harmony. If it leads us to treat virtuous people, especially confessors, with moderation and discretion, it is profitable; but, if the confessor is seen to be tending in any way towards vanity, he should be regarded with grave suspicion, and, in such a case, conversation with him, however edifying, should be avoided, and the sister should make her confession briefly and say nothing more. It would be best for her, indeed, to tell the superior that she does not get on with him and go elsewhere; this is the safest way, providing it can be done without injuring his reputation.[22]

In such cases, and in other difficulties with which the devil might ensnare us, so that we have no idea where to turn, the safest thing will be for the sister to try to speak with some learned person; if necessary, permission to do this can be given her, and she can make her confession to him and act in the matter as he directs her. For he cannot fail to give her some good advice about it, without which she might go very far astray. How often people stray through not taking advice, especially when there is a risk of doing someone harm! The course that must on no account be followed is to do nothing at all; for, when the devil begins to make trouble in this way, he will do a great deal of harm if he is not stopped quickly; the plan I have suggested, then, of trying to consult another confessor is the safest one if it is practicable, and I hope in the Lord that it will be so.

Reflect upon the great importance of this, for it is a dangerous matter, and can be a veritable hell, and a source of harm to everyone. I advise you not to wait until a great deal of harm has been done but to take every possible step that you can think of and stop the trouble at the outset; this you may do with a good conscience. But I hope in the Lord that He will not allow persons who are to spend their lives in prayer to have any attachment save to one who is a great servant of God; and I am quite certain He will not, unless they have no love for prayer and for striving after perfection in the way we try to do here. For, unless they see that he understands their language and likes to speak to them of God, they cannot possibly love him, as he is not like them. If he is such a person, he will have very few opportunities of doing any harm, and, unless he is very simple, he will not seek to disturb his own peace of mind and that of the servants of God.

As I have begun to speak about this, I will repeat that the devil can do a great deal of harm here, which will long remain undiscovered, and thus the soul that is striving after perfection can be gradually ruined without knowing how. For, if a confessor gives occasion for vanity through being vain himself, he will be very tolerant with it in [the consciences of] others. May God, for His Majesty's own sake, deliver us from things of this kind. It would be enough to unsettle all the nuns if their consciences and their confessor should give them exactly opposite advice, and, if it is insisted that they must have one confessor only, they will not know what to do, nor how to pacify their

---

[21] Here begins the passage reproduced in the Appendix to Chapter 4, below.
[22] *Honra.*

minds, since the very person who should be calming them and helping them is the source of the harm. In some places there must be a great deal of trouble of this kind: I always feel very sorry about it and so you must not be surprised if I attach great importance to your understanding this danger.

APPENDIX TO CHAPTER 4

The following variant reading of the Escorial Manuscript seems too important to be relegated to a footnote. It occurs the twelfth paragraph of ch. 4 (cf. n. 24), and deals, as will be seen, with the qualifications and character of the confessor. Many editors substitute it in their text for the corresponding passage in V. As will be seen, however, it is not a pure addition; we therefore reproduce it separately.

The important thing is that these two kinds of mutual love should be untainted by any sort of passion, for such a thing would completely spoil this harmony. If we exercise this love, of which I have spoken, with moderation and discretion, it is wholly meritorious, because what seems to us sensuality is turned into virtue. But the two may be so closely intertwined with one another that it is sometimes impossible to distinguish them, especially where a confessor is concerned. For if persons who are practicing prayer find that their confessor is a holy man and understands the way they behave, they become greatly attached to him. And then forthwith the devil lets loose upon them a whole battery of scruples which produce a terrible disturbance within the soul, this being what he is aiming at. In particular, if the confessor is guiding such persons to greater perfection, they become so depressed that they will go so far as to leave him for another and yet another, only to be tormented by the same temptation every time.

What you can do here is not to let your minds dwell upon whether you like your confessor or not, but just to like him if you feel so inclined. For, if we grow fond of people who are kind to our bodies, why should we not love those who are always striving and toiling to help our souls? Actually, if my confessor is a holy and spiritual man and I see that he is taking great pains for the benefit of my soul, I think it will be a real help to my progress for me to like him. For so weak are we that such affection sometimes helps us a great deal to undertake very great things in God's service.

But, if your confessor is not such a person as I have described, there is a possibility of danger, and for him to know that you like him may do the greatest harm, most of all in houses where the nuns are very strictly enclosed. And as it is a difficult thing to get to know which confessors are good, great care and caution are necessary. The best advice to give would be that you should see he has no idea of your affection for him and is not told about it. But the devil is so active that this is not practicable: you feel as if this is the only thing you have to confess and imagine you are obliged to confess it. For this reason I should like you to think that your affection for him is of no importance and to take no more notice of it.

Follow this advice if you find that everything your confessor says to you profits your soul; if you neither see nor hear him indulge in any vanity (and such things are always noticed except by one who is willfully dull) and if you know him to be a God-fearing man, do not be distressed over any temptation about being too fond of him, and the devil will then grow tired and stop tempting you. But if you notice that the confessor is tending in any way towards vanity in what he says to you, you should regard him with grave suspicion; in such a case conversation with him, even about prayer and about God, should be avoided – the sister should make her confession briefly and say nothing more. It would be best for her to tell the Mother (Superior) that she does not get on with him and go elsewhere. This is the safest way if it is practicable, and I hope in God that it will be, and that you will do all you possibly can to have no relations with him, though this may be very painful for you.

Reflect upon the great importance of this, etc. (pp. 58-9).

CHAPTER 5

Continues speaking of confessors. Explains why it is important that they should be learned men.

May the Lord grant, for His Majesty's own sake, that no one in this house shall experience the trials that have been described, or find herself oppressed in this way in soul and body. I hope the superior will never be so intimate with the confessor that no one will dare to say anything about him to her or about her to him. For this will tempt *unfortunate* penitents to leave very grave sins unconfessed because they will feel uncomfortable about confessing them. God help me! What trouble the devil can make here and how dearly people have to pay for their *miserable* worries and concern about honor! If they consult only one confessor, they think they are acting in the interests of their Order and for the *greater* honor of their convent: and that is the way the devil lays his snares for souls when he can find no other. If the *poor* sisters ask for another confessor, they are told that this would mean the *complete* end of all discipline in the convent; and, if he is not a priest of their Order, even though he be a saint, they are led to believe that they would be disgracing their entire Order by consulting him.

Give great praise to God, Daughters, for this liberty that you have, for, though there are not a great many priests whom you can consult, there are a few, other than your ordinary confessors, who can give you light upon everything. I beg every superior,[23] for the love of the Lord, to allow a holy liberty here: let the Bishop or Provincial be approached for leave for the sisters to go from time to time beyond their ordinary confessors and talk about their souls with persons of learning, especially if the confessors, though good men, have no learning; for learning is a great help in giving light upon everything. It should be possible to find a number of people who combine both learning and spirituality, and the more favors the Lord grants you in prayer, the more needful is it that your good works and your prayers should have a sure foundation.

You already know that the first stone of this foundation must be a good conscience and that you must make every effort to free yourselves from even venial sins and follow the greatest possible perfection. You might suppose that any confessor would know this, but you would be wrong: it happened that I had to go about matters of consciences to a man who had taken a complete course in theology; and he did me a great deal of mischief by telling me that certain things were of no importance. I know that he had no intention of deceiving me, or any reason for doing so: it was simply that he knew no better. And in addition to this instance I have met with two or three similar ones.

Everything depends on our having true light to keep the law of God perfectly. This is a firm basis for prayer; but without this strong foundation the whole building will go awry. In making their confessions, then, the nuns must be free to discuss spiritual matters with such persons as I have described. I will even go farther and say that they should sometimes do as I have said even if their confessor has all these good qualities, for he may quite easily make mistakes and it is a pity that he should be the cause of their going astray. They must try, however, never to act in any way against obedience, for they will find ways of getting all the help they need: it is of great importance to them that they should, and so they must make every possible effort to do so.

All this that I have said has to do with the superior. Since there are no consolations but spiritual ones to be had here, I would beg her once again to see that the sisters get these consolations, for God leads [His handmaidens] by different ways and it is impossible that one confessor should be acquainted with them all. I assure you that, if your souls are as they ought to be, there is no lack of holy persons who will be glad to advise and console you, even though you are poor. For He Who sustains our bodies will awaken and encourage someone to give light to our souls, and thus this evil of which I am so much afraid will be remedied. For if the devil should tempt the confessor, with the result that he leads you astray on any point of doctrine he will go slowly and be more careful about all he is doing when he knows that the penitent is also consulting others.

If the devil is prevented from entering convents in this way, I hope in God that he will never get into this house at all; so, for love of the Lord, I beg whoever is Bishop to allow the sisters this

---

[23] *Lit.:* "I beg her who is in the position of a senior (*mayor*)." *Mayor* was the title given to the superior at the Incarnation, Avila, and many other convents in Spain, at that time.

liberty and not to withdraw it so long as the confessors are persons both of learning and of good lives, a fact which will soon come to be known in a little place like this.

In what I have said here, I am speaking from experience of things that I have seen and heard *in many convents* and gathered from conversation with learned and holy people who have considered what is most fitting for this house, so that it may advance in perfection. Among the perils which exist everywhere, for as long as life lasts, we shall find that this is the least. No vicar should be free to go in and out of the convent, and no confessor should have this freedom either. They are there to watch over the recollectedness and good living of the house and its progress in both interior and exterior matters, so that they may report to the superior whenever needful, but they are never to be superiors themselves. *As I say, excellent reasons have been found why, everything considered, this is the best course, and why, if any priest hears confessions frequently, it should be the chaplain; but, if the nuns think it necessary, they can make their confessions to such persons as have been described, provided the superior is informed of it, and the prioress is such that the Bishop can trust her discretion. As there are very few nuns here, this will not take up much time.*

This is our present practice; and it is not followed merely on my advice. Our present Bishop, Don Alvaro de Mendoza, under whose obedience we live (since for many reasons we have not been placed under the jurisdiction of the Order), is greatly attached to holiness and the religious life, and, besides being of most noble extraction, is a great servant of God. He is always very glad to help this house in every way, and to this very end he brought together persons of learning, spirituality and experience, and this decision was then come to. It will be only right that future superiors should conform to his opinion, since it has been decided on by such good men, and after so many prayers to the Lord that He would enlighten them in every possible way, which, so far as we can at present see, He has certainly done. May the Lord be pleased to promote the advancement of this to His greater glory. Amen.

CHAPTER 6

Returns to the subject of perfect love, already begun.

I have digressed a great deal but no one will blame me who understands the importance of what has been said. Let us now return to the love which it is good [and lawful] for us to feel. This I have described as purely spiritual; I am not sure if I know what I am talking about, but it seems to me that there is no need to speak much of it, since so few, I fear, possess it; let any one of you to whom the Lord has given it praise Him fervently, for she must be a person of the greatest perfection. It is about this that I now wish to write. Perhaps what I say may be of some profit, for if you look at a virtue you desire it and try to gain it, and so become attached to it.

God grant that I may be able to understand this, and even more that I may be able to describe it, for I am not sure that I know when love is spiritual and when there is sensuality mingled with it, or how to begin speaking about it. I am like one who hears a person speaking in the distance and, *though he can hear that he is speaking*, cannot distinguish what he is saying. It is just like that with me: sometimes I cannot understand what I am saying, yet the Lord is pleased to enable me to say it well. If at other times what I say is [ridiculous and] nonsensical, it is only natural for me to go completely astray.

Now it seems to me that, when God has brought someone to a clear knowledge of the world, and of its nature, and of the fact that another world (*or, let us say, another kingdom*) exists, and that there is a great difference between the one and the other, the one being eternal and the other only a dream; and of what it is to love the Creator and what to love the creature (this must be discovered by experience, for it is a very different matter from merely thinking about it and believing it); when one understands by sight and experience what can be gained by the one practice and lost by the other, and what the Creator is and what the creature, and many other things which the Lord teaches to those who are willing to devote themselves to being taught by Him in prayer, or whom His Majesty wishes to teach – then one loves very differently from those of us who have not advanced thus far.

It may be, sisters, that you think it irrelevant for me to treat of this, and you may say that you already know everything that I have said. God grant that this may be so, and that you may indeed know it in the only way which has any meaning, and that it may be graven upon your inmost being, *and that you may never for a moment depart from it,* for, if you know it, you will see that I am telling nothing but the truth when I say that he whom the Lord brings thus far possesses this love. Those whom God brings to this state are, *I think,* generous and royal souls; they are not content with loving anything so miserable as these bodies, however beautiful they be and however numerous the graces they possess. If the sight of the body gives them pleasure they praise the Creator, but as for dwelling upon it *for more than just a moment* – no! When I use that phrase "dwelling upon it", I refer to having love for such things. If they had such love, they would think they were loving something insubstantial and were conceiving fondness for a shadow, they would feel shame for themselves and would not have the effrontery to tell God that they love Him, without feeling great confusion.

You will answer me that such persons cannot love or repay the affection shown to them by others. Certainly they care little about having this affection. They may from time to time experience a natural and momentary pleasure at being loved; yet, as soon as they return to their normal condition, they realize that such pleasure is folly save when the persons concerned can benefit their souls, either by instruction or by prayer. Any other kind of affection wearies them, for they know it can bring them no profit and may well do them harm; none the less they are grateful for it and recompense it by commending those who love them to God. They take this affection as something for which those who love them lay the responsibility upon the Lord, from Whom, since they can see nothing lovable in themselves, they suppose the love comes, and think that others love them because God loves them; and so they leave His Majesty to recompense them for this and beg Him to do so, thus freeing themselves and feeling they have no more responsibility. When I ponder it carefully, I sometimes think this desire for affection is sheer blindness, except when, as I say, it relates to persons who can lead us to do good so that we may gain blessings in perfection.

It should be noted here that, when we desire anyone's affection, we always seek it because of some interest, profit or pleasure of our own. Those who are perfect, however, have trodden all these things beneath their feet – [and have despised] the blessings which may come to them in this world, and its pleasures and delights – in such a way that, even if they wanted to, so to say, they could not love anything outside God, or unless it had to do with God. What profit, then, can come to them from being loved themselves?

When this truth is put to them, they laugh at the distress which had been assailing them in the past as to whether their affection was being returned or no. Of course, however pure our affection may be, it is quite natural for us to wish it to be returned. But, when we come to evaluate the return of affection, we realize that it is insubstantial, like a thing of straw, as light as air and easily carried away by the wind. For, however dearly we have been loved, what is there that remains to us? Such persons, then, except for the advantage that the affection may bring to their souls (because they realize that our nature is such that we soon tire of life without love), care nothing whether they are loved or not. Do you think that such persons will love none and delight in none save God? No; they will love others much more than they did, with a more genuine love, with greater passion and with a love which brings more profit; that, in a word, is what love really is. And such souls are always much fonder of giving than of receiving, even in their relations with the Creator Himself. This [holy affection], I say, merits the name of love, which name has been usurped from it by those other base affections.

Do you ask, again, by what they are attracted if they do not love things they see? They do love what they see and they are greatly attracted by what they hear; but the things which they see are everlasting. If they love anyone they immediately look right beyond the body (*on which, as I say, they cannot dwell*), fix their eyes on the soul and see what there is to be loved in that. If there is nothing, but they see any suggestion or inclination which shows them that, if they dig deep, they will find gold within this mine, they think nothing of the labor of digging, since they have love. There is nothing that suggests itself to them which they will not willingly do for the good of that soul since they desire their love for it to be lasting, and they know quite well that that is impossible unless the loved one has certain good qualities and a great love for God. I really mean that it is impossible, however great their obligations and even if that soul were to die for love of them and do them all the kind actions in its power; even had it all the natural graces joined in one, their wills would not have strength enough to love it nor would they remain fixed upon it. They know and have learned and experienced the worth of all this; no false dice can deceive them. They see that they are not in unison with that soul and that their love for it cannot possibly last; for, unless that soul keeps the law of God, their love will end with life – they know that unless it loves Him they will go to different places.

Those into whose souls the Lord has already infused true wisdom do not esteem this love, which lasts only on earth, at more than its true worth – if, indeed, at so much. Those who like to take pleasure in worldly things, delights, honors and riches, will account it of some worth if their friend is rich and able to afford them pastime *and pleasure* and recreation; but those who already hate all this will care little or nothing for such things. If they have any love for such a person, then, it will be a passion that he may love God so as to be loved by Him; for, as I say, they know that no other kind of affection but this can last, and that this kind will cost them dear, for which reason they do all they possibly can for their friend's profit; they would lose a thousand lives to bring him a small blessing. Oh, precious love, forever imitating the Captain of Love, Jesus, our Good!

CHAPTER 7
Treats of the same subject of spiritual love and gives certain counsels for gaining it.

It is strange to see how impassioned this love is; how many tears, penances and prayers it costs; how careful is the loving soul to commend the object of its affection to all who it thinks may prevail with God and to ask them to intercede with Him for it; and how constant is its longing, so that it cannot be happy unless it sees that its loved one is making progress. If that soul seems to have advanced, and is then seen to fall some way back, her friend seems to have no more pleasure in life: she neither eats nor sleeps, is never free from this fear and is always afraid that the soul whom she loves so much may be lost, and that the two may be parted for ever. She cares nothing for physical death, but she will not suffer herself to be attached to something which a puff of wind may carry away so that she is unable to retain her hold upon it. This, as I have said, is love without any degree whatsoever of self-interest; all that this soul wishes and desires is to see the soul [it loves] enriched with blessings from Heaven. This is love, quite unlike our ill-starred earthly affections – to say nothing of illicit affections, from which may God keep us free.

These last affections are a very hell, and it is needless for us to weary ourselves by saying how evil they are, for the least of the evils which they bring are terrible beyond exaggeration. There is no need for us ever to take such things upon our lips, sisters, *or even to think of them*, or to remember that they exist anywhere in the world; you must never listen to anyone speaking of such affections, either in jest or in earnest, nor allow them to be mentioned or discussed in your presence. No good can come from our doing this and it might do us harm even to hear them mentioned. But with regard to the lawful affections which, as I have said, we may have for each other, or for relatives and friends, it is different. Our whole desire is that they should not die: if their heads ache, our souls seem to ache too; if we see them in distress, we are unable (as people say) to sit still under it;[24] and so on.

This is not so with spiritual affection. Although the weakness of our nature may at first allow us to feel something of all this, our reason soon begins to reflect whether our friend's trials are not good for her, and to wonder if they are making her richer in virtue and how she is bearing them, and then we shall ask God to give her patience so that they may win her merit. If we see that she is being patient, we feel no distress – indeed, we are gladdened and consoled. If all the merit and gain which suffering is capable of producing could be made over to her, we should still prefer suffering her trial ourselves to seeing her suffer it, but we are not worried or disquieted.

---

[24] *Lit.*: "There remains, as people say, no patience"; but, as the phrase "as people say" (which E. omits) suggests that this was a popular phrase, I have translated rather more freely and picturesquely. T. has (after "ache too"): "and it upsets us, and so on."

I repeat once more that this love is a similitude and copy of that which was borne for us by the good Lover, Jesus. It is for that reason that it brings us such immense benefits, for it makes us embrace every kind of suffering, so that others, without having to endure the suffering, may gain its advantages. The recipients of this friendship, then, profit greatly, but their friends should realize that either this intercourse – I mean, this exclusive friendship – must come to an end or that they must prevail upon Our Lord that their friend may walk in the same way as themselves, as Saint Monica prevailed with Him for Saint Augustine. Their heart does not allow them to practice duplicity: if they see their friend straying from the road, or committing any faults, they will speak to her about it; they cannot allow themselves to do anything else. And if after this the loved one does not amend, they will not flatter her or hide anything from her. Either, then, she will amend or their friendship will cease; for otherwise they would be unable to endure it, nor is it in fact endurable. It would mean continual war for both parties. A person may be indifferent to all other people in the world and not worry whether they are serving God or not, since the person she has to worry about is herself. But she cannot take this attitude with her friends: nothing they do can be hidden from her; she sees the smallest mote in them. This, I repeat, is a very heavy cross for her to bear.

Happy the souls that are loved by such as these! Happy the day on which they came to know them! O my Lord, wilt Thou not grant me the favor of giving me many who have such love for me? Truly, Lord, I would rather have this than be loved by all the kings and lords of the world – and rightly so, for such friends use every means in their power to make us lords of the whole world and to have all that is in it subject to us. When you make the acquaintance of any such persons, sisters, the Mother Prioress should employ every possible effort to keep you in touch with them. Love such persons as much as you like. There can be very few of them, but none the less it is the Lord's will that their goodness should be known. When one of you is striving after perfection, she will at once be told that she has no need to know such people – that it is enough for her to have God. But to get to know God's friends is a very good way of "having" Him; as I have discovered by experience, it is most helpful. For, under the Lord, I owe it to such persons that I am not in hell; I was always very fond of asking them to commend me to God, and so I prevailed upon them to do so.

Let us now return to what we were saying. It is this kind of love which I should like us to have; at first it may not be perfect but the Lord will make it increasingly so. Let us begin with the methods of obtaining it. At first it may be mingled with emotion,[25] but this, as a rule, will do no harm. It is sometimes good and necessary for us to show emotion in our love, and also to feel it, and to be distressed by some of our sisters, trials and weaknesses, however trivial they may be. For on one occasion as much distress may be caused by quite a small matter as would be caused on another by some great trial, and there are people whose nature it is to be very much cast down by small things. If you are not like this, do not neglect to have compassion on others; it may be that Our Lord wishes to spare us these sufferings and will give us sufferings of another kind which will seem heavy to us, though to the person already mentioned they may seem light. In these matters, then, we must not judge others by ourselves, nor think of ourselves as we have been at some time when, perhaps without any effort on our part, the Lord has made us stronger than they; let us think of what we were like at the times when we have been weakest.

Note the importance of this advice for those of us who would learn to sympathize with our neighbors' trials, however trivial these may be. It is especially important for such souls as have been described, for, desiring trials as they do, they make light of them all. They must therefore try hard to recall what they were like when they were weak, and reflect that, if they are no longer so, it is not due to themselves. For otherwise, little by little, the devil could easily cool our charity toward our neighbors and make us think that what is really a failing on our part is perfection. In every respect we must be careful and alert, for the devil never slumbers. And the nearer we are to perfection, the more careful we must be, since his temptations are then much more cunning because there are no others that he dare send us; and if, as I say, we are not cautious, the harm is done before we realize it. In short, we must always watch and pray, for there is no better way than prayer of revealing these hidden wiles of the devil and making him declare his presence.

---

25 *Ternura. Lit.*: "tenderness."

Contrive always, even if you do not care for it, to take part in your sisters' necessary recreation and to do so for the whole of the allotted time, for all considerate treatment of them is a part of perfect love. It is a very good thing for us to take compassion on each others' needs. See that you show no lack of discretion about things which are contrary to obedience. Though privately you may think the prioress' orders harsh ones, do not allow this to be noticed or tell anyone about it (except that you may speak of it, with all humility, to the prioress herself), for if you did so you would be doing a great deal of harm. Get to know what are the things in your sisters which you should be sorry to see and those about which you should sympathize with them; and always show your grief at any notorious fault which you may see in one of them. It is a good proof and test of our love if we can bear with such faults and not be shocked by them. Others, in their turn, will bear with your faults, which, if you include those of which you are not aware, must be much more numerous. Often commend to God any sister who is at fault and strive for your own part to practice the virtue which is the opposite of her fault with great perfection. Make determined efforts to do this so that you may teach your sister by your deeds what perhaps she could never learn by words nor gain by punishment.

The habit of performing some conspicuously virtuous action through seeing it performed by another is one which very easily takes root. This is good advice: do not forget it. Oh, how true and genuine will be the love of a sister who can bring profit to everyone by sacrificing her own profit to that of the rest! She will make a great advance in each of the virtues and keep her Rule with great perfection. This will be a much truer kind of friendship than one which uses every possible loving expression (such as are not used, and must not be used, in this house): "My life!" "My love!" "My darling!"[26] and suchlike things, one or another of which people are always saying. Let such endearing words be kept for your Spouse, for you will be so often and so much alone With Him that you will want to make use of them all, and this His Majesty permits you. If you use them among yourselves they will not move the Lord so much; and, quite apart from that, there is no reason why you should do so. They are very effeminate; and I should not like you to be that, or even to appear to be that, in any way, my daughters; I want you to be strong men. If you do all that is in you, the Lord will make you so manly that men themselves will be amazed at you. And how easy is this for His Majesty, Who made us out of nothing at all!

It is also a very clear sign of love to try to spare others household work by taking it upon oneself and also to rejoice and give great praise to the Lord if you see any increase in their virtues. All such things, quite apart from the intrinsic good they bring, add greatly to the peace and concord which we have among ourselves, as, through the goodness of God, We can now see by experience. May His Majesty be pleased ever to increase it, for it would be terrible if it did not exist, and very awkward if, when there are so few of us, we got on badly together. May God forbid that.

If one of you should be cross with another because of some hasty word, the matter must at once be put right and you must betake yourselves to earnest prayer. The same applies to the harboring of any grudge, or to party strife, or to the desire to be greatest, or to any nice point concerning your honor. (My blood seems to run cold, as I write this, at the very idea that this can ever happen, but I know it is the chief trouble in convents.) If it should happen to you, consider yourselves lost. Just reflect and realize that you have driven your Spouse from His home: He will have to go and seek another abode, since you are driving Him from His own house. Cry aloud to His Majesty and try to put things right; and if frequent confessions and communions do not mend them, you may well fear that there is some Judas among you.

For the love of God, let the prioress be most careful not to allow this to occur. She must put a stop to it from the very outset, *and, if love will not suffice, she must use heavy punishments*, for here we have the whole of the mischief and the remedy. If you gather that any of the nuns is making trouble, see that she is sent to some other convent and God will provide them with a dowry for her. Drive away this plague; cut off the branches as well as you can; and, if that is not sufficient, pull up the roots. If you cannot do this, shut up anyone who is guilty of such things and forbid her to leave her cell; far better this than that all the nuns should catch so incurable a plague. Oh, what a great evil is this! God deliver us from a convent into which it enters: I would rather our convent caught fire and we were all burned alive. As this is so important I think I shall say a little more about it

---

26 *Lit.*: "My life!" "My soul!" "My good!"

elsewhere, so I will not write at greater length here, *except to say that, provided they treat each other equally, I would rather that the nuns showed a tender and affectionate love and regard for each other, even though there is less perfection in this than in the love I have described, than that there were a single note of discord to be heard among them. May the Lord forbid this, for His own sake. Amen.*

CHAPTER 8

Treats of the great benefit of self-detachment, both interior and exterior, from all things created.

Let us now come to the detachment which we must practice, for if this is carried out perfectly it includes everything else. I say "it includes everything else" because, if we care nothing for any created things, but embrace the Creator alone, His Majesty will infuse the virtues into us in such a way that, provided we labor to the best of our abilities day by day, we shall not have to wage war much longer, for the Lord will take our defense in hand against the devils and against the whole world. Do you suppose, daughters, that it is a small benefit to obtain for ourselves this blessing of giving ourselves wholly to Him,[27] and keeping nothing for ourselves? Since, as I say, all blessings are in Him, let us give Him hearty praise, sisters, for having brought us together here, where we are occupied in this alone. I do not know why I am saying this, when all of you here are capable of teaching me, for I confess that, in this important respect, I am not as perfect as I should like to be and as I know I ought to be; and I must say the same about all the virtues and about all that I am dealing with here, for it is easier to write of such things than to practice them. I may not even be able to write of them effectively, for sometimes ability to do this comes only from experience – [that is to say, if I have any success, it must be because] I explain the nature of these virtues by describing the contraries of the qualities I myself possess.

As far as exterior matters are concerned, you know how completely cut off we are from everything. *Oh, my Creator and Lord! When have I merited so great an honor? Thou seemest to have searched everywhere for means of drawing nearer to us. May it please Thy goodness that we lose not this through our own fault.* Oh, sisters, for the love of God, try to realize what a great favor the Lord has bestowed on those of us whom He has brought here. Let each of you apply this to herself, since there are only twelve of us[28] and His Majesty has been pleased for you to be one. How many people – *what a multitude of people!* – do I know who are better than myself and would gladly take this place of mine, yet the Lord has granted it to me who so ill deserve it! Blessed be Thou, my God, and let *the angels and* all created things praise Thee, for I can no more repay this favor than all the others Thou hast shown me. It was a wonderful thing to give me the vocation to be a nun; but I have been so wicked, Lord, that Thou couldst not trust me. In a place where there were many good women living together my wickedness would not *perhaps* have been noticed right down to the end of my life: *I should have concealed it, as I did for so many years.* So Thou didst bring me here, where, as there are so few of us that it would seem impossible for it to remain unnoticed, Thou dost remove occasions of sin from me so that I may walk the more carefully. There is no excuse for me, then, O Lord, I confess it, and so I have need of Thy mercy, that Thou mayest pardon me.

Remember, my sisters, that if we are not good we are much more to blame than others. What I earnestly beg of you is that anyone who knows she will be unable to follow our customs will say so [before she is professed]: there are other convents in which the Lord is also well served and she should not remain here and disturb these few of us whom His Majesty has brought together *for His service.* In other convents nuns are free to have the pleasure of seeing their relatives, whereas here, if relatives are ever admitted, it is only for their own pleasure. A nun who [very much] wishes to see her relatives in order to please herself, *and does not get tired of them after the second visit,* must, unless they are spiritual persons *and do her soul some good,* consider herself imperfect and realize

---

[27] *Lit.: de darnos todas a f l todo:* "giving ourselves wholly to Him wholly."
[28] The thirteenth was St. Teresa.

that she is neither detached nor healthy, and will have no freedom of spirit or perfect peace. She needs a physician – and I consider that if this desire does not leave her, and she is not cured, she is not intended for this house.

The best remedy, I think, is that she should not see her relatives again until she feels free in spirit and has obtained this freedom from God by many prayers. When she looks upon such visits as crosses, let her receive them by all means, for then they will do the visitors good and herself no harm. *But if she is fond of the visitors, if their troubles are a great distress to her and if she delights in listening to the stories which they tell her about the world, she may be sure that she will do herself harm and do them no good.*

CHAPTER 9
Treats of the great blessing that shunning their relatives brings to those who have left the world and shows how by doing so they will find truer friends.

Oh, if we religious understood what harm we get from having so much to do with our relatives, how we should shun them! do not see what pleasure they can give us, or how, quite apart from *the harm they do us as touching* our obligations to God, they can bring us any peace or tranquility. For we cannot take part in their recreations, as it is not lawful for us to do so; and, though we can certainly share their troubles, we can never help weeping for them, sometimes more than they do themselves. If they bring us any bodily comforts, there is no doubt that our spiritual life *and our poor souls* will pay for it. From this you are [quite] free here; for, as you have everything in common and none of you may accept any private gift, all the alms given us being held by the community, you are under no obligation to entertain your relatives in return for what they give you, since, as you know, the Lord will provide for us all in common.

I am astounded at the harm which intercourse with our relatives does us: I do not think anyone who had not experience of it would believe it. And how our religious Orders nowadays, *or most of them, at any rate*, seem to be forgetting about perfection, *though all, or most, of the saints wrote about it!* I do not know how much of the world we really leave when we say that we are leaving everything for God's sake, if we do not withdraw ourselves from the chief thing of all – namely, our kinsfolk. The matter has reached such a pitch that some people think, when religious are not fond of their relatives and do not see much of them, it shows a want of virtue in them. And they not only assert this but allege reasons for it.

In this house, daughters, we must be most careful to commend our relatives to God, for that is only right. For the rest, we must keep them out of our minds as much as we can, as it is natural that our desires should be attached to them more than to other people. My own relatives were very fond of me, or so they used to say, and I was so fond of them that I would not let them forget me. But I have learned, by my own experience and by that of others, that it is God's servants who have helped me in trouble; my relatives, apart from my parents, have helped me very little. Parents are different, for they very rarely fail to help their children, and it is right that when they need our comfort we should not refuse it them: if we find our main purpose is not harmed by our so doing we can give it them and yet be completely detached; and this also applies to brothers and sisters.

Believe me, sisters, if you serve God as you should, you will find no better relatives than those [of His servants] whom His Majesty sends you. I know this is so, and, if you keep on as you are doing *here*, and realize that by doing otherwise you will be failing your true Friend and Spouse, you may be sure that you will very soon gain this freedom. Then you will be able to trust those who love you for His sake alone more than all your relatives, and they will not fail you, so that you will find parents and brothers and sisters where you had never expected to find them. For these help us and look for their reward only from God; those who look for rewards from us soon grow tired of helping us when they see that we are poor and can do nothing for them. This cannot be taken as a generalization, but it is the most usual thing to happen in the world, for it is the world all over! If anyone tells you otherwise, and says it is a virtue to do such things, do not believe him. I should have to write at great length, *in view of my lack of skill and my imperfection*, if I were to tell you of all the harm that comes from it; as others have written about it who know what they are talking about better than I, what I have said will suffice. If, imperfect as I am, I have been able to grasp as much as this, how much better will those who are perfect do so!

All the advice which the saints give us about fleeing from the world is, of course, good. Believe me, then, attachment to our relatives is, as I have said, the thing which sticks to us most closely and is hardest to get rid of. People are right, therefore, when they flee from their own part of the country[29] – if it helps them, I mean, for I do not think we are helped so much by fleeing from any place in a physical sense as by resolutely embracing the good Jesus, Our Lord, with the soul. Just as we find everything in Him, so for His sake we forget everything. Still, it is a great help, until we have learned this truth, to keep apart from our kinsfolk; later on, it may be that the Lord will wish us to see them again, so that what used to give us pleasure may be a cross to us.

CHAPTER 10

Teaches that detachment from the things aforementioned is insufficient if we are not detached from our own selves and that this virtue and humility go together.

Once we have detached ourselves from the world, and from our kinsfolk, and are cloistered here, in the conditions already described, it must look as if we have done everything and there is nothing left with which we have to contend. But, oh, my sisters, do not feel secure and fall asleep, or you will be like a man who goes to bed quite peacefully, after bolting all his doors for fear of thieves, when the thieves are already in the house. And you know there is no worse thief *than one who lives in the house.* We ourselves are always the same;[30] unless we take great care and each of us looks well to it that she renounces her self-will, which is the most important business of all, there will be many things to deprive us of the holy freedom of spirit *which our souls* seek in order to soar to their Maker unburdened by the leaden weight of the earth.

It will be a great help towards this if we keep constantly in our thoughts the vanity of all things and the rapidity with which they pass away, so that we may withdraw our affections from things which are so trivial and fix them upon what will never come to an end. This may seem a poor kind of help but it will have the effect of greatly fortifying the soul. With regard to small things, we must be very careful, as soon as we begin to grow fond of them, to withdraw our thoughts from them and turn them to God. His Majesty will help us to do this. He has granted us the great favor of providing that, in this house, most of it is done already; *but it remains for us to become detached from our own selves* and it is a hard thing to withdraw from ourselves and oppose ourselves, because we are very close to ourselves and love ourselves very dearly.

It is here that true humility can enter,[31] for this virtue and that of detachment from self, I think, always go together. They are two sisters, who are inseparable. These are not the kinsfolk whom I counsel you to avoid: no, you must embrace them, and love them, and never be seen without them. Oh, how sovereign are these virtues, mistresses of all created things, empresses of the world, our deliverers from all the snares and entanglements laid by the devil so dearly loved by our Teacher, Christ, Who was never for a moment without them! He that possesses them can safely go out and fight all the united forces of hell and the whole world and its temptations. Let him fear none, for his is the kingdom of the Heavens. There is none whom he need fear, for he cares nothing if he loses everything, nor does he count this as loss: his sole fear is that he may displease his God and he begs Him to nourish these virtues within him lest he lose them through any fault of his own.

These virtues, it is true, have the property of hiding themselves from one who possesses them, in such a way that he never sees them nor can believe that he has any of them, even if he be told so. But he esteems them so much that he is for ever trying to obtain them, and thus he perfects them in himself more and more. And those who possess them soon make the fact clear, even against their

---

[29] *De sus tierras.* The phrase will also bear the interpretation: "from their own countries."

[30] The sense of this passage, especially without the phrase from E. which V. omits, is not very clear. T. remodels thus: "You know there is no worse thief for the perfection of the soul than the love of ourselves, for unless etc."

[31] Here, in the margin, is written: "Humility and mortification, very great virtues."

will, to any with whom they have intercourse. But how inappropriate it is for a person like myself to begin to praise humility and mortification, when these virtues are so highly praised by the King of Glory – a praise exemplified in all the trials He suffered. It is to possess these virtues, then, my daughters, that you must labor if you would leave the land of Egypt, for, when you have obtained them, you will also obtain the manna; all things will taste well to you; and, however much the world may dislike their savor, to you they will be sweet.

The first thing, then, that we have to do, *and that at once*, is to rid ourselves of love for this body of ours – and some of us pamper our natures so much that this will cause us no little labor, *while others* are so concerned about their health that the trouble these things give us (this is especially so of *poor* nuns, but it applies to others as well) is amazing. Some of us, however, seem to think that we embraced the religious life for no other reason than to keep ourselves alive[32] and each nun does all she can to that end. In this house, as a matter of fact, there is very little chance for us to act on such a principle, but I should be sorry if we even wanted to. Resolve, sisters, that it is to die for Christ, and not to practice self-indulgence for Christ, that you have come here. The devil tells us that self-indulgence is necessary if we are to carry out and keep the Rule of our Order, and so many of us, forsooth, try to keep our Rule by looking after our health that we die without having kept it for as long as a month – perhaps even for a day. I really do not know what we are coming to.

No one need be afraid of our committing excesses here, by any chance – for as soon as we do any penances our confessors begin to fear that we shall kill ourselves with them. We are so horrified at our own possible excesses – if only we were as conscientious about everything else! Those who tend to the opposite extreme will I know, not mind my saying this, nor shall I mind if they say I am judging others by myself, for they will be quite right. *I believe – indeed, I am sure – that more nuns are of my way of thinking than are offended by me because they do just the opposite.* My own belief is that it is for this reason that the Lord is pleased to make us such weakly creatures; at least He has shown me great mercy in making me so; for, as I was sure to be self-indulgent in any case, He was pleased to provide me with an excuse for this. It is really amusing to see how some people torture themselves about it, when the real reason lies in themselves; sometimes they get a desire to do penances, as one might say, without rhyme or reason; they go on doing them for a couple of days; and then the devil puts it into their heads that they have been doing themselves harm and so he makes them afraid of penances, after which they dare not do even those that the Order requires – they have tried them once! They do not keep the smallest points in the Rule, such as silence, which is quite incapable of harming us. Hardly have we begun to imagine that our heads are aching than we stay away from choir, though that would not kill us either. *One day we are absent because we had a headache some time ago; another day, because our head has just been aching again; and on the next three days in case it should ache once more.* Then we want to invent penances of our own, with the result that we do neither the one thing nor the other. Sometimes there is very little the matter with us, yet we think that it should dispense us from all our obligations and that if we ask to be excused from them we are doing all we need.

But why, you will say, does the Prioress excuse us? Perhaps she would not if she knew what was going on inside us; but *she sees one of you wailing about a mere nothing as if your heart were breaking, and you come and ask her to excuse you from keeping the whole of your Rule, saying it is a matter of great necessity, and, when there is any substance in what you say*, there is always a physician at hand to confirm it or some friend or relative weeping at your side. *Sometimes the poor Prioress sees that your request is excessive, but* what can she do? She feels a scruple if she thinks she has been lacking in charity and she would rather the fault were yours than hers: *she thinks, too, that it would be unjust of her to judge you harshly.*

Oh, God help me! That there should be complaining like this among nuns! May He forgive me for saying so, but I am afraid it has become quite a habit. I happened to observe this incident once myself: a nun began complaining about her headaches and she went on complaining to me for a long time. In the end I made enquiries and found she had no headache whatever, but was suffering from some pain or other elsewhere.

---

[32] *Lit.*: "to contrive not to die." But the reading of E. ("to think that we came to the convent for no other reason than to serve our bodies and look after them") suggests that this is what is meant.

These are things which may sometimes happen and I put them down here so that you may guard against them; for if once the devil begins to frighten us about losing our health, we shall never get anywhere. The Lord give us light so that we may act rightly in everything! Amen.

CHAPTER 11

Continues to treat of mortification and describes how it may be attained in times of sickness.

These continual moanings which we make about trifling ailments, my sisters, seem to me a sign of imperfection: if you can bear a thing, say nothing about it. When the ailment is serious, it proclaims itself; that is quite another kind of moaning, which draws attention to itself immediately. Remember, there are only a few of you, and if one of you gets into this habit she will worry all the rest – that is, assuming you love each other and there is charity among you. On the other hand, if one of you is really ill, she should say so and take the necessary remedies; and, if you have got rid of your self-love, you will so much regret having to indulge yourselves in any way that there will be no fear of your doing so unnecessarily or of your making a moan without proper cause. When such a reason exists, it would be much worse to say nothing about it than to allow yourselves unnecessary indulgence, and it would be very wrong if everybody were not sorry for you.

However, I am quite sure that where there is *prayer and* charity among you, and your numbers are so small *that you will be aware of each other's needs*, there will never be any lack of care in your being looked after. Do not think of complaining about the weaknesses and minor ailments from which women suffer, for the devil sometimes makes you imagine them. They come and go; and unless you get rid of the habit of talking about them and complaining of everything (except to God) you will never come to the end of them. *I lay great stress on this, for I believe myself it is important, and it is one of the reasons for the relaxation of discipline in religious houses.* For this body of ours has one fault: the more you indulge it, the more things it discovers to be essential to it. It is extraordinary how it likes being indulged; and, if there is any reasonable pretext for indulgence, however little necessity for it there may be, the poor soul is taken in and prevented from making progress. Think how many poor people there must be who are ill and have no one to complain to, for poverty and self-indulgence make bad company. Think, too, how many married women – people of position, as I know – have serious complaints and sore trials and yet dare not complain to their husbands about them for fear of annoying them. Sinner that I am! Surely we have not come here to indulge ourselves more than they! Oh, how free you are from the great trials of the world! Learn to suffer a little for the love of God without telling everyone about it. When a woman has made an unhappy marriage she does not talk about it or complain of it, lest it should come to her husband's knowledge, she has to endure a great deal of misery and yet has no one to whom she may relieve her mind. Cannot we, then, keep secret between God and ourselves some of the ailments which He sends us because of our sins? The more so since talking about them does nothing whatever to alleviate them.

In nothing that I have said am I referring to serious illnesses, accompanied by high fever, though as to these, too, I beg you to observe moderation and to have patience: I am thinking rather of those minor indispositions which you may have and still keep going[33] *without worrying everybody else to death over them.* What would happen if these lines should be seen outside this house? What would all the nuns say of me! And how willingly would I bear what they said if it helped anyone to live a better life! For when there is one person of this kind, the thing generally comes to such a pass that *some suffer on account of others, and* nobody who says she is ill will be believed, however serious her ailment. *As this book is meant only for my daughters, they will put up with everything I say.* Let us remember our holy Fathers of past days, the hermits whose lives we attempt to imitate. What sufferings they bore, what solitude, cold, [thirst] and hunger, what burning sun and heat! And yet they had no one to complain to except God. Do you suppose they were made of iron? No: they were as frail as we are. Believe me, daughters, once we begin to subdue

---

[33] *Lit.*: "which can be suffered on foot."

these miserable bodies of ours, they give us much less trouble. There will be quite sufficient people to see to what you really need,[34] so take no thought for yourselves except when you know it to be necessary. Unless we resolve to put up with death and ill-health once and for all, we shall never accomplish anything.

Try not to fear these and commit yourselves wholly to God, come what may. What does it matter if we die? How many times have our bodies not mocked us? Should we not occasionally mock them in our turn? And, believe me, *slight as it may seem by comparison with other things*, this resolution is much more important than we may think; for, if we continually make it, day by day, by the grace of the Lord, we shall gain dominion over the body. To conquer such an enemy is a great achievement in the battle of life. May the Lord grant, as He is able, that we may do this. I am quite sure that no one who does not enjoy such a victory, which I believe is a great one, will understand what advantage it brings, and no one will regret having gone through trials in order to attain this tranquility and self-mastery.

CHAPTER 12

Teaches that the true lover of God must care little for life and honor.

We now come to some other *little* things which are also of very great importance, though they will appear trifling. All this seems a great task, and so it is, for it means warring against ourselves. But once we begin to work, God, too, works in our souls and bestows such favors on them that the most we can do in this life seems to us very little. And we nuns are doing everything we can, by giving up our freedom for the love of God and entrusting it to another, and in putting up with so many trials – fasts, silence, enclosure, service in choir – that however much we may want to indulge ourselves we can do so only occasionally: perhaps, in all the convents I have seen, I am the only nun guilty of self-indulgence. Why, then, do we shrink from interior mortification, since this is the means by which every other kind of mortification may become much more meritorious and perfect, so that it can then be practiced with greater tranquility and ease? This, as I have said, is acquired by gradual progress and by never indulging our own will and desire, even in small things, until we have succeeded in subduing the body to the spirit.

I repeat that this consists mainly or entirely in our ceasing to care about ourselves and our own pleasures, for the least that anyone who is beginning to serve the Lord truly can offer Him is his life. Once he has surrendered his will to Him, what has he to fear? It is evident that if he is a true religious and a real man of prayer and aspires to the enjoyment of Divine consolations, he must not [turn back or] shrink from desiring to die and suffer martyrdom for His sake. And do you not know, sisters, that the life of a good religious, who wishes to be among the closest friends of God, is one long martyrdom? I say "long", for, by comparison with decapitation, which is over very quickly, it may well be termed so, though life itself is short and some lives are short in the extreme. How do we know but that ours will be so short that it may end only one hour or one moment after the time of our resolving to render our entire service to God? This would be quite possible; and so we must not set store by anything that comes to an end, *least of all by life, since not a day of it is secure*. Who, if he thought that each hour might be his last, would not spend it in labor?

Believe me, it is safest to think that this is so; by so doing we shall learn to subdue our wills in everything; for if, as I have said, you are very careful *about your prayer*, you will soon find yourselves gradually reaching the summit of the mountain without knowing how. But how harsh it sounds to say that we must take pleasure in nothing, unless we also say what consolations and delights this renunciation brings in its train, and what a great gain it is, even in this life! What security it gives us! Here, as you all practice this, you have done the principal part; each of you encourages[35] and helps the rest; and each of you must try to outstrip her sisters.

---

[34] *Lit.*: "to look at (or to) what is needful" – the phrase is ambiguous and might mean: "to worry about their own needs." The word translated "people" is feminine.

[35] *Lit.*: "awakens."

Be very careful about your interior thoughts, especially if they have to do with precedence. May God, by His Passion, keep us from expressing, or dwelling upon, such thoughts as these: "But I am her senior [in the Order]"; "But I am older"; "But I have worked harder"; "But that other sister is being better treated than I am". If these thoughts come, you must quickly check them; if you allow yourselves to dwell on them, or introduce them into your conversation, they will spread like the plague and *in religious houses* they may give rise to great abuses. *Remember, I know a great deal about this.* If you have a prioress who allows such things, however trifling, you must believe that God has permitted her to be given to you because of your sins and that she will be the beginning of your ruin. *Cry to Him, and let your whole prayer be that He may come to your aid by sending you either a religious or a person given to prayer; for, if anyone prays with the resolve to enjoy the favors and consolations which God bestows in prayer, it is always well that he should have this detachment.*

You may ask why I lay such stress on this, and think that I am being too severe about it, and say that God grants consolations to persons less completely detached than that. I quite believe He does; for, in His infinite wisdom, He sees that this will enable Him to lead them to leave everything for His sake. I do not mean, by "leaving" everything, entering the religious life, for there may be obstacles to this, and the soul that is perfect can be detached and humble anywhere. It will find detachment harder in the world, however, for worldly trappings will be a great impediment to it. Still, believe me in this: questions of honor and *desires for* property can arise within convents as well as outside them, and the more temptations of this kind are removed from us, the more we are to blame if we yield to them. Though persons who do so may have spent years in prayer, or rather in meditation (for perfect prayer eventually destroys [all] these attachments), they will never make great progress or come to enjoy the real fruit of prayer.

Ask yourselves, sisters, if these things, *which seem so insignificant*, mean anything to you, for the only reason you are here is that you may detach yourselves from them. Nobody honors you any the more for having them and they lose you advantages which might have gained you more honor; the result is that you get both dishonor and loss at the same time. Let each of you ask herself how much humility she has and she will see what progress she has made. If she is really humble, I do not think the devil will dare to tempt her to take even the slightest interest in matters of precedence, for he is so shrewd that he is afraid of the blow she would strike him. If a humble soul is tempted in this way by the devil, that virtue cannot fail to bring her more fortitude and greater profit. For clearly the temptation will cause her to look into her life, to compare the services she has rendered the Lord with what she owes Him and with the marvelous way in which He abased Himself to give us an example of humility, and to think over her sins and remember where she deserves to be on account of them. Exercises like this bring the soul such profit that on the following day Satan will not dare to come back again lest he should get his head broken.

Take this advice from me and do not forget it: you should see to it that your sisters profit by your temptations, not only interiorly (where it would be very wrong if they did not), but exteriorly as well. If you want to avenge yourself on the devil and free yourselves more quickly from temptation, ask the superior, as soon as a temptation comes to you, to give you some lowly office to do, or do some such thing, as best you can, on our own initiative, studying as you do it how to bend your will to perform tasks you dislike. The Lord will show you ways of doing so and this will soon rid you of the temptation.

God deliver us from people who wish to serve Him yet who are mindful of their own honor. Reflect how little they gain from this; for, as I have said, the very act of desiring honor robs us of it, especially in matters of precedence: there is no poison in the world which is so fatal to perfection. You will say that these are little things which have to do with human nature and are not worth troubling about; do not trifle with them, for *in religious houses* they spread like foam on water, and there is no small matter so extremely dangerous as are punctiliousness about honor and sensitiveness to insult. Do you know one reason, apart from many others, why this is so?[36] It may have its root, perhaps, in some trivial slight – hardly anything, in fact – and the devil will then induce someone else to consider it important, so that she will think it a real charity to tell you about it and to ask how you can allow yourself to be insulted so; and she will pray that God may give you

---

[36] *Lit.*: "Do you know why, apart from other things?"

patience and that you may offer it to Him, for even a saint could not bear more. The devil is simply putting his deceitfulness into this other person's mouth; and, though you yourself are quite ready to bear the slight, you are tempted to vainglory because you have not resisted something else as perfectly as you should.

This human nature of ours is so *wretchedly* weak that, even while we are telling ourselves that there is nothing for us to make a fuss about, we imagine we are doing something virtuous, and begin to feel sorry for ourselves, particularly when we see that other people are sorry for us too. In this way the soul begins to lose the occasions of merit which it had gained; it becomes weaker; and thus a door is opened to the devil by which he can enter on some other occasion with a temptation worse than the last. It may even happen that, when you yourself are prepared to suffer an insult, your sisters come and ask you if you are a beast of burden, and say you ought to be more sensitive about things. Oh, my sisters, for the love of God, never let charity move you to show pity for another in anything to do with these fancied insults, for that is like the pity shown to holy Job by his wife and friends.

CHAPTER 13

Continues to treat of mortification and explains how one must renounce the world's standards of wisdom in order to attain to true wisdom.

I often tell you, sisters, and now I want it to be set down in writing, not to forget that we in this house, and for that matter anyone who would be perfect, must flee a thousand leagues from such phrases as: "I had right on my side"; "They had no right to do this to me"; "The person who treated me like this was not right". God deliver us from such a false idea of right as that! Do you think that it was right for our good Jesus to have to suffer so many insults, and that those who heaped them on Him[37] were right, and that they had any right to do Him those wrongs? I do not know why anyone is in a convent who is willing to bear only the crosses that she has a perfect right to expect: such a person should return to the world, though even there such rights will not be safeguarded. Do you think you can ever possibly have to bear so much that you ought not to have to bear any more? How does right enter into the matter at all? I really do not know.

Before we begin talking about not having our rights, let us wait until we receive some honor or gratification, or are treated kindly, for it is certainly not right that we should have anything in this life like that. When, on the other hand, some offence is done to us (and we do not feel it an offence to us that it should be so described), I do not see what we can find to complain of. Either we are the brides of this great King or we are not. If we are, what wife is there with a sense of honor who does not accept her share in any dishonor done to her spouse, even though she may do so against her will? Each partner, in fact, shares in the honor and dishonor of the other. To desire to share in the kingdom [of our Spouse Jesus Christ], and to enjoy it, and yet not to be willing to have any part in His dishonors and trials, is ridiculous.

God keep us from being like that! Let the sister who thinks that she is accounted the least among all consider herself the [happiest and] most fortunate, as indeed she *really* is, if she lives her life as she should, for in that case she will, *as a rule*, have no lack of honor either in this life or in the next. Believe me when I say this – what an absurdity, though, it is for me to say "Believe me" when the words come from Him Who is true Wisdom, *Who is Truth Itself, and from the Queen of the angels*! Let us, my daughters, in some small degree, imitate the great humility of the most sacred Virgin, whose habit we wear and whose nuns we are ashamed to call ourselves. *Let us at least imitate this humility of hers in some degree – I say "in some degree"* because, however much we may seem to humble ourselves, we fall far short of being the daughters of such a Mother, and the brides of such a Spouse. If, then, the habits I have described are not sternly checked, what seems nothing to-day will perhaps be a venial sin to-morrow, and that is so infectious a tendency that, if you leave it alone, the sin will not be the only one for long; and that is a very bad thing for communities.

---

[37] *Lit.*: "did them to Him."

We who live in a community should consider this very carefully, so as not to harm those who labor to benefit us and to set us a good example. If we realize what great harm is done by the formation of a bad habit of *over-punctiliousness about our honor,* we should rather die *a thousand deaths* than be the cause of such a thing. For only the body would die, whereas the loss of a soul is a great loss which is apparently without end; some of us will die, but others will take our places and perhaps they may all be harmed more by the one bad habit which we started than they are benefited by many virtues. For the devil does not allow a single bad habit to disappear and the very weakness of our mortal nature destroys the virtues in us.

Oh, what a real charity it would be, and what a service would be rendered to God, if any nun who sees that she cannot [endure and] conform to the customs of this house would recognize the fact and go away [before being professed, as I have said elsewhere], *and leave the other sisters in peace! And no convent (at least, if it follows my advice) will take her or allow her to make her profession until they have given her many years' probation to see if she improves. I am not referring to shortcomings affecting penances and fasts, for, although these are wrong, they are not things which do so much harm. I am thinking of nuns who are of such a temperament that they like to be esteemed and made much of; who see the faults of others but never recognize their own; and who are deficient in other ways like these, the true source of which is want of humility. If God does not help such a person by bestowing great spirituality upon her, until after many years she becomes greatly improved, may God preserve you from keeping her in your community. For you must realize that she will neither have peace there herself nor allow you to have any.*

As you do not take dowries, God is very gracious to you in this respect. It grieves me that religious houses should often harbor one who is a thief and robs them of their treasure, either because they are unwilling to return a dowry or out of regard for the relatives. In this house you have risked losing worldly honor and forgone it (for no such honor is paid to those who are poor); do not desire, then, that others should be honored at such a cost to yourselves. Our honor, sisters, must lie in the service of God, and, if anyone thinks to hinder you in this, she had better keep her honor and stay at home. It was with this in mind that our Fathers ordered a year's probation (which in our Order we are free to extend to four years): personally, I should like it to be prolonged to ten years. A humble nun will mind very little if she is not professed: for she knows that if she is good she will not be sent away, and if she is not, why should she wish to do harm to one of Christ's communities?[38]

By not being good, I do not mean being fond of vanities, which, I believe, with the help of God, will be a fault far removed from the nuns in this house. I am referring to a want of mortification and an attachment to worldly things and to self-interest in the matter which I have described. Let anyone who knows that she is not greatly mortified take my advice and not make her profession if she does not wish to suffer a hell on earth, and God grant there may not be another hell awaiting such a nun in the world to come! There are many reasons why she should fear there may belt and possibly neither she nor her sisters may realize this as well as I do.

Believe what I say here; if you will not, I must leave it to time to prove the truth of my words. For the whole manner of life we are trying to live is making us, not only nuns, but hermits [like the holy Fathers our predecessors] and leading us to detachment from all things created. I have observed that anyone whom the Lord has specially chosen for this life is granted that favor. She may not have it in full perfection, but that she has it will be evident from the great joy and gladness that such detachment gives her, and she will never have any more to do with worldly things, for her delight will be in all the practices of the religious life. I say once more that anyone who is inclined to things of the world should leave the convent[39] if she sees she is not making progress. If she still wishes to be a nun she should go to another convent; if she does not, she will see what happens to her. She must not complain of me as the foundress of this convent and say I have not warned her.

This house is another Heaven, if it be possible to have Heaven upon earth. Anyone whose sole pleasure lies in pleasing God and who cares nothing for her own pleasure will find our life a very good one; if she wants anything more, she will lose everything, for there is nothing more that she can have. A discontented soul is like a person suffering from severe nausea, who rejects all food,

---

[38] *Lit.:* "to this college of Christ."
[39] I.e., St. Joseph's, Avila.

however nice it may be; things which persons in good health delight in eating only cause her *the greater* loathing. Such a person will save her soul better elsewhere than here; she may even gradually reach a degree of perfection which she could not have attained here because we expected too much of her all at once. For although we allow time for the attainment of complete detachment and mortification in interior matters, in externals this has to be practiced immediately, *because of the harm which may otherwise befall the rest;* and anyone who sees this being done, and spends all her time in such good company, and yet, at the end of *six months or* a year, has made no progress, will, I fear, make none over a great many years, and will even go backward. I do not say that such a nun must be as perfect as the rest, but she must be sure that her soul is gradually growing healthier – and it will soon become clear if her disease is mortal.

CHAPTER 14
Treats of the great importance of not professing anyone whose spirit is contrary to the things aforementioned.

I feel sure that the Lord bestows great help on anyone who makes good resolutions, and for that reason it is necessary to enquire into the intentions of anyone who enters [the life of religion]. She must not come, as many nuns [now] do, simply to further her own interests, although the Lord can perfect even this intention if she is a person of intelligence. If not intelligent, a person of this kind should on no account be admitted; for she will not understand her own reasons for coming, nor will she understand others who attempt subsequently to improve her. For, in general, a person who has this fault always thinks she knows better than the wisest what is good for her; and I believe this evil is incurable, for it is rarely unaccompanied by malice. In a convent where there are a great many *nuns* it may be tolerated, but it cannot be suffered among a few.

When an intelligent person begins to grow fond of what is good, she clings to it manfully, for she sees that it is the best thing for her; this course may not bring her great spirituality but it will help her to give profitable advice, and to make herself useful in many ways, without being a trouble to anybody. But I do not see how a person lacking in intelligence can be of any use in community life, and she may do a great deal of harm. This defect, *like others*, will not become obvious immediately; for many people are good at talking and bad at understanding, while others speak in a sharp and none too refined a tone,[40] and yet they have intelligence and can do a great deal of good. There are also simple, holy people who are *quite* unversed in business matters and worldly conventions but have great skill in converse with God. Many enquiries, therefore, must be made before novices are admitted, and the period of probation before profession should be a long one. The world must understand once and for an that you are free to send them away *again*, as it is often necessary to do in a convent where the life is one of austerity; and then if you use this right no one will take offence.

I say this because these times are so unhappy, and our weakness is so great, that we are not content to follow the instructions of our predecessors and disregard the current ideas about honor, lest we should give offence to the novices' relatives. God grant that those of us who admit unsuitable persons may not pay for it in the world to come! Such persons are never without a pretext for persuading us to accept them, *though in a matter of such importance no pretext is valid. If the superior is unaffected by her personal likings and prejudices, and considers what is for the good of the house, I do not believe God will ever allow her to go astray. But if she considers other people's feelings and trivial points of detail, I feel sure she will be bound to err.*

This is something which everyone must think out for herself; she must commend it to God and encourage her superior *when her courage fails her*, of such great importance is it. So I beg God to give you light about it. You do very well not to accept dowries; for, if you were to accept them, it might happen that, in order not to have to give back money which you no longer possess, you would keep a thief in the house who was robbing you of your treasure; and that would be no small pity.

---

[40] An untranslatable play upon words: *corto y no muy cortado* – as though "sharpened" could be used in the sense of "refined".

So you must not receive dowries from anyone, for to do so may be to harm the very person to whom you desire to bring profit.

CHAPTER 15

Treats of the great advantage which comes from our not excusing ourselves, even though we find we are unjustly condemned.

But how disconnectedly I am writing! I am just like a person who does not know what she is doing. It is your fault, sisters, for I am doing this at your command. Read it as best you can, for I am writing it as best I can, and, if it is too bad, burn it. I really need leisure, and, as you see, I have so little opportunity for writing that a week passes without my putting down a word, and so I forget what I have said and what I am going to say next. Now what I have just been doing – namely, excusing myself – is very bad for me, and I beg you not to copy it, for to suffer without making excuses is a habit of great perfection, and very edifying and meritorious; and, though I often teach you this, and by God's goodness you practice it, His Majesty has never granted this favor to me. May He be pleased to bestow it on me before I die.

I am greatly confused as I begin to urge this virtue upon you, for I ought myself to have practiced at least something of what I am recommending you with regard to it: but actually I must confess I have made very little progress. I never seem unable to find a reason for thinking I am being virtuous when I make excuses for myself. There are times when this is lawful, and when not to do it would be wrong, but I have not the discretion (or, better, the humility) to do it only when fitting. For, indeed, it takes great humility to find oneself unjustly condemned and be silent, and to do this is to imitate the Lord Who set us free from all our sins. I beg you, then, to study earnestly to do so, for it brings great gain; whereas I can see no gain in our trying to free ourselves from blame: none whatever – save, as I say, in a few cases where hiding the truth might cause offence or scandal. Anyone will understand this who has more discretion than I.

I think it is very important to accustom oneself to practice this virtue and to endeavor to obtain from the Lord the true humility which must result from it. The truly humble person will have a genuine desire to be thought little of, and persecuted, and condemned unjustly, even in serious matters. For, if she desires to imitate the Lord, how can she do so better than in this? And no bodily strength is necessary here, nor the aid of anyone save God.

These are great virtues, my sisters, and I should like us to study them closely, and to make them our penance. As you know, I deprecate [other severe and] excessive penances, which, if practiced indiscreetly, may injure the health. Here, however, there is no cause for fear; for, however great the interior virtues may be, they do not weaken the body so that it cannot serve the Order, while at the same time they strengthen the soul; and, furthermore, they can be applied to very little things, and thus, as I have said on other occasions, they accustom one to gain great victories in *very* important matters. I have not, however, been able to test this particular thing myself, for I never heard anything bad said of me which I did not *clearly* realize fell short of the truth. If I had not *sometimes – often, indeed –* offended God in the ways they referred to, I had done so in many others, and I felt they had treated me far too indulgently in saying nothing about these: I much preferred people to blame me for what was not true than to tell the truth about me. *For I disliked hearing things that were true said about me, whereas these other things, however serious they were, I did not mind at all. In small matters I followed my own inclinations, and I still do so, without paying any affection to what is most perfect. So I should like you to begin to realize this at an early stage, and I want each of you to ponder how much there is to be gained in every way by this virtue, and how, so far as I can see, there is nothing to be lost by it. The chief thing we gain is being able, in some degree, to follow the Lord.*

It is a great help to meditate upon the great gain which in any case this is bound to bring us, and to realize how, properly speaking, we can never be blamed unjustly, since we are always full of faults, and a just man falls seven times a day,[41] so that it would be a falsehood for us to say we

---

[41] Proverbs xxiv, 16.

have no sin. If, then, we are not to blame for the thing that we are accused of, we are never wholly without blame in the way that our good Jesus was.

Oh, my Lord! When I think in how many ways Thou didst suffer, and in all of them undeservedly, I know not what to say for myself, or what I can have been thinking about when I desired not to suffer, or what I am doing when I make excuses for myself. Thou knowest, my Good, that if there is anything good in me it comes from no other hands than Thine own. For what is it to Thee, Lord, to give much instead of little? True, I do not deserve it, but neither have I deserved the favors which Thou hast shown me already. Can it be that I should wish a thing so evil as myself to be thought well of by anyone, when they have said such wicked things of Thee, Who art good above all other good? It is intolerable, my God, it is intolerable; nor would I that Thou shouldst have to tolerate anything displeasing in Thine eyes being found in Thy handmaiden. For see, Lord, mine eyes are blind and very little pleases them. Do Thou give me light and make me truly to desire that all should hate me, since I have so often left Thee, Who hast loved me with such faithfulness.

What is this, my God? What advantage do we think to gain from giving pleasure to creatures? What does it matter to us if we are blamed by them all, provided we are without blame in the sight of the Lord? Oh, my sisters we shall never succeed in understanding this truth and we shall never attain perfection unless we think and meditate upon what is real and upon what is not. If there were no other gain than the confusion which will be felt by the person who has blamed you when she sees that you have allowed yourselves to be condemned unjustly, that would be a very great thing. Such an experience uplifts the soul more than ten sermons. And we must all try to be preachers by our deeds, since both the Apostle and our own lack of ability forbid us to be preachers in word.

Never suppose that either the evil or the good that you do will remain secret, however strict may be your enclosure. Do you suppose, daughter, that, if you do not make excuses for yourself, there will not be someone else who will defend you? Remember how the Lord took the Magdalene's part in the Pharisee's house and also when her sister blamed her. He will not treat you as rigorously as He treated Himself: it was not until He was on the Cross that He had even a thief to defend Him. His Majesty, then, will put it into somebody's mind to defend you; if He does not, it will be because there is no need. This I have myself seen, and it is a fact, although I should not like you to think too much of it, but rather to be glad when you are blamed, and in due time you will see what profit you experience in your souls. For it is in this way that you will begin to gain freedom; soon you will not care if they speak ill or well of you; it will seem like someone else's business. It will be as if two persons are talking *in your presence* and you are quite uninterested in what they are saying because you are not actually being addressed by them. So here: it becomes such a habit with us not to reply that it seems as if they are not addressing us at all. This may seem impossible to those of us who are very sensitive and not capable of great mortification. It is indeed difficult at first, but I know that, with the Lord's help, the *gradual* attainment of this freedom, and of renunciation and self-detachment, is quite possible.

CHAPTER 16

Describes the difference between perfection in the lives of contemplatives and in the lives of those who are content with mental prayer. Explains how it is sometimes possible for God to raise a distracted soul to perfect contemplation and the reason for this. This chapter and that which comes next are to be noted carefully.[42]

I hope you do not think I have written too much about this already; for I have only been placing the board, as they say. You have asked me to tell you about the first steps in prayer; although God did not lead me by them, my daughters I know no others, and even now I can hardly have acquired

---

[42] The first four paragraphs of this chapter originally formed part of V., but, after writing them, St. Teresa tore them out of the manuscript, as though, on consideration, she had decided not to leave on record her knowledge of such a worldly game as chess. The allegory, however, is so expressive and beautiful that it has rightly become famous, and from the time of Fray Luis de Le—n all the editions have included it. The text here followed is that of E.

these elementary virtues. But you may be sure that anyone who cannot set out the pieces in a game of chess will never be able to play well, and, if he does not know how to give check, he will not be able to bring about a checkmate.[43] *Now you will reprove me for talking about games, as we do not play them in this house and are forbidden to do so. That will show you what kind of a mother God has given you – she even knows about vanities like this! However, they say that the game is sometimes legitimate. How legitimate it will be for us to play it in this way, and, if we play it frequently, how quickly we shall give checkmate to this Divine King! He will not be able to move out of our check nor will He desire to do so.*

It is the queen which gives the king most trouble in this game and all the other pieces support her. There is no queen who can beat this King as well as humility can; for humility brought Him down from Heaven into the Virgin's womb and with humility we can draw Him into our souls by a single hair. Be sure that He will give most humility to him who has most already and least to him who has least. I cannot understand how humility exists, or can exist, without love, or love without humility, and it is impossible for these two virtues to exist save where there is great detachment from all created things.

You will ask, my daughters, why I am talking to you about virtues when you have more than enough books to teach you about them and when you want me to tell you only about contemplation. My reply is that, if you had asked me about meditation, I could have talked to you about it, and advised you all to practice it, even if you do not possess the virtues. For this is the first step to be taken towards the acquisition of the virtues and the very life of all Christians depends upon their beginning it. No one, however lost a soul he may be, should neglect so great a blessing if God inspires him to make use of it. All this I have already written elsewhere, and so have many others who know what they are writing about, which I certainly do not: God knows that.

But contemplation, daughters, is another matter. This is an error which we all make: if a person gets so far as to spend a short time each day in thinking about his sins, as he is bound to do if he is a Christian in anything more than name, people at once call him a great contemplative; and then they expect him to have the rare virtues which a great contemplative is bound to possess; he may even think he has them himself, but he will be quite wrong. In his early stages he did not even know how to set out the chess-board, and thought that, in order to give checkmate, it would be enough to be able to recognize the pieces. But that is impossible, for this King does not allow Himself to be taken except by one who surrenders wholly to Him.

Therefore, daughters, if you want me to tell you the way to attain to contemplation, do allow me to speak at some length about these things, even if at the time they do not seem to you very important, for I think myself that they are. If you have no wish either to hear about them or to practice them, continue your mental prayer all your life; but in that case I assure you, and all persons who desire this blessing, that *in my opinion* you will not attain true contemplation. I may, of course, be wrong about this, as I am judging by my own experience, but I have been striving after contemplation for twenty years.

I will now explain what mental prayer is, as some of you will not understand this. God grant that we may practice it as we should! I am afraid, however, that, if we do not achieve the virtues, this can only be done with great labor, although the virtues are not necessary here in such a high degree as they are for contemplation. I mean that the King of glory will not come to our souls – that is, so as to be united with them – unless we strive to gain the greatest virtues.[44] I will explain this, for if you once catch me out in something which is not the truth, you will believe nothing I say – and if I were to say something untrue intentionally, from which may God preserve me, you would be right; but, if I did, it would be because I knew no better or did not understand what I said. I will tell you, then, that God is sometimes pleased to show great favor to persons who are in an evil state [and to raise them to perfect contemplation], so that by this means He may snatch them out of the

---

[43] Chess was very much in vogue in the Spain of St. Teresa's day and it was only in 1561 that its great exponent Ruy Lopez de Segura had published his celebrated treatise, in Spanish, entitled "Book of the liberal invention and art of the game of chess".

[44] *Lit.:* "the great virtues." In V. St. Teresa originally began this sentence thus: "In the last chapter I said that the King of glory, etc.," and ended it: "to gain the virtues which I there described as great." Later she altered it to read as above.

hands of the devil. *It must be understood, I think, that such persons will not be in mortal sin at the time. They may be in an evil state, and yet the Lord will allow them to see a vision, even a very good one, in order to draw them back to Himself. But I cannot believe that He would grant them contemplation. For that is a Divine union, in which the Lord takes His delight in the soul and the soul takes its delight in Him; and there is no way in which the Purity of the Heavens can take pleasure in a soul that is unclean, nor can the Delight of the angels have delight in that which is not His own. And we know that, by committing mortal sin, a soul becomes the property of the devil, and must take its delight in him, since it has given him pleasure; and, as we know, his delights, even in this life, are continuous torture. My Lord will have no lack of children of His own in whom He may rejoice without going and taking the children of others. Yet His Majesty will do what He often does – namely, snatch them out of the devil's hands.*[45]

Oh, my Lord! How often do we cause Thee to wrestle with the devil! Was it not enough that Thou shouldst have allowed him to bear Thee in his arms when he took Thee to the pinnacle of the Temple in order to teach us how to vanquish him? What a sight it would have been, daughters, to see this Sun by the side of the darkness, and what fear that wretched creature must have felt, though he would not have known why, since God did not allow Him to understand!

Blessed be such great pity and mercy; we Christians ought to feel great shame at making Him wrestle daily, in the way I have described, with such an unclean beast. Indeed, Lord, Thine arms had need to be strong, but how was it that they were not weakened by the many [trials and] tortures which Thou didst endure upon the Cross? Oh, how quickly all that is borne for love's sake heals again! I really believe that, if Thou hadst lived longer, the very love which Thou hast for us would have healed Thy wounds again and Thou wouldst have needed no other medicine. Oh, my God, who will give me such medicine for all the things which grieve and try me? How eagerly should I desire them if it were certain that I could be cured by such a health-giving ointment!

Returning to what I was saying, there are souls whom God knows He may gain for Himself by this means; seeing that they are completely lost, His Majesty wants to leave no stone unturned to help them; and therefore, though they are in a sad way and lacking in virtues, He gives them consolations, favors and emotions[46] which begin to move their desires, and occasionally even brings them to a state of contemplation, though rarely and not for long at a time. And this, as I say, He does because He is testing them to see if that favor will not make them anxious to prepare themselves to enjoy it often; if it does not, may they be pardoned; pardon Thou us, Lord, for it is a dreadful thing that a soul whom Thou hast brought near to Thyself should approach any earthly thing and become attached to it.

For my own part I believe there are many souls whom God our Lord tests in this way, and few who prepare themselves to enjoy this favor. When the Lord does this and we ourselves leave nothing undone either, I think it is certain that He never ceases from giving until He has brought us to a very high degree of prayer. If we do not give ourselves to His Majesty as resolutely as He gives Himself to us, He will be doing more than enough for us if He leaves us in mental prayer and from time to time visits us as He would visit servants in His vineyard. But these others are His beloved children, whom He would never want to banish from His side; and, as they have no desire to leave Him, He never does so. He seats them at His table, and feeds them with His own food, almost taking the food from His mouth in order to give it them.

Oh, what blessed care of us is this, my daughters! How happy shall we be if by leaving these few, petty[47] things we can arrive at so high an estate! Even if the whole world should blame you, *and deafen you with its cries*, what matter so long as you are in the arms of God? He is powerful enough to free you from everything; for only once did He command the world to be made and it was done; with Him, to will is to do. Do not be afraid, then, if He is pleased to speak with you, for

---

[45] *Lit.*: "out of his hands", but the meaning, made more explicit in V., is evident. On the doctrinal question involved in this paragraph, see Introduction, above. P. Silverio (III, 75-6), has a more extensive note on the subject than can be given here and cites a number of Spanish authorities, from P. Juan de Jesus Mar'a (*Theologia Mystica*, Chap. III) to P. Seisdedos Sanz (*Principios fundamentales de la m'stica*, Madrid, 1913, II, 61-77.)

[46] *Lit.*: "and tenderness."

[47] *Lit.*: "low", contrasting with "high" at the end of the sentence.

He does this for the greater good of those who love Him. His love for those to whom He is dear is by no means so weak: *He shows it in every way possible.* Why, then, my sisters, do we not show Him love in so far as we can? Consider what a wonderful exchange it is if we give Him our love and receive His. Consider that He can do all things, and we can do nothing here below save as He enables us. And what is it that we do for Thee, O Lord, our Maker? We do hardly anything [at all] – just make some poor weak resolution. And, if His Majesty is pleased that by doing a mere nothing we should win everything, let us not be so foolish as to fail to do it.

O Lord! All our trouble comes to us from not having our eyes fixed upon Thee. If we only looked at the way along which we are walking, we should soon arrive; but we stumble and fall a thousand times and stray from the way because, as I say, we do not set our eyes on the true Way. One would think that no one had ever trodden it before, so new is it to us. It is indeed a pity that this should sometimes happen. *I mean, it hardly seems that we are Christians at all or that we have ever in our lives read about the Passion. Lord help us – that we should be hurt about some small point of honor! And then, when someone tells us not to worry about it, we think he is no Christian. I used to laugh – or sometimes I used to be distressed – at the things I heard in the world, and sometimes, for my sins, in religious Orders.* We refuse to be thwarted over the very smallest matter of precedence: apparently such a thing is quite intolerable. We cry out at once: "Well, I'm no saint"; *I used to say that myself.*

God deliver us, sisters, from saying "We are not angels", or "We are not saints", whenever we commit some imperfection. We may not be; but what a good thing it is for us to reflect that we can be if we will only try and if God gives us His hand! Do not be afraid that He will fail to do His part if we do not fail to do ours. And since we come here for no other reason, let us put our hands to the plough, as they say. Let there be nothing we know of which it would be a service to the Lord for us to do, and which, with His help, we would not venture to take in hand. I should like that kind of venturesomeness to be found in this house, as it always increases humility. We must have a holy boldness, for God helps the strong, being no respecter of persons;[48] *and He will give courage to you and to me.*

I have strayed far from the point. I want to return to what I was saying – that is, to explain the nature of mental prayer and contemplation. It may seem irrelevant, but it is all done for your sakes; you may understand it better as expressed in my rough style than in other books which put it more elegantly. May the Lord grant me His favor, so that this may be so. Amen.

CHAPTER 17

How not all souls are fitted for contemplation and how some take long to attain it.
True humility will walk happily along the road by which the Lord leads it.

I seem now to be beginning my treatment of prayer, but there still remains a little for me to say, which is of great importance because it has to do with humility, and in this house that is necessary. For humility is the principal virtue which must be practiced by those who pray, and, as I have said, it is very fitting that you should try to learn how to practice it often: that is one of the chief things to remember about it and it is very necessary that it should be known by all who practice prayer. How can anyone who is truly humble think herself as good as those who become contemplatives? God, it is true, by His goodness and mercy, can make her so; but my advice is that she should always sit down in the lowest place, for that is what the Lord instructed us to do and taught us by His own example.[49] Let such a one make herself ready for God to lead her by this road if He so wills; if He does not, the whole point of *true* humility is that she should consider herself happy in serving the servants of the Lord and in praising Him. For she deserves to be a slave of the devils in hell; yet His Majesty has brought her here to live among His servants.

I do not say this without good reason, for, as I have said, it is very important for us to realize that God does not lead us all by the same road, and perhaps she who believes herself to be going

---

[48] Acts x, 34.
[49] St. Luke xiv, 10.

along the lowest of roads is the highest in the Lord's eyes. So it does not follow that, because all of us in this house practice prayer, we are all *perforce* to be contemplatives. That is impossible; and those of us who are not would be greatly discouraged if we did not grasp the truth that contemplation is something given by God, and, as it is not necessary for salvation and God does not ask it of us before He gives us our reward, we must not suppose that anyone else will require it of us. We shall not fail to attain perfection if we do what has been said here; we may, in fact, gain much more merit, because what we do will cost us more labor; the Lord will be treating us like those who are strong and will be laying up for us all that we cannot enjoy in this life. Let us not be discouraged, then, and give up prayer or cease doing what the rest do; for the Lord sometimes tarries long, and gives us as great rewards all at once as He has been giving to others over many years.

I myself spent over fourteen years without ever being able to meditate except while reading. There must be many people like this, and others who cannot meditate even after reading, but can only recite vocal prayers, in which they chiefly occupy themselves *and take a certain pleasure.* Some find their thoughts wandering so much that they cannot concentrate upon the same thing, but are always restless, to such an extent that, if they try to fix their thoughts upon God, they are attacked by a thousand foolish ideas and scruples and doubts *concerning the Faith.* I know a very old woman, leading a most excellent life – *I wish mine were like hers* – a penitent and a great servant of God, who for many years has been spending hours and hours in vocal prayer, but from mental prayer can get no help at all; the most she can do is to dwell upon each of her vocal prayers as she says them. There are a great many other people *just* like this; if they are humble, they will not, I think, be any the worse off in the end, but very much in the same state as those who enjoy numerous consolations. In one way they may feel safer, for we cannot tell if consolations come from God or are sent by the devil. If they are not of God, they are the more dangerous; for the chief object of the devil's work on earth is to fill us with pride. If they are of God, there is no reason for fear, for they bring humility with them, as I explained in my other book at great length.

Others[50] walk in humility, and always suspect that if they fail to receive consolations the fault is theirs, and are always most anxious to make progress. They never see a person shedding a tear without thinking themselves very backward in God's service unless they are doing the same, whereas they may perhaps be much more advanced. For tears, though good, are not invariably signs of perfection; there is always greater safety in humility, mortification, detachment and other virtues. There is no reason for fear, and you must not be afraid that you will fail to attain the perfection of the greatest contemplatives.

Saint Martha was holy, but we are not told that she was a contemplative. What more do you want than to be able to grow to be like that blessed woman, who was worthy to receive Christ our Lord so often in her house, and to prepare meals for Him, and to serve Him and perhaps to eat at table with Him? If she had been absorbed in devotion [all the time], as the Magdalene was, there would have been no one to prepare a meal for this Divine Guest. Now remember that this little community is Saint Martha's house and that there must be people of all kinds here. Nuns who are called to the active life must not murmur at others who are very much absorbed in contemplation, for contemplatives know that, though they themselves may be silent, the Lord will speak for them, and this, as a rule, makes them forget themselves and everything else.

Remember that there must be someone to cook the meals and count yourselves happy in being able to serve like Martha. Reflect that true humility consists to a great extent in being ready for what the Lord desires to do with you and happy that He should do it, and in always considering yourselves unworthy to be called His servants. If contemplation and mental and vocal prayer and tending the sick and serving in the house and working at even the lowliest tasks are of service to the Guest who comes to stay with us and to eat and take His recreation with us, what should it matter to us if we do one of these things rather than another?

I do not mean that it is for us to say what we shall do, but that we must do our best in everything, for the choice is not ours but the Lord's. If after many years He is pleased to give each of us her office, it will be a curious kind of humility for you to wish to choose; let the Lord of the house do that, for He is wise and powerful and knows what is fitting for you and for Himself as well. Be sure that, if you do what lies in your power and prepare yourself for *high* contemplation with the

---

[50] *Lit.:* "These others."

perfection aforementioned, then, if He does not grant it you (and I think He will not fail to do so if you have true detachment and humility), it will be because He has laid up this joy for you so as to give it you in Heaven, and because, as I have said elsewhere, He is pleased to treat you like people who are strong and give you a cross to bear on earth like that which His Majesty Himself always bore.

What better sign of friendship is there than for Him to give you what He gave Himself? It might well be that you would not have had so great a reward from contemplation. His judgments are His own; we must not meddle in them. It is indeed a good thing that the choice is not ours; for, if it were, we should think it the more restful life and all become great contemplatives. Oh, how much we gain if we have no desire to gain what seems to us best and so have no fear of losing, since God never permits a truly mortified person to lose anything except when such loss will bring him greater gain!

CHAPTER 18

Continues the same subject and shows how much greater are the trials of contemplatives than those of actives. This chapter offers great consolation to actives.

I tell you, then, daughters – those of you whom God is not leading by this road [of contemplation] – that, as I know from what I have seen and been told by those who are following this road, they are not bearing a lighter cross than you; you would be amazed at all the ways and manners in which God sends them crosses. I know about both types of life and I am well aware that the trials given by God to contemplatives are intolerable; and they are of such a kind that, were He not to feed them with consolations, they could not be borne. It is clear that, since God leads those whom He most loves by the way of trials, the more He loves them, the greater will be their trials; and there is no reason to suppose that He hates contemplatives, since with His own mouth He praises them and calls them friends.

To suppose that He would admit to His close friendship pleasure-loving people who are free from all trials is ridiculous. I feel quite sure that God gives them much greater trials; and that He leads them by a hard and rugged road, so that they sometimes think they are lost and will have to go back and begin again. Then His Majesty is obliged to give them sustenance – not water, but wine, so that they may become inebriated by it and not realize what they are going through and what they are capable of bearing. Thus I find few true contemplatives who are not courageous and resolute in suffering; for, if they are weak, the first thing the Lord does is to give them courage so that they may fear no trials *that may come to them.*

I think, when those who lead an active life occasionally see contemplatives receiving consolations, they suppose that they never experience anything else. But I can assure you that you might not be able to endure their sufferings for as long as a day. The point is that the Lord knows everyone as he really is and gives each his work to do – according to what He sees to be most fitting for his soul, and for His own Self, and for the good of his neighbor. Unless you have omitted to prepare yourselves for your work you need have no fear that it will be lost. Note that I say we must all strive to do this, for we are here for no other purpose; and we must not strive merely for a year, or for two years or ten years, or it will look as if we are abandoning our work like cowards. It is well that the Lord should see we are not leaving anything undone. We are like soldiers who, however long they have served, must always be ready for their captain to send them away on any duty which he wants to entrust to them, since it is he who is paying them. And how much better is the payment given by our King than by people on this earth! *For the unfortunate soldiers die, and God knows who pays them after that!*

When their captain sees they are all present, and anxious for service, he assigns duties to them according to their fitness, *though not so well as our Heavenly Captain.* But if they were not present, He would give them neither pay[51] nor service orders. So practice mental prayer, sisters; or, if any of you cannot do that, vocal prayer, reading and colloquies with God, as I shall explain to you later.

---

[51] *Lit.:* "would give them nothing", but the reference seems to be to payment.

Do not neglect the hours of prayer which are observed by all the nuns; you never know when the Spouse will call you (do not let what happened to the foolish virgins happen to you) and if He will give you fresh trials under the disguise of consolations. If He does not, you may be sure that you are not fit for them and that what you are doing is suitable for you. That is where both merit and humility come in, when you really think that you are not fit for what you are doing.

Go cheerfully about whatever services you are ordered to do, as I have said; if such a servant is truly humble she will be blessed in her active life and will never make any complaint save of herself. *I would much rather be like her than like some contemplatives.* Leave others to wage their own conflicts, which are not light ones. The standard-bearer is not a combatant, yet none the less he is exposed to great danger, and, inwardly, must suffer more than anyone, for he cannot defend himself, as he is carrying the standard, which he must not allow to leave his hands, even if he is cut to pieces. Just so contemplatives have to bear aloft the standard of humility and must suffer all the blows which are aimed at them without striking any themselves. Their duty is to suffer as Christ did, to raise the Cross on high, not to allow it to leave their hands, whatever the perils in which they find themselves, and not to let themselves be found backward in suffering. It is for this reason that they are given such an honorable duty. Let the contemplative consider what he is doing; for, if he lets the standard fall, the battle will be lost. Great harm, I think, is done to those who are not so far advanced if those whom they consider as captains and friends of God let them see them acting in a way unbefitting to their office.

The other soldiers do as best they can; at times they will withdraw from some position of extreme danger, and, as no one observes them, they suffer no loss of honor. But these others have all eyes fixed on them and cannot move. Their office, then, is a noble one, and the King confers great honor and favor upon anyone to whom He gives it, and who, in receiving it, accepts no light obligation. So, sisters, as we *do not understand ourselves and* know not what we ask, let us leave everything to the Lord, *Who knows us better than we know ourselves. True humility consists in our being satisfied with what is given us.* There are some people who seem to want to ask favors from God as a right. A pretty kind of humility that is! He Who knows us all does well in seldom giving things to such persons, He sees clearly that they are unable to drink of His chalice.

If you want to know whether you have made progress or not, sisters, you may be sure that you have if each of you thinks herself the worst of all and shows that she thinks this by acting for the profit and benefit of the rest. Progress has nothing to do with enjoying the greatest number of consolations in prayer, or with raptures, visions or favors [often] given by the Lord, the value of which we cannot estimate until we reach the world to come. The other things I have been describing are current coin, an unfailing source of revenue and a perpetual inheritance – not payments liable at any time to cease, like those favors which are given us and then come to an end. I am referring to the great virtues of humility, mortification and an obedience so *extremely* strict that we never go an inch beyond the superior's orders, knowing that these orders come from God since she is in His place. It is to this duty of obedience that you must attach the greatest importance. It seems to me that anyone who does not have it is not a nun at all, and so I am saying no more about it, as I am speaking to nuns whom I believe to be good, or, at least, desirous of being so. So well known is the matter, and so important, that a single word will suffice to prevent you from forgetting it.

I mean that, if anyone is under a vow of obedience and goes astray through not taking the greatest care to observe these vows with the highest degree of perfection, I do not know why she is in the convent. I can assure her, in any case, that, for so long as she fails in this respect, she will never succeed in leading the contemplative life, or even in leading a good active life: of that I am absolutely certain.[52] And even a person who has not this obligation, but who wishes or tries to achieve contemplation, must, if she would walk safely, be fully resolved to surrender her will to a confessor who is himself a contemplative[53] *and will understand her.* It is a well-known fact that she will make more progress in this way in a year than in a great many years if she acts otherwise. As this does not affect you, however, I will say no more about it.

I conclude, my daughters, [by saying] that these are the virtues which I desire you to possess and to strive to obtain and of which you should cherish a holy envy. Do not be troubled because

---

[52] *Lit.*: "very, very certain" – a typically Theresan repetition.
[53] *Lit.*: "who is such."

you have no experience of those other kinds of devotion: they are very unreliable. It may be that to some people they come from God, and yet that if they came to you it might be because His Majesty had permitted you to be deceived and deluded by the devil, as He has permitted others: *there is danger in this for women*. Why do you want to serve the Lord in so doubtful a way when there are so many ways of [serving Him in] safety? Who wants to plunge you into these perils? I have said a great deal about this, because I am sure it will be useful, for this nature of ours is weak, though His Majesty will strengthen those on whom He wishes to bestow contemplation. With regard to the rest, I am glad to have given them this advice, which will teach contemplatives humility also. *If you say you have no need of it, daughters, some of you may perhaps find it pleasant reading*. May the Lord, for His own sake, give us light to follow His will in all things and we shall have no cause for fear.

CHAPTER 19

Begins to treat of prayer. Addresses souls who cannot reason with the understanding.

It is a long time[54] since I wrote the last chapter and I have had no chance of returning to my writing, so that, without reading through what I have written, I cannot remember what I said. However, I must not spend too much time at this, so it will be best if I go right on[55] without troubling about the connection. For those with orderly minds, and for souls who practice prayer and can be a great deal in their own company, many books have been written, and these are so good and are the work of such competent people that you would be making a mistake if you paid heed to anything about prayer that you learned from me. There are books, as I say, in which the mysteries of the life of the Lord and of His *sacred* Passion are described in short passages, one for each day of the week; there are also meditations on the Judgment, on hell, on our own nothingness and on all that we owe to God, and these books are excellent both as to their teaching and as to the way in which they plan the beginning and the end of the time of prayer.[56] There is no need to tell anyone who is capable of practicing prayer in this way, and has already formed the habit of doing so, that by this good road the Lord will bring her to the harbor of light. If she begins so well, her end will be good also; and all who can walk along this road will walk restfully and securely, for one always walks restfully when the understanding is kept in restraint. It is something else that I wish to treat of and help you about if the Lord is pleased to enable me to do so; if not, you will at least realize that there are many souls who suffer this trial, and you will not be so much distressed at undergoing it yourselves at first, *but will find some comfort in it*.

There are some souls, and some minds, as unruly as horses not yet broken in. No one can stop them: now they go this way, now that way; they are never still. *Although a skilled rider mounted on such a horse may not always be in danger, he will be so sometimes; and, even if he is not concerned about his life, there will always be the risk of his stumbling,*[57] *so that he has to ride with great care.* Some people are either like this by nature or God permits them to become so. I am very sorry for them; they seem to me like people who are very thirsty and see water a long way off, yet, when they try to go to it, find someone who all the time is barring their path – at the beginning of their journey, in the middle and at the end. And when, after all their labor – and the labor is tremendous – they have conquered the first of their enemies, they allow themselves to be conquered by the second, and they prefer to die of thirst rather than drink water which is going to cost them so much trouble. Their strength has come to an end; their courage has failed them; and, though some of them are strong enough to conquer their second enemies as well as their first, when they meet the third group their strength comes to an end, though perhaps they are only a couple of steps from the fountain of living water, of which the Lord said to the Samaritan woman that whosoever drinks

---

[54] *Lit.:* "so many days."

[55] Lit.: "It will have to go as it comes out."

[56] St Teresa is probably referring to the treatises of Luis de Granada and St. Peter of Alcíntara (E. Allison Peers, *Studies of the Spanish Mystics*, 1, 40-52, II, 106-20). Cf. *Constitutions* (Vol. III, p. 236, below).

[57] *Lit.:* "of his doing something on (the horse) which is not graceful."

of it shall not thirst again.[58] How right and *how very* true is that which comes from the lips of Truth Himself! In this life the soul will never thirst for anything more, although its thirst for things in the life to come will exceed any natural thirst that we can imagine here below. How the soul thirsts to experience this thirst! For it knows how very precious it is, and, grievous though it be and exhausting, it creates the very satisfaction by which this thirst is allayed. It is therefore a thirst which quenches nothing but desire for earthly things, and, when God slakes it, satisfies in such a way that one of the greatest favors He can bestow on the soul is to leave it with this longing, so that it has an even greater desire to drink of this water again.

Water has three properties – three relevant properties which I can remember, that is to say, for it must have many more. One of them is that of cooling things; however hot we are, water tempers the heat, and it will even put out a large fire, except when there is tar in the fire, in which case, *they say*, it only burns the more. God help me! What a marvelous thing it is that, when this fire is strong and fierce and subject to none of the elements, water should make it grow fiercer, and, though its contrary element, should not quench it but only cause it to burn the more! It would be very useful to be able to discuss this with someone who understands philosophy; if I knew the properties of things I could explain it myself; but, though I love thinking about it, I cannot explain it – perhaps I do not even understand it.

You will be glad, sisters, if God grants you to drink of this water, as are those who drink of it now, and you will understand how a genuine love of God, if it is really strong, and completely free from earthly things, and able to rise above them, is master of all the elements and of the whole world. And, as water proceeds from the earth, there is no fear of its quenching this fire, which is the love of God; though the two elements are contraries, it has no power over it. The fire is absolute master, and subject to nothing. You will not be surprised, then, sisters, at the way I have insisted in this book that you should strive to obtain this freedom. Is it not a funny thing that a poor *little* nun of Saint Joseph's should attain mastery over the whole earth and all the elements? What wonder that the saints did as they pleased with them by the help of God? Fire and water obeyed Saint Martin; even birds and fishes were obedient to Saint Francis; and similarly with many other saints. *Helped as they were by God, and themselves doing all that was in their power, they could almost have claimed this as a right.* It was clear that they were masters over everything in the world, because they had striven so hard to despise it and subjected themselves to the Lord of the world with all their might. So, as I say, the water, which springs from the earth, has no power over this fire. Its flames rise high and its source is in nothing so base as the earth. There are other fires of love for God – small ones, which may be quenched by the least little thing. But this fire will most certainly not be so quenched.[59] Even should a whole sea of temptations assail it, they will not keep it from burning or prevent it from gaining the mastery over them.

Water which comes down as rain from Heaven will quench the flames even less, for in that case the fire and the water are not contraries, but have the same origin. Do not fear that the one element may harm the other; each helps the other and they produce the same effect. For the water of genuine tears – that is, tears which come from true prayer – is a good gift from the King of Heaven; it fans the flames and keeps them alight, while the fire helps to cool the water. God bless me! What a beautiful and wonderful thing it is that fire should cool water! But it does; and it even freezes all worldly affections, when it is combined with the living water which comes from Heaven, the source of the above-mentioned tears, which are given us, and not acquired by our diligence. Certainly, then, nothing worldly has warmth enough left in it to induce us to cling to it unless it is something which increases this fire, the nature of which is not to be easily satisfied, but, if possible, to enkindle the entire world.

The second property of water is that it cleanses things that are not clean already. What would become of the world if there were no water for washing? Do you know what cleansing properties there are in this living water, this heavenly water, this clear water, when it is unclouded, and free from mud, and comes down from Heaven? Once the soul has drunk of it I am convinced that it makes it pure and clean of all its sins; for, as I have written, God does not allow us to drink of this water of *perfect contemplation* whenever we like: the choice is not ours; this Divine union is

---

[58] St. John iv, 13.
[59] *Lit.*: "But this one – no, no."

something quite supernatural, given that it may cleanse the soul and leave it pure and free from the mud and misery in which it has been plunged because of its sins. Other consolations, excellent as they may be, which come through the intermediacy of the understanding, are like water running all over the ground. This cannot be drunk directly from the source; and its course is never free from clogging impurities, so that it is neither so pure nor so clean as the other. I should not say that this prayer I have been describing, which comes from reasoning with the intellect, is living water – I mean so far as my understanding of it goes. For, despite our efforts, there is always something clinging to the soul, through the influence of the body and of the baseness of our nature, which we should prefer not to be there.

I will explain myself further. We are meditating on the nature of the world, and on the way in which everything will come to an end, so that we may learn to despise it, when, almost without noticing it, we find ourselves ruminating on things in the world that we love. We try to banish these thoughts, but we cannot help being slightly distracted by thinking of things that have happened, or will happen, of things we have done and of things we are going to do. Then we begin to think of how we can get rid of these thoughts; and that sometimes plunges us once again into the same danger. It is not that we ought to omit such meditations; but we need to retain our misgivings about them and not to grow careless. In contemplation the Lord Himself relieves us of this care, for He will not trust us to look after ourselves. So dearly does He love our souls that He prevents them from rushing into things which may do them harm just at this time when He is anxious to help them. So He calls them to His side at once, and in a single moment reveals more truths to them and gives them a clearer insight into the nature of everything than they could otherwise gain in many years. For our sight is poor and the dust which we meet on the road blinds us; but in contemplation the Lord brings us to the end of the day's journey without our understanding how.

The third property of water is that it satisfies and quenches thirst. Thirst, I think, means the desire for something which is very necessary for us – so necessary that if we have none of it we shall die. It is a strange thing that if we have no water we die, and that we can also lose our lives through having too much of it, as happens to many people who get drowned. Oh, my Lord, if only one could be plunged so deeply into this living water that one's life would end! Can that be? Yes: this love and desire for God can increase so much that human nature is unable to bear it, and so there have been persons who have died of it. I knew one person[60] who had this living water in such great abundance that she would almost have been drawn out of herself by raptures if God had not quickly succored her. *She had such a thirst, and her desire grew so greatly, that she realized clearly that she might quite possibly die of thirst if something were not done for her.* I say that she would almost have been drawn out of herself because in this state the soul is in repose. So intolerable does such a soul find the world that it seems to be overwhelmed,[61] but it comes to life again in God; and in this way His Majesty enables it to enjoy experiences which, if it had remained within itself, would perforce have cost it its life.

Let it be understood from this that, as there can be nothing in our supreme Good which is not perfect, all that He gives is for our welfare; and, however abundant this water which He gives may be, in nothing that He gives can there be superfluity. For, if His gift is abundant, He also bestows on the soul, as I have said, an abundant capacity for drinking; just as a glassmaker molds his vessels to the size he thinks necessary, so that there is room for what he wishes to pour into them. As our desires for this water come from ourselves, they are never free from fault; any good that there may be in them comes from the help of the Lord. But we are so indiscreet that, as the pain is sweet and pleasant, we think we can never have too much of it. We have an immeasurable longing for it,[62] and, so far as is possible on earth, we stimulate this longing: sometimes this goes so far as to cause death. How happy is such a death! And yet by living one might perhaps have helped others to die of the desire for it. I believe the devil has something to do with this: knowing how much harm we can do him by living, he tempts us to be indiscreet in our penances and so to ruin our health, which is a matter of no small moment to him.

---

[60] The author probably refers to herself: Cf. *Life*, Chapter XX, and *Relations, passim.*
[61] *Lit.:* "drowned."
[62] *Lit.:* "We eat it without measure."

I advise anyone who attains to an experience of this fierce thirst to watch herself carefully, for I think she will have to contend with this temptation. She may not die of her thirst, but her health will be ruined, and she will involuntarily give her feelings outward expression, which ought at all costs to be avoided. Sometimes, however, all our diligence in this respect is unavailing and we are unable to hide our emotions as much as we should like. Whenever we are assailed by these strong impulses stimulating the increase of our desire, let us take great care not to add to them ourselves but to check them gently[63] by thinking of something else. For our own nature may be playing as great a part in producing these feelings as our love. There are some people *of this type* who have keen desires for all kinds of things, even for bad things, but I do not think such people can have achieved great mortification, for mortification is always profitable. It seems foolish to check so good a thing as this desire, but it is not. I am not saying that the desire should be uprooted – only checked; one may be able to do this by stimulating some other desire which is equally praiseworthy.

In order to explain myself better I will give an illustration. A man has a great desire to be with God, as Saint Paul had, and to be loosed from this prison.[64] This causes him pain which yet is in itself a great joy, and no small degree of mortification will be needed if he is to check it – in fact, he will not always be able to do so. But when he finds it oppressing him so much he may almost lose his reason. I saw this happen to someone not long ago; she was of an impetuous nature, but so accustomed to curbing her own will that, from what I had seen at other times, I thought her will was completely annihilated; yet, when I saw her for a moment, the great stress and strain caused by her efforts to hide her feelings had all but destroyed her reason.[65] In such an extreme case, I think, even did the desire come from the Spirit of God, it would be true humility to be afraid; for we must not imagine that we have sufficient charity to bring us to such a state of oppression.

I shall not think it at all wrong (if it be possible, I mean, for it may not always be so) for us to change our desire by reflecting that, if we live, we have more chance of serving God, and that we might do this by giving light to some soul which otherwise would be lost; as well as that, if we serve Him more, we shall deserve to enjoy Him more, and grieve that we have served Him so little. These are consolations appropriate to such great trials: they will allay our pain and we shall gain a great deal by them if in order to serve the Lord Himself we are willing to spend a long time here below and to live with our grief. It is as if a person were suffering a great trial or a grievous affliction and we consoled him by telling him to have patience and leave himself in God's hands so that His will might be fulfilled in him: it is always best to leave ourselves in God's hands.

And what if the devil had anything to do with these strong desires? This might be possible, as I think is suggested in Cassian's story of a hermit, leading the austerest of lives, who was persuaded by the devil to throw himself down a well so that he might see God the sooner.[66] I do not think this hermit can have served God either humbly or efficiently, for the Lord is faithful and His Majesty would never allow a servant of His to be blinded in a matter in which the truth was so clear. But, of course, if the desire had come from God, it would have done the hermit no harm; for such desires bring with them illumination, moderation and discretion. This is fitting, but our enemy and adversary seeks to harm us wherever he can; and, as he is not unwatchful, we must not be so either. This is an important matter in many respects: for example, we must shorten our time of prayer, however much joy it gives us, if we see our bodily strength waning or find that our headaches: discretion is most necessary in everything.

Why do you suppose, daughters, that I have tried, as people say, to describe the end of the battle before it has begun and to point to its reward by telling you about the blessing which comes from drinking of the heavenly source of this living water? I have done this so that you may not be distressed at the trials and annoyances of the road, and may tread it with courage and not grow weary; for, as I have said, it may be that, when you have arrived, and have only to stoop and drink of the spring, you may fail to do so and lose this blessing, thinking that you have not the strength to attain it and that it is not for you.

---

[63] *Lit.*: "to cut the thread."

[64] Presumably a reminiscence of Romans vii, 24 or Philippians i, 23.

[65] This, too, is generally taken as referring to St. Teresa herself.

[66] Cassian: *Conferences*, II. v.

Remember, the Lord invites us all; and, since He is Truth Itself, we cannot doubt Him. If His invitation were not a general one, He would not have said: "I will give you to drink." He might have said: "Come, all of you, for after all you will lose nothing by coming; and I will give drink to those whom I think fit for it." But, as He said we were all to come, without making this condition, I feel sure that none will fail to receive this living water unless they cannot keep to the path.[67] May the Lord, Who promises it, give us grace, for His Majesty's own sake, to seek it as it must be sought.

CHAPTER 20

Describes how, in one way or another, we never lack consolation on the road of prayer. Counsels the sisters to include this subject continually in their conversation.

In this last chapter I seem to have been contradicting what I had previously said, as, in consoling those who had not reached the contemplative state, I told them that the Lord had different roads by which they might come to Him, just as He also had many mansions.[68] I now repeat this: His Majesty, being Who He is and understanding our weakness, has provided for us. But He did not say: "Some must come by this way and others by that." His mercy is so great that He has forbidden none to strive to come and drink of this fountain of life. Blessed be He for ever! What good reasons there would have been for His forbidding me!

But as He did not order me to cease from drinking when I had begun to do so, but caused me to be plunged into the depths of the water, it is certain that He will forbid no one to come: indeed, He calls us publicly, and in a loud voice, to do so.[69] Yet, as He is so good, He does not force us to drink, but enable those who wish to follow Him to drink in many ways so that none may lack comfort or die of thirst. For from this rich spring flow many streams – some large, others small, and also little pools for children, which they find quite large enough, for the sight of a great deal of water would frighten them: by children, I mean those who are in the early stages.[70] Therefore, sisters, have no fear that you will die of thirst on this road; you will never lack so much of the water of comfort that your thirst will be intolerable; so take my advice and do not tarry on the way, but strive like strong men until you die in the attempt, for you are here for nothing else than to strive. If you always pursue this determination to die rather than fail to reach the end of the road, the Lord may bring you through this life with a certain degree of thirst, but in the life which never ends He will give you great abundance to drink and you will have no fear of its failing you. May the Lord grant us never to fail Him. Amen.

Now, in order to set out upon this aforementioned road so that we do not go astray at the very start, let us consider for a moment how the first stage of our journey is to be begun, for that is the most important thing – or rather, every part of the journey is of importance to the whole. I do not mean to say that no one who has not the resolution that I am going to describe should set out upon the road, for the Lord will gradually bring her nearer to perfection. And even if she did no more than take one step, this alone has such virtue that there is no fear of her losing it or of failing to be very well rewarded. We might compare her to someone who has a rosary with a bead specially indulgenced:[71] one prayer in itself will bring her something, and the more she uses the bead the more she will gain; but if she left it in a box and never took it out it would be better for her not to have it. So, although she may never go any farther along the same road, the short distance she has progressed will give her light and thus help her to go along other roads, and the farther she goes the more light she will gain. In fact, she may be sure that she will do herself no kind of harm through having started on the road, even if she leaves it, for good never leads to evil. So, daughters, whenever you meet people and find them well-disposed and even attracted to the life of prayer, try

---

[67] E. ends the chapter here. This final paragraph appears to be based upon St. John vii, 37.

[68] There is a reference here to St. John xiv, 2.

[69] St. John vii, 37.

[70] *Lit.*: "these are they who are, etc."

[71] *Cuenta de perdones*: a bead larger in size than the remainder in the rosary and carrying special indulgences for the souls in purgatory.

to remove from them all fear of beginning a course which may bring them such great blessings.[72] For the love of God, I beg you always to see to it that your conversation is benefiting those with whom you speak. For your prayers must be for the profit of their souls; and, since you must always pray to the Lord for them, sisters, you would seem to be doing ill if you did not strive to benefit them in every possible way.

If you would be a good kinswoman, this is true friendship; if you would be a good friend, you may be sure that this is the only possible way. Let the truth be in your hearts, as it will be if you practice meditation, and you will see clearly what love we are bound to have for our neighbors. This is no time for child's play, sisters, and these worldly friendships, good though they may be, seem no more than that. Neither with your relatives nor with anyone else must you use such phrases as "If you love me", or "Don't you love me?" unless you have in view some noble end and the profit of the person to whom you are speaking. It may be necessary, in order to get a relative – a brother or some such person – to listen to the truth and accept it, to prepare him for it by using such phrases and showing him signs of love, which are always pleasing to sense. He may possibly be more affected, and influenced, by one kind word, as such phrases are called, than by a great deal which you might say about God, and then there would be plenty of opportunities for you to talk to him about God afterwards. I do not forbid such phrases, therefore, provided you use them in order to bring someone profit. But for no other reason can there be any good in them and they may even do harm without your being aware of it. Everybody knows that you are nuns and that your business is prayer. Do not say to yourselves: "I have no wish to be considered good," for what people see in you is bound to bring them either profit or harm. People like nuns, on whom is laid the obligation to speak of nothing save in the spirit of God,[73] act very wrongly if they dissemble in this way, except occasionally for the purpose of doing greater good. Your intercourse and conversation must be like this: let any who wish to talk to you learn your language; and, if they will not, be careful never to learn theirs: it might lead you to hell.

It matters little if you are considered ill-bred and still less if you are taken for hypocrites: indeed, you will gain by this, because only those who understand your language will come to see you. If one knows no Arabic, one has no desire to talk a great deal with a person who knows no other language. So worldly people will neither weary you nor do you harm – and it would do you no small harm to have to begin to *learn and* talk a new language; you would spend all your time learning it. You cannot know as well as I do, for I have found it out by experience, how very bad this is for the soul; no sooner does it learn one thing than it has to forget another and it never has any rest. This you must at all costs avoid; for peace and quiet in the soul are of great importance on the road which we are about to tread.

If those with whom you converse wish to learn your language, it is not for you to teach it to them, but you can tell them what wealth they will gain by learning it. Never grow tired of this, but do it piously, lovingly and prayerfully, with a view to helping them; they will then realize what great gain *it brings*, and will go and seek a master to teach it them. Our Lord would be doing you no light favor if through your agency He were to arouse some soul to obtain this blessing. When once one begins to describe this road, what a large number of things there are to be said about it, even by those who have trodden it as unsuccessfully as I have! *I only wish I could write with both hands, so as not to forget one thing while I am saying another.* May it please the Lord, sisters, that you may be enabled to speak of it better than I have done.

---

[72] *Lit.*: "of beginning so great a good."

[73] *Lit.*: "save in God" – i.e., save as those whose life is centered in God: not necessarily, I think, only *of* God.

CHAPTER 21

Describes the great importance of setting out upon the practice of prayer with firm resolution and of heeding no difficulties put in the way by the devil.

Do not be dismayed, daughters, at the number of things which you have to consider before setting out on this Divine journey, which is the royal road to Heaven.[74] By taking this road we gain such precious treasures that it is no wonder if the cost seems to us a high one. The time will come when we shall realize that all we have paid has been nothing at all by comparison with the greatness of our prize.

Let us now return to those who wish to travel on this road, and will not halt until they reach their goal, which is the place where they can drink of this water of life. *Although in some book or other – in several, in fact – I have read what a good thing it is to begin in this way, I do not think anything will be lost if I speak of it here.* As I say, it is most important – all-important, indeed – that they should begin well by making an earnest and most determined resolve[75] not to halt until they reach their goal, whatever may come, whatever may happen to them, however hard they may have to labor, whoever may complain of them, whether they reach their goal or die on the road or have no heart to confront the trials which they meet, whether the very world dissolves before them. Yet again and again people will say to us: "It is dangerous", "So-and-so was lost through doing this", "Someone else got into wrong ways", "Some other person, who was always praying, fell just the same", "It is bad for virtue", "It is not meant for women; it may lead them into delusions", "They would do better to stick to their spinning", "These subtleties are of no use to them", "It is quite enough for them to say their Paternoster and Ave Maria."

With this last remark, sisters, I quite agree. Of course it is enough! It is always a great thing to base your prayer on prayers which were uttered by the very lips of the Lord. People are quite right to say this, and, were it not for our great weakness and the lukewarmness of our devotion, there would be no need for any other systems of prayer or for any other books at all. I am speaking to souls who are unable to recollect themselves by meditating upon other mysteries, and who think they need special methods of prayer; some people have such ingenious minds[76] that nothing is good enough for them! So I think I will start to lay down some rules for each part of our prayer – beginning, middle and end – although I shall not spend long on the higher stages. They cannot take books from you, and, if you are studious and humble, you need nothing more.

I have always been fond of the words of the Gospels and have found more recollection in them than in the most carefully planned books – especially books of which the authors were not fully approved, and which I never wanted to read. If I keep close to this Master of wisdom, He may perhaps give me some thoughts[77] which will help you. I do not say that I will explain these Divine prayers, for that I should not presume to do, and there are a great many explanations of them already. Even were there none, it would be ridiculous for me to attempt any. But I will write down a few thoughts on the words of the Paternoster; for sometimes, when we are most anxious to nurture our devotion, consulting a great many books will kill it. When a master is himself giving a lesson, he treats his pupil kindly and likes him to enjoy being taught and does his utmost to help him learn. Just so will this heavenly Master do with us.

Pay no heed, then, to anyone who tries to frighten you or depicts to you the perils of the way. What a strange idea that one could ever expect to travel on a road infested by thieves, for the purpose of gaining some great treasure, without running into danger! Worldly people like to take life peaceably; but they will deny themselves sleep, perhaps for nights on end, in order to gain a farthing's profit, and they will leave you no peace either of body or of soul. If, when you are on the way to gaining this treasure, or to taking it by force (as the Lord says the violent do) and are traveling

---

[74] "Do not be surprised, daughters, for this is the royal road (*camino real*) to Heaven." A more idiomatic translation of *camino real* would be "king's highway".

[75] *Lit.*: "determined determination": this doubling of words is not uncommon in St. Teresa.

[76] *Lit.*: "are such ingenious geniuses."

[77] V.: *alguna consideraci—n*: the use of the singular form in a plural sense, with the shade of meaning which might be conveyed by "some occasional thoughts," is common in Spanish. E. uses one of St. Teresa's characteristic diminutives (see Vol. 1, p. xxi) *alguna consideracioncita* – "some (occasional) trifling thoughts."

by this royal road – this safe road trodden by our King and by His elect and His saints – if even then they tell you it is full of danger and make you so afraid, what will be the dangers encountered by those who think they will be able to gain this treasure and yet are not on the road to it?

Oh, my daughters, how incomparably greater must be the risks they run! And yet they have no idea of this until they fall headlong into some real danger. Having perhaps no one to help them, they lose this water altogether, and drink neither much nor little of it, either from a pool or from a stream. How do you suppose they can do without a drop of this water and yet travel along a road on which there are so many adversaries to fight? Of course, sooner or later, they will die of thirst; for we must all journey to this fountain, my daughters, whether we will or no, though we may not all do so in the same way. Take my advice, then, and let none mislead you by showing you any other road than that of prayer.

I am not now discussing whether or not everyone must practice mental or vocal prayer; but I do say that you yourselves require both. For prayer is the duty of religious. If anyone tells you it is dangerous, look upon that person himself as your principal danger and flee from his company. Do not forget this, for it is advice that you may possibly need. It will be dangerous for you if you do not possess humility and the other virtues; but God forbid that the way of prayer should be a way of danger! This fear seems to have been invented by the devil, who has apparently been very clever in bringing about the fall of some who practice prayer.

See how blind the world is! It never thinks of all the thousands who have fallen into heresies and other great evils through yielding to distractions and not practicing prayer. As against these multitudes there are a few who did practice prayer and whom the devil has been successful enough at his own trade to cause to fall: in doing this he has also caused some to be very much afraid of virtuous practices. Let those who make use of this pretext to absolve themselves from such practices take heed, for in order to save themselves from evil they are fleeing from good. I have never heard of such a wicked invention; it must indeed come from the devil. Oh, my Lord, defend Thyself. See how Thy words are being misunderstood. Permit no such weakness in Thy servants.

There is one great blessing – you will always find a few people ready to help you. For it is a characteristic of the true servant of God, to whom His Majesty has given light to follow the true path, that, when beset by these fears, his desire not to stop only increases. He sees clearly whence the devil's blows are coming, but he parries each blow and breaks his adversary's head. The anger which this arouses in the devil is greater than all the satisfaction which he receives from the pleasures given him by others. When, in troublous times, he has sown his tares, and seems to be leading men everywhere in his train, half-blinded, and [deceiving them into] believing themselves to be zealous for the right, God raises up someone to open their eyes and bid them look at the fog with which the devil has obscured their path. (How great God is! To think that just one man, or perhaps two, can do more by telling the truth than can a great many men all together!) And then they gradually begin to see the path again and God gives them courage. If people say there is danger in prayer, this servant of God, by his deeds if not by his words, tries to make them realize what a good thing it is. If they say that frequent communion is inadvisable, he only practices it the more. So, because just one or two are fearlessly following the better path, the Lord gradually regains what He had lost.

Cease troubling about these fears, then, sisters; and never pay heed to such matters of popular opinion. This is no time for believing everyone; believe only those whom you see modeling their lives on the life of Christ. Endeavor always to have a good conscience; practice humility; despise all worldly things; and believe firmly in the teaching of our Holy Mother [the Roman] Church. You may then be quite sure that you are on a [very] good road. Cease, as I have said, to have fear where no fear is; if any one attempts to frighten you, point out the road to him in all humility. Tell him that you have a Rule which commands you, as it does, to pray without ceasing, and that that rule you must keep. If they tell you that you should practice only vocal prayer, ask whether your mind and heart ought not to be in what you say. If they answer "Yes" – and they cannot do otherwise – you see they are admitting that you are bound to practice mental prayer, and even contemplation, if God should grant it you. [Blessed be He for ever.]

CHAPTER 22

Explains the meaning of mental prayer.

You must know, daughters, that whether or not you are practicing mental prayer has nothing to do with keeping the lips closed. If, while I am speaking with God, I have a clear realization and full consciousness that I am doing so, and if this is more real to me than the words I am uttering, then I am combining mental and vocal prayer. When people tell you that you are speaking with God by reciting the Paternoster and thinking of worldly things – well, words fail me. When you speak, as it is right for you to do, with so great a Lord, it is well that you should think of Who it is that you are addressing, and what you yourself are, if only that you may speak to Him with proper respect. How can you address a king with the deference due to him, or how can you know what ceremonies have to be used when speaking to a grandee, unless you are clearly conscious of the nature of his position and of yours? It is because of this, and because it is the custom to do so, that you must behave respectfully to him, and must learn *what the custom is, and not be careless about such things*, or *you will be dismissed as a simpleton and obtain none of the things you desire. And furthermore, unless you are quite conversant with it, you must get all necessary information, and have what you are going to say written down for you. It once happened to me, when I was not accustomed to*[78] *addressing aristocrats, that I had to go on a matter of urgent business to see a lady who had to be addressed as "Your Ladyship". I was shown that word in writing; but I am stupid, and had never used such a term before; so when I arrived I got it wrong. So I decided to tell her about it and she laughed heartily and told me to be good enough to use the ordinary form of polite address,*[79] *which I did.*

How is it, my Lord, how is it, my Emperor, that Thou canst suffer this, *Prince of all Creation*? For Thou, my God, art a King without end, and Thine is no borrowed Kingdom, *but Thine own, and it will never pass away.* When the Creed says "Whose Kingdom shall have no end" the phrase nearly always makes me feel particularly happy. I praise Thee, Lord, and bless Thee, *and all things praise Thee* for ever – for Thy Kingdom will endure for ever. Do Thou never allow it to be thought right, Lord, for those who *praise Thee and* come to speak with Thee to do so with their lips alone. What do you mean, Christians, when you say that mental prayer is unnecessary? Do you understand what you are saying? I really do not think you can. And so you want us all to go wrong: you cannot know what mental prayer is, or how vocal prayers should be said, or what is meant by contemplation. For, if you knew this, you would not condemn on the one hand what you praise on the other.

Whenever I remember to do so, I shall always speak of mental and vocal prayer together, daughters, so that you may not be alarmed. I know what such fears lead to,[80] for I have suffered a certain number of trials in this respect, and so I should be sorry if anyone were to unsettle you, for it is very bad for you to have misgivings while you are walking on this path. It is most important that you should realize you are making progress; for if a traveler is told that he has taken the wrong road, and has lost his way, he begins to wander to and fro and the constant search for the right road tires him, wastes his time and delays his arrival. Who can say that it is wrong if, before we begin reciting the Hours or the Rosary, we think Whom we are going to address, and who we are that are addressing Him, so that we may do so in the way we should? I assure you, sisters, that if you gave all due attention to a consideration of these two points before beginning the vocal prayers which you are about to say you would be engaging in mental prayer for a very long time. For we cannot approach a prince and address him in the same careless way that we should adopt in speaking to a peasant or to some poor woman like ourselves, whom we may address however we like.

---

[78] This is generally taken as referring to St. Teresa's visit to Do–a Luisa de la Cerda in 1562.

[79] *Lit.*: "to call her 'Honor." The point of this delightfully unaffected reminiscence, omitted in V. and inserted here rather for its attractiveness than for its artistic appropriateness, is that "Your Honor" (*Vuestra Merced*: now abbreviated to Vd. and used as the third personal pronoun of ordinary polite address) was an expression merely of respect and not of rank: the Saint often uses it, for example, in addressing her confessors. It was as though a peer of the realm were to say "Just call me 'Sir."

[80] For "fears" the original has "things"; but that seems to be the meaning.

The reason we sometimes do so is to be found in the humility of this King, Who, unskilled though I am in speaking with Him, does not refuse to hear me or forbid me to approach Him, or command His guards to throw me out. For the angels in His presence know well that their King is such that He prefers the unskilled language of a humble peasant boy, knowing that he would say more if he had more to say, to the speech of the wisest and most learned men, however elegant may be their arguments, if these are not accompanied by humility. But we must not be unmannerly because He is good. If only to show our gratitude to Him for enduring our foul odor and allowing such a one as myself to come near Him, it is well that we should try to realize His purity and His nature. It is true that we recognize this at once when we approach Him, just as we do when we visit the lords of the earth. Once we are told about their fathers' names and their incomes and dignities, there is no more for us to know about them; for on earth one makes account of persons, and honors them, not because of their merits but because of their possessions.

O miserable world! Give hearty praise to God, daughters, that you have left so wretched a place,[81] where people are honored, not for their own selves, but for what they get from their tenants and vassals: if these fail them, they have no honor left. It is a curious thing, and when you go out to recreation together you should laugh about it, for it is a good way of spending your time to reflect how blindly people in the world spend theirs.

O Thou our Emperor! Supreme Power, Supreme Goodness, Wisdom Itself, without beginning, without end and without measure in Thy works: infinite are these and incomprehensible, a fathomless ocean of wonders, O Beauty[82] containing within Thyself all beauties. O Very Strength! God help me! Would that I could command all the eloquence of mortals and all wisdom, so as to understand, as far as is possible here below, that to know nothing is everything, and thus to describe some of the many things on which we may meditate in order to learn something of the nature of this our Lord and Good.

When you approach God, then, try[83] to think and realize Whom you are about to address and continue to do so while you are addressing Him. If we had a thousand lives, we should never fully understand how this Lord merits that we behave toward Him, before Whom even the angels tremble. He orders all things and He can do all things: with Him to will is to perform. It will be right, then, daughters, for us to endeavor to rejoice in these wondrous qualities of our Spouse and to know Whom we have wedded and what our lives should be. Why, God save us, when a woman in this world is about to marry, she knows beforehand whom she is to marry, what sort of a person he is and what property he possesses. Shall not we, then, who are already betrothed, think about our Spouse,[84] before we are wedded to Him and He takes us home to be with Him? If these thoughts are not forbidden to those who are betrothed to men on earth, how can we be forbidden to discover Who this Man is, Who is His Father, what is the country to which He will take me, what are the riches with which He promises to endow me, what is His rank, how I can best make Him happy, what I can do that will give Him pleasure, and how I can bring my rank into line with His. If a woman is to be happy in her marriage, it is just those things that she is advised to see about, even though her husband be a man of very low station.

Shall less respect be paid to Thee, then, my Spouse, than to men? If they think it unfitting to do Thee honor, let them at least leave Thee Thy brides, who are to spend their lives with Thee. A woman is indeed fortunate in her life if her husband is so jealous that he will allow her to speak with no one but himself; it would be a pretty pass if she could not resolve to give him this pleasure, for it is reasonable enough that she should put up with this and not wish to converse with anyone else, since in him she has all that she can desire. To understand these truths, my daughters, is to practice mental prayer. If you wish to learn to understand them, and at the same time to practice vocal prayer, well and good. But do not, I beg you, address God while you are thinking of other things, for to do that is the result of not understanding what mental prayer is. I think I have made this clear. May the Lord grant us to learn how to put it into practice. Amen.

---

81 *Lit.*: "a thing".

82 Lit.: "a Beauty... itself", as though referring to *obras*: "works."

83 *Lit.*: "Yes, approach God, and, in approaching, try."

84 The words "think about our Spouse" appear in no manuscript but were added by Luis de Le—n.

CHAPTER 23

Describes the importance of not turning back when one has set out upon the way of prayer. Repeats how necessary it is to be resolute.

Now, as I have said, it is most important that from the first we should be very resolute, and for this there are so many reasons that if I were to give them all I should have to write at great length. *Some of them are given in other books.* I will tell you just two or three of them, sisters. One is that when we decide to give anything – such as this slight effort of recollection[85] – to Him Who has given us so much, and Who is continually giving, it would be wrong for us not to be entirely resolute in doing so and to act like a person who lends something and expects to get it back again. (Not that we do not receive interest: on the contrary, we gain a great deal.) I do not call this "giving". Anyone who has been lent something always feels slightly displeased when the lender wants it back again, especially if he is using it himself and has come to look upon it as his own. If the two are friends and the lender is indebted to the recipient for many things of which he has made him free gifts, he will think it meanness and a great lack of affection if he will leave not even the smallest thing in his possession, merely as a sign of love.

What wife is there who, after receiving many valuable jewels from her husband, will not give him so much as a ring – which he wants, not because of its value, for all she has is his, but as *a sign of love and* a token that she will be his until she dies? Does the Lord deserve less than this that we should mock Him by taking away the worthless gift[86] which we have given Him? Since we have resolved to devote to Him this very brief period of time – only a small part of what we spend upon ourselves and upon people who are not particularly grateful to us for it – let us give it Him freely, with our minds unoccupied by other things and entirely resolved never to take it back again, whatever we may suffer through trials, annoyances or aridities. Let me realize that this time is being lent me and is not my own, and feel that I can rightly be called to account for it if I am not prepared to devote it wholly to God.

I say "wholly", but we must not be considered as taking it back if we should fail to give it Him for a day, or for a few days, because of legitimate occupations or through some indisposition. Provided the intention remains firm, my God is not in the least meticulous;[87] He does not look at trivial details; and, if you are trying to please Him in any way, He will assuredly accept that as your gift. The other way is suitable for ungenerous souls, so mean that they are not large-hearted enough to give but find it as much as they can do to lend. Still, let them make some effort, for this Lord of ours will reckon everything we do to our credit and accept everything we want to give Him. In drawing up our reckoning, He is not in the least exacting, but generous; however large the amount we may owe Him, it is a small thing for Him to forgive us. And, as to paying us, He is so careful about this that you need have no fear He will leave us without our reward if only we raise our eyes to Heaven and remember Him.

A second reason why we should be resolute is that this will give the devil less opportunity to tempt us. He is very much afraid of resolute souls, knowing by experience that they inflict great injury upon him, and, when he plans to do them harm, he only profits them and others and is himself the loser. We must not become unwatchful, or count upon this, for we have to do with treacherous folk, who are great cowards and dare not attack the wary, but, if they see we are careless, will work us great harm. And if they know anyone to be changeable, and not resolute in *doing* what is good and firmly determined to persevere, they will not leave him alone either by night or by day and will suggest to him endless misgivings and difficulties. This I know very well by experience and so I have been able to tell you about it: I am sure that none of us realize its great importance.

Another reason, very much to the point, is that a resolute person fights more courageously. He knows that, come what may, he must not retreat. He is like a soldier in battle who is aware that if he is vanquished his life will not be spared and that if he escapes death in battle he must die afterwards. *It has been proved, I think, that* such a man will fight more resolutely and will try, as

---

[85] *Este cuidadito: lit.,* "this little attentiveness" – another characteristic diminutive.

[86] *Lit.:* "a nothing at all" (*una nonada*).

[87] *No es nada delicado mi Dios.* "Fastidious" might be nearer to the characteristically bold adjective of the original.

they say, to sell his life dearly, fearing the enemy's blows the less because he understands the importance of victory and knows that his very life depends upon his gaining it. We must also be *firmly* convinced from the start that, if we *fight courageously and* do not allow ourselves to be beaten, we shall get what we want, and there is no doubt that, however small our gains may be, they will make us very rich. Do not be afraid that the Lord Who has called us to drink of this spring will allow you to die of thirst. This I have already said and I should like to repeat it; for people are often timid when they have not learned by experience of the Lord's goodness, even though they know of it by faith. It is a great thing to have experienced what friendship and joy He gives to those who walk on this road and how He takes almost the whole cost of it upon Himself.

I am not surprised that those who have never made this test should want to be sure that they will receive some interest on their outlay. But you already know that even in this life we shall receive a hundredfold, and that the Lord says: "Ask and it shall be given you."[88] If you do not believe His Majesty in those passages of His Gospel where He gives us this assurance, it will be of little help to you, sisters, for me to weary my brains by telling you of it. Still, I will say to anyone who is in doubt that she will lose little by putting the matter to the test; for this journey has the advantage[89] of giving us *very much* more than we ask or shall even get so far as to desire. This is a never-failing truth: I know it; *though, if you do not find it so, do not believe any of the things I tell you.* I can call as witnesses those of you who, by God's goodness, know it from experience.

CHAPTER 24

Describes how vocal prayer may be practiced with perfection and how closely allied it is to mental prayer.

Let us now return to speak of those souls I have mentioned who cannot practice recollection or tie down their minds to mental prayer or make a meditation. We must not talk to them of either of those two things – they will not hear of them; as a matter of fact, there are a great many people who seem terrified at the very name of contemplation or mental prayer.

In case any such person should come to this house (for, as I have said, not all are led by the same path), I want to advise you, or, I might even say, to teach you (for, as your mother, and by the office of prioress which I hold, I have the right to do so) how you must practice vocal prayer, for it is right that you should understand what you are saying. Anyone unable to think of God may find herself wearied by long prayers, and so I will not begin to discuss these, but will speak simply of prayers which, as Christians, we must perforce recite – namely, the Paternoster and the Ave Maria – and then no one will be able to say of us that we are repeating words without understanding what we are saying. We may, of course, consider it enough to say our prayers as a mere habit, repeating the words and thinking that this will suffice. Whether it suffices or no I will not now discuss.[90] Learned men must decide: *they will instruct people to whom God gives light to consult them, and I will not discuss the position of those who have not made a profession like our own.* But what I should like, daughters, is for us not to be satisfied with that alone: when I say the Creed, it seems to me right, *and indeed obligatory*, that I should understand and know what it is that I believe; and, when I repeat the "Our Father", my love should make me want to understand Who this Father of ours is and Who the Master is that taught us this prayer.

If you assert that you know Who He is already, and so there is no need for you to think about Him, you are not right; there is a great deal of difference between one master and another, and it would be very wrong of us not to think about those who teach us, even on earth; if they are holy men and spiritual masters, and we are good pupils, it is impossible for us *not to have great love for them, and indeed to hold them in honor and often to talk about them.* And when it comes to the Master Who taught us this prayer, and Who loves us so much and is so anxious for us to profit by

---

[88] St. Luke xi, 9.
[89] *Lit.:* "the good."
[90] The word rendered "discuss", both here and below, is a strong one, *entrometerse*, to intermeddle.

it, may God forbid that we should fail to think of Him often when we repeat it, although our own weakness may prevent us from doing so every time.

Now, in the first place, you know that His Majesty teaches that this prayer must be made when we are alone, just as He was often alone when He prayed, not because this was necessary for Him, but for our edification. It has already been said that it is impossible to speak to God and to the world at the same time; yet this is just what we are trying to do when we are saying our prayers and at the same time listening to the conversation of others or letting our thoughts wander on any matter that occurs to us, without making an effort to control them. There are occasions when one cannot help doing this: times of ill-health (especially in persons who suffer from melancholia); or times when our heads are tired, and, however hard we try, we cannot concentrate; or times when, for their own good, God allows His servants for days on end to go through great storms. And, although they are distressed and strive to calm themselves, they are unable to do so and incapable of attending to what they are saying, however hard they try, nor can they fix their understanding on anything: they seem to be in a frenzy, so distraught are they.

The very suffering of anyone in this state will show her that she is not to blame, and she must not worry, for that only makes matters worse, nor must she weary herself by trying to put sense into something – namely, her mind – which for the moment is without any. She should pray as best she can: indeed, she need not pray at all, but may try to rest her spirit as though she were ill and busy herself with some other virtuous action. These directions are meant for persons who keep careful guard over themselves and know that they must not speak to God and to the world at the same time. What we can do ourselves is to try to be alone – and God grant that this may suffice, as I say, to make us realize in Whose presence we are and how the Lord answers our petitions. Do you suppose that, because we cannot hear Him, He is silent? He speaks clearly to the heart when we beg Him from our hearts to do so. It would be a good idea for us to imagine[91] that He has taught this prayer to each one of us individually, and that He is continually expounding it to us. The Master is never so far away that the disciple needs to raise his voice in order to be heard: He is always right at his side. I want you to understand that, if you are to recite the Paternoster well, one thing is needful: you must not leave the side of the Master Who has taught it you.

You will say at once that this is meditation, and that you are not capable of it, and do not even wish to practice it, but are content with vocal prayer. For there are impatient people who dislike giving themselves trouble, and it is troublesome at first to practice recollection of the mind when one has not made it a habit. So, in order not to make themselves the least bit tired, they say they are incapable of anything but vocal prayer and do not know how to do anything further. You are right to say that what we have described is mental prayer; but I assure you that I cannot distinguish it from vocal prayer faithfully recited with a realization of Who it is that we are addressing. Further, we are under the obligation of trying to pray attentively: may God grant that, by using these means, we may learn to say the Paternoster well and not find ourselves thinking of something irrelevant. I have sometimes experienced this myself, and the best remedy I have found for it is to try to fix my mind on the Person by Whom the words were first spoken. Have patience, then, and try to make this necessary practice into a habit, *for necessary it is, in my opinion, for those who would be nuns, and indeed for all who would pray like good Christians.*

CHAPTER 25

Describes the great gain which comes to a soul when it practices vocal prayer perfectly. Shows how God may raise it thence to things supernatural.

In case you should think there is little gain to be derived from practicing vocal prayer perfectly, I must tell you that, while you are repeating the Paternoster or some other vocal prayer, it is quite possible for the Lord to grant you perfect contemplation. In this way His Majesty shows that He is listening to the person who is addressing Him, and that, in His greatness, He is addressing her,[92] by

---

[91] More literally: "consider", "reflect".
[92] *Lit.*: "and that His greatness is addressing her."

suspending the understanding, putting a stop to all thought, and, as we say, taking the words out of her mouth, so that even if she wishes to speak she cannot do so, or at any rate not without great difficulty.

Such a person understands that, without any sound of words, she is being taught by this Divine Master, Who is suspending her faculties, which, if they were to work, would be causing her harm rather than profit. The faculties rejoice without knowing how they rejoice; the soul is enkindled in love without understanding how it loves; it knows that it is rejoicing in the object of its love, yet it does not know how it is rejoicing in it. It is well aware that this is not a joy which can be attained by the understanding; the will embraces it, without understanding how; but, in so far as it can understand anything, it perceives that this is a blessing which could not be gained by the merits of all the trials suffered on earth put together. It is a gift of the Lord of earth and Heaven, Who gives it like the God He is. This, daughters, is perfect contemplation.

You will now understand how different it is from mental prayer, which I have already described, and which consists in thinking of what we are saying, understanding it, and realizing Whom we are addressing, and who we are that are daring to address so great a Lord. To think of this and other similar things, such as how little we have served Him and how great is our obligation to serve Him, is mental prayer. Do not think of it as one more thing with an outlandish name[93] and do not let the name frighten you. To recite the Paternoster and the Ave Maria, or any other petition you like, is vocal prayer. But think how harsh your music will be without what must come first; sometimes even the words will get into the wrong order. In these two kinds of prayer, with God's help, we may accomplish something ourselves. In the contemplation which I have just described we can do nothing. It is His Majesty Who does everything; the work is His alone and far transcends human nature.

I described this as well as I was able in the relation which I made of it, as I have said, so that my confessors should see it when they read the account of my life which they had ordered me to write. As I have explained all this about contemplation at such length, therefore, I shall not repeat myself here and I am doing no more than touch upon it. If those of you who have experienced the happiness of being called by the Lord to this state of contemplation can get this book, you will find in it points and counsels which the Lord was pleased to enable me to set down. These should bring you great comfort and profit – in my opinion, at least, and in the opinion of several people who have seen it and who keep it at hand in order to make frequent use of it. I am ashamed to tell you that anything of mine is made such use of and the Lord knows with what confusion I write a great deal that I do. Blessed be He for thus bearing with me. Those of you who, as I say, have experience of supernatural prayer should procure the book after my death; those who have not have no need to do so but they should try to carry out what has been said in this one. Let them leave everything to the Lord, to Whom it belongs to grant this gift, and He will not deny it you if you do not tarry on the road but press forward so as to reach the end of your journey.

CHAPTER 26

Continues the description of a method for recollecting the thoughts. Describes means of doing this. This chapter is very profitable for those who are beginning prayer.

Let us now return to our vocal prayer, so that we may learn to pray in such a way that, without our understanding how, God may give us everything at once: if we do this, as I have said, we shall pray as we ought. As you know, the first things must be examination of conscience, confession of sin and the signing of yourself with the Cross. Then, daughter, as you are alone, you must look for a companion – and who could be a better Companion than the very Master Who taught you the prayer that you are about to say? Imagine that this Lord Himself is at your side and see how lovingly and how humbly He is teaching you – and, believe me, you should stay with so good a Friend for as long as you can before you leave Him. If you become accustomed to having Him at your side,

---

[93] *algarab'a. Lit.*: "Arabic" and hence "gibberish," "jargon."

and if He sees that you love Him to be there and are always trying to please Him, you will never be able, as we put it, to send Him away, nor will He ever fail you. He will help you in all your trials and you will have Him everywhere. Do you think it is a small thing to have such a Friend as that beside you?

O sisters, those of you whose minds cannot reason for long or whose thoughts cannot dwell *upon God* but are *constantly* wandering must at all costs form this habit. I know quite well that you are capable of it – for many years I endured this trial of being unable to concentrate on one subject, and a very sore trial it is. But I know the Lord does not leave us so devoid of help that if we approach Him humbly and ask Him to be with us He will not grant our request. If a whole year passes without our obtaining what we ask, let us be prepared to try for longer. Let us never grudge time so well spent. Who, after all, is hurrying us? I am sure we can form this habit and strive to walk at the side of this true Master.

I am not asking you now to think of Him, or to form numerous conceptions of Him, or to make long and subtle meditations with your understanding. I am asking you only to look at Him. For who can prevent you from turning the eyes of your soul (just for a moment, if you can do no more) upon this Lord? You are capable of looking at very ugly *and loathsome* things: can you not, then, look at the most beautiful thing imaginable? Your Spouse never takes His eyes off you, daughters. He has borne with thousands of foul and abominable sins which you have committed against Him, yet even they have not been enough to make Him cease looking upon you. Is it such a great matter, then, for you to avert the eyes *of your soul* from outward things and sometimes to look at Him? See, He is only waiting for us to look at Him, as He says to the Bride.[94] If you want Him[95] you will find Him. He longs so much for us to look at Him once more that it will not be for lack of effort on His part if we fail to do so.

A wife, they say, must be like this if she is to have a happy married life with her husband. If he is sad, she must show signs of sadness; if he is merry, even though she may not in fact be so, she must appear merry too. See what slavery you have escaped from, sisters! Yet this, without any pretense, is really how we are treated by the Lord. He becomes subject to us and is pleased to let you be the mistress and to conform to your will. If you are happy, look upon your risen Lord, and the very thought of how He rose from the sepulcher will gladden you. How bright and how beautiful was He then! How majestic![96] How victorious! How joyful! He was like one emerging from a battle in which He had gained a great kingdom, all of which He desires you to have – and with it Himself. Is it such a great thing that you should turn your eyes but once and look upon Him Who has made you such great gifts?

If you are suffering trials, or are sad, look upon Him on His way to the Garden. What sore distress He must have borne in His soul, to describe His own suffering as He did and to complain of it! Or look upon Him bound to the Column, full of pain, His flesh all torn to pieces by His great love for you. How much He suffered, persecuted by some, spat upon by others, denied by His friends, and even deserted by them, with none to take His part, frozen with the cold and left so completely alone that you may well comfort each other! Or look upon Him bending under the weight of the Cross and not even allowed to take breath: He will look upon you with His lovely and compassionate eyes, full of tears, and in comforting your grief will forget His own because you are bearing Him company in order to comfort Him and turning your head to look upon Him.

"O Lord of the world, my true Spouse!" you may say to Him, if seeing Him in such a plight has filled your heart with such tenderness that you not only desire to look upon Him but love to speak to Him, not using forms of prayer, but words issuing from the compassion of your heart, which means so much to Him: "Art Thou so needy, my Lord and my Good, that Thou wilt accept poor companionship like mine? Do I read in Thy face that Thou hast found comfort, even in me? How can it be possible, Lord, that the angels are leaving Thee alone and that Thy Father is not comforting Thee?

"If Thou, Lord, art willing to suffer all this for me, what am I suffering for Thee? What have I to complain of? I am ashamed, Lord, when I see Thee in such a plight, and if in any way I can

---

[94] A vague reminiscence of some phrase from Canticles: perhaps ii, 14, 16, v, 2, or vi, 12.

[95] Or "love Him". The verb in the Spanish can have either meaning.

[96] *Lit.*: "With what majesty!"

imitate Thee I will suffer all trials that come to me and count them as a great blessing. Let us go both together, Lord: whither Thou goest, I must go; through whatsoever Thou passest, I must pass." Take up this cross, sisters: never mind if the Jews trample upon you provided you can save Him some of His trials. Take no heed of what they say to you; be deaf to all detraction; stumble and fall with your Spouse, but do not draw back from your cross or give it up. Think often of the weariness of His journey and of how much harder His trials were than those which you have to suffer. However hard you may imagine yours to be, and however much affliction they may cause you, they will be a source of comfort to you, for you will see that they are matters for scorn compared with the trials endured by the Lord.

You will ask me, sisters, how you can possibly do all this, and say that, if you had seen His Majesty with your bodily eyes at the time when He lived in the world, you would have done it willingly and gazed at Him for ever. Do not believe it: anyone who will not make the slight effort necessary for recollection in order to gaze upon this Lord present within her, which she can do without danger and with only the minimum of trouble, would have been far less likely to stand at the foot of the Cross with the Magdalene, who looked death (*as they say*) straight in the face. What the glorious Virgin and this blessed saint must have suffered! What threats, what malicious words, what shocks, what insults! For the people they were dealing with were not exactly polite to them. No, indeed; theirs was the kind of courtesy you might meet in hell, for they were the ministers of the devil himself. Yet, terrible as the sufferings of these women must have been, they would not have noticed them in the presence of pain so much greater.

So do not suppose, sisters, that you would have been prepared to endure such great trials then, if you are not ready for such trifling ones now. Practice enduring these and you may be given others which are greater. *Believe that I am telling the truth when I say that you can do this, for I am speaking from experience.* You will find it very helpful if you can get an image or a picture of this Lord – one that you like – not to wear round your neck and never look at but to use regularly whenever you talk to Him, and He will tell you what to say. If words do not fail you when you talk to people *on earth*, why should they do so when you talk to God? Do not imagine that they will – I shall certainly not believe that they have done so if you once form the habit. For when you never have intercourse with a person he soon becomes a stranger to you, and you forget how to talk to him; and before long, even if he is a kinsman, you feel as if you do not know him, for both kinship and friendship lose their influence when communication ceases.

It is also a great help to have a good book, written in the vernacular, simply as an aid to recollection. With this aid you will learn to say your vocal prayers well, *I mean, as they ought to be said* – and little by little, persuasively and methodically, you will get your soul used to this, so that it will no longer be afraid of it. Remember that many years have passed since it went away from its Spouse, and it needs very careful handling before it will return home. We sinners are like that: we have accustomed our souls and minds to go after their own pleasures (or pains, it would be more correct to say) until the unfortunate soul no longer knows what it is doing. When that has happened, a good deal of skill is necessary before it can be inspired with enough love to make it stay at home; but unless we can gradually do that we shall accomplish nothing. Once again I assure you that, if you are careful to form habits of the kind I have mentioned, you will derive such great profit from them that I could not describe it even if I wished. Keep at the side of this good Master, then, and be most firmly resolved to learn what He teaches you; His Majesty will then ensure you are not failing to be good disciples, and He will never leave you unless you leave Him. Consider the words uttered by those Divine lips: the very first of them will show you at once what love He has for you, and it is no small blessing and joy for the pupil to see that his Master loves Him.

CHAPTER 27

Describes the great love shown us by the Lord in the first words of the Paternoster and the great importance of our making no account of good birth if we truly desire to be the daughters of God.

"Our Father, which art in the Heavens." O my Lord, how Thou dost reveal Thyself as the Father of such a Son, while Thy Son reveals Himself as the Son of such a Father! Blessed be Thou for ever and ever. Ought not so great a favor as this, Lord, to have come at the end of the prayer? Here, at the very beginning, Thou dost fill our hands and grant us so great a favor that it would be a very great blessing if our understanding could be filled with it so that the will would be occupied and we should be unable to say another word. Oh, how appropriate, daughters, would perfect contemplation be here! Oh, how right would the soul be to enter within itself, so as to be the better able to rise above itself, that this holy Son might show it the nature of the place where He says His Father dwells – namely, the Heavens! Let us leave earth, my daughters, for it is not right that a favor like this should be prized so little, and that, after we have realized how great this favor is, we should remain on earth any more.

O Son of God and my Lord! How is it that Thou canst give us so much with Thy first word? It is so wonderful that Thou shouldst descend to such a degree of humility as to join with us when we pray and make Thyself the Brother of creatures so miserable and lowly! How can it be that, in the name of Thy Father, Thou shouldst give us all that there is to be given, by willing Him to have us as His children – and Thy word cannot fail? [It seems that] Thou dost oblige Him to fulfill Thy word, a charge by no means light, since, being our Father, He must bear with us, however great our offences. If we return to Him, He must pardon us, as He pardoned the prodigal son, must comfort us in our trials, and must sustain us, as such a Father is bound to do, for He must needs be better than any earthly father, since nothing good can fail to have its perfection in Him. *He must cherish us; He must sustain us;* and at the last He must make us participants and fellow-heirs with Thee.

Behold, my Lord, with the love that Thou hast for us and with Thy humility, nothing can be an obstacle to Thee. And then, Lord, Thou hast been upon earth and by taking our nature upon Thee hast clothed Thyself with humanity: Thou hast therefore some reason to care for our advantage. But behold, Thy Father is in Heaven, as Thou hast told us, and it is right that Thou shouldst consider His honor. Since Thou hast offered Thyself to be dishonored by us, leave Thy Father free. Oblige Him not to do so much for people as wicked as I, who will make Him such poor acknowledgment.

O good Jesus! How clearly hast Thou shown that Thou art One with Him and that Thy will is His and His is Thine! How open a confession is this, my Lord! What is this love that Thou hast for us? Thou didst deceive the devil, and conceal from him that Thou art the Son of God, but Thy great desire for our welfare overcomes all obstacles to Thy granting us this greatest of favors. Who but Thou could do this, Lord? I cannot think how the devil failed to understand from that word of Thine Who Thou wert, beyond any doubt. I, at least, my Jesus, see clearly that Thou didst speak as a dearly beloved son both for Thyself and for us, and Thou hast such power that what Thou sayest in Heaven shall be done on earth. Blessed be Thou for ever, my Lord, Who lovest so much to give that no obstacle can stay Thee.

Do you not think, daughters, that this is a good Master, since He begins by granting us this great favor so as to make us love to learn what He teaches us? Do you think it would be right for us, while we are repeating this prayer with our lips, to stop trying to think of what we are saying, lest picturing such love should tear our hearts to pieces? No one who realized His greatness could possibly say it would be. What son is there in the world who would not try to learn who his father was if he had one as good, and of as great majesty and dominion, as ours? Were God not all this, it would not surprise me if we had no desire to be known as His children; for the world is such that, if the father is of lower rank than his son, the son feels no honor in recognizing him as his father. This does not apply here: God forbid that such a thing should ever happen in this house – it would turn the place into hell. Let the sister who is of the highest birth speak of her father least; we must all be equals.

O College of Christ, in which the Lord was pleased that Saint Peter, who was a fisherman, should have more authority than Saint Bartholomew, who was the son of a king! His Majesty knew what a fuss would be made in the world about who was fashioned from the finer clay – which is like discussing whether clay is better for bricks or for walls. Dear Lord, what a trouble we make about it! God deliver you, sisters, from such contentions, even if they be carried on only in jest; I hope that His Majesty will indeed deliver you. If anything like this should be going on among you, apply the remedy immediately, and let the sister concerned fear lest she be a Judas among the Apostles. *Do what you can to get rid of such a bad companion. If you cannot*, give her penances *heavier than for anything else* until she realizes that she has not deserved to be even the basest clay. You have a good Father, given you by the good Jesus: let no other father be known or referred to here. Strive, my daughters, to be such that you deserve to find comfort in Him and to throw yourselves into His arms. You know that, if you are good children, He will never send you away. And who would not do anything rather than lose such a Father?

Oh, thank God, what cause for comfort there is here! Rather than write more about it I will leave it for you to think about; for, however much your thoughts may wander, between such a Son and such a Father there must needs be the Holy Spirit. May He enkindle your will and bind you to Himself with the most fervent love, since even the great advantage you gain will not suffice to do so.

CHAPTER 28

Describes the nature of the Prayer of Recollection and sets down some of the means by which we can make it a habit.

Consider now what your Master says next: "Who art in the Heavens." Do you suppose it matters little what Heaven is and where you must seek your most holy Father? I assure you that for minds which wander it is of great importance not only to have a right belief about this but to try to learn it by experience, for it is one of the best ways of concentrating the mind and effecting recollection in the soul.

You know that God is everywhere; and *this is a great truth, for*, of course, wherever the king is, or so they say, the court is too: that is to say, wherever God is, there is Heaven. No doubt you can believe that, in any place where His Majesty is, there is fullness of glory. Remember how Saint Augustine tells us about his seeking God in many places and eventually finding Him within himself. Do you suppose it is of little importance that a soul which is often distracted should come to understand this truth and to find that, in order to speak to its Eternal Father and to take its delight in Him, it has no need to go to Heaven or to speak in a loud voice? However quietly we speak, He is so near that He will hear us: we need no wings to go in search of Him but have only to find a place where we can be alone and look upon Him present within us. Nor need we feel strange in the presence of so kind a Guest; we must talk to Him very humbly, as we should to our father, ask Him for things as we should ask a father, tell Him our troubles, beg Him to put them right, and yet realize that we are not worthy to be called His children.

Avoid being bashful with God, as some people are, in the belief that they are being humble. It would not be humility on your part if the King were to do you a favor and you refused to accept it; but you would be showing humility by taking it, and being pleased with it, yet realizing how far you are from deserving it. A fine humility it would be if I had the Emperor of Heaven and earth in my house, coming to it to do me a favor and to delight in my company, and I were so humble that I would not answer His questions, nor remain with Him, nor accept what He gave me, but left Him alone. Or if He were to speak to me and beg me to ask for what I wanted, and I were so humble that I preferred to remain poor and even let Him go away, so that He would see I had not sufficient resolution.

Have nothing to do with that kind of humility, daughters, but speak with Him as with a Father, a Brother, a Lord and a Spouse – and, sometimes in one way and sometimes in another, He will teach you what you must do to please Him. Do not be foolish; ask Him to let you speak to Him, and, as He is your Spouse, to treat you as His brides. *Remember how important it is for you to have understood this truth – that the Lord is within us and that we should be there with Him.*

If one prays in this way, the prayer may be only vocal, but the mind will be recollected much sooner; and this is a prayer which brings with it many blessings. It is called recollection because the soul collects together all the faculties and enters within itself to be with its God. Its Divine Master comes more speedily to teach it, and to grant it the Prayer of Quiet, than in any other way. For, hidden there within itself, it can think about the Passion, and picture the Son, and offer Him to the Father, without wearying the mind by going to seek Him on Mount Calvary, or in the Garden, or at the Column.

Those who are able to shut themselves up in this way within this little Heaven of the soul, wherein dwells the Maker of Heaven and earth, and who have formed the habit of looking at nothing and staying in no place which will distract these outward senses, may be sure that they are walking on an excellent road, and will come without fail to drink of the water of the fountain, for they will journey a long way in a short time. They are like one who travels in a ship, and, if he has a little good wind, reaches the end of his voyage in a few days, while those who go by land take *much* longer.

These souls have already, as we may say, put out to sea; though they have not sailed quite out of sight of land, they do what they can to get away from it, in the time at their disposal, by recollecting their senses. If their recollection is genuine, the fact becomes very evident, for it produces certain effects which I do not know how to explain but which anyone will recognize who has experience of them. It is as if the soul were rising from play, for it sees that worldly things are nothing but toys; so in due course it rises above them, like a person entering a strong castle, in order that it may have nothing more to fear from its enemies. It withdraws the senses from all outward things and spurns them so completely that, without its understanding how, its eyes close and it cannot see them and the soul's spiritual sight becomes clear. Those who walk along this path almost invariably close their eyes when they say their prayers; this, for many reasons, is an admirable custom, since it means that they are making an effort not to look at things of the world. The effort has to be made only at the beginning; later it becomes unnecessary: eventually, in fact, it would cost a greater effort to open the eyes during prayer than to close them. The soul seems to gather up its strength and to master itself at the expense of the body, which it leaves weakened and alone: in this way it becomes stronger for the fight against it.

This may not be evident at first, if the recollection is not very profound – for at this stage it is sometimes more so and sometimes less. At first it may cause a good deal of trouble, for the body insists on its rights, not understanding that if it refuses to admit defeat it is, as it were, cutting off its own head. But if we cultivate the habit, make the necessary effort and practice the exercises for several days, the benefits will reveal themselves, and when we begin to pray we shall realize that the bees are coming to the hive and entering it to make the honey, and all without any effort of ours. For it is the Lord's will that, in return for the time which their efforts have cost them, the soul and the will should be given this power over the senses. They will only have to make a sign to show that they wish to enter into recollection and the senses will obey and allow themselves to be recollected. Later they may come out again, but it is a great thing that they should ever have surrendered, for if they come out it is as captives and slaves and they do none of the harm that they might have done before. When the will calls them afresh they respond more quickly, until, after they have entered the soul many times, the Lord is pleased that they should remain there altogether in perfect contemplation.

What has been said should be noted with great care, for, though it seems obscure, it will be understood by anyone desirous of putting it into practice. The sea-voyage, then, can be made; and, as it is very important that we should not travel too slowly, let us just consider how we can get accustomed to these good habits. Souls who do so are more secure from many occasions of sin, and the fire of Divine love is the more readily enkindled in them; for they are so near that fire that, however little the blaze has been fanned with the understanding, any small spark that flies out at them will cause them to burst into flame. When no hindrance comes to it from outside, the soul remains alone with its God and is thoroughly prepared to become enkindled.

And now let us imagine that we have within us a palace of priceless worth, built entirely of gold and precious stones – a palace, in short, fit for so great a Lord. Imagine that it is partly your doing that this palace should be what it is – and this is really true, for there is no building so beautiful as a soul that is pure and full of virtues, and, the greater these virtues are, the more brilliantly do the stones shine. Imagine that within the palace dwells this great King, Who has vouchsafed to become your Father and Who is seated upon a throne of supreme price – namely, your heart.

At first you will think this irrelevant – I mean the use of this figure to explain my point – but it may prove very useful, especially to persons like yourselves. For, as we women are not learned *or fine-witted*, we need all these things to help us realize that we actually have something within us incomparably more precious than anything we see outside. Do not let us suppose that the interior of the soul is empty; God grant that only women may be so thoughtless as to suppose that. If we took care always to remember what a Guest we have within us, I think it would be impossible for us to abandon ourselves to *vanities and* things of the world, for we should see how worthless they are by comparison with those which we have within us. What does an animal do beyond satisfying his hunger by seizing whatever attracts him when he sees it? There should surely be a great difference between the brute beasts and ourselves, *as we have such a Father.*

Perhaps you will laugh at me and say that this is obvious enough; and you will be right, though it was some time before I came to see it. I knew perfectly well that I had a soul, but I did not understand what that soul merited, or Who dwelt within it, until I closed my eyes to the vanities of this world in order to see it. I think, if I had understood then, as I do now, how this great King *really* dwells within this little palace of my soul, I should not have left Him alone so often, but should have stayed with Him and never have allowed His dwelling-place to get so dirty. How wonderful it is that He Whose greatness could fill a thousand worlds, and very many more, should confine Himself within so small a space, *just as He was pleased to dwell within the womb of His most holy Mother!* Being the Lord, He has, of course, perfect freedom, and, as He loves us, He fashions Himself to our measure.

When a soul sets out upon this path, He does not reveal Himself to it, lest it should feel dismayed at seeing that its littleness can contain such greatness; but gradually He enlarges it to the extent requisite for what He has to set within it. It is for this reason that I say He has perfect freedom, since He has power to make the whole of this palace great. The important point is that we should be absolutely resolved to give it to Him for His own and should empty it so that He may take out and put in just what He likes, as He would with something of His own. His Majesty is right in demanding this; let us not deny it to Him. And, as He refuses to force our will, He takes what we give Him but does not give Himself wholly until *He sees that* we are giving ourselves wholly to Him. This is certain, and, as it is of such importance, I often remind you of it. Nor does He work within the soul as He does when it is wholly His and keeps nothing back. I do not see how He can do so, since He likes everything to be done in order. If we fill the palace with vulgar people and all kinds of junk, how can the Lord and His Court occupy it? When such a crowd is there it would be a great thing if He were to remain for even a short time.

Do you suppose, daughters, that He is alone when He comes to us? Do you not see that His *most holy* Son says: "Who art in the Heavens"? Surely such a King would not be abandoned by His courtiers. They stay with Him and pray to Him on our behalf and for our welfare, for they are full of charity. Do not imagine that Heaven is like this earth, where, if a lord or prelate shows anyone favors, whether for some particular reason or simply because he likes him, people at once become envious, and, though the poor man has done nothing to them, he is maliciously treated, so that his favors cost him dear.

CHAPTER 29

Continues to describe methods for achieving this Prayer of Recollection. Says what little account we should make of being favored by our superiors.

For the love of God, daughters, avoid making any account of these favors. You should each do your duty; and, if this is not appreciated by your superior, you may be sure that it will be appreciated and rewarded by the Lord. We did not come here to seek rewards in this life, *but only in the life to come.* Let our thoughts always be fixed upon what endures, and not trouble themselves with earthly things which do not endure even for a lifetime. For to-day some other sister will be in your superior's good books; whereas to-morrow, if she sees you exhibiting some additional virtue, it is with you that she will be better pleased – and if she is not it is of little consequence. Never give way to these thoughts, which sometimes begin in a small way but may cost you a great deal of unrest. Check them by remembering that your kingdom is not of this world, and that everything comes quickly to an end, *and that there is nothing in this life that goes on unchangingly.*

But even that is a poor remedy and anything but a perfect one; it is best that this state of things should continue, and that you should be humbled and out of favor, and should wish to be so for the sake of the Lord Who dwells in you. Turn your eyes upon yourself and look at yourself inwardly, as I have said. You will find your Master; He will not fail you: indeed, the less outward comfort you have, the [much] greater the joy He will give you. He is full of compassion and never fails those who are afflicted and out of favor if they trust in Him alone. Thus David tells us *that he never saw the just forsaken*[97], *and again, that* the Lord is with the afflicted.[98] Either you believe this or you do not: if you do, as you should, why do you wear yourselves to death with worry?

O my Lord, if we had a real knowledge of Thee, we should make not the slightest account of anything, since Thou givest so much to those who will set their whole trust on Thee. Believe me, friends, it is a great thing to realize the truth of this so that we may see how deceptive are earthly *things and* favors when they deflect the soul in any way from its course and hinder it from entering within itself.[99] God help me! If only someone could make you realize this! I myself, *Lord,* certainly cannot; I know that [in truth] I owe *Thee* more than anyone else but I cannot realize this myself as well as I should.

Returning to what I was saying, I should like to be able to explain the nature of this holy companionship with our great Companion, the Holiest of the holy, in which there is nothing to hinder the soul and her Spouse from remaining alone together, when the soul desires to enter within herself, to shut the door behind her so as to keep out all that is worldly and to dwell in that Paradise with her God. I say "desires", because you must understand that this is not a supernatural state but depends upon our volition, and that, by God's favor, we can enter it of our own accord: *this condition must be understood of everything that we say in this book can be done,* for without it nothing can be accomplished and we have not the power to think a single good thought. For this is not a silence of the faculties: it is a shutting-up of the faculties within itself by the soul.

There are many ways in which we can gradually acquire this habit, as various books tell us. We must cast aside everything else, they say, in order to approach God inwardly and we must retire within ourselves even during our ordinary occupations. If I can recall the companionship which I have within my soul for as much as a moment, that is of great utility. *But as I am speaking only about the way to recite vocal prayers well, there is no need for me to say as much as this. All I want is that we should know*[100] *and abide with the Person with Whom we are speaking, and not turn our backs upon Him; for that, it seems to me, is what we are doing when we talk to God and yet think of all kinds of vanity. The whole mischief comes from our not really grasping the fact that He is near us, and imagining Him far away – so far, that we shall have to go to Heaven in order to find Him. How is it, Lord, that we do not look at Thy face, when it is so near us? We do not think people are listening to us when we are speaking to them unless we see them looking at us. And do we close our eyes so as not to see that Thou art looking at us? How can we know if Thou hast heard what we say to Thee?*

The great thing I should like to teach you is that, in order to accustom ourselves gradually to giving our minds confidence, so that we may readily understand what we are saying, and with Whom we are speaking, we must recollect our outward senses, take charge of them ourselves and give them something which will occupy them. It is in this way that we have Heaven within ourselves since the Lord of Heaven is there. If once we accustom ourselves to being glad[101] that there is no need to raise our voices in order to speak to Him, since His Majesty will make us conscious that He is there, we shall be able to say the Paternoster and whatever other prayers we like with great peace of mind, and the Lord Himself will help us not to grow tired. Soon after we have begun to force ourselves to remain near the Lord, He will give us indications by which we may understand that, though we have had to say the Paternoster many times, He heard us the first time. For He loves to

---

97 Psalm xxxvi.
98 Psalm xxxiii 20-1.
99 *Lit.* "when they deflect the soul in any way from going within itself."
100 *Lit.*: "see."
101 *Lit.*: "once we begin to be glad."

save us worry; and, even though we may take a whole hour over saying it once, if we can realize that we are with Him, and what it is we are asking Him, and how willing He is, *like any father*, to grant it to us, and how He loves to be with us, *and comfort us*, He has no wish for us to tire our brains by a great deal of talking.

For love of the Lord, then, sisters, accustom yourselves to saying the Paternoster in this recollected way, and before long you will see how you gain by doing so. It is a method of prayer which establishes habits that prevent the soul from going astray and the faculties from becoming restless. This you will find out in time: I only beg you to test it, even at the cost of a little trouble, which always results when we try to form a new habit. I assure you, however, that before long you will have the great comfort of finding it unnecessary to tire yourselves with seeking this holy Father to Whom you pray, for you will discover Him within you.

May the Lord teach this to those of you who do not know it: for my own part I must confess that, until the Lord taught me this method, I never knew what it was to get satisfaction and comfort out of prayer, and it is because I have always gained such great benefits from this custom of interior recollection[102] that I have written about it at such length. *Perhaps you all know this, but some sister may come to you who will not know it, so you must not be vexed at my having spoken about it here.*

I conclude by advising anyone who wishes to acquire it (since, as I say, it is in our power to do so) not to grow weary of trying to get used to the method which has been described, for it is equivalent to a gradual gaining of the mastery over herself and is not vain labor. To conquer oneself for one's own good is to make use of the senses in the service of the interior life. If she is speaking she must try to remember that there is One within her to Whom she can speak; if she is listening, let her remember that she can listen to Him Who is nearer to her than anyone else. Briefly, let her realize that, if she likes, she need never withdraw from this good companionship, and let her grieve when she has left her Father alone for so long though her need of Him is so sore.

If she can, let her practice recollection many times daily; if not, let her do so occasionally. As she grows accustomed to it, she will feel its benefits, either sooner or later. Once the Lord has granted it to her, she would not exchange it for any treasure.

Nothing, sisters, can be learned without a little trouble, so do, for the love of God, look upon any care which you take about this as well spent. I know that, with God's help, if you practice it for a year, or perhaps for only six months, you will be successful in attaining it. Think what a short time that is for acquiring so great a benefit, for you will be laying a good foundation, so that, if the Lord desires to raise you up to achieve great things, He will find you ready, because you will be close to Himself. May His Majesty never allow us to withdraw ourselves from His presence. Amen.

CHAPTER 30

Describes the importance of understanding what we ask for in prayer. Treats of these words in the Paternoster: "Sanctificetur nomen tuum, adveniat regnum tuum."[103] Applies them to the Prayer of Quiet, and begins the explanation of them.

We must now come to consider the next petition in our good Master's prayer, in which He begins to entreat His holy Father on our behalf, and see what it is that He entreats, as it is well that we should know this.

What person, however careless, who had to address someone of importance, would not spend time in thinking how to approach him so as to please him and not be considered tedious? He would also think what he was going to ask for and what use he would make of it, especially if his petition were for some particular thing, as our good Jesus tells us our petitions must be. This point seems to me *very* important. Couldst Thou not, my Lord, have ended this prayer in a single sentence, by saying: "Give us, Father, whatever is good for us"? For, in addressing One Who knows everything, there would seem to be no need to say any more.

---

[102] *Lit.*: "of recollection within me."
[103] "Hallowed be Thy name. Thy kingdom come."

This would have sufficed, O Eternal Wisdom, as between Thee and Thy Father. It was thus that Thou didst address Him in the Garden, telling Him of Thy will and Thy fear, but leaving Thyself in His hands. But Thou knowest us, my Lord, and Thou knowest that we are not as resigned as wert Thou to the will of Thy Father; we needed, therefore, to be taught to ask for particular things so that we should stop *for a moment* to think if what we ask of Thee is good for us, and if it is not, should not ask for it. For, being what we are and having our free will, if we do not receive what we ask for, we shall not accept what the Lord gives us. The gift might be the best one possible – but we never think we are rich unless we actually see money in our hands.

Oh, God help me! What is it that sends our faith to sleep, so that we cannot realize how certain we are, on the one hand, to be punished, and, on the other, to be rewarded? It is for this reason, daughters, that it is good for you to know what you are asking for in the Paternoster, so that, if the Eternal Father gives it you, you shall not cast it back in His face. You must think carefully if what you are about to ask for will be good for you; if it will not, do not ask for it, but ask His Majesty to give you light. For we are blind and often we have such a loathing for life-giving food that we cannot eat it but prefer what will cause us death – and what a death: so terrible and eternal!

Now the good Jesus bids us say these words, in which we pray that this Kingdom may come in us: "Hallowed be Thy Name, Thy Kingdom come in us." Consider now, daughters, how great is our Master's wisdom. I am thinking here of what we are asking in praying for this kingdom, and it is well that we should realize this. His Majesty, knowing of how little we are capable, saw that, unless He provided for us by giving us His Kingdom here on earth, we could neither hallow nor praise nor magnify nor glorify *nor exalt* this holy name of the Eternal Father in a way befitting it. The good Jesus, therefore, places these two petitions next to each other. Let us understand this thing that we are asking for, daughters, and how important it is that we should pray for it without ceasing and do all we can to please Him Who will give it us: it is for that reason that I want to tell you what I know about the matter now. If you do not like the subject, think out some other meditations for yourselves, for our Master will allow us to do this, provided we submit in all things to the teaching of the [Holy Roman] Church, as I do here. *In any case I shall not give you this book to read until persons who understand these matters have seen it: so, if there is anything wrong with it, the reason will be, not wickedness, but my imperfect knowledge.*

To me, then, it seems that, of the many joys to be found in the kingdom of Heaven, the chief is that we shall have no more to do with the things of earth; for in Heaven we shall have an intrinsic tranquility and glory, a joy in the rejoicings of all, a perpetual peace, and a great interior satisfaction which will come to us when we see that all are hallowing and praising the Lord, and are blessing His name, and that none is offending Him. For all love Him there and the soul's one concern is loving Him, nor can it cease from loving Him because it knows Him. And this is how we should love Him on earth, though we cannot do so with the same perfection nor yet all the time; still, if we knew Him, we should love Him very differently from the way we do now.

It looks as though I were going to say that we must be angels to make this petition and to say our vocal prayers well. This would indeed be our Divine Master's wish, since He bids us make so sublime a petition. You may be quite sure that He never tells us to ask for impossibilities, so it must be possible, with God's help, for a soul living in that state of exile to reach such a point, though not as perfectly as those who have been freed from this prison, for we are making a sea-voyage and are still on the journey. But there are times when we are wearied with traveling and the Lord grants our faculties tranquility and our soul quiet, and while they are in that state He gives us a clear understanding of the nature of the gifts He bestows upon those whom He brings to His Kingdom. Those to whom, while they are still on earth, He grants what we are asking Him for receive pledges which will give them a great hope of eventually attaining to a perpetual enjoyment of what on earth He only allows them to taste.

If it were not that you would tell me I am treating of contemplation, it would be appropriate, in writing of this petition, to say a little about the beginning of pure contemplation, which those who experience it call the Prayer of Quiet; but, as I have said, I am discussing vocal prayer here, and anyone ignorant of the subject might think that the two had nothing to do with one another, though I know this is certainly not true. Forgive my wanting to speak of it, for I know there are many people who practice vocal prayer in the manner already described and are raised by God to the higher kind of contemplation without *having had any hand in this themselves or even* knowing

1otionless, for otherwise their peace would be destroyed: for this reason they dare not stir.
g is a distress to them: they will spend a whole hour on a single repetition of the Paternoster.
e so close to God that they know they can make themselves understood by signs. They are
1ace, near to their King, and they see that He is already beginning to give them His Kingdom
   Sometimes tears come to their eyes, but they weep very gently and quite without distress:
ole desire is the hallowing of this name. They seem not to be in the world, and have no
ee or hear anything but their God; nothing distresses them, nor does it seem that anything
ibly do so. In short, for as long as this state lasts, they are so overwhelmed and absorbed
y and delight which they experience that they can think of nothing else to wish for, and
ly say with Saint Peter: "Lord, let us make here three mansions."[105]

asionally, during this Prayer of Quiet, God grants the soul another favor which is hard to
nd if one has not had long experience of it. But any of you who have had this will at once
e it and it will give you great comfort to know what it is. I believe God often grants this
gether with the other. When this quiet is felt in a high degree and lasts for a long time, I do
 that, if the will were not made fast to something, the peace could be of such long duration.
es it goes on for a day, or for two days, and we find ourselves – I mean those who
ce this state – full of this joy without understanding the reason. They see clearly that their
lf is not in what they are doing, but that the most important faculty is absent – namely, the
ich I think is united with its God – and that the other faculties are left free to busy themselves
 service. For this they have much more capacity at such a time, though when attending to
affairs they are dull and sometimes stupid.

 a great favor which the Lord grants to these souls, for it unites the active life with the
lative. At such times they serve the Lord in both these ways at once; the will, while in
lation, is working without knowing how it does so; the other two faculties are serving Him
1a did. Thus Martha and Mary work together. I know someone to whom the Lord often
 this favor; she could not understand it and asked a great contemplative[106] about it, he told
 what she described was quite possible and had happened to himself. I think, therefore, that
ul experiences such satisfaction in this Prayer of Quiet the will must be almost continuously
ith Him Who alone can give it happiness.

ink it will be well, sisters, if I give some advice here to any of you whom the Lord, out of
dness alone, has brought to this state, as I know that this has happened to some of you. First
hen such persons experience this joy, without knowing whence it has come to them, but
g at least that they could not have achieved it of themselves, they are tempted to imagine
y can prolong it and they may even try not to breathe. This is ridiculous: we can no more
this prayer than we can make the day break, or stop night from falling; it is supernatural and
ing we cannot acquire. The most we can do to prolong this favor is to realize that we can
diminish nor add to it, but, being most unworthy and undeserving of it, can only receive it
nksgiving. And we can best give thanks, not with many words, but by lifting up our eyes,
 publican.[107]

 well to seek greater solitude so as to make room for the Lord and allow His Majesty to do
 work in us. The most we should do is occasionally, and quite gently, to utter a single word,
erson giving a little puff to a candle, when he sees it has almost gone out, so as to make it
ain; though, if it were fully alight, I suppose the only result of blowing it would be to put it
ink the puff should be a gentle one because, if we begin to tax our brains by making up long
s, the will may become active again.

---

oradas. The "three tabernacles" of St. Matthew xvii, 4.
 the margin of T. the author adds, in her own hand, that this contemplative was St. Francis Borgia,
f Gand'a. No doubt, then, the other person referred to was St. Teresa herself. The addition reads:
as a religious of the Company of Jesus, who had been Duke of Gand'a," and to this are added some
lso in St. Teresa's hand, but partially scored out and partially cut by the binder, which seem to be:
ew it well by experience."
. Luke xviii, 13. St. Teresa apparently forgot that the publican "would not so much as lift his eyes
 heaven".

how it has happened. *For this reason, daughters, I attach great impor[t]* *vocal prayers well.* I know a nun who could never practice anything but to this and found she had everything else; yet if she omitted saying her p[r] so much that she could not endure it. May we all practice such mental pra a number of Paternosters, corresponding to the number of times Our Lo[r] nothing more than these and a few other prayers she would spend two o[r] me once in great distress, saying that she did not know how to practice m could not contemplate but could only say vocal prayers. *She was quite an an extremely good and religious life.* I asked her what prayers she said, that, though keeping to the Paternoster, she was experiencing pure contem raising her to be with Him in union. She spent her life so well, too, that she was receiving great favors. So I praised the Lord and envied her vo[c] true – and it is – none of you who have had a bad opinion of contemplati will be free from the risk of becoming like them if you say your vocal p said and keep a pure conscience. *I shall have to say still more about thi[s] hear it may pass it over.*

CHAPTER 31

Continues the same subject. Explains what is meant by the Praye[r] several counsels to those who experience it. This chapter is ve[ry]

Now, daughters, I still want to describe this Prayer of Quiet to you, in talked about, and as the Lord has been pleased to teach it to me, perha[p] describe it to you. It is in this kind of prayer, as I have said, that the Lord show us that He is hearing our petition: He begins to give us His Kingdom truly praise Him and hallow His name and strive to make others do so like[wise]

This is a supernatural state, and, however hard we try, we cannot rea[ch] is a state in which the soul enters into peace, or rather in which the Lord gi[ves] presence, as He did to that just man Simeon.[104] In this state all the faculties a way which has nothing to do with the outward senses, realizes that it is no and that, if it were but a little closer, it would become one with Him thr[ough] because it sees Him either with its bodily or with its spiritual eyes. The ju more than the glorious Infant – a poor little Child, Who, to judge from th which He was wrapped and from the small number of the people whom He Him up to the Temple, might well have been the son of these poor people ra Heavenly Father. But the Child Himself revealed to him Who He was. Just does the soul know Who He is. It cannot understand how it knows Him, ye Kingdom (or at least is near to the King Who will give it the Kingdom), and that it dares to ask nothing. It is, as it were, in a swoon, both inwardly and outward man (let me call it the "body", and then you will understand me b move, but rests, like one who has almost reached the end of his journey, s[o] start again upon its way, with redoubled strength for its task.

The body experiences the greatest delight and the soul is conscious of glad is it merely to find itself near the fountain that, even before it has begun fill. There seems nothing left for it to desire. The faculties are stilled and hav[e] any movement they may make appears to hinder the soul from loving God. T[he] lost, however, since, two of them being free, they can realize in Whose Pres will that is in captivity now; and, if while in this state it is capable of experien[ce] comes when it realizes that it will have to resume its liberty. The mind trie[s] only one thing, and the memory has no desire to busy itself with more: they b one thing needful and that anything else will unsettle them. Persons in this st

remain
Speakir
They ar
in the p
on earth
their w
wish to
can pos
by the
will gla
Oc
underst
recogni
favor t
not thir
Someti
experie
whole
will, w
with H
worldly
It
contem
contem
as Mar
grantec
her tha
as the s
united
I
His go
of all,
knowir
that th
contro
somet
neither
with tl
like th
It
His ow
like a
burn a
out. I
speecl

105
106

Duke
"who
words
"who

107

towar

---

104 The allusion is, of course, to St. Luke ii, 25 ("just and devout"), 29.

Note carefully, friends, this piece of advice which I want to give you now. You will often find that these other two faculties are of no help to you. It may come about that the soul is enjoying the highest degree of quiet, and that the understanding has soared so far aloft that what is happening to it seems not to be going on in its own house at all; it *really* seems to be a guest in somebody else's house, looking for other lodgings, since its own lodging no longer satisfies it and it cannot remain there for long together. Perhaps this is only my own experience and other people do not find it so. But, speaking for myself, I sometimes long to die because I cannot cure this wandering of the mind. At other times the mind seems to be settled in its own abode and to be remaining there with the will as its companion. When all three faculties work together it is wonderful. The harmony is like that between husband and wife: if they are happy and love each other, both desire the same thing; but if the husband is unhappy in his marriage he soon begins to make the wife restless. Just so, when the will finds itself in this state of quiet, it must take no more notice of the understanding than it would of a madman, for, if it tries to draw the understanding along with it, it is bound to grow preoccupied and restless, with the result that this state of prayer will be all effort and no gain and the soul will lose what God has been giving it without any effort of its own.

Pay great attention to the following comparison, which *the Lord suggested to me when I was in this state of prayer, and which* seems to me very appropriate. The soul is like an infant still at its mother's breast: such is the mother's care for it that she gives it its milk without its having to ask for it so much as by moving its lips. That is what happens here. The will simply loves, and no effort needs to be made by the understanding, for it is the Lord's pleasure that, without exercising its thought, the soul should realize that it is in His company, and should merely drink the milk which His Majesty puts into its mouth and enjoy its sweetness. The Lord desires it to know that it is He Who is granting it that favor and that in its enjoyment of it He too rejoices. But it is not His will that the soul should try to understand how it is enjoying it, or what it is enjoying; it should lose all thought of itself, and He Who is at its side will not fail to see what is best for it. If it begins to strive with its mind so that the mind may be apprised of what is happening and thus induced to share in it,[108] it will be quite unable to do so, and the soul will perforce lose the milk[109] and forgo that Divine sustenance.

This state of prayer is different from that in which the soul is wholly united with God, for in the latter state it does not even swallow its nourishment: the Lord places this within it, and it has no idea how. But in this state it even seems to be His will that the soul should work a little, though so quietly that it is hardly conscious of doing so. What disturbs it is the understanding and this is not the case when there is union of all the three faculties, since He Who created them suspends them: He keeps them occupied with the enjoyment that He has given them, without their knowing, or being able to understand, the reason. *Anyone who has had experience of this kind of prayer will understand quite well what I am saying if, after reading this, she considers it carefully, and thinks out its meaning: otherwise it will be Greek[110] to her.*

Well, as I say, the soul is conscious of having reached this state of prayer, which is a quiet, deep and Peaceful happiness of the will, without being able to decide precisely what it is, although it can clearly see how it differs from the happiness of the world. To have dominion over the whole world, with all its happiness, would not suffice to bring the soul such inward satisfaction as it enjoys now in the depths of its will. For other kinds of happiness in life, it seems to me, touch only the outward part of the will, which we might describe as its rind.

When one of you finds herself in this sublime state of prayer, which, as I have already said, is most markedly supernatural, and the understanding (or, to put it more clearly, the thought) wanders off after the most ridiculous things in the world, she should laugh at it and treat it as the silly thing it is, and remain in her state of quiet. For thoughts will come and go, but the will is mistress and all-powerful, and will recall them without your having to trouble about it. But if you try to drag the understanding back by force, you lose your power over it, which comes from your taking and receiving that Divine sustenance, and neither will nor understanding will gain,[111] but both will be

---

108 *Lit.*: "and drawn along with it"; the same phrase is found at the end of the preceding paragraph.

109 *Lit.* "let the milk fall out of its mouth."

110 *Algarab'a*. Cf. n. 96 above.

111 *Lit.*: "neither the one nor the other will gain."

losers. There is a saying that, if we try very hard to grasp all, we lose all; and so I think it is here. Experience will show you the truth of this; and I shall not be surprised if those of you who have none think this very obscure and unnecessary. But, as I have said, if you have only a little experience of it you will understand it and be able to profit by it, and you will praise the Lord for being pleased to enable me to explain it.

Let us now conclude by saying that, when the soul is brought to this state of prayer, it would seem that the Eternal Father has already granted its petition that He will give it His Kingdom on earth. O blessed request, in which we ask for so great a good without knowing what we do! Blessed manner of asking! It is for this reason, sisters, that I want us to be careful how we say this prayer, the Paternoster, and all other vocal prayers, *and what we ask for in them*. For *clearly*, when God has shown us this favor, we shall have to forget worldly things, all of which the Lord of the world has come and cast out. I do not mean that everyone who experiences the Prayer of Quiet must perforce be detached from everything in the world; but at least I should like all such persons to know what they lack and to humble themselves *and not to make so great a petition as though they were asking for nothing, and, if the Lord gives them what they ask for, to throw it back in His face.* They must try to become more and more detached from everything, for otherwise they will only remain where they are. If God gives a soul such pledges, it is a sign that He has great things in store for it. It will be its own fault if it does not make great progress. But if He sees that, after He has brought the Kingdom of Heaven into its abode, it returns to earth, not only will He refrain from showing it the secrets of His Kingdom but He will grant it this other favor only for short periods and rarely.

I may be mistaken about this, but I have seen it and know that it happens, and, for my own part, I believe this is why spiritual people are not much more numerous. They do not respond to so great a favor in a practical way: instead of preparing themselves to receive this favor again, they take back from the Lord's hands the will which He considered His own and center it upon base things. So He seeks out others who love Him in order to grant them His greater gifts, although He will not take away all that He has given from those who live in purity of conscience. But there are persons – and I have been one of them – to whom the Lord gives tenderness of devotion and holy inspirations and light on everything. He bestows this Kingdom on them and brings them to this Prayer of Quiet, and yet they deafen their ears to His voice. For they are so fond of talking and of repeating a large number of vocal prayers in a great hurry, as though they were anxious to finish their task of repeating them daily, that when the Lord, as I say, puts His Kingdom into their very hands, *by giving them this Prayer of Quiet and this inward peace*, they do not accept it, but think that they will do better to go on reciting their prayers, which only distract them from their purpose.

Do not be like that, sisters, but be watchful when the Lord grants you this favor. Think what a great treasure you may be losing and realize that you are doing much more by occasionally repeating a single petition of the Paternoster than by repeating the whole of it many times in a hurry *and not thinking what you are saying.* He to Whom you are praying is very near to you and will not fail to hear you; and you may be sure that you are truly praising Him and hallowing His name, since you are glorifying the Lord as a member of His household and praising Him with increasing affection and desire so that it seems you can never forsake His service. *So I advise you to be very cautious about this, for it is of the greatest importance.*

CHAPTER 32

Expounds these words of the Paternoster: "Fiat voluntas tua sicut in coelo et in terra."[112] Describes how much is accomplished by those who repeat these words with full resolution and how well the Lord rewards them for it.

Now that our good Master has asked on our behalf, and has taught us ourselves to ask, for a thing so precious that it includes all we can desire on earth, and has granted us the great favor of making us His brethren, let us see what He desires us to give to His Father, and what He offers Him

---

[112] "Thy will be done: as in Heaven, so on earth."

on our behalf, and what He asks of us, for it is right that we should render Him some service in return for such great favors. O good Jesus! Since Thou givest so little (little, that is to say, on our behalf) how canst Thou ask [so much] for us? What we give is in itself nothing at all by comparison with all that has been given us and with the greatness of Our Lord. But in truth, my Lord, Thou dost not leave us with nothing to give and we give all that we can – I mean if we give in the spirit of these words: "Thy will be done; as in Heaven, so on earth."

Thou didst well, O our good Master, to make this last petition, so that we may be able to accomplish what Thou dost promise in our name. For truly, Lord, hadst Thou not done this, I do not think it would have been possible *for us to accomplish it*. But, since Thy Father does what Thou askest Him in granting us His Kingdom on earth, I know that we can truly fulfill Thy word by giving what Thou dost promise in our name. For since my earth has now become Heaven, it will be possible for Thy will to be done in me. Otherwise, on an earth so wretched as mine, and so barren of fruit, I know not, Lord, how it could be possible. It is a great thing that Thou dost offer.

When I think of this, it amuses me that there should be people who dare not ask the Lord for trials, thinking that His sending them to them depends upon their asking for them! I am not referring to those who omit to ask for them out of humility because they think themselves to be incapable of bearing them, though for my own part I believe that He who gives them love enough to ask for such a stern method of proving it will give them love enough to endure it. I should like to ask those who are afraid to pray for trials lest they should at once be given them what they mean when they beg the Lord to fulfill His will in them. Do they say this because everyone else says it and not because they want it to be done? That would not be right, sisters. Remember that the good Jesus is our Ambassador here, and that His desire has been to mediate between us and His Father at no small cost to Himself: it would not be right for us to refuse to give what He *promises and* offers on our behalf or to say nothing about it. Let me put it in another way. Consider, daughters, that, whether we wish it or no, God's will must be done, and must be done both in Heaven and on earth. Believe me, then, do as I suggest and make a virtue of necessity.

O my Lord, what a great comfort it is to me that Thou didst not entrust the fulfillment of Thy will to one so wretched as I! Blessed be Thou for ever and let all things praise Thee. May Thy name be for ever glorified. I should indeed have had to be good, Lord, if the fulfillment or non-fulfillment of Thy will [in Heaven and on earth] were in my hands. But as it is, though my will is not yet free from self-interest, I give it to Thee freely. For I have proved, by long experience, how much I gain by leaving it freely in Thy hands. O friends, what a great gain is this – and how much we lose through not fulfilling our promises to the Lord in the Paternoster, and giving Him what we offer Him!

Before I tell you in what this gain consists, I will explain to you how much you are offering, lest later you should exclaim that you had been deceived and had not understood what you were saying. Do not behave like some religious among us, who do nothing but promise, and then excuse ourselves for not fulfilling our promises by saying that we had not understood what we were promising. That may well be true, *for it is easy to say things and hard to put them into practice, and anyone who thought that there was no more in the one than in the other certainly did not understand.* It seems very easy to say that we will surrender our will to someone, until we try it and realize that it is the hardest thing we can do if we carry it out as we should. Our superiors do not always treat us strictly when they see we are weak; and sometimes they treat both weak and strong in the same way. That is not so with the Lord; He knows what each of us can bear, and, when He sees that one of us is strong, He does not hesitate to fulfill His will in him.

So I want you to realize with Whom (as they say) you are dealing and what the good Jesus offers on your behalf to the Father, and what you are giving Him when you pray that His will may be done in you: it is nothing else than this that you are praying for. Do not fear that He will give you riches or pleasures or *great* honors or any such earthly things; His love for you is not so poor as that. And He sets a very high value on what you give Him and desires to recompense you for it since He gives you His Kingdom while you are still alive. Would you like to see how He treats those who make this prayer from their hearts? Ask His glorious Son, Who made it thus in the Garden. Think with what resolution and fullness of desire He prayed; and consider if the will of God was not perfectly fulfilled in Him through the trials, sufferings, insults and persecutions which He gave Him, until at last His life ended with death on a Cross.

So you see, daughters, what God gave to His best Beloved, and from that you can understand what His will is. These, then, are His gifts in this world. He gives them in proportion to the love which He bears us. He gives more to those whom He loves most, and less to those He loves least; and He gives in accordance with the courage which He sees that each of us has and the love we bear to His Majesty. When He sees a soul who loves Him greatly, He knows that soul can suffer much for Him, whereas one who loves Him little will suffer little. For my own part, I believe that love is the measure of our ability to bear crosses, whether great or small. So if you have this love, sisters, try not to let the prayers you make to so great a Lord be words of mere politeness but brace yourselves to suffer what His Majesty desires. For if you give Him your will in any other way, you are just showing Him a jewel, making as if to give it to Him and begging Him to take it, and then, when He puts out His hand to do so, taking it back and holding on to it tightly.

Such mockery is no fit treatment for One who endured so much for us. If for no other reason than this, it would not be right to mock Him so often – and it is by no means seldom that we say these words to Him in the Paternoster. Let us give Him once and for all the jewel which we have so often undertaken to give Him. For the truth is that He gives it to us first so that we may give it back to Him. *Ah, my God! How well Jesus knows us and how much He thinks of our good! He did not say we must surrender our wills to the Lord until we had been well paid for this small service. It will be realized from this how much the Lord intends us to gain by rendering it to Him: even in this life He begins to reward us for this, as I shall presently explain.* Worldly people will do a great deal if they sincerely resolve to fulfill the will of God. But you, daughters, must both say and act, and give Him both words and deeds, as I really think we religious do. Yet sometimes not only do we undertake to give God the jewel but we even put it into His hand and then take it back again. We are so generous all of a sudden, and then we become so mean, that it would have been better if we had stopped to think before giving.

The aim of all my advice to you in this book is that we should surrender ourselves wholly to the Creator, place our will in His hands and detach ourselves from the creatures. As you will already have understood how important this is, I will say no more about it, but I will tell you why our good Master puts these words here. He knows how much we shall gain by rendering this service to His Eternal Father. We are preparing ourselves for the time, which will come very soon, when we shall find ourselves at the end of our journey and shall be drinking of living water from the fountain I have described. Unless we make a total surrender of our will to the Lord, *and put ourselves in His hands* so that He may do in all things what is best for us in accordance with His will, He will never allow us to drink of it. This is the perfect contemplation of which you asked me to write to you.

In this matter, as I have already said, we can do nothing of ourselves, either by working hard or by making plans, nor is it needful that we should. For everything else hinders and prevents us from saying [with real resolution], "Fiat voluntas tua": that is, may the Lord fulfill His will in me, in every way and manner which Thou, my Lord, desirest. If Thou wilt do this by means of trials, give me strength and let them come. If by means of persecutions and sickness and dishonor and need, here I am, my Father, I will not turn my face away from Thee nor have I the right to turn my back upon them. For Thy Son gave Thee this will of mine in the name of us all and it is not right that I for my part should fail. Do Thou grant me the grace of bestowing on me Thy Kingdom so that I may do Thy will, since He has asked this of me. Dispose of me as of that which is Thine own, in accordance with Thy will.

Oh, my sisters, what power this gift has! If it be made with due resolution, it cannot fail to draw the Almighty to become one with our lowliness and to transform us into Himself and to effect a union between the Creator and the creature. Ask yourselves if that will not be a rich reward for you, and if you have not a good Master. For, knowing how the good will of His Father is to be gained, He teaches us how and by what means we must serve Him.

The more *resolute we are in soul and the more* we show Him by our actions that the words we use to Him are not words of mere politeness, the more and more does Our Lord draw us to Himself and raise us above all *petty* earthly things, and above ourselves, in order to prepare us to receive great favors *from Him*, for His rewards for our service will not end with this life. So much does He value this service of ours that we do not know for what more we can ask, while His Majesty never wearies of giving. Not content with having made this soul one with Himself, through uniting it to Himself, He begins to cherish it, to reveal secrets to it, to rejoice in its understanding of what it has gained and in the knowledge which it has of all He has yet to give it. He causes it gradually to lose its exterior senses so that nothing may occupy it. This we call rapture. He begins to make such a friend of the soul that not only does He restore its will to it but He gives it His own also. For, now that He is making a friend of it, He is glad to allow it to rule with Him, as we say, turn and turn about. So He does what the soul asks of Him, just as the soul does what He commands, only in a much better way, since He is all-powerful and can do whatever He desires, and His desire never comes to an end.

But the poor soul, despite its desires, is *often* unable to do all it would like, nor can it do anything at all unless it is given the power.[113] And so it grows richer and richer; and the more it serves, the greater becomes its debt; and often, growing weary of finding itself subjected to all the inconveniences and impediments and bonds which it has to endure while it is in the prison of this body, it would gladly pay something of what it owes, for it is quite worn out. But even if we do all that is in us, how can we repay God, since, as I say, we have nothing to give save what we have first received? We can only learn to know ourselves and do what we can – namely, surrender our will and fulfill God's will in us. Anything else must be a hindrance to the soul which the Lord has brought to this state. It causes it, not profit, but harm, for nothing but humility is of any use here, and this is not acquired by the understanding but by a clear perception of the truth, which comprehends in one moment what could not be attained over a long period by the labor of the imagination – namely, that we are nothing and that God is infinitely great.

I will give you one piece of advice: do not suppose that you can reach this state by your own effort or diligence; that would be too much to expect. On the contrary, you would turn what devotion you had quite cold. You must practice simplicity and humility, for those are the virtues which achieve everything. You must say: "Fiat voluntas tua."

CHAPTER 33
Treats of our great need that the Lord should give us what we ask in these words of the Paternoster: "Panem nostrum quotidianum da nobis hodie."[114]

The good Jesus understands, as I have said, how difficult a thing He is offering on our behalf, for He knows our weakness, and how often we show that we do not understand what the will of the Lord is, since we are weak while He is so merciful. He knows that some means must be found by which we shall not omit to give what He has given on our behalf, for if we did that it would be anything but good for us, since everything we gain comes from what we give. Yet He knows that it will be difficult for us to carry this out; for if anyone were to tell some wealthy, pampered person that it is God's will for him to moderate his eating so that others, who are dying of hunger, shall have at least bread to eat, he will discover a thousand reasons for not understanding this but interpreting it in his own way. If one tells a person who speaks ill of others that it is God's will that he should love his neighbor as himself,[115] he will lose patience and no amount of reasoning will convince him. If one tells a religious who is accustomed to liberty and indulgence that he must be careful to set a good example and to remember that when he makes this petition it is his duty to keep what he has sworn and promised, and that not in word alone; that it is the will of God that he should fulfill his vows and see that he gives no occasion for scandal by acting contrarily to them, even though he may not actually break them; that he has taken the vow of poverty and must keep it without evasions, because that is the Lord's will – it would be impossible, in spite of all this, that some religious should not still want their own way. What would be the case, then, if the Lord had not done most of what was necessary by means of the remedy He has given us? There would have been very few who could have fulfilled this petition, which the Lord made to the Father on our behalf: "Fiat voluntas tua." Seeing our need, therefore, the good Jesus has sought the admirable

---

[113] *Lit.* "given it."

[114] "Give us this day our daily bread."

[115] *Lit.*: "should want as much *for himself as for his neighbor, and* for his neighbor as for himself." The italicized phrase is found in E. only.

means whereby He has shown us the extreme love which He has for us, and in His own name and in that of His brethren He has made this petition: "Give us, Lord, this day our daily bread."

For the love of God, sisters, let us realize the meaning of our good Master's petition, for our very life depends on our not disregarding it. Set very little store by what you have given, since there is so much that you will receive. It seems to me, in the absence of a better opinion, that the good Jesus knew what He had given for us and how important it was for us to give this to God, and yet how difficult it would be for us to do so, as has been said, because of our natural inclination to base things and our want of love and courage. He saw that, before we could be aroused, we needed His aid, not once but every day, and it must have been for this reason that He resolved to remain with us. As this was so weighty and important a matter, He wished it to come from the hand of the Eternal Father. Though both Father and Son are one and the same, and He knew that whatever He did on earth God would do in Heaven, and would consider it good, since His will and the Father's will were one, yet the humility of the good Jesus was such that He wanted, as it were, to ask leave of His Father, for He knew that He was His beloved Son and that He was well pleased with Him. He knew quite well that in this petition He was asking for more than He had asked for in the others, but He already knew what death He was to suffer and what dishonors and affronts He would have to bear.

What father could there be, Lord, who, after giving us his son, and such a Son, would allow Him to remain among us day by day to suffer as He had done already? None, Lord, in truth, but Thine: well dost Thou know of Whom Thou art asking this. God help me! What a great love is that of the Son and what a great love is that of the Father! I am not so much amazed at the good Jesus, because, as He had already said "Fiat voluntas tua", He was bound, being Who He is, to put what He had said into practice. Yes, for He is not like us; knowing that He was carrying out His words by loving us as He loves Himself, He went about seeking how He could carry out this commandment more perfectly, even at His own cost. But how, Eternal Father, couldst Thou consent to this? How canst Thou see Thy Son every day in such wicked hands? Since first Thou didst permit it and consent to it, Thou seest how He has been treated. How can Thy Mercy, day by day and every day,[116] see Him affronted? And how many affronts are being offered to-day to this Most Holy Sacrament? How often must the Father see Him in the hands of His enemies? What desecrations these heretics commit!

O Eternal Lord! How canst Thou grant such a petition? How canst Thou consent to it? Consider not His love, which, for the sake of fulfilling Thy will and of helping us, would allow Him to submit day by day to being cut to pieces. It is for Thee to see to this, my Lord, since Thy Son allows no obstacle to stand in His way. Why must all the blessings that we receive be at His cost? How is it that He is silent in face of all, and cannot speak for Himself, but only for us? Is there none who will speak for this most loving Lamb? *Give me permission to speak for Him, Lord, since Thou hast been pleased to leave Him in our power, and let me beseech Thee on His behalf, since He gave Thee such full obedience and surrendered Himself to us with such great love.*

I have been reflecting how in this petition alone the same words are repeated: first of all the Lord speaks of "our daily bread" and asks Thee to give it, and then He says: "Give it us to-day, Lord."[117] He lays the matter before His Father in this way: the Father gave us His Son once and for all to die for us, and thus He is our own; yet He does not want the gift to be taken from us until the end of the world but would have it left to be a help to us every day. Let this melt your hearts, my daughters, and make you love your Spouse, for there is no slave who would willingly call himself by that name, yet the good Jesus seems to think it an honor.

O Eternal Father, how great is the merit of this humility! With what a treasure are we purchasing Thy Son! How to sell Him we already know, for He was sold for thirty pieces of silver; but, if we would purchase Him, no price is sufficient. Being made one with us through the portion of our nature which is His, and being Lord of His own will, He reminds His Father that, as our nature is His, He is able to give it to us, and thus He says "our bread". He makes no difference between Himself and us, though we make one between ourselves and Him through not giving ourselves daily for His Majesty's sake.

---

[116] *Lit.*: "each day, each day."

[117] This, as will be observed from the title to this chapter, is the order of the words in the Latin.

CHAPTER 34

Continues the same subject. This is very suitable for reading after the reception of the Most Holy Sacrament.

We have now reached the conclusion that the good Jesus, being ours, asks His Father to let us have Him daily – which appears to mean "for ever". *While writing this* I have been wondering why, after saying "our 'daily' bread", the Lord repeated the idea in the words "Give us this day, Lord." *I will tell you my own foolish idea: if it really is foolish, well and good – in any case, it is quite bad enough that I should interfere in such a matter at all. Still, as we are trying to understand what we are praying for, let us think carefully what this means, so that we may pray rightly, and thank Him Who is taking such care about teaching us.* This bread, then, is ours daily, it seems to me, because we have Him here on earth, *since He has remained with us here and we receive Him;* and, if we profit by His company, we shall also have Him in Heaven, for the only reason He remains with us is to help and encourage and sustain us so that we shall do that will, which, as we have said, is to be fulfilled in us.

In using the words "this day" He seems to me to be *thinking of a day of the length of this life.* And a day indeed it is! As for the unfortunate souls who *will* bring damnation upon themselves and will not have fruition of Him in the world to come, *they are His own creatures, and He did everything to help them on, and was with them, to strengthen them, throughout the "to-day" of this life, so* it is not His fault if they are vanquished. They will have no excuse to make nor will they be able to complain of the Father for taking this bread from them at the time when they most needed it. Therefore the Son prays the Father that, since this life lasts no more than a day, He will allow Him to spend it in our service.[118] As His Majesty has already given His Son to us, by sending Him, of His will alone, into the world, so now, of that same will, He is pleased not to abandon us, but to remain here with us for the greater glory of His friends and the discomfiture of His enemies. He prays for nothing more than this "to-day" since He has given us this most holy Bread. He has given it to us for ever, as I have said, as the sustenance and manna of humanity. We can have it whenever we please and we shall not die of hunger save through our own fault, for, in whatever way the soul desires to partake of food, it will find joy and comfort in the Most Holy Sacrament. There is no need or trial or persecution that cannot be easily borne if we begin to *partake and* taste of those which He Himself bore, *and to make them the subject of our meditations.*

With regard to other bread[119] – the bread of bodily necessaries and sustenance – I neither like to think that the Lord is always being reminded of it nor would I have you remember it yourselves. Keep on the level of the highest contemplation, for anyone who dwells there no more remembers that he is in the world than if he had already left it – still less does he think about food. Would the Lord ever have insisted upon our asking for food, or taught us to do so by His own example? Not in my opinion. He teaches us to fix our desires upon heavenly things and to pray that we may begin to enjoy these things while here on earth: would He, then, have us trouble about so petty a matter as praying for food? As if He did not know that, once we begin to worry about the needs of the body, we shall forget the needs of the soul! Besides, are we such moderately minded people that we shall be satisfied with just a little and pray only for a little? No: the more food we are given, the less we shall get of the water from Heaven. Let those of you, daughters, who want more of the necessaries of life pray for this.

Join with the Lord, then, daughters, in begging the Father to let you have your Spouse to-day, so that, *as long as you live,* you may never find yourself in this world without Him. Let it suffice to temper your great joy that He should remain disguised beneath these accidents of bread and wine, which is a real torture to those who have nothing else to love and no other consolation. Entreat Him not to fail you but to prepare you to receive Him worthily.

As for that other bread, have no anxiety about it if you have truly resigned yourselves to God's will. I mean that at these hours of prayer you are dealing with more important matters and there is time enough for you to labor and earn your daily bread. Try never at any time to let your thoughts

---

[118] *Lit.:* "in service" – *en servidumbre*, a strong word, better rendered, perhaps, "servitude," and not far removed from "slavery."

[119] The whole of this paragraph is lightly crossed out in the manuscript.

dwell on this; work with your body, for it is good for you to try to support yourselves, but let your soul be at rest. Leave anxiety about this to your Spouse, as has been said at length already, and He will always bear it for you. *Do not fear that He will fail you if you do not fail to do what you have promised and to resign yourselves to God's will. I assure you, daughters, that, if I myself were to fail in this, because of my wickedness, as I have often done in the past, I would not beg Him to give me that bread, or anything else to eat. Let Him leave me to die of hunger. Of what use is life to me if it leads me daily nearer to eternal death?*

If, then, you are really surrendering yourselves to God, as you say, cease to be anxious for yourselves, for He bears your anxiety, and will bear it always. It is as though a servant had gone into service and were anxious to please his master in everything. The master is bound to give him food for so long as he remains in his house, and in his service, unless he is so poor that he has food neither for his servant nor for himself. Here, however, the comparison breaks down, for God is, and will always be, rich and powerful. It would not be right for the servant to go to his master *every day* and ask him for food when he knew that his master would see that it was given him and so he would be sure to receive it. *To do this would be a waste of words.* His master would quite properly tell him that he should look after his own business of serving and pleasing him, for, if he worried himself unnecessarily, he would not do his work as well as he should. So, sisters, those who will may worry about asking for earthly bread; let our own task be to beg the Eternal Father that we may merit our heavenly bread, so that, although our bodily eyes cannot feast themselves on the sight of Him since He is thus hidden from us, He may reveal Himself to the eyes of the soul and may make Himself known to us as another kind of food, full of delight and joy, which sustains our life.

Do you suppose that this most holy food is not *ample* sustenance even for the body and a potent medicine for bodily ills? I am sure that it is. I know a person who was subject to serious illnesses and often suffered great pain; and this pain was taken away from her in a flash[120] and she became quite well again. This often occurs, I believe; and cures are recorded from quite definite illnesses which could not be counterfeited. As the wondrous effects produced by this most holy bread in those who worthily receive it are very well known, I will not describe all the things that could be related about this person I mentioned, though I have been enabled to learn about them and I know that they are not fabrications. The Lord had given this person such a lively faith that, when she heard people say they wished they had lived when Christ walked on this earth, she would smile to herself, for she knew that we have Him as truly with us in the Most Holy Sacrament as people had Him then, and wonder what more they could possibly want.

I know, too, that for many years this person, though by no means perfect, always tried to strengthen her faith, when she communicated, by thinking that it was exactly as if she saw the Lord entering her house, with her own bodily eyes, for she believed in very truth that this Lord was entering her poor abode, and she ceased, as far as she could, to think of outward things, and went into her abode with Him. She tried to recollect her senses so that they might all become aware of this great blessing, or rather, so that they should not hinder the soul from becoming conscious of it. She imagined herself at His feet and wept with the Magdalene exactly as if she had seen Him with her bodily eyes in the Pharisee's house. Even if she felt no devotion, faith told her that it was good for her to be there.

For, unless we want to be foolish and to close our minds to facts, we cannot suppose that this is the work of the imagination, as it is when we think of the Lord on the Cross, or of other incidents of the Passion, and picture within ourselves how these things happened. This is something which is happening now; it is absolutely true; and we have no need to go and seek Him somewhere a long way off. For we know that, until the accidents of bread have been consumed by our natural heat, the good Jesus is with us and we should [not lose so good an opportunity but should] come to Him. If, while He went about in the world, the sick were healed merely by touching His clothes, how can we doubt that He will work miracles when He is within us, if we have faith, or that He will give us what we ask of Him since He is in our house? His Majesty is not wont to offer us too little payment for His lodging if we treat Him well.

If you grieve at not seeing Him with the eyes of the body, remember that that would not be good for us, for it is one thing to see Him glorified and quite another to see Him as He was when

---

[120] *Lit.*: "as if by (someone's) hand." St. Teresa is thought here to be referring to herself.

He lived in the world. So weak is our nature that nobody could endure the sight – in fact, there would be no one left to endure it, for no one would wish to remain in the world any longer. Once having seen this Eternal Truth, people would realize that all the things we prize here are mockery and falsehood. And if such great Majesty could be seen, how could a miserable sinner like myself, after having so greatly offended Him, remain so near to Him? Beneath those accidents of bread, we can approach Him; for, if the King disguises Himself, it would seem that we need not mind coming to Him without so much circumspection and ceremony: by disguising Himself, He has, as it were, obliged Himself to submit to this. Who, otherwise, would dare to approach Him so unworthily, with so many imperfections and with such lukewarm zeal?

Oh, we know not what we ask! How much better does His Wisdom know what we need! He reveals Himself to those who He knows will profit by His presence; though unseen by bodily eyes, He has many ways of revealing Himself to the soul through deep inward emotions and by various other means. Delight to remain with Him; do not lose such an excellent time for talking with Him as the hour after Communion. *Remember that this is a very profitable hour for the soul; if you spend it in the company of the good Jesus, you are doing Him a great service. Be very careful, then, daughters, not to lose it.* If you are compelled by obedience to do something else, try to leave your soul with the Lord. *For He is your Master, and, though it be in a way you may not understand, He will not fail to teach you.* But if you take your thoughts elsewhere, and pay no *more* attention to Him *than if you had not received Him*, and care nothing for His being within you, how can He make Himself known to you? *You must complain, not of Him, but of yourself.* This, then, is a good time for our Master to teach us and for us to listen to Him. *I do not tell you to say no prayers at all, for if I did you would take hold of my words and say I was talking about contemplation, which you need practice only if the Lord brings you to it. No: you should say the Paternoster, realize that you are verily and indeed in the company of Him Who taught it you* and kiss His feet in gratitude to Him for having desired to teach you and beg Him to *show you how to pray and* never to leave you.

You may be in the habit of praying while looking at a picture of Christ, but *at a time like this* it seems foolish to me to turn away from *the living image* – the Person Himself – to look at His picture. Would it not be foolish if we had a portrait of someone whom we dearly loved and, when the person himself came to see us, we refused to talk with him and carried on our entire conversation with the portrait? Do you know when I find the use of a picture an excellent thing, and take great pleasure in it? When the person is absent and we are made to feel his loss by our great aridity, it is then that we find it a great comfort to look at the picture of Him Whom we have such reason to love. *This is a great inspiration*, and *makes us* wish that, in whichever direction we turn our eyes, we could see the picture. What can we look upon that is better or more attractive to the sight than upon Him Who so dearly loves us and contains within Himself all good things? Unhappy are those heretics, who through their own fault have lost this comfort, as well as others.

When you have received the Lord, and are in His very presence, try to shut the bodily eyes and to open the eyes of the soul and to look into your own hearts. I tell you, and tell you again, for I should like to repeat it often, that if you practice this habit *of staying with Him, not just once or twice, but* whenever you communicate, and strive to keep your conscience clear so that you can often rejoice in this your Good, He will not, as I have said, come so much disguised as to be unable to make His presence known to you in many ways, according to the desire which you have of seeing Him. So great, indeed, may be your longing for Him that He will reveal Himself to you wholly.

But if we pay no heed to Him save when we have received Him, and go away from Him in search of other and baser things, what can He do? Will He have to drag us by force to look at Him *and be with Him* because He desires to reveal Himself to us? No; for when He revealed Himself to all men plainly, and told them clearly who He was, they did not treat Him at all well – very few of them, indeed, even believed Him. So He grants us an exceeding great favor when He is pleased to show us that it is He Who is in the Most Holy Sacrament. But He will not reveal Himself openly and communicate His glories and bestow His treasures save on those who He knows greatly desire Him, for these are His true friends. I assure you that anyone who is not a true friend and does not come to receive Him as such, after doing all in his power to prepare for Him, must never importune Him to reveal Himself to him. Hardly is the hour over which such a person has spent in fulfilling the Church's commandment than he goes home and tries to drive Christ out of the house. What with all his other business and occupations and worldly hindrances, he seems to be making all possible haste to prevent the Lord from taking possession of the house which is His own.

CHAPTER 35

Describes the recollection which should be practiced after Communion. Concludes this subject with an exclamatory prayer to the Eternal Father.

I have written at length about this, although, when writing of the Prayer of Recollection, I spoke of the great importance of our entering into solitude with God. When you hear Mass without communicating, daughters, you may communicate spiritually, which is extremely profitable, and afterwards you may practice inward recollection in exactly the same way, for this impresses upon us a deep love of the Lord. If we prepare to receive Him, He never fails to give, and He gives in many ways that we cannot understand. It is as if we were to approach a fire: it might be a very large one, but, if we remained a long way from it and covered our hands, we should get little warmth from it, although we should be warmer than if we were in a place where there was no fire at all. But when we try to approach the Lord there is this difference: if the soul is properly disposed, and comes with the intention of driving out the cold, and stays for some time where it is, it will retain its warmth for several hours, *and if any little spark flies out, it will set it on fire.*

It is of such importance, daughters, for us to prepare ourselves in thy way that you must not be surprised if I often repeat this counsel. If at first you do not get on with this practice (which may happen, for the devil will try to oppress and distress your heart, knowing what great harm he can do in this way), the devil will make you think that you can find more devotion in other things and less in this. But [trust me and] do not give up this method, for the Lord will use it to prove your love for Him. Remember that there are few souls who stay with Him and follow Him in His trials; let us endure something for Him and His Majesty will repay us. Remember, too, that there are actually people who not only have no wish to be with Him but who insult Him and *with great irreverence* drive Him away *from their homes.* We must endure something, therefore, to show Him that we have the desire to see Him. *In many places He is neglected and ill-treated, but* He suffers everything, and will continue to do so, if He finds but one single soul which will receive Him and love to have Him as its Guest.[121] Let this soul be yours, then, for, if there were none, the Eternal Father would rightly refuse to allow Him to remain with us. Yet the Lord is so good a Friend to those who are His friends, and so good a Master to those who are His servants, that, when He knows it to be the will of His Beloved Son, He will not hinder Him in so excellent a work, in which His Son so fully reveals the love which He has for His Father, *as this wonderful way which He seeks of showing how much He loves us and of helping us to bear our trials.*

Since, then, Holy Father, Who art in the Heavens, Thou dost will and accept this (and it is clear that Thou couldst not deny us a thing which is so good for us) there must be someone, as I said at the beginning, who will speak for Thy Son, for He has never defended Himself. Let this be the task for us, daughters, though, having regard to what we are, it is presumptuous of us to undertake it. Let us rely, however, on Our Lord's command to us to pray to Him, and, in fulfillment of our obedience to Him, let us beseech His Majesty, in the name of the good Jesus, that, as He has left nothing undone that He could do for us in granting sinners so great a favor, He may be pleased of His mercy to prevent Him from being so ill-treated. Since His Holy Son has given us this excellent way in which we can offer Him up frequently as a sacrifice, let us make use of this precious gift so that it may stay the advance of such terrible evil and irreverence as in many places is paid to this Most Holy Sacrament. For these Lutherans *seem to want to drive Him out of the world again: they* destroy churches, cause the loss of many priests and abolish the sacraments.[122] *And there is something of this even among Christians, who sometimes go to church meaning to offend Him rather than to worship Him.*

---

[121] *Lit.:* "and have him within itself with love."

[122] The sense of the verb here rendered "cause the loss of" is vague. Literally the phrase reads: "so many priests are lost."

Why is this, my Lord and my God? Do Thou bring the world to an end or give us a remedy for such grievous wrongs, which even our wicked hearts cannot endure. I beseech Thee, Eternal Father, endure it no longer: quench this fire, Lord, for Thou canst do so if Thou wilt. Remember that Thy Son is still in the world; may these dreadful things be stopped out of respect for Him, horrible and abominable and foul as they are. With His beauty and purity He does not deserve to be in a house where such things happen. Do this, Lord, not for our sake, for we do not deserve it, but for the sake of Thy Son. We dare not entreat Thee that He should no longer stay with us, *for Thou hast granted His prayer to Thee to leave Him with us for to-day – that is, until the end of the world.* If He were to go, what would become of us? It would be the end of everything. If anything can placate Thee it is to have on earth such a pledge as this. Since some remedy must be found for this, then, my Lord, I beg Thy Majesty to apply it. *For if Thou wilt, Thou art able.*

O my God, if only I could indeed importune Thee! If only I had served Thee well so that I might be able to beg of Thee this great favor as a reward for my services, for Thou leavest no service unrewarded! But I have not served Thee, Lord; indeed, it may perhaps be for my sins, and because I have so greatly offended Thee, that so many evils come. What, then, can I do, my Creator, but present to Thee this most holy Bread, which, though Thou gavest it to us, I return to Thee, beseeching Thee, by the merits of Thy Son, to grant me this favor, which on so many counts He has merited? Do Thou, Lord, calm this sea, and no longer allow this ship, which is Thy Church, to endure so great a tempest. Save us, my Lord, for we perish.[123]

CHAPTER 36
Treats of these words in the Paternoster: "Dimitte nobis debita nostra."[124]

Our good Master sees that, if we have this heavenly food, everything is easy for us, except when we are ourselves to blame, and that we are well able to fulfill our undertaking to the Father that His will shall be done in us. So He now asks Him to forgive us our debts, as we ourselves forgive others. Thus, continuing the prayer which He is teaching us, He says these words: "And forgive us, Lord, our debts, even as we forgive them to our debtors."

Notice, sisters, that He does not say: "as we shall forgive." We are to understand that anyone who asks for so great a gift as that just mentioned, and has already yielded his own will to the will of God, must have done this already. And so He says: "as we forgive our debtors." Anyone, then, who sincerely repeats this petition, "Fiat voluntas tua", must, at least in intention, have done this already. You see now why the saints rejoiced in insults and persecutions: it was because these gave them something to present to the Lord when they prayed to Him. What can a poor creature like myself do, who has had so little to forgive others and has so much to be forgiven herself? This, sisters, is something which we should consider carefully; it is such a serious and important matter that God should pardon us our sins, which have merited eternal fire, that we must pardon all trifling things which have been done to us *and which are not wrongs at all, or anything else. For how is it possible, either in word or in deed, to wrong one who, like myself, has deserved to be plagued by devils for ever? Is it not only right that I should be plagued*[125] *in this world too?* As I have so few, Lord, even of these trifling things, to offer Thee, Thy pardoning of me must be a free gift: there is abundant scope here for Thy mercy. *Thy Son must pardon me, for no one has done me any injustice, and so there has been nothing that I can pardon for Thy sake. But take my desire to do so, Lord, for I believe I would forgive any wrong if Thou wouldst forgive me and I might unconditionally do Thy will. True, if the occasion were to arise, and I were condemned without cause, I do not know what I should do. But at this moment I see that I am so guilty in Thy sight that everything I might have to suffer would fall short of my deserts, though anyone not knowing, as Thou knowest, what I am, would think I was being wronged.* Blessed be Thou, Who endurest one that is so poor: when Thy

---

[123] St. Matthew viii, 25.
[124] "Forgive us our debts."
[125] *Lit.*: "ill-treated." The same verb is used in the following sentence.

most holy Son makes this petition in the name of all mankind, I cannot be included, being such as I am and having nothing to give.

And supposing, my Lord, that there are others who are like myself but have not realized that this is so? If there are any such, I beg them, in Thy name, to remember this truth, and to pay no heed to little things about which they think they are being slighted, for, if they insist on these nice points of honor, they become like children building houses of straw. Oh, God help me, sisters! If we only knew what honor really is and what is meant by losing it! I am not speaking now about ourselves, for it would indeed be a bad business if we did not understand this; I am speaking of myself as I was when I prided myself on my honor without knowing what honor meant; I just followed the example of others. Oh, how easily I used to feel slighted! I am ashamed to think of it now; and I was not one of those who worried most about such things either. But I never grasped the essence of the matter, because I neither thought nor troubled about true honor, which it is good for us to have because it profits the soul. How truly has someone said: "Honor and profit cannot go together." I do not know if this was what that person was thinking of when he said it; but it is literally true, for the soul's profit and what the world calls honor can never be reconciled. Really, the topsy-turviness of the world is terrible. Blessed be the Lord for taking us out of it! *May His Majesty grant that this house shall always be as far from it as it is now! God preserve us from religious houses where they worry about points of honor! Such places never do much honor to God.*

God help us, how absurd it is for religious to connect their honor with things so trifling that they amaze me! You know nothing about this, sisters, but I will tell you about it so that you may be wary. You see, sisters, the devil has not forgotten us. He has invented honors of his own for religious houses and has made laws by which we go up and down in rank, as people do in the world. Learned men have to observe this with regard to their studies (a matter of which I know nothing): anyone, for example, who has got as far as reading theology must not descend and read philosophy – that is their kind of honor, according to which you must always be going up and never going down. Even if someone were commanded by obedience to take a step down, he would *in his own mind* consider himself slighted; and then someone would take his part [and say] it was an insult; next, the devil would discover reasons for this – and he seems to be an authority even in God's own law. Why, among ourselves, anyone who has been a prioress is thereby incapacitated from holding any lower office *for the rest of her life.* We must defer to the senior among us, and we are not allowed to forget it either: sometimes it would appear to be a positive merit for us to do this, because it is a rule of the Order.

The thing is enough to make one laugh – or, it would be more proper to say, to make one weep. After all, the Order does not command us not to be humble: it commands us to do everything in due form. And in matters which concern my own esteem I ought not to be so formal as to insist that this detail of our Rule shall be kept as strictly as the rest, which we may in fact be observing very imperfectly. We must not put all our effort into observing just this one detail: let my interests be looked after by others – I will forget about myself altogether. The fact is, although we shall never rise as far as Heaven in this way, we are attracted by the thought of rising higher, and we dislike climbing down. O, Lord, Lord, art Thou our Example and our Master? Yes, indeed. And wherein did Thy honor consist, O Lord, Who hast honored us?[126] Didst Thou perchance lose it when Thou wert humbled even to death? No, Lord, rather didst Thou gain it for all.

For the love of God, sisters! We have lost our way; we have taken the wrong path from the very beginning. God grant that no soul be lost through its attention to these wretched niceties about honor, when it has no idea wherein honor consists. We shall get to the point of thinking that we have done something wonderful because we have forgiven a person for some trifling thing, which was neither a slight nor an insult nor anything else. Then we shall ask the Lord to forgive us as people who have done something important, just because we have forgiven someone. Grant us, my God, to understand how little we understand ourselves and how empty our hands are when we come to Thee that Thou, of Thy mercy, mayest forgive us. For in truth, Lord, since all things have an end and punishment is eternal, I can see nothing meritorious which I may present to Thee that Thou

---

[126] *Lit.:* "our Honorer" – *Honrador nuestro*: a rather unusual phrase which T. changes into the quite conventional honrado Maestro – "honored Master."

mayest grant us so great a favor. Do it, then, for the sake of Him Who asks it of Thee, *and Who may well do so, for He is always being wronged and offended.*

How greatly the Lord must esteem this mutual love of ours one for another! *For, having given Him our wills, we have given Him complete rights over us, and we cannot do that without love. See, then, sisters, how important it is for us to love one another and to be at peace.* The good Jesus might have put everything else before our love for one another, and said: "Forgive us, Lord, because we are doing a great deal of penance, or because we are praying often, and fasting, and because we have left all for Thy sake and love Thee greatly." But He has never said: "Because we would lose our lives for Thy sake"; or any of these [numerous] other things which He might have said. He simply says: "Because we forgive." Perhaps *the reason He said* this *rather than anything else* was because He knew that our fondness for this dreadful honor made mutual love the hardest virtue for us to attain, though it is the virtue dearest to His Father. *Because of its very difficulty* He put it where He did, and *after having asked for so many great gifts for us*, He offers it on our behalf to God.

Note particularly, sisters, that He says: "As we forgive." As I have said, He takes this for granted. And observe especially with regard to it that unless, after experiencing the favors granted by God in the prayer that I have called perfect contemplation, a person is very resolute, and makes a point, if the occasion arises, of forgiving, not [only] these mere nothings which people call wrongs, but any wrong, however grave, you need not think much of that person's prayer.[127] For wrongs have no effect upon a soul whom God draws to Himself in such sublime prayer as this, nor does it care if it is highly esteemed or no. That is not quite correct: it does care, for honor distresses much more than dishonor and it prefers trials to a great deal of rest and ease. For anyone to whom the Lord has really given His Kingdom no longer wants a kingdom in this world, knowing that he is going the right way to reign in a much more exalted manner, and having already discovered by experience what great benefits the soul gains and what progress it makes when it suffers for God's sake. For only very rarely does His Majesty grant it such great consolations, and then only to those who have willingly borne many trials for His sake. For contemplatives, as I have said elsewhere in this book, have to bear heavy trials, and therefore the Lord seeks out for Himself souls of great experience.

Understand, then, sisters, that as these persons have already learned to rate everything at its proper valuation, they pay little attention to things which pass away. A great wrong, or a great trial, may cause them some momentary distress, but they will hardly have felt it when reason will intervene, and will seem to raise its standard aloft, and drive away their distress by giving them the joy of seeing how God has entrusted them with the opportunity of gaining, in a single day, more lasting favors and graces in His Majesty's sight than they could gain in ten years by means of trials which they sought on their own account. This, as I understand (and I have talked about it with many contemplatives), is quite usual, and I know for a fact that it happens. Just as other people prize gold and jewels, so these persons prize and desire trials, for they know quite well that trials will make them rich.

Such persons would never on any account esteem themselves: they want their sins to be known and like to speak about them to people who they see have any esteem for them. The same is true of their descent, which they know quite well will be of no advantage to them in the kingdom which has no end. If being of good birth were any satisfaction to them, it would be because this would enable them to serve God better. If they are not well born, it distresses them when people think them better than they are, and it causes them no distress to disabuse them, but only pleasure. The reason for this is that those to whom God grants the favor of possessing such humility and great love for Him forget themselves when there is a possibility of rendering Him greater services, and simply cannot believe that others are troubled by things which they themselves do not consider as wrongs at all.

These last effects which I have mentioned are produced in persons who have reached a high degree of perfection and to whom the Lord commonly grants the favor of uniting them to Himself by perfect contemplation. But the first of these effects – namely, the determination to suffer wrongs even though such suffering brings distress – is very quickly seen in anyone to whom the Lord has

---

[127] St. Teresa left this sentence uncompleted. Luis de Le—n added: "You need not... prayer" in his edition, since when it has always been included. It figures as an anonymous correction in T.

granted this grace of prayer as far as the stage of union. If these effects are not produced in a soul and it is not strengthened by prayer, you may take it that this was not Divine favor but indulgence and illusion coming from the devil, which *he makes us think to be good*, so that we may attach more importance to our honor.

It may be that, when the Lord first grants these favors, the soul will not immediately attain this fortitude. But, if He continues to grant them, He will soon give it fortitude – certainly, at least, as regards forgiveness, if not in the other virtues as well. I cannot believe that a soul which has approached so nearly to Mercy Itself, and has learned to know itself and the greatness of God's pardon, will not immediately and readily forgive, and be mollified and remain on good terms with a person who has done it wrong. For such a soul remembers the consolation and grace which He has shown it, in which it has recognized the signs of great love, and it is glad that the occasion presents itself for showing Him some love in return.

I repeat that I know many persons to whom Our Lord has granted the grace of raising them to supernatural experiences and of giving them this prayer, or contemplation, which has been described; and although I may notice other faults and imperfections in them, I have never seen such a person who had this particular fault, nor do I believe such a person exists, if the favors he has received are of God. If any one of you receives high favors, let her look within herself and see if they are producing these effects, and, if they are not, let her be very fearful, and believe that these consolations are not of God, Who, as I have said, when He visits the soul, always enriches it. That is certain; for, although the grace and the consolations may pass quickly, it can be recognized in due course through the benefits which it bestows on the soul. And, as the good Jesus knows this well, He gives a definite assurance to His Holy Father that we are forgiving our debtors.

CHAPTER 37

Describes the excellence of this prayer called the Paternoster, and the many ways in which we shall find consolation in it.

The sublimity of the perfection of this evangelical prayer is something for which we should give great praise to the Lord. So well composed by the good Master was it, daughters, that each of us may use it in her own way. I am astounded when I consider that in its few words are enshrined all contemplation and perfection, so that if we study it no other book seems necessary. For thus far in the Paternoster the Lord has taught us the whole method of prayer and of high contemplation, from the very beginnings of mental prayer, to Quiet and Union. With so true a foundation to build upon, I could write a great book on prayer if only I knew how to express myself. As you have seen, Our Lord is beginning here to explain to us the effects which it produces, when the favors come from Him.

I have wondered why His Majesty did not expound such obscure and sublime subjects in greater detail so that we might all have understood them. It has occurred to me that, as this prayer was meant to be a general one for the use of all, so that everyone could interpret it as he thought right, ask for what he wanted and find comfort in doing so, He left the matter in doubt;[128] and thus contemplatives, who no longer desire earthly things, and persons greatly devoted to God, can ask for the heavenly favors which, through the great goodness of God, may be given to us on earth. Those who still live on earth, and must conform to the customs of their state, may also ask for the bread which they need for their own maintenance and for that of their households, as is perfectly just and right, and they may also ask for other things according as they need them.

(Blessed be His name for ever and ever. Amen. For His sake I entreat the Eternal Father to forgive my debts and grievous sins: though no one has wronged me, and I have therefore no one to

---

[128] *Lit.:* "He left it thus confused." Here follows in E., in place of the rest of this paragraph, a passage which interrupts the trend of the thought, and therefore, in the text above, is printed in italics and in brackets at the end of this paragraph.

forgive,[129] *I have myself need for forgiveness every day. May He give me grace so that every day I may have some petition to lay before Him.)*

The good Jesus, then, has taught us a sublime method of prayer, and begged that, in this our life of exile, we may be like the angels, if we endeavor, with our whole might, to make our actions conform to our words – in short, to be like the children of such a Father, and the brethren of such a Brother. His Majesty knows that if, as I say, our actions and our words are one, the Lord will unfailingly fulfill our petitions, give us His kingdom and help us by means of supernatural gifts, such as the Prayer of Quiet, perfect contemplation and all the other favors which the Lord bestows on our trifling efforts – and everything is trifling which we can achieve and gain by ourselves alone.

It must be realized, however, that these two things – surrendering our will to God and forgiving others – apply to all. True, some practice them more and some less, as has been said: those who are perfect will surrender their wills like the perfect souls they are and will forgive others with the perfection that has been described. For our own part, sisters, we will do what we can, and the Lord will accept it all. It is as if He were to make a kind of agreement on our behalf with His Eternal Father, and to say: "Do this, Lord, and My brethren shall do that." It is certain that He for His own part will not fail us. Oh, how well He pays us and how limitless are His rewards!

We may say this prayer only once, and yet in such a way that He will know that there is no duplicity about us and that we shall do what we say; and so He will leave us rich. We must never be insincere with Him, for He loves us, in all our dealings with Him, to be honest, and to treat Him frankly and openly, never saying one thing and meaning another; and then He will always give us more than we ask for. Our good Master knows that those who attain real perfection in their petitions will reach this high degree through the favors which the Father will grant them, and is aware that those who are already perfect, or who are on the way to perfection, do not and cannot fear, for they say they have trampled the world beneath their feet, and the Lord of the world is pleased with them. They will derive the greatest hope of His Majesty's pleasure from the effects which He produces in their souls; absorbed in these joys, they wish they were unable to remember that there is any other world at all, and that they have enemies.

O Eternal Wisdom! O good Teacher! What a wonderful thing it is, daughters, to have a wise and prudent Master who foresees our perils! This is the greatest blessing that the spiritual soul still on earth can desire, because it brings complete security. No words could ever exaggerate the importance of this. The Lord, then, saw it was necessary to awaken such souls and to remind them that they have enemies, and how much greater danger they are in if they are unprepared, and, since if they fall it will be from a greater height, how much more help they need from the Eternal Father. So, lest they should fail to realize their danger and suffer deception, He offers these petitions so necessary to us all while we live in this exile: "And lead us not, Lord, into temptation, but deliver us from evil."

CHAPTER 38

Treats of the great need which we have to beseech the Eternal Father to grant us what we ask in these words: "Et ne nos inducas in tentationem, sed libera nos a malo." Explains certain temptations.[130] *This chapter is noteworthy.*

There are great things here for us to meditate upon, sisters, and to learn to understand as we pray. Remember I consider it quite certain that those who attain perfection do not ask the Lord to deliver them from trials, temptations, persecutions and conflicts – and that is another sure and striking sign that these favors and this contemplation which His Majesty gives them are coming from the Spirit of the Lord and are not illusions. For, as I said a little way back, perfect souls *are in no way repelled by trials, but rather* desire them and pray for them and love them. They are like soldiers: the more wars there are, the better they are pleased, because they hope to emerge from

---

[129] The words "though… forgive" are crossed out in the manuscript, as is the following sentence "May He… before Him."

[130] "And lead us not into temptation, but deliver us from evil."

them with the greater riches.[131] If there are no wars, they serve for their pay, but they know they will not get very far on that.

Believe me, sisters, the soldiers of Christ – namely, those who experience contemplation and practice prayer – are always ready for the hour of conflict. They are never very much afraid of their open enemies, for they know who they are and are sure that their strength can never prevail against the strength which they themselves have been given by the Lord: they will always be victorious and gain great riches, so they will never turn their backs on the battle. Those whom they fear, and fear rightly, and from whom they always beg the Lord to deliver them, are enemies who are treacherous, devils who transform themselves and come and visit them in the disguise of angels of light. The soul fails to recognize them until they have done it a great deal of harm; they suck our life-blood and put an end to our virtues and we go on yielding to temptation without knowing it. From these enemies let us pray the Lord often, in the Paternoster, to deliver us: may He not allow us to run into temptations which deceive us; may their poison be detected; and may light and truth not be hidden from us. How rightly does our good Master teach us to pray for this and pray for it in our name!

Consider, daughters, in how many ways these enemies do us harm. Do not suppose that the sole danger lies in their making us believe that the consolations and the favors which they can counterfeit to us come from God. This, I think, in a way, is the least harmful thing they can do; it may even help some whom this sensible devotion entices to spend more time in prayer and thus to make greater progress. Being ignorant that these consolations come from the devil, and knowing themselves to be unworthy of such favors, they will never cease to give thanks to God and will feel the greater obligation to serve Him; further, they will strive to prepare themselves for more favors which the Lord may grant them, since they believe them to come from His hand.

Always strive after humility, sisters, and try to realize that you are not worthy of these graces, and do not seek them. It is because many souls do this, I feel sure, that the devil loses them: he thinks that he has caused their ruin, but out of the evil which he has been trying to do the Lord brings good. For His Majesty regards our intention, which is to please Him and serve Him and keep near to Him in prayer, and the Lord is faithful. We shall do well to be cautious, and not to let our humility break down or to become in any way vainglorious. Entreat the Lord to deliver you from this, daughters, and you need then have no fear that His Majesty will allow you to be comforted much by anyone but Himself.

Where the devil can do great harm without our realizing it is in making us believe that we possess virtues which we do not: that is pestilential. For, when consolations and favors come to us, we feel that we are doing nothing but receive, and have the greater obligation to serve; but when we suffer from this other delusion we think that we are giving and serving, and that the Lord will be obliged to reward us; and this, little by little, does us a great deal of harm. On the one hand, our humility is weakened, while, on the other, we neglect to cultivate that virtue, believing we have already acquired it. *We think we are walking safely, when, without realizing it, we stumble, and fall into a pit from which we cannot escape. Though we may not consciously have committed any mortal sin which would have sent us infallibly to hell, we have sprained our ankles and cannot continue on that road which I began to speak about and which I have not forgotten. You can imagine how much progress will be made by anyone who is at the bottom of a huge pit: it will be the end of him altogether and he will be lucky if he escapes falling right down to hell: at best, he will never get on with his journey. This being so, he will be unable to help either himself or others. It will be a bad thing for others, too, for, once the pit has been dug, a great many passers-by may fall into it. Only if the person who has fallen in gets out of it and fills it up with earth will further harm to himself and others be prevented. But I warn you that this temptation is full of peril. I know a great deal about it from experience, so I can describe it to you, though not as well as I should like.* What can we do about it, sisters? To me the best thing seems to be what our Master teaches us: to pray, and to beseech the Eternal Father not to allow us to fall into temptation.

There is something else, too, which I want to tell you. If we think the Lord has given us a certain grace, we must understand that it is a blessing which we have received but which He may take away from us again, as indeed, in the great providence of God, often happens. Have you never

---

[131] *Lit.*: "gains", as also in the next paragraph. E. has: "because they have hopes of becoming rich." The reference in both manuscripts is, of course, to the spoils and booty of war.

observed this yourselves, sisters? I certainly have: sometimes I think I am extremely detached, and, in fact, when it comes to the test, I am; yet at other times I find I have such attachment to things which the day before I should perhaps have scoffed at that I hardly know myself. At some other time I seem to have so much courage that I should not quail at anything I was asked to do in order to serve God, and, when I am tested, I find that I really can do these things. And then on the next day I discover that I should not have the courage to kill an ant for God's sake if I were to meet with any opposition about it. Sometimes it seems not to matter in the least if people complain or speak ill of me, and, when the test comes, I still feel like this – indeed, I even get pleasure from it. And then there come days when a single word distresses me and I long to leave the world altogether, for everything in it seems to weary me. And I am not the only person to be like this, for I have noticed the same thing in many people better than myself, so I know it can happen.

That being so, who can say that he possesses any virtue, or that he is rich, if at the time when he most needs this virtue he finds himself devoid of it? No, sisters: let us rather think of ourselves as lacking it and not run into debt without having the means of repayment. Our treasure must come from elsewhere and we never know when God will leave us in this prison of our misery without giving us any. If others, thinking we are good, bestow favors and honors upon us, both they and we shall look foolish when, as I say, it becomes clear that our virtues are only lent us. The truth is that, if we serve the Lord with humility, He will sooner or later succor us in our needs. But, if we are not strong in this virtue, the Lord will leave us to ourselves, as they say, at every step. This is a great favor on His part, for it helps us to realize fully that we have nothing which has not been given us.

And now you must take note of this other piece of advice. The devil makes us believe that we have some virtue – patience, let us say – because we have determination and make continual resolutions to suffer a great deal for God's sake. We really and truly believe that we would suffer all this, and the devil encourages us in the belief, and so we are very pleased. I advise you to place no reliance on these virtues: we ought not to think that we know anything about them beyond their names, or to imagine that the Lord has given them to us, until we come to the test. For it may be that at the first annoying word which people say to you your patience will fall to the ground. Whenever you have frequently to suffer, praise God for beginning to teach you this virtue, and force yourself to suffer patiently, for this is a sign that He wants you to repay Him for the virtue which He is giving you, and you must think of it only as a deposit, as has already been said.

The devil has yet another temptation, which is to make us appear very poor in spirit: we are in the habit of saying that we want nothing and care nothing about anything: but as soon as the chance comes of our being given something, even though we do not in the least need it, all our poverty of spirit disappears. Accustoming ourselves to saying this goes far towards making us think it true. It is very important always to be on the watch and to realize that this is a temptation, both in the things I have referred to and in many others. For when the Lord really gives one of these solid virtues, it seems to bring all the rest in its train: that is a very well-known fact. But I advise you once more, even if you think you possess it, to suspect that you may be mistaken; for the person who is truly humble is always doubtful about his own virtues; very often they seem more genuine and of greater worth when he sees them in his neighbors.

The devil makes you think you are poor, and he has some reason for doing so, because you have made (with the lips, of course) a vow of poverty, as have some other people who practice prayer. I say "with the lips" because, if before making the vow we really meant in our hearts what we were going to say, the devil could not possibly lead us into that temptation – not even in twenty years, or in our entire lifetime – for we should see that we were deceiving the whole world, and ourselves into the bargain. Well, we make our vow of poverty, and then one of us, believing herself all the time to be keeping it, says: "I do not want anything, but I am having this because I cannot do without it: after all, if I am to serve God, I must live, and He wants us to keep these bodies of ours alive." So the devil, in his angelic disguise, suggests to her that there are a thousand different things which she needs and that they are all good for her. And all the time he is persuading her to believe that she is still being true to her vow and possesses the virtue of poverty and that what she has done is no more than her duty.

And now let us take a test case, for we can only get to the truth of this by keeping a continual watch on ourselves: then, if there is any cause for anxiety on our part, we shall at once recognize the symptoms. Here is someone who has a larger income than he needs – I mean, needs for the necessaries of life – and, though he could do with a single manservant, he keeps three. Yet, when he is sued in the courts in connection with a part of his property, or some poor peasant omits to pay him his dues, he gets as upset and excited about it as if his life were at stake. He says he must look after his property or he will lose it, and considers that that justifies him. I do not suggest that he ought to neglect his property: whether or no things go well with him, he should look after it. But a person whose profession of poverty is a genuine one makes so little account of these things that, although for various reasons he attends to his own interests, he never worries about them, because he never supposes he will lose everything he has; and, even if he should do so, he would consider it of no great moment, for the matter is one of secondary importance to him and not his principal concern. His thoughts rise high above it and he has to make an effort to occupy himself with it at all.

Now monks and nuns are demonstrably poor – they must be so, for they possess nothing: sometimes because there is nothing for them to possess. But if a religious of the type just mentioned is given anything, it is most unlikely that he will think it superfluous. He always likes to have something laid by; if he can get a habit of good cloth, he will not ask for one of coarse material. He likes to have some trifle, if only books, which he can pawn or sell, for if he falls ill he will need extra comforts. Sinner that I am! Is this the vow of poverty that you took? Stop worrying about yourself and leave God to provide for you, come what may. If you are going about trying to provide for your own future, it would be less trouble for you to have a fixed income. This may not involve any sin, but it is as well that we should learn to recognize our imperfections, so that we can see how far we are from possessing the virtue of poverty, which we must beg and obtain from God. If we think we already possess it, we shall grow careless, and, what is worse, we shall be deceiving ourselves.

The same thing happens with regard to humility.[132] We think that we have no desire for honor and that we care nothing about anything; but as soon as our honor comes to be slighted in some detail our feelings and actions at once show that we are not humble at all. If an opportunity occurs for us to gain more honor, we do not reject it; even those who are poor, and to whom I have just referred, are anxious to have as much profit as possible – God grant we may not go so far as actually to seek it! We always have phrases on our lips about wanting nothing, and caring nothing about anything, and we honestly think them to be true, and get so used to repeating them that we come to believe them more and more firmly. But when, as I say, we keep on the watch, we realize that this is a temptation, as regards both the virtue I have spoken of and all the rest; for when we really have one of these solid virtues, it brings all the rest in its train: that is a very well-known fact.

CHAPTER 39

Continues the same subject and gives counsels concerning different kinds of temptation. Suggests two remedies by which we may be freed from temptations.[133]

Beware also, daughters, of certain kinds of humility which the devil inculcates in us and which make us very uneasy about the gravity of our *past* sins. There are many ways in which he is accustomed to depress us so that in time we withdraw from Communion and give up our private prayer, because the devil suggests to us that we are not worthy to engage in it. When we come to the Most Holy Sacrament, we spend the time during which we ought to be receiving grace in wondering whether we are properly prepared or no. The thing gets to such a pass that a soul can be made to believe that, through being what it is, it has been forsaken by God, and thus it almost doubts His mercy. Everything such a person does appears to her to be dangerous, and all the service she renders, however good it may be, seems to her fruitless. She loses confidence and sits with her

---

[132] It will be noticed that this paragraph is similar to the last paragraph in the text of V. (p. 254, above). The differences, however, are so wide that each of the two is given as it stands.

[133] A marginal addition made, in the autograph, to the title by another hand reads: "This chapter is very noteworthy, both for those tempted by false kinds of humility and for confessors." This is found in T. and in most of the editions.

hands in her lap because she thinks she can do nothing well and that what is good in others is wrong in herself.

Pay great attention, daughters, to this point which I shall now make, because sometimes thinking yourselves so wicked may be humility and virtue and at other times a very great temptation. I have had experience of this, so I know it is true. Humility, however deep it be, neither disquiets nor troubles nor disturbs the soul; it is accompanied by peace, joy and tranquility. Although, on realizing how wicked we are, we can see clearly that we deserve to be in hell, and are distressed by our sinfulness, and rightly think that everyone should hate us, yet, if our humility is true, this distress is accompanied by an interior peace and joy of which we should not like to be deprived. Far from disturbing or depressing the soul, it enlarges it and makes it fit to serve God better. The other kind of distress only disturbs and upsets the mind and troubles the soul, so grievous is it. I think the devil is anxious for us to believe that we are humble, and, if he can, to lead us to distrust God.

When you find yourselves in this state, cease thinking, so far as you can, of your own wretchedness, and think of the mercy of God and of His love and His sufferings for us. If your state of mind is the result of temptation, you will be unable to do even this, for it will not allow you to quiet your thoughts or to fix them on anything but will only weary you the more: it will be a great thing if you can recognize it as a temptation. This is what happens when we perform excessive penances in order to make ourselves believe that, because of what we are doing, we are more penitent than others. If we conceal our penances from our confessor or superior, or if we are told to give them up and do not obey, that is a clear case of temptation. Always try to obey, however much it may hurt you to do so, for that is the greatest possible perfection.

There is another very dangerous kind of temptation: a feeling of security caused by the belief that we shall never again return to our past faults and to the pleasures of the world. "I know all about these things now," we say, "and I realize that they all come to an end and I get more pleasure from the things of God." If this temptation comes to beginners it is very serious; for, having this sense of security, they think nothing of running once more into occasions of sin. They soon come up against these – and then God preserve them from falling back farther than before! The devil, seeing that here are souls which may do him harm and be of great help to others, does all in his power to prevent them from rising again. However many consolations and pledges of love the Lord may give you, therefore, you must never be so sure of yourselves that you cease to be afraid of falling back again, and you must keep yourselves from occasions of sin.

Do all you can to discuss these graces and favors with someone who can give you light and have no secrets from him. However sublime your contemplation may be, take great care both to begin and to end every period of prayer with self-examination. If these favors come from God, you will do this more frequently, without either taking or needing any advice from me, for such favors bring humility with them and always leave us with more light by which we may see our own unworthiness. I will say no more here, for you will find many books which give this kind of advice. I have said all this because I have had experience of the matter and have sometimes found myself in difficulties of this nature. Nothing that can be said about it, however, will give us complete security.

What, then, Eternal Father, can we do but flee to Thee and beg Thee not to allow these enemies of ours to lead us into temptations? If attacks are made upon us publicly, we shall easily surmount them, with Thy help. But how can we be ready for these treacherous assaults,[134] my God? We need constantly to pray for Thy help. Show us, Lord, some way of recognizing them and guarding against them. Thou knowest that there are not many who walk along this road, and if so many fears are to beset them, there will be far fewer.

What a strange thing it is! You might suppose that the devil never tempted those who do not walk along the road of prayer! People get a greater shock when deception overtakes a single one of the many persons who are striving to be perfect than when a hundred thousand others are deceived and fall into open sin, whom there is no need to look at in order to see if they are good or evil, for Satan can be seen at their side a thousand leagues away. But as a matter of fact people are right about this, for very few who say the Paternoster in the way that has been described are deceived by the devil, so that, if the deception of one of them causes surprise, that is because it is a new and an

---

[134] *Lit.*: "these treasons."

unusual thing. For human nature is such that we scarcely notice what we see frequently but are astounded at what we see seldom or hardly at all. And the devils themselves encourage this astonishment, for if a single soul attains perfection it robs them of many others.

It is so strange, I repeat, that I am not surprised if people are amazed at it; for, unless they are altogether at fault, they are much safer on this road than on any other, just as people who watch a bull-fight from the grand-stand are safer than the men who expose themselves to a thrust from the bull's horns. This comparison, which I heard somewhere, seems to me very exact. Do not be afraid to walk on these roads, sisters, for there are many of them in the life of prayer – and some people get most help by using one of them and others by using another, as I have said. This road is a safe one and you will the more readily escape from temptation if you are near the Lord than if you are far away from Him. Beseech and entreat this of Him, as you do so many times each day in the Paternoster.

CHAPTER 40

Describes how, by striving always to walk in the love and fear of God, we shall travel safely amid all these temptations.

Show us, then, O our good Master, some way in which we may live through this most dangerous warfare without frequent surprise. The best way that we can do this, daughters, is to use the love and fear given us by His Majesty. For love will make us quicken our steps, while fear will make us look where we are setting our feet so that we shall not fall on a road where there are so many obstacles. Along that road all living creatures must pass, and if we have these two things we shall certainly not be deceived.

You will ask me how you can tell if you really have these two very, very great virtues.[135] You are right to ask, for we can never be quite definite and certain about it; if we were sure that we possessed love, we should be sure that we were in a state of grace. But you know, sisters, there are some indications which are in no way secret but so evident that even a blind man, as people say, could see them. You may not wish to heed them, but they cry so loud for notice that they make quite an uproar, for there are not many who possess them to the point of perfection and thus they are the more readily noticed. Love and fear of God! These are two strong castles whence we can wage war on the world and on the devils.

Those who really love God love all good, seek all good, help forward all good, praise all good, and invariably join forces with good men and help and defend them. They love only truth and things worthy of love. Do you think it possible that anyone who really and truly loves God can love vanities, riches, worldly pleasures or honors? Can he engage in strife or feel envy? No; for his only desire is to please the Beloved. Such persons die with longing for Him to love them and so they will give their lives to learn how they may please Him better. Will they hide their love? No: if their love for God is genuine love they cannot. Why, think of Saint Paul or the Magdalene. One of these – Saint Paul – found in three days that he was sick with love. The Magdalene discovered this on the very first day. And how certain of it they were! For there are degrees of love for God, which shows itself in proportion to its strength. If there is little of it, it shows itself but little; if there is much, it shows itself a great deal. But it always shows itself, whether little or much, provided it is real love for God.

But to come to what we are chiefly treating of now – the deceptions and illusions practiced against contemplatives by the devil – such souls have no little love; for had they not a great deal they would not be contemplatives, and so their love shows itself plainly and in many ways. Being a great fire, it cannot fail to give out a very bright light. If they have not much love, they should proceed with many misgivings and realize that they have great cause for fear; and they should try to find out what is wrong with them, say their prayers, walk in humility and beseech the Lord not to lead them into temptation, into which, I fear, they will certainly fall unless they bear this sign. But if they walk humbly and strive to discover the truth and do as their confessor bids them and tell

---

[135] *Lit.*: "these two virtues, so great, so great."

him the plain truth, then the Lord is faithful, and, as has been said, by using the very means with which he had thought to give them death, the devil will give them life, with however many fantasies and illusions he tries to deceive them. *If they submit to the teaching of the Church, they need not fear; whatever fantasies and illusions the devil may invent, he will at once betray his presence.*

But if you feel this love for God which I have spoken of, and the fear which I shall now describe, you may go on your way with happiness and tranquility. In order to disturb the soul and keep it from enjoying these great blessings, the devil will suggest to it a thousand false fears and will persuade other people to do the same; for if he cannot win souls he will at least try to make them lose something, and among the losers will be those who might have gained greatly had they believed that such great favors, bestowed upon so miserable a creature, come from God, and that it is possible for them to be thus bestowed, for sometimes we seem to forget His past mercies.

Do you suppose that it is of little use to the devil to suggest these fears? No, it is most useful to him, for there are two *well-known* ways in which he can make use of this means to harm us, *to say nothing of others*. First, he can make those who listen to him fearful of engaging in prayer, because they think that they will be deceived. Secondly, he can dissuade many from approaching God who, as I have said, see that He is so good that He will hold intimate converse with sinners. Many such souls think that He will treat them in the same way, and they are right: I myself know certain persons inspired in this way who began the habit of prayer and in a short time became truly devout and received great favors from the Lord.

Therefore, sisters, when you see someone to whom the Lord is granting these favors, praise Him fervently, yet do not imagine that she is safe, but aid her with more prayer, for no one can be safe in this life amid the engulfing dangers of this stormy sea. Wherever this love is, then, you will not fail to recognize it; I do not know how it could be concealed. For they say that it is impossible for us to hide our love even for creatures, and that, the more we try to conceal it, the more clearly is it revealed. And yet this is so worthless that it hardly deserves the name of love, for it is founded upon nothing at all: *it is loathsome, indeed, to make this comparison.* How, then, could a love like God's be concealed – so strong, so righteous, continually increasing, never seeing cause for ceasing to manifest itself, and resting upon the firm foundation of the love which is its reward? As to the reality of this reward there can be no doubt, for it is manifest in Our Lord's great sorrows, His trials, the shedding of His blood and even the loss of His life. Certainly, then, there is no doubt as to this love. *It is indeed love, and deserves that name, of which worldly vanities have robbed it.* God help me! How different must the one love be from the other to those who have experience of both!

May His Majesty be pleased to grant us *to experience* this before He takes us from this life, for it will be a great thing at the hour of death, *when we are going we know not whither*, to realize that we shall be judged by One Whom we have loved above all things, *and with a passion that makes us entirely forget ourselves*. Once our debts have been paid we shall be able to walls in safety. We shall not be going into a foreign land, but into our own country, for it belongs to Him Whom we have loved so truly and Who Himself loves us. *For this love of His, besides its other properties, is better than all earthly affection in that, if we love Him, we are quite sure that He loves us too.* Remember, my daughters, the greatness of the gain which comes from this love, and of our loss if we do not possess it, for in that case we shall be delivered into the hands of the tempter, hands so cruel and so hostile to all that is good, and so friendly to all that is evil.

What will become of the poor soul when it falls into these hands after emerging from all the pains and trials of death? How little rest it will have! How it will be torn as it goes down to hell! What swarms and varieties of serpents it will meet! How dreadful is that place! How miserable that lodging! Why, a pampered person (and most of those who go to hell are that) can hardly bear to spend a single night in a bad inn: what, then, will be the feelings of that wretched soul when it is condemned to such an inn as this and has to spend eternity there?[136] Let us not try to pamper ourselves, daughters. We are quite well off here: there is only a single night for us to spend in this bad inn. Let us praise God and strive to do penance in this life. How sweet will be the death of those who have done penance for all their sins and have not to go to purgatory! It may be that they will begin to enjoy glory even in this world, and will know no fear, but only peace.

---

[136] *Lit.*: "to an inn for ever, *ever*, for eternity." The repetition of "ever" (*siempre*) reminds one of the famous reminiscence of St. Teresa's childhood, to be found in her *Life*, Chap. I.

Even if we do not attain to this, sisters, let us beseech God that, if in due course we must suffer these pains, it may be with a hope of emerging from them. Then we shall suffer them willingly and lose neither the friendship nor the grace of God. May He grant us these in this life so that we may not unwittingly fall into temptation.

CHAPTER 41

Speaks of the fear of God and of how we must keep ourselves from venial sins.

How I have enlarged on this subject! Yet I have not said as much about it as I should like; for it is a delightful thing to talk about this love *of God*. What, then, must it be to possess it? *May the Lord, for His own sake, give it me! May I not depart from this life till there is nothing in it that I desire, till I have forgotten what it is to love anything but Thee and till I deny the name of love to any other kind of affection – for all love is false but love of Thee, and, unless the foundations of a building are true, the building itself will not endure. I do not know why it surprises us to hear people say: "So-and-so has made me a poor return for something." "Someone else does not like me." I laugh to myself when I hear that. What other sort of return do you expect him to make you? And why do you expect anyone to like you? These things will show you what the world is; your love itself becomes your punishment, and the reason why you are so upset about it is that your will strongly resents your involving it in such childish pastimes.*

Let us now come to the fear of God – *though I am sorry not to be able to say a little about this worldly love, which, for my sins, I know well and should like to acquaint you with, so that you may free yourself from it for ever. But I am straying from my subject and shall have to pass on.*

This fear of God is another thing with which those who possess it and those who have to do with them are very familiar. But I should like you to realize that at first it is not very deep, save in a few people, to whom, as I have said, the Lord grants such great favors as to make them rich in virtues *and to raise them, in a very short time, to great heights of prayer.* It is not recognizable, therefore, at first, in everyone. As it increases, it grows stronger each day, and then, of course, it can be recognized, for those who possess it forsake sin, and occasions of sin, and bad company, and other signs of it are visible in them. When at last the soul attains to contemplation, of which we are chiefly treating at the moment, its fear of God is plainly revealed, and its love is not dissembled even outwardly. However narrowly we watch such persons, we shall not find them growing careless; for, close as our watch on them may be, the Lord so preserves them that they would not knowingly commit one venial sin even to further their own interests, and, as for mortal sin, they fear it like fire. These are the illusions, sisters, which I should like you always to fear; let us always beseech God that temptation may not be strong enough for us to offend Him but that He may send it to us in proportion to the strength which He gives us to conquer it. *If we keep a pure conscience, we can suffer little or no harm.* That is the important point; and that is the fear which I hope will never be taken from us, for it is that fear which will stand us in good stead.

Oh, what a great thing it is not to have offended the Lord, so that the servants and slaves of hell[137] may be kept under control! In the end, whether willingly or no, we shall all serve Him – they by compulsion and we with our whole heart. So that, if we please Him, they will be kept at bay and will do nothing that can harm us, however much they lead us into temptation and lay secret snares for us.

Keep this in mind, for it is very important advice, so do not neglect it until you find you have such a fixed determination not to offend the Lord that you would rather lose a thousand lives *and be persecuted by the whole world*, than commit one mortal sin, and until you are most careful not to commit venial sins. I am referring now to sins committed knowingly: as far as those of the other kind are concerned, who can fail to commit them frequently? But it is one thing to commit a sin knowingly and after long deliberation, and quite another to do it so suddenly that the knowledge of its being a venial sin and its commission are one and the same thing, and we hardly realize what we have done, *although we do to some extent realize it.* From any sin, however small, committed with

---

[137] *Lit.*: "the infernal slaves."

full knowledge, may God deliver us, especially since we are sinning against so great a Sovereign and realizing that He is watching us! That seems to me to be a sin committed of malice aforethought; it is as though one were to say: "Lord, although this displeases Thee, I shall do it. I know that Thou seest it and I know that Thou wouldst not have me do it; but, though I understand this, I would rather follow my own whim and desire than Thy will." If we commit a sin in this way, however slight, it seems to me that our offence is not small but very, very great.

For the love of God, sisters, *never be careless about this – and, glory be to the Lord, you are not so at present.* If you would gain this fear of God, *remember the importance of habit and of starting to realize what a serious thing it is to offend Him. Do your utmost to learn this and to turn it over in your minds*; for our life, and much more than our life, depends upon this virtue being firmly planted in our souls. Until you are conscious within your soul of possessing it, you need always to exercise very great care and to avoid all occasions of sin and any kind of company which will not help you to get nearer to God. Be most careful, in all that you do, to bend your will to it; see that all you say tends to edification; flee from all places where there is conversation which is not pleasing to God. Much care is needed if this fear of God is to be thoroughly impressed upon the soul; though, if one has true love, it is quickly acquired. Even when the soul has that firm inward determination which I have described, not to offend God for the sake of any creature, *or from fear of a thousand deaths*, it may subsequently fall from time to time, for we are weak and cannot trust ourselves, and, the more determined we are, the less self-confidence we should have, for confidence must come from God. But, when we find ourselves in this state, we need not feel constrained or depressed, for the Lord will help us and the habits we have formed will be of assistance to us so that we shall not offend Him; we shall be able to walk in holy freedom, and associate with anyone, as seems right to us, even with dissolute people. *These will do you no harm, if you hate sin.* Before we had this true fear of God worldly people would have been poisonous to us and would have helped to ruin our souls; but now they will often help us to love God more and to praise Him for having delivered us from what we see to be a notorious danger. And whereas we for our part may previously have helped to foster their weaknesses, we shall now be helping to repress them, because they will restrain themselves in our presence, and this is a compliment which they will pay us without our desiring it.

I often praise the Lord (though I also wonder why it should be so) that merely by his presence, and without saying a word, a servant of God should frequently prevent people from speaking against Him. It may be as it is in worldly intercourse: a person is always spoken of with respect, even in his absence, before those who are known to be his friends, lest they should be offended. Since this servant of God is in a state of grace, this grace must cause him to be respected, however lowly his station, for people will not distress him in a matter about which they know him to feel so strongly as giving offence to God. I really do not know the reason for this but I do know that it very commonly happens. Do not be too strict with yourselves, then, for, if your spirit begins to quail, it will do great harm to what is good in you and may sometimes lead to scrupulosity, which is a hindrance to progress both in yourselves and in others. Even if things are not as bad as this, a person, however good in herself, will not lead many souls to God if they see that she is so strict and timorous. Human nature is such that these characteristics will frighten and oppress it and lead people to avoid the road you are taking, even if they are quite clear it is the best one.

Another source of harm is this: we may judge others unfavorably, though they may be holier than ourselves, because they do not walk as we do, but, in order to profit their neighbors, talk freely and without restraint. You think such people are imperfect; and if they are good and yet at the same time of a lively disposition, you think them dissolute. This is especially true of those of us who are unlearned and are not sure what we can speak about without committing sin. It is a very dangerous state of mind, leading to great uneasiness and to continual temptation, because it is unfair to our neighbor. It is very wrong to think that everyone who does not follow in your own timorous footsteps has something the matter with her. Another danger is that, when it is your duty to speak, and right that you should speak, you may not dare to do so lest you say too much and may perhaps speak well of things that you ought to hate.

Try, then, sisters, to be as pleasant as you can, without offending God, and to get on as well as you can with those you have to deal with, so that they may like talking to you and want to follow your way of life and conversation, and not be frightened and put off by virtue. This is very important for nuns: the holier they are, the more sociable they should be with their sisters. Although you may be very sorry if all your sisters' conversation is not just as you would like it to be, never keep aloof from them if you wish to help them and to have their love. We must try hard to be pleasant, and to humor the people we deal with and make them like us, especially our sisters.

So try, my daughters, to bear in mind that God does not pay great attention to all the trifling matters which occupy you, and do not allow these things to make your spirit quail and your courage fade, for if you do that you may lose many blessings. As I have said, let your intention be upright and your will determined not to offend God. But do not let your soul dwell in seclusion, or, instead of acquiring holiness, you will develop many imperfections, which the devil will implant in you in other ways, in which case, as I have said, you will not do the good that you might, either to yourselves or to others.

You see that, with these two things – love and fear of God – we can travel along this road in peace and quietness, *and not think at every step that we can see some pitfall, and that we shall never reach our goal.*[138] *Yet we cannot be sure of reaching it, so* fear will always lead the way, and then we shall not grow careless, for, as long as we live, we must never feel completely safe or we shall be in great danger. And that was our Teacher's meaning when at the end of this prayer He said these words to His Father, knowing how necessary they were: "*But deliver us from evil. Amen.*"

CHAPTER 42
Treats of these last words of the Paternoster: "Sed libera nos a malo. Amen." "But deliver us from evil. Amen."

I think the good Jesus was right to ask this for Himself, for we know how weary of this life He was when at the Supper He said to His Apostles: "With desire I have desired to sup with you"[139] – and that was the last supper of His life. From this it can be seen how weary He must have been of living; yet nowadays people are not weary even at a hundred years old, but always want to live longer. It is true, however, that we do not live so difficult a life or suffer such trials or such poverty as His Majesty had to bear. What was His whole life but a continuous death, with the picture of the cruel death that He was to suffer always before His eyes? And this was the least important thing, with so many offenses being committed against His Father and such a multitude of souls being lost. If to any human being full of charity this is a great torment, what must it have been to the boundless and measureless charity of the Lord? And how right He was to beseech the Father to deliver Him from so many evils and trials and to give Him rest for ever in His Kingdom, of which He was the true heir.

By the word "Amen," as it comes at the end of every prayer, I understand that the Lord is begging that we may be delivered from all evil for ever. *It is useless, sisters, for us to think that, for so long as we live, we can be free from numerous temptations and imperfections and even sins; for it is said that whosoever thinks himself to be without sin deceives himself, and that is true. But if we try to banish bodily ills and trials – and who is without very many and various trials of such kinds? – is it not right that we should ask to be delivered from sin?*

Still, let us realize that what we are asking here – this deliverance from all evil – seems an impossibility, whether we are thinking of bodily ills, as I have said, or of imperfections and faults in God's service. I am referring, not to the saints, who, as Saint Paul said, can do all things in Christ[140] *but to sinners like myself. When I find myself trammeled by weakness, lukewarmness, lack of mortification and many other things, I realize that I must beg for help from the Lord.*

You, daughters, must ask as you think best. Personally, I shall find no redress in this life, so I ask the Lord to deliver me from all evil "for ever." What good thing shall we find in this life, sisters, in which we are deprived of our great Good and are absent from Him? Deliver me, Lord, from this shadow of death; deliver me from all these trials; deliver me from all these pains; deliver me from

---

[138] Or "for [if we do this] we shall never reach our goal."
[139] St. Luke xxii, 15.
[140] Philippians iv, 13.

all these changes, from all the formalities with which we are forced to comply for as long as we live, from all the many, many, many things which weary and depress me, and the enumeration of all of which would weary the reader if I were to repeat them. This life is unendurable. The source of my own depression must be my own wicked life and the realization that even now I am not living as I should, so great are my obligations.

I beseech the Lord, then, to deliver me from all evil for ever, since I cannot pay what I owe, and may perhaps run farther into debt each day. And the hardest thing to bear, Lord, is that I cannot know with any certainty if I love Thee and if my desires are acceptable in Thy sight. O my God and Lord, deliver me from all evil and be pleased to lead me to that place where all good things are to be found. What can be looked for on earth by those to whom Thou hast given some knowledge of what the world is and those who have a living faith in what the Eternal Father has laid up for them *because His Son asks it of Him and teaches us to ask Him for it too?*

When contemplatives ask for this with fervent desire and full determination it is a *very* clear sign that *their contemplation is genuine and that* the favors which they receive in prayer are from God. Let those who have these favors,[141] then, prize them highly. But if I myself make this request it is not for that reason (I mean, it must not be taken as being for that reason); it is because I am wearied by so many trials and because my life has been so wicked that I am afraid of living any longer. It is not surprising if those who share in the favors of God should wish to pass to a life where they no longer enjoy mere sips at them: *being already partakers in some knowledge of His greatness, they would fain see it in its entirety. They have no desire to remain* where there are so many hindrances to the enjoyment of so many blessings; nor that they should desire to be where the Sun of justice never sets. Henceforward all the things they see on earth seem dim to them and I wonder that they can live for even an hour. No one can be content to do so who has begun to enjoy such things, and has been given the Kingdom of God on earth, and must live to do, not his own will, but the will of the King.

Oh, far other must be that life in which we no longer desire death! How differently shall we then incline our wills towards the will of God! His will is for us to desire truth, whereas we desire falsehood; His will is for us to desire the eternal, whereas we prefer that which passes away; His will is for us to desire great and sublime things, whereas we desire the base things of earth; He would have us desire only what is certain, whereas here on earth we love what is doubtful. What a mockery it all is, my daughters, unless we beseech God to deliver us from these perils for ever and to keep us from all evil! And although our desire for this may not be perfect, let us strive to make the petition. What does it cost us to ask it, since we ask it of One Who is so powerful? *It would be insulting a great emperor to ask him for a farthing.* Since we have already given Him our will, let us leave the giving to His will, so that we may be the more surely heard; and may His name be for ever hallowed in the Heavens and on the earth and may His will be ever done in me. Amen.

You see now, friends, what is meant by perfection in vocal prayer, in which we consider and know to Whom the prayer is being made, Who is making it and what is its object. When you are told that it is not good for you to practice any but vocal prayer, do not be discouraged, but read this with great care and beg God to explain to you anything about prayer which you cannot understand. For no one can deprive you of vocal prayer or make you say the Paternoster hurriedly, without understanding it. If anyone tries to do so, or advises you to give up your prayer, take no notice of him. You may be sure he is a false prophet; and in these days, remember, you must not believe everyone, for, though you may be told now that you have nothing to fear, you do not know what is in store for you. I had intended, as well as saying this, to talk to you a little about how you should say the Ave Maria, but I have written at such length that that will have to be left over. If you have learned how to say the Paternoster well, you will know enough to enable you to say all the other vocal prayers you may have to recite.

Now let us go back and finish the journey which I have been describing, for the Lord seems to have been saving me labor by teaching both you and me the Way which I began to outline to you and by showing me how much we ask for when we repeat this evangelical prayer. May He be for ever blessed, for it had certainly never entered my mind that there were such great secrets in it. You have now seen that it comprises the whole spiritual road, right from the beginning, until God

---

[141] *Lit.:* "Let those who are so."

absorbs the soul and gives it to drink abundantly of the fountain of living water which I told you was at the end of the road. It seems, sisters, that the Lord's will has been to teach us what great consolation is comprised in it, and this is a great advantage to those who cannot read. If they understood this prayer, they could derive a great deal of sound instruction from it and would find it a real comfort. *Our books may be taken from us, but this is a book which no one can take away, and it comes from the lips of the Truth Himself, Who cannot err.*

As we repeat the Paternoster so many times daily, then, as I have said, let us delight in it and strive to learn from so excellent a Master the humility with which He prays, and all the other things that have been described. May His Majesty forgive me for having dared to speak of such high matters. Well does His Majesty know that *I should not have ventured to do so, and that* my understanding would not have been capable of it, had He not taught me what I have said. Give thanks to Him for this, sisters, for He must have done it because of the humility with which you asked me to write it for you in your desire to be instructed by one so unworthy.

Well, sisters, Our Lord seems not to want me to write any more, for, although I had intended to go on, I can think of nothing to say. The Lord has shown you the road and has taught me what I wrote in the book which, as I say, I have already written.[142] *This tells you how to conduct yourselves on reaching this fount of living water and what the soul experiences when there, and how God satiates it and takes away its thirst for earthly things, and makes it grow in things pertaining to God's service. This will be very helpful to those who have reached the fount, and will give them a great deal of light.*

Before you see this book I shall give it to my confessor, Father Presentado Domingo Baez *of the Order of Saint Dominic.* If he thinks you will benefit by it, and gives it you to read, and if you find it of any comfort, I, too, shall be comforted. *If he gives you this book, he will give you the other*[143] *as well.* Should it be found unsuitable for anyone to read, you must take the will for the deed, as I have obeyed your command by writing it.[144] I consider myself well repaid for my labor in writing, though it has certainly been no labor to me to think about what I have been going to say, as the Lord has taught me the secrets of this evangelical prayer, which has been a great comfort to me. Blessed and praised be the Lord, from Whom comes all the good that we speak and think and do. Amen.

---

[142] The *Life.*

[143] The *Life.* I do not know what reason St. Teresa had to suppose this, but the Spanish of E. ("tambian os dari el otro") is quite definite.

[144] *Lit.:* "you will take my will, as I have obeyed your command with the work" [i.e. in deed].

.

The Book of Her Life

The Autobiography of
St. Teresa of Avila

By

Saint Teresa of Avila

The Life of St. Teresa of Jesus,
of the Order of Our Lady of Carmel
Translated by David Lewis

Table of Contents

THE LIFE OF THE HOLY MOTHER TERESA OF JESUS 208

The Life of the Holy Mother Teresa of Jesus

Written by Herself.

Prologue.

As I have been commanded and left at liberty to describe at length my way of prayer, and the workings of the grace of our Lord within me, I could wish that I had been allowed at the same time to speak distinctly and in detail of my grievous sins and wicked life. But it has not been so willed; on the contrary, I am laid herein under great restraint; and therefore, for the love of our Lord, I beg of every one who shall read this story of my life[1] to keep in mind how wicked it has been; and how, among the Saints who were converted to God, I have never found one in whom I can have any comfort. For I see that they, after our Lord had called them, never fell into sin again; I not only became worse, but, as it seems to me, deliberately withstood the graces of His Majesty, because I saw that I was thereby bound to serve Him more earnestly, knowing, at the same time, that of myself I could not pay the least portion of my debt.

May He be blessed for ever Who waited for me so long! I implore Him with my whole heart to send me His grace, so that in all clearness and truth I may give this account of myself which my confessors command me to give; and even our Lord Himself, I know it, has also willed it should be given for some time past, but I had not the courage to attempt it. And I pray it may be to His praise and glory, and a help to my confessors; who, knowing me better, may succor my weakness, so that I may render to our Lord some portion of the service I owe Him. May all creatures praise Him for ever! Amen.

Chapter I.

Childhood and Early Impressions. The Blessing of Pious Parents. Desire of Martyrdom. Death of the Saint's Mother.

In all that I shall say in this Book, I submit to what is taught by Our Mother, the Holy Roman Church; if there is anything in it contrary to this, it will be without my knowledge. Therefore, for the love of Our Lord, I beg the learned men who are to revise it to look at it very carefully and to amend any faults of this nature which there may be in it and the many others which it will have of other kinds. If there is anything good in it, let this be to the glory and honor of God and in the service of His most sacred Mother, our Patroness and Lady, whose habit, though all unworthily, I wear.

1. I had a father and mother, who were devout and feared God. Our Lord also helped me with His grace. All this would have been enough to make me good, if I had not been so wicked. My father was very much given to the reading of good books; and so he had them in Spanish, that his children might read them. These books, with my mother's carefulness to make us say our prayers, and to bring us up devout to our Lady and to certain Saints, began to make me think seriously when I was, I believe, six or seven years old. It helped me, too, that I never saw my father and mother respect anything but goodness. They were very good themselves. My father was a man of great charity towards the poor, and compassion for the sick, and also for servants; so much so, that he

---

[1] The Saint, in a letter written November 19, 1581, to Don Pedro de Castro, then canon of Avila, speaking of this book, calls it the book "Of the compassions of God"—Y ansi intitule ese libro De las Misericordias de Dios. That letter is the 358th in the edition of Don Vicente de la Fuente, and the 8th of the fourth volume of the Doblado edition of Madrid. "Vitam igitur suam internam et supernaturalem magis pandit quam narrat actiones suas mere humanas" (Bollandists, n. 2).

never could be persuaded to keep slaves, for he pitied them so much: and a slave belonging to one of his brothers being once in his house, was treated by him with as much tenderness as his own children. He used to say that he could not endure the pain of seeing that she was not free. He was a man of great truthfulness; nobody ever heard him swear or speak ill of any one; his life was most pure.

2. My mother also was a woman of great goodness, and her life was spent in great infirmities. She was singularly pure in all her ways. Though possessing great beauty, yet was it never known that she gave reason to suspect that she made any account whatever of it; for, though she was only three-and-thirty years of age when she died, her apparel was already that of a woman advanced in years. She was very calm, and had great sense. The sufferings she went through during her life were grievous, her death most Christian.[2]

3. We were three sisters and nine brothers.[3] All, by the mercy of God, resembled their parents in goodness except myself, though I was the most cherished of my father. And, before I began to offend God, I think he had some reason,—for I am filled with sorrow whenever I think of the good desires with which our Lord inspired me, and what a wretched use I made of them. Besides, my brothers never in any way hindered me in the service of God.

4. One of my brothers was nearly of my own age;[4] and he it was whom I most loved, though I was very fond of them all, and they of me. He and I used to read Lives of Saints together. When I read of martyrdom undergone by the Saints for the love of God, it struck me that the vision of God was very cheaply purchased; and I had a great desire to die a martyr's death,—not out of any love of Him of which I was conscious, but that I might most quickly attain to the fruition of those great joys of which I read that they were reserved in Heaven; and I used to discuss with my brother how we could become martyrs. We settled to go together to the country of the Moors,[5] begging our way for the love of God, that we might be there beheaded;[6] and our Lord, I believe, had given us courage enough, even at so tender an age, if we could have found the means to proceed; but our greatest difficulty seemed to be our father and mother.

5. It astonished us greatly to find it said in what we were reading that pain and bliss were everlasting. We happened very often to talk about this; and we had a pleasure in repeating

---

[2] See ch. xxxvii. § 1; where the Saint says that she saw them in a vision both in Heaven.

[3] Alfonso Sanchez de Cepeda, father of the Saint, married first Catalina del Peso y Henao, and had three children—one daughter, Maria de Cepeda, and two sons. After the death of Catalina, he married Beatriz Davila y Ahumada, by whom he had nine children—seven boys and two girls. The third of these, and the eldest of the daughters, was the Saint, Doña Teresa Sanchez Cepeda Davila y Ahumada. In the Monastery of the Incarnation, where she was a professed nun for twenty-eight years, she was known as Doña Teresa; but in the year 1563, when she left her monastery for the new foundation of St. Joseph, of the Reform of the Carmelites, she took for the first time the name of Teresa of Jesus (De la Fuente). The Saint was born March 28, 1515, and baptized on the 4th of April, in the church of St. John; on which day Mass was said for the first time in the Monastery of the Incarnation, where the Saint made her profession. Her godfather was Vela Nuñez, and her godmother Doña Maria del Aguila. The Bollandists and Father Bouix say that she was baptized on the very day of her birth. But the testimony of Doña Maria de Pinel, a nun in the Monastery of the Incarnation, is clear: and Don Vicente de La Fuente, quoting it, vol. i. p. 549, says that this delay of baptism was nothing singular in those days, provided there was no danger of death.

[4] Rodrigo de Cepeda, four years older than the Saint, entered the army, and, serving in South America, was drowned in the river Plate, Rio de la Plata. St. Teresa always considered him a martyr, because he died in defense of the Catholic faith (Ribera, lib. i. ch. iii.). Before he sailed for the Indies, he made his will, and left all his property to the Saint, his sister (Reforma de los Descalços, vol. i. lib. i. ch. iii. § 4).

[5] The Bollandists incline to believe that St. Teresa may not have intended to quit Spain, because all the Moors were not at that time driven out of the country. The Bull of the Saint's canonization, and the Lections of the Breviary, say that she left her father's house, ut in Africam trajiceret.

[6] The two children set out on their strange journey—one of them seven, the other eleven, years old— through the Adaja Gate; but when they had crossed the bridge, they were met by one of their uncles, who brought them back to their mother, who had already sent through Avila in quest of them. Rodrigo, like Adam, excused himself, and laid the blame on the woman (Ribera, lib. i. ch. iii.). Francisco de Santa Maria, chronicler of the Order, says that the uncle was Francisco Alvarez de Cepeda (Reforma de los Descalços, lib. i. ch. v. § 4).

frequently, "For ever, ever, ever." Through the constant uttering of these words, our Lord was pleased that I should receive an abiding impression of the way of truth when I was yet a child.

6. As soon as I saw it was impossible to go to any place where people would put me to death for the sake of God, my brother and I set about becoming hermits; and in an orchard belonging to the house we contrived, as well as we could, to build hermitages, by piling up small stones one on the other, which fell down immediately; and so it came to pass that we found no means of accomplishing our wish. Even now, I have a feeling of devotion when I consider how God gave me in my early youth what I lost by my own fault. I gave alms as I could—and I could but little. I contrived to be alone, for the sake of saying my prayers⁷—and they were many—especially the Rosary, to which my mother had a great devotion, and had made us also in this like herself. I used to delight exceedingly, when playing with other children, in the building of monasteries, as if we were nuns; and I think I wished to be a nun, though not so much as I did to be a martyr or a hermit.

7. I remember that, when my mother died,⁸ I was about twelve years old—a little less. When I began to understand my loss, I went in my affliction to an image of our Lady,⁹ and with many tears implored her to be my mother. I did this in my simplicity, and I believe that it was of service to me; for I have by experience found the royal Virgin help me whenever I recommended myself to her; and at last she has brought me back to herself. It distresses me now, when I think of, and reflect on, that which kept me from being earnest in the good desires with which I began.

8. O my Lord, since Thou art determined to save me—may it be the pleasure of Thy Majesty to effect it!—and to bestow upon me so many graces, why has it not been Thy pleasure also—not for my advantage, but for Thy greater honor—that this habitation, wherein Thou has continually to dwell, should not have contracted so much defilement? It distresses me even to say this, O my Lord, because I know the fault is all my own, seeing that Thou has left nothing undone to make me, even from my youth, wholly Thine. When I would complain of my parents, I cannot do it; for I saw nothing in them but all good, and carefulness for my welfare. Then, growing up, I began to discover the natural gifts which our Lord had given me—they were said to be many; and, when I should have given Him thanks for them, I made use of every one of them, as I shall now explain, to offend Him.

Chapter II.

Early Impressions. Dangerous Books and Companions. The Saint Is Placed in a Monastery.

1. What I shall now speak of was, I believe, the beginning of great harm to me. I often think how wrong it is of parents not to be very careful that their children should always, and in every way, see only that which is good; for though my mother was, as I have just said, so good herself, nevertheless I, when I came to the use of reason, did not derive so much good from her as I ought to have done—almost none at all; and the evil I learned did me much harm. She was very fond of books of chivalry; but this pastime did not hurt her so much as it hurt me, because she never wasted her time on them; only we, her children, were left at liberty to read them; and perhaps she did this to distract her thoughts from her great sufferings, and occupy her children, that they might not go astray in other ways. It annoyed my father so much, that we had to be careful he never saw us. I contracted a habit of reading these books; and this little fault which I observed in my mother was

---

⁷ She was also marvelously touched by the story of the Samaritan woman at the well, of whom there was a picture in her room (*Ribera*, lib. i. ch. iv.). She speaks of this later on. (See ch. xxx. § 24.)

⁸ The last will and testament of Doña Beatriz de Ahumada was made November 24, 1528 and she may have died soon after. If there be no mistake in the copy of that instrument, the Saint must have been more than twelve years old at that time. Don Vicente, in a note, says, with the Bollandists, that Doña Beatriz died at the end of the year 1526, or in the beginning of 1527; but it is probable that, when he wrote that note, he had not read the copy of the will, which he has printed in the first volume of the Saint's writings, p. 550.

⁹ Our Lady of Charity, in the church of the hospital where the poor and pilgrims were received in Avila (*Bouix*).

the beginning of lukewarmness in my good desires, and the occasion of my falling away in other respects. I thought there was no harm in it when I wasted many hours night and day in so vain an occupation, even when I kept it a secret from my father. So completely was I mastered by this passion, that I thought I could never be happy without a new book.

2. I began to make much of dress, to wish to please others by my appearance. I took pains with my hands and my hair, used perfumes, and all vanities within my reach—and they were many, for I was very much given to them. I had no evil intention, because I never wished any one to offend God for me. This fastidiousness of excessive neatness[10] lasted some years; and so also did other practices, which I thought then were not at all sinful; now, I see how wrong all this must have been.

3. I had some cousins; for into my father's house no others were allowed an entrance. In this he was very cautious; and would to God he had been cautious about them!—for I see now the danger of conversing, at an age when virtue should begin to grow, with persons who, knowing nothing themselves of the vanity of the world, provoke others to throw themselves into the midst of it. These cousins were nearly of mine own age—a little older, perhaps. We were always together; and they had a great affection for me. In everything that gave them pleasure, I kept the conversation alive,—listened to the stories of their affections and childish follies, good for nothing; and, what was still worse, my soul began to give itself up to that which was the cause of all its disorders. If I were to give advice, I would say to parents that they ought to be very careful whom they allow to mix with their children when young; for much mischief thence ensues, and our natural inclinations are unto evil rather than unto good.

4. So it was with me; for I had a sister much older than myself,[11] from whose modesty and goodness, which were great, I learned nothing; and learned every evil from a relative who was often in the house. She was so light and frivolous, that my mother took great pains to keep her out of the house, as if she foresaw the evil I should learn from her; but she could not succeed, there being so many reasons for her coming. I was very fond of this person's company, gossiped and talked with her; for she helped me in all the amusements I liked, and, what is more, found some for me, and communicated to me her own conversations and her vanities. Until I knew her, I mean, until she became friendly with me, and communicated to me her own affairs—I was then about fourteen years old, a little more, I think—I do not believe that I turned away from God in mortal sin, or lost the fear of Him, though I had a greater fear of disgrace. This latter fear had such sway over me, that I never wholly forfeited my good name—and, as to that, there was nothing in the world for which I would have bartered it, and nobody in the world I liked well enough who could have persuaded me to do it. Thus I might have had the strength never to do anything against the honor of God, as I had it by nature not to fail in that wherein I thought the honor of the world consisted; and I never observed that I was failing in many other ways. In vainly seeking after it I was extremely careful; but in the use of the means necessary for preserving it I was utterly careless. I was anxious only not to be lost altogether.

5. This friendship distressed my father and sister exceedingly. They often blamed me for it; but, as they could not hinder that person from coming into the house, all their efforts were in vain; for I was very adroit in doing anything that was wrong. Now and then, I am amazed at the evil one bad companion can do,—nor could I believe it if I did not know it by experience,—especially when we are young: then is it that the evil must be greatest. Oh, that parents would take warning by me, and look carefully to this! So it was; the conversation of this person so changed me, that no trace was left of my soul's natural disposition to virtue, and I became a reflection of her and of another who was given to the same kind of amusements.

---

[10] The Saint throughout her life was extremely careful of cleanliness. In one of her letters to Father Jerome Gratian of the Mother of God (No. 323, Letter 28, vol. iii. ed. Doblado), she begs him, for the love of God, to see that the Fathers had clean cells and table; and the Ven. Mother Anne of St. Bartholomew, in her life (Bruxelles, 1708, p. 40), says that she changed the Saint's linen on the day of her death, and was thanked by her for her carefulness. "Her soul was so pure," says the Ven. Mother, "that she could not bear anything that was not clean."

[11] Maria de Cepeda, half-sister of the Saint. She was married to Don Martin de Guzman y Barrientos; and the contract for the dowry was signed January 11, 1531 (*Reforma de los Descalços* lib. i. ch. vii. § 4).

6. I know from this the great advantage of good companions; and I am certain that if at that tender age I had been thrown among good people, I should have persevered in virtue; for if at that time I had found any one to teach me the fear of God, my soul would have grown strong enough not to fall away. Afterwards, when the fear of God had utterly departed from me, the fear of dishonor alone remained, and was a torment to me in all I did. When I thought that nobody would ever know, I ventured upon many things that were neither honorable nor pleasing unto God.

7. In the beginning, these conversations did me harm—I believe so. The fault was perhaps not hers, but mine; for afterwards my own wickedness was enough to lead me astray, together with the servants about me, whom I found ready enough for all evil. If any one of these had given me good advice, I might perhaps have profited by it; but they were blinded by interest, as I was by passion. Still, I was never inclined to much evil,—for I hated naturally anything dishonorable,—but only to the amusement of a pleasant conversation. The occasion of sin, however, being present, danger was at hand, and I exposed to it my father and brothers. God delivered me out of it all, so that I should not be lost, in a manner visibly against my will, yet not so secretly as to allow me to escape without the loss of my good name and the suspicions of my father.

8. I had not spent, I think, three months in these vanities, when they took me to a monastery[12] in the city where I lived, in which children like myself were brought up, though their way of life was not so wicked as mine. This was done with the utmost concealment of the true reason, which was known only to myself and one of my kindred. They waited for an opportunity which would make the change seem nothing out of the way; for, as my sister was married, it was not fitting I should remain alone, without a mother, in the house.

9. So excessive was my father's love for me, and so deep my dissembling, that he never would believe me to be so wicked as I was; and hence I was never in disgrace with him. Though some remarks were made, yet, as the time had been short, nothing could be positively asserted; and, as I was so much afraid about my good name, I had taken every care to be secret; and yet I never considered that I could conceal nothing from Him Who sees all things. O my God, what evil is done in the world by disregarding this, and thinking that anything can be kept secret that is done against Thee! I am quite certain that great evils would be avoided if we clearly understood that what we have to do is, not to be on our guard against men, but on our guard against displeasing Thee.

10. For the first eight days, I suffered much; but more from the suspicion that my vanity was known, than from being in the monastery; for I was already weary of myself—and, though I offended God, I never ceased to have a great fear of Him, and contrived to go to confession as quickly as I could. I was very uncomfortable; but within eight days, I think sooner, I was much more contented than I had been in my father's house. All the nuns were pleased with me; for our Lord had given me the grace to please every one, wherever I might be. I was therefore made much of in the monastery. Though at this time I hated to be a nun, yet I was delighted at the sight of nuns so good; for they were very good in that house—very prudent, observant of the rule, and recollected.

11. Yet, for all this, the devil did not cease to tempt me; and people in the world sought means to trouble my rest with messages and presents. As this could not be allowed, it was soon over, and my soul began to return to the good habits of my earlier years; and I recognized the great mercy of God to those whom He places among good people. It seems as if His Majesty had sought and sought again how to convert me to Himself. Blessed be Thou, O Lord, for having borne with me so long! Amen.

12. Were it not for my many faults, there was some excuse for me, I think, in this: that the conversation I shared in was with one who, I thought, would do well in the estate of matrimony;[13] and I was told by my confessors, and others also, whom in many points I consulted, used to say,

---

[12] The Augustinian Monastery of Our Lady of Grace. It was founded in 1509 by the venerable Fra Juan of Seville, Vicar-General of the Order (*Reforma de los Descalços* lib. i. ch. vii. n. 2). There were forty nuns in the house at this time (*De la Fuente*).

[13] Some have said that the Saint at this time intended, or wished, to be married; and Father Bouix translates the passage thus: "une alliance honorable pour moi." But it is more probable that the Saint had listened only to the story of her cousin's intended marriage; for in ch. v. § 11, she says that our Lord had always kept her from seeking to be loved of men.

that I was not offending God. One of the nuns[14] slept with us who were seculars, and through her it pleased our Lord to give me light, as I shall now explain.

Chapter III.

The Blessing of Being with Good People. How Certain Illusions Were Removed.

1. I began gradually to like the good and holy conversation of this nun. How well she used to speak of God! for she was a person of great discretion and sanctity. I listened to her with delight. I think there never was a time when I was not glad to listen to her. She began by telling me how she came to be a nun through the mere reading of the words of the Gospel "Many are called, and few are chosen."[15] She would speak of the reward which our Lord gives to those who forsake all things for His sake. This good companionship began to root out the habits which bad companionship had formed, and to bring my thoughts back to the desire of eternal things, as well as to banish in some measure the great dislike I had to be a nun, which had been very great; and if I saw any one weep in prayer, or devout in any other way, I envied her very much; for my heart was now so hard, that I could not shed a tear, even if I read the Passion through. This was a grief to me.

2. I remained in the monastery a year and a half, and was very much the better for it. I began to say many vocal prayers, and to ask all the nuns to pray for me, that God would place me in that state wherein I was to serve Him; but, for all this, I wished not to be a nun, and that God would not be pleased I should be one, though at the same time I was afraid of marriage. At the end of my stay there, I had a greater inclination to be a nun, yet not in that house, on account of certain devotional practices which I understood prevailed there, and which I thought overstrained. Some of the younger ones encouraged me in this my wish; and if all had been of one mind, I might have profited by it. I had also a great friend[16] in another monastery; and this made me resolve, if I was to be a nun, not to be one in any other house than where she was. I looked more to the pleasure of sense and vanity than to the good of my soul. These good thoughts of being a nun came to me from time to time. They left me very soon; and I could not persuade myself to become one.

3. At this time, though I was not careless about my own good, our Lord was much more careful to dispose me for that state of life which was best for me. He sent me a serious illness, so that I was obliged to return to my father's house.

4. When I became well again, they took me to see my sister[17] in her house in the country village where she dwelt. Her love for me was so great, that, if she had had her will, I should never have left her. Her husband also had a great affection for me—at least, he showed me all kindness. This too I owe rather to our Lord, for I have received kindness everywhere; and all my service in return is, that I am what I am.

5. On the road lived a brother of my father[18]—a prudent and most excellent man, then a widower. Him too our Lord was preparing for Himself. In his old age, he left all his possessions and became a religious. He so finished his course, that I believe him to have the vision of God. He would have me stay with him some days. His practice was to read good books in Spanish; and his ordinary conversation was about God and the vanity of the world. These books he made me read to him; and, though I did not much like them, I appeared as if I did; for in giving pleasure to others I have been most particular, though it might be painful to myself—so much so, that what in others might have been a virtue was in me a great fault, because I was often extremely indiscreet. O my God, in how many ways did His Majesty prepare me for the state wherein it was His will I should

---

[14] Doña Maria Brizeño, mistress of the secular children who were educated in the monastery (*Reforma*, lib. i. ch. vii. § 3).

[15] St. Matt. xx. 16: "Multi enim sunt vocati, pauci vero electi."

[16] Juana Suarez, in the Monastery of the incarnation, Avila (*Reforma*, lib. i. ch. vii. § 7).

[17] Maria de Cepeda, married to Don Martin Guzman y Barrientos. They lived in Castellanos de la Cañada, where they had considerable property; but in the later years of their lives they were in straitened circumstances (*De la Fuente*). See below, ch. xxxiv. § 24.

[18] Don Pedro Sanchez de Cepeda. He lived in Hortigosa, four leagues from Avila (*De la Fuente*).

serve Him!—how, against my own will, He constrained me to do violence to myself! May He be blessed for ever! Amen.

6. Though I remained here but a few days, yet, through the impression made on my heart by the words of God both heard and read, and by the good conversation of my uncle, I came to understand the truth I had heard in my childhood, that all things are as nothing, the world vanity, and passing rapidly away. I also began to be afraid that, if I were then to die, I should go down to hell. Though I could not bend my will to be a nun, I saw that the religious state was the best and the safest. And thus, by little and little, I resolved to force myself into it.

7. The struggle lasted three months. I used to press this reason against myself: The trials and sufferings of living as a nun cannot be greater than those of purgatory, and I have well deserved to be in hell. It is not much to spend the rest of my life as if I were in purgatory, and then go straight to Heaven—which was what I desired. I was more influenced by servile fear, I think, than by love, to enter religion.

8. The devil put before me that I could not endure the trials of the religious life, because of my delicate nurture. I defended myself against him by alleging the trials which Christ endured, and that it was not much for me to suffer something for His sake; besides, He would help me to bear it. I must have thought so, but I do not remember this consideration. I endured many temptations during these days. I was subject to fainting-fits, attended with fever,—for my health was always weak. I had become by this time fond of good books, and that gave me life. I read the Epistles of St. Jerome, which filled me with so much courage, that I resolved to tell my father of my purpose,—which was almost like taking the habit; for I was so jealous of my word, that I would never, for any consideration, recede from a promise when once my word had been given.

9. My father's love for me was so great, that I could never obtain his consent; nor could the prayers of others, whom I persuaded to speak to him, be of any avail. The utmost I could get from him was that I might do as I pleased after his death. I now began to be afraid of myself, and of my own weakness—for I might go back. So, considering that such waiting was not safe for me, I obtained my end in another way, as I shall now relate.

Chapter IV.
Our Lord Helps Her to Become a Nun. Her Many Infirmities.

1. In those days, when I was thus resolved, I had persuaded one of my brothers,[19] by speaking to him of the vanity of the world, to become a friar; and we agreed together to set out one day very early in the morning for the monastery where that friend of mine lived for whom I had so great an affection:[20] though I would have gone to any other monastery, if I thought I should serve God better in it, or to any one my father liked, so strong was my resolution now to become a nun—for I thought more of the salvation of my soul now, and made no account whatever of mine own ease. I remember perfectly well, and it is quite true, that the pain I felt when I left my father's house was so great, that I do not believe the pain of dying will be greater—for it seemed to me as if every bone in my body were wrenched asunder; for, as I had no love of God to destroy my love of father and of kindred, this latter love came upon me with a violence so great that, if our Lord had not been my keeper, my own resolution to go on would have failed me. But He gave me courage to fight against myself, so that I executed my purpose.[21]

---

[19] Antonio de Ahumada; who, according to the most probable opinion, entered the Dominican monastery of St. Thomas, Avila. It is said that he died before he was professed. Some said he joined the Hieronymites; but this is not so probable (*De la Fuente*). Ribera, however, says that he did enter the novitiate of the Hieronymites, but died before he was out of it (lib. i. ch. vi.).

[20] Juana Suarez, in the Monastery of the Incarnation, Avila.

[21] The nuns sent word to the father of his child's escape, and of her desire to become a nun, but without any expectation of obtaining his consent. He came to the monastery forthwith, and "offered up his Isaac on Mount Carmel" (*Reforma*, lib. i. ch. viii. § 5).

2. When I took the habit,[22] our Lord at once made me understand how He helps those who do violence to themselves in order to serve Him. No one observed this violence in me; they saw nothing but the greatest good will. At that moment, because I was entering on that state, I was filled with a joy so great, that it has never failed me to this day; and God converted the aridity of my soul into the greatest tenderness. Everything in religion was a delight unto me; and it is true that now and then I used to sweep the house during those hours of the day which I had formerly spent on my amusements and my dress; and, calling to mind that I was delivered from such follies, I was filled with a new joy that surprised me, nor could I understand whence it came.

3. Whenever I remember this, there is nothing in the world, however hard it may be, that, if it were proposed to me, I would not undertake without any hesitation whatever; for I know now, by experience in many things, that if from the first I resolutely persevere in my purpose, even in this life His Majesty rewards it in a way which he only understands who has tried it. When the act is done for God only, it is His will before we begin it that the soul, in order to the increase of its merits, should be afraid; and the greater the fear, if we do but succeed, the greater the reward, and the sweetness thence afterwards resulting. I know this by experience, as I have just said, in many serious affairs; and so, if I were a person who had to advise anybody, I would never counsel any one, to whom good inspirations from time to time may come, to resist them through fear of the difficulty of carrying them into effect; for if a person lives detached for the love of God only, that is no reason for being afraid of failure, for He is omnipotent. May He be blessed for ever! Amen.

4. O supreme Good, and my Rest, those graces ought to have been enough which Thou has given me hitherto, seeing that Thy compassion and greatness had drawn me through so many windings to a state so secure, to a house where there are so many servants of God, from whom I might learn how I may advance in Thy service. I know not how to go on, when I call to mind the circumstances of my profession, the great resolution and joy with which I made it, and my betrothal unto Thee. I cannot speak of it without tears; and my tears ought to be tears of blood, my heart ought to break, and that would not be much to suffer because of the many offences against Thee which I have committed since that day. It seems to me now that I had good reasons for not wishing for this dignity, seeing that I have made so sad a use of it. But Thou, O my Lord, has been willing to bear with me for almost twenty years of my evil using of Thy graces, till I might become better. It seems to me, O my God, that I did nothing but promise never to keep any of the promises then made to Thee. Yet such was not my intention: but I see that what I have done since is of such a nature, that I know not what my intention was. So it was and so it happened, that it may be the better known, O my Bridegroom, Who Thou art and what I am.

5. It is certainly true that very frequently the joy I have in that the multitude of Thy mercies is made known in me, softens the bitter sense of my great faults. In whom, O Lord, can they shine forth as they do in me, who by my evil deeds have shrouded in darkness Thy great graces, which Thou has begun to work in me? Woe is me, O my Maker! If I would make an excuse, I have none to offer; and I only am to blame. For if I could return to Thee any portion of that love which Thou has begun to show unto me, I would give it only unto Thee, and then everything would have been safe. But, as I have not deserved this, nor been so happy as to have done it, let Thy mercy, O Lord, rest upon me.

6. The change in the habits of my life, and in my food, proved hurtful to my health; and though my happiness was great, that was not enough. The fainting-fits began to be more frequent; and my heart was so seriously affected, that every one who saw it was alarmed; and I had also many other ailments. And thus it was I spent the first year, having very bad health, though I do not think I offended God in it much. And as my illness was so serious—I was almost insensible at all times, and frequently wholly so—my father took great pains to find some relief; and as the physicians who attended me had none to give, he had me taken to a place which had a great reputation for the cure of other infirmities. They said I should find relief there.[23] That friend of whom I have spoken as

---

[22] The Saint entered the Monastery of the Incarnation Nov. 2, 1533, and made her profession Nov. 3, 1534 (*Bollandists* and *Bouix*). Ribera says she entered November 2, 1535; and the chronicler of the Order, relying on the contract by which her father bound himself to the monastery, says that she took the habit Nov. 2, 1536, and that Ribera had made a mistake.

[23] Her father took her from the monastery in the autumn of 1535, according to the Bollandists, but of

being in the house went with me. She was one of the elder nuns. In the house where I was a nun, there was no vow of enclosure.[24]

7. I remained there nearly a year, for three months of it suffering most cruel tortures—effects of the violent remedies which they applied. I know not how I endured them; and indeed, though I submitted myself to them, they were, as I shall relate,[25] more than my constitution could bear.

8. I was to begin the treatment in the spring, and went thither when winter commenced. The intervening time I spent with my sister, of whom I spoke before,[26] in her house in the country, waiting for the month of April, which was drawing near, that I might not have to go and return. The uncle of whom I have made mention before,[27] and whose house was on our road, gave me a book called *Tercer Abecedario*,[28] which treats of the prayer of recollection. Though in the first year I had read good books—for I would read no others, because I understood now the harm they had done me—I did not know how to make my prayer, nor how to recollect myself. I was therefore much pleased with the book, and resolved to follow the way of prayer it described with all my might. And as our Lord had already bestowed upon me the gift of tears, and I found pleasure in reading, I began to spend a certain time in solitude, to go frequently to confession, and make a beginning of that way of prayer, with this book for my guide; for I had no master—I mean, no confessor—who understood me, though I sought for such a one for twenty years afterwards: which did me much harm, in that I frequently went backwards, and might have been even utterly lost; for, anyhow, a director would have helped me to escape the risks I ran of sinning against God.

9. From the very beginning, God was most gracious unto me. Though I was not so free from sin as the book required, I passed that by; such watchfulness seemed to me almost impossible. I was on my guard against mortal sin—and would to God I had always been so!—but I was careless about venial sins, and that was my ruin. Yet, for all this, at the end of my stay there—I spent nearly nine months in the practice of solitude—our Lord began to comfort me so much in this way of prayer, as in His mercy to raise me to the prayer of quiet, and now and then to that of union, though I understood not what either the one or the other was, nor the great esteem I ought to have had of them. I believe it would have been a great blessing to me if I had understood the matter. It is true that the prayer of union lasted but a short time: I know not if it continued for the space of an *Ave Maria*; but the fruits of it remained; and they were such that, though I was then not twenty years of age, I seemed to despise the world utterly; and so I remember how sorry I was for those who followed its ways, though only in things lawful.

10. I used to labor with all my might to imagine Jesus Christ, our Good and our Lord, present within me. And this was the way I prayed. If I meditated on any mystery of His life, I represented it to myself as within me, though the greater part of my time I spent in reading good books, which was all my comfort; for God never endowed me with the gift of making reflections with the understanding, or with that of using the imagination to any good purpose: my imagination is so sluggish,[29] that even if I would think of, or picture to myself, as I used to labor to picture, our Lord's Humanity, I never could do it.

11. And though men may attain more quickly to the state of contemplation, if they persevere, by this way of inability to exert the intellect, yet is the process more laborious and painful; for if the will have nothing to occupy it, and if love have no present object to rest on, the soul is without support and without employment—its isolation and dryness occasion great pain, and the thoughts assail it most grievously. Persons in this condition must have greater purity of conscience than those who can make use of their understanding; for he who can use his intellect in the way of meditation on what the world is, on what he owes to God, on the great sufferings of God for him, his own

1538, according to the chronicler, who adds, that she was taken to her uncle's house—Pedro Sanchez de Cepeda—in Hortigosa, and then to Castellanos de la Cañada, to the house of her sister, Doña Maria, where she remained till the spring, when she went to Bezadas for her cure (*Reforma*, lib. i. ch. xi. § 2).

[24] It was in 1563 that all nuns were compelled to observe enclosure (*De la Fuente*).

[25] Ch. v. § 15.

[26] Ch. iii. § 4.

[27] Ch. iii. § 5.

[28] By Fray Francisco de Osuna, of the Order of St. Francis (*Reforma*, lib. i. ch. xi. § 2).

[29] See ch. ix. §§ 4, 7.

scanty service in return, and on the reward God reserves for those who love Him, learns how to defend himself against his own thoughts, and against the occasions and perils of sin. On the other hand, he who has not that power is in greater danger, and ought to occupy himself much in reading, seeing that he is not in the slightest degree able to help himself.

12. This way of proceeding is so exceedingly painful, that if the master who teaches it insists on cutting off the succors which reading gives, and requires the spending of much time in prayer, then, I say, it will be impossible to persevere long in it: and if he persists in his plan, health will be ruined, because it is a most painful process. Reading is of great service towards procuring recollection in any one who proceeds in this way; and it is even necessary for him, however little it may be that he reads, if only as a substitute for the mental prayer which is beyond his reach.

13. Now I seem to understand that it was the good providence of our Lord over me that found no one to teach me. If I had, it would have been impossible for me to persevere during the eighteen years of my trial and of those great aridities because of my inability to meditate. During all this time, it was only after Communion that I ever ventured to begin my prayer without a book—my soul was as much afraid to pray without one, as if it had to fight against a host. With a book to help me—it was like a companion, and a shield whereon to receive the blows of many thoughts—I found comfort; for it was not usual with me to be in aridity: but I always was so when I had no book; for my soul was disturbed, and my thoughts wandered at once. With one, I began to collect my thoughts, and, using it as a decoy, kept my soul in peace, very frequently by merely opening a book—there was no necessity for more. Sometimes, I read but little; at other times, much—according as our Lord had pity on me.

14. It seemed to me, in these beginnings of which I am speaking, that there could be no danger capable of withdrawing me from so great a blessing, if I had but books, and could have remained alone; and I believe that, by the grace of God, it would have been so, if I had had a master or any one to warn me against those occasions of sin in the beginning, and, if I fell, to bring me quickly out of them. If the devil had assailed me openly then, I believe I should never have fallen into any grievous sin; but he was so subtle, and I so weak, that all my good resolutions were of little service—though, in those days in which I served God, they were very profitable in enabling me, with that patience which His Majesty gave me, to endure the alarming illnesses which I had to bear. I have often thought with wonder of the great goodness of God; and my soul has rejoiced in the contemplation of His great magnificence and mercy. May He be blessed for ever!—for I see clearly that He has not omitted to reward me, even in this life, for every one of my good desires. My good works, however wretched and imperfect, have been made better and perfected by Him Who is my Lord: He has rendered them meritorious. As to my evil deeds and my sins, He hid them at once. The eyes of those who saw them, He made even blind; and He has blotted them out of their memory. He gilds my faults, makes virtue to shine forth, giving it to me Himself, and compelling me to possess it, as it were, by force.

15. I must now return to that which has been enjoined me. I say, that if I had to describe minutely how our Lord dealt with me in the beginning, it would be necessary for me to have another understanding than that I have: so that I might be able to appreciate what I owe to Him, together with my own ingratitude and wickedness; for I have forgotten it all.

May He be blessed for ever Who has borne with me so long! Amen.

Chapter V.

Illness and Patience of the Saint. The Story of a Priest Whom She Rescued from a Life of Sin.

1. I forgot to say how, in the year of my novitiate, I suffered much uneasiness about things in themselves of no importance; but I was found fault with very often when I was blameless. I bore it painfully and with imperfection; however, I went through it all, because of the joy I had in being a nun. When they saw me seeking to be alone, and even weeping over my sins at times, they thought I was discontented, and said so.

2. All religious observances had an attraction for me, but I could not endure any which seemed to make me contemptible. I delighted in being thought well of by others, and was very exact in everything I had to do. All this I thought was a virtue, though it will not serve as any excuse for me, because I knew what it was to procure my own satisfaction in everything, and so ignorance does not blot out the blame. There may be some excuse in the fact that the monastery was not founded in great perfection. I, wicked as I was, followed after that which I saw was wrong, and neglected that which was good.

3. There was then in the house a nun laboring under a most grievous and painful disorder, for there were open ulcers in her body, caused by certain obstructions, through which her food was rejected. Of this sickness she soon died. All the sisters, I saw, were afraid of her malady. I envied her patience very much; I prayed to God that He would give me a like patience; and then, whatever sickness it might be His pleasure to send, I do not think I was afraid of any, for I was resolved on gaining eternal good, and determined to gain it by any and by every means.

4. I am surprised at myself, because then I had not, as I believe, that love of God which I think I had after I began to pray. Then, I had only light to see that all things that pass away are to be lightly esteemed, and that the good things to be gained by despising them are of great price, because they are for ever. His Majesty heard me also in this, for in less than two years I was so afflicted myself that the illness which I had, though of a different kind from that of the sister, was, I really believe, not less painful and trying for the three years it lasted, as I shall now relate.

5. When the time had come for which I was waiting in the place I spoke of before[30]—I was in my sister's house, for the purpose of undergoing the medical treatment—they took me away with the utmost care of my comfort; that is, my father, my sister, and the nun, my friend, who had come from the monastery with me,—for her love for me was very great. At that moment, Satan began to trouble my soul; God, however, brought forth a great blessing out of that trouble.

6. In the place to which I had gone for my cure lived a priest of good birth and understanding, with some learning, but not much. I went to confession to him, for I was always fond of learned men, although confessors indifferently learned did my soul much harm; for I did not always find confessors whose learning was as good as I could wish it was. I know by experience that it is better, if the confessors are good men and of holy lives, that they should have no learning at all, than a little; for such confessors never trust themselves without consulting those who are learned—nor would I trust them myself: and a really learned confessor never deceived me.[31] Neither did the others willingly deceive me, only they knew no better; I thought they were learned, and that I was not under any other obligation than that of believing them, as their instructions to me were lax, and left me more at liberty—for if they had been strict with me, I am so wicked, I should have sought for others. That which was a venial sin, they told me was no sin at all; of that which was most grievously mortal, they said it was venial.[32]

7. This did me so much harm, that it is no wonder I should speak of it here as a warning to others, that they may avoid an evil so great; for I see clearly that in the eyes of God I was without excuse, that the things I did being in themselves not good, this should have been enough to keep me from them. I believe that God, by reason of my sins, allowed those confessors to deceive themselves and to deceive me. I myself deceived many others by saying to them what had been said to me.

---

[30] Ch. iv. § 6. The person to whom she was taken was a woman famous for certain cures she had wrought, but whose skill proved worse than useless to the Saint (*Reforma*, lib. i. ch. xi. § 2).

[31] Schram, *Theolog. Mystic.*, § 483. "Magni doctores scholastici, si non sint spirituales, vel omni rerum spiritualium experientia careant, non solent esse magistri spirituales idonei—nam theologia scholastica est perfectio intellectus; mystica, perfectio intellectus et voluntatis: unde bonus theologus scholasticus potest esse malus theologus mysticus. In rebus tamen difficilibus, dubiis, spiritualibus, præstat mediocriter spiritualem theologum consulere quam spiritualem idiotam."

[32] See *Way of Perfection*, ch. viii. § 2.

8. I continued in this blindness, I believe, more than seventeen years, till a most learned Dominican Father[33] undeceived me in part, and those of the Company of Jesus made me altogether so afraid, by insisting on the erroneousness of these principles, as I shall hereafter show.[34]

9. I began, then, by going to confession to that priest of whom I spoke before.[35] He took an extreme liking to me, because I had then but little to confess in comparison with what I had afterwards; and I had never much to say since I became a nun. There was no harm in the liking he had for me, but it ceased to be good, because it was in excess. He clearly understood that I was determined on no account whatever to do anything whereby God might be seriously offended. He, too, gave me a like assurance about himself, and accordingly our conferences were many. But at that time, through the knowledge and fear of God which filled my soul, what gave me most pleasure in all my conversations with others was to speak of God; and, as I was so young, this made him ashamed; and then, out of that great goodwill he bore me, he began to tell me of his wretched state. It was very sad, for he had been nearly seven years in a most perilous condition, because of his affection for, and conversation with, a woman of that place; and yet he used to say Mass. The matter was so public, that his honor and good name were lost, and no one ventured to speak to him about it. I was extremely sorry for him, because I liked him much. I was then so imprudent and so blind as to think it a virtue to be grateful and loyal to one who liked me. Cursed be that loyalty which reaches so far as to go against the law of God. It is a madness common in the world, and it makes me mad to see it. We are indebted to God for all the good that men do to us, and yet we hold it to be an act of virtue not to break a friendship of this kind, though it lead us to go against Him. Oh, blindness of the world! Let me, O Lord, be most ungrateful to the world; never at all unto Thee. But I have been altogether otherwise through my sins.

10. I procured further information about the matter from members of his household; I learned more of his ruinous state, and saw that the poor man's fault was not so grave, because the miserable woman had had recourse to enchantments, by giving him a little image made of copper, which she had begged him to wear for love of her around his neck; and this no one had influence enough to persuade him to throw away. As to this matter of enchantments, I do not believe it to be altogether true; but I will relate what I saw, by way of warning to men to be on their guard against women who will do things of this kind. And let them be assured of this, that women—for they are more bound to purity than men—if once they have lost all shame before God, are in nothing whatever to be trusted; and that in exchange for the gratification of their will, and of that affection which the devil suggests, they will hesitate at nothing.

11. Though I have been so wicked myself, I never fell into anything of this kind, nor did I ever attempt to do evil; nor, if I had the power, would I have ever constrained any one to like me, for our Lord kept me from this. But if He had abandoned me, I should have done wrong in this, as I did in other things—for there is nothing in me whereon anyone may rely.

12. When I knew this, I began to show him greater affection: my intention was good, but the act was wrong, for I ought not to do the least wrong for the sake of any good, how great so ever it may be. I spoke to him most frequently of God; and this must have done him good—though I believe that what touched him most was his great affection for me, because, to do me a pleasure, he gave me that little image of copper, and I had it at once thrown into a river. When he had given it up, like a man roused from deep sleep, he began to consider all that he had done in those years; and then, amazed at himself, lamenting his ruinous state, that woman came to be hateful in his eyes. Our Lady must have helped him greatly, for he had a very great devotion to her Conception, and used to keep the feast thereof with great solemnity. In short, he broke off all relations with that woman utterly, and was never weary of giving God thanks for the light He had given him; and at the end of the year from the day I first saw him, he died.

13. He had been most diligent in the service of God; and as for that great affection he had for me, I never observed anything wrong in it, though it might have been of greater purity. There were also occasions wherein he might have most grievously offended, if he had not kept himself in the

---

[33] F. Vicente Barron (*Bouix*).

[34] See ch. xxiii.

[35] § 6.

near presence of God. As I said before,[36] I would not then have done anything I knew was a mortal sin. And I think that observing this resolution in me helped him to have that affection for me; for I believe that all men must have a greater affection for those women whom they see disposed to be good; and even for the attainment of earthly ends, women must have more power over men because they are good, as I shall show hereafter. I am convinced that the priest is in the way of salvation. He died most piously, and completely withdrawn from that occasion of sin. It seems that it was the will of our Lord he should be saved by these means.

14. I remained three months in that place, in the most grievous sufferings; for the treatment was too severe for my constitution. In two months—so strong were the medicines—my life was nearly worn out; and the severity of the pain in the heart,[37] for the cure of which I was there was much more keen: it seemed to me, now and then, as if it had been seized by sharp teeth. So great was the torment, that it was feared it might end in madness. There was a great loss of strength, for I could eat nothing whatever, only drink. I had a great loathing for food, and a fever that never left me. I was so reduced, for they had given me purgatives daily for nearly a month, and so parched up, that my sinews began to shrink. The pains I had were unendurable, and I was overwhelmed in a most deep sadness, so that I had no rest either night or day.

15. This was the result; and thereupon my father took me back. Then the physicians visited me again. All gave me up; they said I was also consumptive. This gave me little or no concern; what distressed me were the pains I had—for I was in pain from my head down to my feet. Now, nervous pains, according to the physicians, are intolerable; and all my nerves were shrunk. Certainly, if I had not brought this upon myself by my sins, the torture would have been unendurable.

16. I was not more than three months in this cruel distress, for it seemed impossible that so many ills could be borne together. I now am astonished at myself, and the patience His Majesty gave me—for it clearly came from Him—I look upon as a great mercy of our Lord. It was a great help to me to be patient, that I had read the story of Job, in the *Morals* of St. Gregory (our Lord seems to have prepared me thereby); and that I had begun the practice of prayer, so that I might bear it all, conforming my will to the will of God. All my conversation was with God. I had continually these words of Job in my thoughts and in my mouth: "If we have received good things of the hand of our Lord, why should we not receive evil things?"[38] This seemed to give me courage.

17. The feast of our Lady, in August, came round; from April until then I had been in great pain, but more especially during the last three months. I made haste to go to confession, for I had always been very fond of frequent confession. They thought I was driven by the fear of death; and so my father, in order to quiet me, would not suffer me to go. Oh, the unreasonable love of flesh and blood! Though it was that of a father so Catholic and so wise—he was very much so, and this act of his could not be the effect of any ignorance on his part—what evil it might have done me!

18. That very night my sickness became so acute, that for about four days I remained insensible. They administered the Sacrament of the last Anointing, and every hour, or rather every moment, thought I was dying; they did nothing but repeat the *Credo*, as if I could have understood anything they said. They must have regarded me as dead more than once, for I found afterwards drops of wax on my eyelids. My father, because he had not allowed me to go to confession, was grievously distressed. Loud cries and many prayers were made to God: blessed be He Who heard them.

19. For a day-and-a-half the grave was open in my monastery, waiting for my body;[39] and the Friars of our Order, in a house at some distance from this place, performed funeral solemnities. But it pleased our Lord I should come to myself. I wished to go to confession at once. I communicated with many tears; but I do not think those tears had their source in that pain and sorrow only for having offended God, which might have sufficed for my salvation—unless, indeed, the delusion which I labored under were some excuse for me, and into which I had been led by those who had told me that some things were not mortal sins which afterwards I found were so certainly.

---

[36] § 9.

[37] Ch. iv. § 6.

[38] Job ii. 10: "Si bona suscepimus de manu Dei, mala quare non suscipiamus?"

[39] Some of the nuns of the Incarnation were in the house, sent thither from the monastery; and, but for the father's disbelief in her death, would have taken her home for burial (*Ribera*, lib. i. ch. iv.).

20. Though my sufferings were unendurable, and my perceptions dull, yet my confession, I believe, was complete as to all matters wherein I understood myself to have offended God. This grace, among others, did His Majesty bestow on me, that ever since my first Communion never in confession have I failed to confess anything I thought to be a sin, though it might be only a venial sin. But I think that undoubtedly my salvation was in great peril, if I had died at that time—partly because my confessors were so unlearned, and partly because I was so very wicked. It is certainly true that when I think of it, and consider how our Lord seems to have raised me up from the dead, I am so filled with wonder, that I almost tremble with fear.[40]

21. And now, O my soul, it were well for thee to look that danger in the face from which our Lord delivered thee; and if thou does not cease to offend Him out of love thou should do so out of fear. He might have slain thee a thousand times, and in a far more perilous state. I believe I exaggerate nothing if I say a thousand times again, though he may rebuke me who has commanded me to restrain myself in recounting my sins; and they are glossed over enough. I pray him, for the love of God, not to suppress one of my faults, because herein shines forth the magnificence of God, as well as His long-suffering towards souls. May He be blessed for evermore, and destroy me utterly, rather than let me cease to love Him any more!

Chapter VI.

The Great Debt She Owed to Our Lord for His Mercy to Her. She Takes St. Joseph for Her Patron.

1. After those four days, during which I was insensible, so great was my distress, that our Lord alone knows the intolerable sufferings I endured. My tongue was bitten to pieces; there was a choking in my throat because I had taken nothing, and because of my weakness, so that I could not swallow even a drop of water; all my bones seemed to be out of joint, and the disorder of my head was extreme. I was bent together like a coil of ropes—for to this was I brought by the torture of those days—unable to move either arm, or foot, or hand, or head, any more than if I had been dead, unless others moved me; I could move, however, I think, one finger of my right hand. Then, as to touching me, that was impossible, for I was so bruised that I could not endure it. They used to move me in a sheet, one holding one end, and another the other. This lasted till Palm Sunday.[41]

2. The only comfort I had was this—if no one came near me, my pains frequently ceased; and then, because I had a little rest, I considered myself well, for I was afraid my patience would fail: and thus I was exceedingly happy when I saw myself free from those pains which were so sharp and constant, though in the cold fits of an intermittent fever, which were most violent, they were still unendurable. My dislike of food was very great.

3. I was now so anxious to return to my monastery, that I had myself conveyed thither in the state I was in. There they received alive one whom they had waited for as dead; but her body was worse than dead: the sight of it could only give pain. It is impossible to describe my extreme weakness, for I was nothing but bones. I remained in this state, as I have already said,[42] more than eight months; and was paralytic, though getting better, for about three years. I praised God when I began to crawl on my hands and knees. I bore all this with great resignation, and, if I except the beginning of my illness, with great joy; for all this was as nothing in comparison with the pains and tortures I had to bear at first. I was resigned to the will of God, even if He left me in this state for

---

[40] *Ribera*, lib. i. ch. iv., says he heard Fra Bañes, in a sermon, say that the Saint told him she had, during these four days, seen hell in a vision. And the chronicler says that though there was bodily illness, yet it was a trance of the soul at the same time (vol. i. lib. i. ch. xii. § 3).

[41] March 25, 1537.

[42] Ch. v. § 17. The Saint left her monastery in 1535; and in the spring of 1536 went from her sister's house to Bezadas; and in July of that year was brought back to her father's house in Avila, wherein she remained till Palm Sunday, 1537, when she returned to the Monastery of the Incarnation. She had been seized with paralysis there, and labored under it nearly three years, from 1536 to 1539, when she was miraculously healed through the intercession of St. Joseph (*Bolland*, n. 100, 101). The dates of the Chronicler are different from these.

ever. My anxiety about the recovery of my health seemed to be grounded on my desire to pray in solitude, as I had been taught; for there were no means of doing so in the infirmary. I went to confession most frequently, spoke much about God, and in such a way as to edify everyone; and they all marveled at the patience which our Lord gave me—for if it had not come from the hand of His Majesty, it seemed impossible to endure so great an affliction with so great a joy.

4. It was a great thing for me to have had the grace of prayer which God had wrought in me; it made me understand what it is to love Him. In a little while, I saw these virtues renewed within me; still they were not strong, for they were not sufficient to sustain me in justice. I never spoke ill in the slightest degree whatever of any one, and my ordinary practice was to avoid all detraction; for I used to keep most carefully in mind that I ought not to assent to, nor say of another, anything I should not like to have said of myself. I was extremely careful to keep this resolution on all occasions though not so perfectly, upon some great occasions that presented themselves, as not to break it sometimes. But my ordinary practice was this: and thus those who were about me, and those with whom I conversed, became so convinced that it was right, that they adopted it as a habit. It came to be understood that where I was, absent persons were safe; so they were also with my friends and kindred, and with those whom I instructed. Still, for all this, I have a strict account to give unto God for the bad example I gave in other respects. May it please His Majesty to forgive me, for I have been the cause of much evil; though not with intentions as perverse as were the acts that followed.

5. The longing for solitude remained, and I loved to discourse and speak of God; for if I found any one with whom I could do so, it was a greater joy and satisfaction to me than all the refinements—or rather to speak more correctly, the real rudeness—of the world's conversation. I communicated and confessed more frequently still, and desired to do so; I was extremely fond of reading good books; I was most deeply penitent for having offended God; and I remember that very often I did not dare to pray, because I was afraid of that most bitter anguish which I felt for having offended God, dreading it as a great chastisement. This grew upon me afterwards to so great a degree, that I know of no torment wherewith to compare it; and yet it was neither more nor less because of any fear I had at any time, for it came upon me only when I remembered the consolations of our Lord which He gave me in prayer, the great debt I owed Him, the evil return I made: I could not bear it. I was also extremely angry with myself on account of the many tears I shed for my faults, when I saw how little I improved, seeing that neither my good resolutions, nor the pains I took, were sufficient to keep me from falling whenever I had the opportunity. I looked on my tears as a delusion; and my faults, therefore, I regarded as the more grievous, because I saw the great goodness of our Lord to me in the shedding of those tears, and together with them such deep compunction.

6. I took care to go to confession as soon as I could; and, as I think, did all that was possible on my part to return to a state of grace. But the whole evil lay in my not thoroughly avoiding the occasions of sin, and in my confessors, who helped me so little. If they had told me that I was travelling on a dangerous road, and that I was bound to abstain from those conversations, I believe, without any doubt, that the matter would have been remedied, because I could not bear to remain even for one day in mortal sin, if I knew it.

7. All these tokens of the fear of God came to me through prayer; and the greatest of them was this, that fear was swallowed up of love—for I never thought of chastisement. All the time I was so ill, my strict watch over my conscience reached to all that is mortal sin.

8. O my God! I wished for health, that I might serve Thee better; that was the cause of all my ruin. For when I saw how helpless I was through paralysis, being still so young, and how the physicians of this world had dealt with me, I determined to ask those of heaven to heal me—for I wished, nevertheless, to be well, though I bore my illness with great joy. Sometimes, too, I used to think that if I recovered my health, and yet were lost for ever, I was better as I was. But, for all that, I thought I might serve God much better if I were well. This is our delusion; we do not resign ourselves absolutely to the disposition of our Lord, Who knows best what is for our good.

9. I began by having Masses and prayers said for my intention—prayers that were highly sanctioned; for I never liked those other devotions which some people, especially women, make use of with a ceremoniousness to me intolerable, but which move them to be devout. I have been given to understand since that they were unseemly and superstitious; and I took for my patron and

lord the glorious St. Joseph, and recommended myself earnestly to him. I saw clearly that both out of this my present trouble, and out of others of greater importance, relating to my honor and the loss of my soul, this my father and lord delivered me, and rendered me greater services than I knew how to ask for. I cannot call to mind that I have ever asked him at any time for anything which he has not granted; and I am filled with amazement when I consider the great favors which God hath given me through this blessed Saint; the dangers from which he hath delivered me, both of body and of soul. To other Saints, our Lord seems to have given grace to succor men in some special necessity; but to this glorious Saint, I know by experience, to help us in all: and our Lord would have us understand that as He was Himself subject to him upon earth—for St. Joseph having the title of father, and being His guardian, could command Him—so now in heaven He performs all his petitions. I have asked others to recommend themselves to St. Joseph, and they too know this by experience; and there are many who are now of late devout to him,[43] having had experience of this truth.

10. I used to keep his feast with all the solemnity I could, but with more vanity than spirituality, seeking rather too much splendor and effect, and yet with good intentions. I had this evil in me, that if our Lord gave me grace to do any good, that good became full of imperfections and of many faults; but as for doing wrong, the indulgence of curiosity and vanity, I was very skillful and active therein. Our Lord forgive me!

11. Would that I could persuade all men to be devout to this glorious Saint; for I know by long experience what blessings he can obtain for us from God. I have never known any one who was really devout to him, and who honored him by particular services, who did not visibly grow more and more in virtue; for he helps in a special way those souls who commend themselves to him. It is now some years since I have always on his feast asked him for something, and I always have it. If the petition be in any way amiss, he directs it aright for my greater good.

12. If I were a person who had authority to write, it would be a pleasure to me to be diffusive in speaking most minutely of the graces which this glorious Saint has obtained for me and for others. But that I may not go beyond the commandment that is laid upon me, I must in many things be more brief than I could wish, and more diffusive than is necessary in others; for, in short, I am a person who, in all that is good, has but little discretion. But I ask, for the love of God, that he who does not believe me will make the trial for himself—when he will see by experience the great good that results from commending oneself to this glorious patriarch, and being devout to him. Those who give themselves to prayer should in a special manner have always a devotion to St. Joseph; for I know not how any man can think of the Queen of the angels, during the time that she suffered so much with the Infant Jesus, without giving thanks to St. Joseph for the services he rendered them then. He who cannot find any one to teach him how to pray, let him take this glorious Saint for his master, and he will not wander out of the way.

13. May it please our Lord that I have not done amiss in venturing to speak about St. Joseph; for, though I publicly profess my devotion to him, I have always failed in my service to him and imitation of him. He was like himself when he made me able to rise and walk, no longer a paralytic; and I, too, am like myself when I make so bad a use of this grace.

14. Who could have said that I was so soon to fall, after such great consolations from God—after His Majesty had implanted virtues in me which of themselves made me serve Him—after I had been, as it were, dead, and in such extreme peril of eternal damnation—after He had raised me up, soul and body, so that all who saw me marveled to see me alive? What can it mean, O my Lord? The life we live is so full of danger! While I am writing this—and it seems to me, too, by Thy grace and mercy—I may say with St. Paul, though not so truly as he did: "It is not I who live now, but Thou, my Creator, lives in me."[44] For some years past, so it seems to me, Thou has held me by the hand; and I see in myself desires and resolutions—in some measure tested by experience, in many

[43] Of the devotion to St. Joseph, F. Faber (*The Blessed Sacrament*, bk. ii. p. 199, 3rd ed.) says that it took its rise in the West, in a confraternity in Avignon. "Then it spread over the church. Gerson was raised up to be its doctor and theologian, and St. Teresa to be its Saint, and St. Francis of Sales to be its popular teacher and missionary. The houses of Carmel were like the holy house of Nazareth to it; and the colleges of the Jesuits, its peaceful sojourns in dark Egypt."

[44] Galat. ii. 20: "Vivo autem, jam non ego; vivit vero in me Christus."

ways, during that time—never to do anything, however slight it may be, contrary to Thy will, though I must have frequently offended Thy Divine Majesty without being aware of it; and I also think that nothing can be proposed to me that I should not with great resolution undertake for Thy love. In some things Thou has Thyself helped me to succeed therein. I love neither the world, nor the things of the world; nor do I believe that anything that does not come from Thee can give me pleasure; everything else seems to me a heavy cross.

15. Still, I may easily deceive myself, and it may be that I am not what I say I am; but Thou knows, O my Lord, that, to the best of my knowledge, I lie not. I am afraid, and with good reason, lest Thou should abandon me; for I know now how far my strength and little virtue can reach, if Thou be not ever at hand to supply them, and to help me never to forsake Thee. May His Majesty grant that I be not forsaken of Thee even now, when I am thinking all this of myself!

16. I know not how we can wish to live, seeing that everything is so uncertain. Once, O Lord, I thought it impossible to forsake Thee so utterly; and now that I have forsaken Thee so often, I cannot help being afraid; for when Thou did withdraw but a little from me, I fell down to the ground at once. Blessed for ever be Thou! Though I have forsaken Thee, Thou has not forsaken me so utterly but that Thou has come again and raised me up, giving me Thy hand always. Very often, O Lord, I would not take it: very often I would not listen when Thou wert calling me again, as I am going to show.

Chapter VII.

Lukewarmness. The Loss of Grace. Inconvenience of Laxity in Religious Houses.

1. So, then, going on from pastime to pastime, from vanity to vanity, from one occasion of sin to another, I began to expose myself exceedingly to the very greatest dangers: my soul was so distracted by many vanities, that I was ashamed to draw near unto God in an act of such special friendship as that of prayer.[45] As my sins multiplied, I began to lose the pleasure and comfort I had in virtuous things: and that loss contributed to the abandonment of prayer. I see now most clearly, O my Lord, that this comfort departed from me because I had departed from Thee.

2. It was the most fearful delusion into which Satan could plunge me—to give up prayer under the pretense of humility. I began to be afraid of giving myself to prayer, because I saw myself so lost. I thought it would be better for me, seeing that in my wickedness I was one of the most wicked, to live like the multitude—to say the prayers which I was bound to say, and that vocally: not to practice mental prayer nor commune with God so much; for I deserved to be with the devils, and was deceiving those who were about me, because I made an outward show of goodness; and therefore the community in which I dwelt is not to be blamed; for with my cunning I so managed matters, that all had a good opinion of me; and yet I did not seek this deliberately by simulating devotion; for in all that relates to hypocrisy and ostentation—glory be to God!—I do not remember that I ever offended Him, so far as I know. The very first movements herein gave me such pain, that the devil would depart from me with loss, and the gain remained with me; and thus, accordingly, he never tempted me much in this way. Perhaps, however, if God had permitted Satan to tempt me as sharply herein as he tempted me in other things, I should have fallen also into this; but His Majesty has preserved me until now. May He be blessed for evermore! It was rather a heavy affliction to me that I should be thought so well of; for I knew my own secret.

3. The reason why they thought I was not so wicked was this: they saw that I, who was so young, and exposed to so many occasions of sin, withdrew myself so often into solitude for prayer, read much, spoke of God, that I liked to have His image painted in many places, to have an oratory of my own, and furnish it with objects of devotion, that I spoke ill of no one, and other things of the same kind in me which have the appearance of virtue. Yet all the while—I was so vain—I knew how to procure respect for myself by doing those things which in the world are usually regarded with respect.

---

[45] See *Way of Perfection*, ch. xl.; but ch. xxvii. of the former editions.

4. In consequence of this, they gave me as much liberty as they did to the oldest nuns, and even more, and had great confidence in me; for as to taking any liberty for myself, or doing anything without leave—such as conversing through the door, or in secret, or by night—I do not think I could have brought myself to speak with anybody in the monastery in that way, and I never did it; for our Lord held me back. It seemed to me—for I considered many things carefully and of set purpose—that it would be a very evil deed on my part, wicked as I was, to risk the credit of so many nuns, who were all good—as if everything else I did was well done! In truth, the evil I did was not the result of deliberation, as this would have been, if I had done it, although it was too much so.

5. Therefore, I think that it did me much harm to be in a monastery not enclosed. The liberty which those who were good might have with advantage—they not being obliged to do more than they do, because they had not bound themselves to enclosure—would certainly have led me, who am wicked, straight to hell, if our Lord, by so many remedies and means of His most singular mercy, had not delivered me out of that danger—and it is, I believe, the very greatest danger—namely, a monastery of women unenclosed—yes, more, I think it is, for those who will be wicked, a road to hell, rather than a help to their weakness. This is not to be understood of my monastery; for there are so many there who in the utmost sincerity, and in great perfection, serve our Lord, so that His Majesty, according to His goodness, cannot but be gracious unto them; neither is it one of those which are most open for all religious observances are kept in it; and I am speaking only of others which I have seen and known.

6. I am exceedingly sorry for these houses, because our Lord must of necessity send His special inspirations not merely once, but many times, if the nuns therein are to be saved, seeing that the honors and amusements of the world are allowed among them, and the obligations of their state are so ill-understood. God grant they may not count that to be virtue which is sin, as I did so often! It is very difficult to make people understand this; it is necessary our Lord Himself should take the matter seriously into His own hands.

7. If parents would take my advice, now that they are at no pains to place their daughters where they may walk in the way of salvation without incurring a greater risk than they would do if they were left in the world, let them look at least at that which concerns their good name. Let them marry them to persons of a much lower degree, rather than place them in monasteries of this kind, unless they be of extremely good inclinations, and God grant that these inclinations may come to good! or let them keep them at home. If they will be wicked at home, their evil life can be hidden only for a short time; but in monasteries it can be hidden long, and, in the end, it is our Lord that discovers it. They injure not only themselves, but all the nuns also. And all the while the poor things are not in fault; for they walk in the way that is shown them. Many of them are to be pitied; for they wished to withdraw from the world, and, thinking to escape from the dangers of it, and that they were going to serve our Lord, have found themselves in ten worlds at once, without knowing what to do, or how to help themselves. Youth and sensuality and the devil invite them and incline them to follow certain ways which are of the essence of worldliness. They see these ways, so to speak, considered as safe there.

8. Now, these seem to me to be in some degree like those wretched heretics who will make themselves blind, and who will consider that which they do to be good, and so believe, but without really believing; for they have within themselves something that tells them it is wrong.

9. Oh, what utter ruin! utter ruin of religious persons—I am not speaking now more of women than of men—where the rules of the Order are not kept; where the same monastery offers two roads: one of virtue and observance, the other of inobservance, and both equally frequented! I have spoken incorrectly: they are not equally frequented; for, on account of our sins, the way of the greatest imperfection is the most frequented; and because it is the broadest, it is also the most in favor. The way of religious observance is so little used, that the friar and the nun who would really begin to follow their vocation thoroughly have reason to fear the members of their communities more than all the devils together. They must be more cautious, and dissemble more, when they would speak of that friendship with God which they desire to have, than when they would speak of those friendships and affections which the devil arranges in monasteries. I know not why we are astonished that the Church is in so much trouble, when we see those, who ought to be an example of every virtue to others, so disfigure the work which the spirit of the Saints departed wrought in

their Orders. May it please His Divine Majesty to apply a remedy to this, as He sees it to be needful! Amen.

10. So, then, when I began to indulge in these conversations, I did not think, seeing they were customary, that my soul must be injured and dissipated, as I afterwards found it must be, by such conversations. I thought that, as receiving visits was so common in many monasteries, no more harm would befall me thereby than befell others, whom I knew to be good. I did not observe that they were much better than I was, and that an act which was perilous for me was not so perilous for them; and yet I have no doubt there was some danger in it, were it nothing else but a waste of time.

11. I was once with a person—it was at the very beginning of my acquaintance with her when our Lord was pleased to show me that these friendships were not good for me: to warn me also, and in my blindness, which was so great, to give me light. Christ stood before me, stern and grave, giving me to understand what in my conduct was offensive to Him. I saw Him with the eyes of the soul more distinctly than I could have seen Him with the eyes of the body. The vision made so deep an impression upon me, that, though it is more than twenty-six years ago,[46] I seem to see Him present even now. I was greatly astonished and disturbed, and I resolved not to see that person again.

12. It did me much harm that I did not then know it was possible to see anything otherwise than with the eyes of the body;[47] so did Satan too, in that he helped me to think so: he made me understand it to be impossible, and suggested that I had imagined the vision—that it might be Satan himself—and other suppositions of that kind. For all this, the impression remained with me that the vision was from God, and not an imagination; but, as it was not to my liking, I forced myself to lie to myself; and as I did not dare to discuss the matter with any one, and as great importunity was used, I went back to my former conversation with the same person, and with others also, at different times; for I was assured that there was no harm in seeing such a person, and that I gained, instead of losing, reputation by doing so. I spent many years in this pestilent amusement; for it never appeared to me, when I was engaged in it, to be so bad as it really was, though at times I saw clearly it was not good. But no one caused me the same distraction which that person did of whom I am speaking; and that was because I had a great affection for her.

13. At another time, when I was with that person, we saw, both of us, and others who were present also saw, something like a great toad crawling towards us, more rapidly than such a creature is in the habit of crawling. I cannot understand how a reptile of that kind could, in the middle of the day, have come forth from that place; it never had done so before,[48] but the impression it made on me was such, that I think it must have had a meaning; neither have I ever forgotten it. Oh, the greatness of God! with what care and tenderness didst Thou warn me in every way! and how little I profited by those warnings!

14. There was in that house a nun, who was related to me, now grown old, a great servant of God, and a strict observer of the rule. She too warned me from time to time; but I not only did not listen to her, but was even offended, thinking she was scandalized without cause. I have mentioned this in order that my wickedness and the great goodness of God might be understood, and to show how much I deserved hell for ingratitude so great, and, moreover, if it should be our Lord's will and pleasure that any nun at any time should read this, that she might take warning by me. I beseech them all, for the love of our Lord, to flee from such recreations as these.

15. May His Majesty grant I may undeceive some one of the many I led astray when I told them there was no harm in these things, and assured them there was no such great danger therein. I did so because I was blind myself; for I would not deliberately lead them astray. By the bad example I set before them—I spoke of this before[49]—I was the occasion of much evil, not thinking I was doing so much harm.

---

[46] A.D. 1537, when the Saint was twenty-two years old (*Bouix*). This passage, therefore, must be one of the additions to the second Life; for the first was written in 1562, twenty-five years only after the vision.

[47] See ch. xxvii. § 3.

[48] In the parlor of the monastery of the Incarnation, Avila, a painting of this is preserved to this day (*De la Fuente*).

[49] Ch. vi. § 4.

16. In those early days, when I was ill, and before I knew how to be of use to myself, I had a very strong desire to further the progress of others:[50] a most common temptation of beginners. With me, however, it had good results. Loving my father so much, I longed to see him in the possession of that good which I seemed to derive myself from prayer. I thought that in this life there could not be a greater good than prayer; and by roundabout ways, as well as I could, I contrived make him enter upon it; I gave him books for that end. As he was so good—I said so before[51]—this exercise took such a hold upon him, that in five or six years, I think it was, he made so great a progress that I used to praise our Lord for it. It was a very great consolation to me. He had most grievous trials of diverse kinds; and he bore them all with the greatest resignation. He came often to see me; for it was a comfort to him to speak of the things of God.

17. And now that I had become so dissipated, and had ceased to pray, and yet saw that he still thought I was what I used to be, I could not endure it, and so undeceived him. I had been a year and more without praying, thinking it an act of greater humility to abstain. This—I shall speak of it again[52]—was the greatest temptation I ever had, because it very nearly wrought my utter ruin;[53] for, when I used to pray, if I offended God one day, on the following days I would recollect myself, and withdraw farther from the occasions of sin.

18. When that blessed man, having that good opinion of me, came to visit me, it pained me to see him so deceived as to think that I used to pray to God as before. So I told him that I did not pray; but I did not tell him why. I put my infirmities forward as an excuse; for though I had recovered from that which was so troublesome, I have always been weak, even very much so; and though my infirmities are somewhat less troublesome now than they were, they still afflict me in many ways; specially, I have been suffering for twenty years from sickness every morning,[54] so that I could not take any food till past mid-day, and even occasionally not till later; and now, since my Communions have become more frequent, it is at night, before I lie down to rest, that the sickness occurs, and with greater pain; for I have to bring it on with a feather, or other means. If I do not bring it on, I suffer more; and thus I am never, I believe, free from great pain, which is sometimes very acute, especially about the heart; though the fainting-fits are now but of rare occurrence. I am also, these eight years past, free from the paralysis, and from other infirmities of fever, which I had so often. These afflictions I now regard so lightly, that I am even glad of them, believing that our Lord in some degree takes His pleasure in them.

19. My father believed me when I gave him that for a reason, as he never told a lie himself; neither should I have done so, considering the relation we were in. I told him, in order to be the more easily believed, that it was much for me to be able to attend in choir, though I saw clearly that this was no excuse whatever; neither, however, was it a sufficient reason for giving up a practice which does not require, of necessity, bodily strength, but only love and a habit thereof; yet our Lord always furnishes an opportunity for it, if we but seek it. I say always; for though there may be times, as in illness, and from other causes, when we cannot be much alone, yet it never can be but there must be opportunities when our strength is sufficient for the purpose; and in sickness itself, and amidst other hindrances, true prayer consists, when the soul loves, in offering up its burden, and in thinking of Him for Whom it suffers, and in the resignation of the will, and in a thousand ways which then present themselves. It is under these circumstances that love exerts itself for it is not necessarily prayer when we are alone; and neither is it not prayer when we are not.

20. With a little care, we may find great blessings on those occasions when our Lord, by means of afflictions, deprives us of time for prayer; and so I found it when I had a good conscience. But my father, having that opinion of me which he had, and because of the love he bore me, believed all I told him; moreover, he was sorry for me; and as he had now risen to great heights of prayer himself, he never remained with me long; for when he had seen me, he went his way, saying that he was wasting his time. As I was wasting it in other vanities, I cared little about this.

---

50 See *Interior Castle*, v. iii. § 1.

51 Ch. i. § i.

52 Ch. xix. §§ 9, 17.

53 See § 2, above.

54 See ch. xi. § 23: *Interior Castle*, vi. i. § 8.

21. My father was not the only person whom I prevailed upon to practice prayer, though I was walking in vanity myself. When I saw persons fond of reciting their prayers, I showed them how to make a meditation, and helped them and gave them books; for from the time I began myself to pray, as I said before,[55] I always had a desire that others should serve God. I thought, now that I did not myself serve our Lord according to the light I had, that the knowledge His Majesty had given me ought not to be lost, and that others should serve Him for me.[56] I say this in order to explain the great blindness I was in: going to ruin myself, and laboring to save others.

22. At this time, that illness befell my father of which he died;[57] it lasted some days. I went to nurse him, being more sick in spirit than he was in body, owing to my many vanities—though not, so far as I know, to the extent of being in mortal sin—through the whole of that wretched time of which I am speaking; for, if I knew myself to be in mortal sin, I would not have continued in it on any account. I suffered much myself during his illness. I believe I rendered him some service in return for what he had suffered in mine. Though I was very ill, I did violence to myself; and though in losing him I was to lose all the comfort and good of my life—he was all this to me—I was so courageous, that I never betrayed my sorrows, concealing them till he was dead, as if I felt none at all. It seemed as if my very soul were wrenched when I saw him at the point of death—my love for him was so deep.

23. It was a matter for which we ought to praise our Lord—the death that he died, and the desire he had to die; so also was the advice he gave us after the last anointing, how he charged us to recommend him to God, and to pray for mercy for him, how he bade us serve God always, and consider how all things come to an end. He told us with tears how sorry he was that he had not served Him himself; for he wished he was a friar—I mean, that he had been one in the Strictest Order that is. I have a most assured conviction that our Lord, some fifteen days before, had revealed to him he was not to live; for up to that time, though very ill, he did not think so; but now, though he was somewhat better, and the physicians said so, he gave no heed to them, but employed himself in the ordering of his soul.

24. His chief suffering consisted in a most acute pain of the shoulders, which never left him: it was so sharp at times, that it put him into great torture. I said to him, that as he had so great a devotion to our Lord carrying His cross on His shoulders, he should now think that His Majesty wished him to feel somewhat of that pain which He then suffered Himself. This so comforted him, that I do not think I heard him complain afterwards.

25. He remained three days without consciousness; but on the day he died, our Lord restored him so completely, that we were astonished: he preserved his understanding to the last; for in the middle of the creed, which he repeated himself, he died. He lay there like an angel—such he seemed to me, if I may say so, both in soul and disposition: he was very good.

26. I know not why I have said this, unless it be for the purpose of showing how much the more I am to be blamed for my wickedness; for after seeing such a death, and knowing what his life had been, I, in order to be in any wise like unto such a father, ought to have grown better. His confessor, a most learned Dominican,[58] used to say that he had no doubt he went straight to heaven.[59] He had heard his confession for some years, and spoke with praise of the purity of his conscience.

27. This Dominican father, who was a very good man, fearing God, did me a very great service; for I confessed to him. He took upon himself the task of helping my soul in earnest, and of making me see the perilous state I was in.[60] He sent me to Communion once a fortnight;[61] and I, by degrees beginning to speak to him, told him about my prayer. He charged me never to omit it: that, anyhow, it could not do me anything but good. I began to return to it—though I did not cut off the occasions

---

[55] § 16.

[56] See *Interior Castle*, v. iii. § 1.

[57] In 1541, when the Saint was twenty-five years of age (*Bouix*).

[58] F. Vicente Barron (*Reforma*, lib. i. ch. xv.).

[59] See ch. xxxviii. § 1.

[60] See ch. xix. § 19.

[61] The Spanish editor calls attention to this as a proof of great laxity in those days—that a nun like St. Teresa should be urged to communicate as often as once in a fortnight.

of sin—and never afterwards gave it up. My life became most wretched, because I learned in prayer more and more of my faults. On one side, God was calling me; on the other, I was following the world. All the things of God gave me great pleasure; and I was a prisoner to the things of the world. It seemed as if I wished to reconcile two contradictions, so much at variance one with another as are the life of the spirit and the joys and pleasures and amusements of sense.[62]

28. I suffered much in prayer; for the spirit was slave, and not master; and so I was not able to shut myself up within myself—that was my whole method of prayer—without shutting up with me a thousand vanities at the same time. I spent many years in this way; and I am now astonished that any one could have borne it without abandoning either the one or the other. I know well that it was not in my power then to give up prayer, because He held me in His hand Who sought me that He might show me greater mercies.

29. O my God! if I might, I would speak of the occasions from which God delivered me, and how I threw myself into them again; and of the risks I ran of losing utterly my good name, from which He delivered me. I did things to show what I was; and our Lord hid the evil, and revealed some little virtue—if so be I had any—and made it great in the eyes of all, so that they always held me in much honor. For although my follies came occasionally into light, people would not believe it when they saw other things, which they thought good. The reason is, that He Who knows all things saw it was necessary it should be so, in order that I might have some credit given me by those to whom in after years I was to speak of His service. His supreme munificence regarded not my great sins, but rather the desires I frequently had to please Him, and the pain I felt because I had not the strength to bring those desires to good effect.

30. O Lord of my soul! how shall I be able to magnify the graces which Thou, in those years, did bestow upon me? Oh, how, at the very time that I offended Thee most, Thou did prepare me in a moment, by a most profound compunction, to taste of the sweetness of Thy consolations and mercies! In truth, O my King, Thou did administer to me the most delicate and painful chastisement it was possible for me to bear; for Thou knew well what would have given me the most pain. Thou did chastise my sins with great consolations. I do not believe I am saying foolish things, though it may well be that I am beside myself whenever I call to mind my ingratitude and my wickedness.

31. It was more painful for me, in the state I was in, to receive graces, when I had fallen into grievous faults, than it would have been to receive chastisement; for one of those faults, I am sure, used to bring me low, shame and distress me, more than many diseases, together with many heavy trials, could have done. For, as to the latter, I saw that I deserved them; and it seemed to me that by them I was making some reparation for my sins, though it was but slight, for my sins are so many. But when I see myself receive graces anew, after being so ungrateful for those already received, that is to me—and, I believe, to all who have any knowledge or love of God—a fearful kind of torment. We may see how true this is by considering what a virtuous mind must be. Hence my tears and vexation when I reflected on what I felt, seeing myself in a condition to fall at every moment, though my resolutions and desires then—I am speaking of that time—were strong.

32. It is a great evil for a soul to be alone in the midst of such great dangers; it seems to me that if I had had any one with whom I could have spoken of all this, it might have helped me not to fall. I might, at least, have been ashamed before him—and yet I was not ashamed before God.

33. For this reason, I would advise those who give themselves to prayer, particularly at first, to form friendships; and converse familiarly, with others who are doing the same thing. It is a matter of the last importance, even if it lead only to helping one another by prayer: how much more, seeing that it has led to much greater gain! Now, if in their intercourse one with another, and in the indulgence of human affections even not of the best kind, men seek friends with whom they may refresh themselves, and for the purpose of having greater satisfaction in speaking of their empty joys, I know no reason why it should not be lawful for him who is beginning to love and serve God in earnest to confide to another his joys and sorrows; for they who are given to prayer are thoroughly accustomed to both.

34. For if that friendship with God which he desires be real, let him not be afraid of vain-glory; and if the first movements thereof assail him, he will escape from it with merit; and I believe that he who will discuss the matter with this intention will profit both himself and those who hear him,

---

[62] See ch. xiii. §§ 7, 8.

and thus will derive more light for his own understanding, as well as for the instruction of his friends. He who in discussing his method of prayer falls into vain-glory will do so also when he hears Mass devoutly, if he is seen of men, and in doing other good works, which must be done under pain of being no Christian; and yet these things must not be omitted through fear of vain-glory.

35. Moreover, it is a most important matter for those souls who are not strong in virtue; for they have so many people, enemies as well as friends, to urge them the wrong way, that I do not see how this point is capable of exaggeration. It seems to me that Satan has employed this artifice— and it is of the greatest service to him—namely, that men who really wish to love and please God should hide the fact, while others, at his suggestion, make open show of their malicious dispositions; and this is so common, that it seems a matter of boasting now, and the offences committed against God are thus published abroad.

36. I do not know whether the things I am saying are foolish or not. If they be so, your reverence will strike them out. I entreat you to help my simplicity by adding a good deal to this, because the things that relate to the service of God are so feebly managed, that it is necessary for those who would serve Him to join shoulder to shoulder, if they are to advance at all; for it is considered safe to live amidst the vanities and pleasures of the world, and few there be who regard them with unfavorable eyes. But if any one begins to give himself up to the service of God, there are so many to find fault with him, that it becomes necessary for him to seek companions, in order that he may find protection among them till he grows strong enough not to feel what he may be made to suffer. If he does not, he will find himself in great straits.

37. This, I believe, must have been the reason why some of the Saints withdrew into the desert. And it is a kind of humility in man not to trust to himself, but to believe that God will help him in his relations with those with whom he converses; and charity grows by being diffused; and there are a thousand blessings herein which I would not dare to speak of, if I had not known by experience the great importance of it. It is very true that I am the most wicked and the basest of all who are born of women; but I believe that he who, humbling himself, though strong, yet trusts not in himself, and believes another who in this matter has had experience, will lose nothing. Of myself I may say that, if our Lord had not revealed to me this truth, and given me the opportunity of speaking very frequently to persons given to prayer, I should have gone on falling and rising till I tumbled into hell. I had many friends to help me to fall; but as to rising again, I was so much left to myself, that I wonder now I was not always on the ground. I praise God for His mercy; for it was He only Who stretched out His hand to me. May He be blessed for ever! Amen.

Chapter VIII.

The Saint Ceases Not to Pray. Prayer the Way to Recover What Is Lost. All Exhorted to Pray. The Great Advantage of Prayer, Even to Those Who May Have Ceased from It.

1. It is not without reason that I have dwelt so long on this portion of my life. I see clearly that it will give no one pleasure to see anything so base; and certainly I wish those who may read this to have me in abhorrence, as a soul so obstinate and so ungrateful to Him Who did so much for me. I could wish, too, I had permission to say how often at this time I failed in my duty to God, because I was not leaning on the strong pillar of prayer. I passed nearly twenty years on this stormy sea, falling and rising, but rising to no good purpose, seeing that I went and fell again. My life was one of perfection; but it was so mean, that I scarcely made any account whatever of venial sins; and though of mortal sins I was afraid, I was not so afraid of them as I ought to have been, because I did not avoid the perilous occasions of them. I may say that it was the most painful life that can be imagined, because I had no sweetness in God, and no pleasure in the world.

2. When I was in the midst of the pleasures of the world, the remembrance of what I owed to God made me sad; and when I was praying to God, my worldly affections disturbed me. This is so painful a struggle, that I know not how I could have borne it for a month, let alone for so many years. Nevertheless, I can trace distinctly the great mercy of our Lord to me, while thus immersed

in the world, in that I had still the courage to pray. I say courage, because I know of nothing in the whole world which requires greater courage than plotting treason against the King, knowing that He knows it, and yet never withdrawing from His presence; for, granting that we are always in the presence of God, yet it seems to me that those who pray are in His presence in a very different sense; for they, as it were, see that He is looking upon them; while others may be for days together without even once recollecting that God sees them.

3. It is true, indeed, that during these years there were many months, and, I believe, occasionally a whole year, in which I so kept guard over myself that I did not offend our Lord, gave myself much to prayer, and took some pains, and that successfully, not to offend Him. I speak of this now, because all I am saying is strictly true; but I remember very little of those good days, and so they must have been few, while my evil days were many. Still, the days that passed over without my spending a great part of them in prayer were few, unless I was very ill, or very much occupied.

4. When I was ill, I was well with God. I contrived that those about me should be so, too, and I made supplications to our Lord for this grace, and spoke frequently of Him. Thus, with the exception of that year of which I have been speaking, during eight-and-twenty years of prayer, I spent more than eighteen in that strife and contention which arose out of my attempts to reconcile God and the world. As to the other years, of which I have now to speak, in them the grounds of the warfare, though it was not slight, were changed; but inasmuch as I was—at least, I think so— serving God, and aware of the vanity of the world, all has been pleasant, as I shall show hereafter.[63]

5. The reason, then, of my telling this at so great a length is that, as I have just said,[64] the mercy of God and my ingratitude, on the one hand, may become known; and, on the other, that men may understand how great is the good which God works in a soul when He gives it a disposition to pray in earnest, though it may not be so well prepared as it ought to be. If that soul perseveres in spite of sins, temptations, and relapses, brought about in a thousand ways by Satan, our Lord will bring it at last—I am certain of it—to the harbor of salvation, as He has brought me myself; for so it seems to me now. May His Majesty grant I may never go back and be lost! He who gives himself to prayer is in possession of a great blessing, of which many saintly and good men have written—I am speaking of mental prayer—glory be to God for it; and, if they had not done so, I am not proud enough, though I have but little humility, to presume to discuss it.

6. I may speak of that which I know by experience; and so I say, let him never cease from prayer who has once begun it, be his life ever so wicked; for prayer is the way to amend it, and without prayer such amendment will be much more difficult. Let him not be tempted by Satan, as I was, to give it up, on the pretense of humility;[65] let him rather believe that His words are true Who says that, if we truly repent, and resolve never to offend Him, He will take us into His favor again,[66] give us the graces He gave us before, and occasionally even greater, if our repentance deserve it. And as to him who has not begun to pray, I implore him by the love of our Lord not to deprive himself of so great a good.

7. Herein there is nothing to be afraid of, but everything to hope for. Granting that such a one does not advance, nor make an effort to become perfect, so as to merit the joys and consolations which the perfect receive from God, yet he will by little and little attain to a knowledge of the road which leads to heaven. And if he perseveres, I hope in the mercy of God for him, seeing that no one ever took Him for his friend that was not amply rewarded; for mental prayer is nothing else, in my opinion, but being on terms of friendship with God, frequently conversing in secret with Him Who, we know, loves us. Now, true love and lasting friendship require certain dispositions: those of our Lord, we know, are absolutely perfect; ours, vicious, sensual, and thankless; and you cannot therefore, bring yourselves to love Him as He loves you, because you have not the disposition to do so; and if you do not love Him, yet, seeing how much it concerns you to have His friendship, and how great is His love for you, rise above that pain you feel at being much with Him Who is so different from you.

---

[63] Ch. ix. § 10.

[64] § 1, above.

[65] Ch. vii. § 17; ch. xix. § 8.

[66] Ezech. xviii. 21: "Si autem impius egerit poenitentiam,… vita vivet, et non morietur. Omnium iniquitatum ejus… non recordabor."

8. O infinite goodness of my God! I seem to see Thee and myself in this relation to one another. O Joy of the angels! when I consider it, I wish I could wholly die of love! How true it is that Thou endures those who will not endure Thee! Oh, how good a friend art Thou, O my Lord! how Thou comforts and endures, and also waits for them to make themselves like unto Thee, and yet, in the meanwhile, art Thyself so patient of the state they are in! Thou takes into account the occasions during which they seek Thee, and for a moment of penitence forgets their offences against Thyself.

9. I have seen this distinctly in my own case, and I cannot tell why the whole world does not labor to draw near to Thee in this particular friendship. The wicked, who do not resemble Thee, ought to do so, in order that Thou mayest make them good, and for that purpose should permit Thee to remain with them at least for two hours daily, even though they may not remain with Thee but, as I used to do, with a thousand distractions, and with worldly thoughts. In return for this violence which they offer to themselves for the purpose of remaining in a company so good as Thine—for at first they can do no more, and even afterwards at times—Thou, O Lord, defend them against the assaults of evil spirits, whose power Thou restrains, and even lessens daily, giving to them the victory over these their enemies. So it is, O Life of all lives, Thou slays none that put their trust in Thee, and seek Thy friendship; yes, rather, Thou sustains their bodily life in greater vigor, and makes their soul to live.

10. I do not understand what there can be to make them afraid who are afraid to begin mental prayer, nor do I know what it is they dread. The devil does well to bring this fear upon us, that he may really hurt us by putting me in fear, he can make me cease from thinking of my offences against God, of the great debt I owe Him, of the existence of heaven and hell, and of the great sorrows and trials He underwent for me. That was all my prayer, and had been, when I was in this dangerous state, and it was on those subjects I dwelt whenever I could; and very often, for some years, I was more occupied with the wish to see the end of the time I had appointed for myself to spend in prayer, and in watching the hour-glass, than with other thoughts that were good. If a sharp penance had been laid upon me, I know of none that I would not very often have willingly undertaken, rather than prepare myself for prayer by self-recollection. And certainly the violence with which Satan assailed me was so irresistible, or my evil habits were so strong, that I did not betake myself to prayer; and the sadness I felt on entering the oratory was so great, that it required all the courage I had to force myself in. They say of me that my courage is not slight, and it is known that God has given me a courage beyond that of a woman; but I have made a bad use of it. In the end, our Lord came to my help; and then, when I had done this violence to myself, I found greater peace and joy than I sometimes had when I had a desire to pray.

11. If, then, our Lord bore so long with me, who was so wicked—and it is plain that it was by prayer all my evil was corrected—why should any one, how wicked so ever he may be, have any fear? Let him be ever so wicked, he will not remain in his wickedness so many years as I did, after receiving so many graces from our Lord. Is there any one who can despair, when He bore so long with me, only because I desired and contrived to find some place and some opportunities for Him to be alone with me—and that very often against my will? for I did violence to myself, or rather our Lord Himself did violence to me.

12. If, then, to those who do not serve God, but rather offend Him, prayer be all this, and so necessary, and if no one can really find out any harm it can do him, and if the omission of it be not a still greater harm, why, then, should they abstain from it who serve and desire to serve God? Certainly I cannot comprehend it, unless it be that men have a mind to go through the troubles of this life in greater misery, and to shut the door in the face of God, so that He shall give them no comfort in it. I am most truly sorry for them, because they serve God at their own cost; for of those who pray, God Himself defrays the charges, seeing that for a little trouble He gives sweetness, in order that, by the help it supplies, they may bear their trials.

13. But because I have much to say hereafter of this sweetness, which our Lord gives to those who persevere in prayer,[67] I do not speak of it here; only this will I say: prayer is the door to those great graces which our Lord bestowed upon me. If this door be shut, I do not see how He can bestow them; for even if He entered into a soul to take His delight therein, and to make that soul also delight in Him, there is no way by which He can do so; for His will is, that such a soul should be lonely

---

[67] See ch. x. § 2, and ch. xi. § 22.

and pure, with a great desire to receive His graces. If we put many hindrances in the way, and take no pains whatever to remove them, how can He come to us, and how can we have any desire that He should show us His great mercies?

14. I will speak now—for it is very important to understand it—of the assaults which Satan directs against a soul for the purpose of taking it, and of the contrivances and compassion wherewith our Lord labors to convert it to Himself, in order that men may behold His mercy, and the great good it was for me that I did not give up prayer and spiritual reading, and that they may be on their guard against the dangers against which I was not on my guard myself. And, above all, I implore them for the love of our Lord, and for the great love with which He goes about seeking our conversion to Himself, to beware of the occasions of sin; for once placed therein, we have no ground to rest on—so many enemies then assail us, and our own weakness is such, that we cannot defend ourselves.

15. Oh, that I knew how to describe the captivity of my soul in those days! I understood perfectly that I was in captivity, but I could not understand the nature of it; neither could I entirely believe that those things which my confessors did not make so much of were so wrong as I in my soul felt them to be. One of them—I had gone to him with a scruple—told me that, even if I were raised to high contemplation, those occasions and conversations were not unfitting for me. This was towards the end, when, by the grace of God, I was withdrawing more and more from those great dangers, but not wholly from the occasions of them.

16. When they saw my good desires, and how I occupied myself in prayer, I seemed to them to have done much; but my soul knew that this was not doing what I was bound to do for Him to Whom I owed so much. I am sorry for my poor soul even now, because of its great sufferings, and the little help it had from any one except God, and for the wide door that man opened for it, that it might go forth to its pastimes and pleasures, when they said that these things were lawful.

17. Then there was the torture of sermons, and that not a slight one; for I was very fond of them. If I heard any one preach well and with unction, I felt, without my seeking it, a particular affection for him, neither do I know whence it came. Thus, no sermon ever seemed to me so bad, but that I listened to it with pleasure; though, according to others who heard it, the preaching was not good. If it was a good sermon, it was to me a most special refreshment. To speak of God, or to hear Him spoken of, never wearied me. I am speaking of the time after I gave myself to prayer. At one time I had great comfort in sermons, at another they distressed me, because they made me feel that I was very far from being what I ought to have been.

18. I used to pray to our Lord for help; but, as it now seems to me, I must have committed the fault of not putting my whole trust in His Majesty, and of not thoroughly distrusting myself. I sought for help, took great pains; but it must be that I did not understand how all is of little profit if we do not root out all confidence in ourselves, and place it wholly in God. I wished to live, but I saw clearly that I was not living, but rather wrestling with the shadow of death; there was no one to give me life, and I was not able to take it. He Who could have given it me had good reasons for not coming to my aid, seeing that He had brought me back to Himself so many times, and I as often had left Him.

Chapter IX.

The Means Whereby Our Lord Quickened Her Soul, Gave Her Light in Her Darkness, and Made Her Strong in Goodness.

1. My soul was now grown weary; and the miserable habits it had contracted would not suffer it to rest, though it was desirous of doing so. It came to pass one day, when I went into the oratory, that I saw a picture which they had put by there, and which had been procured for a certain feast observed in the house. It was a representation of Christ most grievously wounded; and so devotional, that the very sight of it, when I saw it, moved me—so well did it show forth that which He suffered for us. So keenly did I feel the evil return I had made for those wounds, that I thought my heart was breaking. I threw myself on the ground beside it, my tears flowing plenteously, and implored Him to strengthen me once for all, so that I might never offend Him any more.

2. I had a very great devotion to the glorious Magdalene, and very frequently used to think of her conversion—especially when I went to Communion. As I knew for certain that our Lord was then within me, I used to place myself at His feet, thinking that my tears would not be despised. I did not know what I was saying; only He did great things for me, in that He was pleased I should shed those tears, seeing that I so soon forgot that impression. I used to recommend myself to that glorious Saint, that she might obtain my pardon.

3. But this last time, before that picture of which I am speaking, I seem to have made greater progress; for I was now very distrustful of myself, placing all my confidence in God. It seems to me that I said to Him then that I would not rise up till He granted my petition. I do certainly believe that this was of great service to me, because I have grown better ever since.[68]

4. This was my method of prayer: as I could not make reflections with my understanding, I contrived to picture Christ as within me;[69] and I used to find myself the better for thinking of those mysteries of His life during which He was most lonely. It seemed to me that the being alone and afflicted, like a person in trouble, must needs permit me to come near unto Him.

5. I did many simple things of this kind; and in particular I used to find myself most at home in the prayer in the Garden, whither I went in His company. I thought of the bloody sweat, and of the affliction He endured there; I wished, if it had been possible, to wipe away that painful sweat from His face; but I remember that I never dared to form such a resolution—my sins stood before me so grievously. I used to remain with Him there as long as my thoughts allowed me, and I had many thoughts to torment me. For many years, nearly every night before I fell asleep, when I recommended myself to God, that I might sleep in peace, I used always to think a little of this mystery of the prayer in the Garden—yes, even before I was a nun, because I had been told that many indulgences were to be gained thereby. For my part, I believe that my soul gained very much in this way, because I began to practice prayer without knowing what it was; and now that it had become my constant habit, I was saved from omitting it, as I was from omitting to bless myself with the sign of the cross before I slept.

6. And now to go back to what I was saying of the torture which my thoughts inflicted upon me. This method of praying, in which the understanding makes no reflections, hath this property: the soul must gain much, or lose. I mean, that those who advance without meditation, make great progress, because it is done by love. But to attain to this involves great labor, except to those persons whom it is our Lord's good pleasure to lead quickly to the prayer of quiet. I know of some. For those who walk in this way, a book is profitable, that by the help thereof they may the more quickly recollect themselves. It was a help to me also to look on fields, water, and flowers. In them I saw traces of the Creator—I mean, that the sight of these things was as a book unto me; it roused me, made me recollected, and reminded me of my ingratitude and of my sins. My understanding was so dull, that I could never represent in the imagination either heavenly or high things in any form whatever until our Lord placed them before me in another way.[70]

7. I was so little able to put things before me by the help of my understanding, that, unless I saw a thing with my eyes, my imagination was of no use whatever. I could not do as others do, who can put matters before themselves so as to become thereby recollected. I was able to think of Christ only as man. But so it was; and I never could form any image of Him to myself, though I read much of His beauty, and looked at pictures of Him. I was like one who is blind, or in the dark, who, though speaking to a person present, and feeling his presence, because he knows for certain that he is present—I mean, that he understands him to be present, and believes it—yet does not see him. It was thus with me when I used to think of our Lord. This is why I was so fond of images. Wretched are they who, through their own fault, have lost this blessing; it is clear enough that they do not love our Lord—for if they loved Him, they would rejoice at the sight of His picture, just as men find pleasure when they see the portrait of one they love.

8. At this time, the *Confessions* of St. Augustine were given me. Our Lord seems to have so ordained it, for I did not seek them myself, neither had I ever seen them before. I had a very great devotion to St. Augustine, because the monastery in which I lived when I was yet in the world was

---

[68] In the year 1555 (*Bouix*).

[69] See ch. iv. § 10; ch. x. § 1.

[70] See ch. iv. § 11.

of his Order;[71] and also because he had been a sinner—for I used to find great comfort in those Saints whom, after they had sinned, our Lord converted to Himself. I thought they would help me, and that, as our Lord had forgiven them, so also He would forgive me. One thing, however, there was that troubled me—I have spoken of it before[72]—our Lord had called them but once, and they never relapsed; while my relapses were now so many. This it was that vexed me. But calling to mind the love that He bore me, I took courage again. Of His mercy I never doubted once, but I did very often of myself.

9. O my God, I amazed at the hardness of my heart amidst so many succors from Thee. I am filled with dread when I see how little I could do with myself, and how I was clogged, so that I could not resolve to give myself entirely to God. When I began to read the *Confessions*, I thought I saw myself there described, and began to recommend myself greatly to this glorious Saint. When I came to his conversion, and read how he heard that voice in the garden, it seemed to me nothing less than that our Lord had uttered it for me: I felt so in my heart. I remained for some time lost in tears, in great inward affliction and distress. O my God, what a soul has to suffer because it has lost the liberty it had of being mistress over itself! and what torments it has to endure! I wonder now how I could live in torments so great: God be praised Who gave me life, so that I might escape from so fatal a death! I believe that my soul obtained great strength from His Divine Majesty, and that He must have heard my cry, and had compassion upon so many tears.

10. A desire to spend more time with Him began to grow within me, and also to withdraw from the occasions of sin: for as soon as I had done so, I turned lovingly to His Majesty at once. I understood clearly, as I thought, that I loved Him; but I did not understand, as I ought to have understood it, wherein the true love of God consists. I do not think I had yet perfectly disposed myself to seek His service when His Majesty turned towards me with His consolations. What others strive after with great labor, our Lord seems to have looked out for a way to make me willing to accept—that is, in these later years to give me joy and comfort. But as for asking our Lord to give me either these things or sweetness in devotion, I never dared to do it; the only thing I prayed Him to give me was the grace never to offend Him, together with the forgiveness of my great sins. When I saw that my sins were so great, I never ventured deliberately to ask for consolation or for sweetness. He had compassion enough upon me, I think—and, in truth, He dealt with me according to His great mercy—when He allowed me to stand before Him, and when He drew me into His presence; for I saw that, if He had not drawn me, I should not have come at all.

11. Once only in my life do I remember asking for consolation, being at the time in great aridities. When I considered what I had done, I was so confounded, that the very distress I suffered from seeing how little humility I had, brought me that which I had been so bold as to ask for. I knew well that it was lawful to pray for it; but it seemed to me that it is lawful only for those who are in good dispositions, who have sought with all their might to attain to true devotion—that is, not to offend God, and to be disposed and resolved for all goodness. I looked upon those tears of mine as womanish and weak, seeing that I did not obtain my desires by them; nevertheless, I believe that they did me some service; for, especially after those two occasions of great compunction and sorrow of heart,[73] accompanied by tears, of which I am speaking, I began in an especial way to give myself more to prayer, and to occupy myself less with those things which did me harm—though I did not give them up altogether. But God Himself, as I have just said, came to my aid, and helped me to turn away from them. As His Majesty was only waiting for some preparation on my part, the spiritual graces grew in me as I shall now explain. It is not the custom of our Lord to give these graces to any but to those who keep their consciences in greater pureness.[74]

---

[71] Ch. ii. § 8.
[72] In the Prologue.
[73] § 1.
[74] Ch. iv. § 11.

Chapter X.

The Graces She Received in Prayer. What We Can Do Ourselves. The Great Importance of Understanding What Our Lord Is Doing for Us. She Desires Her Confessors to Keep Her Writings Secret, Because of the Special Graces of Our Lord to Her, Which They Had Commanded Her to Describe.

1. I used to have at times, as I have said,[75] though it used to pass quickly away—certain commencements of that which I am going now to describe. When I formed those pictures within myself of throwing myself at the feet of Christ, as I said before,[76] and sometimes even when I was reading, a feeling of the presence of God would come over me unexpectedly, so that I could in no wise doubt either that He was within me, or that I was wholly absorbed in Him. It was not by way of vision; I believe it was what is called mystical theology. The soul is suspended in such a way that it seems to be utterly beside itself. The will loves; the memory, so it seems to me, is as it were lost; and the understanding, so I think, makes no reflections—yet is not lost: as I have just said, it is not at work, but it stands as if amazed at the greatness of the things it understands; for God wills it to understand that it understands nothing whatever of that which His Majesty places before it.

2. Before this, I had a certain tenderness of soul which was very abiding, partially attainable, I believe, in some measure, by our own efforts: a consolation which is not wholly in the senses, nor yet altogether in the spirit, but is all of it the gift of God. However, I think we can contribute much towards the attaining of it by considering our vileness and our ingratitude towards God—the great things He has done for us—His Passion, with its grievous pains—and His life, so full of sorrows; also, by rejoicing in the contemplation of His works, of His greatness, and of the love that He bears us. Many other considerations there are which he who really desires to make progress will often stumble on, though he may not be very much on the watch for them. If with this there be a little love, the soul is comforted, the heart is softened, and tears flow. Sometimes it seems that we do violence to ourselves and weep; at other times, our Lord seems to do so, so that we have no power to resist Him. His Majesty seems to reward this slight carefulness of ours with so grand a gift as is this consolation which He ministers to the soul of seeing itself weeping for so great a Lord. I am not surprised; for the soul has reason enough, and more than enough, for its joy. Here it comforts itself—here it rejoices.

3. The comparison which now presents itself seems to me to be good. These joys in prayer are like what those of heaven must be. As the vision of the saints, which is measured by their merits there, reaches no further than our Lord wills, and as the blessed see how little merit they had, every one of them is satisfied with the place assigned him: there being the very greatest difference between one joy and another in heaven, and much greater than between one spiritual joy and another on earth—which is, however, very great. And in truth, in the beginning, a soul in which God works this grace thinks that now it has scarcely anything more to desire, and counts itself abundantly rewarded for all the service it has rendered Him. And there is reason for this: for one of those tears—which, as I have just said, are almost in our own power, though without God nothing can be done—cannot, in my opinion, be purchased with all the labors of the world, because of the great gain it brings us. And what greater gain can we have than some testimony of our having pleased God? Let him, then, who shall have attained to this, give praise unto God—acknowledge himself to be one of His greatest debtors; because it seems to be His will to take him into His house, having chosen him for His kingdom, if he does not turn back.

4. Let him not regard certain kinds of humility which exist, and of which I mean to speak.[77] Some think it humility not to believe that God is bestowing His gifts upon them. Let us clearly understand this, and that it is perfectly clear God bestows His gifts without any merit whatever on our part; and let us be grateful to His Majesty for them; for if we do not recognize the gifts received at His hands, we shall never be moved to love Him. It is a most certain truth, that the richer we see

---

[75] The Saint interrupts her history here to enter on the difficult questions of mystical theology, and resumes it in ch. xxiii.

[76] Ch. ix. § 4.

[77] Ch. xxx. §§ 10 and 11.

ourselves to be, confessing at the same time our poverty, the greater will be our progress, and the more real our humility.

5. An opposite course tends to take away all courage; for we shall think ourselves incapable of great blessings, if we begin to frighten ourselves with the dread of vain-glory when our Lord begins to show His mercy upon us.[78] Let us believe that He Who gives these gifts will also, when the devil begins to tempt us herein, give us the grace to detect him, and the strength to resist him—that is, He will do so if we walk in simplicity before God, aiming at pleasing Him only, and not men. It is a most evident truth, that our love for a person is greater, the more distinctly we remember the good he has done us.

6. If, then, it is lawful, and so meritorious, always to remember that we have our being from God, that He has created us out of nothing, that He preserves us, and also to remember all the benefits of His death and Passion, which He suffered long before He made us for every one of us now alive—why should it not be lawful for me to discern, confess, and consider often that I was once accustomed to speak of vanities, and that now our Lord has given me the grace to speak only of Himself?

7. Here, then, is a precious pearl, which, when we remember that it is given us, and that we have it in possession, powerfully invites us to love. All this is the fruit of prayer founded on humility. What, then, will it be when we shall find ourselves in possession of other pearls of greater price, such as contempt of the world and of self, which some servants of God have already received? It is clear that such souls must consider themselves greater debtors—under greater obligations to serve Him: we must acknowledge that we have nothing of ourselves, and confess the munificence of our Lord, Who, on a soul so wretched and poor, and so utterly undeserving, as mine is,—for whom the first of these pearls was enough, and more than enough,—would bestow greater riches than I could desire.

8. We must renew our strength to serve Him, and strive not to be ungrateful, because it is on this condition that our Lord dispenses His treasures; for if we do not make a good use of them, and of the high estate to which He raises us, He will return and take them from us, and we shall be poorer than ever. His Majesty will give the pearls to him who shall bring them forth and employ them usefully for himself and others. For how shall he be useful, and how shall he spend liberally, who does not know that he is rich? It is not possible, I think, our nature being what it is, that he can have the courage necessary for great things who does not know that God is on his side; for so miserable are we, so inclined to the things of this world, that he can hardly have any real abhorrence of, with great detachment from, all earthly things who does not see that he holds some pledges for those things that are above. It is by these gifts that our Lord gives us that strength which we through our sins have lost.

9. A man will hardly wish to be held in contempt and abhorrence, nor will he seek after the other great virtues to which the perfect attain, if he has not some pledges of the love which God bears him, together with a living faith. Our nature is so dead, that we go after that which we see immediately before us; and it is these graces, therefore, that quicken and strengthen our faith. It may well be that I, who am so wicked, measure others by myself, and that others require nothing more than the verities of the faith, in order to render their works most perfect; while I, wretched that I am! have need of everything.

10. Others will explain this. I speak from my own experience, as I have been commanded; and if what I say be not correct, let him[79] to whom I send it destroy it; for he knows better than I do what is wrong in it. I entreat him, for the love of our Lord, to publish abroad what I have thus far said of my wretched life, and of my sins. I give him leave to do so; and to all my confessors, also,—of whom he is one—to whom this is to be sent, if it be their pleasure, even during my life, so that I may no longer deceive people who think there must be some good in me.[80] Certainly, I speak in all sincerity, so far as I understand myself. Such publication will give me great comfort.

11. But as to that which I am now going to say, I give no such leave; nor, if it be shown to any one, do I consent to its being said who the person is whose experience it describes, nor who wrote

---

[78] See ch. xiii. § 5.
[79] 5. F. Pedro Ybañez, of the Order of St. Dominic.
[80] See ch. xxxi. § 17.

it. This is why I mention neither my own name, nor that of any other person whatever. I have written it in the best way I could, in order not to be known; and this I beg of them for the love of God. Persons so learned and grave as they are[81] have authority enough to approve of whatever right things I may say, should our Lord give me the grace to do so; and if I should say anything of the kind, it will be His, and not mine—because I am neither learned nor of good life, and I have no person of learning or any other to teach me; for they only who ordered me to write know that I am writing, and at this moment they are not here. I have, as it were, to steal the time, and that with difficulty, because my writing hinders me from spinning. I am living in a house that is poor, and have many things to do.[82] If, indeed, our Lord had given me greater abilities and a better memory, I might then profit by what I have seen and read; but my abilities are very slight. If, then, I should say anything that is right, our Lord will have it said for some good purpose; that which may be wrong will be mine, and your reverence will strike it out.

12. In neither case will it be of any use to publish my name: during my life, it is clear that no good I may have done ought to be told; after death, there is no reason against it, except that it will lose all authority and credit, because related of a person so vile and so wicked as I am. And because I think your reverence and the others who may see this writing will do this that I ask of you, for the love of our Lord, I write with freedom. If it were not so, I should have great scruples, except in declaring my sins: and in that matter I should have none at all. For the rest, it is enough that I am a woman to make my sails droop: how much more, then, when I am a woman, and a wicked one?

13. So, then, everything here beyond the simple story of my life your reverence must take upon yourself—since you have so pressed me to give some account of the graces which our Lord bestowed upon me in prayer—if it be consistent with the truths of our holy Catholic faith; if it be not, your reverence must burn it at once—for I give my consent. I will recount my experience, in order that, if it be consistent with those truths, your reverence may make some use of it; if not, you will deliver my soul from delusion, so that Satan may gain nothing there where I seemed to be gaining myself. Our Lord knows well that I, as I shall show hereafter,[83] have always labored to find out those who could give me light.

14. How clear so ever I may wish to make my account of that which relates to prayer, it will be obscure enough for those who are without experience. I shall speak of certain hindrances, which, as I understand it, keep men from advancing on this road—and of other things which are dangerous, as our Lord has taught me by experience. I have also discussed the matter with men of great learning, with persons who for many years had lived spiritual lives, who admit that, in the twenty-seven years only during which I have given myself to prayer—though I walked so ill, and stumbled so often on the road—His Majesty granted me that experience which others attain to in seven-and-thirty, or seven-and-forty, years; and they, too, being persons who ever advanced in the way of penance and of virtue.

15. Blessed be God for all, and may His infinite Majesty make use of me! Our Lord knows well that I have no other end in this than that He may be praised and magnified a little, when men shall see that on a dunghill so foul and rank He has made a garden of flowers so sweet. May it please His Majesty that I may not by my own fault root them out, and become again what I was before. And I entreat your reverence, for the love of our Lord, to beg this of Him for me, seeing that you have a clearer knowledge of what I am than you have allowed me to give of myself here.

---

[81] See ch. xv. § 12.
[82] See ch. xiv. § 12.
[83] See ch. xxiv. § 5.

Chapter XI.

Why Men Do Not Attain Quickly to the Perfect Love of God. Of Four Degrees of
Prayer. Of the First Degree. The Doctrine Profitable for Beginners, and for Those
Who Have No Sensible Sweetness.

1. I speak now of those who begin to be the servants of love; that seems to me to be nothing else but to resolve to follow Him in the way of prayer, who has loved us so much. It is a dignity so great, that I have a strange joy in thinking of it; for servile fear vanishes at once, if we are, as we ought to be, in the first degree. O Lord of my soul, and my good, how is it that, when a soul is determined to love Thee—doing all it can, by forsaking all things, in order that it may the better occupy itself with the love of God—it is not Thy will it should have the joy of ascending at once to the possession of perfect love? I have spoken amiss; I ought to have said, and my complaint should have been, why is it we do not? for the fault is wholly our own that we do not rejoice at once in a dignity so great, seeing that the attaining to the perfect possession of this true love brings all blessings with it.

2. We think so much of ourselves, and are so dilatory in giving ourselves wholly to God, that, as His Majesty will not let us have the fruition of that which is so precious but at a great cost, so neither do we perfectly prepare ourselves for it. I see plainly that there is nothing by which so great a good can be procured in this world. If, however, we did what we could, not clinging to anything upon earth, but having all our thoughts and conversation in Heaven, I believe that this blessing would quickly be given us, provided we perfectly prepared ourselves for it at once, as some of the saints have done. We think we are giving all to God; but, in fact, we are offering only the revenue or the produce, while we retain the fee-simple of the land in our own possession.

3. We resolve to become poor, and it is a resolution of great merit; but we very often take great care not to be in want, not simply of what is necessary, but of what is superfluous: yes, and to make for ourselves friends who may supply us; and in this way we take more pains, and perhaps expose ourselves to greater danger, in order that we may want nothing, than we did formerly, when we had our own possessions in our own power.

4. We thought, also, that we gave up all desire of honor when we became religious, or when we began the spiritual life, and followed after perfection; and yet, when we are touched on the point of honor, we do not then remember that we had given it up to God. We would seize it again, and take it, as they say, out of His Hands, even after we had made Him, to all appearance, the Lord of our own will. So is it in every thing else.

5. A pleasant way this of seeking the love of God! we retain our own affections, and yet will have that love, as they say, by handfuls. We make no efforts to bring our desires to good effect, or to raise them resolutely above the earth; and yet, with all this, we must have many spiritual consolations. This is not well, and we are seeking things that are incompatible one with the other. So, because we do not give ourselves up wholly and at once, this treasure is not given wholly and at once to us. May it be the good pleasure of our Lord to give it us drop by drop, though it may cost us all the trials in the world.

6. He shows great mercy unto him to whom He gives the grace and resolution to strive for this blessing with all his might; for God withholds Himself from no one who perseveres. He will by little and little strengthen that soul, so that it may come forth victorious. I say resolution, because of the multitude of those things which Satan puts before it at first, to keep it back from beginning to travel on this road; for he knows what harm will befall him thereby—he will lose not only that soul, but many others also. If he who enters on this road does violence to himself, with the help of God, so as to reach the summit of perfection, such a one, I believe, will never go alone to Heaven; he will always take many with him: God gives to him, as to a good captain, those who shall be of his company.

7. Thus, then, the dangers and difficulties which Satan puts before them are so many, that they have need, not of a little, but of a very great, resolution, and great grace from God, to save them from falling away.

8. Speaking, then, of their beginnings who are determined to follow after this good, and to succeed in their enterprise—what I began to say[84] of mystical theology—I believe they call it by that name—I shall proceed with hereafter—I have to say that the labor is greatest at first; for it is they who toil, our Lord, indeed, giving them strength. In the other degrees of prayer, there is more of fruition; although they who are in the beginning, the middle, and the end, have their crosses to carry: the crosses, however, are different. They who would follow Christ, if they do not wish to be lost, must walk in the way He walked Himself. Blessed labors! even here, in this life, so superabundantly rewarded!

9. I shall have to make use of a comparison; I should like to avoid it, because I am a woman, and write simply what I have been commanded. But this language of spirituality is so difficult of utterance for those who are not learned, and such am I. I have therefore to seek for some means to make the matter plain. It may be that the comparison will very rarely be to the purpose—your reverence will be amused when you see my stupidity. I think, now, I have either read or heard of this comparison; but as my memory is bad, I know not where, nor on what occasion; however, I am satisfied with it for my present purpose.[85]

10. A beginner must look upon himself as making a garden, wherein our Lord may take His delight, but in a soil unfruitful, and abounding in weeds. His Majesty roots up the weeds, and has to plant good herbs. Let us, then, take for granted that this is already done when a soul is determined to give itself to prayer, and has begun the practice of it. We have, then, as good gardeners, by the help of God, to see that the plants grow, to water them carefully, that they may not die, but produce blossoms, which shall send forth much fragrance, refreshing to our Lord, so that He may come often for His pleasure into this garden, and delight Himself in the midst of these virtues.

11. Let us now see how this garden is to be watered, that we may understand what we have to do: how much trouble it will cost us, whether the gain be greater than the trouble, or how long a time it will take us. It seems to me that the garden may be watered in four ways: by water taken out of a well, which is very laborious; or with water raised by means of an engine and buckets, drawn by a windlass—I have drawn it this way sometimes—it is a less troublesome way than the first, and gives more water; or by a stream or brook, whereby the garden is watered in a much better way—for the soil is more thoroughly saturated, and there is no necessity to water it so often, and the labor of the gardener is much less; or by showers of rain, when our Lord Himself waters it, without labor on our part—and this way is incomparably better than all the others of which I have spoken.

12. Now, then, for the application of these four ways of irrigation by which the garden is to be maintained; for without water it must fail. The comparison is to my purpose, and it seems to me that by the help of it I shall be able to explain, in some measure, the four degrees of prayer to which our Lord, of His goodness, has occasionally raised my soul. May He graciously grant that I may so speak as to be of some service to one of those who has commanded me to write, whom our Lord has raised in four months to a greater height than I have reached in seventeen years! He prepared himself better than I did, and therefore is his garden without labor on his part, irrigated by these four waters—though the last of them is only drop by drop; but it is growing in such a way, that soon, by the help of our Lord, he will be swallowed up therein, and it will be a pleasure to me, if he finds my explanation absurd, that he should laugh at it.

13. Of those who are beginners in prayer, we may say, that they are those who draw the water up out of the well—a process which, as I have said, is very laborious; for they must be wearied in keeping the senses recollected, and this is a great labor, because the senses have been hitherto accustomed to distractions. It is necessary for beginners to accustom themselves to disregard what they hear or see, and to put it away from them during the time of prayer; they must be alone, and in retirement think over their past life. Though all must do this many times, beginners as well as those more advanced; all, however, must not do so equally, as I shall show hereafter.[86] Beginners at first suffer much, because they are not convinced that they are penitent for their sins; and yet they are, because they are so sincerely resolved on serving God. They must strive to meditate on the life of

---

[84] Ch. x. § 1.

[85] *Vide* St. Bernard, *in Cantic.* Serm. 30. n. 7, ed. Ben.

[86] Ch. xiii. § 23.

Christ, and the understanding is wearied thereby. Thus far we can advance of ourselves—that is, by the grace of God—for without that, as every one knows, we never can have one good thought.

14. This is beginning to draw water up out of the well. God grant there may be water in it! That, however, does not depend on us; we are drawing it, and doing what we can towards watering the flowers. So good is God, that when, for reasons known to His Majesty—perhaps for our greater good—it is His will the well should be dry, He Himself preserves the flowers without water—we, like good gardeners, doing what lies in our power—and makes our virtues grow. By water here I mean tears, and if there be none, then tenderness and an inward feeling of devotion.

15. What, then, will he do here who sees that, for many days, he is conscious only of aridity, disgust, dislike, and so great an unwillingness to go to the well for water, that he would give it up altogether, if he did not remember that he has to please and serve the Lord of the garden; if he did not trust that his service was not in vain, and did not hope for some gain by a labor so great as that of lowering the bucket into the well so often, and drawing it up without water in it? It will happen that he is often unable to move his arms for that purpose, or to have one good thought: working with the understanding is drawing water out of the well.

16. What, then, once more, will the gardener do now? He must rejoice and take comfort, and consider it as the greatest favor to labor in the garden of so great an Emperor; and as he knows that he is pleasing Him in the matter—and his purpose must not be to please himself, but Him—let him praise Him greatly for the trust He has in him—for He sees that, without any recompense, he is taking so much care of that which has been confided to him; let him help Him to carry the Cross, and let him think how He carried it all His life long; let him not seek his kingdom here, nor ever intermit his prayer; and so let him resolve, if this aridity should last even his whole life long, never to let Christ fall down beneath the Cross.[87]

17. The time will come when he shall be paid once for all. Let him have no fear that his labor is in vain: he serves a good Master, Whose eyes are upon him. Let him make no account of evil thoughts, but remember that Satan suggested them to St. Jerome also in the desert.[88] These labors have their reward, I know it; for I am one who underwent them for many years. When I drew but one drop of water out of this blessed well, I considered it was a mercy of God. I know these labors are very great, and require, I think, greater courage than many others in this world; but I have seen clearly that God does not leave them without a great recompense, even in this life; for it is very certain that in one hour, during which our Lord gave me to taste His sweetness, all the anxieties which I had to bear when persevering in prayer seem to me ever afterwards perfectly rewarded.

18. I believe that it is our Lord's good pleasure frequently in the beginning, and at times in the end, to send these torments, and many other incidental temptations, to try those who love Him, and to ascertain if they will drink the chalice,[89] and help Him to carry the Cross, before He entrusts them with His great treasures. I believe it to be for our good that His Majesty should lead us by this way, so that we may perfectly understand how worthless we are; for the graces which He gives afterwards are of a dignity so great, that He will have us by experience know our wretchedness before He grants them, that it may not be with us as it was with Lucifer.

19. What canst Thou do, O my Lord, that is not for the greater good of that soul which Thou knows to be already Thine, and which gives itself up to Thee to follow Thee whithersoever Thou goes, even to the death of the Cross; and which is determined to help Thee to carry that Cross, and not to leave Thee alone with it? He who shall discern this resolution in himself has nothing to fear: no, no; spiritual people have nothing to fear. There is no reason why he should be distressed who is already raised to so high a degree as this is of wishing to converse in solitude with God, and to abandon the amusements of the world. The greater part of the work is done; give praise to His

[87] See ch. xv. § 17.

[88] Epist. 22, *ad Eustochium*. "O quoties ego ipse in eremo constitutus, et in illa vasta solitudine quæ exusta solis ardoribus horridum monachis præstat habitaculum putabam me Romanis interesse deliciis. Sedebam solus... Horrebant sacco membra deformia... Ille igitur ego, qui ob Gehennæ metum tali me carcere damnaveram, scorpionum tantum socius et ferarum, sæpe choris intereram puellarum, pallebant ora jejuniis, et mens desideriis æstuabat in frigido corpore, et ante hominem sua jam carne præmortuum sola libidinum incendia bulliebant."

[89] St. Matt. xx. 22: "Potestis bibere calicem?"

Majesty for it, and trust in His goodness who has never failed those who love Him. Close the eyes of your imagination, and do not ask why He gives devotion to this person in so short a time, and none to me after so many years. Let us believe that all is for our greater good; let His Majesty guide us whithersoever He will: we are not our own, but His. He shows us mercy enough when it is His pleasure we should be willing to dig in His garden, and to be so near the Lord of it: He certainly is near to us. If it be His will that these plants and flowers should grow—some of them when He gives water we may draw from the well, others when He gives none—what is that to me? Do Thou, O Lord, accomplish Thy will; let me never offend Thee, nor let my virtues perish; if Thou has given me any, it is out of Thy mere goodness. I wish to suffer, because Thou, O Lord, has suffered; do Thou in every way fulfil Thy will in me, and may it never be the pleasure of Thy Majesty that a gift of so high a price as that of Thy love, be given to people who serve Thee only because of the sweetness they find thereby.

20. It is much to be observed, and I say so because I know by experience, that the soul which, begins to walk in the way of mental prayer with resolution, and is determined not to care much, neither to rejoice nor to be greatly afflicted, whether sweetness and tenderness fail it, or our Lord grants them, has already travelled a great part of the road. Let that soul, then, have no fear that it is going back, though it may frequently stumble; for the building is begun on a firm foundation. It is certain that the love of God does not consist in tears, nor in this sweetness and tenderness which we for the most part desire, and with which we console ourselves; but rather in serving Him in justice, fortitude, and humility. That seems to me to be a receiving rather than a giving of anything on our part.

21. As for poor women, such as I am, weak and infirm of purpose, it seems to me to be necessary that I should be led on through consolations, as God is doing now, so that I might be able to endure certain afflictions which it has pleased His Majesty I should have. But when the servants of God, who are men of weight, learning, and sense, make so much account, as I see they do, whether God gives them sweetness in devotion or not, I am disgusted when I listen to them. I do not say that they ought not to accept it, and make much of it, when God gives it—because, when He gives it, His Majesty sees it to be necessary for them—but I do say that they ought not to grow weary when they have it not. They should then understand that they have no need of it, and be masters of themselves, when His Majesty does not give it. Let them be convinced of this, there is a fault here; I have had experience of it, and know it to be so. Let them believe it as an imperfection: they are not advancing in liberty of spirit, but shrinking like cowards from the assault.

22. It is not so much to beginners that I say this—though I do insist upon it, because it is of great importance to them that they should begin with this liberty and resolution—as to others, of whom there are many, who make a beginning, but never come to the end; and that is owing, I believe, in great measure, to their not having embraced the Cross from the first. They are distressed, thinking they are doing nothing; the understanding ceases from its acts, and they cannot bear it. Yet, perhaps, at that very time, the will is feeding and gathering strength, and they know it not.

23. We must suppose that our Lord does not regard these things; for though they seem to us to be faults, yet they are not. His Majesty knows our misery and natural vileness better than we do ourselves. He knows that these souls long to be always thinking of Him and loving Him. It is this resolution that He seeks in us; the other anxieties which we inflict upon ourselves serve to no other end but to disquiet the soul—which, if it be unable to derive any profit in one hour, will by them be disabled for four. This comes most frequently from bodily indisposition—I have had very great experience in the matter, and I know it is true; for I have carefully observed it and discussed it afterwards with spiritual persons—for we are so wretched, that this poor prisoner of a soul shares in the miseries of the body. The changes of the seasons, and the alterations of the humors, very often compel it, without fault of its own, not to do what it would, but rather to suffer in every way. Meanwhile, the more we force the soul on these occasions, the greater the mischief, and the longer it lasts. Some discretion must be used, in order to ascertain whether ill-health be the occasion or not. The poor soul must not be stifled. Let those who thus suffer understand that they are ill; a change should be made in the hour of prayer, and oftentimes that change should be continued for some days. Let souls pass out of this desert as they can, for it is very often the misery of one that loves God to see itself living in such wretchedness, unable to do what it would, because it has to keep so evil a guest as the body.

24. I spoke of discretion, because sometimes the devil will do the same work; and so it is not always right to omit prayer when the understanding is greatly distracted and disturbed, nor to torment the soul to the doing of that which is out of its power. There are other things then to be done—exterior works, as of charity and spiritual reading—though at times the soul will not be able to do them. Take care, then, of the body, for the love of God, because at many other times the body must serve the soul; and let recourse be had to some recreations—holy ones—such as conversation, or going out into the fields, as the confessor shall advise. Altogether, experience is a great matter, and it makes us understand what is convenient for us. Let God be served in all things—His yoke is sweet;[90] and it is of great importance that the soul should not be dragged, as they say, but carried gently, that it may make greater progress.

25. So, then, I come back to what I advised before[91]—and though I repeat it often, it matters not; it is of great importance that no one should distress himself on account of aridities, or because his thoughts are restless and distracted; neither should he be afflicted thereat, if he would attain to liberty of spirit, and not be always in trouble. Let him begin by not being afraid of the Cross, and he will see how our Lord will help him to carry it, how joyfully he will advance, and what profit he will derive from it all. It is now clear, if there is no water in the well, that we at least can put none into it. It is true we must not be careless about drawing it when there is any in it, because at that time it is the will of God to multiply our virtues by means thereof.

Chapter XII.

What We Can Ourselves Do. The Evil of Desiring to Attain to Supernatural States Before Our Lord Calls Us.

1. My aim in the foregoing chapter—though I digressed to many other matters, because they seemed to me very necessary—was to explain how much we may attain to of ourselves; and how, in these beginnings of devotion, we are able in some degree to help ourselves: because thinking of, and pondering on, the sufferings of our Lord for our sakes moves us to compassion, and the sorrow and tears which result therefrom are sweet. The thought of the blessedness we hope for, of the love our Lord bore us, and of His resurrection, kindle within us a joy which is neither wholly spiritual nor wholly sensual; but the joy is virtuous, and the sorrow is most meritorious.

2. Of this kind are all those things which produce a devotion acquired in part by means of the understanding, though it can neither be merited nor had, if God grants it not. It is best for a soul which God has not raised to a higher state than this not to try to rise of itself. Let this be well considered, because all the soul will gain in that way will be a loss. In this state it can make many acts of good resolutions to do much for God, and enkindle its love; other acts also, which may help the growth of virtues, according to that which is written in a book called *The Art of Serving God*,[92] a most excellent work, and profitable for those who are in this state, because the understanding is active now.

3. The soul may also place itself in the presence of Christ, and accustom itself to many acts of love directed to His sacred Humanity, and remain in His presence continually, and speak to Him, pray to Him in its necessities, and complain to Him of its troubles; be merry with Him in its joys, and yet not forget Him because of its joys. All this it may do without set prayers, but rather with words befitting its desires and its needs.

4. This is an excellent way whereby to advance, and that very quickly. He that will strive to have this precious companionship, and will make much of it, and will sincerely love our Lord, to whom we owe so much, is one, in my opinion, who has made some progress. There is therefore no reason why we should trouble ourselves because we have no sensible devotion, as I said before.[93]

---

[90] St. Matt. xi. 30: "Jugum enim meum suave est."

[91] § 18

[92] *Arte de servir a Dios*, by Rodrigue de Solis, friar of the Augustinian Order (*Bouix*). *Arte para servir a Dios*, by Fra. Alonso de Madrid (*De la Fuente*).

[93] Ch. xi. §§ 20, 25.

But let us rather give thanks to our Lord, who allows us to have a desire to please Him, though our works be poor. This practice of the presence of Christ is profitable in all states of prayer, and is a most safe way of advancing in the first state, and of attaining quickly to the second; and as for the last states, it secures us against those risks which the devil may occasion.

5. This, then, is what we can do. He who would pass out of this state, and upraise his spirit, in order to taste consolations denied him, will, in my opinion, lose both the one and the other.[94] These consolations being supernatural, and the understanding inactive, the soul is then left desolate and in great aridity. As the foundation of the whole building is humility, the nearer we draw unto God the more this virtue should grow; if it does not, everything is lost. It seems to be a kind of pride when we seek to ascend higher, seeing that God descends so low, when He allows us, being what we are, to draw near unto Him.

6. It must not be supposed that I am now speaking of raising our thoughts to the consideration of the high things of heaven and of its glory, or unto God and His great wisdom. I never did this myself, because I had not the capacity for it—as I said before;[95] and I was so worthless, that, as to thinking even of the things of earth, God gave me grace to understand this truth: that in me it was no slight boldness to do so. How much more, then, the thinking of heavenly things? Others, however, will profit in that way, particularly those who are learned; for learning, in my opinion, is a great treasury in the matter of this exercise, if it be accompanied with humility. I observed this a few days ago in some learned men who had shortly before made a beginning, and had made great progress. This is the reason why I am so very anxious that many learned men may become spiritual. I shall speak of this by and by.[96]

7. What I am saying—namely, let them not rise if God does not raise them—is the language of spirituality. He will understand me who has had any experience; and I know not how to explain it, if what I have said does not make it plain.

8. In mystical theology—of which I spoke before[97]—the understanding ceases from its acts, because God suspends it—as I shall explain by and by, if I can;[98] and God give me the grace to do so. We must neither imagine nor think that we can of ourselves bring about this suspension. That is what I say must not be done; nor must we allow the understanding to cease from its acts; for in that case we shall be stupid and cold, and the result will be neither the one nor the other. For when our Lord suspends the understanding, and makes it cease from its acts, He puts before it that which astonishes and occupies it: so that without making any reflections, it shall comprehend in a moment[99] more than we could comprehend in many years with all the efforts in the world.

9. To have the powers of the mind occupied, and to think that you can keep them at the same time quiet, is folly. I repeat it, though it be not so understood, there is no great humility in this; and, if it be blameless, it is not left unpunished—it is labor thrown away, and the soul is a little disgusted: it feels like a man about to take a leap, and is held back. Such a one seems to have used up his strength already, and finds himself unable to do that which he wished to have done: so here, in the scanty gain that remains, he who will consider the matter will trace that slight want of humility of which I have spoken;[100] for that virtue has this excellence: there is no good work attended by humility that leaves the soul disgusted. It seems to me that I have made this clear enough; yet, after all, perhaps only for myself. May our Lord open their eyes who read this, by giving them experience; and then however slight that experience may be, they will immediately understand it.

10. For many years I read much, and understood nothing; and for a long time, too, though God gave me understanding herein, I never could utter a word by which I might explain it to others. This was no little trouble to me. When His Majesty pleases, He teaches everything in a moment, so that

---

[94] That is, he will lose the prayer of acquired quiet, because he voluntarily abandons it before the time; and will not attain to the prayer of infused quiet, because he attempts to rise into it before he is called (Francis. de Sancto Thoma, *Medulla Mystica*, tr. iv. ch. xi. n. 69).

[95] Ch. iv. § 10.

[96] Ch. xxxiv. § 9.

[97] Ch. x. § 1.

[98] Ch. xvi. § 4.

[99] "En un credo."

[100] § 5.

I am lost in wonder. One thing I can truly say: though I conversed with many spiritual persons, who sought to make me understand what our Lord was giving me, in order that I might be able to speak of it, the fact is, that my dullness was so great, that I derived no advantage whatever, much or little, from their teaching.

11. Or it may be, as His Majesty has always been my Master—may He be blessed for ever! for I am ashamed of myself that I can say so with truth—that it was His good pleasure I should meet with no one to whom I should be indebted in this matter. So, without my wishing or asking it—I never was careful about this, for that would have been a virtue in me, but only about vanity—God gave me to understand with all distinctness in a moment, and also enabled me to express myself, so that my confessors were astonished but I more than they, because I knew my own dullness better. It is not long since this happened. And so that which our Lord has not taught me, I seek not to know it, unless it be a matter that touches my conscience.

12. Again I repeat my advice: it is of great moment not to raise our spirit ourselves, if our Lord does not raise it for us; and if He does, there can be no mistaking it. For women, it is specially wrong, because the devil can delude them—though I am certain our Lord will never allow him to hurt any one who labors to draw near unto God in humility. On the contrary, such a one will derive more profit and advantage out of that attack by which Satan intended to hurt him.

13. I have dwelt so long upon this matter because this way of prayer is the most common with beginners, and because the advice I have given is very important. It will be found much better given elsewhere: that I admit; and I admit, also, that in writing it I am ashamed of myself, and covered with confusion—though not so much so as I ought to be. Blessed for ever be our Lord, of whose will and pleasure it is that I am allowed, being what I am, to speak of things which are His, of such a nature, and so deep.

Chapter XIII.

Of Certain Temptations of Satan. Instructions Relating Thereto.

1. I have thought it right to speak of certain temptations I have observed to which beginners are liable—some of them I have had myself—and to give some advice about certain things which to me seem necessary. In the beginning, then, we should strive to be cheerful and unconstrained; for there are people who think it is all over with devotion if they relax themselves ever so little. It is right to be afraid of self; so that, having no confidence in ourselves, much or little, we may not place ourselves in those circumstances wherein men usually sin against God; for it is a most necessary fear, till we become very perfect in virtue. And there are not many who are so perfect as to be able to relax themselves on those occasions which offer temptations to their natural temper; for always while we live, were it only to preserve humility, it is well we should know our own miserable nature; but there are many occasions on which it is permitted us—as I said just now[101]—to take some recreation, in order that we may with more vigor resume our prayer.

2. Discretion is necessary throughout. We must have great confidence; because it is very necessary for us not to contract our desires, but put our trust in God; for, if we do violence to ourselves by little and little, we shall, though not at once, reach that height which many Saints by His grace have reached. If they had never resolved to desire, and had never by little and little acted upon that resolve, they never could have ascended to so high a state.

3. His Majesty seeks and loves courageous souls; but they must be humble in their ways, and have no confidence in themselves. I never saw one of those lag behind on the road; and never a cowardly soul, though aided by humility, make that progress in many years which the former makes in a few. I am astonished at the great things done on this road by encouraging oneself to undertake great things, though we may not have the strength for them at once; the soul takes a flight upwards and ascends high, though, like a little bird whose wings are weak, it grows weary and rests.

---

[101] Ch. xi. § 24.

4. At one time I used often to think of those words of St. Paul: "That all things are possible in God."[102] I saw clearly that of myself I could do nothing. This was of great service to me. So also was the saying of St. Augustine: "Give me, O Lord, what Thou commands, and command what Thou will."[103] I was often thinking how St. Peter lost nothing by throwing himself into the sea, though he was afterwards afraid.[104] These first resolutions are a great matter—although it is necessary in the beginning that we should be very reserved, controlled by the discretion and authority of a director; but we must take care that he be one who does not teach us to crawl like toads, nor one who may be satisfied when the soul shows itself fit only to catch lizards. Humility must always go before: so that we may know that this strength can come out of no strength of our own.

5. But it is necessary we should understand what manner of humility this should be, because Satan, I believe, does great harm; for he hinders those who begin to pray from going onwards, by suggesting to them false notions of humility. He makes them think it is pride to have large desires, to wish to imitate the Saints, and to long for martyrdom. He tells us forthwith, or he makes us think, that the actions of the Saints are to be admired, not to be imitated, by us who are sinners. I, too, say the same thing; but we must see what those actions are which we are to admire, and what those are which we are to imitate; for it would be wrong in a person who is weak and sickly to undertake much fasting and sharp penances to retire into the desert, where he could not sleep, nor find anything to eat; or, indeed, to undertake any austerities of this kind.

6. But we ought to think that we can force ourselves, by the grace of God, to hold the world in profound contempt—to make light of honor, and be detached from our possessions. Our hearts, however, are so mean that we think the earth would fail us under our feet, if we were to cease to care even for a moment for the body, and give ourselves up to spirituality. Then we think that to have all we require contributes to recollection, because anxieties disturb prayer. It is painful to me that our confidence in God is so scanty, and our self-love so strong, as that any anxiety about our own necessities should disturb us. But so it is; for when our spiritual progress is so slight, a mere nothing will give us as much trouble as great and important matters will give to others. And we think ourselves spiritual!

7. Now, to me, this way of going on seems to betray a disposition to reconcile soul and body together, in order that we may not miss our ease in this world, and yet have the fruition of God in the next; and so it will be if we walk according to justice, clinging to virtue; but it is the pace of a hen—it will never bring us to liberty of spirit. It is a course of proceeding, as it seems to me, most excellent for those who are in the married state, and who must live according to their vocation; but for the other state, I by no means wish for such a method of progress, neither can I be made to believe it to be sound; for I have tried it, and I should have remained in that way, if our Lord in His goodness had not taught me another and a shorter road.

8. Though, in the matter of desires, I always had generous ones; but I labored, as I said before,[105] to make my prayer, and, at the same time, to live at my ease. If there had been any one to rouse me to a higher flight, he might have brought me, so I think, to a state in which these desires might have had their effects; but, for our sins, so few and so rare are they whose discretion in that matter is not excessive. That, I believe, is reason enough why those who begin do not attain more quickly to great perfection; for our Lord never fails us, and it is not His fault; the fault and the wretchedness of this being all our own.

9. We may also imitate the Saints by striving after solitude and silence, and many other virtues that will not kill these wretched bodies of ours, which insist on being treated so orderly, that they may disorder the soul; and Satan, too, helps much to make them unmanageable. When he sees us a little anxious about them, he wants nothing more to convince us that our way of life must kill us, and destroy our health; even if we weep, he makes us afraid of blindness. I have passed through this, and therefore I know it; but I know of no better sight or better health that we can desire, than the loss of both in such a cause. Being myself so sickly, I was always under constraint, and good

---

102 Philipp. iv. 13; "Omnia possum in Eo."
103 *Confess.* x. ch. 29: "Da quod jubes, et jube quod vis."
104 St. Matt. xiv. 30: "Videns vero ventum validum, timuit."
105 Ch. vii. §§ 27, 31.

for nothing, till I resolved to make no account of my body nor of my health; even now I am worthless enough.

10. But when it pleased God to let me find out this device of Satan, I used to say to the latter, when he suggested to me that I was ruining my health, that my death was of no consequence; when he suggested rest, I replied that I did not want rest, but the Cross. His other suggestions I treated in the same way. I saw clearly that in most things, though I was really very sickly, it was either a temptation of Satan, or a weakness on my part. My health has been much better since I have ceased to look after my ease and comforts. It is of great importance not to let our own thoughts frighten us in the beginning, when we set ourselves to pray. Believe me in this, for I know it by experience. As a warning to others, it may be that this story of my failures may be useful.

11. There is another temptation, which is very common: when people begin to have pleasure in the rest and the fruit of prayer, they will have everybody else be very spiritual also. Now, to desire this is not wrong, but to try to bring it about may not be right, except with great discretion and with much reserve, without any appearance of teaching. He who would do any good in this matter ought to be endowed with solid virtues, that he may not put temptation in the way of others. It happened to me—that is how I know it—when, as I said before,[106] I made others apply themselves to prayer, to be a source of temptation and disorder; for, on the one hand, they heard me say great things of the blessedness of prayer, and, on the other, saw how poor I was in virtue, notwithstanding my prayer. They had good reasons on their side, and afterwards they told me of it; for they knew not how these things could be compatible one with the other. This it was that made them not to regard that as evil which was really so in itself, namely, that they saw me do it myself, now and then, during the time that they thought well of me in some measure.

12. This is Satan's work: he seems to take advantage of the virtues we may have, for the purpose of giving a sanction, so far as he can, to the evil he aims at; how slight so ever that evil may be, his gain must be great, if it prevail in a religious house. How much, then, must his gain have been, when the evil I did was so very great! And thus, during many years, only three persons were the better for what I said to them; but now that our Lord has made me stronger in virtue, in the course of two or three years many persons have profited, as I shall show hereafter.[107]

13. There is another great inconvenience in addition to this: the loss to our own soul; for the utmost we have to do in the beginning is to take care of our own soul only, and consider that in the whole world there is only God and our soul. This is a point of great importance.

14. There is another temptation—we ought to be aware of it, and be cautious in our conduct: persons are carried away by a zeal for virtue, through the pain which the sight of the sins and failings of others occasions them. Satan tells them that this pain arises only out of their desire that God may not be offended, and out of their anxiety about His honor; so they immediately seek to remedy the evil. This so disturbs them, that they cannot pray. The greatest evil of all is their thinking this an act of virtue, of perfection, and of a great zeal for God. I am not speaking of the pain which public sins occasion, if they be habitual in any community, nor of wrongs done to the Church, nor of heresies by which so many souls are visibly lost; for this pain is most wholesome, and being wholesome is no source of disquiet. The security, therefore, of that soul which would apply itself to prayer lies in casting away from itself all anxiety about persons and things, in taking care of itself, and in pleasing God. This is the most profitable course.

15. If I were to speak of the mistakes which I have seen people make, in reliance on their own good intentions, I should never come to an end. Let us labor, therefore, always to consider the virtues and the good qualities which we discern in others, and with our own great sins cover our eyes, so that we may see none of their failings. This is one way of doing our work; and though we may not be perfect in it at once, we shall acquire one great virtue—we shall look upon all men as better than ourselves; and we begin to acquire that virtue in this way, by the grace of God, which is necessary in all things—for when we have it not, all our endeavors are in vain—and by imploring Him to give us this virtue; for He never fails us, if we do what we can.

16. This advice, also, they must take into their consideration who make much use of their understanding, eliciting from one subject many thoughts and conceptions. As to those who, like

---

[106] Ch. vii. § 16.
[107] See ch. xxxi. § 7, and ch. xxxix. § 14.

myself, cannot do it, I have no advice to give, except that they are to have patience, until our Lord shall send them both matter and light; for they can do so little of themselves, that their understanding is a hindrance to them rather than a help.

17. To those, then, who can make use of their understanding, I say that they are not to spend the whole time in that way; for though it be most meritorious, yet they must not, when prayer is sweet, suppose that there never will be a Sunday or a time when no work ought to be done. They think it lost time to do otherwise; but I think that loss their greatest gain. Let them rather, as I have said,[108] place themselves in the presence of Christ, and, without fatiguing the understanding, converse with Him, and in Him rejoice, without wearying themselves in searching out reasons; but let them rather lay their necessities before Him, and the just reasons there are why He should not suffer us in His presence: at one time this, at another time that, lest the soul should be wearied by always eating of the same food. These meats are most savory and wholesome, if the palate be accustomed to them; they will furnish a great support for the life of the soul, and they have many other advantages also.

18. I will explain myself further; for the doctrine of prayer is difficult, and, without a director, very hard to understand. Though I would willingly be concise, and though a mere hint is enough for his clear intellect who has commanded me to write on the subject of prayer, yet so it is, my dullness does not allow me to say or explain in a few words that which it is so important to explain well. I, who have gone through so much, am sorry for those who begin only with books; for there is a strange difference between that which we learn by reading, and that which we learn by experience.

19. Going back, then, to what I was saying. We set ourselves to meditate upon some mystery of the Passion: let us say, our Lord at the pillar. The understanding goes about seeking for the sources out of which came the great dolors and the bitter anguish which His Majesty endured in that desolation. It considers that mystery in many lights, which the intellect, if it be skilled in its work, or furnished with learning, may there obtain. This is a method of prayer which should be to everyone the beginning, the middle, and the end: a most excellent and safe way, until our Lord shall guide them to other supernatural ways.

20. I say to all, because there are many souls who make greater progress by meditation on other subjects than on the Sacred Passion; for as there are many mansions in heaven, so there are also many roads leading thither. Some persons advance by considering themselves in hell, others in heaven—and these are distressed by meditations on hell. Others meditate on death; some persons, if tender-hearted, are greatly fatigued by continual meditations on the Passion; but are consoled and make progress when they meditate on the power and greatness of God in His creatures, and on His love visible in all things. This is an admirable method—not omitting, however, from time to time, the Passion and Life of Christ, the Source of all good that ever came, and that ever shall come.

21. He who begins is in need of instruction, whereby he may ascertain what profits him most. For this end it is very necessary he should have a director, who ought to be a person of experience; for if he be not, he will make many mistakes, and direct a soul without understanding its ways, or suffering it to understand them itself; for such a soul, knowing that obedience to a director is highly meritorious, dares not transgress the commandments it receives. I have met with souls cramped and tormented, because he who directed them had no experience: that made me sorry for them. Some of them knew not what to do with themselves; for directors who do not understand the spirit of their penitents afflict them soul and body, and hinder their progress.[109]

22. One person I had to do with had been kept by her director for eight years, as it were, in prison; he would not allow her to quit the subject of self-knowledge; and yet our Lord had already raised her to the prayer of quiet; so she had much to suffer.

23. Although this matter of self-knowledge must never be put aside—for there is no soul so great a giant on this road but has frequent need to turn back, and be again an infant at the breast; and this must never be forgotten. I shall repeat it,[110] perhaps, many times, because of its great importance—for among all the states of prayer, however high they may be, there is not one in which

---

[108] Ch. xii. § 3.
[109] See St. John of the Cross, *Living Flame*, pp. 267, 278-284, Engl. trans.
[110] See ch. xv. § 20.

it is not often necessary to go back to the beginning. The knowledge of our sins, and of our own selves, is the bread which we have to eat with all the meats, however delicate they may be, in the way of prayer; without this bread, life cannot be sustained, though it must be taken by measure. When a soul beholds itself resigned, and clearly understands that there is no goodness in it—when it feels itself abashed in the presence of so great a King, and sees how little it pays of the great debt it owes Him—why should it be necessary for it to waste its time on this subject? Why should it not rather proceed to other matters which our Lord places before it, and for neglecting which there is no reason? His Majesty surely knows better than we do what kind of food is proper for us.

24. So, then, it is of great consequence that the director should be prudent—I mean, of sound understanding—and a man of experience. If, in addition to this, he is a learned man, it is a very great matter. But if these three qualities cannot be had together, the first two are the most important, because learned men may be found with whom we can communicate when it is necessary. I mean, that for beginners learned men are of little use, if they are not men of prayer. I do not say that they are to have nothing to do with learned men, because a spirituality, the foundations of which are not resting on the truth, I would rather were not accompanied with prayer. Learning is a great thing, for it teaches us who know so little, and enlightens us; so when we have come to the knowledge of the truths contained in the holy writings, we do what we ought to do. From silly devotions, God deliver us!

25. I will explain myself further, for I am meddling, I believe, with too many matters. It has always been my failing that I could never make myself understood—as I said before[111]—but at the cost of many words. A nun begins to practice prayer; if her director be silly, and if he should take it into his head, he will make her feel that it is better for her to obey him than her own superior. He will do all this without any evil purpose, thinking that he is doing right. For if he be not a religious himself, he will think this right enough. If his penitent be a married woman, he will tell her that it is better for her to give herself unto prayer, when she ought to attend to her house, although she may thereby displease her husband. And so it is, he knows not how to make arrangements for time and business, so that everything may be done as it ought to be done; he has no light himself, and can therefore give none to others, however much he may wish to do so.

26. Though learning does not seem necessary for discretion, my opinion has always been, and will be, that every Christian should continue to be guided by a learned director if he can, and the more learned the better. They who walk in the way of prayer have the greater need of learning; and the more spiritual they are the greater is that need. Let them not say that learned men not given to prayer are not fit counsellors for those who pray: that is a delusion. I have conversed with many; and now for some years I have sought them the more, because of my greater need of them. I have always been fond of them; for though some of them have no experience, they do not dislike spirituality, neither are they ignorant of what it is, because in the sacred writings with which they are familiar they always find the truth about spirituality. I am certain myself that a person given to prayer, who treats of these matters with learned men, unless he is deceived with his own consent, will never be carried away by any illusions of the devil. I believe that the evil spirits are exceedingly afraid of learned men who are humble and virtuous, knowing that they will be found out and defeated by them.

27. I have said this because there are opinions held to the effect that learned men, if they are not spiritual, are not suited for persons given to prayer. I have just said that a spiritual director is necessary; but if he be not a learned man, he is a great hindrance. It will help us much if we consult those who are learned, provided they be virtuous; even if they be not spiritual, they will be of service to me, and God will enable them to understand what they should teach; He will even make them spiritual, in order that they may help us on. I do not say this without having had experience of it; and I have met with more than two.

28. I say, then, that a person who shall resign his soul to be wholly subject to one director will make a great mistake, if he is in religion, unless he finds a director of this kind, because of the obedience due to his own superior. His director may be deficient in the three requisites I speak of,[112] and that will be no slight cross, without voluntarily subjecting the understanding to one whose

---

[111] § 18.
[112] Prudence, experience, and learning; see § 24.

understanding is none of the best. At least, I have never been able to bring myself to do it, neither does it seem to me to be right.

29. But if he be a person living in the world, let him praise God for the power he has of choosing whom he will obey, and let him not lose so excellent a liberty; yes, rather let him be without a director till he finds him—for our Lord will give him one, if he is really humble, and has a desire to meet with the right person. I praise God greatly—we women, and those who are unlearned, ought always to render Him unceasing thanks—because there are persons who, by labors so great, have attained to the truth, of which we unlearned people are ignorant. I often wonder at learned men—particularly those who are in religion—when I think of the trouble they have had in acquiring that which they communicate to me for my good, and that without any more trouble to me than the asking for it. And yet there are people who will not take advantage of their learning: God grant it may not be so!

30. I see them undergo the poverty of the religious life, which is great, together with its penances, its meagre food, the yoke of obedience, which makes me ashamed of myself at times; and with all this, interrupted sleep, trials everywhere, everywhere the Cross. I think it would be a great evil for any one to lose so great a good by his own fault. It may be some of us, who are exempted from these burdens—who have our food put into our mouths, as they say, and live at our ease—may think, because we give ourselves a little more to prayer, that we are raised above the necessity of such great hardships. Blessed be Thou, O Lord, who has made me so incapable and so useless; but I bless Thee still more for this—that Thou quickens so many to quicken us. Our prayer must therefore be very earnest for those who give us light. What should we be without them in the midst of these violent storms which now disturb the Church? If some have fallen, the good will shine more and more.[113] May it please our Lord to hold them in His hand, and help them, that they may help us.

31. I have gone far away from the subject I began to speak of; but all is to the purpose for those who are beginners, that they may begin a journey which is so high in such a way as that they shall go on by the right road. Coming back, then, to what I spoke of before,[114] the meditation on Christ bound to the pillar, it is well we should make reflections for a time, and consider the sufferings He there endured, for whom He endured them, who He is who endured them, and the love with which He bore them. But a person should not always fatigue himself in making these reflections, but rather let him remain there with Christ, in the silence of the understanding.

32. If he is able, let him employ himself in looking upon Christ, who is looking upon him; let him accompany Him, and make his petitions to Him; let him humble himself, and delight himself in Christ, and keep in mind that he never deserved to be there. When he shall be able to do this, though it may be in the beginning of his prayer, he will find great advantage; and this way of prayer brings great advantages with it—at least, so my soul has found it. I do not know whether I am describing it aright; you, my father, will see to it. May our Lord grant me to please Him rightly for ever! Amen.

Chapter XIV.

The Second State of Prayer. Its Supernatural Character.

1. Having spoken of the toilsome efforts and of the strength required for watering the garden when we have to draw the water out of the well, let us now speak of the second manner of drawing the water, which the Lord of the vineyard has ordained; of the machine of wheel and buckets whereby the gardener may draw more water with less labor, and be able to take some rest without being continually at work. This, then, is what I am now going to describe; and I apply it to the prayer called the prayer of quiet.

2. Herein the soul begins to be recollected; it is now touching on the supernatural—for it never could by any efforts of its own attain to this. True, it seems at times to have been wearied at the

---

[113] Dan. xii. 3: "Qui autem docti fuerint, fulgebunt quasi splendor firmamenti."
[114] § 19.

wheel, laboring with the understanding, and filling the buckets; but in this second degree the water is higher, and accordingly the labor is much less than it was when the water had to be drawn up out of the well; I mean, that the water is nearer to it, for grace reveals itself more distinctly to the soul.

3. This is a gathering together of the faculties of the soul within itself, in order that it may have the fruition of that contentment in greater sweetness; but the faculties are not lost, neither are they asleep: the will alone is occupied in such a way that, without knowing how it has become a captive, it gives a simple consent to become the prisoner of God; for it knows well what is to be the captive of Him it loves. O my Jesus and my Lord, how pressing now is Thy love![115] It binds our love in bonds so straightly, that it is not in its power at this moment to love anything else but Thee.

4. The other two faculties help the will, that it may render itself capable of the fruition of so great a good; nevertheless, it occasionally happens, even when the will is in union, that they hinder it very much: but then it should never heed them at all, simply abiding in its fruition and quiet.[116] For if it tried to make them recollected, it would miss its way together with them, because they are at this time like doves which are not satisfied with the food the master of the dovecot gives them without any laboring for it on their part, and which go forth in quest of it elsewhere, and so hardly find it that they come back. And so the memory and the understanding come and go, seeking whether the will is going to give them that into the fruition of which it has entered itself.

5. If it be our Lord's pleasure to throw them any food, they stop; if not, they go again to seek it. They must be thinking that they are of some service to the will; and now and then the memory or the imagination, seeking to represent to it that of which it has the fruition, does it harm. The will, therefore, should be careful to deal with them as I shall explain. Everything that takes place now in this state brings the very greatest consolation; and the labor is so slight, that prayer, even if persevered in for some time, is never wearisome. The reason is, that the understanding is now working very gently, and is drawing very much more water than it drew out of the well. The tears, which God now sends, flow with joy; though we feel them, they are not the result of any efforts of our own.

6. This water of grand blessings and graces, which our Lord now supplies, makes the virtues thrive much more, beyond all comparison, than they did in the previous state of prayer; for the soul is already ascending out of its wretched state, and some little knowledge of the blissfulness of glory is communicated to it. This, I believe, is it that makes the virtues grow the more, and also to draw nearer to essential virtue, God Himself, from Whom all virtues proceed; for His Majesty has begun to communicate Himself to this soul, and will have it feel how He is communicating Himself.

7. As soon as the soul has arrived thus far, it begins to lose the desire of earthly things, and no wonder; for it sees clearly that, even for a moment, this joy is not to be had on earth; that there are no riches, no dominion, no honors, no delights, that can for one instant, even for the twinkling of an eye, minister such a joy; for it is a true satisfaction, and the soul sees that it really does satisfy. Now, we who are on earth, as it seems to me, scarcely ever understand wherein our satisfaction lies, for it is always liable to disappointment; but in this, at that time, there is none: the disappointment comes afterwards, when the soul sees that all is over, and that it has no power to recover it, neither does it know how; for if it cut itself in pieces by penance and prayer, and every other kind of austerities, all would be of little use, if our Lord did not grant it. God, in His great mercy, will have the soul comprehend that His Majesty is so near to it, that it need not send messengers to Him, but may speak to Him itself, and not with a loud crying, because so near is He already, that He understands even the movements of its lips.

8. It seems absurd to say this, seeing that we know that God understands us always, and is present with us. It is so, and there can be no doubt of it; but our Emperor and Lord will have us now understand that He understands us; and also have us understand what His presence brings about, and that He means in a special way to begin a work in the soul, which is manifested in the great joy, inward and outward, which He communicates, and in the difference there is, as I said just now, between this joy and delight and all the joys of earth; for He seems to be filling up the void in our souls occasioned by our sins.

---

[115] 2 Cor. v. 14: "Charitas enim Christi urget nos."
[116] See ch. xvii. § 12; *Way of Perfection*, ch. liii., but xxxi. of the old editions.

9. This satisfaction lies in the innermost part of the soul, and the soul knows not whence, nor how, it came, very often it knows not what to do, or wish, or pray for. It seems to find all this at once, and knows not what it hath found; nor do I know how to explain it, because learning is necessary for many things. Here, indeed, learning would be very much to the purpose, in order to explain the general and particular helps of grace; for there are many who know nothing about them. Learning would serve to show how our Lord now will have the soul to see, as it were, with the naked eye, as men speak, this particular help of grace, and be also useful in many other ways wherein I am likely to go astray. But as what I write is to be seen by those who have the learning to discover whether I make mistakes or not, I go on without anxiety; for I know I need have none whatever about either the letter or the spirit, because it is in their power to whom it is to be sent to do with it as they will: they will understand it, and blot out whatever may be amiss.

10. I should like them to explain this, because it is a principal point, and because a soul, when our Lord begins to bestow these graces upon it, does not understand them, and does not know what to do with itself; for if God leads it by the way of fear, as He led me, its trial will be heavy, if there be no one who understands the state it is in; and to see itself as in a picture is a great comfort; and then it sees clearly that it is travelling on that road. The knowledge of what it has to do is a great blessing for it, so that it may advance forwards in every one of these degrees of prayer; for I have suffered greatly, and lost much time, because I did not know what to do; and I am very sorry for those souls who find themselves alone when they come to this state; for though I read many spiritual books, wherein this very matter is discussed, they threw very little light upon it. And if it be not a soul much exercised in prayer, it will find it enough to understand its state, be the books ever so clear.

11. I wish much that our Lord would help me to describe the effects on the soul of these things, now that they begin to be supernatural, so that men might know by these effects whether they come from the Spirit of God. I mean, known as things are known here below—though it is always well to live in fear, and on our guard; for even if they do come from God, now and then the devil will be able to transform himself into an angel of light;[117] and the soul, if not experienced herein, will not understand the matter; and it must have so much experience for the understanding thereof, that it is necessary it should have attained to the highest perfection of prayer.

12. The little time I have helps me but little, and it is therefore necessary His Majesty should undertake it Himself; for I have to live in community, and have very many things to employ me, as I am in a house which is newly founded—as will appear hereafter;[118] and so I am writing, with very many interruptions, by little and little at a time. I wish I had leisure; for when our Lord gives the spirit, it is more easily and better done; it is then as with a person working embroidery with the pattern before her; but if the spirit be wanting, there is no more meaning in the words than in gibberish, so to speak, though many years may have been spent in prayer. And thus I think it a very great advantage to be in this state of prayer when I am writing this; for I see clearly that it is not I who speak, nor is it I who with her understanding has arranged it; and afterwards I do not know how I came to speak so accurately.[119] It has often happened to me thus.

13. Let us now return to our orchard, or flower-garden, and behold now how the trees begin to fill with sap for the bringing forth of the blossoms, and then of the fruit—the flowers and the plants, also, their fragrance. This illustration pleases me; for very often, when I was beginning—and our

---

117 2 Cor. xi. 14: "Ipse enim Satanas transfigurat se in angelum lucis."

118 See ch. x. § 11. As that passage refers probably to the monastery of the Incarnation, this must refer to that of St. Joseph, newly founded in Avila; for that of the Incarnation was founded a short time before the Saint was born; and she could hardly say of it, now that she was at least in her forty-seventh year, that it was newly founded. The house, however, was poor; for she says, ch. xxxii. § 12, that the nuns occasionally quitted the monastery for a time, because of its poverty.

119 See ch. xviii. § 10. In the second Report of the Rota, p. 477—quoted by Benedict XIV., *De Canoniz*. iii. 26, n. 12, and by the Bollandists in the *Acta*, 1315—we have these words, and they throw great light on the text: "Sunt et alli testes de visu affirmantes quod quando beata Teresa scribebat libros, facies ejus resplendebat." In the information taken in Granada, the Mother Anne of the Incarnation says she saw the Saint one night, while writing the *Fortress of the Soul*, with her face shining; and Mary of St. Francis deposes to the same effect in the informations taken in Medina (*De la Fuente*, vol. ii. pp. 389, 392).

Lord grant that I have really begun to serve His Majesty—I mean, begun in relation to what I have to say of my life,—it was to me a great joy to consider my soul as a garden, and our Lord as walking in it. I used to beseech Him to increase the fragrance of the little flowers of virtues—which were beginning, as it seemed to bud—and preserve them, that they might be to His glory; for I desired nothing for myself. I prayed Him to cut those He liked, because I already knew that they would grow the better.

14. I say cut; for there are times in which the soul has no recollection of this garden—everything seems parched, and there is no water to be had for preserving it—and in which it seems as if the soul had never possessed any virtue at all. This is the season of heavy trials; for our Lord will have the poor gardener suppose all the trouble he took in maintaining and watering the garden to have been taken to no purpose. Then is the time really for weeding and rooting out every plant, however small it may be, that is worthless, in the knowledge that no efforts of ours are sufficient, if God withholds from us the waters of His grace; and in despising ourselves as being nothing, and even less than nothing. In this way we gain great humility—the flowers grow afresh.

15. O my Lord and my Good! I cannot utter these words without tears, and rejoicing in my soul; for Thou will be thus with us, and art with us, in the Sacrament. We may believe so most truly; for so it is, and the comparison I make is a great truth; and, if our sins stand not in the way, we may rejoice in Thee, because Thou rejoices in us; for Thou has told us that Thy delight is to be with the children of men.[120] O my Lord, what does it mean? Whenever I hear these words, they always give me great consolation, and did so even when I was most wicked.

16. Is it possible, O Lord, that there can be a soul which, after attaining to this state wherein Thou bestows upon it the like graces and consolations, and wherein it understands that Thou delights to be with it, can yet fall back and offend Thee after so many favors, and such great demonstrations of the love Thou bares it, and of which there cannot be any doubt, because the effect of it is so visible? Such a soul there certainly is; for I have done so, not once, but often. May it please Thy goodness, O Lord, that I may be alone in my ingratitude—the only one who has committed so great an iniquity, and whose ingratitude has been so immeasurable! But even out of my ingratitude Thine infinite goodness has brought forth some good; and the greater my wickedness, the greater the splendor of the great mercy of Thy compassions. Oh, what reasons have I to magnify them for ever!

17. May it be so, I beseech Thee, O my God, and may I sing of them for ever, now that Thou has been pleased to show mercies so great unto me that they who see them are astonished, mercies which draw me out of myself continually, that I may praise Thee more and more! for, remaining in myself, without Thee, I could do nothing, O my Lord, but be as the withered flowers of the garden; so that this miserable earth of mine becomes a heap of refuse, as it was before. Let it not be so, O Lord!—let not a soul which Thou has purchased with so many labors be lost, one which Thou has so often ransomed anew, and delivered from between the teeth of the hideous dragon!

18. You, my father, must forgive me for wandering from the subject; and, as I am speaking to the purpose I have in view, you must not be surprised. What I write is what my soul has understood; and it is very often hard enough to abstain from the praises of God when, in the course of writing, the great debt I owe Him presents itself before me. Nor do I think that it can be disagreeable to you; because both of us, I believe, may sing the same song, though in a different way; for my debt is much the greater, seeing that God has forgiven me more, as you, my father, know.

Chapter XV.

Instructions for Those Who Have Attained to the Prayer of Quiet. Many Advance So Far, But Few Go Farther.

1. Let us now go back to the subject. This quiet and recollection of the soul makes itself in great measure felt in the satisfaction and peace, attended with very great joy and repose of the

---

[120] Prov. viii. 31: "Deliciæ meæ esse cum filiis hominum."

faculties, and most sweet delight, wherein the soul is established.[121] It thinks, because it has not gone beyond it, that there is nothing further to wish for, but that its abode might be there, and it would willingly say so with St. Peter.[122] It dares not move nor stir, because it thinks that this blessing it has received must then escape out of its hands; now and then, it could wish it did not even breathe.[123] The poor little soul is not aware that, as of itself it could do nothing to draw down this blessing on itself, it is still less able to retain it a moment longer than our Lord wills it should remain.

2. I have already said that, in the prior recollection and quiet,[124] there is no failure of the powers of the soul; but the soul is so satisfied in God that, although two of its powers be distracted, yet, while the recollection lasts, as the will abides in union with God, so its peace and quiet are not disturbed; on the contrary, the will by degrees brings the understanding and the memory back again; for though the will is not yet altogether absorbed, it continues still occupied without knowing how, so that, notwithstanding all the efforts of the memory and the understanding, they cannot rob it of its delight and joy[125]—yes, rather, it helps without any labor at all to keep this little spark of the love of God from being quenched.

3. Oh, that His Majesty would be gracious unto me, and enable me to give a clear account of the matter; for many are the souls who attain to this state, and few are they who go farther: and I know not who is in fault; most certainly it is not God; for when His Majesty shows mercy unto a soul, so that it advances so far, I believe that He will not fail to be more merciful still, if there be no shortcomings on our part.

4. And it is of great importance for the soul that has advanced so far as this to understand the great dignity of its state, the great grace given it by our Lord, and how in all reason it should not belong to earth; because He, of His goodness, seems to make it here a denizen of heaven, unless it be itself in fault. And miserable will that soul be if it turns back; it will go down, I think so, even to the abyss, as I was going myself, if the mercy of our Lord had not brought me back; because, for the most part, it must be the effect of grave faults—that is my opinion: nor is it possible to forsake so great a good otherwise than through the blindness occasioned by much evil.

5. Therefore, for the love of our Lord, I implore those souls to whom His Majesty has given so great a grace—the attainment of this state—to know and make much of themselves, with a humble and holy presumption, in order that they may never return to the flesh-pots of Egypt. And if through weakness and wickedness, and a mean and wretched nature, they should fall, as I did, let them always keep in mind the good they have lost; let them suspect and fear—they have reason to do so—that, if they do not resume their prayer, they may go on from bad to worse. I call that a real fall which makes us hate the way by which so great a good was obtained. I address myself to those souls; but I am not saying that they will never offend God, nor fall into sin,—though there are good reasons why those who have received these graces should keep themselves carefully from sin; but we are miserable creatures. What I earnestly advise is this: let there be no giving up of prayer; it is by prayer they will understand what they are doing, and obtain from our Lord the grace to repent, and strength to rise again; they must believe and believe again that, if they cease from praying, they run—so I think—into danger. I know not if I understand what I am saying; for, as I said before, I measure others by myself.[126]

6. The prayer of quiet, then, is a little spark of the true love of Himself, which our Lord begins to enkindle in the soul; and His will is, that the soul should understand what this love is by the joy it brings. This quiet and recollection and little spark, if it is the work of the Spirit of God, and not a sweetness supplied by Satan, or brought about by ourselves, produces great results. A person of experience, however, cannot possibly fail to understand at once that it is not a thing that can be acquired, were it not that our nature is so greedy of sweetness, that it seeks for it in every way. But it becomes cold very soon; for, however much we try to make the fire burn, in order to obtain this sweetness, it does not appear that we do anything else but throw water on it, to put it out. This spark,

---

[121] See *Way of Perfection*, ch. liii., but ch. xxxii of the old edition.

[122] St. Matt. xvii. 4: "Bonum est nos hic esse."

[123] See ch. xvii. § 6.

[124] Ch. x. § 1.

[125] Ch. xiv. §§ 3, 4.

[126] Ch. x. § 9.

then, given of God, however slight it may be, causes a great crackling; and if men do not quench it by their faults, it is the beginning of the great fire, which sends forth—I shall speak of it in the proper place[127]—the flames of that most vehement love of God which His Majesty will have perfect souls to possess.

7. This little spark is a sign or pledge which God gives to a soul, in token of His having chosen it for great things, if it will prepare to receive them. It is a great gift, much too great for me to be able to speak of it. It is a great sorrow to me; because, as I said before,[128] I know that many souls come thus far, and that those who go farther, as they ought to go, are so few, that I am ashamed to say it. I do not mean that they are absolutely few: there must be many, because God is patient with us, for some reasons; I speak of what I have seen.

8. I should like much to recommend these souls to take care that they do not hide their talent; for it may be that God has chosen them to be the edification of many others, especially in these days, when the friends of God should be strong, in order that they may support the weak. Those who discern in themselves this grace, must look upon themselves as such friends, if they would fulfil the law which even the honorable friendship of the world respects; if not, as I said just now,[129] let them fear and tremble, lest they should be doing mischief to themselves—and God grant it be to themselves only!

9. What the soul has to do at those seasons wherein it is raised to the prayer of quiet is nothing more than to be gentle and without noise. By noise, I mean going about with the understanding in search of words and reflections whereby to give God thanks for this grace, and heaping up its sins and imperfections together to show that it does not deserve it. All this commotion takes place now, and the understanding comes forward, and the memory is restless, and certainly to me these powers bring much weariness at times; for, though my memory is not strong, I cannot control it. Let the will quietly and wisely understand that it is not by dint of labor on our part that we can converse to any good purpose with God, and that our own efforts are only great logs of wood, laid on without discretion to quench this little spark; and let it confess this, and in humility say, O Lord, what can I do here? what has the servant to do with her Lord, and earth with heaven? or words of love that suggest themselves now, firmly grounded in the conviction that what it says is truth; and let it make no account of the understanding, which is simply tiresome.

10. And if the will wishes to communicate to the understanding any portion of that the fruition of which itself has entered on, or if it labors to make the understanding recollected, it shall not succeed; for it will often happen that the will is in union and at rest, while the understanding is in extreme disorder. It is better for it to leave it alone, and not to run after it—I am speaking of the will; for the will should abide in the fruition of that grace, recollected itself, like the prudent bee; for if no bees entered the hive, and each of them wandered abroad in search of the rest, the honey would hardly be made. In the same way, the soul will lose much if it be not careful now, especially if the understanding be acute; for when it begins to make reflections and search for reasons, it will think at once that it is doing something if its reasons and reflections are good.

11. The only reason that ought to be admitted now is to understand clearly that there is no reason whatever, except His mere goodness, why God should grant us so great a grace, and to be aware that we are so near Him, and to pray to His Majesty for mercies, to make intercession for the Church, for those who had been recommended to us, and for the souls in purgatory,—not, however, with noise of words, but with a heartfelt desire to be heard. This is a prayer that contains much, and by it more is obtained than by many reflections of the understanding. Let the will stir up some of those reasons, which proceed from reason itself, to quicken its love, such as the fact of its being in a better state, and let it make certain acts of love, as what it will do for Him to whom it owes so much,—and that, as I said just now, without any noise of the understanding, in the search after profound reflections. A little straw,—and it will be less than straw, if we bring it ourselves,—laid on with humility, will be more effectual here, and will help to kindle a fire more than many fagots of most learned reasons, which, in my opinion, will put it out in a moment.

---

[127] Ch. xviii. § 4, and ch. xxi. § 9.

[128] § 3.

[129] § 5.

12. This is good for those learned men who have commanded me to write,[130] and who all, by the goodness of God, have come to this state; for it may be that they spend the time in making applications of passages of the Scriptures. And though learning could not fail to be of great use to them, both before and after prayer, still, in the very time of prayer itself, there is little necessity for it, in my opinion, unless it be for the purpose of making the will tepid; for the understanding then, because of its nearness to the light, is itself illuminated; so that even I, who am what I am, seem to be a different person. And so it is; for it has happened to me, who scarcely understand a word of what I read in Latin, and especially in the Psalms, when in the prayer of quiet, not only to understand the Latin as if it were Spanish, but, still more, to take a delight in dwelling on the meaning of that I knew through the Spanish. We must make an exception: if these learned men have to preach or to teach, they will do well to take advantage of their learning, that they may help poor people of little learning, of whom I am one. Charity is a great thing; and so always is ministering unto souls, when done simply for God.

13. So, then, when the soul is in the prayer of quiet, let it repose in its rest—let learning be put on one side. The time will come when they may make use of it in the service of our Lord—when they that possess it will appreciate it so highly as to be glad that they had not neglected it even for all the treasures of the world, simply because it enables them to serve His Majesty; for it is a great help. But in the eyes of Infinite Wisdom, believe me, a little striving after humility, and a single act thereof, are worth more than all the science in the world. This is not the time for discussing, but for understanding plainly what we are, and presenting ourselves in simplicity before God, who will have the soul make itself as a fool—as, indeed, it is—in His presence, seeing that His Majesty so humbles Himself as to suffer it to be near Him, we being what we are.

14. Moreover, the understanding bestirs itself to make its thanksgiving in phrases well arranged; but the will, in peace, not daring to lift up its eyes with the publican,[131] makes perhaps a better act of thanksgiving than the understanding, with all the tropes of its rhetoric. In a word, mental prayer is not to be abandoned altogether now, nor even vocal prayer, if at any time we wish, or can, to make use of either of them; for if the state of quiet be profound, it becomes difficult to speak, and it can be done only with great pain.

15. I believe myself that we know whether this proceeds from the Spirit of God, or is brought about by endeavors of our own, in the commencement of devotion which God gives; and we seek of ourselves, as I said before,[132] to pass onwards to this quiet of the will. Then, no effect whatever is produced; it is quickly over, and aridity is the result. If it comes from Satan, the practiced soul, in my opinion, will detect it, because it leaves trouble behind, and scant humility and poor dispositions for those effects which are wrought if it comes from God; it leaves neither light in the understanding nor steadiness in the truth.[133]

16. Here Satan can do little or no harm, if the soul directs unto God the joy and sweetness it then feels; and if it fixes the thoughts and desires on Him, according to the advice already given, the devil can gain nothing whatever—on the contrary, by the permission of God, he will lose much by that very joy which he causes in the soul, because that joy will help the soul, inasmuch as it thinks the joy comes from God, to betake itself often to prayer in its desire for it. And if the soul is humble, indifferent to, and detached from, all joy, however spiritual, and if it loves the cross, it will make no account of the sweetness which Satan sends. But it cannot so deal with that which comes from the Spirit of God; of that it will make much. Now, when Satan sends it, as he is nothing but a lie, and when he sees that the soul humbles itself through that joy and sweetness—and here, in all things relating to prayer and sweetness, we must be very careful to endeavor to make ourselves humble,—Satan will not often repeat his work, when he sees that he loses by it.

---

[130] Ch. x. § 1.

[131] St. Luke xviii. 13: "Nolebat nec oculos ad coelum levare."

[132] Ch. xii. § 5.

[133] "Firmeza en la verdad." Francisco de St. Thoma, in his *Medulla Mystica*, p. 204, quoting this passage, has, "firmeza en la voluntad." Philip a SS. Trinitate, *Theolog. Mystic.* p. 354, and his Abbreviator, Anton. a Sp. Sancto, *Direct. Mystic.* tr. iv. disp. i. § 11, n. 94, seem also to have preferred "voluntad" to "verdad;" for the words they use are, "nec intellectui lux nec voluntati firmitas;" and, "defectus lucis in intellectu, et firmitatis in voluntate."

17. For this and for many other reasons, when I was speaking of the first degree of prayer, and of the first method of drawing the water,[134] I insisted upon it that the great affair of souls is, when they begin to pray, to begin also to detach themselves from every kind of joy, and to enter on it resolved only on helping to carry the cross of Christ like good soldiers, willing to serve their King without present pay, because they are sure of it at last, having their eyes directed to the true and everlasting kingdom at the conquest of which we are aiming.

18. It is a very great matter to have this always before our eyes, especially in the beginning; afterwards, it becomes so clear, that it is rather a matter of necessity to forget it, in order to live on. Now, laboring to keep in mind that all things here below are of short duration, that they are all nothing, that the rest we have here is to be accounted as none,—all this, I say, seems to be exceedingly low; and so, indeed, it is,—because those who have gone on to greater perfection would look upon it as a reproach, and be ashamed of themselves, if they thought that they were giving up the goods of this world because they are perishable, or that they would not be glad to give them up for God—even if they were to last for ever. The greater the perfection of these persons, the greater their joy, and the greater also would that joy be if the duration of these worldly goods were greater.

19. In these persons, thus far advanced, love is already grown, and love is that which does this work. But as to beginners, to them it is of the utmost importance, and they must not regard this consideration as unbecoming, for the blessings to be gained are great,—and that is why I recommend it so much to them; for they will have need of it—even those who have attained to great heights of prayer—at certain times, when God will try them, and when His Majesty seems to have forsaken them.

20. I have said as much already, and I would not have it forgotten,[135] in this our life on earth, the growth of the soul is not like that of the body. We, however, so speak of it—and, in truth, it does grow. A youth that is grown up, whose body is formed, and who is become a man, does not ungrow, nor does his body lessen in size; but as to the soul, it so is by our Lord's will, so far as I have seen it in my own experience,—but I know nothing of it in any other way. It must be in order to humble us for our greater good, and to keep us from being careless during our exile; seeing that he who has ascended the higher has the more reason to be afraid, and to be less confident in himself. A time may come when they whose will is so wrapped up in the will of God—and who, rather than fall into a single imperfection, would undergo torture and suffer a thousand deaths—will find it necessary, if they would be delivered from offending God, and from the commission of sin, to make use of the first armor of prayer, to call to mind how everything is coming to an end, that there is a heaven and a hell, and to make use of other reflections of that nature, when they find themselves assailed by temptations and persecutions.

21. Let us go back to what I was saying. The great source of our deliverance from the cunning devices and the sweetness which Satan sends is to begin with a resolution to walk in the way of the Cross from the very first, and not to desire any sweetness at all, seeing that our Lord Himself has pointed out to us the way of perfection, saying, "Take up thy cross and follow Me."[136] He is our example; and whosoever follows His counsels only to please Him has nothing to fear. In the improvement which they detect in themselves, they who do so will see that this is no work of Satan and if they fall, they have a sign of the presence of our Lord in their rising again at once. They have other signs, also, of which I am going to speak.

22. When it is the work of the Spirit of God, there is no necessity for going about searching for reasons, on the strength of which we may elicit acts of humility and of shame, because our Lord Himself supplies them in a way very different from that by which we could acquire them by our own poor reflections, which are as nothing in comparison with that real humility arising out of the light which our Lord here gives us, and which begets a confusion of face that undoes us. The knowledge with which God supplies us, in order that we may know that of ourselves we have no good in us, is perfectly apprehended—and the more perfectly, the greater the graces. It fills us with a great desire of advancing in prayer, and of never giving it up, whatever troubles may arise. The

---

[134] Ch. xi. § 16.

[135] Ch. xiii. § 23.

[136] St. Matt. xvi. 24: "Tollat crucem suam et sequatur Me."

soul offers to suffer everything. A certain security, joined with humility and fear concerning our salvation, casts out servile fear at once from the soul, and in its place plants a loyal fear[137] of more perfect growth.[138] There is a visible beginning of a love of God, utterly divested of all self-interest, together with a longing after seasons of solitude, in order to obtain a greater fruition of this good.

23. In short, not to weary myself, it is the beginning of all good; the flowers have so thriven, that they are on the point of budding. And this the soul sees most clearly, and it is impossible to persuade it now that God was not with it, till it turns back upon itself, and beholds its own failings and imperfections. Then it fears for everything; and it is well it should do so—though there are souls whom the certain conviction that God is with them benefits more than all the fear they may ever have. If a soul love greatly, and is thankful naturally, the remembrance of the mercies of God makes it turn to Him more effectually than all the chastisements of hell it can ever picture to itself— at least, it was so with me, though I am so wicked.

24. As I shall speak at greater length of the signs of a good spirit[139]—it has cost me much labor to be clear about them—I do not treat of them here. I believe, too, that, with the help of God, I shall be able to speak somewhat to the point, because—setting aside the experience I have had, and by which I learned much—I have had the help of some most learned men and persons of great holiness, whom we may reasonably believe in the matter. Souls, therefore, are not to weary themselves so much as I did, when, by the goodness of our Lord, they may have come to this state.

Chapter XVI.
The Third State of Prayer. Deep Matters. What the Soul Can Do That Has Reached It. Effects of the Great Graces of Our Lord.

1. Let us now speak of the third water wherewith this garden is watered,—water running from a river or from a brook,—whereby the garden is watered with very much less trouble, although there is some in directing the water.[140] In this state our Lord will help the gardener, and in such a way as to be, as it were, the Gardener Himself, doing all the work. It is a sleep of the powers of the soul, which are not wholly lost, nor yet understanding how they are at work. The pleasure, sweetness, and delight are incomparably greater than in the former state of prayer; and the reason is, that the waters of grace have risen up to the neck of the soul, so that it can neither advance nor retreat—nor does it know how to do so; it seeks only the fruition of exceeding bliss. It is like a dying man with the candle in his hand, on the point of dying the death desired. It is rejoicing in this agony with unutterable joy; to me it seems to be nothing else but a death, as it were, to all the things of this world, and a fruition of God. I know of no other words whereby to describe it or to explain it; neither does the soul then know what to do,—for it knows not whether to speak or be silent, whether it should laugh or weep. It is a glorious folly, a heavenly madness, wherein true wisdom is acquired; and to the soul a kind of fruition most full of delight.[141]

2. It is now some five or six years, I believe, since our Lord raised me to this state of prayer, in its fulness, and that more than once,—and I never understood it, and never could explain it; and so I was resolved, when I should come thus far in my story, to say very little or nothing at all. I knew well enough that it was not altogether the union of all the faculties, and yet most certainly it was higher than the previous state of prayer; but I confess that I could not determine and understand the difference.

---

[137] "Fiel temor." In the previous editions it was *filial*.

[138] Ch. xi. § 1.

[139] See ch. xxv.

[140] "The third degree, or third water, of the Saint, must begin, I think, with the prayer of infused recollection, include that of infused quiet, and end in that of inebriation; because it is not in our power to draw this water—all we can do is to direct the stream." (Francis. de St. Thoma, *Medulla Mystica*, tr. iv. ch. xii. p. 208).

[141] See St. John of the Cross, *Spirit. Canticle*, stanza xvii. vol. ii. p. 98, Engl. trans.

3. The humility of your reverence, willing to be helped by a simplicity so great as mine, has been the cause, I believe, why our Lord, to-day, after Communion, admitted me to this state of prayer, without the power of going further, and suggested to me these comparisons, and taught me how to speak of it, and of what the soul must do therein. Certainly, I was amazed, and in a moment understood it all. I have often been thus, as it were, beside myself, drunk with love, and yet never could understand how it was. I knew well that it was the work of God, but I never was able to understand the manner of His working here; for, in fact, the faculties are almost all completely in union, yet not so absorbed that they do not act. I have been singularly delighted in that I have been able to comprehend the matter at last. Blessed be our Lord, who has thus consoled me!

4. The faculties of the soul now retain only the power of occupying themselves wholly with God; not one of them ventures to stir, neither can we move one of them without making great efforts to distract ourselves—and, indeed, I do not think we can do it at all at this time. Many words are then uttered in praise of God—but disorderly, unless it be that our Lord orders them himself. At least, the understanding is utterly powerless here; the soul longs to send forth words of praise, but it has no control over itself,—it is in a state of sweet restlessness. The flowers are already opening; they are beginning to send forth their fragrance.

5. The soul in this state would have all men behold and know of its bliss, to the praise of God, and help it to praise Him. It would have them to be partakers of its joy; for its joy is greater than it can bear. It seems to me that it is like the woman in the Gospel, who would, or used to, call in her neighbors.[142] The admirable spirit of David, the royal prophet, must have felt in the same way, so it seems to me, when he played on the harp, singing the praises of God. I have a very great devotion to this glorious king;[143] and I wish all had it, particularly those who are sinners like myself.

6. O my God, what must that soul be when it is in this state? It wishes it were all tongue, in order that it may praise our Lord. It utters a thousand holy follies, striving continually to please Him by whom it is thus possessed. I know one[144] who, though she was no poet, yet composed, without any preparation, certain stanzas, full of feeling, most expressive of her pain: they were not the work of her own understanding; but, in order to have a greater fruition of that bliss which so sweet a pain occasioned her, she complained of it in that way to God. She was willing to be cut in pieces, soul and body, to show the delight she felt in that pain. To what torments could she be then exposed, that would not be delicious to endure for her Lord? She sees clearly that the martyrs did little or nothing, so far as they were concerned, when they endured their tortures, because the soul is well aware that its strength is derived from another source.

7. But what will be its sufferings when it returns to the use of the senses, to live in the world, and go back to the anxieties and the fashions thereof? I do not think that I have exaggerated in any way, but rather have fallen short, in speaking of that joy, which our Lord, of His good pleasure, gives to the soul in this its exile. Blessed for ever be Thou, O Lord! and may all created things praise Thee for ever!

8. O my King, seeing that I am now, while writing this, still under the power of this heavenly madness, an effect of Thy mercy and goodness,—and it is a mercy I never deserved,—grant, I beseech Thee, that all those with whom I may have to converse may become mad through Thy love, or let me converse with none, or so order it that I may have nothing to do in the world, or take me away from it. This Thy servant, O my God, is no longer able to endure sufferings so great as those are which she must bear when she sees herself without Thee if she must live, she seeks no repose in this life,—and do Thou give her none. This my soul longs to be free—eating is killing it, and sleep is wearisome; it sees itself wasting the time of this life in comforts, and that there is no comfort for it now but in Thee; it seems to be living contrary to nature—for now, it desires to live not in itself, but in Thee.

9. O my true Lord and my happiness! what a cross has Thou prepared for those who attain to this state!—light and most heavy at the same time: light, because sweet; heavy, because now and then there is no patience left to endure it—and yet the soul never wishes to be delivered from it, unless it be that it may come to Thee. When the soul remembers that it has never served Thee at all,

142 St. Luke xv. 9: "Convocat amicas et vicinas."
143 *Foundations*, ch. xxix. § 9.
144 The Saint herself (*De la Fuente*).

and that by living on it may do Thee some service, it longs for a still heavier cross, and never to die before the end of the world. Its own repose it counts as nothing in comparison with doing a slight service to Thee. It knows not what to desire; but it clearly understands that it desires nothing else but Thee.

10. O my son,[145] so humble is he to whom this writing is directed, and who has commanded me to write, that he suffers himself to be thus addressed,—you, my father, only must see these things, in which I seem to have transgressed all bounds; for no reason can keep me reasonable when our Lord draws me out of myself. Since my communion this morning,[146] I do not believe that I am the person who is speaking; I seem to be dreaming the things I see, and I wish I might never see any but people ill, as I am now. I beseech you, my father, let us all be mad, for the love of Him who for our sakes suffered men to say of Him that He was mad.[147]

11. You, my father, say that you wish me well. I wish you would prove it by disposing yourself so that God may bestow this grace upon you; for I see very few people who have not too much sense for everything they have to do: and it may be that I have more than anybody else. Your reverence must not allow it; you are my father, for you are my confessor, and the person to whom I have trusted my soul; disperse my delusions by telling the truth; for truths of this sort are very rarely told.

12. I wish we five, who now love one another in our Lord, had made some such arrangement as this: as others in these times have met together in secret[148] to plot wickedness and heresies against His Majesty, so we might contrive to meet together now and then, in order to undeceive one another, to tell each other wherein we might improve ourselves, and be more pleasing unto God; for there is no one that knows himself as well as he is known of others who see him, if it be with eyes of love and the wish to do him good. I say; in secret; for language of this kind is no longer in use; even preachers go about arranging their sermons so as to displease no one.[149] They have a good intention, and their work is good; yet still few amend their lives. But how is it that they are not many who, in consequence of these sermons, abstain from public sins? Well, I think it is because the preachers are highly sensible men. They are not burning with the great fire of the love of God, as the Apostles were, casting worldly prudence aside; and so their fire throws out but little heat. I do not say that their fire ought to burn like that of the Apostles, but I do wish it were a stronger fire than I see it is. Do you, my father, know wherein much of this fire consists? In the hatred of this life, in the desertion of its honors, in being utterly indifferent whether we lose or gain anything or everything, provided the truth be told and maintained for the glory of God; for he who is courageously in earnest for God, looks upon loss or gain indifferently. I do not say that I am a person of this kind, but I wish I was.

13. Oh, grand freedom, to regard it as a captivity to be obliged to live and converse with men according to the laws of the world! It is the gift of our Lord; there is not a slave who would not imperil everything that he might escape and return to his country; and as this is the true road, there is no reason why we should linger; for we shall never effectually gain a treasure so great, so long as this life is not ended. May our Lord give us His grace for that end! You, my father, if it shall seem good to you, will tear up what I have written, and consider it as a letter for yourself alone, and forgive me that I have been very bold.

---

[145] This was either F. Ybañez or the Inquisitor Soto, if the expression did not occur in the first Life. F. Dom. Bañes struck out "son," and wrote "father" in its place, omitting the words, "so humble is he" (*De la Fuente*).

[146] See § 3, above.

[147] St. John x. 20: "Dæmonium habet et insanit."

[148] The Saint refers to the secret meetings of heretics in Valladolid, under the direction of a fallen priest, the Doctor Agostino Cazalla, whose vanity led him to imitate Luther. Some nuns in Valladolid were imprisoned, Cazalla strangled, and his body burnt, in 1559 (*De la Fuente*).

[149] Father Bañes wrote here on the margin of the Saint's MS, "Legant prædicatores" (*De la Fuente*).

Chapter XVII.

The Third State of Prayer. The Effects Thereof. The Hindrance Caused by the Imagination and the Memory.

1. Enough has been said of this manner of prayer, and of what the soul has to do, or rather, to speak more correctly, of what God is doing within it; for it is He who now takes upon Himself the gardener's work, and who will have the soul take its ease; except that the will is consenting to the graces, the fruition of which it has, and that it must resign itself to all that the True Wisdom would accomplish in it—for which it is certain it has need of courage; because the joy is so great, that the soul seems now and then to be on the very point of going forth out of the body: and what a blessed death that would be! Now, I think it is for the soul's good—as you, my father, have been told—to abandon itself into the arms of God altogether; if He will take it to heaven, let it go; if to hell, no matter, as it is going thither with its sovereign Good. If life is to come to an end for ever, so it wills; if it is to last a thousand years, it wills that also: His Majesty may do with it as with His own property,—the soul no longer belongs to itself, it has been given wholly to our Lord; let it cast all care utterly away.

2. My meaning is that, in a state of prayer, so high as this, the soul understands that God is doing His work without any fatiguing of the understanding, except that, as it seems to me, it is as if amazed in beholding our Lord taking upon Himself the work of the good gardener, refusing to let the soul undergo any labor whatever, but that of taking its pleasure in the flowers beginning to send forth their fragrance; for when God raises a soul up to this state, it can do all this, and much more,—for these are the effects of it.

3. In one of these visits, how brief so ever it may be, the Gardener, being who He is,—in a word, the Creator of the water,—pours the water without stint; and what the poor soul, with the labor, perhaps, of twenty years in fatiguing the understanding, could not bring about, that the heavenly Gardener accomplishes in an instant, causing the fruit both to grow and ripen; so that the soul, such being the will of our Lord, may derive its sustenance from its garden. But He allows it not to divide the fruit with others, until by eating thereof, it is strong enough not to waste it in the mere tasting of it,—giving to Him none of the produce, nor making any compensation for it to Him who supplies it,—lest it should be maintaining others, feeding them at its own cost, and itself perhaps dying of hunger.[150] The meaning of this is perfectly clear for those who have understanding enough to apply it—much more clear than I can make it; and I am tired.

4. Finally, the virtues are now stronger than they were during the preceding prayer of quiet; for the soul sees itself to be other than it was, and it knows not how it is beginning to do great things in the odor which the flowers send forth; it being our Lord's will that the flowers should open, in order that the soul may believe itself to be in possession of virtue; though it sees most clearly that it cannot, and never could, acquire them in many years, and that the heavenly Gardener has given them to it in that instant. Now, too, the humility of the soul is much greater and deeper than it was before; because it sees more clearly that it did neither much nor little, beyond giving its consent that our Lord might work those graces in it, and then accepting them willingly.

5. This state of prayer seems to me to be a most distinct union of the whole soul with God, but for this, that His Majesty appears to give the faculties leave to be intent upon, and have the fruition of, the great work He is doing then. It happens at times, and indeed very often, that, the will being in union, the soul should be aware of it, and see that the will is a captive and in joy, that the will alone is abiding in great peace,—while, on the other hand, the understanding and the memory are so free, that they can be employed in affairs and be occupied in works of charity. I say this, that you, my father, may see it is so, and understand the matter when it shall happen to yourself; at least, it carried me out of myself, and that is the reason why I speak of it here.

6. It differs from the prayer of quiet, of which I have spoken,[151] though it does seem as if it were all one with it. In that prayer, the soul, which would willingly neither stir nor move, is delighting in the holy repose of Mary; but in this prayer it can be like Martha also.[152] Accordingly,

---

[150] See ch. xix. § 4.
[151] Ch. xv. § 1.
[152] See *Way of Perfection*, ch. liii., but ch xxxi. of former editions.

the soul is, as it were, living the active and contemplative life at once, and is able to apply itself to works of charity and the affairs of its state, and to spiritual reading. Still, those who arrive at this state, are not wholly masters of themselves, and are well aware that the better part of the soul is elsewhere. It is as if we were speaking to one person, and another speaking to us at the same time, while we ourselves are not perfectly attentive either to the one or the other. It is a state that is most easily ascertained, and one, when attained to, that ministers great joy and contentment, and that prepares the soul in the highest degree, by observing times of solitude, or of freedom from business, for the attainment of the most tranquil quietude. It is like the life of a man who is full, requiring no food, with his appetite satisfied, so that he will not eat of everything set before him, yet not so full either as to refuse to eat if he saw any desirable food. So the soul has no satisfaction in the world, and seeks no pleasure in it then; because it has in itself that which gives it a greater satisfaction, greater joys in God, longings for the satisfaction of its longing to have a deeper joy in being with Him—this is what the soul seeks.

7. There is another kind of union, which, though not a perfect union, is yet more so than the one of which I have just spoken; but not so much so as this spoken of as the third water. You, my father, will be delighted greatly if our Lord should bestow them all upon you, if you have them not already, to find an account of the matter in writing, and to understand it; for it is one grace that our Lord gives grace; and it is another grace to understand what grace and what gift it is; and it is another and further grace to have the power to describe and explain it to others. Though it does not seem that more than the first of these—the giving of the grace—is necessary to enable the soul to advance without confusion and fear, and to walk with the greater courage in the way of our Lord, trampling under foot all the things of this world, it is a great advantage and a great grace to understand it; for every one who has it has great reason to praise our Lord; and so, also, has he who has it not: because His Majesty has bestowed it upon some person living who is to make us profit by it.

8. This union, of which I would now speak, frequently occurs, particularly to myself. God has very often bestowed such a grace upon me, whereby He constrains the will, and even the understanding, as it seems to me, seeing that it makes no reflections, but is occupied in the fruition of God: like a person who looks on, and sees so many things, that he knows not where to look—one object puts another out of sight, and none of them leaves any impression behind.

9. The memory remains free, and it must be so, together with the imagination; and so, when it finds itself alone, it is marvelous to behold what war it makes on the soul, and how it labors to throw everything into disorder. As for me, I am wearied by it, and I hate it; and very often do I implore our Lord to deprive me of it on these occasions, if I am to be so much troubled by it. Now and then, I say to Him: O my God, when shall my soul praise Thee without distraction, not dissipated in this way, unable to control itself! I understand now the mischief that sin has done, in that it has rendered us unable to do what we desire—to be always occupied in God.

10. I say that it happens to me from time to time,—it has done so this very day, and so I remember it well,—to see my soul tear itself, in order to find itself there where the greater part of it is, and to see, at the same time, that it is impossible: because the memory and the imagination assail it with such force, that it cannot prevail against them; yet, as the other faculties give them no assistance, they are not able to do it any harm—none whatever; they do enough when they trouble its rest. When I say they do no harm, my meaning is, that they cannot really hurt it, because they have not strength enough, and because they are too discursive. As the understanding gives no help, neither much nor little, in the matters put before the soul, they never rest anywhere, but hurry to and fro, like nothing else but gnats at night, troublesome and unquiet: and so they go about from one subject to another.

11. This comparison seems to me to be singularly to the purpose; for the memory and the imagination, though they have no power to do any harm, are very troublesome. I know of no remedy for it; and, hitherto, God has told me of none. If He had, most gladly would I make use of it; for I am, as I say, tormented very often. This shows our wretchedness and brings out most distinctly the great power of God, seeing that the faculty which is free hurts and wearies us so much; while the others, occupied with His Majesty, give us rest.

12. The only remedy I have found, after many years of weariness, is that I spoke of when I was describing the prayer of quiet:[153] to make no more account of it than of a madman, but let it go with its subject; for God alone can take it from it,—in short, it is a slave here. We must bear patiently with it, as Jacob bore with Lia; for our Lord shows us mercy enough when we are allowed to have Rachel with us.

13. I say that it remains a slave; for, after all, let it do what it will, it cannot drag the other faculties in its train; on the contrary, they, without taking any trouble, compel it to follow after them. Sometimes God is pleased to take pity on it, when He sees it so lost and so unquiet, through the longing it has to be united with the other faculties, and His Majesty consents to its burning itself in the flame of that divine candle by which the others are already reduced to ashes, and their nature lost, being, as it were, supernaturally in the fruition of blessings so great.

14. In all these states of prayer of which I have spoken, while explaining this last method of drawing the water out of the well, so great is the bliss and repose of the soul, that even the body most distinctly shares in its joy and delight,—and this is most plain; and the virtues continue to grow, as I said before.[154] It seems to have been the good pleasure of our Lord to explain these states of prayer, wherein the soul finds itself, with the utmost clearness possible, I think, here on earth.

15. Do you, my father, discuss it with any spiritual person who has arrived at this state, and is learned. If he says of it, it is well, you may believe that God has spoken it, and you will give thanks to His Majesty; for, as I said just now,[155] in the course of time you will rejoice greatly in that you have understood it. Meanwhile, if He does not allow you to understand what it is, though He does give you the possession of it, yet, with your intellect and learning, seeing that His Majesty has given you the first, you will know what it is, by the help of what I have written here. Unto Him be praise for ever and ever! Amen.

Chapter XVIII.

The Fourth State of Prayer. The Great Dignity of the Soul Raised to It by Our Lord. Attainable on Earth, Not by Our Merit, But by the Goodness of Our Lord.

1. May our Lord teach me words whereby I may in some measure describe the fourth water.[156] I have great need of His help—even more than I had while speaking of the last; for in that the soul still feels that it is not dead altogether. We may thus speak, seeing that to the world it is really dead. But, as I have said,[157] it retains the sense to see that it is in the world, and to feel its own loneliness; and it makes use of that which is outward for the purpose of manifesting its feelings, at least by signs. In the whole of the prayer already spoken of, and in all the states of it, the gardener undergoes some labor: though in the later states the labor is attended with so much bliss and comfort of the soul, that the soul would never willingly pass out of it,—and thus the labor is not felt as labor, but as bliss.

2. In this the fourth state there is no sense of anything, only fruition, without understanding what that is the fruition of which is granted. It is understood that the fruition is of a certain good containing in itself all good together at once; but this good is not comprehended. The senses are all occupied in this fruition in such a way that not one of them is at liberty, so as to be able to attend to anything else, whether outward or inward.

3. The senses were permitted before, as I have said,[158] to give some signs of the great joy they feel; but now, in this state, the joy of the soul is incomparably greater, and the power of showing it is still less; for there is no power in the body, and the soul has none, whereby this fruition can be made known. Everything of that kind would be a great hindrance, a torment, and a disturbance of

[153] Ch. xiv. § 4. See also *Way of Perfection*, ch. liii., but ch. xxxi. of the old editions.
[154] Ch. xiv. § 6.
[155] § 7.
[156] See ch. xi. § 11.
[157] Ch. xvi. §§ 7, 8.
[158] Ch. xvii. § 5.

its rest. And I say, if it really be a union of all the faculties, that the soul, even if it wished,—I mean, when it is in union,—cannot make it known; and if it can, then it is not union at all.

4. How this, which we call union, is effected, and what it is, I cannot tell. Mystical theology explains it, and I do not know the terms of that science; nor can I understand what the mind is, nor how it differs from the soul or the spirit either: all three seem to me but one; though I do know that the soul sometimes leaps forth out of itself, like a fire that is burning and is become a flame; and occasionally this fire increases violently—the flame ascends high above the fire; but it is not therefore a different thing: it is still the same flame of the same fire. Your learning, my fathers, will enable you to understand the matter; I can go no further.

5. What I undertake to explain is that which the soul feels when it is in the divine union. It is plain enough what union is—two distinct things becoming one. O my Lord, how good Thou art! Blessed be Thou for ever, O my God! Let all creatures praise Thee, Who has so loved us that we can truly speak of this communication which Thou has with souls in this our exile! Yes, even if they be good souls, it is on Thy part great munificence and magnanimity,—in a word, it is Thy munificence, O my Lord, seeing that Thou gives like Thyself. O infinite Munificence!—how magnificent are Thy works! Even he whose understanding is not occupied with the things of earth is amazed that he is unable to understand these truths. Why, then, give graces so high to souls who have been such great sinners? Truly, this passes my understanding; and when I come to think of it, I can get no further. Is there any way at all for me to go on which is not a going back? For, as to giving Thee thanks for mercies so great, I know not how to do it. Sometimes I relieve myself by giving utterance to follies. It often happens to me, either when I receive these graces, or when God is about to bestow them,—for, in the midst of them, I have already said,[159] I was able to do nothing,—that I would break out into words like these.

6. O Lord, consider what Thou art doing; forget not so soon the great evils that I have done. To forgive me, Thou must already have forgotten them; yet, in order that there may be some limit to Thy graces, I beseech Thee remember them. O my Creator, pour not a liquor so precious into a vessel so broken; for Thou has already seen how on other occasions I allowed it to run waste. Lay not up treasure like this, where the longing after the consolations of this life is not so mortified as it ought to be; for it will be utterly lost. How canst Thou commit the defense of the city, and the keys of its fortress to a commander so cowardly, who at the first assault will let the enemy enter within? Oh, let not Thy love be so great, O King Eternal, as to imperil jewels so precious! O my Lord, to me it seems that it becomes a ground for undervaluing them, when Thou putts them in the power of one so wretched, so vile, so frail, so miserable, and so worthless as I am, who, though she may labor not to lose them, by the help of Thy grace,—and I have need of no little grace for that end, being what I am,—is not able to win over any one to Thee,—in short, I am a woman, not good, but wicked. It seems to me that the talents are not only hidden, but buried, when they are committed to earth so vile. It is not Thy wont, O Lord, to bestow graces and mercies like these upon a soul, unless it be that it may edify many.

7. Thou, O my God, knows already that I beg this of Thee with my whole will, from the bottom of my heart, and that I have done so more than once, and I account it a blessing to lose the greatest blessings which may be had on earth, if Thou wouldst but bestow these graces upon him who will make a better use of them to the increase of Thy glory. These, and expressions like these, it has happened to me often to utter. I saw afterwards my own foolishness and want of humility; for our Lord knows well what is expedient, and that there is no strength in my soul to be saved, if His Majesty did not give it with graces so great.

8. I purpose also to speak of the graces and effects which abide in the soul, and of that which the soul itself can do, or rather, if it can do anything of itself towards attaining to a state so high. The elevation of the spirit, or union, comes together with heavenly love but, as I understand it, union is a different thing from elevation in union itself. To him who may not have had any experience of the latter, it must seem that it is not; and, according to my view of it, even if they are both one, the operations of our Lord therein are different: there is a growth of the soul's detachment from creatures more abundantly still in the flight of the spirit.[160] I have clearly seen that this is a particular

---

[159] § 3.
[160] See ch. xx. § 10; and *Relation*, viii. § 10.

grace, though, as I say, it may be the same, or seem to be so, with the other; but a little fire, also, is as much fire as a great fire—and yet there is a visible difference between them. Before a small piece of iron is made red-hot in a little fire, some time must pass; but if the fire be great, the iron very quickly, though bulky, loses its nature altogether in appearance.

9. So, it seems to me, is it with these two kinds of graces which our Lord bestows. He who has had raptures will, I am sure, understand it well; to him who has not had that experience, it must appear folly. And, indeed, it may well be so; for if a person like myself should speak of a matter of this kind, and give any explanation at all of that for the description of which no words ever can possibly be found, it is not to be wondered at that I may be speaking foolishly.

10. But I have this confidence in our Lord, that He will help me here; for His Majesty knows that my object in writing—the first is to obey—is to inspire souls with a longing after so high a good. I will speak of nothing that I do not know by great experience: and so, when I began to describe the last kind of water, I thought it more impossible for me to speak of it at all than to speak Greek. It is a very difficult matter; so I left it, and went to Communion. Blessed be our Lord, who is merciful to the ignorant! Oh, virtue of obedience! it can do everything! God enlightened my understanding—at one time suggesting the words, at another showing me how to use them; for, as in the preceding state of prayer, so also now, His Majesty seems to utter what I can neither speak nor understand.[161]

11. What I am saying is the simple truth; and therefore whatever is good herein is His teaching; what is erroneous, clearly comes out of that sea of evil—myself. If there be any—and there must be many—who, having attained to these states of prayer whereunto our Lord in His mercy has brought me—wretch that I am!—and who, thinking they have missed their way, desire to treat of these matters with me, I am sure that our Lord will help His servant to declare the truth more plainly.

12. I am now speaking of the water which comes down from heaven to fill and saturate in its abundance the whole of this garden with water. If our Lord never ceased to pour it down whenever it was necessary, the gardener certainly would have plenty of rest; and if there were no winter, but an ever temperate season, fruits and flowers would never fail. The gardener would have his delight therein; but in this life that is impossible. We must always be careful, when one water fails, to obtain another. This water from heaven comes down very often when the gardener least expects it.

13. The truth is that, in the beginning, this almost always happens after much mental prayer. Our Lord advances step by step to lay hold of the little bird, and to lay it in the nest where it may repose. He observed it fluttering for a long time, striving with the understanding and the will, and with all its might, to seek God and to please Him; so now it is His pleasure to reward it even in this life. And what a reward!—one moment is enough to repay all the possible trials of this life.

14. The soul, while thus seeking after God, is conscious, with a joy excessive and sweet, that it is, as it were, utterly fainting away in a kind of trance: breathing, and all the bodily strength, fail it, so that it cannot even move the hands without great pain; the eyes close involuntarily, and if they are open, they are as if they saw nothing; nor is reading possible,—the very letters seem strange, and cannot be distinguished,—the letters, indeed, are visible, but, as the understanding furnishes no help, all reading is impracticable, though seriously attempted. The ear hears; but what is heard is not comprehended. The senses are of no use whatever, except to hinder the soul's fruition; and so they rather hurt it. It is useless to try to speak, because it is not possible to conceive a word; nor, if it were conceived, is there strength sufficient to utter it; for all bodily strength vanishes, and that of the soul increases, to enable it the better to have the fruition of its joy. Great and most perceptible, also, is the outward joy now felt.

15. This prayer, however long it may last, does no harm—at least, it has never done any to me; nor do I remember, however ill I might have been when our Lord had mercy upon me in this way, that I ever felt the worse for it—on the contrary, I was always better afterwards. But so great a blessing, what harm can it do? The outward effects are so plain as to leave no doubt possible that there must have been some great cause, seeing that it thus robs us of our bodily powers with so much joy, in order to leave them greater.

16. The truth is, it passes away so quickly in the beginning—at least, so it was with me—that neither by the outward signs, nor by the failure of the senses, can it be perceived when it passes so

---

[161] See ch. xiv. § 12.

quickly away. But it is plain, from the overflowing abundance of grace, that the brightness of the sun which had shone there must have been great, seeing that it has thus made the soul to melt away. And this is to be considered; for, as it seems to me, the period of time, however long it may have been, during which the faculties of the soul were entranced, is very short; if half an hour, that would be a long time. I do not think that I have ever been so long. The truth of the matter is this: it is extremely difficult to know how long, because the senses are in suspense; but I think that at any time it cannot be very long before some one of the faculties recovers itself. It is the will that persists in the work; the other two faculties quickly begin to molest it. As the will is calm, it entrances them again; they are quiet for another moment, and then they recover themselves once more.

17. In this way, some hours may be, and are, passed in prayer; for when the two faculties begin to drink deep, and to perceive the taste of this divine wine, they give themselves up with great readiness, in order to be the more absorbed: they follow the will, and the three rejoice together. But this state of complete absorption, together with the utter rest of the imagination,—for I believe that even the imagination is then wholly at rest,—lasts only for a short time; though the faculties do not so completely recover themselves as not to be for some hours afterwards as if in disorder: God, from time to time, drawing them to Himself.

18. Let us now come to that which the soul feels interiorly. Let him describe it who knows it; for as it is impossible to understand it, much more is it so to describe it. When I purposed to write this, I had just communicated, and had risen from the very prayer of which I am speaking. I am thinking of what the soul was then doing. Our Lord said to me: It undoes itself utterly, My daughter, in order that it may give itself more and more to Me: it is not itself that then lives, it is I. As it cannot comprehend what it understands, it understands by not understanding.

19. He who has had experience of this will understand it in some measure, for it cannot be more clearly described, because what then takes place is so obscure. All I am able to say is, that the soul is represented as being close to God; and that there abides a conviction thereof so certain and strong, that it cannot possibly help believing so. All the faculties fail now, and are suspended in such a way that, as I said before,[162] their operations cannot be traced. If the soul is making a meditation on any subject, the memory of it is lost at once, just as if it had never been thought of. If it reads, what is read is not remembered nor dwelt upon; neither is it otherwise with vocal prayer. Accordingly, the restless little butterfly of the memory has its wings burnt now, and it cannot fly. The will must be fully occupied in loving, but it understands not how it loves; the understanding, if it understands, does not understand how it understands—at least, it can comprehend nothing of that it understands: it does not understand, as it seems to me, because, as I said just now, this cannot be understood. I do not understand it at all myself.

20. In the beginning, it happened to me that I was ignorant of one thing—I did not know that God was in all things:[163] and when He seemed to me to be so near, I thought it impossible. Not to believe that He was present, was not in my power; for it seemed to me, as it were, evident that I felt there His very presence. Some unlearned men used to say to me, that He was present only by His grace. I could not believe that, because, as I am saying, He seemed to me to be present Himself: so I was distressed. A most learned man, of the Order of the glorious Patriarch St. Dominic, delivered me from this doubt; for he told me that He was present, and how He communed with us: this was a great comfort to me.

21. It is to be observed and understood that this water from heaven,—this greatest grace of our Lord—always leaves in the soul the greatest fruits, as I shall now show.

---

[162] Ch. x. § 1, and ch. xviii. § 16.
[163] See *Interior Castle*, v. ch. i. § 11.

Chapter XIX.

The Effects of This Fourth State of Prayer. Earnest Exhortations to Those Who Have Attained to It Not to Go Back, Nor to Cease from Prayer, Even If They Fall. The Great Calamity of Going Back.

1. There remains in the soul, when the prayer of union is over, an exceedingly great tenderness; so much so, that it would undo itself—not from pain, but through tears of joy it finds itself bathed therein, without being aware of it, and it knows not how or when it wept them. But to behold the violence of the fire subdued by the water, which yet makes it burn the more, gives it great delight. It seems as if I were speaking an unknown language. So it is, however.

2. It has happened to me occasionally, when this prayer was over, to be so beside myself as not to know whether I had been dreaming, or whether the bliss I felt had really been mine; and, on finding myself in a flood of tears—which had painlessly flowed, with such violence and rapidity that it seemed as if a cloud from heaven[164] had shed them—to perceive that it was no dream. Thus it was with me in the beginning, when it passed quickly away. The soul remains possessed of so much courage, that if it were now hewn in pieces for God, it would be a great consolation to it. This is the time of resolutions, of heroic determinations, of the living energy of good desires, of the beginning of hatred of the world, and of the most clear perception of its vanity. The soul makes greater and higher progress than it ever made before in the previous states of prayer; and grows in humility more and more, because it sees clearly that neither for obtaining nor for retaining this grace, great beyond all measure, has it ever done, or ever been able to do, anything of itself. It looks upon itself as most unworthy—for in a room into which the sunlight enters strongly, not a cobweb can be hid; it sees its own misery; self-conceit is so far away, that it seems as if it never could have had any—for now its own eyes behold how very little it could ever do, or rather, that it never did anything, that it hardly gave even its own consent, but that it rather seemed as if the doors of the senses were closed against its will in order that it might have more abundantly the fruition of our Lord. It is abiding alone with Him: what has it to do but to love Him? It neither sees nor hears, unless on compulsion: no thanks to it. Its past life stands before it then, together with the great mercy of God, in great distinctness; and it is not necessary for it to go forth to hunt with the understanding, because what it has to eat and ruminate upon, it sees now ready prepared. It sees, so far as itself is concerned, that it has deserved hell, and that its punishment is bliss. It undoes itself in the praises of God, and I would gladly undo myself now.

3. Blessed be Thou, O my Lord, who, out of a pool so filthy as I am, brings forth water so clean as to be meet for Thy table! Praised be Thou, O Joy of the Angels, who has been thus pleased to exalt so vile a worm!

4. The good effects of this prayer abide in the soul for some time. Now that it clearly apprehends that the fruit is not its own, the soul can begin to share it with others, and that without any loss to itself. It begins to show signs of its being a soul that is guarding the treasures of heaven, and to be desirous of communicating them to others,[165] and to pray to God that itself may not be the only soul that is rich in them. It begins to benefit its neighbors, as it were, without being aware of it, or doing anything consciously: its neighbors understand the matter, because the odor of the flowers has grown so strong as to make them eager to approach them. They understand that this soul is full of virtue: they see the fruit, how delicious it is, and they wish to help that soul to eat it.

5. If this ground be well dug by troubles, by persecutions, detractions, and infirmities,—they are few who ascend so high without this,—if it be well broken up by great detachment from all self-interest, it will drink in so much water that it can hardly ever be parched again. But if it be ground which is mere waste, and covered with thorns (as I was when I began); if the occasions of sin be not avoided; if it be an ungrateful soil, unfitted for so great a grace,—it will be parched up again. If the gardener become careless,—and if our Lord, out of His mere goodness, will not send down rain upon it,—the garden is ruined. Thus has it been with me more than once, so that I am amazed at it; and if I had not found it so by experience, I could not have believed it.

---

[164] See ch. xx. § 2.
[165] See ch. xvii. § 3.

6. I write this for the comfort of souls which are weak, as I am, that they may never despair, nor cease to trust in the power of God; even if they should fall after our Lord has raised them to so high a degree of prayer as this is, they must not be discouraged, unless they would lose themselves utterly. Tears gain everything, and one drop of water attracts another.

7. One of the reasons that move me, who am what I am, under obedience to write this, and give an account of my wretched life, and of the graces our Lord has wrought in me,—though I never served Him, but offended Him rather,—is what I have just given: and, certainly, I wish I was a person of great authority, that people might believe what I say. I pray to our Lord that His Majesty would be pleased to grant me this grace. I repeat it, let no one who has begun to give himself to prayer be discouraged, and say: If I fall into sin, it will be worse for me if I go on now with the practice of prayer. I think so too, if he gives up prayer, and does not correct his evil ways; but if he does not give up prayer, let him be assured of this—prayer will bring him to the haven of light.

8. In this the devil turned his batteries against me, and I suffered so much because I thought it showed but little humility if I persevered in prayer when I was so wicked, that—as I have already said[166]—I gave it up for a year and a half—at least, for a year, but I do not remember distinctly the other six months. This could not have been, neither was it, anything else but to throw myself down into hell; there was no need of any devils to drag me thither. O my God, was there ever blindness so great as this? How well Satan prepares his measures for his purpose, when he pursues us in this way! The traitor knows that he has already lost that soul which perseveres in prayer, and that every fall which he can bring about helps it, by the goodness of God, to make greater progress in His service. Satan has some interest in this.

9. O my Jesus, what a sight that must be—a soul so highly exalted falling into sin, and raised up again by Thee; who, in Thy mercy, stretches forth Thine hand to save! How such a soul confesses Thy greatness and compassion and its own wretchedness! It really looks on itself as nothingness, and confesses Thy power. It dares not lift up its eyes; it raises them, indeed, but it is to acknowledge how much it owes unto Thee. It becomes devout to the Queen of Heaven, that she may propitiate Thee; it invokes the Saints, who fell after Thou has called them, for succor. Thou seems now to be too bountiful in Thy gifts, because it feels itself to be unworthy of the earth it treads on. It has recourse to the Sacraments, to a quickened faith, which abides in it at the contemplation of the power which Thou has lodged in them. It praises Thee because Thou has left us such medicines and ointment for our wounds, which not only heal them on the surface, but remove all traces whatever of them.

10. The soul is amazed at it. Who is there, O Lord of my soul, that is not amazed at compassion so great and mercy so surpassing, after treason so foul and so hateful? I know not how it is that my heart does not break when I write this, for I am wicked. With these scanty tears which I am now weeping, but yet Thy gift,—water out of a well, so far as it is mine, so impure,—I seem to make Thee some recompense for treachery so great as mine, in that I was always doing evil, laboring to make void the graces Thou has given me. Do Thou, O Lord, make my tears available; purify the water which is so muddy; at least, let me not be to others a temptation to rash judgments, as I have been to myself, when I used to think such thoughts as these. Why, O Lord, does Thou pass by most holy persons, who have always served Thee, and who have been tried; who have been brought up in religion, and are really religious—not such as I am, having only the name—so as to make it plain that they are not recipients of those graces which Thou has bestowed upon me?

11. I see clearly now, O Thou my Good, Thou has kept the reward to give it them all at once: my weakness has need of these succors. They, being strong, serve Thee without them, and Thou deals with them as with a strong race, free from all self-interest. But yet Thou knows, O my Lord, that I have often cried unto Thee, making excuses for those who murmured against me; for I thought they had reason on their side. This I did then when Thou of Thy goodness has kept me back from offending Thee so much, and when I was departing from everything which I thought displeasing unto Thee. It was when I did this that Thou, O Lord, did begin to lay open Thy treasures for Thy servant. It seemed as if Thou wert looking for nothing else but that I should be willing and ready to receive them; accordingly, Thou did begin at once, not only to give them, but also to make others know that Thou wert giving them.

---

[166] Ch. vii. § 17, and ch. viii. § 5.

12. When this was known, there began to prevail a good opinion of her, of whom all had not yet clearly understood how wicked she was, though much of that wickedness was plain enough. Calumny and persecution began at once, and, as I think, with good reason; so I looked on none of them as an enemy, but made my supplications to Thee, imploring Thee to consider the grounds they had. They said that I wished to be a saint, and that I invented novelties; but I had not then attained in many things even to the observance of my rule; nor had I come near those excellent and holy nuns who were in the house,—and I do not believe I ever shall, if God of His goodness will not do that for me Himself; on the contrary, I was there only to do away with what was good, and introduce customs which were not good; at least, I did what I could to bring them in, and I was very powerful for evil. Thus it was that they were blameless, when they blamed me. I do not mean the nuns only, but the others as well: they told me truths; for it was Thy will.

13. I was once saying the Office,—I had had this temptation for some time,—and when I came to these words, "Justus es, Domine, et rectum judicium tuum,"[167] I began to think what a deep truth it was. Satan never was strong enough to tempt me in any way to doubt of Thy goodness, or of any article of the faith: on the contrary, it seems to me that the more these truths were above nature, the more firmly I held them, and my devotion grew; when I thought of Thy omnipotence, I accepted all Thy wonderful works, and I say it again, I never had a doubt. Then, as I was thinking how it could be just in Thee to allow so many, who, as I said, are Thy most faithful servants, to remain without those consolations and graces which Thou has given to me, who am what I am, Thou, O my Lord, did answer me: Serve thou Me, and meddle not with this.

14. This was the first word which I ever heard Thee speak to me, and it made me greatly afraid. But as I shall speak hereafter[168] of this way of hearing, and of other matters, I say nothing here; for to do so would be to digress from my subject, and I have already made digressions enough. I scarcely know what I have said, nor can it be otherwise; but you, my father, must bear with these interruptions; for when I consider what God must have borne with from me, and when I see the state I am in, it is not strange that I should wander in what I am saying, and what I have still to say.

15. May it please our Lord that my wanderings may be of this kind, and may His Majesty never suffer me to have strength to resist Him even in the least; yes, rather than that, may He destroy me this moment. It is evidence enough of His great compassions, that He has forgiven so much ingratitude, not once, but often. He forgave St. Peter once; but I have been forgiven many times. Satan had good reasons for tempting me: I ought never to have pretended to a strict friendship with One, my hatred of whom I made so public. Was there ever blindness so great as mine? Where could I think I should find help but in Thee? What folly to run away from the light, to be for ever stumbling! What a proud humility was that which Satan devised for me, when I ceased to lean upon the pillar, and threw the staff away which supported me, in order that my fall might not be great![169]

16. I make the sign of the cross this moment. I do not think I ever escaped so great a danger as this device of Satan, which he would have imposed upon me in the disguise of humility.[170] He filled me with such thoughts as these: How could I make my prayer, who was so wicked, and yet had received so many mercies? It was enough for me to recite the Office, as all others did; but as I did not that much well, how could I desire to do more? I was not reverential enough, and made too little of the mercies of God. There was no harm in these thoughts and feelings in themselves; but to act upon them, that was an exceedingly great wickedness. Blessed be Thou, O Lord; for Thou came to my help. This seems to me to be in principle the temptation of Judas, only that Satan did not dare to tempt me so openly. But he might have led me by little and little, as he led Judas, to the same pit of destruction.

17. Let all those who give themselves to prayer, for the love of God, look well to this. They should know that when I was neglecting it, my life was much worse than it had ever been; let them reflect on the excellent help and the pleasant humility which Satan provided for me: it was a grave interior disquietude. But how could my spirit be quiet? It was going away in its misery from its true rest. I remembered the graces and mercies I had received, and felt that the joys of this world were

[167] Psalm cxviii. 137: "Thou art just, O Lord, and Thy judgment is right."
[168] See ch. xxv.
[169] See ch. viii. § 1.
[170] Ch. vii. § 17.

loathsome. I am astonished that I was able to bear it. It must have been the hope I had; for, as well as I can remember now, it is more than twenty-one years ago. I do not think I ever gave up my purpose of resuming my prayer; but I was waiting to be very free from sin first.

18. Oh, how deluded I was in this expectation! The devil would have held it out before me till the day of judgment, that he might then take me with him to hell. Then, when I applied myself to prayer and to spiritual reading,—whereby I might perceive these truths, and the evil nature of the way I was walking in, and was often importunate with our Lord in tears,—I was so wicked, that it availed me nothing; when I gave that up, and wasted my time in amusing myself, in great danger of falling into sin, and with scanty helps,—and I may venture to say no help at all, unless it was a help to my ruin,—what could I expect but that of which I have spoken?

19. I believe that a certain Dominican friar, a most learned man, has greatly merited in the eyes of God; for it was he who roused me from this slumber. He made me—I think I said so before[171]— go to Communion once a fortnight, and be less given to evil; I began to be converted, though I did not cease to offend our Lord all at once: however, as I had not lost my way, I walked on in it, though slowly, falling and rising again; and he who does not cease to walk and press onwards, arrives at last, even if late. To lose one's way is—so it seems to me—nothing else but the giving up of prayer. God, of His mercy, keeps us from this!

20. It is clear from this,—and, for the love of God, consider it well,—that a soul, though it may receive great graces from God in prayer, must never rely on itself, because it may fall, nor expose itself in any way whatever to any risks of sin. This should be well considered because much depends on it; for the delusion here, wherein Satan is able to entangle us afterwards, though the grace be really from God, lies in the traitor's making use of that very grace, so far as he can, for his own purpose, and particularly against persons not grown strong in virtues, who are neither mortified nor detached; for these are not at present strong enough—as I shall explain hereafter[172]—to expose themselves to dangerous occasions, notwithstanding the noble desires and resolutions they may have.

21. This doctrine is excellent, and not mine, but the teaching of God, and accordingly I wish ignorant people like myself knew it; for even if a soul were in this state, it must not rely so much upon itself as to go forth to the battle, because it will have enough to do in defending itself. Defensive armor is the present necessity; the soul is not yet strong enough to assail Satan, and to trample him under foot, as those are who are in the state of which I shall speak further on.[173]

22. This is the delusion by which Satan prevails: when a soul sees itself so near unto God, when it sees the difference there is between the things of heaven and those of earth, and when it sees the love which our Lord bears it, there grows out of that love a certain trust and confidence that there is to be no falling away from that the fruition of which it then possesses. It seems to see the reward distinctly, as if it were impossible for it to abandon that which, even in this life, is so delicious and sweet, for anything so mean and impure as worldly joy. Through this confidence, Satan robs it of that distrust which it ought to have in itself; and so, as I have just said, the soul exposes itself to dangers, and begins, in the fulness of its zeal, to give away without discretion the fruit of its garden, thinking that now it has no reason to be afraid for itself. Yet this does not come out of pride; for the soul clearly understands that of itself it can do no good thing; but rather out of an excessive confidence in God, without discretion: because the soul does not see itself to be unfledged. [174]It can go forth out of its nest, and God Himself may take it out, but still it cannot fly, because the virtues are not strong, and itself has no experience wherewith to discern the dangers; nor is it aware of the evil which trusting to itself may do it.

23. This it was that ruined me. Now, to understand this, and everything else in the spiritual life, we have great need of a director, and of conference with spiritual persons. I fully believe, with respect to that soul which God raises to this state, that He will not cease to be gracious to it, nor suffer it to be lost, if it does not utterly forsake His Majesty. But when that soul—as I said—falls, let it look to it again and again, for the love of our Lord, that Satan deceive it not by tempting it to

[171] Ch. vii. § 27.

[172] Ch. xxxi. § 21.

[173] Ch. xx. § 33, and ch. xxv. § 24.

[174] Ch. xix. § 4.

give up prayer, as he tempted me, through that false humility of which I have spoken before,[175] and would gladly speak of again and again. Let it rely on the goodness of God, which is greater than all the evil we can do. When we, acknowledging our own vileness, desire to return into His grace, He remembers our ingratitude no more,—no, not even the graces He has given us, for the purpose of chastising us, because of our misuse of them; yes, rather, they help to procure our pardon the sooner, as of persons who have been members of His household, and who, as they say, have eaten of His bread.

24. Let them remember His words, and behold what He hath done unto me, who grew weary of sinning before He grew weary of forgiving. He is never weary of giving, nor can His compassion be exhausted. Let us not grow weary ourselves of receiving. May He be blessed for ever, Amen; and may all created things praise Him!

Chapter XX.

The Difference Between Union and Rapture. What Rapture Is. The Blessing It Is to the Soul. The Effects of It.

1. I wish I could explain, with the help of God, wherein union differs from rapture, or from transport, or from flight of the spirit, as they speak, or from a trance, which are all one.[176] I mean, that all these are only different names for that one and the same thing, which is also called ecstasy.[177] It is more excellent than union, the fruits of it are much greater, and its other operations more manifold; for union is uniform in the beginning, the middle, and the end, and is so also interiorly. But as raptures have ends of a much higher kind, they produce effects both within and without. As our Lord has explained the other matters, so also may He explain this; for certainly, if He had not shown me in what way and by what means this explanation was in some measure possible, I should never have been able to do it.

2. Consider we now that this last water, of which I am speaking, is so abundant that, were it not that the ground refuses to receive it, we might suppose that the cloud of His great Majesty is here raining down upon us on earth. And when we are giving Him thanks for this great mercy, drawing near to Him in earnest, with all our might, then it is our Lord draws up the soul, as the clouds, so to speak, gather the mists from the face of the earth, and carries it away out of itself,—I have heard it said that the clouds, or the sun, draw the mists together,[178]—and as a cloud, rising up to heaven, takes the soul with Him, and begins to show it the treasures of the kingdom which He has prepared for it. I know not whether the comparison be accurate or not; but the fact is, that is the way in which it is brought about. During rapture, the soul does not seem to animate the body, the natural heat of which is perceptibly lessened; the coldness increases, though accompanied with exceeding joy and sweetness.[179]

---

[175] See § 16.

[176] See *Interior Castle*, vi. ch. v.; Philippus a SS. Trinitate, *Theolog. Mystic.* par. iii. tr. i, disp. iii., art. 3; "Hæc oratio raptus superior est præcedentibus orationis gradibus, etiam oratione unionis ordinariæ, et habet effectus multoexcellentiores et multas alias operationes."

[177] "She says that rapture is more excellent than union; that is, that the soul in a rapture has a greater fruition of God, and that God takes it then more into His own hands. That is evidently so; because in a rapture the soul loses the use of its exterior and interior faculties. When she says that union is the beginning, middle, and end, she means that pure union is almost always uniform; but that there are degrees in rapture, of which some are, as it were, the beginning, some the middle, others the end. That is the reason why it is called by different names; some of which denote the least, others the most, perfect form of it, as it will appear hereafter."—Note in the Spanish edition of Lopez (*De la Fuente*).

[178] The words between the dashes are in the handwriting of the Saint—not however, in the text, but on the margin (*De la Fuente*).

[179] See *Interior Castle*, vi. ch. v. "Primus effectus orationis ecstaticæ est in corpore, quod ita remanet, ac si per animam non informaretur, infrigidatur enim calore naturali deficiente, clauduntur suaviter oculi, et alii sensus amittuntur: contingit tamen quod corpus infirmum in hac oratione sanitatem recuperat." Anton. a Spirit. Sancto, *Direct. Mystic.* tr. iv. d. 2, § 4, n. 150.

3. A rapture is absolutely irresistible; whilst union, inasmuch as we are then on our own ground, may be hindered, though that resistance be painful and violent; it is, however, almost always impossible. But rapture, for the most part, is irresistible. It comes, in general, as a shock, quick and sharp, before you can collect your thoughts, or help yourself in any way, and you see and feel it as a cloud, or a strong eagle rising upwards, and carrying you away on its wings.

4. I repeat it: you feel and see yourself carried away, you know not whither. For though we feel how delicious it is, yet the weakness of our nature makes us afraid at first, and we require a much more resolute and courageous spirit than in the previous states, in order to risk everything, come what may, and to abandon ourselves into the hands of God, and go willingly whither we are carried, seeing that we must be carried away, however painful it may be; and so trying is it, that I would very often resist, and exert all my strength, particularly at those times when the rapture was coming on me in public. I did so, too, very often when I was alone, because I was afraid of delusions. Occasionally I was able, by great efforts, to make a slight resistance; but afterwards I was worn out, like a person who had been contending with a strong giant; at other times it was impossible to resist at all: my soul was carried away, and almost always my head with it,—I had no power over it,—and now and then the whole body as well, so that it was lifted up from the ground.

5. This has not happened to me often: once, however, it took place when we were all together in choir, and I, on my knees, on the point of communicating. It was a very sore distress to me; for I thought it a most extraordinary thing, and was afraid it would occasion much talk; so I commanded the nuns—for it happened after I was made Prioress—never to speak of it. But at other times, the moment I felt that our Lord was about to repeat the act, and once, in particular, during a sermon,—it was the feast of our house, some great ladies being present,—I threw myself on the ground; then the nuns came around me to hold me; but still the rapture was observed.

6. I made many supplications to our Lord, that He would be pleased to give me no more of those graces which were outwardly visible; for I was weary of living under such great restraint, and because His Majesty could not bestow such graces on me without their becoming known. It seems that, of His goodness, He has been pleased to hear my prayer; for I have never been enraptured since. It is true that it was not long ago.[180]

7. It seemed to me, when I tried to make some resistance, as if a great force beneath my feet lifted me up. I know of nothing with which to compare it; but it was much more violent than the other spiritual visitations, and I was therefore as one ground to pieces; for it is a great struggle, and, in short, of little use, whenever our Lord so wills it. There is no power against His power.

8. At other times He is pleased to be satisfied when He makes us see that He is ready to give us this grace, and that it is not He that withholds it. Then, when we resist it out of humility, He produces those very effects which would have resulted if we had fully consented to it.

9. The effects of rapture are great: one is that the mighty power of our Lord is manifested; and as we are not strong enough, when His Majesty wills it, to control either soul or body, so neither have we any power over it; but, whether we like it or not, we see that there is one mightier than we are, that these graces are His gifts, and that of ourselves we can do nothing whatever; and humility is deeply imprinted in us. And further, I confess that it threw me into great fear, very great indeed at first; for when I saw my body thus lifted up from the earth, how could I help it? Though the spirit draws it upwards after itself, and that with great sweetness, if unresisted, the senses are not lost; at least, I was so much myself as to be able to see that I was being lifted up. The majesty of Him who can effect this so manifests itself, that the hairs of my head stand upright,[181] and a great fear comes upon me of offending God, who is so mighty. This fear is bound up in exceedingly great love, which is acquired anew, and directed to Him, who, we see, bears so great a love to a worm so vile, and who seems not to be satisfied with attracting the soul to Himself in so real a way, but who will have the body also, though it be mortal and of earth so foul, such as it is through our sins, which are so great.

---

[180] This passage could not have been in the first Life; for that was written before she had ever been Prioress.

[181] Job. iv. 15: "Inhorruerunt pili carnis meæ." (See St. John of the Cross. *Spiritual Canticle*, sts. 14, 15, vol. ii p. 83, Engl. trans.)

10. Rapture leaves behind a certain strange detachment also, which I shall never be able to describe; I think I can say that it is in some respects different from—yes, higher than—the other graces, which are simply spiritual; for though these effect a complete detachment in spirit from all things, it seems that in this of rapture our Lord would have the body itself to be detached also: and thus a certain singular estrangement from the things of earth is wrought, which makes life much more distressing. Afterwards it causes a pain, which we can never inflict of ourselves, nor remove when once it has come.

11. I should like very much to explain this great pain, and I believe I shall not be able; however, I will say something if I can. And it is to be observed that this is my present state, and one to which I have been brought very lately, after all the visions and revelations of which I shall speak, and after that time, wherein I gave myself to prayer, in which our Lord gave me so much sweetness and delight.[182] Even now I have that sweetness occasionally; but it is the pain of which I speak that is the most frequent and the most common. It varies in its intensity. I will now speak of it when it is sharpest; for I shall speak later on[183] of the great shocks I used to feel when our Lord would throw me into those trances, and which are, in my opinion, as different from this pain as the most corporeal thing is from the most spiritual; and I believe that I am not exaggerating much. For though the soul feels that pain, it is in company with the body;[184] both soul and body apparently share it, and it is not attended with that extremity of abandonment which belongs to this.

12. As I said before,[185] we have no part in causing this pain; but very often there springs up a desire unexpectedly,—I know not how it comes,—and because of this desire, which pierces the soul in a moment, the soul begins to be wearied, so much so that it rises upwards above itself, and above all created things. God then so strips it of everything, that, do what it may, there is nothing on earth that can be its companion. Neither, indeed, would it wish to have any; it would rather die in that loneliness. If people spoke to it, and if itself made every effort possible to speak, it would be of little use: the spirit, notwithstanding all it may do, cannot be withdrawn from that loneliness; and though God seems, as it were, far away from the soul at that moment, yet He reveals His grandeurs at times in the strangest way conceivable. That way is indescribable; I do not think any one can believe or comprehend it who has not previously had experience of it. It is a communication made, not to console, but to show the reason why the soul must be weary; because it is far away from the Good which in itself comprehends all good.

13. In this communication the desire grows, so also does the bitterness of that loneliness wherein the soul beholds itself, suffering a pain so sharp and piercing that, in that very loneliness in which it dwells, it may literally say of itself,—and perhaps the royal prophet said so, being in that very loneliness himself, except that our Lord may have granted to him, being a saint, to feel it more deeply,— "Vigilavi, et factus sum sicut passer solitarius in tecto."[186] These words presented themselves to me in such a way that I thought I saw them fulfilled in myself. It was a comfort to know that others had felt this extreme loneliness; how much greater my comfort, when these persons were such as David was! The soul is then—so I think—not in itself, but on the house-top, or on the roof, above itself, and above all created things; for it seems to me to have its dwelling higher than even in the highest part of itself.

14. On other occasions, the soul seems to be, as it were, in the utmost extremity of need, asking itself, and saying, "Where is Thy God?"[187] And it is to be remembered, that I did not know how to express in Spanish the meaning of those words. Afterwards, when I understood what it was, I used to console myself with the thought, that our Lord, without any effort of mine, had made me remember them. At other times, I used to recollect a saying of St. Paul's, to the effect that he was crucified to the world.[188] I do not mean that this is true of me: I know it is not; but I think it is the state of the enraptured soul. No consolation reaches it from heaven, and it is not there itself; it wishes

---

[182] See ch. xxix.

[183] See ch. xx. § 21.

[184] § 9, *supra.*

[185] § 10.

[186] Psalm ci. 8: "I have watched, and become as a sparrow alone on the house-top."

[187] Psalm xli. 4: "Ubi est Deus tuus?"

[188] Galat. vi. 14: "In cruce Jesu Christi: per quem mihi mundus crucifixus est, et ego mundo."

for none from earth, and it is not there either; but it is, as it were, crucified between heaven and earth, enduring its passion: receiving no succor from either.

15. Now, the succor it receives from heaven—which, as I have said,[189] is a most marvelous knowledge of God, above all that we can desire—brings with it greater pain; for the desire then so grows, that, in my opinion, its intense painfulness now and then robs the soul of all sensation; only, it lasts but for a short time after the senses are suspended. It seems as if it were the point of death; only, the agony carries with it so great a joy, that I know of nothing wherewith to compare it. It is a sharp martyrdom, full of sweetness; for if any earthly thing be then offered to the soul, even though it may be that which it habitually found most sweet, the soul will have none of it; yes, it seems to throw it away at once. The soul sees distinctly that it seeks nothing but God; yet its love dwells not on any attribute of Him in particular; it seeks Him as He is, and knows not what it seeks. I say that it knows not, because the imagination forms no representation whatever; and, indeed, as I think, during much of that time the faculties are at rest. Pain suspends them then, as joy suspends them in union and in a trance.

16. O Jesus! oh, that some one would clearly explain this to you, my father, were it only that you may tell me what it means, because this is the habitual state of my soul! Generally, when I am not particularly occupied, I fall into these agonies of death, and I tremble when I feel them coming on, because they are not unto death. But when I am in them, I then wish to spend therein all the rest of my life, though the pain be so very great, that I can scarcely endure it. Sometimes my pulse ceases, as it were, to beat at all,—so the sisters say, who sometimes approach me, and who now understand the matter better,—my bones are racked, and my hands become so rigid, that I cannot always join them. Even on the following day I have a pain in my wrists, and over my whole body, as if my bones were out of joint.[190] Well, I think sometimes, if it continues as at present, that it will end, in the good pleasure of our Lord, by putting an end to my life; for the pain seems to me sharp enough to cause death; only, I do not deserve it.

17. All my anxiety at these times is that I should die: I do not think of purgatory, nor of the great sins I have committed, and by which I have deserved hell. I forget everything in my eagerness to see God; and this abandonment and loneliness seem preferable to any company in the world. If anything can be a consolation in this state, it is to speak to one who has passed through this trial, seeing that, though the soul may complain of it, no one seems disposed to believe in it.

18. The soul is tormented also because the pain has increased so much, that it seeks solitude no longer, as it did before, nor companionship, unless it be that of those to whom it may make its complaint. It is now like a person, who, having a rope around his neck, and being strangled, tries to breathe. This desire of companionship seems to me to proceed from our weakness; for, as pain brings with it the risk of death,—which it certainly does; for I have been occasionally in danger of death, in my great sickness and infirmities, as I have said before,[191] and I think I may say that this pain is as great as any,—so the desire not to be parted, which possesses soul and body, is that which raises the cry for succor in order to breathe, and by speaking of it, by complaining, and distracting itself, causes the soul to seek means of living very much against the will of the spirit, or the higher part of the soul, which would not wish to be delivered from this pain.

19. I am not sure that I am correct in what I say, nor do I know how to express myself, but to the best of my knowledge it comes to pass in this way. See, my father, what rest I can have in this life, now that what I once had in prayer and loneliness—therein our Lord used to comfort me—has become in general a torment of this kind; while, at the same time, it is so full of sweetness, that the soul, discerning its inestimable worth, prefers it to all those consolations which it formerly had. It seems also to be a safer state, because it is the way of the cross; and involves, in my opinion, a joy of exceeding worth, because the state of the body in it is only pain. It is the soul that suffers and exults alone in that joy and contentment which suffering supplies.

---

[189] §§ 9 and 12.

[190] Daniel x. 16: "In visione tua dissolutæ sunt compages meæ." See St. John of the Cross, *Spiritual Canticle*, st. 14, vol. ii. p. 84, Engl. trans.; and also *Relation*, viii. § 13, where this is repeated.

[191] Ch. v. § 18.

20. I know not how this can be, but so it is; it comes from the hand of our Lord, and, as I said before,[192] is not anything that I have acquired myself, because it is exceedingly supernatural, and I think I would not barter it for all the graces of which I shall speak further on: I do not say for all of them together, but for any one of them separately. And it must not be forgotten that, as I have just said, these impetuosities came upon me after I had received those graces from our Lord[193] which I am speaking of now, and all those described in this book, and it is in this state our Lord keeps me at this moment.[194]

21. In the beginning I was afraid—it happens to me to be almost always so when our Lord leads me by a new way, until His Majesty reassures me as I proceed—and so our Lord bade me not to fear, but to esteem this grace more than all the others He had given me; for the soul was purified by this pain—burnished, or refined as gold in the crucible, so that it might be the better enameled with His gifts, and the dross burnt away in this life, which would have to be burnt away in purgatory.

22. I understood perfectly that this pain was a great grace; but I was much more certain of it now and my confessor tells me I did well. And though I was afraid, because I was so wicked, I never could believe it was anything wrong: on the other hand, the exceeding greatness of the blessing made me afraid, when I called to mind how little I had deserved it. Blessed be our Lord, who is so good! Amen.

23. I have, it seems, wandered from my subject; for I began by speaking of raptures, and that of which I have been speaking is even more than a rapture, and the effects of it are what I have described. Now let us return to raptures, and speak of their ordinary characteristics. I have to say that, when the rapture was over, my body seemed frequently to be buoyant, as if all weight had departed from it; so much so, that now and then I scarcely knew that my feet touched the ground. But during the rapture itself the body is very often as if it were dead, perfectly powerless. It continues in the position it was in when the rapture came upon it—if sitting, sitting; if the hands were open, or if they were shut, they will remain open or shut. For though the senses fail but rarely, it has happened to me occasionally to lose them wholly—seldom, however, and then only for a short time. But in general they are in disorder; and though they have no power whatever to deal with outward things, there remains the power of hearing and seeing; but it is as if the things heard and seen were at a great distance, far away.

24. I do not say that the soul sees and hears when the rapture is at the highest,—I mean by at the highest, when the faculties are lost, because profoundly united with God,—for then it neither sees, nor hears, nor perceives, as I believe; but, as I said of the previous prayer of union,[195] this utter transformation of the soul in God continues only for an instant; yet while it continues no faculty of the soul is aware of it, or knows what is passing there. Nor can it be understood while we are living on the earth—at least, God will not have us understand it, because we must be incapable of understanding it. I know it by experience.

25. You, my father, will ask me: How comes it, then, that a rapture occasionally lasts so many hours? What has often happened to me is this,—I spoke of it before, when writing of the previous state of prayer,[196]—the rapture is not continuous, the soul is frequently absorbed, or, to speak more correctly, our Lord absorbs it in Himself; and when He has held it thus for a moment, the will alone remains in union with Him. The movements of the two other faculties seem to me to be like those of the needle of sun-dials, which is never at rest; yet when the Sun of Justice will have it so, He can hold it still.

26. This I speak of lasts but a moment; yet, as the impulse and the upraising of the spirit were vehement, and though the other faculties bestir themselves again, the will continues absorbed, and causes this operation in the body, as if it were the absolute mistress; for now that the two other faculties are restless, and attempt to disturb it, it takes care—for if it is to have enemies, the fewer the better—that the senses also shall not trouble it: and thus it comes to pass that the senses are

---

[192] § 12.

[193] The words from "I have just said" to "our Lord" are in the margin of the text, but in the handwriting of the Saint (*De la Fuente*).

[194] See § 11.

[195] Ch. xviii. § 16.

[196] Ch. xviii. § 17.

suspended; for so our Lord wills it. And for the most part the eyes are closed, though we may not wish to close them; and if occasionally they remain open, as I said just now, the soul neither discerns nor considers what it sees.

27. What the body then can do here is still less in order that, when the faculties come together again, there may not be so much to do. Let him, therefore, to whom our Lord has granted this grace, be not discouraged when he finds himself in this state—the body under constraint for many hours, the understanding and the memory occasionally astray. The truth is that, in general, they are inebriated with the praises of God, or with searching to comprehend or understand that which has passed over them. And yet even for this they are not thoroughly awake, but are rather like one who has slept long, and dreamed, and is hardly yet awake.

28. I dwell so long on this point because I know that there are persons now, even in this place,[197] to whom our Lord is granting these graces; and if their directors have had no experience in the matter, they will think, perhaps, that they must be as dead persons during the trance—and they will think so the more if they have no learning. It is piteous to see what those confessors who do not understand this make people suffer. I shall speak of it by and by.[198] Perhaps I do not know what I am saying. You, my father, will understand it, if I am at all correct; for our Lord has admitted you to the experience of it: yet, because that experience is not very great, it may be, perhaps, that you have not considered the matter so much as I have done.

29. So then, though I do all I can, my body has no strength to move for some time; the soul took it all away. Very often, too, he who was before sickly and full of pain remains healthy, and even stronger; for it is something great that is given to the soul in rapture; and sometimes, as I have said already,[199] our Lord will have the body rejoice, because it is obedient in that which the soul requires of it. When we recover our consciousness, the faculties may remain, if the rapture has been deep, for a day or two, and even for three days, so absorbed, or as if stunned,—so much so, as to be in appearance no longer themselves.

30. Here comes the pain of returning to this life; here it is the wings of the soul grew, to enable it to fly so high: the weak feathers are fallen off. Now the standard of Christ is raised up aloft, which seems to be nothing else but the going up, or the carrying up, of the Captain of the fort to the highest tower of it, there to raise up the standard of God. The soul, as in a place of safety, looks down on those below; it fears no dangers now—yes, rather, it courts them, as one assured beforehand of victory. It sees most clearly how lightly are the things of this world to be esteemed, and the nothingness thereof. The soul now seeks not, and possesses not, any other will but that of doing our Lord's will,[200] and so it prays Him to let it be so; it gives to Him the keys of its own will. Lo, the gardener is now become the commander of a fortress! The soul will do nothing but the will of our Lord; it will not act as the owner even of itself, nor of anything, not even of a single apple in the orchard; only, if there be any good thing in the garden, it is at His Majesty's disposal; for from henceforth the soul will have nothing of its own,—all it seeks is to do everything for His glory, and according to His will.

31. This is really the way in which these things come to pass; if the raptures be true raptures, the fruits and advantages spoken of abide in the soul; but if they did not, I should have great doubts about their being from God—yes, rather, I should be afraid they were those frenzies of which St. Vincent speaks. I have seen it myself, and I know it by experience, that the soul in rapture is mistress of everything, and acquires such freedom in one hour, and even in less, as to be unable to recognize itself. It sees distinctly that all this does not belong to it, neither knows it how it came to possess so great a good; but it clearly perceives the very great blessing which every one of these raptures always brings. No one will believe this who has not had experience of it, and so they do not believe the poor soul: they saw it lately so wicked, and now they see it pretend to things of so high an order; for it is not satisfied with serving our Lord in the common way,—it must do so forthwith in the

---

[197] Avila.

[198] Ch. xxv. § 18.

[199] § 9

[200] "Other will… Lord's will." These words—in Spanish, "Otra voluntad, sino hacer la de nuestro Señor"—are not in the handwriting of the Saint; perhaps it was Father Bañes who wrote them. The MS. is blurred, and the original text seems to have been, "libre alvedrio ni guerra" (*De la Fuente*).

highest way it can. They consider this a temptation and a folly; yet they would not be astonished, if they knew that it comes not from the soul, but from our Lord, to whom it has given up the keys of its will.

32. For my part, I believe that a soul which has reached this state neither speaks nor acts of itself, but rather that the supreme King takes care of all it has to do. O my God, how clear is the meaning of those words, and what good reason the Psalmist had, and all the world will ever have, to pray for the wings of a dove![201] It is plain that this is the flight of the spirit rising upwards above all created things, and chiefly above itself: but it is a sweet flight, a delicious flight—a flight without noise.

33. Oh, what power that soul possesses which our Lord raises to this state! how it looks down upon everything, entangled by nothing! how ashamed it is of the time when it was entangled! how it is amazed at its own blindness! how it pities those who are still in darkness, especially if they are men of prayer, and have received consolations from God! It would like to cry out to them, that they might be made to see the delusions they are in: and, indeed, it does so now and then; and then a thousand persecutions fall upon it as a shower. People consider it wanting in humility, and think it means to teach those from whom it should learn, particularly if it be a woman. Hence its condemnation; and not without reason; because they know not how strong the influence is that moves it. The soul at times cannot help itself; nor can it refrain from undeceiving those it loves, and whom it longs to see delivered out of the prison of this life; for that state in which the soul itself had been before neither is, nor seems to be, anything else but a prison.

34. The soul is weary of the days during which it respected points of honor, and the delusion which led it to believe that to be honor which the world calls by that name; now it sees it to be the greatest lie, and that we are all walking therein. It understands that true honor is not delusive, but real, esteeming that which is worthy of esteem, and despising that which is despicable; for everything is nothing, and less than nothing, whatever passes away, and is not pleasing unto God. The soul laughs at itself when it thinks of the time in which it regarded money, and desired to possess it,—though, as to this, I verily believe that I never had to confess such a fault; it was fault enough to have regarded money at all. If I could purchase with money the blessings which I possess, I should make much of it; but it is plain that these blessings are gained by abandoning all things.

35. What is there that is procurable by this money which we desire? Is it anything of worth, and anything lasting? Why, then, do we desire it? A dismal resting place it provides, which costs so dear! Very often it obtains for us hell itself, fire everlasting, and torments without end. Oh, if all men would but regard it as profitless dross, how peaceful the world would be! how free from bargaining! How friendly all men would be one with another, if no regard were paid to honor and money! I believe it would be a remedy for everything.

36. The soul sees how blind men are to the nature of pleasure—how by means of it they provide for themselves trouble and disquietude even in this life. What restlessness! how little satisfaction! what labor in vain! It sees, too, not only the cobwebs that cover it, and its great faults, but also the specks of dirt, however slight they may be; for the sun shines most clearly; and thus, however much the soul may have labored at its own perfection, it sees itself to be very unclean, if the rays of the sun fall really upon it. The soul is like water in a vessel, which appears pellucid when the sun does not shine through it; but if it does, the water then is found to be full of motes.

37. This comparison is literally correct. Before the soul fell into the trance, it thought itself to be careful about not offending God, and that it did what it could in proportion to its strength; but now that it has attained to this state, in which the Sun of Justice shines upon it, and makes it open its eyes, it beholds so many motes, that it would gladly close them again. It is not so truly the child of the noble eagle, that it can gaze upon the sun; but, for the few instants it can keep them open, it beholds itself wholly unclean. It remembers the words: "Who shall be just in Thy presence?"[202] When it looks on this Divine Sun, the brightness thereof dazzles it,—when it looks on itself, its eyes are blinded by the dust: the little dove is blind. So it happens very often: the soul is utterly blinded, absorbed, amazed, dizzy at the vision of so much grandeur.

---

[201] Psalm liv. 7: "Quis dabit mihi pennas sicut columbæ?"
[202] Job iv. 17: "Numquid homo Dei comparatione justificabitur?"

38. It is in rapture that true humility is acquired—humility that will never say any good of self, nor suffer others to do so. The Lord of the garden, not the soul, distributes the fruit thereof, and so none remains in its hands; all the good it has, it refers to God; if it says anything about itself, it is for His glory. It knows that it possesses nothing here; and even if it wished, it cannot continue ignorant of that. It sees this, as it were, with the naked eye; for, whether it will or not, its eyes are shut against the things of this world, and open to see the truth.

Chapter XXI.
Conclusion of the Subject. Pain of the Awakening. Light Against Delusions.

1. To bring this matter to an end, I say that it is not necessary for the soul to give its consent here; it is already given: the soul knows that it has given up its will into His hands,[203] and that it cannot deceive Him, because He knows all things. It is not here as it is in the world, where all life is full of deceit and double-dealing. When you think you have gained one man's good will, because of the outward show he makes, you afterwards learn that all was a lie. No one can live in the midst of so much scheming, particularly if there be any interests at stake.

2. Blessed, then, is that soul which our Lord draws on to the understanding of the truth! Oh, what a state for kings! How much better it would be for them if they strove for this, rather than for great dominions! How justice would prevail under their rule! What evils would be prevented, and might have been prevented already! Here no man fears to lose life or honor for the love of God. What a grand thing this would be to him who is more bound than those beneath him to regard the honor of our Lord!—for it is kings whom the crowd must follow. To make one step in the propagation of the faith, and to give one ray of light to heretics, I would forfeit a thousand kingdoms. And with good reason: for it is another thing altogether to gain a kingdom that shall never end, because one drop of the water of that kingdom, if the soul but tastes it, renders the things of this world utterly loathsome.

3. If, then, the soul should be wholly engulfed, what then? O Lord, if Thou wert to give me the right to publish this abroad, people would not believe me—as they do not believe many who are able to speak of it in a way very different from mine; but I should satisfy myself, at least. I believe I should count my life as nothing, if I might make others understand but one of these truths. I know not what I shall do afterwards, for I cannot trust myself; though I am what I am, I have a violent desire, which is wasting me, to say this to those who are in authority. And now that I can do no more, I betake myself to Thee, O my Lord, to implore a remedy for all. Thou knows well that I would gladly divest myself of all the graces which Thou has given me,—provided I remained in a condition never to offend Thee,—and give them up to those who are kings; for I know it would then be impossible for them to allow what they allow now, or fail to receive the very greatest blessings.

4. O my God, make kings to understand how far their obligations reach! Thou has been pleased to distinguish them on earth in such a way that—so I have heard—Thou shows signs in the heavens when Thou takes any of them away. Certainly, when I think of this, my devotion is stirred, because Thou will have them learn, O my King, even from this, that they must imitate Thee in their lives, seeing that, when they die, signs are visible in the heavens, as it was when Thou wert dying Thyself.

5. I am very bold; if it be wrong, you, my father, will tear this out: only believe that I should speak much more to the purpose in the presence of kings,—if I might, or thought they would listen to me,—for I recommend them greatly to God, and I wish I might be of service to them. All this makes one risk life; for I long frequently to lose mine,—and that would be to lose a little for the chance of gaining much; for surely it is not possible to live, when we see with our eyes the great delusion wherein we are walking, and the blindness in which we are living.

6. A soul that has attained to this is not limited to the desires it has to serve God; for His Majesty gives it strength to bring those desires to good effect. Nothing can be put before it into which it will not throw itself, if only it thinks that God may be served thereby: and yet it is doing nothing,

---

[203] Ch. xx. § 30.

because, as I said before,[204] it sees clearly that all is nothing, except pleasing God. The trial is, that those who are so worthless as I am, have no trial of the kind. May it be Thy good pleasure, O my God, that the time may come in which I may be able to pay one farthing at least, of the heavy debt I owe Thee! Do Thou, O Lord, so dispose matters according to Thy will, that this Thy servant may do Thee some service. Other women there have been who did heroic deeds for Thee; I am good only to talk; and so it has not been Thy pleasure, O my God, that I should do any thing: all ends in talk and desires—that is all my service. And yet even in this I am not free, because it is possible I might fail altogether.

7. Strengthen Thou my soul, and prepare it, O Good of all good; and, my Jesus, then ordain Thou the means whereby I may do something for Thee, so that there may be not even one who can bear to receive so much, and make no payment in return. Cost what it may, O Lord, let me not come before Thee with hands so empty,[205] seeing that the reward of every one will be according to his works.[206] Behold my life, behold my good name and my will; I have given them all to Thee; I am Thine: dispose of me according to Thy will. I see well enough, O Lord, how little I can do; but now, having drawn near to Thee,—having ascended to this watchtower, from which the truth may be seen,—and while Thou departs not from me, I can do all things; but if Thou departs from me, were it but for a moment, I shall go thither where I was once—that is, to hell.[207]

8. Oh, what it is for a soul in this state to have to return to the commerce of the world, to see and look on the farce of this life, so ill-ordered; to waste its time in attending to the body by sleeping and eating![208] All is wearisome; it cannot run away,—it sees itself chained and imprisoned; it feels then most keenly the captivity into which the body has brought us, and the wretchedness of this life. It understands the reason why St. Paul prayed to God to deliver him from it.[209] The soul cries with the Apostle, and calls upon God to deliver it, as I said on another occasion.[210] But here it often cries with so much violence, that it seems as if it would go out of the body in search of its freedom, now that they do not take it away. It is as a slave sold into a strange land; and what distresses it most is, that it cannot find many who make the same complaint and the same prayer: the desire of life is more common.

9. Oh, if we were utterly detached,—if we never placed our happiness in anything of this world,—how the pain, caused by living always away from God, would temper the fear of death with the desire of enjoying the true life! Sometimes I consider, if a person like myself—because our Lord has given this light to me, whose love is so cold, and whose true rest is so uncertain, for I have not deserved it by my works—frequently feels her banishment so much, what the feelings of the Saints must have been. What must St. Paul and the Magdalene, and others like them, have suffered, in whom the fire of the love of God has grown so strong? Their life must have been a continual martyrdom. It seems to me that they who bring me any comfort, and whose conversation is any relief, are those persons in whom I find these desires—I mean, desires with acts. I say with acts, for there are people who think themselves detached, and who say so of themselves,—and it must be so, for their vocation demands it, as well as the many years that are passed since some of them began to walk in the way of perfection,—but my soul distinguishes clearly, and afar off, between those who are detached in words, and those who make good those words by deeds. The little progress of the former, and the great progress of the latter, make it plain. This is a matter which a person of any experience can see into most clearly.

10. So far, then, of the effects of those raptures which come from the Spirit of God. The truth is, that these are greater or less. I say less, because in the beginning, though the effects are wrought, they are not tested by works, and so it cannot be clear that a person has them; and perfection, too, is a thing of growth, and of laboring after freedom from the cobwebs of memory; and this requires some time. Meanwhile, the greater the growth of love and humility in the soul, the stronger the

---

[204] Ch. xx. § 34.

[205] Exod. xxiii. 15: "Non apparebis in conspectu meo vacuus."

[206] Apoc. ii. 23: "Dabo unicuique vestrum secundum opera sua."

[207] See ch. xxxii. § 1.

[208] *Interior Castle*, iv. ch. i. § 11.

[209] Rom. vii. 24: "Quis me liberabit de corpore mortis hujus?"

[210] Ch. xvi. § 7.

perfume of the flowers of virtues is for itself and for others. The truth is, that our Lord can so work in the soul in an instant during these raptures, that but little remains for the soul to do in order to attain to perfection. No one, who has not had experience of it, will ever be able to believe what our Lord now bestows on the soul. No effort of ours—so I think—can ever reach so far.

11. However, I do not mean to say that those persons who during many years make use of the method prescribed by writers on prayer,—who discuss the principles thereof, and the means whereby it may be acquired,—will not, by the help of our Lord, attain to perfection and great detachment with much labor; but they will not attain to it so rapidly as by the way of raptures, in which our Lord works independently of us, draws the soul utterly away from earth, and gives it dominion over all things here below, though the merits of that soul may not be greater than mine were: I cannot use stronger language, for my merits are as nothing. Why His Majesty does this is, because it is His pleasure, and He does it according to His pleasure; even if the soul be without the fitting disposition, He disposes it for the reception of that blessing which He is giving to it. Although it be most certain that He never fails to comfort those who do well, and strive to be detached, still He does not always give these effects because they have deserved them at His hands by cultivating the garden, but because it is His will to show His greatness at times in a soil which is most worthless, as I have just said, and to prepare it for all good: and all this in such a way that it seems as if the soul was now, in a manner, unable to go back and live in sin against God, as it did before.

12. The mind is now so inured to the comprehension of that which is truth indeed, that everything else seems to it to be but child's play. It laughs to itself, at times, when it sees grave men—men given to prayer, men of religion—make much of points of honor, which itself is trampling beneath its feet. They say that discretion, and the dignity of their callings, require it of them as a means to do more good; but that soul knows perfectly well that they would do more good in one day by preferring the love of God to this their dignity, than they will do in ten years by considering it.

13. The life of this soul is a life of trouble: the cross is always there, but the progress it makes is great. When those who have to do with it think it has arrived at the summit of perfection, within a little while they see it much more advanced; for God is ever giving it grace upon grace. God is the soul of that soul now; it is He who has the charge of it; and so He enlightens it; for He seems to be watching over it, always attentive to it, that it may not offend Him,—giving it grace, and stirring it up in His service. When my soul reached this state, in which God showed me mercy so great, my wretchedness came to an end, and our Lord gave me strength to rise above it. The former occasions of sin, as well as the persons with whom I was accustomed to distract myself, did me no more harm than if they had never existed; on the contrary, that which ordinarily did me harm, helped me on. Everything contributed to make me know God more, and to love Him; to make me see how much I owed Him, as well as to be sorry for being what I had been.

14. I saw clearly that this did not come from myself, that I had not brought it about by any efforts of my own, and that there was not time enough for it. His Majesty, of His mere goodness, had given me strength for it. From the time our Lord began to give me the grace of raptures, until now, this strength has gone on increasing. He, of His goodness, hath held me by the hand, that I might not go back. I do not think that I am doing anything myself—certainly I do not; for I see distinctly that all this is the work of our Lord. For this reason, it seems to me that the soul in which our Lord works these graces,—if it walks in humility and fear, always acknowledging the work of our Lord, and that we ourselves can do, as it were, nothing,—may be thrown among any companions, and, however distracted and wicked these may be, will neither be hurt nor disturbed in any way; on the contrary, as I have just said, that will help it on, and be a means unto it whereby it may derive much greater profit.

15. Those souls are strong which are chosen by our Lord to do good to others; still, this their strength is not their own. When our Lord brings a soul on to this state, He communicates to it of His greatest secrets by degrees. True revelations—the great gifts and visions—come by ecstasies, all tending to make the soul humble and strong, to make it despise the things of this world, and have a clearer knowledge of the greatness of the reward which our Lord has prepared for those who serve Him.[211]

---

[211] 1 Cor. ii. 9: "Quæ præparavit Deus his qui diligunt Illum."

16. May it please His Majesty that the great munificence with which He hath dealt with me, miserable sinner that I am, may have some weight with those who shall read this, so that they may be strong and courageous enough to give up everything utterly for God. If His Majesty repays us so abundantly, that even in this life the reward and gain of those who serve Him become visible, what will it be in the next?

Chapter XXII.

The Security of Contemplatives Lies in Their Not Ascending to High Things if Our Lord Does Not Raise Them. The Sacred Humanity Must Be the Road to the Highest Contemplation. A Delusion in Which the Saint Was Once Entangled.

1. There is one thing I should like to say—I think it important: and if you, my father, approve, it will serve for a lesson that possibly may be necessary; for in some books on prayer the writers say that the soul, though it cannot in its own strength attain to this state,—because it is altogether a supernatural work wrought in it by our Lord,—may nevertheless succeed, by lifting up the spirit above all created things, and raising it upwards in humility, after some years spent in a purgative life, and advancing in the illuminative. I do not very well know what they mean by illuminative: I understand it to mean the life of those who are making progress. And they advise us much to withdraw from all bodily imagination, and draw near to the contemplation of the Divinity; for they say that those who have advanced so far would be embarrassed or hindered in their way to the highest contemplation, if they regarded even the Sacred Humanity itself.[212] They defend their opinion[213] by bringing forward the words[214] of our Lord to the Apostles, concerning the coming of the Holy Ghost; I mean that Coming which was after the Ascension. If the Apostles had believed, as they believed after the Coming of the Holy Ghost, that He is both God and Man, His bodily Presence would, in my opinion, have been no hindrance; for those words were not said to the Mother of God, though she loved Him more than all.[215] They think that, as this work of contemplation is wholly spiritual, any bodily object whatever can disturb or hinder it. They say that the contemplative should regard himself as being within a definite space, God everywhere around, and himself absorbed in Him. This is what we should aim at.

2. This seems to me right enough now and then; but to withdraw altogether from Christ, and to compare His divine Body with our miseries or with any created thing whatever, is what I cannot endure. May God help me to explain myself! I am not contradicting them on this point, for they are learned and spiritual persons, understanding what they say: God, too, is guiding souls by many ways and methods, as He has guided mine. It is of my own soul that I wish to speak now,—I do not intermeddle with others,—and of the danger I was in because I would comply with the directions I was reading. I can well believe that he who has attained to union, and advances no further,—that is, to raptures, visions, and other graces of God given to souls,—will consider that opinion to be best, as I did myself: and if I had continued in it, I believe I should never have reached the state I am in now. I hold it to be a delusion: still, it may be that it is I who am deluded. But I will tell you what happened to me.

3. As I had no director, I used to read these books, where, by little and little, I thought I might understand something. I found out afterwards that, if our Lord had not shown me the way, I should have learned but little from books; for I understood really nothing till His Majesty made me learn by experience: neither did I know what I was doing. So, in the beginning, when I attained to some

---

[212] See *Interior Castle*, vi. 7, § 4.

[213] This opinion is supposed to be justified by the words of St. Thomas, 3 Sent. dist. 22, qu. 3, art. 1, *ad quintum.* "Corporalis præsentia Christi in duobus poterat esse nociva. Primo, quantum ad fidem, quia videntes Eum in forma in qua erat minor Patre, non ita de facili crederent Eum æqualem Patri, ut dicit glossa super Joannem. Secundo, quantum ad dilectionem, quia Eum non solum spiritualiter, sed etiam carnaliter diligeremus, conversantes cum Ipso corporaliter, et hoc est de imperfectione dilectionis."

[214] St. John xvi. 7: "Expedit vobis ut Ego vadam; si enim non abiero, Paracletus non veniet ad vos."

[215] This sentence is in the margin of the original MS., not in the text, but in the handwriting of the Saint (*De la Fuente*).

degree of supernatural prayer,—I speak of the prayer of quiet,—I labored to remove from myself every thought of bodily objects; but I did not dare to lift up my soul, for that I saw would be presumption in me, who was always so wicked. I thought, however, that I had a sense of the presence of God: this was true, and I contrived to be in a state of recollection before Him. This method of prayer is full of sweetness, if God helps us in it, and the joy of it is great. And so, because I was conscious of the profit and delight which this way furnished me, no one could have brought me back to the contemplation of the Sacred Humanity; for that seemed to me to be a real hindrance to prayer.

4. O Lord of my soul, and my Good! Jesus Christ crucified! I never think of this opinion, which I then held, without pain; I believe it was an act of high treason, though done in ignorance. Hitherto, I had been all my life long so devout to the Sacred Humanity—for this happened but lately; I mean by lately, that it was before our Lord gave me the grace of raptures and visions. I did not continue long of this opinion,[216] and so I returned to my habit of delighting in our Lord, particularly at Communion. I wish I could have His picture and image always before my eyes, since I cannot have Him graven in my soul as deeply as I wish.

5. Is it possible, O my Lord, that I could have had the thought, if only for an hour, that Thou could be a hindrance to my greatest good? Whence are all my blessings? are they not from Thee? I will not think that I was blamable, for I was very sorry for it, and it was certainly done in ignorance. And so it pleased Thee, in Thy goodness, to succor me, by sending me one who has delivered me from this delusion; and afterwards by showing Thyself to me so many times, as I shall relate hereafter,[217] that I might clearly perceive how great my delusion was, and also tell it to many persons; which I have done, as well as describe it as I am doing now. I believe myself that this is the reason why so many souls, after advancing to the prayer of union, make no further progress, and do not attain to very great liberty of spirit.

6. It seems to me, that there are two considerations on which I may ground this opinion. Perhaps I am saying nothing to the purpose, yet what I say is the result of experience; for my soul was in a very evil plight, till our Lord enlightened it: all its joys were but sips; and when it had come forth therefrom, it never found itself in that company which afterwards it had in trials and temptations.

7. The first consideration is this: there is a little absence of humility—so secret and so hidden, that we do not observe it. Who is there so proud and wretched as I, that, even after laboring all his life in penances and prayers and persecutions, can possibly imagine himself not to be exceedingly rich, most abundantly rewarded, when our Lord permits him to stand with St. John at the foot of the cross? I know not into whose head it could have entered to be not satisfied with this, unless it be mine, which has gone wrong in every way where it should have gone right onwards.

8. Then, if our constitution—or perhaps sickness—will not permit us always to think of His Passion, because it is so painful, who is to hinder us from thinking of Him risen from the grave, seeing that we have Him so near us in the Sacrament, where he is glorified, and where we shall not see Him in His great weariness—scourged, streaming with blood, faint by the way, persecuted by those to whom He had done good, and not believed in by the Apostles? Certainly it is not always that one can bear to meditate on sufferings so great as were those He underwent. Behold Him here, before His ascension into heaven, without pain, all-glorious, giving strength to some and courage to others. In the most Holy Sacrament, He is our companion, as if it was not in His power to withdraw Himself for a moment from us. And yet it was in my power to withdraw from Thee, O my Lord, that I might serve Thee better! It may be that I knew Thee not when I sinned against Thee; but how could I, having once known Thee, ever think I should gain more in this way? O Lord, what an evil way I took! and I was going out of the way, if Thou has not brought me back to it. When I see Thee near me, I see all good things together. No trial befalls me that is not easy to bear, when I think of Thee standing before those who judged Thee.

9. With so good a Friend and Captain ever present, Himself the first to suffer, everything can be borne. He helps, He strengthens, He never fails, He is the true Friend. I see clearly, and since

---

[216] "I mean by lately… and visions" is in the margin of the MS., but in the handwriting of the Saint (*De la Fuente*).

[217] Ch. xxviii. § 4.

then have always seen, that if we are to please God, and if He is to give us His great graces, everything must pass through the hands of His most Sacred Humanity, in whom His Majesty said that He is well pleased.[218] I know this by repeated experience: our Lord has told it me. I have seen clearly that this is the door[219] by which we are to enter, if we would have His supreme Majesty reveal to us His great secrets.

10. So, then, I would have your reverence seek no other way, even if you were arrived at the highest contemplation. This way is safe. Our Lord is He by whom all good things come to us; He will teach you. Consider His life; that is the best example. What more can we want than so good a Friend at our side, who will not forsake us when we are in trouble and distress, as they do who belong to this world! Blessed is he who truly loves Him, and who always has Him near him! Let us consider the glorious St. Paul, who seems as if Jesus was never absent from his lips, as if he had Him deep down in his heart. After I had heard this of some great Saints given to contemplation, I considered the matter carefully; and I see that they walked in no other way. St. Francis with the stigmata proves it, St. Antony of Padua with the Infant Jesus; St. Bernard rejoiced in the Sacred Humanity; so did St. Catherine of Siena, and many others, as your reverence knows better than I do.

11. This withdrawing from bodily objects must no doubt be good, seeing that it is recommended by persons who are so spiritual; but, in my opinion, it ought to be done only when the soul has made very great progress; for until then it is clear that the Creator must be sought for through His creatures. All this depends on the grace which our Lord distributes to every soul. I do not intermeddle here. What I would say is, that the most Sacred Humanity of Christ is not to be counted among the objects from which we have to withdraw. Let this be clearly understood. I wish I knew how to explain it.[220]

12. When God suspends all the powers of the soul,—as we see He does in the states of prayer already described,—it is clear that, whether we wish it or not, this presence is withdrawn. Be it so, then. The loss is a blessed one, because it takes place in order that we may have a deeper fruition of what we seem to have lost; for at that moment the whole soul is occupied in loving Him whom the understanding has toiled to know; and it loves what it has not comprehended, and rejoices in what it could not have rejoiced in so well, if it had not lost itself, in order, as I am saying, to gain itself the more. But that we should carefully and laboriously accustom ourselves not to strive with all our might to have always—and please God it be always!—the most Sacred Humanity before our eyes,—this, I say, is what seems to me not to be right: it is making the soul, as they say, to walk in the air; for it has nothing to rest on, how full so ever of God it may think itself to be.

13. It is a great matter for us to have our Lord before us as Man while we are living and in the flesh. This is that other inconvenience which I say must be met with. The first—I have already begun to describe it—is a little failure in humility, in that the soul desires to rise of itself before our Lord raises it, and is not satisfied with meditation on so excellent a subject,—seeking to be Mary before it has labored with Martha. If our Lord will have a soul to be Mary, even on the first day, there is nothing to be afraid of; but we must not be self-invited guests, as I think I said on another occasion.[221] This little mote of want of humility, though in appearance a mere nothing, does a great deal of harm to those who wish to advance in contemplation.

14. I now come back to the second consideration. We are not angels, for we have a body; to seek to make ourselves angels while we are on the earth, and so much on the earth as I was, is an act of folly. In general, our thoughts must have something to rest on, though the soul may go forth out of itself now and then, or it may be very often so full of God as to be in need of no created thing by the help of which it may recollect itself. But this is not so common a case; for when we have many things to do, when we are persecuted and in trouble, when we cannot have much rest, and when we have our seasons of dryness, Christ is our best Friend; for we regard Him as Man, and behold Him faint and in trouble, and He is our Companion; and when we shall have accustomed

---

[218] St. Matt. iii. 17: "Hic est Filius Meus dilectus, in quo Mihi complacui."

[219] St. John x. 7, 9: "Ego sum ostium."

[220] See St. John of the Cross, *Mount Carmel*, bk. iii. ch. i. p. 212.

[221] Ch. xii. §§ 5, 7.

ourselves in this way, it is very easy to find Him near us, although there will be occasions from time to time when we can do neither the one nor the other.

15. For this end, that is useful which I spoke of before:[222] we must not show ourselves as laboring after spiritual consolations; come what may, to embrace the cross is the great thing. The Lord of all consolation was Himself forsaken: they left Him alone in His sorrows. Do not let us forsake Him; for His hand will help us to rise more than any efforts we can make; and He will withdraw Himself when He sees it be expedient for us, and when He pleases will also draw the soul forth out of itself, as I said before.[223]

16. God is greatly pleased when He beholds a soul in its humility making His Son a Mediator between itself and Him, and yet loving Him so much as to confess its own unworthiness, even when He would raise it up to the highest contemplation, and saying with St. Peter:[224] "Go Thou away from me, O Lord, for I am a sinful man." I know this by experience: it was thus that God directed my soul. Others may walk, as I said before,[225] by another and a shorter road. What I have understood of the matter is this: that the whole foundation of prayer must be laid in humility, and that the more a soul humbles itself in prayer, the more God lifts it up. I do not remember that He ever showed me any of those marvelous mercies, of which I shall speak hereafter,[226] at any other time than when I was as one brought to nothing,[227] by seeing how wicked I was. Moreover, His Majesty contrived to make me understand matters that helped me to know myself, but which I could never have even imagined of myself.

17. I believe myself that if a soul makes any efforts of its own to further itself in the way of the prayer of union, and though it may seem to make immediate progress, it will quickly fall back, because the foundations were not duly laid. I fear, too, that such a soul will never attain to true poverty of spirit, which consists in seeking consolation or sweetness, not in prayer,—the consolations of the earth are already abandoned,—but rather in sorrows, for the love of Him who always lived in sorrows Himself;[228] and in being calm in the midst of sorrows and aridities. Though the soul may feel it in some measure, there is no disquiet, nor any of that pain which some persons suffer, who, if they are not always laboring with the understanding and with a sense of devotion, think everything lost,—as if their efforts merited so great a blessing!

18. I am not saying that men should not seek to be devout, nor that they should not stand with great reverence in the presence of God, but only that they are not to vex themselves if they cannot find even one good thought, as I said in another place;[229] for we are unprofitable servants.[230] What do we think we can do? Our Lord grant that we understand this, and that we may be those little asses who drive the windlass I spoke of:[231] these, though their eyes are bandaged, and they do not understand what they are doing, yet draw up more water than the gardener can draw with all his efforts. We must walk in liberty on this road, committing ourselves into the hands of God. If it be His Majesty's good pleasure to raise us and place us among His chamberlains and secret councilors, we must go willingly; if not, we must serve Him in the lower offices of His house, and not sit down on the upper seats.[232] As I have sometimes said,[233] God is more careful of us than we are ourselves, and knows what each one of us is fit for.

19. What use is there in governing oneself by oneself, when the whole will has been given up to God? I think this less endurable now than in the first state of prayer, and it does much greater

[222] Ch. xv. § 21.

[223] Ch. xx. § 2.

[224] St. Luke v. 8: "Exi a me, quia homo peccator sum, Domine."

[225] Ch. xii. § 6.

[226] Ch. xxviii.

[227] Psalm lxxii. 22: "Et ego ad nihilum redactus sum, et nescivi."

[228] Isaias liii. 3: "Virum dolorum, et scientem infirmitatem."

[229] Ch. xi. § 15.

[230] St. Luke xvii. 10: "Servi inutiles sumus."

[231] Ch. xi. § 11.

[232] St. Luke xiv. 8: "Non discumbas in primo loco." See *Way of Perfection*, ch. xxvi. § 1; but ch. xvii. of the old editions.

[233] Ch. xi. § 23, ch. xviii. § 6

harm; for these blessings are supernatural. If a man has a bad voice, let him force himself ever so much to sing, he will never improve it; but if God gives him a good voice, he has no need to try it twice. Let us, then, pray Him always to show His mercy upon us, with a submissive spirit, yet trusting in the goodness of God. And now that the soul is permitted to sit at the feet of Christ, let it contrive not to quit its place, but keep it anyhow. Let it follow the example of the Magdalene; and when it shall be strong enough, God will lead it into the wilderness.[234]

20. You, then, my father, must be content with this until you meet with some one of more experience and better knowledge than I am. If you see people who are beginning to taste of God, do not trust them if they think that they advance more, and have a deeper fruition of God, when they make efforts of their own. Oh, when God wills it, how He discovers Himself without these little efforts of ours! We may do what we like, but He throws the spirit into a trance as easily as a giant takes up a straw; no resistance is possible. What a thing to believe, that God will wait till the toad shall fly of itself, when He has already willed it should do so! Well, it seems to me still more difficult and hard for our spirit to rise upwards, if God does not raise it, seeing that it is burdened with earth, and hindered in a thousand ways. Its willingness to rise is of no service to it; for, though an aptness for flying be more natural to it than to a toad, yet is it so sunk in the mire as to have lost it by its own fault.

21. I come, then, to this conclusion: whenever we think of Christ, we should remind ourselves of the love that made Him bestow so many graces upon us, and also how great that love is which our Lord God has shown us, in giving us such a pledge of the love He bears us; for love draws forth love. And though we are only at the very beginning, and exceedingly wicked, yet let us always labor to keep this in view, and stir ourselves up to love; for if once our Lord grants us this grace, of having this love imprinted in our hearts, everything will be easy, and we shall do great things in a very short time, and with very little labor. May His Majesty give us that love,—He knows the great need we have of it,—for the sake of that love which He bore us, and of His glorious Son, to whom it cost so much to make it known to us! Amen.

22. There is one thing I should like to ask you, my father. How is it that, when our Lord begins to bestow upon a soul a grace so great as this of perfect contemplation, it is not, as it ought to be, perfect at once? Certainly, it seems it should be so; for he who receives a grace so great ought never more to seek consolations on earth. How is it, I ask, that a soul which has ecstasies and so far is more accustomed to receive graces, should yet seem to bring forth fruits still higher and higher,—and the more so, the more it is detached,—when our Lord might have sanctified it at once, the moment He came near it? How is it, I ask again, that the same Lord brings it to the perfection of virtue only in the course of time? I should be glad to learn the reason, for I know it not. I do know, however, that in the beginning, when a trance lasts only the twinkling of an eye, and is almost imperceptible but for the effects it produces, the degree of strength which God then gives is very different from that which He gives when this grace is a trance of longer duration.

23. Very often, when thinking of this, have I imagined the reason might be, that the soul does not despise itself all at once, till our Lord instructs it by degrees, and makes it resolute, and gives it the strength of manhood, so that it may trample utterly upon everything. He gave this strength to the Magdalene in a moment. He gives the same grace to others, according to the measure of their abandonment of themselves into the hands of His Majesty, that He may do with them as He will. We never thoroughly believe that God rewards a hundredfold even in this life.[235]

24. I also thought of this comparison: supposing grace given to those who are far advanced to be the same with that given to those who are but beginners, we may then liken it to a certain food of which many persons partake: they who eat a little retain the savor of it for a moment, they who eat more are nourished by it, but those who eat much receive life and strength. Now, the soul may eat so frequently and so abundantly of this food of life as to have no pleasure in eating any other food, because it sees how much good it derives from it. Its taste is now so formed upon it, that it would rather not live than have to eat any other food; for all food but this has no other effect than to take away the sweet savor which this good food leaves behind.

---

[234] Os. ii. 14: "Ducam eam in solitudinem."

[235] St. Matt. xix. 29: "Qui reliquerit domum,... centuplum accipiet."

25. Further, the conversation of good people does not profit us in one day as much as it does in many; and we may converse with them long enough to become like them, by the grace of God. In short, the whole matter is as His Majesty wills. He gives His grace to whom He pleases; but much depends on this: he who begins to receive this grace must make a firm resolution to detach himself from all things, and esteem this grace according to reason.

26. It seems also to me as if His Majesty were going about to try those who love Him,—now one, now another,—revealing Himself in supreme joy, so as to quicken our belief, if it should be dead, in what He will give us, saying, Behold! this is but a drop of the immense sea of blessings; for He leaves nothing undone for those He loves; and as He sees them receive it, so He gives, and He gives Himself. He loves those who love Him. Oh, how dear He is!—how good a Friend! O my soul's Lord, who can find words to describe what Thou gives to those who trust in Thee, and what they lose who come to this state, and yet dwell in themselves! Oh, let not this be so, O my Lord! for Thou does more than this when Thou comes to a lodging so mean as mine. Blessed be Thou for ever and ever!

27. I now humbly ask you, my father, if you mean to discuss what I have written on prayer with spiritual persons, to see that they are so really; for if they be persons who know only one way, or who have stood still midway, they will not be able to understand the matter. There are also some whom God leads at once by the highest way; these think that others might advance in the same manner—quiet the understanding, and make bodily objects none of their means; but these people will remain dry as a stick. Others, also, there are who, having for a moment attained to the prayer of quiet, think forthwith that, as they have had the one, so they may have the other. These instead of advancing, go back, as I said before.[236] So, throughout, experience and discretion are necessary. May our Lord, of His goodness, bestow them on us!

Chapter XXIII.

The Saint Resumes the History of Her Life. Aiming at Perfection. Means Whereby It May Be Gained. Instructions for Confessors.

1. I shall now return to that point in my life where I broke off,[237] having made, I believe, a longer digression than I need have made, in order that what is still to come may be more clearly understood. Henceforth, it is another and a new book,—I mean, another and a new life. Hitherto, my life was my own; my life, since I began to explain these methods of prayer, is the life which God lived in me,—so it seems to me; for I feel it to be impossible that I should have escaped in so short a time from ways and works that were so wicked. May our Lord be praised, who has delivered me from myself!

2. When, then, I began to avoid the occasions of sin, and to give myself more unto prayer, our Lord also began to bestow His graces upon me, as one who desired, so it seemed, that I too should be willing to receive them. His Majesty began to give me most frequently the grace of the prayer of quiet, and very often that of union, which lasted some time. But as, in these days, women have fallen into great delusions and deceits of Satan,[238] I began to be afraid, because the joy and sweetness which I felt were so great, and very often beyond my power to avoid. On the other hand, I felt in myself a very deep conviction that God was with me, especially when I was in prayer. I saw, too, that I grew better and stronger thereby.

3. But if I was a little distracted, I began to be afraid, and to imagine that perhaps it was Satan that suspended my understanding, making me think it to be good, in order to withdraw me from mental prayer, hinder my meditation on the Passion, and debar me the use of my understanding: this seemed to me, who did not comprehend the matter, to be a grievous loss but, as His Majesty was pleased to give me light to offend Him no more, and to understand how much I owed Him, this

---

[236] Ch. xii. § 5.

[237] At the end of ch. ix. The thirteen chapters interposed between that and this—the twenty-third—are a treatise on mystical theology.

[238] She refers to Magdalene of the Cross (*Reforma de los Descalços*, vol. i. lib. i. c. xix. § 2).

fear so grew upon me, that it made me seek diligently for spiritual persons with whom I might treat of my state. I had already heard of some; for the Fathers of the Society of Jesus had come hither;[239] and I, though I knew none of them, was greatly attracted by them, merely because I had heard of their way of life and of prayer; but I did not think myself fit to speak to them, or strong enough to obey them; and this made me still more afraid; for to converse with them, and remain what I was, seemed to me somewhat rude.

4. I spent some time in this state, till, after much inward contention and fear, I determined to confer with some spiritual person, to ask him to tell me what that method of prayer was which I was using, and to show me whether I was in error. I was also resolved to do everything I could not to offend God; for the want of courage of which I was conscious, as I said before,[240] made me so timid. Was there ever delusion so great as mine, O my God, when I withdrew from good in order to become good! The devil must lay much stress on this in the beginning of a course of virtue; for I could not overcome my repugnance. He knows that the whole relief of the soul consists in conferring with the friends of God. Hence it was that no time was fixed in which I should resolve to do this. I waited to grow better first, as I did before when I ceased to pray,[241]—and perhaps I never should have become better; for I had now sunk so deeply into the petty ways of an evil habit,—I could not convince myself that they were wrong,—that I needed the help of others, who should hold out a hand to raise me up. Blessed be Thou, O Lord!—for the first hand outstretched to me was Thine.

5. When I saw that my fear was going so far, it struck me—because I was making progress in prayer—that this must be a great blessing, or a very great evil; for I understood perfectly that what had happened was something supernatural, because at times I was unable to withstand it; to have it when I would was also impossible. I thought to myself that there was no help for it, but in keeping my conscience pure, avoiding every occasion even of venial sins; for if it was the work of the Spirit of God, the gain was clear; and if the work of Satan, so long as I strove to please, and did not offend, our Lord, Satan could do me little harm; on the contrary, he must lose in the struggle. Determined on this course, and always praying God to help me, striving also after purity of conscience for some days, I saw that my soul had not strength to go forth alone to a perfection so great. I had certain attachments to trifles, which, though not very wrong in themselves, were yet enough to ruin all.

6. I was told of a learned ecclesiastic,[242] dwelling in this city, whose goodness and pious life our Lord was beginning to make known to the world. I contrived to make his acquaintance through a saintly nobleman[243] living in the same place. This latter is a married man; but his life is so edifying and virtuous, so given to prayer, and so full of charity, that the goodness and perfection of it shine forth in all he does: and most justly so; for many souls have been greatly blessed through him, because of his great gifts, which, though his condition of a layman be a hindrance to him, never lie idle. He is a man of great sense, and very gentle with all people; his conversation is never wearisome, but so sweet and gracious, as well as upright and holy, that he pleases everybody very much with whom he has any relations. He directs it all to the great good of those souls with whom he converses and he seems to have no other end in view but to do all he may be permitted to do for all men, and make them content.

---

[239] The college of the Society at Avila was founded in 1555; but some of the Fathers had come thither in 1553 (*De la Fuente*).

[240] Ch. vii. § 37.

[241] Ch. xix. §§ 7, 8.

[242] Gaspar Daza had formed a society of priests in Avila, and was a very laborious and holy man. It was he who said the first Mass in the monastery of St. Joseph, founded by St. Teresa, whom he survived, dying Nov. 24, 1592. He committed the direction of his priests to F. Baltasar Alvarez (*Bouix*). Juan of Avila acted much in the same way when the Jesuits settled in Avila (*De la Fuente*).

[243] Don Francisco de Salcedo. After the death of his wife, he became a priest, and was chaplain and confessor of the Carmelite nuns of St. Joseph. For twenty years of his married life he attended regularly the theological lectures of the Dominicans, in the house of St. Thomas. His death took place Sept. 12, 1580, when he had been a priest for ten years (*St. Teresa's Letters*, vol. iv. letter 43, note 13: letter 368, ed. of De la Fuente).

7. This blessed and holy man, then, seems to me, by the pains he took, to have been the beginning of salvation to my soul. His humility in his relations with me makes me wonder; for he had spent, I believe, nearly forty years in prayer,—it may be two or three years less,—and all his life was ordered with that perfection which his state admitted. His wife is so great a servant of God, and so full of charity, that nothing is lost to him on her account,[244]—in short, she was the chosen wife of one who God knew would serve Him so well. Some of their kindred are married to some of mine. Besides, I had also much communication with another great servant of God, married to one of my first cousins.

8. It was thus I contrived that the ecclesiastic I speak of, who was so great a servant of God, and his great friend, should come to speak to me, intending to confess to him, and to take him for my director. When he had brought him to speak to me, I, in the greatest confusion at finding myself in the presence of so holy a man, revealed to him the state of my soul, and my way of prayer. He would not be my confessor; he said that he was very much occupied: and so, indeed, he was. He began with a holy resolution to direct me as if I was strong,—I ought to have been strong, according to the method of prayer which he saw I used,—so that I should in nothing offend God. When I saw that he was resolved to make me break off at once with the petty ways I spoke of before,[245] and that I had not the courage to go forth at once in the perfection he required of me, I was distressed; and when I perceived that he ordered the affairs of my soul as if I ought to be perfect at once, I saw that much more care was necessary in my case. In a word, I felt that the means he would have employed were not those by which my soul could be helped onwards; for they were fitted for a soul more perfect than mine; and though the graces I had received from God were very many, I was still at the very beginning in the matter of virtue and of mortification.

9. I believe certainly, if I had only had this ecclesiastic to confer with, that my soul would have made no progress; for the pain it gave me to see that I was not doing—and, as I thought, could not do—what he told me, was enough to destroy all hope, and make me abandon the matter altogether. I wonder at times how it was that he, being one who had a particular grace for the direction of beginners in the way of God, was not permitted to understand my case, or to undertake the care of my soul. I see it was all for my greater good, in order that I might know and converse with persons so holy as the members of the Society of Jesus.

10. After this, I arranged with that saintly nobleman that he should come and see me now and then. It shows how deep his humility was; for he consented to converse with a person so wicked as I was. He began his visits, he encouraged me, and told me that I ought not to suppose I could give up everything in one day; God would bring it about by degrees: he himself had for some years been unable to free himself from some very slight imperfections. O humility! what great blessings thou brings to those in whom thou dwells, and to them who draw near to those who possess thee! This holy man—for I think I may justly call him so—told me of weaknesses of his own, in order to help me. He, in his humility, thought them weaknesses; but, if we consider his state, they were neither faults nor imperfections; yet, in my state, it was a very great fault to be subject to them.

11. I am not saying this without a meaning, though I seem to be enlarging on trifles; but these trifles contribute so much towards the beginning of the soul's progress and its flight upwards, though it has no wings, as they say; and yet no one will believe it who has not had experience of it; but, as I hope in God that your reverence will help many a soul, I speak of it here. My whole salvation depended on his knowing how to treat me, on his humility, on the charity with which he conversed with me, and on his patient endurance of me when he saw that I did not mend my ways at once. He went on discreetly, by degrees showing me how to overcome Satan. My affection for him so grew upon me, that I never was more at ease than on the day I used to see him. I saw him, however, very rarely. When he was long in coming, I used to be very much distressed, thinking that he would not see me because I was so wicked.

12. When he found out my great imperfections, they might well have been sins, though since I conversed with him I am somewhat improved,—and when I recounted to him, in order to obtain light from him, the great graces which God had bestowed upon me, he told me that these things

---

[244] Doña Mencia del Aguila (*De la Fuente*, in a note on letter 10, vol. ii. p. 9, where he corrects himself,—having previously called her Mencia de Avila).

[245] § 4.

were inconsistent one with another; that these consolations were given to people who had made great progress, and led mortified lives; that he could not help being very much afraid—he thought that the evil spirit might have something to do in my case; he would not decide that question, however, but he would have me carefully consider my whole method of prayer, and then tell him of it. That was the difficulty: I did not understand it myself, and so I could tell him nothing of my prayer; for the grace to understand it—and, understanding it, to describe it—has only lately been given me of God. This saying of his, together with the fear I was in, distressed me exceedingly, and I cried; for certainly I was anxious to please God, and I could not persuade myself that Satan had anything to do with it. But I was afraid, on account of my great sins, that God might leave me blind, so that I should understand nothing.

13. Looking into books to see if I could find anything there by which I might recognize the prayer I practiced, I found in one of them, called the *Ascent of the Mount*, and in that part of it which relates to the union of the soul with God, all those marks which I had in myself, in that I could not think of anything. This is what I most dwelt on—that I could think of nothing when I was in prayer. I marked that passage, and gave him the book, that he, and the ecclesiastic mentioned before,[246] saint and servant of God, might consider it, and tell me what I should do. If they thought it right, I would give up that method of prayer altogether; for why should I expose myself to danger, when, at the end of nearly twenty years, during which I had used it, I had gained nothing, but had fallen into a delusion of the devil? It was better for me to give it up. And yet this seemed to me hard; for I had already discovered what my soul would become without prayer. Everything seemed full of trouble. I was like a person in the middle of a river, who, in whatever direction he may turn, fears a still greater danger, and is well-nigh drowned. This is a very great trial, and I have gone through many like it, as I shall show hereafter;[247] and though it does not seem to be of any importance, it will perhaps be advantageous to understand how the spirit is to be tried.

14. And certainly the affliction to be borne is great, and caution is necessary, particularly in the case of women,—for our weakness is great,—and much evil may be the result of telling them very distinctly that the devil is busy with them; yes, rather, the matter should be very carefully considered, and they should be removed out of reach of the dangers that may arise. They should be advised to keep things secret; and it is necessary, also, that their secret should be kept. I am speaking of this as one to whom it has been a sore trouble; for some of those with whom I spoke of my prayer did not keep my secret, but, making inquiries one of another, for a good purpose, did me much harm; for they made things known which might well have remained secret, because not intended for every one and it seemed as if I had made them public myself.[248]

15. I believe that our Lord permitted this to be done without sin on their part, in order that I might suffer. I do not say that they revealed anything I discussed with them in confession; still, as they were persons to whom, in my fears, I gave a full account of myself, in order that they might give me light, I thought they ought to have been silent. Nevertheless, I never dared to conceal anything from such persons. My meaning, then, is, that women should be directed with much discretion; their directors should encourage them, and bide the time when our Lord will help them, as He has helped me. If He had not, the greatest harm would have befallen me, for I was in great fear and dread; and as I suffered from disease of the heart,[249] I am astonished that all this did not do me a great deal of harm.

16. Then, when I had given him the book, and told the story of my life and of my sins, the best way I could in general,—for I was not in confession, because he was a layman; yet I gave him clearly to understand how wicked I was,—those two servants of God, with great charity and affection, considered what was best for me. When they had made up their minds what to say,—I was waiting for it in great dread, having begged many persons to pray to God for me, and I too had prayed much during those days,—the nobleman came to me in great distress, and said that, in the opinion of both, I was deluded by an evil spirit; that the best thing for me to do was to apply to a certain father of the Society of Jesus, who would come to me if I sent for him, saying I had need of

[246] § 6.
[247] See ch. xxv. § 18.
[248] See ch. xxviii. § 18.
[249] See ch. iv. § 6.

him; that I ought, in a general confession, to give him an account of my whole life, and of the state I was in,—and all with great clearness: God would, in virtue of the Sacrament of Confession, give him more light concerning me; for those fathers were very experienced men in matters of spirituality. Further, I was not to swerve in a single point from the counsels of that father; for I was in great danger, if I had no one to direct me.

17. This answer so alarmed and distressed me, that I knew not what to do—I did nothing but cry. Being in an oratory in great affliction, not knowing what would become of me, I read in a book—it seemed as if our Lord had put it into my hands—that St. Paul said, God is faithful;[250] that He will never permit Satan to deceive those who love Him. This gave me great consolation. I began to prepare for my general confession, and to write out all the evil and all the good: a history of my life, as clearly as I understood it, and knew how to make it, omitting nothing whatever. I remember, when I saw I had written so much evil, and scarcely anything that was good, that I was exceedingly distressed and sorrowful. It pained me, also, that the nuns of the community should see me converse with such holy persons as those of the Society of Jesus; for I was afraid of my own wickedness, and I thought I should be obliged to cease from it, and give up my amusements; and that if I did not do so, I should grow worse: so I persuaded the sacristan and the portress to tell no one of it. This was of little use, after all; for when I was called down there was one at the door, as it happened, who told it to the whole convent. But what difficulties and what terrors Satan troubles them with who would draw near unto God!

18. I communicated the whole state of my soul to that servant of God[251] and he was a great servant of His, and very prudent. He understood all I told him, explained it to me, and encouraged me greatly. He said that all was very evidently the work of the Spirit of God; only it was necessary for me to go back again to my prayer, because I was not well grounded, and had not begun to understand what mortification meant,—that was true, for I do not think I knew it even by name,— that I was by no means to give up prayer; on the contrary, I was to do violence to myself in order to practice it, because God had bestowed on me such special graces as made it impossible to say whether it was, or was not, the will of our Lord to do good to many through me. He went further, for he seems to have prophesied of that which our Lord afterwards did with me, and said that I should be very much to blame if I did not correspond with the graces which God bestowed upon me. It seems to me that the Holy Ghost was speaking by his mouth in order to heal my soul, so deep was the impression he made. He made me very much ashamed of myself, and directed me by a way which seemed to change me altogether. What a grand thing it is to understand a soul! He told me to make my prayer every day on some mystery of the Passion, and that I should profit by it, and to fix my thoughts on the Sacred Humanity only, resisting to the utmost of my power those recollections and delights, to which I was not to yield in any way till he gave me further directions in the matter.

19. He left me consoled and fortified: our Lord came to my succor and to his, so that he might understand the state I was in, and how he was to direct me. I made a firm resolution not to swerve from anything he might command me, and to this day I have kept it. Our Lord be praised, who has given me grace to be obedient to my confessors, however imperfectly!—and they have almost always been those blessed men of the Society of Jesus; though, as I said, I have but imperfectly obeyed them. My soul began to improve visibly, as I am now going to say.

---

250 1 Cor. x. 13: "Fidelis autem Deus est, qui non patietur vos tentari supra id quod potestis."

251 F. Juan de Padranos, whom St. Francis de Borja had sent in 1555, with F. Fernando Alvarez del Aguila, to found the house of the Society in Avila (*De la Fuente*). Ribera, i. 5, says he heard that F. Juan de Padranos gave in part the Exercises of St. Ignatius to the Saint.

Chapter XXIV.

Progress Under Obedience. Her Inability to Resist the Graces of God. God Multiplies His Graces.

1. After this my confession, my soul was so docile that, as it seems to me, there was nothing in the world I was not prepared to undertake. I began at once to make a change in many things, though my confessor never pressed me—on the contrary, he seemed to make light of it all. I was the more influenced by this, because he led me on by the way of the love of God; he left me free, and did not press me, unless I did so myself, out of love. I continued thus nearly two months, doing all I could to resist the sweetness and graces that God sent. As to my outward life, the change was visible; for our Lord gave me courage to go through with certain things, of which those who knew me—and even those in the community—said that they seemed to them extreme; and, indeed, compared with what I had been accustomed to do, they were extreme: people, therefore, had reason to say so. Yet, in those things which were of obligation, considering the habit I wore, and the profession I had made, I was still deficient. By resisting the sweetness and joys which God sent me, I gained this, that His Majesty taught me Himself; for, previously, I used to think that, in order to obtain sweetness in prayer, it was necessary for me to hide myself in secret places, and so I scarcely dared to stir. Afterwards, I saw how little that was to the purpose; for the more I tried to distract myself, the more our Lord poured over me that sweetness and joy which seemed to me to be flowing around me, so that I could not in any way escape from it: and so it was. I was so careful about this resistance, that it was a pain to me. But our Lord was more careful to show His mercies, and during those two months to reveal Himself more than before, so that I might the better comprehend that it was no longer in my power to resist Him.

2. I began with a renewed love of the most Sacred Humanity; my prayer began to be solid, like a house, the foundations of which are strong; and I was inclined to practice greater penance, having been negligent in this matter hitherto because of my great infirmities. The holy man who heard my confession told me that certain penances would not hurt me, and that God perhaps sent me so much sickness because I did no penance; His Majesty would therefore impose it Himself. He ordered me to practice certain acts of mortification not very pleasant for me.[252] I did so, because I felt that our Lord was enjoining it all, and giving him grace to command me in such a way as to make me obedient unto him.

3. My soul was now sensitive to every offence I committed against God, however slight it might be; so much so, that if I had any superfluity about me, I could not recollect myself in prayer till I had got rid of it. I prayed earnestly that our Lord would hold me by the hand, and not suffer me to fall again, now that I was under the direction of His servants. I thought that would be a great evil, and that they would lose their credit through me.

4. At this time, Father Francis, who was Duke of Gandia,[253] came here; he had left all he possessed some years before, and had entered the Society of Jesus. My confessor, and the nobleman of whom I spoke before,[254] contrived that he should visit me, in order that I might speak to him, and give him an account of my way of prayer; for they knew him to be greatly favored and comforted of God: he had given up much, and was rewarded for it even in this life. When he had heard me, he said to me that it was the work of the Spirit of God, and that he thought it was not right now to prolong that resistance; that hitherto it had been safe enough,—only, I should always begin my prayer by meditating on some part of the Passion and that if our Lord should then raise up my spirit, I should make no resistance, but suffer His Majesty to raise it upwards, I myself not seeking it. He gave both medicine and advice, as one who had made great progress himself; for experience is very important in these matters. He said that further resistance would be a mistake. I was exceedingly consoled; so, too, was the nobleman, who rejoiced greatly when he was told that it was

---

[252] The Saint now treated her body with extreme severity, disciplining herself even unto blood (*Reforma*, vol. i. lib. i. c. xx. § 4).

[253] St. Francis de Borja came to Avila, where St. Teresa lived, in 1557 (*De la Fuente*). This passage must have been written after the foundation of St. Joseph, for it was not in the first Life, as the Saint says, ch. x. § 11, that he kept secret the names of herself and all others.

[254] Ch. xxiii. § 6.

the work of God. He always helped me and gave me advice according to his power,—and that power was great.

5. At this time, they changed my confessor's residence. I felt it very much, for I thought I should go back to my wickedness, and that it was not possible to find another such as he. My soul was, as it were, in a desert, most sorrowful and afraid. I knew not what to do with myself. One of my kinswomen contrived to get me into her house, and I contrived at once to find another confessor,[255] in the Society of Jesus. It pleased our Lord that I should commence a friendship with a noble lady,[256] a widow, much given to prayer, who had much to do with the fathers. She made her own confessor[257] hear me, and I remained in her house some days. She lived near, and I delighted in the many conferences I had with the fathers; for merely by observing the holiness of their way of life, I felt that my soul profited exceedingly.

6. This father began by putting me in the way of greater perfection. He used to say to me, that I ought to leave nothing undone that I might be wholly pleasing unto God. He was, however, very prudent and very gentle at the same time; for my soul was not at all strong, but rather very weak, especially as to giving up certain friendships, though I did not offend God by them: there was much natural affection in them, and I thought it would be an act of ingratitude if I broke them off. And so, as I did not offend God, I asked him if I must be ungrateful. He told me to lay the matter before God for a few days, and recite the hymn, "Veni, Creator," that God might enlighten me as to the better course. One day, having prayed for some time, and implored our Lord to help me to please Him in all things, I began the hymn; and as I was saying it, I fell into a trance—so suddenly, that I was, as it were, carried out of myself. I could have no doubt about it, for it was most plain.

7. This was the first time that our Lord bestowed on me the grace of ecstasy. I heard these words: "I will not have thee converse with men, but with angels." This made me wonder very much; for the commotion of my spirit was great, and these words were uttered in the very depth of my soul. They made me afraid,—though, on the other hand, they gave me great comfort, which, when I had lost the fear,—caused, I believe, by the strangeness of the visitation,—remained with me.

8. Those words have been fulfilled; for I have never been able to form friendship with, nor have any comfort in, nor any particular love for, any persons whatever except those who, as I believe, love God, and who strive to serve Him. It has not been in my power to do it. It is nothing to me that they are my kindred, or my friends, if I do not know them to be lovers of God, or persons given to prayer. It is to me a painful cross to converse with any one. This is the truth, so far as I can judge. From that day forth, I have had courage so great as to leave all things for God, who in one moment—and it seems to me but a moment—was pleased to change His servant into another person. Accordingly, there was no necessity for laying further commands upon me in this matter. When my confessor saw how much I clung to these friendships, he did not venture to bid me distinctly to give them up. He must have waited till our Lord did the work—as He did Himself. Nor did I think myself that I could succeed; for I had tried before, and the pain it gave me was so great that I abandoned the attempt, on the ground that there was nothing unseemly in those attachments. Now our Lord set me at liberty, and gave me strength also to use it.

9. So I told my confessor of it, and gave up everything, according to his advice. It did a great deal of good to those with whom I used to converse, to see my determination. God be blessed for ever! Who in one moment set me free, while I had been for many years making many efforts, and had never succeeded, very often also doing such violence to myself as injured my health; but, as it was done by Him Who is almighty, and the true Lord of all, it gave me no pain whatever.

---

[255] Who he was is not certainly known. The Bollandists decline to give an opinion: but F. Bouix thinks it was F. Ferdinand Alvarez, who became her confessor on the removal of F. Juan de Padranos, and that it was to him she confessed till she placed herself under the direction of F. Baltasar Alvarez, the confessor of Doña Guiomar, as it is stated in the next paragraph,—unless the confessor there mentioned was F. Ferdinand.

[256] Doña Guiomar de Ulloa. See below, ch. xxxii. § 13.

[257] If this confessor was F. Baltasar Alvarez, the Saint, F. Bouix observes, passes rapidly over the history of the year 1557, and the greater part, perhaps, of 1558; for F. Baltasar was ordained priest only in the latter year.

Chapter XXV.

Divine Locutions. Discussions on That Subject.

1. It will be as well, I think, to explain these locutions of God, and to describe what the soul feels when it receives them, in order that you, my father, may understand the matter; for ever since that time of which I am speaking, when our Lord granted me that grace, it has been an ordinary occurrence until now, as will appear by what I have yet to say.

2. The words are very distinctly formed; but by the bodily ear they are not heard. They are, however, much more clearly understood than they would be if they were heard by the ear. It is impossible not to understand them, whatever resistance we may offer. When we wish not to hear anything in this world, we can stop our ears, or give attention to something else: so that, even if we do hear, at least we can refuse to understand. In this locution of God addressed to the soul there is no escape, for in spite of ourselves we must listen; and the understanding must apply itself so thoroughly to the comprehension of that which God wills we should hear, that it is nothing to the purpose whether we will it or not; for it is His will, Who can do all things. We should understand that His will must be done; and He reveals Himself as our true Lord, having dominion over us. I know this by much experience; for my resistance lasted nearly two years,[258] because of the great fear I was in: and even now I resist occasionally; but it is of no use.

3. I should like to explain the delusions which may happen here, though he who has had much experience will run little or no risk, I think; but the experience must be great. I should like to explain also how those locutions which come from the Good Spirit differ from those which come from an evil spirit; and, further, how they may be but an apprehension of the understanding,—for that is possible,—or even words which the mind addressed to itself. I do not know if it be so but even this very day I thought it possible. I know by experience in many ways, when these locutions come from God. I have been told things two or three years beforehand, which have all come to pass; and in none of them have I been hitherto deceived. There are also other things in which the Spirit of God may be clearly traced, as I shall relate by and by.[259]

4. It seems to me that a person commending a matter to God with great love and earnestness may think that he hears in some way or other whether his prayer will be granted or not, and this is quite possible; but he who has heard the divine locution will see clearly enough what this is, because there is a great difference between the two. If it be anything which the understanding has fashioned, however cunningly it may have done so, he sees that it is the understanding which has arranged that locution, and that it is speaking of itself. This is nothing else but a word uttered by one, and listened to by another: in that case, the understanding will see that it has not been listening only, but also forming the words; and the words it forms are something indistinct, fantastic, and not clear like the divine locutions. It is in our power to turn away our attention from these locutions of our own, just as we can be silent when we are speaking; but, with respect to the former, that cannot be done.

5. There is another test more decisive still. The words formed by the understanding effect nothing; but, when our Lord speaks, it is at once word and work; and though the words may not be meant to stir up our devotion, but are rather words of reproof, they dispose a soul at once, strengthen it, make it tender, give it light, console and calm it; and if it should be in dryness, or in trouble and uneasiness, all is removed, as if by the action of a hand, and even better; for it seems as if our Lord would have the soul understand that He is all-powerful, and that His words are deeds.

6. It seems to me that there is as much difference between these two locutions as there is between speaking and listening, neither more nor less; for when I speak, as I have just said,[260] I go on with my understanding arranging what I am saying; but if I am spoken to by others, I do nothing else but listen, without any labor. The human locution is as something which we cannot well make out, as if we were half asleep; but the divine locution is a voice so clear that not a syllable of its utterance is lost. It may occur, too, when the understanding and the soul are so troubled and distracted that they cannot form one sentence correctly; and yet grand sentences, perfectly arranged,

---

[258] From 1555 to 1557, when the Saint was advised by St. Francis de Borja to make no further resistance (*Bouix*).

[259] See ch. xxvii. § 4.

[260] § 4.

such as the soul in its most recollected state never could have formed, are uttered, and at the first word, as I said,[261] change it utterly. Still less could it have formed them if they are uttered in an ecstasy, when the faculties of the soul are suspended; for how should the soul then comprehend anything, when it remembers nothing?—yes, rather, how can it remember them then, when the memory can hardly do anything at all, and the imagination is, as it were, suspended?

7. But it is to be observed, that if we see visions and hear words it never is as at the time when the soul is in union in the very rapture itself,—so it seems to me. At that moment, as I have shown,— I think it was when I was speaking of the second water,[262]—all the faculties of the soul are suspended; and, as I think, neither vision, nor understanding, nor hearing, is possible at that time. The soul is then wholly in the power of another; and in that instant—a very brief one, in my opinion—our Lord leaves it free for nothing whatever; but when this instant is passed, the soul continuing still entranced, then is the time of which I am speaking; for the faculties, though not completely suspended, are so disposed that they are scarcely active, being, as it were, absorbed, and incapable of making any reflections.

8. There are so many ways of ascertaining the nature of these locutions, that if a person be once deceived, he will not be deceived often. I mean, that a soul accustomed to them, and on its guard, will most clearly see what they are; for, setting other considerations aside which prove what I have said, the human locution produces no effect, neither does the soul accept it,—though it must admit the other, whether we like it or not,—nor does it believe it; on the contrary, it is known to be a delusion of the understanding, and is therefore put away as we would put away the ravings of a lunatic.

9. But as to the divine locution, we listen to that as we do to a person of great holiness, learning, or authority, whom we know to be incapable of uttering a falsehood. And yet this is an inadequate illustration; for these locutions proceed occasionally in such great majesty that, without our recollecting who it is that utters them, they make us tremble if they be words of reproof, and die of love if words of love. They are also, as I have said,[263] matters of which the memory has not the least recollection; and expressions so full are uttered so rapidly, that much time must have been spent in arranging them, if we formed them ourselves; and so it seems to me that we cannot possibly be ignorant at the time that we have never formed them ourselves at all.

10. There is no reason, therefore, why I should dwell longer on this matter. It is a wonder to me that any experienced person, unless he deliberately chooses to do so, can fall into delusions. It has often happened to me, when I had doubts, to distrust what I had heard, and to think that it was all imagination,—but this I did afterwards: for at the moment that is impossible,—and at a later time to see the whole fulfilled; for our Lord makes the words dwell in the memory so that they cannot be forgotten. Now, that which comes forth from our understanding is, as it were, the first movement of thought, which passes away and is forgotten; but the divine locution is a work done; and though some of it may be forgotten, and time have lapsed, yet is not so wholly forgotten that the memory loses all traces of what was once spoken,—unless, indeed, after very long time, or unless the locution were words of grace or of instruction. But as to prophetic words, they are never forgotten, in my opinion; at least, I have never forgotten any,—and yet my memory is weak.

11. I repeat it, unless a soul be so wicked as to pretend that it has these locutions, which would be a great sin, and say that it hears divine words when it hears nothing of the kind, it cannot possibly fail to see clearly that itself arranges the words, and utters them to itself. That seems to me altogether impossible for any soul that has ever known the Spirit of God. If it has not, it may continue all its life long in this delusion, and imagine that it hears and understands, though I know not how that can be. A soul desires to hear these locutions, or it does not; if it does not, it is distressed because it hears them, and is unwilling to listen to them, because of a thousand fears which they occasion, and for many other reasons it has for being quiet in prayer without these interruptions. How is it that the understanding has time enough to arrange these locutions? They require time.

---

[261] § 5.

[262] The doctrine here laid down is not that of the second water,—chs. xiv. and xv.,—but that of the third, ch. xvi. The Saint herself speaks doubtfully; and as she had but little time for writing, she could not correct nor read again what she had written (*De la Fuente*).

[263] § 6.

12. But, on the other side, the divine locutions instruct us without loss of time, and we understand matters which seem to require a month on our part to arrange. The understanding itself, and the soul, stand amazed at some of the things we understand. So it is; and he who has any experience of it will see that what I am saying is literally true. I give God thanks that I have been able thus to explain it. I end by saying that, in my opinion, we may hear the locutions that proceed from the understanding whenever we like, and think that we hear them whenever we pray. But it is not so with the divine locutions: for many days I may desire to hear them, and I cannot; and at other times, even when I would not, as I said before,[264] hear them, I must. It seems to me that any one disposed to deceive people by saying that he heard from God that which he has invented himself, might as easily say that he heard it with his bodily ears. It is most certainly true that I never imagined there was any other way of hearing or understanding till I had proof of it in myself; and so, as I have said before,[265] it gave me trouble enough.

13. Locutions that come from Satan not only do not leave any good effects behind, but do leave evil effects. This has happened to me; but not more than two or three times. Our Lord warned me at once that they came from Satan. Over and above the great aridity which remains in the soul after these evil locutions, there is also a certain disquiet, such as I have had on many other occasions, when, by our Lord's permission, I fell into great temptations and travail of soul in diverse ways; and though I am in trouble often enough, as I shall show hereafter,[266] yet this disquiet is such that I know not whence it comes; only the soul seems to resist, is troubled and distressed, without knowing why; for the words of Satan are good, and not evil. I am thinking whether this may not be so because one spirit is conscious of the presence of another.

14. The sweetness and joy which Satan gives are, in my opinion, of a very different kind. By means of these sweetnesses he may deceive any one who does not, or who never did, taste of the sweetness of God,—by which I mean a certain sweet, strong, impressive, delightsome, and calm refreshing. Those little, fervid bursts of tears, and other slight emotions,—for at the first breath of persecution these flowers wither,—I do not call devotion, though they are a good beginning, and are holy impressions; but they are not a test to determine whether these locutions come from a good or an evil spirit. It is therefore best for us to proceed always with great caution; for those persons who have advanced in prayer only so far as this may most easily fall into delusions, if they have visions or revelations. For myself, I never had a single vision or revelation till God had led me on to the prayer of union,—unless it be on that occasion, of which I have spoken before,[267] now many years ago, when I saw our Lord. Oh, that His Majesty had been pleased to let me then understand that it was a true vision, as I have since understood it was! it would have been no slight blessing to me.

15. After these locutions of the evil one, the soul is never gentle, but is, as it were, terrified, and greatly disgusted.

16. I look upon it as a most certain truth, that the devil will never deceive, and that God will not suffer him to deceive, the soul which has no confidence whatever in itself; which is strong in faith, and resolved to undergo a thousand deaths for any one article of the creed; which in its love of the faith, infused of God once for all,—a faith living and strong,—always labors, seeking for further light on this side and on that, to mold itself on the teaching of the Church, as one already deeply grounded in the truth. No imaginable revelations, not even if it saw the heavens open, could make that soul swerve in any degree from the doctrine of the Church. If, however, it should at any time find itself wavering even in thought on this point, or stopping to say to itself, If God says this to me, it may be true, as well as what He said to the Saints—the soul must not be sure of it. I do not mean that it so believes, only that Satan has taken the first step towards tempting it; and the giving way to the first movements of a thought like this is evidently most wrong. I believe, however, that these first movements will not take place if the soul is so strong in the matter—as that soul is to whom our Lord sends these graces—that it seems as if it could crush the evil spirits in defense of the very least of the truths which the Church holds.

---

[264] § 2.
[265] Ch. vii. § 12.
[266] Ch. xxviii. § 6, ch. xxx. § 10.
[267] Ch. vii. § 11.

17. If the soul does not discern this great strength in itself, and if the particular devotion or vision help it not onwards, then it must not look upon it as safe. For though at first the soul is conscious of no harm, great harm may by degrees ensue; because, so far as I can see, and by experience understand, that which purports to come from God is received only in so far as it corresponds with the sacred writings; but if it varies therefrom ever so little, I am incomparably more convinced that it comes from Satan than I am now convinced it comes from God, however deep that conviction may be. In this case, there is no need to ask for signs, nor from what spirit it proceeds, because this varying is so clear a sign of the devil's presence, that if all the world were to assure me that it came from God, I would not believe it. The fact is, that all good seems to be lost out of sight, and to have fled from the soul, when the devil has spoken to it; the soul is thrown into a state of disgust, and is troubled, able to do no good thing whatever—for if it conceives good desires, they are not strong; its humility is fictitious, disturbed, and without sweetness. Any one who has ever tasted of the Spirit of God will, I think, understand it.

18. Nevertheless, Satan has many devices; and so there is nothing more certain than that it is safer to be afraid, and always on our guard, under a learned director, from whom nothing is concealed. If we do this, no harm can befall us, though much has befallen me through the excessive fears which possessed some people. For instance, it happened so once to me, when many persons in whom I had great confidence, and with good reason, had assembled together,—five or six in number, I think,—and all very great servants of God. It is true, my relations were with one of them only; but by his orders made my state known to the others. They had many conferences together about my necessities; for they had great affection for me, and were afraid I was under a delusion. I, too, was very much afraid whenever I was not occupied in prayer; but when I prayed, and our Lord bestowed His graces upon me, I was instantly reassured. My confessor told me they were all of opinion that I was deceived by Satan; that I must communicate less frequently, and contrive to distract myself in such a way as to be less alone.

19. I was in great fear myself, as I have just said, and my disease of the heart[268] contributed thereto, so that very often I did not dare to remain alone in my cell during the day. When I found so many maintain this, and myself unable to believe them, I had at once a most grievous scruple; for it seemed to me that I had very little humility, especially as they all led lives incomparably better than mine: they were also learned men. Why should I not believe them? I did all I could to believe them. I reflected on my wicked life, and therefore what they said to me must be true.

20. In this distress, I quitted the church,[269] and entered an oratory. I had not been to Communion for many days, nor had I been alone, which was all my comfort. I had no one to speak to, for every one was against me. Some, I thought, made a mock of me when I spoke to them of my prayer, as if I were a person under delusions of the imagination; others warned my confessor to be on his guard against me; and some said it was clear the whole was an operation of Satan. My confessor, though he agreed with them for the sake of trying me, as I understood afterwards, always comforted me: and he alone did so. He told me that, if I did not offend God, my prayer, even if it was the work of Satan, could do me no harm; that I should be delivered from it. He bade me pray much to God: he himself, and all his penitents, and many others did so earnestly; I, too, with all my might, and as many as I knew to be servants of God, prayed that His Majesty would be pleased to lead me by another way. This lasted, I think, about two years; and this was the subject of my continual prayer to our Lord.

21. But there was no comfort for me when I thought of the possibility that Satan could speak to me so often. Now that I was never alone for prayer, our Lord made me recollected even during conversation: He spoke what He pleased,—I could not avoid it; and, though it distressed me, I was forced to listen. I was by myself, having no one in whom I could find any comfort; unable to pray or read, like a person stunned by heavy trials, and by the dread that the evil one had deluded me; utterly disquieted and wearied, not knowing what would become of me. I have been occasionally— yes, very often—in distress, but never before in distress so great. I was in this state for four or five hours; there was no comfort for me, either from heaven or on earth—only our Lord left me to suffer, afraid of a thousand dangers.

---

[268] Ch. iv. § 6, ch. v. § 14.
[269] It was the church of the Jesuits (*Bouix*).

22. O my Lord, how true a friend art Thou! how powerful! Thou shows Thy power when Thou will; and Thou does will it always, if only we will it also. Let the whole creation praise Thee, O Thou Lord of the world! Oh, that a voice might go forth over all the earth, proclaiming Thy faithfulness to those who love Thee! All things fail; but Thou, Lord of all, never fails! They who love Thee, oh, how little they have to suffer! oh, how gently, how tenderly, how sweetly Thou, O my Lord, deals with them! Oh, that no one had ever been occupied with any other love than Thine! It seems as if Thou did subject those who love Thee to a severe trial: but it is in order that they may learn, in the depths of that trial, the depths of Thy love. O my God, oh, that I had understanding and learning, and a new language, in order to magnify Thy works, according to the knowledge of them which my soul possesses! Everything fails me, O my Lord; but if Thou will not abandon me, I will never fail Thee. Let all the learned rise up against me,—let the whole creation persecute me,—let the evil spirits torment me,—but do Thou, O Lord, fail me not; for I know by experience now the blessedness of that deliverance which Thou does effect for those who trust only in Thee. In this distress,—for then I had never had a single vision,—these Thy words alone were enough to remove it, and give me perfect peace: "Be not afraid, my daughter: it is I; and I will not abandon thee. Fear not."[270]

23. It seems to me that, in the state I was in then, many hours would have been necessary to calm me, and that no one could have done it. Yet I found myself, through these words alone, tranquil and strong, courageous and confident, at rest and enlightened; in a moment, my soul seemed changed, and I felt I could maintain against all the world that my prayer was the work of God. Oh, how good is God! how good is our Lord, and how powerful! He gives not counsel only, but relief as well. His words are deeds. O my God! as He strengthens our faith, love grows. So it is, in truth; for I used frequently to recollect how our Lord, when the tempest arose, commanded the winds to be still over the sea.[271] So I said to myself: Who is He, that all my faculties should thus obey Him? Who is He, that gives light in such darkness in a moment; who softens a heart that seemed to be made of stone; who gives the waters of sweet tears, where for a long time great dryness seems to have prevailed; who inspires these desires; who bestows this courage? What have I been thinking of? what am I afraid of? what is it? I desire to serve this my Lord; I aim at nothing else but His pleasure; I seek no joy, no rest, no other good than that of doing His will. I was so confident that I had no other desire, that I could safely assert it.

24. Seeing, then, that our Lord is so powerful,—as I see and know He is,—and that the evil spirits are His slaves, of which there can be no doubt, because it is of faith,—and I a servant of this our Lord and King,—what harm can Satan do unto me? Why have I not strength enough to fight against all hell? I took up the cross in my hand,—I was changed in a moment into another person, and it seemed as if God had really given me courage enough not to be afraid of encountering all the evil spirits. It seemed to me that I could, with the cross, easily defeat them altogether. So I cried out, Come on, all of you; I am the servant of our Lord: I should like to see what you can do against me.

25. And certainly they seemed to be afraid of me, for I was left in peace: I feared them so little, that the terrors, which until now oppressed me, quitted me altogether; and though I saw them occasionally,—I shall speak of this by and by,[272]—I was never again afraid of them—on the contrary, they seemed to be afraid of me.[273] I found myself endowed with a certain authority over them, given me by the Lord of all, so that I cared no more for them than for flies. They seem to be such cowards; for their strength fails them at the sight of any one who despises them. These enemies have not the courage to assail any but those whom they see ready to give in to them, or when God permits them to do so, for the greater good of His servants, whom they may try and torment.

26. May it please His Majesty that we fear Him whom we ought to fear,[274] and understand that one venial sin can do us more harm than all hell together; for that is the truth. The evil spirits keep us in terror, because we expose ourselves to the assaults of terror by our attachments to honors, possessions, and pleasures. For then the evil spirits, uniting themselves with us,—we become our

[270] See *Interior Castle*, vi. 3, § 5.
[271] St. Matt. viii. 26; "Imperavit ventis et mari, et facta est tranquillitas magna."
[272] Ch. xxxi. § 2.
[273] St. John of the Cross, *Spiritual Canticle*, st. 24, p. 128, Eng. trans.
[274] St. Matt. x. 26, 28; "Ne ergo timueritis eos,... sed potius timete Eum."

own enemies when we love and seek what we ought to hate,—do us great harm. We ourselves put weapons into their hands, that they may assail us; those very weapons with which we should defend ourselves. It is a great pity. But if, for the love of God, we hated all this, and embraced the cross, and set about His service in earnest, Satan would fly away before such realities, as from the plague. He is the friend of lies, and a lie himself.[275] He will have nothing to do with those who walk in the truth. When he sees the understanding of any one obscured, he simply helps to pluck out his eyes; if he sees any one already blind, seeking peace in vanities,—for all the things of this world are so utterly vanity, that they seem to be but the playthings of a child,—he sees at once that such a one is a child; he treats him as a child, and ventures to wrestle with him—not once, but often.

27. May it please our Lord that I be not one of these; and may His Majesty give me grace to take that for peace which is really peace, that for honor which is really honor, and that for delight which is really a delight. Let me never mistake one thing for another—and then I snap my fingers at all the devils, for they shall be afraid of me. I do not understand those terrors which make us cry out, Satan, Satan! when we may say, God, God! and make Satan tremble. Do we not know that he cannot stir without the permission of God? What does it mean? I am really much more afraid of those people who have so great a fear of the devil, than I am of the devil himself. Satan can do me no harm whatever, but they can trouble me very much, particularly if they be confessors. I have spent some years of such great anxiety, that even now I am amazed that I was able to bear it. Blessed be our Lord, who has so effectually helped me!

Chapter XXVI.

How the Fears of the Saint Vanished. How She Was Assured That Her Prayer Was the Work of the Holy Spirit.

1. I look upon the courage which our Lord has implanted in me against evil spirits as one of the greatest mercies which He has bestowed upon me; for a cowardly soul, afraid of anything but sin against God, is a very unseemly thing, when we have on our side the King omnipotent, our Lord most high, who can do all things, and subjects all things to Himself. There is nothing to be afraid of if we walk, as I said before,[276] in the truth, in the sight of His Majesty, with a pure conscience. And for this end, as I said in the same place, I would have myself all fears, that I may not for one instant offend Him who in that instant is able to destroy us. If His Majesty is pleased with us, whoever resists us—be he who he may—will be utterly disappointed.

2. It may be so, you will say; but, then, where is that soul so just as to please Him in everything?—and that is the reason why we are afraid. Certainly it is not my soul, which is most wretched, unprofitable, and full of misery. God is not like man in His ways; He knows our weakness. But the soul perceives, by the help of certain great signs, whether it loves God of a truth; for the love of those souls who have come to this state is not hidden as it was at first, but is full of high impulses, and of longings for the vision of God, as I shall show hereafter—or rather, as I have shown already.[277] Everything wearies, everything distresses, everything torments the soul, unless it be suffered with God, or for God. There is no rest which is not a weariness, because the soul knows itself to be away from its true rest; and so love is made most manifest, and, as I have just said, impossible to hide.

3. It happened to me, on another occasion to be grievously tried, and much spoken against on account of a certain affair,—of which I will speak hereafter,[278]—by almost everybody in the place where I am living, and by the members of my Order. When I was in this distress, and afflicted by many occasions of disquiet wherein I was placed, our Lord spoke to me, saying: "What art thou afraid of? knows thou not that I am almighty? I will do what I have promised thee." And so, afterwards, was it done. I found myself at once so strong, that I could have undertaken anything, so

---

[275] St. John viii. 44: "Mendax est, et pater ejus."

[276] Ch. xxv. § 26.

[277] Ch. xv. § 6.

[278] Ch. xxxiii.; the foundation of the house of St. Joseph.

it seemed, immediately, even if I had to endure greater trials for His service, and had to enter on a new state of suffering. These locutions are so frequent, that I cannot count them; many of them are reproaches, and He sends them when I fall into imperfections. They are enough to destroy a soul. They correct me, however; for His Majesty—as I said before[279]—gives both counsel and relief. There are others which bring my former sins into remembrance,—particularly when He is about to bestow upon me some special grace,—in such a way that the soul beholds itself as being really judged; for those reproaches of God put the truth before it so distinctly, that it knows not what to do with itself. Some are warnings against certain dangers to myself or others; many of them are prophecies of future things, three or four years beforehand; and all of them have been fulfilled: some of them I could mention. Here, then, are so many reasons for believing that they come from God, as make it impossible, I believe, for anybody to mistake them.

4. The safest course in these things is to declare, without fail, the whole state of the soul, together with the graces our Lord gives me, to a confessor who is learned, and obey him. I do so; and if I did not, I should have no peace. Nor is it right that we women, who are unlearned, should have any: there can be no danger in this, but rather great profit. This is what our Lord has often commanded me to do, and it is what I have often done. I had a confessor[280] who mortified me greatly, and now and then distressed me: he tried me heavily, for he disquieted me exceedingly; and yet he was the one who, I believe, did me the most good. Though I had a great affection for him, I was occasionally tempted to leave him; I thought that the pain he inflicted on me disturbed my prayer. Whenever I was resolved on leaving him, I used to feel instantly that I ought not to do so; and one reproach of our Lord would press more heavily upon me than all that my confessor did. Now and then, I was worn out—torture on the one hand, reproaches on the other. I required it all, for my will was but little subdued. Our Lord said to me once, that there was no obedience where there was no resolution to suffer; that I was to think of His sufferings, and then everything would be easy.

5. One of my confessors, to whom I went in the beginning, advised me once, now that my spiritual state was known to be the work of God, to keep silence, and not speak of these things to any one, on the ground that it was safer to keep these graces secret. To me, the advice seemed good, because I felt it so much whenever I had to speak of them to my confessor; I was also so ashamed of myself, that I felt it more keenly at times to speak of them than I should have done in confessing grave sins, particularly when the graces I had to reveal were great. I thought they did not believe me, and that they were laughing at me. I felt it so much,—for I look on this as an irreverent treatment of the marvels of God,—that I was glad to be silent. I learned then that I had been ill-advised by that confessor, because I ought never to hide anything from my confessor; for I should find great security if I told everything; and if I did otherwise, I might at any time fall into delusions.[281]

6. Whenever our Lord commanded me to do one thing in prayer, and if my confessor forbade it, our Lord Himself told me to obey my confessor. His Majesty afterwards would change the mind of that confessor, so that he would have me do what he had forbidden before. When we were deprived of many books written in Spanish, and forbidden to read them,—I felt it deeply, for some of these books were a great comfort to me, and I could not read them in Latin,—our Lord said to me, "Be not troubled; I will give thee a living book." I could not understand why this was said to me, for at that time I had never had a vision.[282] But, a very few days afterwards, I understood it well enough; for I had so much to think of, and such reasons for self-recollection in what I saw before me and our Lord dealt so lovingly with me, in teaching me in so many ways, that I had little or no need whatever of books. His Majesty has been to me a veritable Book, in which I saw all truth. Blessed be such a Book, which leaves behind an impression of what is read therein, and in such a way that it cannot be forgotten!

---

[279] Ch. xxv. § 23.

[280] The Bollandists, n. 185, attribute some of the severity with which her confessor treated the Saint to the spirit of desolation with which he was then tried himself; and, in proof of it, refer to the account which F. Baltasar Alvarez gave of his own prayer to the General of the Society.

[281] St. John of the Cross, *Mount Carmel*, bk. ii. ch. 22, § 14.

[282] The visions of the Saint began in 1558 (*De la Fuente*) or, according to Father Bouix, in 1559.

7. Who can look upon our Lord, covered with wounds, and bowed down under persecutions, without accepting, loving, and longing for them? Who can behold but a part of that glory which He will give to those who serve Him without confessing that all he may do, and all he may suffer, are altogether as nothing, when we may hope for such a reward? Who can look at the torments of lost souls without acknowledging the torments of this life to be joyous delights in comparison, and confessing how much they owe to our Lord in having saved them so often from the place of torments?[283] But as, by the help of God, I shall speak more at large of certain things, I wish now to go on with the story of my life. Our Lord grant that I have been clear enough in what I have hitherto said! I feel assured that he will understand me who has had experience herein, and that he will see I have partially succeeded; but as to him who has had no such experience, I should not be surprised if he regarded it all as folly. It is enough for him that it is I who say it, in order to be free from blame; neither will I blame any one who shall so speak of it. Our Lord grant that I may never fail to do His will! Amen.

Chapter XXVII.

The Saint Prays to Be Directed by a Different Way. Intellectual Visions.

1. I now resume the story of my life. I was in great pain and distress; and many prayers, as I said,[284] were made on my behalf, that our Lord would lead me by another and a safer way; for this, they told me, was so suspicious. The truth is, that though I was praying to God for this, and wished I had a desire for another way, yet, when I saw the progress I was making, I was unable really to desire a change,—though I always prayed for it,—excepting on those occasions when I was extremely cast down by what people said to me, and by the fears with which they filled me.

2. I felt that I was wholly changed; I could do nothing but put myself in the hands of God: He knew what was expedient for me; let Him do with me according to His will in all things. I saw that by this way I was directed heavenwards, and that formerly I was going down to hell. I could not force myself to desire a change, nor believe that I was under the influence of Satan. Though I was doing all I could to believe the one and to desire the other, it was not in my power to do so. I offered up all my actions, if there should be any good in them, for this end; I had recourse to the Saints for whom I had a devotion, that they might deliver me from the evil one; I made novenas; I commended myself to St. Hilarion, to the Angel St. Michael, to whom I had recently become devout, for this purpose; and many other Saints I importuned, that our Lord might show me the way,—I mean, that they might obtain this for me from His Majesty.

3. At the end of two years spent in prayer by myself and others for this end, namely, that our Lord would either lead me by another way, or show the truth of this,—for now the locutions of our Lord were extremely frequent,—this happened to me. I was in prayer one day,—it was the feast of the glorious St. Peter,[285]—when I saw Christ close by me, or, to speak more correctly, felt Him; for I saw nothing with the eyes of the body, nothing with the eyes of the soul. He seemed to me to be close beside me; and I saw, too, as I believe, that it was He who was speaking to me. As I was utterly ignorant that such a vision was possible,[286] I was extremely afraid at first, and did nothing but weep; however, when He spoke to me but one word to reassure me, I recovered myself, and was, as usual, calm and comforted, without any fear whatever. Jesus Christ seemed to be by my side continually, and, as the vision was not imaginary, I saw no form; but I had a most distinct feeling that He was always on my right hand, a witness of all I did; and never at any time, if I was but slightly recollected, or not too much distracted, could I be ignorant of His near presence.

---

[283] St. Luke xvi. 28: "Ne et ipsi veniant in hunc locum tormentorum."

[284] Ch. xxv. § 20.

[285] See ch. xxviii. § 5, and ch. xxix. § 1. The vision took place, it seems, on the 29th June. See ch. xxix. § 6.

[286] See ch. vii. § 12.

4. I went at once to my confessor,[287] in great distress, to tell him of it. He asked in what form I saw our Lord. I told him I saw no form. He then said: "How did you know that it was Christ?" I replied, that I did not know how I knew it; but I could not help knowing that He was close beside me,—that I saw Him distinctly, and felt His presence,—that the recollection of my soul was deeper in the prayer of quiet, and more continuous,—that the effects thereof were very different from what I had hitherto experienced,—and that it was most certain. I could only make comparisons in order to explain myself; and certainly there are no comparisons, in my opinion, by which visions of this kind can be described. Afterwards I learnt from Friar Peter of Alcantara, a holy man of great spirituality,—of whom I shall speak by and by,[288]—and from others of great learning, that this vision was of the highest order, and one with which Satan can least interfere; and therefore there are no words whereby to explain,—at least, none for us women, who know so little: learned men can explain it better.

5. For if I say that I see Him neither with the eyes of the body, nor with those of the soul,—because it was not an imaginary vision,—how is it that I can understand and maintain that He stands beside me, and be more certain of it than if I saw Him? If it be supposed that it is as if a person were blind, or in the dark, and therefore unable to see another who is close to him, the comparison is not exact. There is a certain likelihood about it, however, but not much, because the other senses tell him who is blind of that presence: he hears the other speak or move, or he touches him; but in these visions there is nothing like this. The darkness is not felt; only He renders Himself present to the soul by a certain knowledge of Himself which is more clear than the sun. I do not mean that we now see either a sun or any brightness, only that there is a light not seen, which illumines the understanding so that the soul may have the fruition of so great a good. This vision brings with it great blessings.

6. It is not like that presence of God which is frequently felt, particularly by those who have attained to the prayer of union and of quiet, when we seem, at the very commencement of our prayer, to find Him with whom we would converse, and when we seem to feel that He hears us by the effects and the spiritual impressions of great love and faith of which we are then conscious, as well as by the good resolutions, accompanied by sweetness, which we then make. This is a great grace from God; and let him to whom He has given it esteem it much, because it is a very high degree of prayer; but it is not vision. God is understood to be present there by the effects He works in the soul: that is the way His Majesty makes His presence felt; but here, in this vision, it is seen clearly that Jesus Christ is present, the Son of the Virgin. In the prayer of union and of quiet, certain inflowings of the Godhead are present; but in the vision, the Sacred Humanity also, together with them, is pleased to be our visible companion, and to do us good.

7. My confessor next asked me, who told me it was Jesus Christ.[289] I replied that He often told me so Himself; but, even before He told me so, there was an impression on my understanding that it was He; and before this He used to tell me so, and I saw Him not. If a person whom I had never seen, but of whom I had heard, came to speak to me, and I were blind or in the dark, and told me who he was, I should believe him; but I could not so confidently affirm that he was that person, as I might do if I had seen him. But in this vision I could do so, because so clear a knowledge is impressed on the soul that all doubt seems impossible, though He is not seen. Our Lord wills that this knowledge be so graven on the understanding, that we can no more question His presence than we can question that which we see with our eyes: not so much even; for very often there arises a suspicion that we have imagined things we think we see; but here, though there may be a suspicion in the first instant, there remains a certainty so great, that the doubt has no force whatever. So also is it when God teaches the soul in another way, and speaks to it without speaking, in the way I have described.

8. There is so much of heaven in this language, that it cannot well be understood on earth, though we may desire ever so much to explain it, if our Lord will not teach it experimentally. Our Lord impresses in the innermost soul that which He wills that soul to understand; and He manifests it there without images or formal words, after the manner of the vision I am speaking of. Consider

[287] See *Interior Castle*, vi. 8, § 3.

[288] § 17, *infra*.

[289] *Interior Castle*, vi. 8, § 3.

well this way in which God works, in order that the soul may understand what He means—His great truths and mysteries; for very often what I understand, when our Lord explains to me the vision, which it is His Majesty's pleasure to set before me, is after this manner; and it seems to me that this is a state with which the devil can least interfere, for these reasons; but if these reasons are not good, I must be under a delusion. The vision and the language are matters of such pure spirituality, that there is no toil of the faculties, or of the senses, out of which—so seems to me—the devil can derive any advantage.

9. It is only at intervals, and for an instant, that this occurs; for generally—so I think—the senses are not taken away, and the faculties are not suspended: they preserve their ordinary state. It is not always so in contemplation; on the contrary, it is very rarely so; but when it is so, I say that we do nothing whatever ourselves: no work of ours is then possible; all that is done is apparently the work of our Lord. It is as if food had been received into the stomach which had not first been eaten, and without our knowing how it entered; but we do know well that it is there, though we know not its nature, nor who it was that placed it there. In this vision, I know who placed it; but I do not know how He did it. I neither saw it, nor felt it; I never had any inclination to desire it, and I never knew before that such a thing was possible.

10. In the locutions of which I spoke before,[290] God makes the understanding attentive, though it may be painful to understand what is said; then the soul seems to have other ears wherewith it hears; and He forces it to listen, and will not let it be distracted. The soul is like a person whose hearing was good, and who is not suffered to stop his ears, while people standing close beside him speak to him with a loud voice. He may be unwilling to hear, yet hear he must. Such a person contributes something of his own; for he attends to what is said to him; but here there is nothing of the kind: even that little, which is nothing more than the bare act of listening, which is granted to it in the other case, is now out of its power. It finds its food prepared and eaten; it has nothing more to do but to enjoy it. It is as if one without ever learning, without taking the pains even to learn to read, and without studying any subject whatever, should find himself in possession of all knowledge, not knowing how or whence it came to him, seeing that he had never taken the trouble even to learn the alphabet. This last comparison seems to me to throw some light on this heavenly gift; for the soul finds itself learned in a moment, and the mystery of the most Holy Trinity so clearly revealed to it, together with other most deep doctrines, that there is no theologian in the world with whom it would hesitate to dispute for the truth of these matters.

11. It is impossible to describe the surprise of the soul when it finds that one of these graces is enough to change it utterly, and make it love nothing but Him who, without waiting for anything itself might do, renders it fit for blessings so high, communicates to it His secrets, and treats it with so much affection and love. Some of the graces He bestows are liable to suspicion because they are so marvelous, and given to one who has deserved them so little—incredible, too, without a most lively faith. I intend, therefore, to mention very few of those graces which our Lord has wrought in me, if I should not be ordered otherwise; but there are certain visions of which I shall speak, an account of which may be of some service. In doing so, I shall either dispel his fears to whom our Lord sends them, and who, as I used to do, thinks them impossible, or I shall explain the way or the road by which our Lord has led me; and that is what I have been commanded to describe.

12. Now, going back to speak of this way of understanding, what it is seems to me to be this: it is our Lord's will in every way that the soul should have some knowledge of what passes in heaven; and I think that, as the blessed there without speech understand one another,—I never knew this for certain till our Lord of His goodness made me see it; He showed it to me in a trance,—so is it here: God and the soul understand one another, merely because His Majesty so wills it, without the help of other means, to express the love there is between them both. In the same way on earth, two persons of sound sense, if they love each other much, can even, without any signs, understand one another only by their looks. It must be so here, though we do not see how, as these two lovers earnestly regard each other: the bridegroom says so to the bride in the Canticle, so I believe, and I have heard that it is spoken of there.[291]

---

[290] Ch. xxv. § 1.

[291] Cant. vi. 4: "Averte oculos tuos a me, quia ipsi me avolare fecerunt." St. John of the Cross, *Mount Carmel*, bk. ii. ch. xxix. n. 6, Engl. trans.

13. Oh, marvelous goodness of God, in that Thou permits eyes which have looked upon so much evil as those of my soul to look upon Thee! May they never accustom themselves, after looking on Thee, to look upon vile things again! and may they have pleasure in nothing but in Thee, O Lord! Oh, ingratitude of men, how far will it go! I know by experience that what I am saying is true, and that all we can say is exceedingly little, when we consider what Thou does to the soul which Thou has led to such a state as this. O souls, you who have begun to pray, and you who possess the true faith, what can you be in search of even in this life, let alone that which is for ever, that is comparable to the least of these graces? Consider, and it is true, that God gives Himself to those who give up everything for Him. God is not an accepter of persons.[292] He loves all; there is no excuse for any one, however wicked he may be, seeing that He hath thus dealt with me, raising me to the state I am in. Consider, that what I am saying is not even an iota of what may be said; I say only that which is necessary to show the kind of the vision and of the grace which God bestows on the soul; for that cannot be told which it feels when our Lord admits it to the understanding of His secrets and of His mighty works. The joy of this is so far above all conceivable joys, that it may well make us loathe all the joys of earth; for they are all but dross; and it is an odious thing to make them enter into the comparison, even if we might have them for ever. Those which our Lord gives, what are they? One drop only of the waters of the overflowing river which He is reserving for us.

14. It is a shame! And, in truth, I am ashamed of myself; if shame could have a place in heaven, I should certainly be the most ashamed there. Why do we seek blessings and joys so great, bliss without end, and all at the cost of our good Jesus? Shall we not at least weep with the daughters of Jerusalem,[293] if we do not help to carry his cross with the Cyrenean?[294] Is it by pleasure and idle amusements that we can attain to the fruition of what He purchased with so much blood? It is impossible. Can we think that we can, by preserving our honor, which is vanity, recompense Him for the sufferings He endured, that we might reign with Him for ever? This is not the way; we are going by the wrong road utterly, and we shall never arrive there. You, my father, must lift up your voice, and utter these truths aloud, seeing that God has taken from me the power of doing it. I should like to utter them to myself for ever. I listened to them myself, and came to the knowledge of God so late, as will appear by what I have written, that I am ashamed of myself when I speak of this; and so I should like to be silent.

15. Of one thing, however, I will speak, and I think of it now and then,—may it be the good pleasure of our Lord to bring me on, so that I may have the fruition of it!—what will be the accidental glory and the joy of the blessed who have entered on it, when they see that, though they were late, yet they left nothing undone which it was possible for them to do for God, who kept nothing back they could give Him, and who gave what they gave in every way they could, according to their strength and their measure,—they who had more gave more. How rich will he be who gave up all his riches for Christ! How honorable will he be who, for His sake, sought no honors whatever, but rather took pleasure in seeing himself abased! How wise he will be who rejoiced when men accounted him as mad!—they did so of Wisdom Itself![295] How few there are of this kind now, because of our sins! Now, indeed, they are all gone whom people regarded as mad,[296] because they saw them perform heroic acts, as true lovers of Christ.

16. O world, world! how thou art gaining credit because they are few who know thee! But do we suppose that God is better pleased when men account us wise and discreet persons? We think forthwith that there is but little edification given when people do not go about, every one in his degree, with great gravity, in a dignified way. Even in the friar, the ecclesiastic, and the nun, if they wear old and patched garments, we think it a novelty, and a scandal to the weak; and even if they are very recollected and given to prayer. Such is the state of the world, and so forgotten are matters of perfection, and those grand impetuosities of the Saints. More mischief, I think, is done in this way, than by any scandal that might arise if the religious showed in their actions, as they proclaim it in words, that the world is to be held in contempt. Out of scandals such as this, our Lord obtains

---

292 Acts x. 34: "Non est personarum acceptor Deus."

293 St. Luke xxiii. 28: "Filiæ Jerusalem, nolite flere super Me, sed super vos ipsas flete."

294 St. Matt. xxvii. 32: "Hunc angariaverunt ut tolleret crucem Ejus."

295 St. John x. 20: "Dæmonium habet et insanit: quid Eum auditis?"

296 Sap. v. 4: "Nos insensati vitam illorum æstimabamus insaniam."

great fruit. If some people took scandal, others are filled with remorse: anyhow, we should have before us some likeness of that which our Lord and His Apostles endured; for we have need of it now more than ever.

17. And what an excellent likeness in the person of that blessed friar, Peter of Alcantara, God has just taken from us![297] The world cannot bear such perfection now; it is said that men's health is grown feebler, and that we are not now in those former times. But this holy man lived in our day; he had a spirit strong as those of another age, and so he trampled on the world. If men do not go about barefooted, nor undergo sharp penances, as he did, there are many ways, as I have said before,[298] of trampling on the world; and our Lord teaches them when He finds the necessary courage. How great was the courage with which His Majesty filled the Saint I am speaking of! He did penance—oh, how sharp it was!—for seven-and-forty years, as all men know. I should like to speak of it, for I know it to be all true.

18. He spoke of it to me and to another person, from whom he kept few or no secrets. As for me, it was the affection he bore me that led him to speak; for it was our Lord's will that he should undertake my defense, and encourage me, at a time when I was in great straits, as I said before, and shall speak of again.[299] He told me, I think, that for forty years he slept but an hour and a half out of the twenty-four, and that the most laborious penance he underwent, when he began, was this of overcoming sleep. For that purpose, he was always either kneeling or standing. When he slept, he sat down, his head resting against a piece of wood driven into the wall. Lie down he could not, if he wished it; for his cell, as every one knows, was only four feet and a half in length. In all these years, he never covered his head with his hood, even when the sun was hottest, or the rain heaviest. He never covered his feet: the only garment he wore was made of sackcloth, and that was as tight as it could be, with nothing between it and his flesh; over this, he wore a cloak of the same stuff. He told me that, in the severe cold, he used to take off his cloak, and open the door and the window of his cell, in order that when he put his cloak on again, after shutting the door and the window, he might give some satisfaction to his body in the pleasure it might have in the increased warmth. His ordinary practice was to eat but once in three days. He said to me, "Why are you astonished at it? it is very possible for any one who is used to it." One of his companions told me that he would be occasionally eight days without eating: that must have been when he was in prayer; for he was subject to trances, and to the impetuosities of the love of God, of which I was once a witness myself.

19. His poverty was extreme; and his mortification, from his youth, was such,—so he told me,—that he was three years in one of the houses of his Order without knowing how to distinguish one friar from another, otherwise than by the voice; for he never raised his eyes: and so, when he was obliged to go from one part of the house to the other, he never knew the way, unless he followed the friars. His journeys, also, were made in the same way. For many years, he never saw a woman's face. He told me that it was nothing to him then whether he saw it or not: but he was an aged man when I made his acquaintance; and his weakness was so great, that he seemed like nothing else but the roots of trees. With all his sanctity, he was very agreeable; though his words were few, unless when he was asked questions; he was very pleasant to speak to, for he had a most clear understanding.

20. Many other things I should like to say of him, if I were not afraid, my father, that you will say, Why does she meddle here? and it is in that fear I have written this. So I leave the subject, only saying that his last end was like his life—preaching to, and exhorting, his brethren. When he saw that the end was comes he repeated the Psalm,[300] "Lætatus sum in his quæ dicta sunt mihi;" and then, kneeling down, he died.

21. Since then, it has pleased our Lord that I should find more help from him than during his life. He advises me in many matters. I have often seen him in great glory. The first time he appeared to me, he said: "O blessed penance, which has merited so great a reward!" with other things. A year before his death, he appeared to me being then far away. I knew he was about to die, and so I sent

---

[297] 18th Oct. 1562. As the Saint finished the first relation of her life in June, 1562, this is one of the additions subsequently made.

[298] Ch. xiv. § 7.

[299] Ch. xxvi. § 3, ch. xxxii. § 16.

[300] Psalm cxxi. The words in the MS. are: "Letatun sun yn is que dita sun miqui" (*De la Fuente*).

him word to that effect, when he was some leagues from here. When he died, he appeared to me, and said that he was going to his rest. I did not believe it. I spoke of it to some persons, and within eight days came the news that he was dead—or, to speak more correctly, he had begun to live for evermore.[301]

22. Behold here, then, how that life of sharp penance is perfected in such great glory: and now he is a greater comfort to me, I do believe, than he was on earth. Our Lord said to me on one occasion, that persons could not ask Him anything in his name, and He not hear them. I have recommended many things to him that he was to ask of our Lord, and I have seen my petitions granted. God be blessed for ever! Amen.

23. But how I have been talking in order to stir you up never to esteem anything in this life!—as if you did not know this, or as if you were not resolved to leave everything, and had already done it! I see so much going wrong in the world, that though my speaking of it is of no other use than to weary me by writing of it, it is some relief to me that all I am saying makes against myself. Our Lord forgive me all that I do amiss herein; and you too, my father, for wearying you to no purpose. It seems as if I would make you do penance for my sins herein.

Chapter XXVIII.

Visions of the Sacred Humanity, and of the Glorified Bodies. Imaginary Visions. Great Fruits Thereof When They Come from God.

1. I now resume our subject. I spent some days, not many, with that vision[302] continually before me. It did me so much good, that I never ceased to pray. Even when I did cease, I contrived that it should be in such a way as that I should not displease Him whom I saw so clearly present, an eye-witness of my acts. And though I was occasionally afraid, because so much was said to me about delusions, that fear lasted not long, because our Lord reassured me.

2. It pleased our Lord, one day that I was in prayer, to show me His Hands, and His Hands only. The beauty of them was so great, that no language can describe it. This put me in great fear; for everything that is strange, in the beginning of any new grace from God, makes me very much afraid. A few days later, I saw His divine Face, and I was utterly entranced. I could not understand why our Lord showed Himself in this way, seeing that, afterwards, He granted me the grace of seeing His whole Person. Later on, I understood that His Majesty was dealing with me according to the weakness of my nature. May He be blessed for ever! A glory so great was more than one so base and wicked could bear; and our merciful Lord, knowing this, ordered it in this way.

3. You will think, my father, that it required no great courage to look upon Hands and Face so beautiful. But so beautiful are glorified bodies, that the glory which surrounds them renders those who see that which is so supernatural and beautiful beside themselves. It was so with me: I was in such great fear, trouble, and perplexity at the sight. Afterwards there ensued a sense of safety and certainty, together with other results, so that all fear passed immediately away.[303]

4. On one of the feasts of St. Paul,[304] when I was at Mass, there stood before me the most Sacred Humanity,[305] as painters represent Him after the resurrection, in great beauty and majesty, as I particularly described it to you, my father, when you had insisted on it. It was painful enough to have to write about it, for I could not describe it without doing great violence to myself. But I

---

[301] See ch. xxx. § 2.

[302] Ch. xxvii. § 3.

[303] St. John of the Cross, *Spiritual Canticle*, st. 14, p. 84: "In the spiritual passage from the sleep of natural ignorance to the wakefulness of the supernatural understanding, which is the beginning of trance or ecstasy, the spiritual vision then revealed makes the soul fear and tremble."

[304] See ch. xxix. § 4.

[305] "The holy Mother, Teresa of Jesus, had these imaginary visions for many years, seeing our Lord continually present before her in great beauty, risen from the dead, with His wounds and the crown of thorns. She had a picture made of Him, which she gave to me, and which I gave to Don Fernando de Toledo, Duke of Alva" (Jerome Gratian, *Union del Alma*, cap. 5. Madrid, 1616).

described it as well as I could, and there is no reason why I should now recur to it. One thing, however, I have to say: if in heaven itself there were nothing else to delight our eyes but the great beauty of glorified bodies, that would be an excessive bliss, particularly the vision of the Humanity of Jesus Christ our Lord. If here below, where His Majesty shows Himself to us according to the measure which our wretchedness can bear, it is so great, what must it be there, where the fruition of it is complete!

5. This vision, though imaginary, I never saw with my bodily eyes, nor, indeed, any other, but only with the eyes of the soul. Those who understand these things better than I do, say that the intellectual vision is more perfect than this; and this, the imaginary vision, much more perfect than those visions which are seen by the bodily eyes. The latter kind of visions, they say, is the lowest; and it is by these that the devil can most delude us. I did not know it then; for I wished, when this grace had been granted me, that it had been so in such a way that I could see it with my bodily eyes, in order that my confessor might not say to me that I indulged in fancies.

6. After the vision was over, it happened that I too imagined—the thought came at once—I had fancied these things; so I was distressed, because I had spoken of them to my confessor, thinking that I might have been deceiving him. There was another lamentation: I went to my confessor, and told him of my doubts. He would ask me whether I told him the truth so far as I knew it; or, if not, had I intended to deceive him? I would reply, that I told the truth; for, to the best of my belief, I did not lie, nor did I mean anything of the kind; neither would I tell a lie for the whole world.[306] This he knew well enough; and, accordingly, he contrived to quiet me; and I felt so much the going to him with these doubts, that I cannot tell how Satan could have put it into my head that I invented those things for the purpose of tormenting myself.

7. But our Lord made such haste to bestow this grace upon me, and to declare the reality of it, that all doubts of the vision being a fancy on my part were quickly taken away, and ever since I see most clearly how silly I was. For if I were to spend many years in devising how to picture to myself anything so beautiful, I should never be able, nor even know how, to do it for it is beyond the reach of any possible imagination here below: the whiteness and brilliancy alone are inconceivable. It is not a brilliancy which dazzles, but a delicate whiteness and a brilliancy infused, furnishing the most excessive delight to the eyes, never wearied thereby, nor by the visible brightness which enables us to see a beauty so divine. It is a light so different from any light here below, that the very brightness of the sun we see, in comparison with the brightness and light before our eyes, seems to be something so obscure, that no one would ever wish to open his eyes again.

8. It is like most pellucid water running in a bed of crystal, reflecting the rays of the sun, compared with most muddy water on a cloudy day, flowing on the surface of the earth. Not that there is anything like the sun present here, nor is the light like that of the sun: this light seems to be natural; and, in comparison with it, every other light is something artificial. It is a light which knows no night; but rather, as it is always light, nothing ever disturbs it. In short, it is such that no man, however gifted he may be, can ever, in the whole course of his life, arrive at any imagination of what it is. God puts it before us so instantaneously, that we could not open our eyes in time to see it, if it were necessary for us to open them at all. But whether our eyes be open or shut, it makes no difference whatever; for when our Lord wills, we must see it, whether we will or not. No distraction can shut it out, no power can resist it, nor can we attain to it by any diligence or efforts of our own. I know this by experience well, as I shall show you.

9. That which I wish now to speak of is the manner in which our Lord manifests Himself in these visions. I do not mean that I am going to explain how it is that a light so strong can enter the interior sense, or so distinct an image the understanding, so as to seem to be really there; for this must be work for learned men. Our Lord has not been pleased to let me understand how it is. I am so ignorant myself, and so dull of understanding, that, although people have very much wished to explain it to me, I have never been able to understand how it can be.

10. This is the truth: though you, my father, may think that I have a quick understanding, it is not so; for I have found out, in many ways, that my understanding can take in only, as they say, what is given to it to eat. Sometimes my confessor used to be amazed at my ignorance: and he never explained to me—nor, indeed, did I desire to understand—how God did this, nor how it could be.

---

[306] See ch. xxx. § 18.

Nor did I ever ask; though, as I have said,[307] I had converse for many years with men of great learning. But I did ask them if this or that were a sin or not: as for everything else, the thought that God did it all was enough for me. I saw there was no reason to be afraid, but great reason to praise Him. On the other hand, difficulties increase my devotion; and the greater the difficulty the greater the increase.

11. I will therefore relate what my experience has shown me; but how our Lord brought it about, you, my father, will explain better than I can, and make clear all that is obscure, and beyond my skill to explain. Now and then it seemed to me that what I saw was an image; but most frequently it was not so. I thought it was Christ Himself, judging by the brightness in which He was pleased to show Himself. Sometimes the vision was so indistinct, that I thought it was an image; but still not like a picture, however well painted—and I have seen many good pictures. It would be absurd to suppose that the one bears any resemblance whatever to the other, for they differ as a living person differs from his portrait, which, however well drawn, cannot be lifelike, for it is plain that it is a dead thing. But let this pass, though to the purpose, and literally true.

12. I do not say this by way of comparison, for comparisons are never exact, but because it is the truth itself, as there is the same difference here that there is between a living subject and the portrait thereof, neither more nor less: for if what I saw was an image, it was a living image,—not a dead man, but the living Christ: and He makes me see that He is God and man,—not as He was in the sepulcher, but as He was when He had gone forth from it, risen from the dead. He comes at times in majesty so great, that no one can have any doubt that it is our Lord Himself, especially after Communion: we know that He is then present, for faith says so. He shows Himself so clearly to be the Lord of that little dwelling-place, that the soul seems to be dissolved and lost in Christ. O my Jesus, who can describe the majesty wherein Thou shows Thyself! How utterly Thou art the Lord of the whole world, and of heaven, and of a thousand other and innumerable worlds and heavens, the creation of which is possible to Thee! The soul understands by that majesty wherein Thou shows Thyself that it is nothing for Thee to be Lord of all this.

13. Here it is plain, O my Jesus, how slight is the power of all the devils in comparison with Thine, and how he who is pleasing unto Thee is able to tread all hell under his feet. Here we see why the devils trembled when Thou did go down to Limbus, and why they might have longed for a thousand hells still lower, that they might escape from Thy terrible Majesty. I see that it is Thy will the soul should feel the greatness of Thy Majesty, and the power of Thy most Sacred Humanity, united with Thy Divinity. Here, too, we see what the day of judgment will be, when we shall behold the King in His Majesty, and in the rigor of His justice against the wicked. Here we learn true humility, imprinted in the soul by the sight of its own wretchedness, of which now it cannot be ignorant. Here, also, is confusion of face, and true repentance for sins; for though the soul sees that our Lord shows how He loves it, yet it knows not where to go, and so is utterly dissolved.

14. My meaning is, that so exceedingly great is the power of this vision, when our Lord shows the soul much of His grandeur and majesty, that it is impossible, in my opinion, for any soul to endure it, if our Lord did not succor it in a most supernatural way, by throwing it into a trance or ecstasy, whereby the vision of the divine presence is lost in the fruition thereof. It is true that afterwards the vision is forgotten; but there remains so deep an impression of the majesty and beauty of God, that it is impossible to forget it, except when our Lord is pleased that the soul should suffer from aridity and desolation, of which I shall speak hereafter;[308] for then it seems to forget God Himself. The soul is itself no longer, it is always inebriated; it seems as if a living love of God, of the highest kind, made a new beginning within it; for though the former vision, which I said represented God without any likeness of Him,[309] is of a higher kind, yet because of our weakness, in order that the remembrance of the vision may last, and that our thoughts may be well occupied, it is a great matter that a presence so divine should remain and abide in our imagination. These two kinds of visions come almost always together, and they do so come; for we behold the excellency and beauty and glory of the most Holy Humanity with the eyes of the soul. And in the other way I

---

[307] Ch. xxv. § 18.

[308] Ch. xxx. §§ 9, 10. See St. John of the Cross, *Obscure Night*, bk. ii. ch. 7.

[309] Ch. xxvii. § 3.

have spoken of,—that of intellectual vision,—we learn how He is God, is mighty, can do all things, commands all things, governs all things, and fills all things with His love.

15. This vision is to be esteemed very highly; nor is there, in my opinion, any risk in it, because the fruits of it show that the devil has no power here. I think he tried three or four times to represent our Lord to me, in this way, by a false image of Him. He takes the appearance of flesh, but he cannot counterfeit the glory which it has when the vision is from God. Satan makes his representations in order to undo the true vision which the soul has had: but the soul resists instinctively; is troubled, disgusted, and restless; it loses that devotion and joy it previously had, and cannot pray at all. In the beginning, it so happened to me three or four times. These satanic visions are very different things; and even he who shall have attained to the prayer of quiet only will, I believe, detect them by those results of them which I described when I was speaking of locutions.[310] They are most easily recognized; and if a soul consents not to its own delusion, I do not think that Satan will be able to deceive it, provided it walks in humility and singleness of heart. He who shall have had the true vision, coming from God, detects the false visions at once; for, though they begin with a certain sweetness and joy, the soul rejects them of itself; and the joy which Satan ministers must be, I think, very different—it shows no traces of pure and holy love: Satan very quickly betrays himself.

16. Thus, then, as I believe, Satan can do no harm to anyone who has had experience of these things; for it is the most impossible of all impossible things that all this may be the work of the imagination. There is no ground whatever for the supposition; for the very beauty and whiteness of one of our Lord's Hands[311] are beyond our imagination altogether. How is it that we see present before us, in a moment, what we do not remember, what we have never thought of, and, moreover, what, in a long space of time, the imagination could not compass, because, as I have just said,[312] it far transcends anything we can comprehend in this life? This, then, is not possible. Whether we have any power in the matter or not will appear by what I am now going to say.

17. If the vision were the work of a man's own understanding,—setting aside that such a vision would not accomplish the great results of the true one, nor, indeed, any at all,—it would be as the act of one who tries to go to sleep, and yet continues awake, because sleep has not come. He longs for it, because of some necessity or weakness in his head: and so he lulls himself to sleep, and makes efforts to procure it, and now and then thinks he has succeeded; but, if the sleep be not real, it will not support him, nor supply strength to his head: on the contrary, his head will very often be the worse for it. So will it be here, in a measure; the soul will be dissipated, neither sustained nor strengthened; on the contrary, it will be wearied and disgusted. But, in the true vision, the riches which abide in the soul cannot be described; even the body receives health and comfort.

18. I urged this argument, among others, when they told me that my visions came from the evil one, and that I imagined them myself,—and it was very often,—and made use of certain illustrations, as well as I could, and as our Lord suggested to me. But all was to little purpose; for as there were most holy persons in the place,—in comparison with whom I was a mass of perdition,—whom God did not lead by this way, they were at once filled with fear; they thought it all came through my sins. And so my state was talked about, and came to the knowledge of many; though I had spoken of it to no one, except my confessor, or to those to whom he commanded[313] me to speak of it.

19. I said to them once, If they who thus speak of my state were to tell me that a person with whom I had just conversed, and whom I knew well, was not that person, but that I was deluding myself, and that they knew it, I should certainly trust them rather than my own eyes. But if that person left with me certain jewels,—and if, possessing none previously, I held the jewels in my hand as pledges of a great love,—and if I were now rich, instead of poor as before,—I should not be able to believe this that they said, though I might wish it. These jewels I could now show them, for all who knew me saw clearly that my soul was changed,—and so my confessor said; for the difference was very great in every way—not a pretense, but such as all might most clearly observe. As I was formerly so wicked, I said, I could not believe that Satan, if he wished to deceive me and

---

[310] Ch. xxv. § 8.

[311] See § 2.

[312] § 7, *supra*.

[313] See ch. xxiii. § 14.

take me down to hell, would have recourse to means so adverse to his purpose as this, of rooting out my faults, implanting virtues and spiritual strength; for I saw clearly that I had become at once another person through the instrumentality of these visions.

20. My confessor, who was, as I said before,[314] one of the fathers of the Society of Jesus, and a really holy man, answered them in the same way,—so I learnt afterwards. He was a most discreet man, and of great humility; but this great humility of his brought me into serious trouble: for, though he was a man much given to prayer, and learned, he never trusted his own judgment, because our Lord was not leading him by this way. He had, therefore, much to suffer on my account, in many ways. I knew they used to say to him that he must be on his guard against me, lest Satan should delude him through a belief in anything I might say to him. They gave instances of others who were deluded.[315] All this distressed me. I began to be afraid I should find no one to hear my confession,[316] and that all would avoid me. I did nothing but weep.

21. It was a providence of God that he was willing to stand by me and hear my confession. But he was so great a servant of God, that he would have exposed himself to anything for His sake. So he told me that if I did not offend God, nor swerve from the instructions he gave me, there was no fear I should be deserted by him. He encouraged me always, and quieted me. He bade me never to conceal anything from him; and I never did.[317] He used to say that, so long as I did this, the devil, if it were the devil, could not hurt me; on the contrary, out of that evil which Satan wished to do me, our Lord would bring forth good. He labored with all his might to make me perfect. As I was very much afraid myself, I obeyed him in everything, though imperfectly. He had much to suffer on my account during three years of trouble and more, because he heard my confession all that time; for in the great persecutions that fell upon me, and the many harsh judgments of me which our Lord permitted,—many of which I did not deserve,—everything was carried to him, and he was found fault with because of me,—he being all the while utterly blameless.

22. If he had not been so holy a man, and if our Lord had not been with him, it would have, been impossible for him to bear so much; for he had to answer those who regarded me as one going to destruction; and they would not believe what he said to them. On the other hand, he had to quiet me, and relieve me of my fears; when my fears increased, he had again to reassure me; for, after every vision which was strange to me, our Lord permitted me to remain in great fear. All this was the result of my being then, and of having been, a sinner. He used to console me out of his great compassion; and, if he had trusted to his own convictions, I should not have had so much to suffer; for God revealed the whole truth to him. I believe that he received this light from the Blessed Sacrament.

23. Those servants of God who were not satisfied had many conversations with me.[318] As I spoke to them carelessly, so they misunderstood my meaning in many things. I had a great regard for one of them; for my soul owed him more than I can tell. He was a most holy man, and I felt it most acutely when I saw that he did not understand me. He had a great desire for my improvement, and hoped our Lord would enlighten me. So, then, because I spoke, as I was saying, without careful consideration, they looked upon me as deficient in humility; and when they detected any of my faults—they might have detected many—they condemned me at once. They used to put certain questions to me, which I answered simply and carelessly. Then they concluded forthwith that I wished to teach them, and that I considered myself to be a learned woman. All this was carried to my confessor,—for certainly they desired my amendment—and so he would reprimand me. This lasted some time, and I was distressed on many sides; but, with the graces which our Lord gave me, I bore it all.

24. I relate this in order that people may see what a great trial it is not to find any one who knows this way of the spirit by experience. If our Lord had not dealt so favorably with me, I know not what would have become of me. There were some things that were enough to take away my

---

[314] Ch. xxiv. § 5.

[315] 15. There were in Spain, and elsewhere, many women who were hypocrites, or deluded. Among others was the prioress of Lisbon, afterwards notorious, who deceived Luis of Granada (*De la Fuente*).

[316] *Interior Castle*, vi. 1, § 4.

[317] Ch. xxvi. § 5; *Interior Castle*, vi. 9, § 7.

[318] See ch. xxv. § 18.

reason; and now and then I was reduced to such straits that I could do nothing but lift up my eyes to our Lord. The contradiction of good people, which a wretched woman, weak, wicked, and timid as I am, must bear with, seems to be nothing when thus described; but I, who in the course of my life passed through very great trials, found this one of the heaviest.[319]

25. May our Lord grant that I may have pleased His Majesty a little herein; for I am sure that they pleased Him who condemned and rebuked me, and that it was all for my great good.

Chapter XXIX.

Of Visions. The Graces Our Lord Bestowed on the Saint. The Answers Our Lord Gave Her for Those Who Tried Her.

1. I have wandered far from the subject; for I undertook to give reasons why the vision was no work of the imagination. For how can we, by any efforts of ours, picture to ourselves the Humanity of Christ, and imagine His great beauty? No little time is necessary, if our conception is in any way to resemble it. Certainly, the imagination may be able to picture it, and a person may for a time contemplate that picture,—the form and the brightness of it,—and gradually make it more perfect, and so lay up that image in his memory. Who can hinder this, seeing that it could be fashioned by the understanding? But as to the vision of which I am speaking, there are no means of bringing it about; only we must behold it when our Lord is pleased to present it before us, as He wills and what He wills; and there is no possibility of taking anything away from it, or of adding anything to it; nor is there any way of effecting it, whatever we may do, nor of seeing it when we like, nor of abstaining from seeing; if we try to gaze upon it—part of the vision in particular—the vision of Christ is lost at once.

2. For two years and a half God granted me this grace very frequently; but it is now more than three years since He has taken away from me its continual presence, through another of a higher nature, as I shall perhaps explain hereafter.[320] And though I saw Him speaking to me, and though I was contemplating His great beauty, and the sweetness with which those words of His came forth from His divine mouth,—they were sometimes uttered with severity,—and though I was extremely desirous to behold the color of His eyes, or the form of them, so that I might be able to describe them, yet I never attained to the sight of them, and I could do nothing for that end; on the contrary, I lost the vision altogether. And though I see that He looks upon me at times with great tenderness, yet so strong is His gaze, that my soul cannot endure it; I fall into a trance so deep, that I lose the beautiful vision, in order to have a greater fruition of it all.

3. Accordingly, willing or not willing, the vision has nothing to do with it. Our Lord clearly regards nothing but humility and confusion of face, the acceptance of what He wishes to give, and the praise of Himself, the Giver. This is true of all visions without exception: we can contribute nothing towards them—we cannot add to them, nor can we take from them; our own efforts can neither make nor unmake them. Our Lord would have us see most clearly that it is no work of ours, but of His Divine Majesty; we are therefore the less able to be proud of it: on the contrary, it makes us humble and afraid; for we see that, as our Lord can take from us the power of seeing what we would see, so also can He take from us these mercies and His grace, and we may be lost for ever. We must therefore walk in His fear while we are living in this our exile.

4. Our Lord showed Himself to me almost always as He is after His resurrection. It was the same in the Host; only at those times when I was in trouble, and when it was His will to strengthen me, did He show His wounds. Sometimes I saw Him on the cross, in the Garden, crowned with thorns,—but that was rarely; sometimes also carrying His cross because of my necessities,—I may say so,—or those of others; but always in His glorified body. Many reproaches and many vexations have I borne while telling this—many suspicions and much persecution also. So certain were they to whom I spoke that I had an evil spirit, that some would have me exorcised. I did not care much

---

[319] See ch. xxx. § 6.
[320] Ch. xl.

for this; but I felt it bitterly when I saw that my confessors were afraid to hear me, or when I knew that they were told of anything about me.

5. Notwithstanding all this, I never could be sorry that I had had these heavenly visions; nor would I exchange even one of them for all the wealth and all the pleasures of the world. I always regarded them as a great mercy from our Lord; and to me they were the very greatest treasure,—of this our Lord assured me often. I used to go to Him to complain of all these hardships; and I came away from prayer consoled, and with renewed strength. I did not dare to contradict those who were trying me; for I saw that it made matters worse, because they looked on my doing so as a failure in humility. I spoke of it to my confessor; he always consoled me greatly when he saw me in distress.

6. As my visions grew in frequency, one of those who used to help me before—it was to him I confessed when the father-minister[321] could not hear me—began to say that I was certainly under the influence of Satan. He bade me, now that I had no power of resisting, always to make the sign of the cross when I had a vision, to point my finger at it by way of scorn, and be firmly persuaded of its diabolic nature. If I did this, the vision would not recur. I was to be without fear on the point; God would watch over me, and take the vision away.[322] This was a great hardship for me; for, as I could not believe that the vision did not come from God, it was a fearful thing for me to do; and I could not wish, as I said before, that the visions should be withheld. However, I did at last as I was bidden. I prayed much to our Lord, that He would deliver me from delusions. I was always praying to that effect, and with many tears. I had recourse also to St. Peter and St. Paul; for our Lord had said to me—it was on their feast that He had appeared to me the first time[323]—that they would preserve me from delusion. I used to see them frequently most distinctly on my left hand; but that vision was not imaginary. These glorious Saints were my very good lords.

7. It was to me a most painful thing to make a show of contempt whenever I saw our Lord in a vision; for when I saw Him before me, if I were to be cut in pieces, I could not believe it was Satan. This was to me, therefore, a heavy kind of penance; and accordingly, that I might not be so continually crossing myself, I used to hold a crucifix in my hand. This I did almost always; but I did not always make signs of contempt, because I felt that too much. It reminded me of the insults which the Jews heaped upon Him; and so I prayed Him to forgive me, seeing that I did so in obedience to him who stood in His stead, and not to lay the blame on me, seeing that he was one of those whom He had placed as His ministers in His Church. He said to me that I was not to distress myself—that I did well to obey; but He would make them see the truth of the matter. He seemed to me to be angry when they made me give up my prayer.[324] He told me to say to them that this was tyranny. He gave me reasons for believing that the vision was not satanic; some of them I mean to repeat by and by.

8. On one occasion, when I was holding in my hand the cross of my rosary, He took it from me into His own hand. He returned it; but it was then four large stones incomparably more precious than diamonds; for nothing can be compared with what is supernatural. Diamonds seem counterfeits and imperfect when compared with these precious stones. The five wounds were delineated on them with most admirable art. He said to me, that for the future that cross would appear so to me always; and so it did. I never saw the wood of which it was made, but only the precious stones. They were seen, however, by no one else,—only by myself.[325]

9. When they had begun to insist on my putting my visions to a test like this, and resisting them, the graces I received were multiplied more and more. I tried to distract myself; I never ceased to be in prayer: even during sleep my prayer seemed to be continual; for now my love grew, I made piteous complaints to our Lord, and told Him I could not bear it. Neither was it in my power—

[321] Baltasar Alvarez was father-minister of the house of St. Giles, Avila, in whose absence she had recourse to another father of that house (*Ribera*, i. ch. 6).

[322] See *Book of the Foundations*, ch. viii. § 3, where the Saint refers to this advice, and to the better advice given her later by F. Dominic Bañes, one of her confessors. See also *Interior Castle*, vi. 9, § 7.

[323] See ch. xxvii. § 3, and ch. xxviii. § 4.

[324] Ch. xxv. § 18.

[325] The cross was made of ebony (*Ribera*). It is not known where that cross is now. The Saint gave it to her sister, Doña Juana de Ahumada, who begged it of her. Some say that the Carmelites of Madrid possess it; and others, those of Valladolid (*De la Fuente*).

though I desired, and, more than that, even strove—to give up thinking of Him. Nevertheless, I obeyed to the utmost of my power; but my power was little or nothing in the matter; and our Lord never released me from that obedience; but though He bade me obey my confessor, He reassured me in another way, and taught me what I was to say. He has continued to do so until now; and He gave me reasons so sufficient, that I felt myself perfectly safe.

10. Not long afterwards His Majesty began, according to His promise, to make it clear that it was He Himself who appeared, by the growth in me of the love of God so strong, that I knew not who could have infused it; for it was most supernatural, and I had not attained to it by any efforts of my own. I saw myself dying with a desire to see God, and I knew not how to seek that life otherwise than by dying. Certain great impetuosities of love, though not so intolerable as those of which I have spoken before,[326] nor yet of so great worth, overwhelmed me. I knew not what to do; for nothing gave me pleasure, and I had no control over myself. It seemed as if my soul were really torn away from myself. Oh, supreme artifice of our Lord! how tenderly did Thou deal with Thy miserable slave! Thou did hide Thyself from me, and did yet constrain me with Thy love, with a death so sweet, that my soul would never wish it over.

11. It is not possible for any one to understand these impetuosities if he has not experienced them himself. They are not an upheaving of the breast, nor those devotional sensations, not uncommon, which seem on the point of causing suffocation, and are beyond control. That prayer is of a much lower order; and those agitations should be avoided by gently endeavoring to be recollected; and the soul should be kept in quiet. This prayer is like the sobbing of little children, who seem on the point of choking, and whose disordered senses are soothed by giving them to drink. So here reason should draw in the reins, because nature itself may be contributing to it and we should consider with fear that all this may not be perfect, and that much sensuality may be involved in it. The infant soul should be soothed by the caresses of love, which shall draw forth its love in a gentle way, and not, as they say, by force of blows. This love should be inwardly under control, and not as a caldron, fiercely boiling because too much fuel has been applied to it, and out of which everything is lost. The source of the fire must be kept under control, and the flame must be quenched in sweet tears, and not with those painful tears which come out of these emotions, and which do so much harm.

12. In the beginning, I had tears of this kind. They left me with a disordered head and a wearied spirit, and for a day or two afterwards unable to resume my prayer. Great discretion, therefore, is necessary at first, in order that everything may proceed gently, and that the operations of the spirit may be within; all outward manifestations should be carefully avoided.

13. These other impetuosities are very different. It is not we who apply the fuel; the fire is already kindled, and we are thrown into it in a moment to be consumed. It is by no efforts of the soul that it sorrows over the wound which the absence of our Lord has inflicted on it; it is far otherwise; for an arrow is driven into the entrails to the very quick,[327] and into the heart at times, so that the soul knows not what is the matter with it, nor what it wishes for. It understands clearly enough that it wishes for God, and that the arrow seems tempered with some herb which makes the soul hate itself for the love of our Lord, and willingly lose its life for Him. It is impossible to describe or explain the way in which God wounds the soul, nor the very grievous pain inflicted, which deprives it of all self-consciousness; yet this pain is so sweet, that there is no joy in the world which gives greater delight. As I have just said,[328] the soul would wish to be always dying of this wound.

14. This pain and bliss together carried me out of myself, and I never could understand how it was. Oh, what a sight a wounded soul is!—a soul, I mean, so conscious of it, as to be able to say of itself that it is wounded for so good a cause; and seeing distinctly that it never did anything whereby this love should come to it, and that it does come from that exceeding love which our Lord bears it. A spark seems to have fallen suddenly upon it, that has set it all on fire. Oh, how often do I remember, when in this state, those words of David: "Quemadmodum desiderat cervus ad fontes aquarum"![329] They seem to me to be literally true of myself.

---

326 Ch. xx. § 11.

327 *Interior Castle*, vi. 11, § 2; St. John of the Cross, *Spiritual Canticle*, st. 1, p. 22, Engl. trans.

328 § 10.

329 Psalm xli. 2: "As the longing of the hart for the fountains of waters, so is the longing of my soul for

15. When these impetuosities are not very violent they seem to admit of a little mitigation—at least, the soul seeks some relief, because it knows not what to do—through certain penances; the painfulness of which, and even the shedding of its blood, are no more felt than if the body were dead. The soul seeks for ways and means to do something that may be felt, for the love of God; but the first pain is so great, that no bodily torture I know of can take it away. As relief is not to be had here, these medicines are too mean for so high a disease. Some slight mitigation may be had, and the pain may pass away a little, by praying God to relieve its sufferings: but the soul sees no relief except in death, by which it thinks to attain completely to the fruition of its good. At other times, these impetuosities are so violent, that the soul can do neither this nor anything else; the whole body is contracted, and neither hand nor foot can be moved: if the body be upright at the time, it falls down, as a thing that has no control over itself. It cannot even breathe; all it does is to moan—not loudly, because it cannot: its moaning, however, comes from a keen sense of pain.

16. Our Lord was pleased that I should have at times a vision of this kind: I saw an angel close by me, on my left side, in bodily form. This I am not accustomed to see, unless very rarely. Though I have visions of angels frequently, yet I see them only by an intellectual vision, such as I have spoken of before.[330] It was our Lord's will that in this vision I should see the angel in this wise. He was not large, but small of stature, and most beautiful—his face burning, as if he were one of the highest angels, who seem to be all of fire: they must be those whom we call cherubim.[331] Their names they never tell me; but I see very well that there is in heaven so great a difference between one angel and another, and between these and the others, that I cannot explain it.

17. I saw in his hand a long spear of gold, and at the iron's point there seemed to be a little fire. He appeared to me to be thrusting it at times into my heart, and to pierce my very entrails; when he drew it out, he seemed to draw them out also, and to leave me all on fire with a great love of God. The pain was so great, that it made me moan; and yet so surpassing was the sweetness of this excessive pain, that I could not wish to be rid of it. The soul is satisfied now with nothing less than God. The pain is not bodily, but spiritual; though the body has its share in it, even a large one. It is a caressing of love so sweet which now takes place between the soul and God, that I pray God of His goodness to make him experience it who may think that I am lying.[332]

18. During the days that this lasted, I went about as if beside myself. I wished to see, or speak with, no one, but only to cherish my pain, which was to me a greater bliss than all created things could give me.[333]

19. I was in this state from time to time, whenever it was our Lord's pleasure to throw me into those deep trances, which I could not prevent even when I was in the company of others, and which, to my deep vexation, came to be publicly known. Since then, I do not feel that pain so much, but only that which I spoke of before,—I do not remember the chapter,[334]—which is in many ways very different from it, and of greater worth. On the other hand, when this pain, of which I am now speaking, begins, our Lord seems to lay hold of the soul, and to throw it into a trance, so that there is no time for me to have any sense of pain or suffering, because fruition ensues at once. May He be blessed for ever, who hath bestowed such great graces on one who has responded so ill to blessings so great!

Thee, O my God."

[330] Ch. xxvii. § 3.

[331] In the MS. of the Saint preserved in the Escurial, the word is "cherubines;" but all the editors before Don Vicente de la Fuente have adopted the suggestion, in the margin, of Bañes, who preferred "seraphim." F. Bouix, in his translation, corrected the mistake; but, with his usual modesty, did not call the reader's attention to it.

[332] "The most probable opinion is, that the piercing of the heart of the Saint took place in 1559. The hymn which she composed on that occasion was discovered in Seville in 1700 ("En las internas entrañas"). On the high altar of the Carmelite church in Alba de Tormes, the heart of the Saint thus pierced is to be seen; and I have seen it myself more than once" (*De la Fuente*).

[333] 17. *Brev. Rom.* in fest. S. Teresiæ, Oct. 15, Lect. v.: "Tanto autem divini amoris incendio cor ejus conflagravit, ut merito viderit Angelum ignito jaculo sibi præcordia transverberantem." The Carmelites keep the feast of this piercing of the Saint's heart on the 27th of August.

[334] Ch. xx. § 11.

Chapter XXX.

St. Peter of Alcantara Comforts the Saint. Great Temptations and Interior Trials.

1. When I saw that I was able to do little or nothing towards avoiding these great impetuosities, I began also to be afraid of them, because I could not understand how this pain and joy could subsist together. I knew it was possible enough for bodily pain and spiritual joy to dwell together; but the coexistence of a spiritual pain so excessive as this, and of joy so deep, troubled my understanding. Still, I tried to continue my resistance; but I was so little able, that I was now and then wearied. I used to take up the cross for protection, and try to defend myself against Him who, by the cross, is the Protector of us all. I saw that no one understood me. I saw it very clearly myself, but I did not dare to say so to any one except my confessor; for that would have been a real admission that I had no humility.

2. Our Lord was pleased to succor me in a great measure,—and, for the moment, altogether,— by bringing to the place where I was that blessed friar, Peter of Alcantara. Of him I spoke before, and said something of his penance.[335] Among other things, I have been assured that he wore continually, for twenty years, a girdle made of iron. He is the author of certain little books, in Spanish, on prayer, which are now in common use; for, as he was much exercised therein, his writings are very profitable to those who are given to prayer. He kept the first rule of the blessed St. Francis in all its rigor, and did those things besides of which I spoke before.

3. When that widow, the servant of God and my friend, of whom I have already spoken,[336] knew that so great a man had come, she took her measures. She knew the straits I was in, for she was an eye-witness of my afflictions, and was a great comfort to me. Her faith was so strong, that she could not help believing that what others said was the work of the devil was really the work of the Spirit of God; and as she is a person of great sense and great caution, and one to whom our Lord is very bountiful in prayer, it pleased His Majesty to let her see what learned men failed to discern. My confessors gave me leave to accept relief in some things from her, because in many ways she was able to afford it. Some of those graces which our Lord bestowed on me fell to her lot occasionally, together with instructions most profitable for her soul. So, then, when she knew that the blessed man was come, without saying a word to me, she obtained leave from the Provincial for me to stay eight days in her house, in order that I might the more easily confer with him. In that house, and in one church or another, I had many conversations with him the first time he came here; for, afterwards, I had many communications with him at diverse times.

4. I gave him an account, as briefly as I could, of my life, and of my way of prayer, with the utmost clearness in my power. I have always held to this, to be perfectly frank and exact with those to whom I make known the state of my soul.[337] Even my first impulses I wish them to know; and as for doubtful and suspicious matters, I used to make the most of them by arguing against myself. Thus, then, without equivocation or concealment, I laid before him the state of my soul. I saw almost at once that he understood me, by reason of his own experience. That was all I required; for at that time I did not know myself as I do now, so as to give an account of my state. It was at a later time that God enabled me to understand myself, and describe the graces which His Majesty bestows upon me. It was necessary, then, that he who would clearly understand and explain my state should have had experience of it himself.

5. The light he threw on the matter was of the clearest; for as to these visions, at least, which were not imaginary, I could not understand how they could be. And it seemed that I could not understand, too, how those could be which I saw with the eyes of the soul; for, as I said before,[338] those visions only seemed to me to be of consequence which were seen with the bodily eyes: and of these I had none. The holy man enlightened me on the whole question, explained it to me, and bade me not to be distressed, but to praise God, and to abide in the full conviction that this was the work of the Spirit of God; for, saving the faith, nothing could be more true, and there was nothing on which I could more firmly rely. He was greatly comforted in me, was most kind and serviceable,

---

[335] Ch. xxvii. §§ 17, 18, 19.
[336] Ch. xxiv. § 5. Doña Guiomar de Ulloa.
[337] Ch. xxvi. § 5.
[338] Ch. vii. § 12.

and ever afterwards took great care of me, and told me of his own affairs and labors; and when he saw that I had those very desires which in himself were fulfilled already,—for our Lord had given me very strong desires,—and also how great my resolution was, he delighted in conversing with me.

6. To a person whom our Lord has raised to this state, there is no pleasure or comfort equal to that of meeting with another whom our Lord has begun to raise in the same way. At that time, however, it must have been only a beginning with me, as I believe; and God grant I may not have gone back now. He was extremely sorry for me. He told me that one of the greatest trials in this world was that which I had borne,—namely, the contradiction of good people,[339]—and that more was in reserve for me: I had need, therefore, of some one—and there was no one in this city—who understood me; but he would speak to my confessor, and to that married nobleman, already spoken of,[340] who was one of those who tormented me most, and who, because of his great affection for me, was the cause of all these attacks. He was a holy but timid man, and could not feel safe about me, because he had seen how wicked I was, and that not long before. The holy man did so; he spoke to them both, explained the matter, and gave them reasons why they should reassure themselves, and disturb me no more. My confessor was easily satisfied,—not so the nobleman; for though they were not enough to keep him quiet, yet they kept him in some measure from frightening me so much as he used to do.

7. We made an agreement that I should write to him and tell him how it fared with me, for the future, and that we should pray much for each other. Such was his humility, that he held to the prayers of a wretch like me. It made me very much ashamed of myself. He left me in the greatest consolation and joy, bidding me continue my prayer with confidence, and without any doubt that it was the work of God. If I should have any doubts, for my greater security, I was to make them known to my confessor, and, having done so, be in peace. Nevertheless, I was not able at all to feel that confidence, for our Lord was leading me by the way of fear; and so, when they told me that the devil had power over me, I believed them. Thus, then, not one of them was able to inspire me with confidence on the one hand, or fear on the other, in such a way as to make me believe either of them, otherwise than as our Lord allowed me. Accordingly, though the holy friar consoled and calmed me, I did not rely so much on him as to be altogether without fear, particularly when our Lord forsook me in the afflictions of my soul, of which I will now speak. Nevertheless, as I have said, I was very much consoled.

8. I could not give thanks enough to God, and to my glorious father St. Joseph, who seemed to me to have brought him here. He was the commissary-general of the custody[341] of St. Joseph, to whom, and to our Lady, I used to pray much.

9. I suffered at times—and even still, though not so often—the most grievous trials, together with bodily pains and afflictions arising from violent sicknesses; so much so, that I could scarcely control myself. At other times, my bodily sickness was more grievous; and as I had no spiritual pain, I bore it with great joy: but, when both pains came upon me together, my distress was so heavy, that I was reduced to sore straits.

10. I forgot all the mercies our Lord had shown me, and remembered them only as a dream, to my great distress; for my understanding was so dull, that I had a thousand doubts and suspicions whether I had ever understood matters aright, thinking that perhaps all was fancy, and that it was enough for me to have deceived myself, without also deceiving good men. I looked upon myself as so wicked as to have been the cause, by my sins, of all the evils and all the heresies that had sprung up. This is but a false humility, and Satan invented it for the purpose of disquieting me, and trying whether he could thereby drive my soul to despair. I have now had so much experience, that I know this was his work; so he, seeing that I understand him, does not torment me in the same way as much as he used to do. That it is his work is clear from the restlessness and discomfort with which it begins, and the trouble it causes in the soul while it lasts; from the obscurity and distress, the

---

[339] See ch. xxviii. § 24.

[340] Ch. xxiii. § 7.

[341] A "custody" is a division of the province, in the Order of St. Francis, comprising a certain number of convents.

aridity and indisposition for prayer and for every good work, which it produces. It seems to stifle the soul and trammel the body, so as to make them good for nothing.

11. Now, though the soul acknowledges itself to be miserable, and though it is painful to us to see ourselves as we are, and though we have most deep convictions of our own wickedness,—deep as those spoken of just now,[342] and really felt,—yet true humility is not attended with trouble; it does not disturb the soul; it causes neither obscurity nor aridity: on the contrary, it consoles. It is altogether different, bringing with it calm, sweetness, and light. It is no doubt painful; but, on the other hand, it is consoling, because we see how great is the mercy of our Lord in allowing the soul to have that pain, and how well the soul is occupied. On the one hand, the soul grieves over its offences against God; on the other, His compassion makes it glad. It has light, which makes it ashamed of itself; and it gives thanks to His Majesty, who has borne with it so long. That other humility, which is the work of Satan, furnishes no light for any good work; it pictures God as bringing upon everything fire and sword; it dwells upon His justice; and the soul's faith in the mercy of God—for the power of the devil does not reach so far as to destroy faith—is of such a nature as to give me no consolation: on the contrary, the consideration of mercies so great helps to increase the pain, because I look upon myself as bound to render greater service.

12. This invention of Satan is one of the most painful, subtle, and crafty that I have known him to possess; I should therefore like to warn you, my father, of it, in order that, if Satan should tempt you herein, you may have some light, and be aware of his devices, if your understanding should be left at liberty: because you must not suppose that learning and knowledge are of any use here; for though I have none of them myself, yet now that I have escaped out of his hands I see clearly that this is folly. What I understood by it is this: that it is our Lord's pleasure to give him leave and license, as He gave him of old to tempt Job;[343] though in my case, because of my wretchedness, the temptation is not so sharp.

13. It happened to me to be tempted once in this way; and I remember it was on the day before the vigil of Corpus Christi,—a feast to which I have great devotion, though not so great as I ought to have. The trial then lasted only till the day of the feast itself. But, on other occasions, it continued one, two, and even three weeks and—I know not—perhaps longer. But I was specially liable to it during the Holy Weeks, when it was my habit to make prayer my joy. Then the devil seizes on my understanding in a moment; and occasionally, by means of things so trivial that I should laugh at them at any other time, he makes it stumble over anything he likes. The soul, laid in fetters, loses all control over itself, and all power of thinking of anything but the absurdities he puts before it, which, being more or less unsubstantial, inconsistent, and disconnected, serve only to stifle the soul, so that it has no power over itself; and accordingly—so it seems to me—the devils make a football of it, and the soul is unable to escape out of their hands. It is impossible to describe the sufferings of the soul in this state. It goes about in quest of relief, and God suffers it to find none. The light of reason, in the freedom of its will, remains, but it is not clear; it seems to me as if its eyes were covered with a veil. As a person who, having travelled often by a particular road, knows, though it be night and dark, by his past experience of it, where he may stumble, and where he ought to be on his guard against that risk, because he has seen the place by day, so the soul avoids offending God: it seems to go on by habit—that is, if we put out of sight the fact that our Lord holds it by the hand, which is the true explanation of the matter.

14. Faith is then as dead, and asleep, like all the other virtues; not lost, however,—for the soul truly believes all that the church holds; but its profession of the faith is hardly more than an outward profession of the mouth. And, on the other hand, temptations seem to press it down, and make it dull, so that its knowledge of God becomes to it as that of something which it hears of far away. So tepid is its love that, when it hears God spoken of, it listens and believes that He is what He is, because the Church so teaches; but it recollects nothing of its own former experience. Vocal prayer or solitude is only a greater affliction, because the interior suffering—whence it comes, it knows not—is unendurable, and, as it seems to me, in some measure a counterpart of hell. So it is, as our Lord showed me in a vision;[344] for the soul itself is then burning in the fire, knowing not who has

---

[342] § 10.
[343] Job i.
[344] See ch. xxxii. § 1, &c.

kindled it, nor whence it comes, nor how to escape it, nor how to put it out: if it seeks relief from the fire by spiritual reading, it cannot find any, just as if it could not read at all. On one occasion, it occurred to me to read a life of a Saint, that I might forget myself, and be refreshed with the recital of what he had suffered. Four or five times, I read as many lines; and, though they were written in Spanish, I understood them less at the end than I did when I began: so I gave it up. It so happened to me on more occasions than one, but I have a more distinct recollection of this.

15. To converse with any one is worse, for the devil then sends so offensive a spirit of bad temper, that I think I could eat people up; nor can I help myself. I feel that I do something when I keep myself under control; or rather our Lord does so, when He holds back with His hand any one in this state from saying or doing something that may be hurtful to his neighbors and offensive to God. Then, as to going to our confessor, that is of no use; for the certain result is—and very often has it happened to me—what I shall now describe. Though my confessors, with whom I had to do then, and have to do still, are so holy, they spoke to me and reproved me with such harshness, that they were astonished at it afterwards when I told them of it. They said that they could not help themselves; for, though they had resolved not to use such language, and though they pitied me also very much,—yes, even had scruples on the subject, because of my grievous trials of soul and body,—and were, moreover, determined to console me, they could not refrain. They did not use unbecoming words—I mean, words offensive to God; yet their words were the most offensive that could be borne with in confession. They must have aimed at mortifying me. At other times, I used to delight in this, and was prepared to bear it; but it was then a torment altogether. I used to think, too, that I deceived them; so I went to them, and cautioned them very earnestly to be on their guard against me, for it might be that I deceived them. I saw well enough that I would not do so advisedly, nor tell them an untruth;[345] but everything made me afraid. One of them, on one occasion, when he had heard me speak of this temptation, told me not to distress myself; for, even if I wished to deceive him, he had sense enough not to be deceived. This gave me great comfort.

16. Sometimes, almost always,—at least, very frequently,—I used to find rest after Communion; now and then, even, as I drew near to the most Holy Sacrament, all at once my soul and body would be so well, that I was amazed.[346] It seemed to be nothing else but an instantaneous dispersion of the darkness that covered my soul: when the sun rose, I saw how silly I had been.

17. On other occasions, if our Lord spoke to me but one word, saying only, "Be not distressed, have no fear,"—as I said before,[347]—I was made whole at once; or, if I saw a vision, I was as if I had never been amiss. I rejoiced in God, and made my complaint to Him, because He permitted me to undergo such afflictions; yet the recompense was great; for almost always, afterwards, His mercies descended upon me in great abundance. The soul seemed to come forth as gold out of the crucible, most refined, and made glorious to behold, our Lord dwelling within it. These trials afterwards are light, though they once seemed to be unendurable; and the soul longs to undergo them again, if that be more pleasing to our Lord. And though trials and persecutions increase, yet, if we bear them without offending our Lord, rejoicing in suffering for His sake, it will be all the greater gain: I, however, do not bear them as they ought to be borne, but rather in a most imperfect way. At other times, my trials came upon me—they come still—in another form; and then it seems to me as if the very possibility of thinking a good thought, or desiring the accomplishment of it, were utterly taken from me: both soul and body are altogether useless and a heavy burden. However, when I am in this state, I do not suffer from the other temptations and disquietudes, but only from a certain loathing of I know not what, and my soul finds pleasure in nothing.

18. I used to try exterior good works, in order to occupy myself partly by violence; and I know well how weak a soul is when grace is hiding itself. It did not distress me much, because the sight of my own meanness gave me some satisfaction. On other occasions, I find myself unable to pray or to fix my thoughts with any distinctness upon God, or anything that is good, though I may be alone; but I have a sense that I know Him. It is the understanding and the imagination, I believe, which hurt me here; for it seems to me that I have a good will, disposed for all good; but the

---

[345] See ch. xxviii. § 6.

[346] See *Way of Perfection*, ch. lxi. § 2; but ch. xxxiv. § 8 of the earlier editions.

[347] Ch. xx. § 21, ch. xxv. § 22, ch. xxvi. § 3.

understanding is so lost, that it seems to be nothing else but a raving lunatic, which nobody can restrain, and of which I am not mistress enough to keep it quiet for a minute.[348]

19. Sometimes I laugh at myself, and recognize my wretchedness: I watch my understanding, and leave it alone to see what it will do. Glory be to God, for a wonder, it never runs on what is wrong, but only on indifferent things, considering what is going on here, or there, or elsewhere. I see then, more and more, the exceeding great mercy of our Lord to me, when He keeps this lunatic bound in the chains of perfect contemplation. I wonder what would happen if those people who think I am good knew of my extravagance. I am very sorry when I see my soul in such bad company; I long to see it delivered therefrom, and so I say to our Lord: When, O my God, shall I see my whole soul praising Thee, that it may have the fruition of Thee in all its faculties? Let me be no longer, O Lord, thus torn to pieces, and every one of them, as it were, running in a different direction. This has been often the case with me, but I think that my scanty bodily health was now and then enough to bring it about.

20. I dwell much on the harm which original sin has done us; that is, I believe, what has rendered us incapable of the fruition of so great a good. My sins, too, must be in fault; for, if I had not committed so many, I should have been more perfect in goodness. Another great affliction which I suffered was this: all the books which I read on the subject of prayer, I thought I understood thoroughly, and that I required them no longer, because our Lord had given me the gift of prayer. I therefore ceased to read those books, and applied myself to lives of Saints, thinking that this would improve me and give me courage; for I found myself very defective in every kind of service which the Saints rendered unto God. Then it struck me that I had very little humility, when I could think that I had attained to this degree of prayer; and so, when I could not come to any other conclusion, I was greatly distressed, until certain learned persons, and the blessed friar, Peter of Alcantara, told me not to trouble myself about the matter.

21. I see clearly enough that I have not yet begun to serve God, though He showers down upon me those very graces which He gives to many good people. I am a mass of imperfection, except in desire and in love; for herein I see well that our Lord has been gracious to me, in order that I may please Him in some measure. I really think that I love Him; but my conduct, and the many imperfections I discern in myself, make me sad.

22. My soul, also, is subject occasionally to a certain foolishness,—that is the right name to give it,—when I seem to be doing neither good nor evil, but following in the wake of others, as they say, without pain or pleasure, indifferent to life and death, pleasure and pain. I seem to have no feeling. The soul seems to me like a little ass, which feeds and thrives, because it accepts the food which is given it, and eats it without reflection. The soul in this state must be feeding on some great mercies of God, seeing that its miserable life is no burden to it, and that it bears it patiently but it is conscious of no sensible movements or results, whereby it may ascertain the state it is in.

23. It seems to me now like sailing with a very gentle wind, when one makes much way without knowing how; for in the other states, so great are the effects, that the soul sees almost at once an improvement in itself, because the desires instantly are on fire, and the soul is never satisfied. This comes from those great impetuosities of love, spoken of before,[349] in those to whom God grants them. It is like those little wells I have seen flowing, wherein the upheaving of the sand never ceases. This illustration and comparison seem to me to be a true description of those souls who attain to this state; their love is ever active, thinking what it may do; it cannot contain itself, as the water remains not in the earth, but is continually welling upwards. So is the soul, in general; it is not at rest, nor can it contain itself, because of the love it has: it is so saturated therewith, that it would have others drink of it, because there is more than enough for itself, in order that they might help it to praise God.

24. I call to remembrance—oh, how often!—that living water of which our Lord spoke to the Samaritan woman. That Gospel[350] has a great attraction for me; and, indeed, so it had even when I was a little child, though I did not understand it then as I do now. I used to pray much to our Lord

---

[348] "Un Credo."

[349] Ch. xxix. § 11.

[350] St. John iv. 5-42: the Gospel of Friday after the Third Sunday in Lent, where the words are, "hanc aquam."

for that living water; and I had always a picture of it, representing our Lord at the well, with this inscription, "Domine, da mihi aquam."[351]

25. This love is also like a great fire, which requires fuel continually, in order that it may not burn out. So those souls I am speaking of, however much it may cost them, will always bring fuel, in order that the fire may not be quenched. As for me, I should be glad, considering what I am, if I had but straw even to throw upon it. And so it is with me occasionally—and, indeed, very often. At one time, I laugh at myself; and at another, I am very much distressed. The inward stirring of my love urges me to do something for the service of God; and I am not able to do more than adorn images with boughs and flowers, clean or arrange an oratory, or some such trifling acts, so that I am ashamed of myself. If I undertook any penitential practice, the whole was so slight, and was done in such a way, that if our Lord did not accept my good will, I saw it was all worthless, and so I laughed at myself. The failure of bodily strength, sufficient to do something for God, is no light affliction for those souls to whom He, in His goodness, has communicated this fire of His love in its fulness. It is a very good penance; for when souls are not strong enough to heap fuel on this fire, and die of fear that the fire may go out, it seems to me that they become fuel themselves, are reduced to ashes, or dissolved in tears, and burn away: and this is suffering enough, though it be sweet.

26. Let him, then, praise our Lord exceedingly, who has attained to this state; who has received the bodily strength requisite for penance; who has learning, ability, and power to preach, to hear confessions, and to draw souls unto God. Such a one neither knows nor comprehends the blessing he possesses, unless he knows by experience what it is to be powerless to serve God in anything, and at the same time to be receiving much from Him. May He be blessed for ever, and may the angels glorify Him! Amen.

27. I know not if I do well to write so much in detail. But as you, my father, bade me again not to be troubled by the minuteness of my account, nor to omit anything, I go on recounting clearly and truly all I can call to mind. But I must omit much; for if I did not, I should have to spend more time—and, as I said before,[352] I have so little to spend, and perhaps, after all, nothing will be gained.

Chapter XXXI.

Of Certain Outward Temptations and Appearances of Satan. Of the Sufferings Thereby Occasioned. Counsels for Those Who Go on Unto Perfection.

1. Now that I have described certain temptations and troubles, interior and secret, of which Satan was the cause, I will speak of others which he wrought almost in public, and in which his presence could not be ignored.[353]

2. I was once in an oratory, when Satan, in an abominable shape, appeared on my left hand. I looked at his mouth in particular, because he spoke, and it was horrible. A huge flame seemed to issue out of his body, perfectly bright, without any shadow. He spoke in a fearful way, and said to me that, though I had escaped out of his hands, he would yet lay hold of me again. I was in great terror, made the sign of the cross as well as I could, and then the form vanished—but it reappeared instantly. This occurred twice; I did not know what to do; there was some holy water at hand; I took some, and threw it in the direction of the figure, and then Satan never returned.

3. On another occasion, I was tortured for five hours with such terrible pains, such inward and outward sufferings, that it seemed to me as if I could not bear them. Those who were with me were frightened; they knew not what to do, and I could not help myself. I am in the habit, when these pains and my bodily suffering are most unendurable, to make interior acts as well as I can, imploring our Lord, if it be His will, to give me patience, and then to let me suffer on, even to the end of the world. So, when I found myself suffering so cruelly, I relieved myself by making those acts and resolutions, in order that I might be able to endure the pain. It pleased our Lord to let me understand

---

[351] "Lord, give me this water" (St. John iv. 15). See ch. i. § 6; and *Way of Perfection*, ch. xxix. § 5; ch. xix. § 5 of the earlier editions.

[352] Ch. xiv. § 12.

[353] 2 Cor. ii. 11: "Non enim ignoramus cogitationes ejus."

that it was the work of Satan; for I saw close beside me a most frightful little negro, gnashing his teeth in despair at losing what he attempted to seize. When I saw him, I laughed, and had no fear; for there were some then present who were helpless, and knew of no means whereby so great a pain could be relieved. My body, head, and arms were violently shaken; I could not help myself: but the worst of all was the interior pain, for I could find no ease in any way. Nor did I dare to ask for holy water, lest those who were with me should be afraid, and find out what the matter really was.

4. I know by frequent experience that there is nothing which puts the devils to flight like holy water. They run away before the sign of the cross also, but they return immediately: great, then, must be the power of holy water. As for me, my soul is conscious of a special and most distinct consolation whenever I take it. Indeed, I feel almost always a certain refreshing, which I cannot describe, together with an inward joy, which comforts my whole soul. This is no fancy, nor a thing which has occurred once only; for it has happened very often, and I have watched it very carefully. I may compare what I feel with that which happens to a person in great heat, and very thirsty, drinking a cup of cold water—his whole being is refreshed. I consider that everything ordained by the Church is very important; and I have a joy in reflecting that the words of the Church are so mighty, that they endow water with power, so that there shall be so great a difference between holy water and water that has never been blessed. Then, as my pains did not cease, I told them, if they would not laugh, I would ask for some holy water. They brought me some, and sprinkled me with it; but I was no better. I then threw some myself in the direction of the negro, when he fled in a moment. All my sufferings ceased, just as if some one had taken them from me with his hand; only I was wearied, as if I had been beaten with many blows. It was of great service to me to learn that if, by our Lord's permission, Satan can do so much evil to a soul and body not in his power, he can do much more when he has them in his possession. It gave me a renewed desire to be delivered from a fellowship so dangerous.

5. Another time, and not long ago, the same thing happened to me, though it did not last so long, and I was alone at the moment. I asked for holy water; and they who came in after the devil had gone away,—they were two nuns, worthy of all credit, and would not tell a lie for anything,—perceived a most offensive smell, like that of brimstone. I smelt nothing myself; but the odor lasted long enough to become sensible to them.

6. On another occasion, I was in choir, when, in a moment, I became profoundly recollected. I went out in order that the sisters might know nothing of it; yet those who were near heard the sound of heavy blows where I was, and I heard voices myself, as of persons in consultation, but I did not hear what they said: I was so absorbed in prayer that I understood nothing, neither was I at all afraid. This took place almost always when our Lord was pleased that some soul or other, persuaded by me, advanced in the spiritual life. Certainly, what I am now about to describe happened to me once; there are witnesses to testify to it, particularly my present confessor, for he saw the account in a letter. I did not tell him from whom the letter came, but he knew perfectly who the person was.

7. There came to me a person who, for two years and a half, had been living in mortal sin of the most abominable nature I ever heard. During the whole of that time, he neither confessed it nor ceased from it; and yet he said Mass. He confessed his other sins but of this one he used to say, How can I confess so foul a sin? He wished to give it up, but he could not prevail on himself to do so. I was very sorry for him, and it was a great grief to me to see God offended in such a way. I promised him that I would pray to God for his amendment, and get others who were better than I to do the same. I wrote to one person, and the priest undertook to get the letter delivered. It came to pass that he made a full confession at the first opportunity; for our Lord God was pleased, on account of the prayers of those most holy persons to whom I had recommended him, to have pity on this soul. I, too, wretched as I am, did all I could for the same end.

8. He wrote to me, and said that he was so far improved, that he had not for some days repeated his sin; but he was so tormented by the temptation, that it seemed to him as if he were in hell already, so great were his sufferings. He asked me to pray to God for him. I recommended him to my sisters, through whose prayers I must have obtained this mercy from our Lord; for they took the matter greatly to heart; and he was a person whom no one could find out. I implored His Majesty to put an end to these torments and temptations, and to let the evil spirits torment me instead, provided I did not offend our Lord. Thus it was that for one month I was most grievously tormented; and then it was that these two assaults of Satan, of which I have just spoken, took place.

9. Our Lord was pleased to deliver him out of this temptation, so I was informed; for I told him what happened to myself that month. His soul gained strength, and he continued free; he could never give thanks enough to our Lord and to me as if I had been of any service—unless it be that the belief he had that our Lord granted me such graces was of some advantage to him. He said that, when he saw himself in great straits, he would read my letters, and then the temptation left him. He was very much astonished at my sufferings, and at the manner of his own deliverance: even I myself am astonished, and I would suffer as much for many years for the deliverance of that soul. May our Lord be praised for ever! for the prayers of those who serve Him can do great things; and I believe the sisters of this house do serve Him. The devils must have been more angry with me only because I asked them to pray, and because our Lord permitted it on account of my sins. At that time, too, I thought the evil spirits would have suffocated me one night, and when the sisters threw much holy water about I saw a great troop of them rush away as if tumbling over a precipice. These cursed spirits have tormented me so often, and I am now so little afraid of them,—because I see they cannot stir without our Lord's permission,—that I should weary both you, my father, and myself, if I were to speak of these things in detail.

10. May this I have written be of use to the true servant of God, who ought to despise these terrors, which Satan sends only to make him afraid! Let him understand that each time we despise those terrors, their force is lessened, and the soul gains power over them. There is always some great good obtained; but I will not speak of it, that I may not be too diffuse. I will speak, however, of what happened to me once on the night of All Souls. I was in an oratory, and, having said one Nocturn, was saying some very devotional prayers at the end of our Breviary, when Satan put himself on the book before me, to prevent my finishing my prayer. I made the sign of the cross, and he went away. I then returned to my prayer, and he, too, came back; he did so, I believe, three times, and I was not able to finish the prayer without throwing holy water at him. I saw certain souls at that moment come forth out of purgatory—they must have been near their deliverance, and I thought that Satan might in this way have been trying to hinder their release. It is very rarely that I saw Satan assume a bodily form; I know of his presence through the vision I have spoken of before,[354] the vision wherein no form is seen.

11. I wish also to relate what follows, for I was greatly alarmed at it: on Trinity Sunday, in the choir of a certain monastery, and in a trance, I saw a great fight between evil spirits and the angels. I could not make out what the vision meant. In less than a fortnight, it was explained clearly enough by the dispute that took place between persons given to prayer and many who were not, which did great harm to that house; for it was a dispute that lasted long and caused much trouble. On another occasion, I saw a great multitude of evil spirits round about me, and, at the same time, a great light, in which I was enveloped, which kept them from coming near me. I understood it to mean that God was watching over me, that they might not approach me so as to make me offend Him. I knew the vision was real by what I saw occasionally in myself. The fact is, I know now how little power the evil spirits have, provided I am not out of the grace of God; I have scarcely any fear of them at all, for their strength is as nothing, if they do not find the souls they assail give up the contest, and become cowards; it is in this case that they show their power.

12. Now and then, during the temptations I am speaking of, it seemed to me as if all my vanity and weakness in times past had become alive again within me; so I had reason enough to commit myself into the hands of God. Then I was tormented by the thought that, as these things came back to my memory, I must be utterly in the power of Satan, until my confessor consoled me; for I imagined that even the first movement towards an evil thought ought not to have come near one who had received from our Lord such great graces as I had.

13. At other times, I was much tormented—and even now I am tormented—when I saw people make much of me, particularly great people, and when they spoke well of me. I have suffered, and still suffer, much in this way. I think at once of the life of Christ and of the Saints, and then my life seems the reverse of theirs, for they received nothing but contempt and ill-treatment. All this makes me afraid; I dare not lift up my head, and I wish nobody saw me at all. It is not thus with me when I am persecuted; then my soul is so conscious of strength, though the body suffers, and though I am

---

[354] Ch. xxvii. § 4.

322   St. Teresa of Avila

in other ways afflicted, that I do not know how this can be; but so it is,—and my soul seems then to be a queen in its kingdom, having everything under its feet.

14. I had such a thought now and then—and, indeed, for many days together. I regarded it as a sign of virtue and of humility; but I see clearly now it was nothing else but a temptation. A Dominican friar, of great learning, showed it to me very plainly. When I considered that the graces which our Lord had bestowed upon me might come to the knowledge of the public, my sufferings became so excessive as greatly to disturb my soul. They went so far, that I made up my mind, while thinking of it, that I would rather be buried alive than have these things known. And so, when I began to be profoundly recollected, or to fall into a trance, which I could not resist even in public, I was so ashamed of myself, that I would not appear where people might see me.

15. Once, when I was much distressed at this, our Lord said to me, What was I afraid of? one of two things must happen—people would either speak ill of me, or give glory to Him. He made me understand by this, that those who believed in the truth of what was going on in me would glorify Him; and that those who did not would condemn me without cause: in both ways I should be the gainer, and I was therefore not to distress myself.[355] This made me quite calm, and it comforts me whenever I think of it.

16. This temptation became so excessive, that I wished to leave the house, and take my dower to another monastery, where enclosure was more strictly observed than in that wherein I was at this time. I had heard great things of that other house, which was of the same Order as mine; it was also at a great distance, and it would have been a great consolation to me to live where I was not known; but my confessor would never let me go. These fears deprived me in a great measure of all liberty of spirit; and I understood afterwards that this was not true humility, because it disturbed me so much. And our Lord taught me this truth; if I was convinced, and certainly persuaded, that all that was good in me came wholly and only from God, and if it did not distress me to hear the praises of others,—yes, rather, if I was pleased and comforted when I saw that God was working in them,—then neither should I be distressed if He showed forth His works in me.

17. I fell, too, into another extreme. I begged of God, and made it a particular subject of prayer, that it might please His Majesty, whenever any one saw any good in me, that such a one might also become acquainted with my sins, in order that he might see that His graces were bestowed on me without any merit on my part: and I always greatly desire this. My confessor told me not to do it. But almost to this day, if I saw that any one thought well of me, I used in a roundabout way, or any how, as I could, to contrive he should know of my sins:[356] that seemed to relieve me. But they have made me very scrupulous on this point. This, it appears to me, was not an effect of humility, but oftentimes the result of temptation. It seemed to me that I was deceiving everybody—though, in truth, they deceived themselves, by thinking that there was any good in me.[357] I did not wish to deceive them, nor did I ever attempt it, only our Lord permitted it for some end; and so, even with my confessors, I never discussed any of these matters if I did not see the necessity of it, for that would have occasioned very considerable scruples.

18. All these little fears and distresses, and semblance of humility, I now see clearly were mere imperfections, and the result of my unmortified life; for a soul left in the hands of God cares nothing about evil or good report, if it clearly comprehends, when our Lord is pleased to bestow upon it His grace, that it has nothing of its own. Let it trust the Giver; it will know hereafter why He reveals His gifts, and prepare itself for persecution, which in these times is sure to come, when it is our Lord's will it should be known of any one that He bestows upon him graces such as these; for a thousand eyes are watching that soul, while a thousand souls of another order are observed of none. In truth, there was no little ground for fear, and that fear should have been mine: I was therefore not humble, but a coward; for a soul which God permits to be thus seen of men may well prepare itself to be the world's martyr—because, if it will not die to the world voluntarily, that very world will kill it.

---

[355] See *Interior Castle*, vi. ch. iv. § 12.

[356] *Way of Perfection*, ch. lxv. § 2; but ch. xxxvi. of the previous editions. 5. See ch. x. § 10.

[357] *Way of Perfection*, ch. lxv. § 2; but ch. xxxvi. of the previous editions. 5. See ch. x. § 10.

19. Certainly, I see nothing in the world that seems to me good except this, that it tolerates no faults in good people, and helps them to perfection by dint of complaints against them. I mean, that it requires greater courage in one not yet perfect to walk in the way of perfection than to undergo an instant martyrdom; for perfection is not attained to at once, unless our Lord grant that grace by a special privilege: yet the world, when it sees any one beginning to travel on that road, insists on his becoming perfect at once, and a thousand leagues off detects in him a fault, which after all may be a virtue. He who finds fault is doing the very same thing,—but, in his own case, viciously,—and he pronounces it to be so wrong in the other. He who aims at perfection, then, must neither eat nor sleep,—nor, as they say, even breathe; and the more men respect such a one, the more do they forget that he is still in the body; and, though they may consider him perfect, he is living on the earth, subject to its miseries, however much he may tread them under his feet. And so, as I have just said, great courage is necessary here for, though the poor soul have not yet begun to walk, the world will have it fly; and, though its passions be not wholly overcome, men will have it that they must be under restraint, even upon trying occasions, as those of the Saints are, of whom they read, after they are confirmed in grace.

20. All this is a reason for praising God, and also for great sorrow of heart, because very many go backwards who, poor souls, know not how to help themselves; and I too, I believe, would have gone back also, if our Lord had not so mercifully on His part done everything for me. And until He, of His goodness, had done all, nothing was done by me, as you, my father, may have seen already, beyond falling and rising again. I wish I knew how to explain it, because many souls, I believe, delude themselves in this matter; they would fly before God gives them wings.

21. I believe I have made this comparison on another occasion,[358] but it is to the purpose here, for I see certain souls are very greatly afflicted on that ground. When these souls begin, with great fervor, courage, and desire, to advance in virtue,—some of them, at least outwardly, giving up all for God,—when they see in others, more advanced than themselves, greater fruits of virtue given them by our Lord,—for we cannot acquire these of ourselves,—when they see in all the books written on prayer and on contemplation an account of what we have to do in order to attain thereto, but which they cannot accomplish themselves,—they lose heart. For instance, they read that we must not be troubled when men speak ill of us, that we are to be then more pleased than when they speak well of us; that we must despise our own good name, be detached from our kindred; avoid their company, which should be wearisome to us, unless they be given to prayer; with many other things of the same kind. The disposition to practice this must be, in my opinion, the gift of God; for it seems to me a supernatural good, contrary to our natural inclinations. Let them not distress themselves; let them trust in our Lord: what they now desire, His Majesty will enable them to attain to by prayer, and by doing what they can themselves; for it is very necessary for our weak nature that we should have great confidence, that we should not be fainthearted, nor suppose that, if we do our best, we shall fail to obtain the victory at last. And as my experience here is large, I will say, by way of caution to you, my father, do not think—though it may seem so—that a virtue is acquired when we have not tested it by its opposing vice: we must always be suspicious of ourselves, and never negligent while we live; for much evil clings to us if, as I said before,[359] grace be not given to us fully to understand what everything is: and in this life there is nothing without great risks.

22. I thought a few years ago, not only that I was detached from my kindred, but that they were a burden to me; and certainly it was so, for I could not endure their conversation. An affair of some importance had to be settled, and I had to remain with a sister of mine, for whom I had always before had a great affection. The conversation we had together, though she is better than I am, did not please me; for it could not always be on subjects I preferred, owing to the difference of our conditions—she being married. I was therefore as much alone as I could; yet I felt that her troubles gave me more trouble than did those of my neighbors, and even some anxiety. In short, I found out that I was not so detached as I thought, and that it was necessary for me to flee from dangerous occasions, in order that the virtue which our Lord had begun to implant in me might grow; and so, by His help, I have striven to do from that time till now.

---

[358] Ch. xiii. § 3.
[359] Ch. xx. § 38.

23. If our Lord bestows any virtue upon us, we must make much of it, and by no means run the risk of losing it; so it is in those things which concern our good name, and many other matters. You, my father, must believe that we are not all of us detached, though we think we are; it is necessary for us never to be careless on this point. If any one detects in himself any tenderness about his good name, and yet wishes to advance in the spiritual life, let him believe me and throw this embarrassment behind his back, for it is a chain which no file can sever; only the help of God, obtained by prayer and much striving on his part, can do it. It seems to me to be a hindrance on the road, and I am astonished at the harm it does. I see some persons so holy in their works, and they are so great as to fill people with wonder. O my God, why is their soul still on the earth? Why has it not arrived at the summit of perfection? What does it mean? What keeps him back who does so much for God? Oh, there it is!—self-respect! and the worst of it is, that these persons will not admit that they have it, merely because Satan now and then convinces them that they are under an obligation to observe it.

24. Well, then, let them believe me: for the love of our Lord, let them give heed to the little ant, who speaks because it is His pleasure. If they take not this caterpillar away, though it does not hurt the whole tree, because some virtues remain, the worm will eat into every one of them. Not only is the tree not beautiful, but it also never thrives, neither does it suffer the others near it to thrive; for the fruit of good example which it bears is not sound, and endures but a short time. I say it again and again, let our self-respect be ever so slight, it will have the same result as the missing of a note on the organ when it is played,—the whole music is out of tune. It is a thing which hurts the soul exceedingly in every way, but it is a pestilence in the way of prayer.

25. Are we striving after union with God? and do we wish to follow the counsels of Christ,— who was loaded with reproaches and falsely accused,—and, at the same time, to keep our own reputation and credit untouched? We cannot succeed, for these things are inconsistent one with another. Our Lord comes to the soul when we do violence to ourselves, and strive to give up our rights in many things. Some will say, I have nothing that I can give up, nor have I any opportunity of doing so. I believe that our Lord will never suffer any one who has made so good a resolution as this to miss so great a blessing. His Majesty will make so many arrangements for him, whereby he may acquire this virtue,—more frequently, perhaps, than he will like. Let him put his hand to the work. I speak of the little nothings and trifles which I gave up when I began—or, at least, of some of them: the straws which I said[360] I threw into the fire; for I am not able to do more. All this our Lord accepted: may He be blessed for evermore!

26. One of my faults was this: I had a very imperfect knowledge of my Breviary and of my duties in choir, simply because I was careless and given to vanities; and I knew the other novices could have taught me. But I never asked them, that they might not know how little I knew. It suggested itself to me at once, that I ought to set a good example: this is very common. Now, however, that God has opened my eyes a little, even when I know a thing, but yet am very slightly in doubt about it, I ask the children. I have lost neither honor nor credit by it—on the contrary, I believe our Lord has been pleased to strengthen my memory. My singing of the Office was bad, and I felt it much if I had not learned the part entrusted to me,—not because I made mistakes before our Lord, which would have been a virtue, but because I made them before the many nuns who heard me. I was so full of my own reputation, that I was disturbed, and therefore did not sing what I had to sing even so well as I might have done. Afterwards, I ventured, when I did not know it very well, to say so. At first, I felt it very much; but afterwards I found pleasure in doing it. So, when I began to be indifferent about its being known that I could not sing well, it gave me no pain at all, and I sang much better. This miserable self-esteem took from me the power of doing that which I regarded as an honor, for every one regards as honorable that which he likes.

27. By trifles such as these, which are nothing,—and I am altogether nothing myself, seeing that this gave me pain,—by little and little, doing such actions, and by such slight performances,— they become of worth because done for God,—His Majesty helps us on towards greater things; and so it happened to me in the matter of humility. When I saw that all the nuns except myself were making great progress,—I was always myself good for nothing,—I used to fold up their mantles when they left the choir. I looked on myself as doing service to angels who had been there praising

---

[360] Ch. xxx. § 25.

God. I did so till they—I know not how—found it out; and then I was not a little ashamed, because my virtue was not strong enough to bear that they should know of it. But the shame arose, not because I was humble, but because I was afraid they would laugh at me, the matter being so trifling.

28. O Lord, what a shame for me to lay bare so much wickedness, and to number these grains of sand, which yet I did not raise up from the ground in Thy service without mixing them with a thousand meannesses! The waters of Thy grace were not as yet flowing beneath them, so as to make them ascend upwards. O my Creator, oh, that I had anything worth recounting amid so many evil things, when I am recounting the great mercies I received at Thy hands! So it is, O my Lord. I know not how my heart could have borne it, nor how any one who shall read this can help having me in abhorrence when he sees that mercies so great had been so ill-requited, and that I have not been ashamed to speak of these services. Ah! they are only mine, O my Lord; but I am ashamed I have nothing else to say of myself; and that it is that makes me speak of these wretched beginnings, in order that he who has begun more nobly may have hope that our Lord, who has made much of mine, will make more of his. May it please His Majesty to give me this grace, that I may not remain for ever at the beginning! Amen.[361]

Chapter XXXII.

Our Lord Shows St. Teresa the Place Which She Had by Her Sins Deserved in Hell. The Torments There. How the Monastery of St. Joseph Was Founded.

1. Some considerable time after our Lord had bestowed upon me the graces I have been describing, and others also of a higher nature, I was one day in prayer when I found myself in a moment, without knowing how, plunged apparently into hell. I understood that it was our Lord's will I should see the place which the devils kept in readiness for me, and which I had deserved by my sins. It was but a moment, but it seems to me impossible I should ever forget it even if I were to live many years.

2. The entrance seemed to be by a long narrow pass, like a furnace, very low, dark, and close. The ground seemed to be saturated with water, mere mud, exceedingly foul, sending forth pestilential odors, and covered with loathsome vermin. At the end was a hollow place in the wall, like a closet, and in that I saw myself confined. All this was even pleasant to behold in comparison with what I felt there. There is no exaggeration in what I am saying.

3. But as to what I then felt, I do not know where to begin, if I were to describe it; it is utterly inexplicable. I felt a fire in my soul. I cannot see how it is possible to describe it. My bodily sufferings were unendurable. I have undergone most painful sufferings in this life, and, as the physicians say, the greatest that can be borne, such as the contraction of my sinews when I was paralyzed,[362] without speaking of others of different kinds, yes, even those of which I have also spoken,[363] inflicted on me by Satan; yet all these were as nothing in comparison with what I felt then, especially when I saw that there would be no intermission, nor any end to them.

4. These sufferings were nothing in comparison with the anguish of my soul, a sense of oppression, of stifling, and of pain so keen, accompanied by so hopeless and cruel an infliction, that I know not how to speak of it. If I said that the soul is continually being torn from the body, it would be nothing, for that implies the destruction of life by the hands of another but here it is the soul itself that is tearing itself in pieces. I cannot describe that inward fire or that despair, surpassing all torments and all pain. I did not see who it was that tormented me, but I felt myself on fire, and torn to pieces, as it seemed to me; and, I repeat it, this inward fire and despair are the greatest torments of all.

---

[361] Don Vicente de la Fuente thinks the first "Life" ended here; that which follows was written under obedience to her confessor, F. Garcia of Toledo, and after the foundation of the monastery of St. Joseph, Avila.

[362] See ch. v. § 14, ch. vi. § 1.

[363] Ch. xxxi. § 3.

5. Left in that pestilential place, and utterly without the power to hope for comfort, I could neither sit nor lie down: there was no room. I was placed as it were in a hole in the wall; and those walls, terrible to look on of themselves, hemmed me in on every side. I could not breathe. There was no light, but all was thick darkness. I do not understand how it is; though there was no light, yet everything that can give pain by being seen was visible.

6. Our Lord at that time would not let me see more of hell. Afterwards, I had another most fearful vision, in which I saw the punishment of certain sins. They were most horrible to look at; but, because I felt none of the pain, my terror was not so great. In the former vision, our Lord made me really feel those torments, and that anguish of spirit, just as if I had been suffering them in the body there. I know not how it was, but I understood distinctly that it was a great mercy that our Lord would have me see with mine own eyes the very place from which His compassion saved me. I have listened to people speaking of these things, and I have at other times dwelt on the various torments of hell, though not often, because my soul made no progress by the way of fear; and I have read of the diverse tortures, and how the devils tear the flesh with red-hot pincers. But all is as nothing before this; it is a wholly different matter. In short, the one is a reality, the other a picture; and all burning here in this life is as nothing in comparison with the fire that is there.

7. I was so terrified by that vision,—and that terror is on me even now while I am writing,—that, though it took place nearly six years ago,[364] the natural warmth of my body is chilled by fear even now when I think of it. And so, amid all the pain and suffering which I may have had to bear, I remember no time in which I do not think that all we have to suffer in this world is as nothing. It seems to me that we complain without reason. I repeat it, this vision was one of the grandest mercies of our Lord. It has been to me of the greatest service, because it has destroyed my fear of trouble and of the contradiction of the world, and because it has made me strong enough to bear up against them, and to give thanks to our Lord, who has been my Deliverer, as it now seems to me, from such fearful and everlasting pains.

8. Ever since that time, as I was saying, everything seems endurable in comparison with one instant of suffering such as those I had then to bear in hell. I am filled with fear when I see that, after frequently reading books which describe in some manner the pains of hell, I was not afraid of them, nor made any account of them. Where was I? How could I possibly take any pleasure in those things which led me directly to so dreadful a place? Blessed for ever be Thou, O my God! and, oh, how manifest is it that Thou did love me much more than I did love Thee! How often, O Lord, did Thou save me from that fearful prison! and how I used to get back to it contrary to Thy will.

9. It was that vision that filled me with the very great distress which I feel at the sight of so many lost souls,—especially of the Lutherans,—for they were once members of the Church by baptism,—and also gave me the most vehement desires for the salvation of souls; for certainly I believe that, to save even one from those overwhelming torments, I would most willingly endure many deaths. If here on earth we see one whom we specially love in great trouble or pain, our very nature seems to bid us compassionate him; and if those pains be great, we are troubled ourselves. What, then, must it be to see a soul in danger of pain, the most grievous of all pains, for ever? Who can endure it? It is a thought no heart can bear without great anguish. Here we know that pain ends with life at last, and that there are limits to it; yet the sight of it moves our compassion so greatly. That other pain has no ending; and I know not how we can be calm, when we see Satan carry so many souls daily away.

10. This also makes me wish that, in a matter which concerns us so much, we did not rest satisfied with doing less than we can do on our part,—that we left nothing undone. May our Lord vouchsafe to give us His grace for that end! When I consider that, notwithstanding my very great wickedness, I took some pains to please God, and abstained from certain things which I know the world makes light of,—that, in short, I suffered grievous infirmities, and with great patience, which our Lord gave me; that I was not inclined to murmur or to speak ill of anybody; that I could not—I believe so—wish harm to any one; that I was not, to the best of my recollection, either avaricious or envious, so as to be grievously offensive in the sight of God; and that I was free from many other faults,—for, though so wicked, I had lived constantly in the fear of God,—I had to look at the very place which the devils kept ready for me. It is true that, considering my faults, I had deserved a still

---

[364] In 1558 (*De la Fuente*).

heavier chastisement; but for all that, I repeat it, the torment was fearful, and we run a great risk whenever we please ourselves. No soul should take either rest or pleasure that is liable to fall every moment into mortal sin. Let us, then, for the love of God, avoid all occasions of sin, and our Lord will help us, as He has helped me. May it please His Majesty never to let me out of His hands, lest I should turn back and fall, now that I have seen the place where I must dwell if I do. I entreat our Lord, for His Majesty's sake, never to permit it. Amen.

11. When I had seen this vision, and had learned other great and hidden things which our Lord, of His goodness, was pleased to show me,—namely, the joy of the blessed and the torment of the wicked,—I longed for the way and the means of doing penance for the great evil I had done, and of meriting in some degree, so that I might gain so great a good; and therefore I wished to avoid all society, and to withdraw myself utterly from the world. I was in spirit restless, yet my restlessness was not harassing, but rather pleasant. I saw clearly that it was the work of God, and that His Majesty had furnished my soul with fervor, so that I might be able to digest other and stronger food than I had been accustomed to eat. I tried to think what I could do for God, and thought that the first thing was to follow my vocation to a religious life, which His Majesty had given me, by keeping my rule in the greatest perfection possible.

12. Though in that house in which I then lived there were many servants of God, and God was greatly served therein, yet, because it was very poor, the nuns left it very often and went to other places, where, however, we could serve God in all honor and observances of religion. The rule also was kept, not in its original exactness, but according to the custom of the whole Order, authorized by the Bull of Mitigation. There were other inconveniences also: we had too many comforts, as it seemed to me; for the house was large and pleasant. But this inconvenience of going out, though it was I that took most advantage of it, was a very grievous one for me; for many persons, to whom my superiors could not say no, were glad to have me with them. My superiors, thus importuned, commanded me to visit these persons; and thus it was so arranged that I could not be long together in the monastery. Satan, too, must have had a share in this, in order that I might not be in the house, where I was of great service to those of my sisters to whom I continually communicated the instructions which I received from my confessors.

13. It occurred once to a person with whom I was speaking to say to me and the others that it was possible to find means for the foundation of a monastery, if we were prepared to become nuns like those of the Barefooted Orders.[365] I, having this desire, began to discuss the matter with that widowed lady who was my companion,—I have spoken of her before,[366]—and she had the same wish that I had. She began to consider how to provide a revenue for the home. I see now that this was not the way,—only the wish we had to do so made us think it was; but I, on the other hand, seeing that I took the greatest delight in the house in which I was then living, because it was very pleasant to me, and, in my own cell, most convenient for my purpose, still held back. Nevertheless, we agreed to commit the matter with all earnestness to God.

14. One day, after Communion, our Lord commanded me to labor with all my might for this end. He made me great promises,—that the monastery would be certainly built; that He would take great delight therein; that it should be called St. Joseph's; that St. Joseph would keep guard at one door, and our Lady at the other; that Christ would be in the midst of us; that the monastery would be a star shining in great splendor; that, though the religious Orders were then relaxed, I was not to suppose that He was scantily served in them,—for what would become of the world, if there were no religious in it?—I was to tell my confessor what He commanded me, and that He asked him not to oppose nor thwart me in the matter.

15. So efficacious was the vision, and such was the nature of the words our Lord spoke to me, that I could not possibly doubt that they came from Him. I suffered most keenly, because I saw in part the great anxieties and troubles that the work would cost me, and I was also very happy in the house I was in then; and though I used to speak of this matter in past times, yet it was not with resolution nor with any confidence that the thing could ever be done. I saw that I was now in a great

---

[365] This was said by Maria de Ocampo, niece of St. Teresa, then living in the monastery of the Incarnation, but not a religious; afterwards Maria Bautista, Prioress of the Carmelites at Valladolid (*Ribera*, i. 7).

[366] Ch. xxiv. § 5. Doña Guiomar de Ulloa.

strait; and when I saw that I was entering on a work of great anxiety, I hesitated; but our Lord spoke of it so often to me, and set before me so many reasons and motives, which I saw could not be gainsaid,—I saw, too, that such was His will; so I did not dare do otherwise than put the whole matter before my confessor, and give him an account in writing of all that took place.

16. My confessor did not venture definitely to bid me abandon my purpose; but he saw that naturally there was no way of carrying it out; because my friend, who was to do it, had very little or no means available for that end. He told me to lay the matter before my superior,[367] and do what he might bid me do. I never spoke of my visions to my superior, but that lady who desired to found the monastery communicated with him. The Provincial was very much pleased, for he loves the whole Order, gave her every help that was necessary, and promised to acknowledge the house. Then there was a discussion about the revenues of the monastery, and for many reasons we never would allow more than thirteen sisters together. Before we began our arrangements, we wrote to the holy friar, Peter of Alcantara, telling him all that was taking place; and he advised us not to abandon our work, and gave us his sanction on all points.

17. As soon as the affair began to be known here, there fell upon us a violent persecution, which cannot be very easily described—sharp sayings and keen jests. People said it was folly in me, who was so well off in my monastery; as to my friend, the persecution was so continuous, that it wearied her. I did not know what to do, and I thought that people were partly in the right. When I was thus heavily afflicted, I commended myself to God, and His Majesty began to console and encourage me. He told me that I could then see what the Saints had to go through who founded the religious Orders: that I had much heavier persecutions to endure than I could imagine, but I was not to mind them. He told me also what I was to say to my friend; and what surprised me most was, that we were consoled at once as to the past, and resolved to withstand everybody courageously. And so it came to pass; for among people of prayer, and indeed in the whole neighborhood, there was hardly one who was not against us, and who did not think our work the greatest folly.

18. There was so much talking and confusion in the very monastery wherein I was, that the Provincial began to think it hard for him to set himself against everybody; so he changed his mind, and would not acknowledge the new house. He said that the revenue was not certain, and too little, while the opposition was great. On the whole, it seemed that he was right; he gave it up at last, and would have nothing to do with it. It was a very great pain to us,—for we seemed now to have received the first blow,—and in particular to me, to find the Provincial against us; for when he approved of the plan, I considered myself blameless before all. They would not give absolution to my friend, if she did not abandon the project; for they said she was bound to remove the scandal.

19. She went to a very learned man, and a very great servant of God, of the Order of St. Dominic, to whom she gave an account of all this matter. This was even before the Provincial had withdrawn his consent; for in this place we had no one who would give us advice; and so they said that it all proceeded solely from our obstinacy. That lady gave an account of everything, and told the holy man how much she received from the property of her husband. Having a great desire that he would help us,—for he was the most learned man here, and there are few in his Order more learned than he,—I told him myself all we intended to do, and some of my motives. I never said a word of any revelation whatever, speaking only of the natural reasons which influenced me; for I would not have him give an opinion otherwise than on those grounds. He asked us to give him eight days before he answered, and also if we had made up our minds to abide by what he might say. I said we had; but though I said so, and though I thought so, I never lost a certain confidence that the monastery would be founded. My friend had more faith than I; nothing they could say could make her give it up. As for myself, though, as I said, it seemed to me impossible that the work should be finally abandoned, yet my belief in the truth of the revelation went no further than in so far as it was not against what is contained in the sacred writings, nor against the laws of the Church, which we are bound to keep. Though the revelation seemed to me to have come really from God, yet, if that learned man had told me that we could not go on without offending God and going against our conscience, I believe I should have given it up, and looked out for some other way; but our Lord showed me no other way than this.

---

[367] The Provincial of the Carmelites: F. Angel de Salasar (*De la Fuente*).

20. The servant of God told me afterwards that he had made up his mind to insist on the abandonment of our project, for he had already heard the popular cry: moreover, he, as everybody did, thought it folly; and a certain nobleman also, as soon as he knew that we had gone to him, had sent him word to consider well what he was doing, and to give us no help; that when he began to consider the answer he should make us, and to ponder on the matter, the object we had in view, our manner of life, and the Order, he became convinced that it was greatly for the service of God, and that we must not give it up. Accordingly, his answer was that we should make haste to settle the matter. He told us how and in what way it was to be done; and if our means were scanty, we must trust somewhat in God. If anyone made any objections, they were to go to him—he would answer them; and in this way he always helped us, as I shall show by and by.[368]

21. This answer was a great comfort to us; so also was the conduct of certain holy persons who were usually against us: they were now pacified, and some of them even helped us. One of them was the saintly nobleman[369] of whom I spoke before;[370] he looked on it—so, indeed, it was—as a means of great perfection, because the whole foundation was laid in prayer. He saw also very many difficulties before us, and no way out of them,—yet he gave up his own opinion, and admitted that the work might be of God. Our Lord Himself must have touched his heart, as He also did that of the doctor, the priest and servant of God, to whom, as I said before,[371] I first spoke, who is an example to the whole city,—being one whom God maintains there for the relief and progress of many souls: he, too, came now to give us his assistance.

22. When matters had come to this state, and always with the help of many prayers, we purchased a house in a convenient spot; and though it was small, I cared not at all for that, for our Lord had told me to go into it as well as I could,—that I should see afterwards what He would do; and how well I have seen it! I saw, too, how scanty were our means; and yet I believed our Lord would order these things by other ways, and be gracious unto us.

Chapter XXXIII.
The Foundation of the Monastery Hindered. Our Lord Consoles the Saint.

1. When the matter was in this state—so near its conclusion, that on the very next day the papers were to be signed—then it was that the Father Provincial changed his mind. I believe that the change was divinely ordered—so it appeared afterwards; for while so many prayers were made, our Lord was perfecting His work and arranging its execution in another way. When the Provincial refused us, my confessor bade me forthwith to think no more of it, notwithstanding the great trouble and distress which our Lord knows it cost me to bring it to this state. When the work was given up and abandoned, people were the more convinced that it was altogether the foolishness of women; and the complaints against me were multiplied, although I had until then this commandment of my Provincial to justify me.

2. I was now very much disliked throughout the whole monastery, because I wished to found another with stricter enclosure. It was said I insulted my sisters; that I could serve God among them as well as elsewhere, for there were many among them much better than I; that I did not love the house, and that it would have been better if I had procured greater resources for it than for another. Some said I ought to be put in prison; others—but they were not many—defended me in some degree. I saw well enough that they were for the most part right, and now and then I made excuses for myself; though, as I could not tell them the chief reason, which was the commandment of our Lord, I knew not what to do, and so was silent.

3. In other respects God was most merciful unto me, for all this caused me no uneasiness; and I gave up our design with much readiness and joy, as if it cost me nothing. No one could believe it, not even those men of prayer with whom I conversed; for they thought I was exceedingly pained

---

[368] Ch. xxxiii. § 8.
[369] Francis de Salcedo.
[370] Ch. xxiii. § 6.
[371] Gaspar Daza. See ch. xxiii. § 6.

and sorry: even my confessor himself could hardly believe it. I had done, as it seemed to me, all that was in my power. I thought myself obliged to do no more than I had done to fulfil our Lord's commandment, and so I remained in the house where I was, exceedingly happy and joyful; though, at the same time, I was never able to give up my conviction that the work would be done. I had now no means of doing it, nor did I know how or when it would be done; but I firmly believed in its accomplishment.

4. I was much distressed at one time by a letter which my confessor wrote to me, as if I had done anything in the matter contrary to his will. Our Lord also must have meant that suffering should not fail me there where I should feel it most; and so, amid the multitude of my persecutions, when, as it seemed to me, consolations should have come from my confessor, he told me that I ought to recognize in the result that all was a dream; that I ought to lead a new life by ceasing to have anything to do for the future with it, or even to speak of it any more, seeing the scandal it had occasioned. He made some further remarks, all of them very painful. This was a greater affliction to me than all the others together. I considered whether I had done anything myself, and whether I was to blame for anything that was an offence unto God; whether all my visions were illusions, all my prayers a delusion, and I, therefore, deeply deluded and lost. This pressed so heavily upon me, that I was altogether disturbed and most grievously distressed. But our Lord, who never failed me in all the trials I speak of, so frequently consoled and strengthened me, that I need not speak of it here. He told me then not to distress myself; that I had pleased God greatly, and had not sinned against Him throughout the whole affair; that I was to do what my confessors required of me, and be silent on the subject till the time came to resume it. I was so comforted and so happy, that the persecution which had befallen me seemed to be as nothing at all.

5. Our Lord now showed me what an exceedingly great blessing it is to be tried and persecuted for His sake; for the growth of the love of God in my soul, which I now discerned, as well as of many other virtues, was such as to fill me with wonder. It made me unable to abstain from desiring trials, and yet those about me thought I was exceedingly disheartened; and I must have been so, if our Lord in that extremity had not succored me with His great compassion. Now was the beginning of those more violent impetuosities of the love of God of which I have spoken before,[372] as well as of those profounder trances. I kept silence, however, and never spoke of those graces to any one. The saintly Dominican[373] was as confident as I was that the work would be done; and as I would not speak of it, in order that nothing might take place contrary to the obedience I owed my confessor, he communicated with my companion, and they wrote letters to Rome and made their preparations.

6. Satan also contrived now that persons should hear one from another that I had had a revelation in the matter; and people came to me in great terror, saying that the times were dangerous, that something might be laid to my charge, and that I might be taken before the Inquisitors. I heard this with pleasure, and it made me laugh, because I never was afraid of them; for I knew well enough that in matters of faith I would not break the least ceremony of the Church, that I would expose myself to die a thousand times rather than that any one should see me go against it or against any truth of Holy Writ. So I told them I was not afraid of that, for my soul must be in a very bad state if there was anything the matter with it of such a nature as to make me fear the Inquisition; I would go myself and give myself up, if I thought there was anything amiss; and if I should be denounced, our Lord would deliver me, and I should gain much.

7. I had recourse to my Dominican father; for I could rely upon him, because he was a learned man. I told him all about my visions, my way of prayer, the great graces our Lord had given me, as clearly as I could, and I begged him to consider the matter well, and tell me if there was anything therein at variance with the Holy Writings, and give me his opinion on the whole matter. He reassured me much, and, I think, profited himself; for though he was exceedingly good, yet, from this time forth, he gave himself more and more to prayer, and retired to a monastery of his Order which was very lonely, that he might apply himself more effectually to prayer, where he remained more than two years. He was dragged out of his solitude by obedience, to his great sorrow: his superiors required his services; for he was a man of great ability. I, too, on my part, felt his retirement very much, because it was a great loss to me, though I did not disturb him. But I knew it

---

372 Ch. xxi. § 6, ch. xxix. §§ 10, 11.
373 Pedro Ibañez. See ch. xxxviii. § 15.

was a gain to him; for when I was so much distressed at his departure, our Lord bade me be comforted, not to take it to heart, for he was gone under good guidance.

8. So, when he came back, his soul had made such great progress, and he was so advanced in the ways of the spirit, that he told me on his return he would not have missed that journey for anything in the world. And I, too, could say the same thing; for where he reassured and consoled me formerly by his mere learning, he did so now through that spiritual experience he had gained of supernatural things. And God, too, brought him here in time; for He saw that his help would be required in the foundation of the monastery, which His Majesty willed should be laid.

9. I remained quiet after this for five or six months, neither thinking nor speaking of the matter; nor did our Lord once speak to me about it. I know not why, but I could never rid myself of the thought that the monastery would be founded. At the end of that time, the then Rector[374] of the Society of Jesus having gone away, His Majesty brought into his place another,[375] of great spirituality, high courage, strong understanding, and profound learning, at the very time when I was in great straits. As he who then heard my confession had a superior over him—the fathers of the Society are extremely strict about the virtue of obedience and never stir but in conformity with the will of their superiors,—so he would not dare, though he perfectly understood my spirit, and desired the accomplishment of my purpose, to come to any resolution; and he had many reasons to justify his conduct. I was at the same time subject to such great impetuosities of spirit, that I felt my chains extremely heavy; nevertheless, I never swerved from the commandment he gave me.

10. One day, when in great distress, because I thought my confessor did not trust me, our Lord said to me, Be not troubled; this suffering will soon be over. I was very much delighted, thinking I should die shortly; and I was very happy whenever I recalled those words to remembrance. Afterwards I saw clearly that they referred to the coming of the rector of whom I am speaking, for never again had I any reason to be distressed. The rector that came never interfered with the father-minister who was my confessor. On the contrary, he told him to console me,—that there was nothing to be afraid of,—and not to direct me along a road so narrow, but to leave the operations of the Spirit of God alone; for now and then it seemed as if these great impetuosities of the spirit took away the very breath of the soul.

11. The rector came to see me, and my confessor bade me speak to him in all freedom and openness. I used to feel the very greatest repugnance to speak of this matter; but so it was, when I went into the confessional, I felt in my soul something, I know not what. I do not remember to have felt so either before or after towards any one. I cannot tell what it was, nor do I know of anything with which I could compare it. It was a spiritual joy, and a conviction in my soul that his soul must understand mine, that it was in unison with it, and yet, as I have said, I knew not how. If I had ever spoken to him, or had heard great things of him, it would have been nothing out of the way that I should rejoice in the conviction that he would understand me; but he had never spoken to me before, nor I to him, and, indeed, he was a person of whom I had no previous knowledge whatever.

12. Afterwards, I saw clearly that my spirit was not deceived; for my relations with him were in every way of the utmost service to me and my soul, because his method of direction is proper for those persons whom our Lord seems to have led far on the way, seeing that He makes them run, and not to crawl step by step. His plan is to render them thoroughly detached and mortified, and our Lord has endowed him with the highest gifts herein as well as in many other things beside. As soon as I began to have to do with him, I knew his method at once, and saw that he had a pure and holy soul, with a special grace of our Lord for the discernment of spirits. He gave me great consolation. Shortly after I had begun to speak to him, our Lord began to constrain me to return to the affair of the monastery, and to lay before my confessor and the father-rector many reasons and considerations why they should not stand in my way. Some of these reasons made them afraid, for the father-rector never had a doubt of its being the work of the Spirit of God, because he regarded

---

[374] Dionisio Vasquez. Of him the Bollandists say that he was very austere and harsh to his subjects, notwithstanding his great learning: "homini egregie docto ac rebus gestis claro, sed in subditos, ut ex historia Societatis Jesu liquet, valde immiti" (n. 309).

[375] Gaspar de Salazar was made rector of the house in Avila in 1561, therein succeeding Vasquez (*Bollandists, ibid.*).

the fruits of it with great care and attention. At last, after much consideration, they did not dare to hinder me.[376]

13. My confessor gave me leave to prosecute the work with all my might. I saw well enough the trouble I exposed myself to, for I was utterly alone, and able to do so very little. We agreed that it should be carried on with the utmost secrecy; and so I contrived that one of my sisters,[377] who lived out of the town, should buy a house, and prepare it as if for herself, with money which our Lord provided for us.[378] I made it a great point to do nothing against obedience; but I knew that if I spoke of it to my superiors all was lost, as on the former occasion, and worse even might happen. In holding the money, in finding the house, in treating for it, in putting it in order, I had so much to suffer; and, for the most part, I had to suffer alone, though my friend did what she could: she could do but little, and that was almost nothing. Beyond giving her name and her countenance, the whole of the trouble was mine; and that fell upon me in so many ways, that I am astonished now how I could have borne it.[379] Sometimes, in my affliction, I used to say: O my Lord, how is it that Thou commands me to do that which seems impossible?—for, though I am a woman, yet, if I were free, it might be done; but when I am tied in so many ways, without money, or the means of procuring it, either for the purpose of the Brief or for any other,—what, O Lord, can I do?

14. Once when I was in one of my difficulties, not knowing what to do, unable to pay the workmen, St. Joseph, my true father and lord, appeared to me, and gave me to understand that money would not be wanting, and I must hire the workmen. So I did, though I was penniless; and our Lord, in a way that filled those who heard of it with wonder, provided for me. The house offered me was too small,—so much so, that it seemed as if it could never be made into a monastery,—and I wished to buy another, but had not the means, and there was neither way nor means to do so. I knew not what to do. There was another little house close to the one we had, which might have formed a small church. One day, after Communion, our Lord said to me, I have already bidden thee to go in anyhow. And then, as if exclaiming, said: Oh, covetousness of the human race, thinking that even the whole earth is too little for it! how often have I slept in the open air, because I had no place to shelter Me![380] I was alarmed, and saw that He had good reasons to complain. I went to the little house, arranged the divisions of it, and found that it would make a sufficient, though small, monastery. I did not care now to add to the site by purchase, and so I did nothing but contrive to have it prepared in such a way that it could be lived in. Everything was coarse, and nothing more was done to it than to render it not hurtful to health—and that must be done everywhere.

15. As I was going to Communion on her feast, St. Clare appeared to me in great beauty, and bade me take courage, and go on with what I had begun; she would help me. I began to have a great devotion to St. Clare; and she has so truly kept her word, that a monastery of nuns of her Order in our neighborhood helped us to live; and, what is of more importance, by little and little she so perfectly fulfilled my desire, that the poverty which the blessed Saint observes in her own house is observed in this, and we are living on alms. It cost me no small labor to have this matter settled by the plenary sanction and authority of the Holy Father,[381] so that it shall never be otherwise, and we possess no revenues. Our Lord is doing more for us—perhaps we owe it to the prayers of this

---

[376] St. Teresa was commanded by our Lord to ask Father Baltasar Alvarez to make a meditation on Psalm xci. 6: "Quam magnificata sunt opera Tua." The Saint obeyed, and the meditation was made. From that moment, as F. Alvarez afterwards told Father de Ribera (*Life of St. Teresa*, i. ch. vii.), there was no further hesitation on the part of the Saint's confessor.

[377] Juana de Ahumada, wife of Juan de Ovalle.

[378] The money was a present from her brother, Don Lorenzo de Cepeda; and the Saint acknowledges the receipt of it, and confesses the use made of it, in a letter to her brother, written in Avila, Dec. 31, 1561 (*De la Fuente*).

[379] One day, she went with her sister—she was staying in her house—to hear a sermon in the church of St. Thomas. The zealous preacher denounced visions and revelations; and his observations were so much to the point, that there was no need of his saying that they were directed against St. Teresa, who was present. Her sister was greatly hurt, and persuaded the Saint to return to the monastery at once (*Reforma*, i. ch. xlii. § 1).

[380] St. Luke ix. 58: "Filius autem hominis non habet ubi caput reclinet."

[381] Pius IV., on Dec. 5, 1562, (*Bouix*). See ch. xxxix. § 19.

blessed Saint; for, without our asking anybody, His Majesty supplies most abundantly all our wants. May He be blessed for ever! Amen.

16. On one of these days—it was the Feast of the Assumption of our Lady—I was in the church of the monastery of the Order of the glorious St. Dominic, thinking of the events of my wretched life, and of the many sins which in times past I had confessed in that house. I fell into so profound a trance, that I was as it were beside myself. I sat down, and it seemed as if I could neither see the Elevation nor hear Mass. This afterwards became a scruple to me. I thought then, when I was in that state, that I saw myself clothed with a garment of excessive whiteness and splendor. At first I did not see who was putting it on me. Afterwards I saw our Lady on my right hand, and my father St. Joseph on my left, clothing me with that garment. I was given to understand that I was then cleansed from my sins. When I had been thus clad—I was filled with the utmost delight and joy— our Lady seemed at once to take me by both hands. She said that I pleased her very much by being devout to the glorious St. Joseph; that I might rely on it my desires about the monastery were accomplished, and that our Lord and they too would be greatly honored in it; that I was to be afraid of no failure whatever, though the obedience under which it would be placed might not be according to my mind, because they would watch over us, and because her Son had promised to be with us[382]—and, as a proof of this, she would give me that jewel. She then seemed to throw around my neck a most splendid necklace of gold, from which hung a cross of great value. The stones and gold were so different from any in this world, that there is nothing wherewith to compare them. The beauty of them is such as can be conceived by no imagination,—and no understanding can find out the materials of the robe, nor picture to itself the splendors which our Lord revealed, in comparison with which all the splendors of earth, so to say, are a daubing of soot. This beauty, which I saw in our Lady, was exceedingly grand, though I did not trace it in any particular feature, but rather in the whole form of her face. She was clothed in white and her garments shone with excessive luster that was not dazzling, but soft. I did not see St. Joseph so distinctly, though I saw clearly that he was there, as in the visions of which I spoke before,[383] in which nothing is seen. Our Lady seemed to be very young.

17. When they had been with me for a while,—I, too, in the greatest delight and joy, greater than I had ever had before, as I think, and with which I wished never to part,—I saw them, so it seemed, ascend up to heaven, attended by a great multitude of angels. I was left in great loneliness, though so comforted and raised up, so recollected in prayer and softened, that I was for some time unable to move or speak—being, as it were, beside myself. I was now possessed by a strong desire to be consumed for the love of God, and by other affections of the same kind. Everything took place in such a way that I could never have a doubt—though I often tried—that the vision came from God.[384] It left me in the greatest consolation and peace.

18. As to that which the Queen of the Angels spoke about obedience, it is this: it was painful to me not to subject the monastery to the Order, and our Lord had told me that it was inexpedient to do so. He told me the reasons why it was in no wise convenient that I should do it but I must send to Rome in a certain way, which He also explained; He would take care that I found help there: and so I did. I sent to Rome, as our Lord directed me,—for we should never have succeeded otherwise,—and most favorable was the result.

19. And as to subsequent events, it was very convenient to be under the Bishop,[385] but at that time I did not know him, nor did I know what kind of a superior he might be. It pleased our Lord that he should be as good and favorable to this house as it was necessary he should be on account of the great opposition it met with at the beginning, as I shall show hereafter,[386] and also for the sake of bringing it to the condition it is now in. Blessed be He who has done it all! Amen.

---

[382] Ch. xxxii. § 14.

[383] See ch. xxvii. § 7.

[384] "Nuestro Señor," "our Lord," though inserted in the printed editions after the word "God," is not in the MS., according to Don V. de la Fuente.

[385] Don Alvaro de Mendoza, Bishop of Avila, afterwards of Palencia.

[386] See ch. xxxvi. § 15; *Way of Perfection*, ch. v. § 10; *Foundations*, ch. xxxi. § 1.

Chapter XXXIV.

*The Saint Leaves Her Monastery of the Incarnation for a Time, at the Command
of Her Superior. Consoles an Afflicted Widow.*

1. Now, though I was very careful that no one should know what we were doing, all this work could not be carried on so secretly as not to come to the knowledge of divers persons; some believed, in it, others did not, I was in great fear lest the Provincial should be spoken to about it when he came, and find himself compelled to order me to give it up; and if he did so, it would have been abandoned at once. Our Lord provided against it in this way. In a large city, more than twenty leagues distant, was a lady in great distress on account of her husband's death.[387] She was in such extreme affliction, that fears were entertained about her life. She had heard of me, a poor sinner,— for our Lord had provided that,—and men spoke well to her of me, for the sake of other good works which resulted from it. This lady knew the Provincial well; and as she was a person of some consideration, and knew that I lived in a monastery the nuns of which were permitted to go out, our Lord made her desire much to see me. She thought that my presence would be a consolation to her, and that she could not be comforted otherwise. She therefore strove by all the means in her power to get me into her house, sending messages to the Provincial, who was at a distance far away.

2. The Provincial sent me an order, charging me in virtue of my obedience to go immediately, with one companion. I knew of it on Christmas night. It caused me some trouble and much suffering to see that they sent for me because they thought there was some good in me; I, knowing myself to be so wicked, could not bear it. I commended myself earnestly to God, and during Matins, or the greater part of them, was lost in a profound trance. Our Lord told me I must go without fail, and give no heed to the opinions of people, for they were few who would not be rash in their counsel; and though I should have troubles, yet God would be served greatly: as to the monastery, it was expedient I should be absent till the Brief came, because Satan had contrived a great plot against the coming of the Provincial; that I was to have no fear,—He would help me. I repeated this to the rector, and he told me that I must go by all means, though others were saying I ought not to go, that it was a trick of Satan to bring some evil upon me there, and that I ought to send word to the Provincial.

3. I obeyed the rector, and went without fear, because of what I had understood in prayer, though in the greatest confusion when I thought of the reasons why they sent for me, and how very much they were deceived. It made me more and more importunate with our Lord that He would not abandon me. It was a great comfort that there was a house of the Society of Jesus there whither I was going, and so I thought I should be in some degree safe under the direction of those fathers, as I had been here.

4. It was the good pleasure of our Lord that the lady who sent for me should be so much consoled that a visible improvement was the immediate result she was comforted every day more and more. This was very remarkable, because, as I said before, her suffering had reduced her to great straits. Our Lord must have done this in answer to the many prayers which the good people of my acquaintance made for me, that I might prosper in my work. She had a profound fear of God, and was so good, that her great devotion supplied my deficiencies. She conceived a great affection for me—I, too, for her, because of her goodness; but all was as it were a cross for me; for the comforts of her house were a great torment, and her making so much of me made me afraid. I kept my soul continually recollected—I did not dare to be careless: nor was our Lord careless of me; for while I was there, He bestowed the greatest graces upon me, and those graces made me so free, and filled me with such contempt for all I saw,—and the more I saw, the greater my contempt,—that I never failed to treat those ladies, whom to serve would have been a great honor for me, with as much freedom as if I had been their equal.

5. I derived very great advantages from this, and I said so. I saw that she was a woman, and as much liable to passion and weakness as I was; that rank is of little worth, and the higher it is, the greater the anxiety and trouble it brings. People must be careful of the dignity of their state, which

---

[387] Doña Luisa de la Cerda, sister of the Duke of Medina-Coeli, was now the widow of Arias Pardo, Marshal of Castille, Lord of Malagon and Paracuellos. Don Arias was nephew of Cardinal Tabera, Archbishop of Toledo (*De la Fuente*).

will not suffer them to live at ease; they must eat at fixed hours and by rule, for everything must be according to their state, and not according to their constitutions; and they have frequently to take food fitted more for their state than for their liking.

6. So it was that I came to hate the very wish to be a great lady. God deliver me from this wicked, artificial life!—though I believe that this lady, notwithstanding that she was one of the chief personages of the realm, was a woman of great simplicity, and that few were more humble than she was. I was very sorry for her, for I saw how often she had to submit to much that was disagreeable to her, because of the requirements of her rank. Then, as to servants, though this lady had very good servants, how slight is that little trust that may be put in them! One must not be conversed with more than another; otherwise, he who is so favored is envied by the rest. This of itself is a slavery, and one of the lies of the world is that it calls such persons masters, who, in my eyes, are nothing else but slaves in a thousand ways.

7. It was our Lord's pleasure that the household of that lady improved in the service of His Majesty during my stay there, though I was not exempted from some trials and some jealousies on the part of some of its members, because of the great affection their mistress had for me. They perhaps must have thought I had some personal interest to serve. Our Lord must have permitted such matters, and others of the same kind, to give me trouble, in order that I might not be absorbed in the comforts which otherwise I had there; and He was pleased to deliver me out of it all with great profit to my soul.

8. When I was there, a religious person of great consideration, and with whom I had conversed occasionally some years ago,[388] happened to arrive. When I was at Mass, in a monastery of his Order, near the house in which I was staying, I felt a longing to know the state of his soul,—for I wished him to be a great servant of God,—and I rose up in order to go and speak to him. But as I was then recollected in prayer, it seemed to me a waste of time—for what had I to do in that matter?—and so I returned to my place. Three times, I think I did this, and at last my good angel prevailed over the evil one, and I went and asked for him; and he came to speak to me in one of the confessionals. We began by asking one another of our past lives, for we had not seen one another for many years. I told him that my life had been one in which my soul had had many trials. He insisted much on my telling him what those trials were. I said that they were not to be told, and that I was not to tell them. He replied that the Dominican father,[389] of whom I have spoken, knew them, and that, as they were great friends, he could learn them from him, and so I had better tell them without hesitation.

9. The fact is, that it was not in his power not to insist, nor in mine, I believe, to refuse to speak; for notwithstanding all the trouble and shame I used to feel formerly, I spoke of my state, to him, and to the rector whom I have referred to before,[390] without any difficulty whatever; on the contrary, it was a great consolation to me; and so I told him all in confession. He seemed to me then more prudent than ever; though I had always looked upon him as a man of great understanding. I considered what high gifts and endowments for great services he had, if he gave himself wholly unto God. I had this feeling now for many years, so that I never saw any one who pleased me much without wishing at once he were given wholly unto God; and sometimes I feel this so keenly, that I can hardly contain myself. Though I long to see everybody serve God, yet my desire about those who please me is very vehement, and so I importune our Lord on their behalf.

10. So it happened with respect to this religious. He asked me to pray much for him to God. There was no necessity for his doing so, because I could not do anything else, and so I went back to my place where I was in the habit of praying alone, and began to pray to our Lord, being extremely recollected, in that my simple, silly way, when I speak without knowing very often what I am saying. It is love that speaks, and my soul is so beside itself, that I do not regard the distance between it and God. That love which I know His Majesty has for it makes it forget itself, and think

---

[388] F. Vicente Barron, Dominican (see ch. v. § 8), according to F. Bouix, on the authority of Ribera and Yepez; but the Carmelite Father, Fr. Antonio of St. Joseph, in his note on the first Fragment (*Letters*, vol. iv. p. 408), says that it was Fr. Garcia of Toledo, brother of Don Fernando, Duke of Alva; and Don Vicente de la Fuente thinks the opinion of Fr. Antonio the more probable.

[389] Pedro Ibañez (*Bouix*).

[390] Ch. xxxiii. § 11.

itself to be one with Him; and so, as being one with Him, and not divided from Him, the soul speaks foolishly. When I had prayed with many tears that the soul of this religious might serve Him truly,—for, though I considered it good, it was not enough for me; I would have it much better,—I remember I said, "O Lord, Thou must not refuse me this grace; behold him,—he is a fit person to be our friend."

11. Oh, the great goodness and compassion of God! How He regards not the words, but the desire and the will with which they are spoken! How He suffered such a one as I am to speak so boldly before His Majesty! May He be blessed for evermore!

12. I remember that during those hours of prayer on that very night I was extremely distressed by the thought whether I was in the grace of God, and that I could never know whether I was so or not,—not that I wished to know it; I wished, however, to die, in order that I might not live a life in which I was not sure that I was not dead in sin, for there could be no death more dreadful for me than to think that I had sinned against God. I was in great straits at this thought. I implored Him not to suffer me to fall into sin, with great sweetness, dissolved in tears. Then I heard that I might console myself, and trust[391] that I was in a state of grace, because a love of God like mine, together with the graces and feelings with which His Majesty filled my soul, was of such a nature as to be inconsistent with a state of mortal sin.

13. I was now confident that our Lord would grant my prayer as to that religious. He bade me repeat certain words to him. This I felt much, because I knew not how to speak to him; for this carrying messages to a third person, as I have said,[392] is what I have always felt the most, especially when I did not know how that person would take them, nor whether he would not laugh at me. This placed me in great difficulties, but at last I was so convinced I ought to do it, that I believe I made a promise to God I would not neglect that message; and because of the great shame I felt, I wrote it out, and gave it in that way. The result showed clearly enough that it was a message from God, for that religious resolved with great earnestness to give himself to prayer, though he did not do so at once. Our Lord would have him for Himself, so He sent me to tell him certain truths which, without my understanding them, were so much to the purpose that he was astonished. Our Lord must have prepared him to receive them as from His Majesty; and though I am but a miserable sinner myself, yet I made many supplications to our Lord to convert him thoroughly, and to make him hate the pleasures and the things of this life. And so he did—blessed be God!—for every time that he spoke to me I was in a manner beside myself; and if I had not seen it, I should never have believed that our Lord would have given him in so short a time graces so matured, and filled him so full of God, that he seemed to be alive to nothing on earth.

14. May His Majesty hold him in His hand! If he will go on—and I trust in our Lord he will do so, now that he is so well grounded in the knowledge of himself—he will be one of the most distinguished servants of God, to the great profit of many souls, because he has in a short time had great experience in spiritual things: that is a gift of God, which He gives when He will and as He will, and it depends not on length of time nor extent of service. I do not mean that time and service, are not great helps, but very often our Lord will not give to some in twenty years the grace of contemplation, while He gives it to others in one,—His Majesty knows why. We are under a delusion when we think that in the course of years we shall come to the knowledge of that which we can in no way attain to but by experience; and thus many are in error, as I have said[393] when they would understand spirituality without being spiritual themselves. I do not mean that a man

---

[391] Father Bouix says that here the word "confiar," "trust," in the printed text, has been substituted by some one for the words "estar cierta," "be certain," which he found in the MS. But Don Vicente de la Fuente retains the old reading "confiar," and makes no observation on the alleged discrepancy between the MS. and the printed text. The observation of F. Bouix, however, is more important, and deserves credit,—for Don Vicente may have failed, through mere inadvertence, to see what F. Bouix saw; and it is also to be remembered that Don Vicente does not say that the MS. on this point has been so closely inspected as to throw any doubt on the positive testimony of F. Bouix. Six years after this note was written Don Vicente published a facsimile by photography of the original text in the handwriting of the Saint, preserved in the Escurial. The words are not "confiar," but "estar cierta."

[392] Ch. xxxiii. § 12.

[393] Ch. xiv. § 10.

who is not spiritual, if he is learned, may not direct one that is spiritual; but it must be understood that in outward and inward things, in the order of nature, the direction must be an act of reason; and in supernatural things, according to the teaching of the sacred writings. In other matters, let him not distress himself, nor think that he can understand that which he understands not; neither let him quench the Spirit;[394] for now another Master, greater than he, is directing these souls, so that they are not left without authority over them.

15. He must not be astonished at this, nor think it impossible: all things are possible to our Lord;[395] he must strive rather to strengthen his faith, and humble himself, because in this matter our Lord imparts perhaps a deeper knowledge to some old woman than to him, though he may be a very learned man. Being thus humble, he will profit souls and himself more than if he affected to be a contemplative without being so; for, I repeat it, if he have no experience, if he have not a most profound humility, whereby he may see that he does not understand, and that the thing is not for that reason impossible, he will do himself but little good, and still less to his penitent. But if he is humble, let him have no fear that our Lord will allow either the one or the other to fall into delusion.

16. Now as to this father I am speaking of, as our Lord has given him light in many things, so has he labored to find out by study that which in this matter can be by study ascertained; for he is a very learned man, and that of which he has no experience himself he seeks to find out from those who have it,—and our Lord helps him by increasing his faith, and so he has greatly benefited himself and some other souls, of whom mine is one. As our Lord knew the trials I had to undergo, His Majesty seems to have provided that, when He took away unto Himself some of those who directed me, others might remain, who helped me in my great afflictions, and rendered me great services.

17. Our Lord wrought a complete change in this father, so much so that he scarcely knew himself, so to speak. He has given him bodily health, so that he may do penance, such as he never had before; for he was sickly. He has given him courage to undertake good works, with other gifts, so that he seems to have received a most special vocation from our Lord. May He be blessed for ever!

18. All these blessings, I believe, came to him through the graces our Lord bestowed upon him in prayer; for they are real. It has been our Lord's pleasure already to try him in certain difficulties, out of which he has come forth like one who knows the true worth of that merit which is gained by suffering persecutions. I trust in the munificence of our Lord that great good will, by his means, accrue to some of his Order and to the Order itself. This is beginning to be understood. I have had great visions on the subject, and our Lord has told me wonderful things of him and of the Rector of the Society of Jesus, whom I am speaking of,[396] and also of two other religious of the Order of St. Dominic, particularly of one who, to his own profit, has actually learned of our Lord certain things which I had formerly understood of him. But there were greater things made known of him to whom I am now referring: one of them I will now relate.

19. I was with him once in the parlor, when in my soul and spirit I felt what great love burned within him, and became as it were lost in ecstasy by considering the greatness of God, who had raised that soul in so short a time to a state so high. It made me ashamed of myself when I saw him listen with so much humility to what I was saying about certain matters of prayer, when I had so little myself that I could speak on the subject to one like him. Our Lord must have borne with me in this on account of the great desire I had to see that religious making great progress. My interview with him did me great good,—it seems as if it left a new fire in my soul, burning with desire to serve our Lord as in the beginning. O my Jesus! what is a soul on fire with Thy love! How we ought to prize it, and implore our Lord to let it live long upon earth! He who has this love should follow after such souls, if it be possible.

20. It is a great thing for a person ill of this disease to find another struck down by it,—it comforts him much to see that he is not alone; they help one another greatly to suffer and to merit. They are strong with a double strength who are resolved to risk a thousand lives for God, and who long for an opportunity of losing them. They are like soldiers who, to acquire booty, and therewith

394 1 Thess. v. 19: "Spiritum nolite extinguere."
395 St. Matt. xix. 26: "Apud Deum autem omnia possibilia sunt."
396 F. Gaspar de Salazar.

enrich themselves, wish for war, knowing well that they cannot become rich without it. This is their work—to suffer. Oh, what a blessing it is when our Lord gives light to understand how great is the gain of suffering for Him! This is never understood till we have left all things; for if anybody is attached to any one thing, that is a proof that he sets some value upon it; and if he sets any value upon it, it is painful to be compelled to give it up. In that case, everything is imperfect and lost. The saying is to the purpose here,—he who follows what is lost, is lost himself; and what greater loss, what greater blindness, what greater calamity, can there be than making much of that which is nothing!

21. I now return to that which I had begun to speak of. I was in the greatest joy, beholding that soul. It seemed as if our Lord would have me see clearly the treasures He had laid up in it; and so, when I considered the favor our Lord had shown me, in that I should be the means of so great a good, I recognized my own unworthiness for such an end. I thought much of the graces our Lord had given him, and held myself as indebted for them more than if they had been given to myself. So I gave thanks to our Lord, when I saw that His Majesty had fulfilled my desires and heard my petition that He would raise up persons like him. And now my soul, no longer able to bear the joy that filled it, went forth out of itself, losing itself that it might gain the more. It lost sight of the reflections it was making; and the hearing of that divine language which the Holy Ghost seemed to speak threw me into a deep trance, which almost deprived me of all sense, though it did not last long. I saw Christ, in exceeding great majesty and glory, manifesting His joy at what was then passing. He told me as much, and it was His pleasure that I should clearly see that He was always present at similar interviews, and how much He was pleased when people thus found their delight in speaking of Him.

22. On another occasion, when far away from this place, I saw him carried by angels in great glory. I understood by that vision that his soul was making great progress: so it was; for an evil report was spread abroad against him by one to whom he had rendered a great service, and whose reputation and whose soul he had saved. He bore it with much joy. He did also other things greatly to the honor of God, and underwent more persecutions. I do not think it expedient now to speak further on this point; if, however, you, my father, who know all, should hereafter think otherwise, more might be said to the glory of our Lord.

23. All the prophecies spoken of before,[397] relating to this house, as well as others, of which I shall speak hereafter, relating to it and to other matters, have been accomplished. Some of them our Lord revealed to me three years before they became known, others earlier and others later. But I always made them known to my confessor, and to the widow my friend; for I had leave to communicate with her, as I said before.[398] She, I know, repeated them to others, and these know that I lie not. May God never permit me, in any matter whatever,—much more in things of this importance,—to say anything but the whole truth!

24. One of my brothers-in-law[399] died suddenly; and as I was in great distress at this, because he had no opportunity of making his confession, our Lord said to me in prayer that my sister also was to die in the same way; that I must go to her, and make her prepare herself for such an end. I told this to my confessor; but as he would not let me go, I heard the same warning again; and now, when he saw this, he told me I might go, and that I should lose nothing by going. My sister was living in the country; and as I did not tell her why I came, I gave her what light I could in all things. I made her go frequently to confession, and look to her soul in everything. She was very good, and did as I asked her. Four or five years after she had begun this practice, and keeping a strict watch over her conscience, she died, with nobody near her, and without being able to go to confession. This was a blessing to her, for it was little more than a week since she had been to her accustomed confession. It was a great joy to me when I heard of her death. She was but a short time in purgatory.

25. I do not think it was quite eight days afterwards when, after Communion, our Lord appeared to me, and was pleased that I should see Him receive my sister into glory. During all those years, after our Lord had spoken to me, until her death, what I then learnt with respect to her was never forgotten either by myself or by my friend, who, when my sister was thus dead, came to me

---

[397] Ch. xxvi. § 3.

[398] Ch. xxx. § 3. Doña Guiomar de Ulloa.

[399] Don Martin de Guzman y Barrientos, husband of Maria de Cepeda, the Saint's sister.

in great amazement at the fulfilment of the prophecy. God be praised for ever, who takes such care of souls that they may not be lost!

Chapter XXXV.

The Foundation of the House of St. Joseph. The Observation of Holy Poverty Therein. How the Saint Left Toledo.

1. When I was staying with this lady,[400] already spoken of, in whose house I remained more than six months, our Lord ordained that a holy woman[401] of our Order should hear of me, who was more than seventy leagues away from the place. She happened to travel this way, and went some leagues out of her road that she might see me. Our Lord had moved her in the same year, and in the same month of the year, that He had moved me, to found another monastery of the Order; and as He had given her this desire, she sold all she possessed, and went to Rome to obtain the necessary faculties. She went on foot, and barefooted. She is a woman of great penance and prayer, and one to whom our Lord gave many graces; and our Lady appeared to her, and commanded her to undertake this work. Her progress in the service of our Lord was so much greater than mine, that I was ashamed to stand in her presence. She showed me Briefs she brought from Rome, and during the fortnight she remained with me we laid our plan for the founding of these monasteries.

2. Until I spoke to her, I never knew that our rule, before it was mitigated, required of us that we should possess nothing;[402] nor was I going to found a monastery without revenue,[403] for my intention was that we should be without anxiety about all that was necessary for us, and I did not think of the many anxieties which the possession of property brings in its train. This holy woman, taught of our Lord, perfectly understood—though she could not read—what I was ignorant of, notwithstanding my having read the Constitutions[404] so often; and when she told me of it, I thought it right, though I feared they would never consent to this, but would tell me I was committing follies, and that I ought not to do anything whereby I might bring suffering upon others. If this concerned only myself, nothing should have kept me back,—on the contrary, it would have been my great joy to think that I was observing the counsels of Christ our Lord; for His Majesty had already given me great longings for poverty.

3. As for myself, I never doubted that this was the better part; for I had now for some time wished it were possible in my state to go about begging, for the love of God—to have no house of my own, nor anything else. But I was afraid that others—if our Lord did not give them the same

---

[400] Doña Luisa de la Cerda.

[401] Maria of Jesus was the daughter of a Reporter of Causes in the Chancery of Granada; but his name and that of his wife are not known. Maria married, but became a widow soon afterwards. She then became a novice in the Carmelite monastery in Granada, and during her noviciate had revelations, like those of St. Teresa, about a reform of the Order. Her confessor made light of her revelations, and she then referred them to F. Gaspar de Salazar, a confessor of St. Teresa, who was then in Granada. He approved of them, and Maria left the noviciate, and went to Rome with two holy women of the Order of St. Francis. The three made the journey on foot, and, moreover, barefooted. Pope Pius IV. heard her prayer, and, looking at her torn and bleeding feet, said to her, "Woman of strong courage, let it be as thou wilt." She returned to Granada, but both the Carmelites and the city refused her permission to found her house there, and some went so far as to threaten to have her publicly whipped. Doña Leonor de Mascareñas gave her a house in Alcala de Henares, of which she took possession Sept. 11, 1562; but the house was formally constituted July 23, 1563, and subjected to the Bishop ten days after (*Reforma*, i. c. 59; and *Don Vicente*, vol. i. p. 255). The latter says that the Chronicler is in error when he asserts that this monastery of Maria of Jesus was endowed.

[402] The sixth chapter of the rule is: "Nullus fratrum sibi aliquid proprium, esse dicat, sed sint vobis omnia communia."

[403] See ch. xxxii. § 13.

[404] The Constitutions which the Saint read in the Monastery of the Incarnation must have been the Constitutions grounded on the Mitigated Rule which was sanctioned by Eugenius IV. (*Romani Pontificis*, A.D. 1432).

desire—might live in discontent. Moreover, I feared that it might be the cause of some distraction: for I knew some poor monasteries not very recollected, and I did not consider that their not being recollected was the cause of their poverty, and that their poverty was not the cause of their distraction: distraction never makes people richer, and God never fails those who serve Him. In short, I was weak in faith; but not so this servant of God.

4. As I took the advice of many in everything, I found scarcely any one of this opinion—neither my confessor, nor the learned men to whom I spoke of it. They gave me so many reasons the other way, that I did not know what to do. But when I saw what the rule required, and that poverty was the more perfect way, I could not persuade myself to allow an endowment. And though they did persuade me now and then that they were right, yet, when I returned to my prayer, and saw Christ on the cross, so poor and destitute, I could not bear to be rich, and I implored Him with tears so to order matters that I might be poor as He was.

5. I found that so many inconveniences resulted from an endowment, and saw that it was the cause of so much trouble, and even distraction, that I did nothing but dispute with the learned. I wrote to that Dominican friar[405] who was helping us, and he sent back two sheets by way of reply, full of objections and theology against my plan, telling me that he had thought much on the subject. I answered that, in order to escape from my vocation, the vow of poverty I had made, and the perfect observance of the counsels of Christ, I did not want any theology to help me, and in this case I should not thank him for his learning. If I found any one who would help me, it pleased me much. The lady in whose house I was staying was a great help to me in this matter. Some at first told me that they agreed with me; afterwards, when they had considered the matter longer, they found in it so many inconveniences that they insisted on my giving it up. I told them that, though they changed their opinion so quickly, I would abide by the first.

6. At this time, because of my entreaties,—for the lady had never seen the holy friar, Peter of Alcantara,—it pleased our Lord to bring him to her house. As he was a great lover of poverty, and had lived in it for so many years, he knew well the treasures it contains, and so he was a great help to me; he charged me on no account whatever to give up my purpose. Now, having this opinion and sanction,—no one was better able to give it, because he knew what it was by long experience,—I made up my mind to seek no further advice.

7. One day, when I was very earnestly commending the matter to God, our Lord told me that I must by no means give up my purpose of founding the monastery in poverty; it was His will, and the will of His Father: He would help me. I was in a trance; and the effects were such, that I could have no doubt it came from God. On another occasion, He said to me that endowments bred confusion, with other things in praise of poverty; and assured me that whosoever served Him would never be in want of the necessary means of living: and this want, as I have said,[406] I never feared myself. Our Lord changed the dispositions also of the licentiate,—I am speaking of the Dominican friar,[407]—who, as I said, wrote to me that I should not found the monastery without an endowment. Now, I was in the greatest joy at hearing this; and having these opinions in my favor, it seemed to me nothing less than the possession of all the wealth of the world, when I had resolved to live in poverty for the love of God.

8. At this time, my Provincial withdrew the order and the obedience, in virtue of which I was staying in that house.[408] He left it to me to do as I liked: if I wished to return I might do so; if I wished to remain I might also do so for a certain time. But during that time the elections in my monastery[409] would take place and I was told that many of the nuns wished to lay on me the burden of superiority. The very thought of this alone was a great torment to me; for though I was resolved to undergo readily any kind of martyrdom for God, I could not persuade myself at all to accept this; for, putting aside the great trouble it involved,—because the nuns were so many,—and other reasons, such as that I never wished for it, nor for any other office,—on the contrary, had always

---

405 F. Pedro Ibañez.

406 Ch. xi. § 3.

407 F. Pedro Ibañez.

408 The house of Doña Luisa, in Toledo.

409 The monastery of the Incarnation, Avila.

refused them,—it seemed to me that my conscience would be in great danger; and so I praised God that I was not then in my convent. I wrote to my friends and asked them not to vote for me.

9. When I was rejoicing that I was not in that trouble, our Lord said to me that I was on no account to keep away; that as I longed for a cross, there was one ready for me, and that a heavy one: that I was not to throw it away, but go on with resolution; He would help me, and I must go at once. I was very much distressed, and did nothing but weep, because I thought that my cross was to be the office of prioress; and, as I have just said, I could not persuade myself that it would be at all good for my soul—nor could I see any means by which it would be. I told my confessor of it, and he commanded me to return at once: that to do so was clearly the most perfect way; and that, because the heat was very great,—it would be enough if I arrived before the election,—I might wait a few days, in order that my journey might do me no harm.

10. But our Lord had ordered it otherwise. I had to go at once, because the uneasiness I felt was very great; and I was unable to pray, and thought I was failing in obedience to the commandments of our Lord, and that as I was happy and contented where I was, I would not go to meet trouble. All my service of God there was lip-service: why did I, having the opportunity of living in greater perfection, neglect it? If I died on the road, let me die. Besides, my soul was in great straits, and our Lord had taken from me all sweetness in prayer. In short, I was in such a state of torment, that I begged the lady to let me go; for my confessor, when he saw the plight I was in, had already told me to go, God having moved him as He had moved me. The lady felt my departure very much, and that was another pain to bear; for it had cost her much trouble, and diverse importunities of the Provincial, to have me in her house.

11. I considered it a very great thing for her to have given her consent, when she felt it so much; but, as she was a person who feared God exceedingly,—and as I told her, among many other reasons, that my going away tended greatly to His service, and held out the hope that I might possibly return,—she gave way, but with much sorrow. I was now not sorry myself at coming away, for I knew that it was an act of greater perfection, and for the service of God. So the pleasure I had in pleasing God took away the pain of quitting that lady,—whom I saw suffering so keenly,—and others to whom I owed much, particularly my confessor of the Society of Jesus, in whom I found all I needed. But the greater the consolations I lost for our Lord's sake, the greater was my joy in losing them. I could not understand it, for I had a clear consciousness of these two contrary feelings—pleasure, consolation, and joy in that which weighed down my soul with sadness. I was joyful and tranquil, and had opportunities of spending many hours in prayer; and I saw that I was going to throw myself into a fire; for our Lord had already told me that I was going to carry a heavy cross,—though I never thought it would be so heavy as I afterwards found it to be,—yet I went forth rejoicing. I was distressed because I had not already begun the fight, since it was our Lord's will that I should be in it. Thus His Majesty gave me strength, and established it in my weakness.[410]

12. As I have just said, I could not understand how this could be. I thought of this illustration: if I were possessed of a jewel, or any other thing which gave me great pleasure, and it came to my knowledge that a person whom I loved more than myself, and whose satisfaction I preferred to my own, wished to have it, it would give me great pleasure to deprive myself of it, because I would give all I possessed to please that person. Now, as the pleasure of giving pleasure to that person surpasses any pleasure I have in that jewel myself, I should not be distressed in giving away that or anything else I loved, nor at the loss of that pleasure which the possession of it gave me. So now, though I wished to feel some distress when I saw that those whom I was leaving felt my going so much, yet, notwithstanding my naturally grateful disposition,—which, under other circumstances, would have been enough to have caused me great pain,—at this time, though I wished to feel it, I could feel none.

13. The delay of another day was so serious a matter in the affairs of this holy house, that I know not how they would have been settled if I had waited. Oh, God is great! I am often lost in wonder when I consider and see the special help which His Majesty gave me towards the establishment of this little cell of God,—for such I believe it to be,—the lodging wherein His Majesty delights; for once, when I was in prayer, He told me that this house was the paradise of his

---

[410] 2 Cor. xii. 9: "Virtus in infirmitate perficitur."

delight.[411] It seems, then, that His Majesty has chosen these whom he has drawn hither, among whom I am living very much ashamed of myself. I could not have even wished for souls such as they are for the purpose of this house, where enclosure, poverty, and prayer are so strictly observed; they submit with so much joy and contentment, that every one of them thinks herself unworthy of the grace of being received into it,—some of them particularly; for our Lord has called them out of the vanity and dissipation of the world, in which, according to its laws, they might have lived contented. Our Lord has multiplied their joy, so that they see clearly how He had given them a hundredfold for the one thing they have left,[412] and for which they cannot thank His Majesty enough. Others He has advanced from well to better. To the young He gives courage and knowledge, so that they may desire nothing else, and also to understand that to live away from all things in this life is to live in greater peace even here below. To those who are no longer young, and whose health is weak, He gives—and has given—the strength to undergo the same austerities and penance with all the others.

14. O my Lord! how Thou does show Thy power! There is no need to seek reasons for Thy will; for with Thee, against all natural reason, all things are possible: so that thou teaches clearly there is no need of anything but of loving Thee[413] in earnest, and really giving up everything for Thee, in order that Thou, O my Lord, might make everything easy. It is well said that Thou feigns to make Thy law difficult:[414] I do not see it, nor do I feel that the way that leads unto Thee is narrow. I see it as a royal road, and not a pathway; a road upon which whosoever really enters, travels most securely. No mountain passes and no cliffs are near it: these are the occasions of sin. I call that a pass,—a dangerous pass,—and a narrow road, which has on one side a deep hollow, into which one stumbles, and on the other a precipice, over which they who are careless fall, and are dashed to pieces. He who loves Thee, O my God, travels safely by the open and royal road, far away from the precipice: he has scarcely stumbled at all, when Thou stretches forth Thy hand to save him. One fall—yes, many falls—if he does but love Thee, and not the things of the world, are not enough to make him perish; he travels in the valley of humility. I cannot understand what it is that makes men afraid of the way of perfection.

15. May our Lord of His mercy make us see what a poor security we have in the midst of dangers so manifest, when we live like the rest of the world; and that true security consists in striving to advance in the way of God! Let us fix our eyes upon Him, and have no fear that the Sun of justice will ever set, or suffer us to travel to our ruin by night, unless we first look away from Him. People are not afraid of living in the midst of lions, every one of whom seems eager to tear them: I am speaking of honors, pleasures, and the like joys, as the world calls them: and herein the devil seems to make us afraid of ghosts. I am astonished a thousand times, and ten thousand times would I relieve myself by weeping, and proclaim aloud my own great blindness and wickedness, if, perchance, it might help in some measure to open their eyes. May He, who is almighty, of His goodness open their eyes, and never suffer mine to be blind again!

---

[411] See *Way of Perfection*, ch. xxii.; but ch. xiii. ed. Doblado.

[412] St. Matt. xix. 29: "Et omnis qui reliquerit domum… propter nomen Meum, centuplum accipiet, et vitam æternam possidebit."

[413] When the workmen were busy with the building, a nephew of the Saint, the child of her sister and Don Juan de Ovalle, was struck by some falling stones and killed. The workmen took the child to his mother: and the Saint, then in the house of Doña Guiomar de Ulloa, was sent for. Doña Guiomar took the dead boy into her arms, gave him to the Saint, saying that it was a grievous blow to the father and mother, and that she must obtain his life from God. The Saint took the body, and, laying it in her lap, ordered those around her to cease their lamentations, of whom her sister was naturally the loudest, and be silent. Then, covering her face and her body with her veil, she prayed to God, and God gave the child his life again. The little boy soon after ran up to his aunt and thanked her for what she had done. In after years the child used to say to the Saint that, as she had deprived him of the bliss of heaven by bringing him back to life, she was bound to see that he did not suffer loss. Don Gonzalo died three years after St. Teresa, when he was twenty-eight years of age (*Reforma*, i. c. 42, § 2).

[414] Psalm xciii. 20: "Qui fingis laborem in præcepto."

Chapter XXXVI.

The Foundation of the Monastery of St. Joseph. Persecution and Temptations.
Great Interior Trial of the Saint, and Her Deliverance.

1. Having now left that city,[415] I travelled in great joy, resolved to suffer most willingly whatever our Lord might be pleased to lay upon me. On the night of my arrival here,[416] came also from Rome the commission and the Brief for the erection of the monastery.[417] I was astonished myself, and so were those who knew how our Lord hastened my coming, when they saw how necessary it was, and in what a moment our Lord had brought me back.[418] I found here the Bishop and the holy friar,[419] Peter of Alcantara, and that nobleman,[420] the great servant of God, in whose house the holy man was staying; for he was a man who was in the habit of receiving the servants of God in his house. These two prevailed on the Bishop to accept the monastery, which was no small thing, because it was founded in poverty; but he was so great a lover of those whom he saw determined to serve our Lord, that he was immediately drawn to give them His protection. It was the approbation of the holy old man,[421] and the great trouble he took to make now this one, now that one, help us, that did the whole work. If I had not come at the moment, as I have just said, I do not see how it could have been done; for the holy man was here but a short time,—I think not quite eight days,—during which he was also ill; and almost immediately afterwards our Lord took him to Himself.[422] It seems as if His Majesty reserved him till this affair was ended, because now for some time—I think for more than two years—he had been very ill.

2. Everything was done in the utmost secrecy; and if it had not been so, I do not see how anything could have been done at all; for the people of the city were against us, as it appeared afterwards. Our Lord ordained that one of my brothers-in-law[423] should be ill, and his wife away, and himself in such straits that my superiors gave me leave to remain with him. Nothing, therefore, was found out, though some persons had their suspicions;—still, they did not believe. It was very wonderful, for his illness lasted only no longer than was necessary for our affair; and when it was necessary he should recover his health, that I might be disengaged, and he leave the house empty, our Lord restored him; and he was astonished at it himself.[424]

3. I had much trouble in persuading this person and that to allow the foundation; I had to nurse the sick man, and obtain from the workmen the hasty preparation of the house, so that it might have the form of a monastery; but much remained still to be done. My friend was not here,[425] for we thought it best she should be away, in order the better to hide our purpose. I saw that everything depended on haste, for many, reasons, one of which was that I was afraid I might be ordered back to my monastery at any moment. I was troubled by so many things, that I suspected my cross had been sent me, though it seemed but a light one in comparison with that which I understood our Lord meant me to carry.

4. When everything was settled, our Lord was pleased that some of us should take the habit on St. Bartholomew's Day. The most Holy Sacrament began to dwell in the house at the same time.[426] With full sanction and authority, then, our monastery of our most glorious father St. Joseph was

---

[415] Toledo.

[416] Avila. In the beginning of June, 1562.

[417] See ch. xxxiv. § 2. The Brief was dated Feb. 7, 1562, the third year of Pius IV. (*De la Fuente*).

[418] The Brief was addressed to Doña Aldonza de Guzman, and to Doña Guiomar de Ulloa, her daughter.

[419] Don Alvaro de Mendoza (*De la Fuente*).

[420] Don Francisco de Salcedo.

[421] St. Peter of Alcantara. "Truly this is the house of St. Joseph," were the Saint's words when he saw the rising monastery; "for I see it is the little hospice of Bethlehem" (*De la Fuente*).

[422] In less than three months, perhaps; for St. Peter died in the sixty-third year of his age, Oct. 18, 1562, and in less than eight weeks after the foundation of the monastery of St. Joseph.

[423] Don Juan de Ovalle.

[424] When he saw that the Saint had made all her arrangements, he knew the meaning of his illness, and said to her, "It is not necessary I should be ill any longer" (*Ribera*, i. c. 8).

[425] Doña Guiomar de Ulloa was now in her native place, Ciudad Toro.

[426] The Mass was said by Gaspar Daza. See *infra*, § 18; *Reforma*, i. c. xlvi. § 3.

founded in the year 1562.[427] I was there myself to give the habit, with two nuns[428] of the house to which we belonged, who happened then to be absent from it. As the house which thus became a monastery was that of my brother-in-law—I said before[429] that he had bought it, for the purpose of concealing our plan—I was there myself with the permission of my superiors; and I did nothing without the advice of learned men, in order that I might not break, in a single point, my vow of obedience. As these persons considered what I was doing to be most advantageous for the whole Order, on many accounts, they told me—though I was acting secretly, and taking care my superiors should know nothing—that I might go on. If they had told me that there was the slightest imperfection in the whole matter, I would have given up the founding of a thousand monasteries,—how much more, then, this one! I am certain of this; for though I longed to withdraw from everything more and more, and to follow my rule and vocation in the greatest perfection and seclusion, yet I wished to do so only conditionally: for if I should have learnt that it would be for the greater honor of our Lord to abandon it, I would have done so, as I did before on one occasion,[430] in all peace and contentment.

5. I felt as if I were in bliss, when I saw the most Holy Sacrament reserved, with four poor orphans,[431]—for they were received without a dowry,—and great servants of God, established in the house. It was our aim from the beginning to receive only those who, by their example, might be the foundation on which we could build up what we had in view—great perfection and prayer—and effect a work which I believed to be for the service of our Lord, and to the honor of the habit of His glorious Mother. This was my anxiety. It was also a great consolation to me that I had done that which our Lord had so often commanded me to do, and that there was one church more in this city dedicated to my glorious father St. Joseph. Not that I thought I had done anything myself, for I have never thought so, and do not think so even now; I always looked upon it as the work of our Lord. My part in it was so full of imperfections, that I look upon myself rather as a person in fault than as one to whom any thanks are due. But it was a great joy to me when I saw His Majesty make use of me, who am so worthless, as His instrument in so grand a work. I was therefore in great joy,—so much so, that I was, as it were, beside myself, lost in prayer.

6. When all was done—it might have been about three or four hours afterwards—Satan returned to the spiritual fight against me, as I shall now relate. He suggested to me that perhaps I had been wrong in what I had done; perhaps I had failed in my obedience, in having brought it about without the commandment of the Provincial. I did certainly think that the Provincial would be displeased because I had placed the monastery under the jurisdiction of the Bishop[432] without telling him of it beforehand; though, as he would not acknowledge the monastery himself, and as I had not changed mine, it seemed to me that perhaps he would not care much about the matter. Satan also suggested whether the nuns would be contented to live in so strict a house, whether they could always find food, whether I had not done a silly thing, and what had I to do with it, when I was

---

[427] The bell which the Saint had provided for the convent weighed less than three pounds, and remained in the monastery for a hundred years, till it was sent, by order of the General, to the monastery of Pastrana, where the general chapters were held. There the friars assembled at the sound of the bell, which rang for the first Mass of the Carmelite Reform (*Reforma*, i. c. xlvi. § 1).

[428] They were Doña Ines and Doña Ana de Tapia, cousins of the Saint. There were present also Don Gonzalo de Aranda, Don Francisco Salcedo, Julian of Avila, priest; Doña Juana de Ahumada, the Saint's sister; with her husband, Juan de Ovalle. The Saint herself retained her own habit, making no change, because she had not the permission of her superiors (*Reforma*, i. c. xlvi. § 2).

[429] Ch. xxxiii. § 13.

[430] Ch. xxxiii. § 3.

[431] The first of these was Antonia de Henao, a penitent of St. Peter of Alcantara, and who wished to enter a religious house far away from Avila, her home. St. Peter kept her for St. Teresa. She was called from this day forth Antonia of the Holy Ghost. The second was Maria de la Paz, brought up by Doña Guiomar de Ulloa. Her name was Maria of the Cross. The third was Ursola de los Santos. She retained her family name as Ursola of the Saints. It was Gaspar Daza who brought her to the Saint. The fourth was Maria de Avila, sister of Julian the priest, and she was called Mary of St. Joseph. It was at this house, too, that the Saint herself exchanged her ordinary designation of Doña Teresa de Ahumada for Teresa of Jesus (*Reforma*, i. c. xlvi. § 2).

[432] See *Foundations*, ch. ii. § 1, and ch. xxxi, § 1.

already in a monastery? All our Lord had said to me, all the opinions I had heard, and all the prayers which had been almost uninterrupted for more than two years, were completely blotted out of my memory, just as if they had never been. The only thing I remembered was my own opinion; and every virtue, with faith itself, was then suspended within me, so that I was without strength to practice any one of them, or to defend myself against so many blows.

7. The devil also would have me ask myself how I could think of shutting myself up in so strict a house, when I was subject to so many infirmities; how could I bear so penitential a life, and leave a house large and pleasant, where I had been always so happy, and where I had so many friends?—perhaps I might not like those of the new monastery; I had taken on myself a heavy obligation, and might possibly end in despair. He also suggested that perhaps it was he himself who had contrived it, in order to rob me of my peace and rest, so that, being unable to pray, I might be disquieted, and so lose my soul. Thoughts of this kind he put before me; and they were so many, that I could think of nothing else; and with them came such distress, obscurity, and darkness of soul as I can never describe. When I found myself in this state, I went and placed myself before the most Holy Sacrament, though I could not pray to Him; so great was my anguish, that I was like one in the agony of death. I could not make the matter known to any one, because no confessor had as yet been appointed.

8. O my God, how wretched is this life! No joy is lasting; everything is liable to change. Only a moment ago, I do not think I would have exchanged my joy with any man upon earth; and the very grounds of that joy so tormented me now, that I knew not what to do with myself. Oh, if we did but consider carefully the events of our life, every one of us would learn from experience how little we ought to make either of its pleasures or of its pains! Certainly this was, I believe, one of the most distressing moments I ever passed in all my life; my spirit seemed to forecast the great sufferings in store for me, though they never were so heavy as this was, if it had continued. But our Lord would not let His poor servant suffer, for in all my troubles He never failed to succor me; so it was now. He gave me a little light, so that I might see it was the work of the devil, and might understand the truth,—namely, that it was nothing else but an attempt on his part to frighten me with his lies. So I began to call to mind my great resolutions to serve our Lord, and my desire to suffer for His sake; and I thought that if I carried them out, I must not seek to be at rest; that if I had my trials, they would be meritorious; and that if I had troubles, and endured them in order to please God, it would serve me for purgatory. What was I, then, afraid of? If I longed for tribulations, I had them now; and my gain lay in the greatest opposition. Why, then, did I fail in courage to serve One to whom I owed so much?

9. After making these and other reflections, and doing great violence to myself, I promised before the most Holy Sacrament to do all in my power to obtain permission to enter this house, and, if I could do it with a good conscience, to make a vow of enclosure. When I had done this, the devil fled in a moment, and left me calm and peaceful, and I have continued so ever since; and the enclosure, penances, and other rules of this house are to me, in their observance, so singularly sweet and light, the joy I have is so exceedingly great, that I am now and then thinking what on earth I could have chosen which should be more delightful. I know not whether this may not be the cause of my being in better health than I was ever before, or whether it be that our Lord, because it is needful and reasonable that I should do as all the others do, gives me this comfort of keeping the whole rule, though with some difficulty. However, all who know my infirmities, are astonished at my strength. Blessed be He who gives it all, and in whose strength I am strong!

10. Such a contest left me greatly fatigued, and laughing at Satan; for I saw clearly it was he. As I have never known what it is to be discontented because I am a nun—no, not for an instant—during more than twenty-eight years of religion, I believe that our Lord suffered me to be thus tempted, that I might understand how great a mercy He had shown me herein, and from what torment He had delivered me, and that if I saw any one in like trouble I might not be alarmed at it, but have pity on her, and be able to console her.

11. Then, when this was over, I wished to rest myself a little after our dinner; for during the whole of that night I had scarcely rested at all, and for some nights previously I had had much trouble and anxiety, while every day was full of toil; for the news of what we had done had reached my monastery, and was spread through the city. There arose a great outcry, for the reasons I

mentioned before,[433] and there was some apparent ground for it. The prioress[434] sent for me to come to her immediately. When I received the order, I went at once, leaving the nuns in great distress. I saw clearly enough that there were troubles before me; but as the work was really done, I did not care much for that. I prayed and implored our Lord to help me, and my father St. Joseph to bring me back to his house. I offered up to him all I was to suffer, rejoicing greatly that I had the opportunity of suffering for his honor and of doing him service. I went persuaded that I should be put in prison at once but this would have been a great comfort, because I should have nobody to speak to, and might have some rest and solitude, of which I was in great need; for so much intercourse with people had worn me out.

12. When I came and told the prioress what I had done, she was softened a little. They all sent for the Provincial, and the matter was reserved for him. When he came, I was summoned to judgment, rejoicing greatly at seeing that I had something to suffer for our Lord. I did not think I had offended against His Majesty, or against my Order, in anything I had done; on the contrary, I was striving with all my might to exalt my Order, for which I would willingly have died,—for my whole desire was that its rule might be observed in all perfection. I thought of Christ receiving sentence, and I saw how this of mine would be less than nothing. I confessed my fault, as if I had been very much to blame; and so I seemed to every one who did not know all the reasons. After the Provincial had rebuked me sharply—though not with the severity which my fault deserved, nor according to the representations made to him—I would not defend myself, for I was determined to bear it all; on the contrary, I prayed him to forgive and punish, and be no longer angry with me.

13. I saw well enough that they condemned me on some charges of which I was innocent, for they said I had founded the monastery that I might be thought much of, and to make myself a name, and for other reasons of that kind. But on other points I understood clearly that they were speaking the truth, as when they said that I was more wicked than the other nuns. They asked, how could I, who had not kept the rule in that house, think of keeping it in another of stricter observance? They said I was giving scandal in the city, and setting up novelties. All this neither troubled nor distressed me in the least, though I did seem to feel it, lest I should appear to make light of what they were saying.

14. At last the Provincial commanded me to explain my conduct before the nuns, and I had to do it. As I was perfectly calm, and our Lord helped me, I explained everything in such a way that neither the Provincial nor those who were present found any reason to condemn me. Afterwards I spoke more plainly to the Provincial alone; he was very much satisfied, and promised, if the new monastery prospered, and the city became quiet, to give me leave to live in it. Now the outcry in the city was very great, as I am going to tell. Two or three days after this, the governor, certain members of the council of the city and of the Chapter, came together, and resolved that the new monastery should not be allowed to exist, that it was a visible wrong to the state, that the most Holy Sacrament should be removed, and that they would not suffer us to go on with our work.

15. They assembled all the Orders—that is, two learned men from each—to give their opinion. Some were silent, others condemned; in the end, they resolved that the monastery should be broken up. Only one[435]—he was of the Order of St. Dominic, and objected, not to the monastery itself, but to the foundation of it in poverty—said that there was no reason why it should be thus dissolved, that the matter ought to be well considered, that there was time enough, that it was the affair of the bishop, with other things of that kind. This was of great service to us, for they were angry enough to proceed to its destruction at once, and it was fortunate they did not. In short, the monastery must

---

[433] Ch. xxxiii. §§ 1, 2.

[434] Of the Incarnation.

[435] F. Domingo Bañes, the great commentator on St. Thomas. On the margin of the MS., Bañes has with his own hand written: "This was at the end of August, 1562. I was present, and gave this opinion. I am writing this in May" (the day of the month is not legible) "1575, and the mother has now founded nine monasteries *en gran religion*" (*De la Fuente*). At this time Bañes did not know, and had never seen, the Saint; he undertook her defense simply because he saw that her intentions were good, and the means she made use of for founding the monastery lawful, seeing that she had received the commandment to do so from the Pope. Bañes testifies thus in the depositions made in Salamanca in 1591 in the Saint's process. See vol. ii. p. 376 of Don Vicente's edition.

exist; our Lord was pleased to have it, and all of them could do nothing against His will. They gave their reasons, and showed their zeal for good, and thus, without offending God, made me suffer together with all those who were in favor of the monastery; there were not many, but they suffered much persecution. The inhabitants were so excited, that they talked of nothing else; every one condemned me, and hurried to the Provincial and to my monastery.

16. I was no more distressed by what they said of me than if they had said nothing; but I was afraid the monastery would be destroyed: that was painful; so also was it to see those persons who helped me lose their credit and suffer so much annoyance. But as to what was said of myself I was rather glad, and if I had had any faith I should not have been troubled at all. But a slight failing in one virtue is enough to put all the others to sleep. I was therefore extremely distressed during the two days on which those assemblies of which I have spoken were held. In the extremity of my trouble, our Lord said to me: "Knows thou not that I am the Almighty? what art thou afraid of?" He made me feel assured that the monastery would not be broken up, and I was exceedingly comforted. The informations taken were sent up to the king's council, and an order came back for a report on the whole matter.

17. Here was the beginning of a grand lawsuit: the city sent delegates to the court, and some must be sent also to defend the monastery: but I had no money, nor did I know what to do. Our Lord provided for us for the Father Provincial never ordered me not to meddle in the matter. He is so great a lover of all that is good, that, though he did not help us, he would not be against our work. Neither did he authorize me to enter the house till he saw how it would end. Those servants of God who were in it were left alone, and did more by their prayers than I did with all my negotiations, though the affair needed the utmost attention. Now and then everything seemed to fail; particularly one day, before the Provincial came, when the prioress ordered me to meddle no more with it, and to give it up altogether. I betook myself to God, and said, "O Lord, this house is not mine; it was founded for Thee; and now that there is no one to take up the cause, do Thou protect it." I now felt myself in peace, and as free from anxiety as if the whole world were on my side in the matter; and at once I looked upon it as safe.[436]

18. A very great servant of God, and a lover of all perfection, a priest[437] who had helped me always, went to the court on this business, and took great pains. That holy nobleman[438] of whom I have often spoken labored much on our behalf, and helped us in every way. He had much trouble and persecution to endure, and I always found a father in him, and do so still. All those who helped us, our Lord filled with such fervor as made them consider our affair as their own, as if their own life and reputation were at stake; and yet it was nothing to them, except in so far as it regarded the service of our Lord. His Majesty visibly helped the priest I have spoken of before,[439] who was also one of those who gave us great help when the Bishop sent him as his representative to one of the great meetings. There he stood alone against all; at last he pacified them by means of certain propositions, which obtained us a little respite. But that was not enough; for they were ready to spend their lives, if they could but destroy the monastery. This servant of God was he who gave the habit and reserved the most Holy Sacrament, and he was the object of much persecution. This attack lasted about six months: to relate in detail the heavy trials we passed through would be too tedious.

19. I wondered at what Satan did against a few poor women, and also how all people thought that merely twelve women, with a prioress, could be so hurtful to the city,—for they were not to be more,—I say this to those who opposed us,—and living such austere lives; for if any harm or error came of it, it would all fall upon them. Harm to the city there could not be in any way; and yet the people thought there was so much in it, that they opposed us with a good conscience. At last they resolved they would tolerate us if we were endowed, and in consideration of that would suffer us to remain. I was so distressed at the trouble of all those who were on our side—more than at my own—that I thought it would not be amiss, till the people were pacified, to accept an endowment, but afterwards to resign it. At other times, too, wicked and imperfect as I am, I thought that perhaps

436 See Ch. xxxix. § 25.
437 Gonzalo de Aranda (*De la Fuente*).
438 Don Francisco de Salcedo (*ibid.*).
439 Ch. xxiii. § 6; Gaspar Daza (*ibid.*).

our Lord wished it to be so, seeing that, without accepting it, we could not succeed; and so I consented to the compromise.

20. The night before the settlement was to be made, I was in prayer,—the discussion of the terms of it had already begun,—when our Lord said to me that I must do nothing of the kind; for if we began with an endowment, they would never allow us to resign it. He said some other things also. The same night, the holy friar, Peter of Alcantara, appeared to me. He was then dead.[440] But he had written to me before his death—for he knew the great opposition and persecution we had to bear—that he was glad the foundation was so much spoken against; it was a sign that our Lord would be exceedingly honored in the monastery, seeing that Satan was so earnest against it; and that I was by no means to consent to an endowment. He urged this upon me twice or thrice in that letter, and said that if I persisted in this everything would succeed according to my wish.

21. At this time I had already seen him twice since his death, and the great glory he was in, and so I was not afraid,—on the contrary, I was very glad; for he always appeared as a glorified body in great happiness, and the vision made me very happy too. I remember that he told me, the first time I saw him, among other things, when speaking of the greatness of his joy, that the penance he had done was a blessed thing for him, in that it had obtained so great a reward. But, as I think I have spoken of this before,[441] I will now say no more than that he showed himself severe on this occasion: he merely said that I was on no account to accept an endowment, and asked why it was I did not take his advice. He then disappeared. I remained in astonishment, and the next day told the nobleman—for I went to him in all my trouble, as to one who did more than others for us in the matter,—what had taken place, and charged him not to consent to the endowment, but to let the lawsuit go on. He was more firm on this point than I was, and was therefore greatly pleased; he told me afterwards how much he disliked the compromise.

22. After this, another personage—a great servant of God, and with good intentions—came forward, who, now that the matter was in good train, advised us to put it in the hands of learned men. This brought on trouble enough; for some of those who helped me agreed to do so; and this plot of Satan was one of the most difficult of all to unravel. Our Lord was my helper throughout. Writing thus briefly, it is impossible for me to explain what took place during the two years that passed between the beginning and the completion of the monastery: the last six months and the first six months were the most painful.

23. When at last the city was somewhat calm, the licentiate father, the Dominican friar[442] who helped us, exerted himself most skillfully on our behalf. Though not here at the time, our Lord brought him here at a most convenient moment for our service, and it seems that His Majesty brought him for that purpose only. He told me afterwards that he had no reasons for coming, and that he heard of our affair as if by chance. He remained here as long as we wanted him, and on going away he prevailed, by some means, on the Father Provincial to permit me to enter this house, and to take with me some of the nuns[443]—such a permission seemed impossible in so short a time for the performance of the Divine Office—and the training of those who were in this house: the day of our coming was a most joyful day for me.[444]

24. While praying in the church, before I went into the house, and being as it were in a trance, I saw Christ; who, as it seemed to me, received me with great affection, placed a crown on my head, and thanked me for what I had done for His Mother. On another occasion, when all of us remained in the choir in prayer after Compline, I saw our Lady in exceeding glory, in a white mantle, with

---

[440] 26. He died Oct. 18, 1562.

[441] Ch. xxvii. § 21.

[442] "El Padre Presentado, Dominico. Presentado en algunas Religiones es cierto titulo de grado que es respeto del Maestro como Licenciado" (*Cobarruvias, in voce* Presente). The father was Fra Pedro Ibañez. See ch. xxxviii. § 15.

[443] From the monastery of the Incarnation. These were Ana of St. John, Ana of All the Angels, Maria Isabel, and Isabel of St. Paul. St. Teresa was a simple nun, living under obedience to the prioress of St. Joseph, Ana of St. John, and intended so to remain. But the nuns applied to the Bishop of Avila and to the Provincial of the Order, who, listening to the complaints of the sisters, compelled the Saint to be their prioress. See *Reforma*, i. c. xlix. § 4.

[444] Mid-Lent of 1563.

which she seemed to cover us all. I understood by that the high degree of glory to which our Lord would raise the religious of this house.

25. When we had begun to sing the Office, the people began to have a great devotion to the monastery; more nuns were received, and our Lord began to stir up those who had been our greatest persecutors to become great benefactors, and give alms to us. In this way they came to approve of what they had condemned; and so, by degrees, they withdrew from the lawsuit, and would say that they now felt it to be a work of God, since His Majesty had been pleased to carry it on in the face of so much opposition. And now there is not one who thinks that it would have been right not to have founded the monastery: so they make a point of furnishing us with alms; for without any asking on our part, without begging of any one, our Lord moves them to, succor us; and so we always have what is necessary for us, and I trust in our Lord it will always be so.[445] As the sisters are few in number, if they do their duty as our Lord at present by His grace enables them to do, I am confident that they will always have it, and that they need not be a burden nor troublesome to anybody; for our Lord will care for them, as He has hitherto done.

26. It is the greatest consolation to me to find myself among those who are so detached. Their occupation is to learn how they may advance in the service of God. Solitude is their delight; and the thought of being visited by any one, even of their nearest kindred, is a trial, unless it helps them to kindle more and more their love of the Bridegroom. Accordingly, none come to this house who do not aim at this; otherwise they neither give nor receive any pleasure from their visits. Their conversation is of God only; and so he whose conversation is different does not understand them, and they do not understand him.

27. We keep the rule of our Lady of Carmel, not the rule of the Mitigation, but as it was settled by Fr. Hugo, Cardinal of Santa Sabina, and given in the year 1248, in the fifth year of the pontificate of Innocent IV., Pope. All the trouble we had to go through, as it seems to me, will have been endured to good purpose.

28. And now, though the rule be somewhat severe,—for we never eat flesh except in cases of necessity, fast eight months in the year, and practice some other austerities besides, according to the primitive rule,[446]—yet the sisters think it light on many points, and so they have other observances, which we have thought necessary for the more perfect keeping of it. And I trust in our Lord that what we have begun will prosper more and more, according to the promise of His Majesty.

29. The other house, which the holy woman of whom I spoke before[447] labored to establish, has been also blessed of our Lord, and is founded in Alcala: it did not escape serious opposition, nor fail to endure many trials. I know that all duties of religion are observed in it, according to our primitive rule. Our Lord grant that all may be to the praise and glory of Himself and of the glorious Virgin Mary, whose habit we wear. Amen.

30. I think you must be wearied, my father, by the tedious history of this monastery; and yet it is most concise, if you compare it with our labors, and the wonders which our Lord has wrought here. There are many who can bear witness to this on oath. I therefore beg of your reverence, for the love of God, should you think fit to destroy the rest of this my writing, to preserve that part of it which relates to this monastery, and give it, when I am dead, to the sisters who may then be living in it. It will encourage them greatly, who shall come here both to serve God and to labor, that what has been thus begun may not fall to decay, but ever grow and thrive, when they see how much our Lord has done through one so mean and vile as I. As our Lord has been so particularly gracious to us in the foundation of this house it seems to me that she will do very wrong, and that she will be

---

[445] See *Way of Perfection*, ch. ii.

[446] "Jejunium singulis diebus, exceptis Dominicis, observetis a Festo Exaltationis Sanctæ Crucis usque ad diem Dominicæ Resurrectionis, nisi infirmitas vel debilitas corporis, aut alia justa causa, jejunium solvi suadeat; quia necessitas non habet legem. Ab esu carnium abstineatis, nisi pro infirmitatis aut debilitatis remedio sint sumantur." That is the tenth section of the rule.

[447] See ch. xxxv. § 1. Maria of Jesus had founded her house in Alcala de Henares; but the austerities practiced in it, and the absence of the religious mitigations which long experience had introduced, were too much for the fervent nuns there assembled. Maria of Jesus begged Doña Leonor de Mascareñas to persuade St. Teresa to come to Alcala. The Saint went to the monastery, and was received there with joy, and even entreated to take the house under her own government (*Reforma*, ii. c. x. §§ 3, 4).

heavily chastised of God, who shall be the first to relax the perfect observance of the rule, which our Lord has here begun and countenanced, so that it may be kept with so much sweetness: it is most evident that the observance of it is easy, and that it can be kept with ease, by the arrangement made for those who long to be alone with their Bridegroom Christ, in order to live for ever in Him.

31. This is to be the perpetual aim of those who are here, to be alone with Him alone. They are not to be more in number than thirteen: I know this number to be the best, for I have had many opinions about it; and I have seen in my own experience, that to preserve our spirit, living on alms, without asking of anyone, a larger number would be inexpedient. May they always believe one who with much labor, and by the prayers of many people, accomplished that which must be for the best! That this is most expedient for us will be seen from the joy and cheerfulness, and the few troubles, we have all had in the years we have lived in this house, as well as from the better health than usual of us all. If any one thinks the rule hard, let her lay the fault on her want of the true spirit, and not on the rule of the house, seeing that delicate persons, and those not saints,—because they have the true spirit,—can bear it all with so much sweetness. Let others go to another monastery, where they may save their souls in the way of their own spirit.

Chapter XXXVII.

The Effects of the Divine Graces in the Soul. The Inestimable Greatness of One Degree of Glory.

1. It is painful to me to recount more of the graces which our Lord gave me than these already spoken of; and they are so many, that nobody can believe they were ever given to one so wicked: but in obedience to our Lord, who has commanded me to do it,[448] and you, my fathers, I will speak of some of them to His glory. May it please His Majesty it may be to the profit of some soul! For if our Lord has been thus gracious to so—miserable a thing as myself, what will He be to those who shall serve Him truly? Let all people resolve to please His Majesty, seeing that He gives such pledges as these even in this life.[449]

2. In the first place, it must be understood that, in those graces which God bestows on the soul, there are diverse degrees of joy: for in some visions the joy and sweetness and comfort of them so far exceed those of others, that I am amazed at the different degrees of fruition even in this life; for it happens that the joy and consolation which God gives in a vision or a trance are so different, that it seems impossible for the soul to be able to desire anything more in this world: and, so, in fact, the soul does not desire, nor would it ask for, a greater joy. Still, since our Lord has made me understand how great a difference there is in heaven itself between the fruition of one and that of another, I see clearly enough that here also, when our Lord wills, He gives not by measure;[450] and so I wish that I myself observed no measure in serving His Majesty, and in using my whole life and strength and health therein; and I would not have any fault of mine rob me of the slightest degree of fruition.

3. And so I say that if I were asked which I preferred, to endure all the trials of the world until the end of it, and then receive one slight degree of glory additional, or without any suffering of any kind to enter into glory of a slightly lower degree, I would accept—oh, how willingly!—all those trials for one slight degree of fruition in the contemplation of the greatness of God; for I know that he who understands Him best, loves Him and praises Him best. I do not mean that I should not be satisfied, and consider myself most blessed, to be in heaven, even if I should be in the lowest place; for as I am one who had that place in hell, it would be a great mercy of our Lord to admit me at all; and may it please His Majesty to bring me thither, and take away His eyes from beholding my grievous sins. What I mean is this,—if it were in my power, even if it cost me everything, and our

---

[448] The Saint, having interrupted her account of her interior life in order to give the history of the foundation of the monastery of St. Joseph, Avila,—the first house of the Reformed Carmelites,—here resumes that account broken off at the end of § 10 of ch. xxxii.

[449] Ephes. i. 14: "Pignus hæreditatis nostræ."

[450] St. John iii. 34: "Non enim ad mensuram dat Deus spiritum."

Lord gave me the grace to endure much affliction, I would not through any fault of mine lose one degree of glory. Ah, wretched that I am, who by so many faults had forfeited all!

4. It is also to be observed that, in every vision or revelation which our Lord in His mercy sent me, a great gain accrued to my soul, and that in some of the visions this gain was very great. The vision of Christ left behind an impression of His exceeding beauty, and it remains with me to this day. One vision alone of Him is enough to effect this; what, then, must all those visions have done, which our Lord in His mercy sent me? One exceedingly great blessing has resulted therefrom, and it is this,—I had one very grievous fault, which was the source of much evil; namely, whenever I found anybody well disposed towards myself, and I liked him, I used to have such an affection for him as compelled me always to remember and think of him, though I had no intention of offending God: however, I was pleased to see him, to think of him and of his good qualities. All this was so hurtful, that it brought my soul to the very verge of destruction.

5. But ever since I saw the great beauty[451] of our Lord, I never saw any one who in comparison with Him seemed even endurable, or that could occupy my thoughts. For if I but turn mine eyes inwardly for a moment to the contemplation of the image which I have within me, I find myself so free, that from that instant everything I see is loathsome in comparison with the excellences and graces of which I had a vision in our Lord. Neither is there any sweetness, nor any kind of pleasure, which I can make any account of, compared with that which comes from hearing but one word from His divine mouth. What, then, must it be when I hear so many? I look upon it as impossible— unless our Lord, for my sins, should permit the loss of this remembrance—that I should have the power to occupy myself with anything in such a way as that I should not instantly recover my liberty by thinking of our Lord.

6. This has happened to me with some of my confessors, for I always have a great affection for those who have the direction of my soul. As I really saw in them only the representatives of God, I thought my will was always there where it is most occupied; and as I felt very safe in the matter, I always showed myself glad to see them.[452] They, on the other hand, servants of God, and fearing Him, were afraid that I was attaching and binding myself too much to them, though in a holy way, and treated me with rudeness. This took place after I had become so ready to obey them; for before that time I had no affection whatever for them. I used to laugh to myself, when I saw how much they were deceived. Though I was not always putting before them how little I was attached to anybody, as clearly as I was convinced of it myself, yet I did assure them of it; and they, in their further relations with me, acknowledged how much I owed to our Lord in the matter. These suspicions of me always arose in the beginning.

7. My love of, and trust in, our Lord, after I had seen Him in a vision, began to grow, for my converse with Him was so continual. I saw that, though He was God, He was man also; that He is not surprised at the frailties of men, that He understands our miserable nature, liable to fall continually, because of the first sin, for the reparation of which He had come. I could speak to Him as to a friend, though He is my Lord, because I do not consider Him as one of our earthly Lords, who affect a power they do not possess, who give audience at fixed hours, and to whom only certain persons may speak. If a poor man have any business with these, it will cost him many goings and comings, and currying favor with others, together with much pain and labor before he can speak to them. Ah, if such a one has business with a king! Poor people, not of gentle blood, cannot approach him, for they must apply to those who are his friends, and certainly these are not persons who tread the world under their feet; for they who do this speak the truth, fear nothing, and ought to fear nothing; they are not courtiers, because it is not the custom of a court, where they must be silent about those things they dislike, must not even dare to think about them, lest they should fall into disgrace.

8. O King of glory, and Lord of all kings! oh, how Thy kingly dignity is not hedged about by trifles of this kind! Thy kingdom is for ever. We do not require chamberlains to introduce us into Thy presence. The very vision of Thy person shows us at once that Thou alone art to be called Lord. Thy Majesty is so manifest that there is no need of a retinue or guard to make us confess that Thou art King. An earthly king without attendants would be hardly acknowledged; and though he might

---

[451] Ch. xxviii. §§ 1-5.
[452] See ch. xl. § 24; *Way of Perfection*, ch. vii. § 1; but ch. iv. of the previous editions.

wish ever so much to be recognized, people will not own him when he appears as others; it is necessary that his dignity should be visible, if people are to believe in it. This is reason enough why kings should affect so much state; for if they had none, no one would respect them; this their semblance of power is not in themselves, and their authority must come to them from others.

9. O my Lord! O my King! who can describe Thy Majesty? It is impossible not to see that Thou art Thyself the great Ruler of all, that the beholding of Thy Majesty fills men with awe. But I am filled with greater awe, O my Lord, when I consider Thy humility, and the love Thou has for such as I am. We can converse and speak with Thee about everything whenever we will; and when we lose our first fear and awe at the vision of Thy Majesty, we have a greater dread of offending Thee,—not arising out of the fear of punishment, O my Lord, for that is as nothing in comparison with the loss of Thee!

10. Thus far of the blessings of this vision, without speaking of others, which abide in the soul when it is past. If it be from God, the fruits thereof show it, when the soul receives light; for, as I have often said,[453] the will of our Lord is that the soul should be in darkness, and not see this light. It is, therefore, nothing to be wondered at that I, knowing myself to be so wicked as I am, should be afraid.

11. It is only just now it happened to me to be for eight days in a state wherein it seemed that I did not, and could not, confess my obligations to God, or remember His mercies; but my soul was so stupefied, and occupied with I know not what nor how: not that I had any bad thoughts; only I was so incapable of good thoughts, that I was laughing at myself, and even rejoicing to see how mean a soul can be if God is not always working in it.[454] The soul sees clearly that God is not away from it in this state, and that it is not in those great tribulations which I have spoken of as being occasionally mine. Though it heaps up fuel, and does the little it can do of itself, it cannot make the fire of the love of God burn: it is a great mercy that even the smoke is visible, showing that it is not altogether quenched. Our Lord will return and kindle it; and until then the soul—though it may lose its breath in blowing and arranging the fuel—seems to be doing nothing but putting it out more and more.

12. I believe that now the best course is to be absolutely resigned, confessing that we can do nothing, and so apply ourselves—as I said before[455]—to something else which is meritorious. Our Lord, it may be, takes away from the soul the power of praying, that it may betake itself to something else, and learn by experience how little it can do in its own strength.

13. It is true I have this day been rejoicing in our Lord, and have dared to complain of His Majesty. I said unto Him: How is it, O my God, that it is not enough for Thee to detain me in this wretched life, and that I should have to bear with it for the love of Thee, and be willing to live where everything hinders the fruition of Thee; where, besides, I must eat and sleep, transact business, and converse with every one, and all for Thy love? how is it, then,—for Thou well knows, O my Lord, all this to be the greatest torment unto me,—that, in the rare moments when I am with Thee, Thou hides Thyself from me? How is this consistent with Thy compassion? How can that love Thou has for me endure this? I believe, O Lord, if it were possible for me to hide myself from Thee, as Thou hides Thyself from me—I think and believe so—such is Thy love, that Thou would not endure it at my hands. But Thou art with me, and see me always. O my Lord, I beseech Thee look to this; it must not be; a wrong is done to one who loves Thee so much.

14. I happened to utter these words, and others of the same kind, when I should have been thinking rather how my place in hell was pleasant in comparison with the place I deserved. But now and then my love makes me foolish, so that I lose my senses; only it is with all the sense I have that I make these complaints, and our Lord bears it all. Blessed be so good a King!

15. Can we be thus bold with the kings of this world? And yet I am not surprised that we dare not thus speak to a king, for it is only reasonable that men should be afraid of him, or even to the great lords who are his representatives. The world is now come to such a state, that men's lives ought to be longer than they are if we are to learn all the new customs and ceremonies of good breeding, and yet spend any time in the service of God. I bless myself at the sight of what is going

---

453 See ch. xx. § 14.
454 See ch. xxx. § 19.
455 See ch. xxx. §§ 18, 25.

on. The fact is, I did not know how I was to live when I came into this house. Any negligence in being much more ceremonious with people than they deserve is not taken as a jest; on the contrary, they look upon it as an insult deliberately offered; so that it becomes necessary for you to satisfy them of your good intentions, if there happens, as I have said, to have been any negligence; and even then, God grant they may believe you.

16. I repeat it,—I certainly did not know how to live; for my poor soul was worn out. It is told to employ all its thoughts always on God, and that it is necessary to do so if it would avoid many dangers. On the other hand, it finds it will not do to fail in any one point of the world's law, under the penalty of affronting those who look upon these things as touching their honor. I was worn out in unceasingly giving satisfaction to people; for, though I tried my utmost, I could not help failing in many ways in matters which, as I have said, are not slightly thought of in the world.

17. Is it true that in religious houses no explanations are necessary, for it is only reasonable we should be excused these observances? Well, that is not so; for there are people who say that monasteries ought to be courts in politeness and instruction. I certainly cannot understand it. I thought that perhaps some saint may have said that they ought to be courts to teach those who wish to be the courtiers of heaven, and that these people misunderstood their meaning; for if a man be careful to please God continually, and to hate the world, as he ought to do, I do not see how he can be equally careful to please those who live in the world in these matters which are continually changing. If they could be learnt once for all, it might be borne with: but as to the way of addressing letters, there ought to be a professor's chair founded, from which lectures should be given, so to speak, teaching us how to do it; for the paper should on one occasion be left blank in one corner, and on another in another corner; and a man must be addressed as the illustrious who was not hitherto addressed as the magnificent.

18. I know not where this will stop: I am not yet fifty, and yet I have seen so many changes during my life, that I do not know how to live. What will they do who are only just born, and who may live many years? Certainly I am sorry for those spiritual people who, for certain holy purposes, are obliged to live in the world; the cross they have to carry is a dreadful one. If they could all agree together, and make themselves ignorant, and be willing to be considered so in these sciences, they would set themselves free from much trouble. But what folly am I about! from speaking of the greatness of God I am come to speak of the meanness of the world! Since our Lord has given me the grace to quit it, I wish to leave it altogether. Let them settle these matters who maintain these follies with so much labor. God grant that in the next life, where there is no changing, we may not have to pay for them! Amen.

Chapter XXXVIII.

Certain Heavenly Secrets, Visions, and Revelations. The Effects of Them in Her Soul.

1. One night I was so unwell that I thought I might be excused making my prayer; so I took my rosary, that I might employ myself in vocal prayer, trying not to be recollected in my understanding, though outwardly I was recollected, being in my oratory. These little precautions are of no use when our Lord will have it otherwise. I remained there but a few moments thus, when I was rapt in spirit with such violence that I could make no resistance whatever. It seemed to me that I was taken up to heaven; and the first persons I saw there were my father and my mother. I saw other things also; but the time was no longer than that in which the *Ave Maria* might be said, and I was amazed at it, looking on it all as too great a grace for me. But as to the shortness of the time, it might have been longer, only it was all done in a very short space.

2. I was afraid it might be an illusion; but as I did not think so, I knew not what to do, because I was very much ashamed to go to my confessor about it. It was not, as it seemed to me, because I was humble, but because I thought he would laugh at me, and say: Oh, what a St. Paul!—she sees the things of heaven; or a St. Jerome. And because these glorious Saints had had such visions, I was so much the more afraid, and did nothing but cry; for I did not think it possible for me to see what they saw. At last, though I felt it exceedingly, I went to my confessor; for I never dared to keep

secret anything of this kind, however much it distressed me to speak of them, owing to the great fear I had of being deceived. When my confessor saw how much I was suffering, he consoled me greatly, and gave me plenty of good reasons why I should have no fear.

3. It happened, also, as time went on, and it happens now from time to time, that our Lord showed me still greater secrets. The soul, even if it would, has neither the means not the power to see more than what He shows it; and so, each time, I saw nothing more than what our Lord was pleased to let me see. But such was the vision, that the least part of it was enough to make my soul amazed, and to raise it so high that it esteems and counts as nothing all the things of this life. I wish I could describe, in some measure, the smallest portion of what I saw; but when I think of doing it, I find it impossible; for the mere difference alone between the light we have here below, and that which is seen in a vision,—both being light,—is so great, that there is no comparison between them; the brightness of the sun itself seems to be something exceedingly loathsome. In a word, the imagination, however strong it may be, can neither conceive nor picture to itself this light, nor any one of the things which our Lord showed me in a joy so supreme that it cannot be described; for then all the senses exult so deeply and so sweetly that no description is possible; and so it is better to say nothing more.

4. I was in this state once for more than an hour, our Lord showing me wonderful things. He seemed as if He would not leave me. He said to me, "See, My daughter, what they lose who are against Me; do not fail to tell them of it." Ah, my Lord, how little good my words will do them, who are made blind by their own conduct, if Thy Majesty will not give them light! Some, to whom Thou has given it, there are, who have profited by the knowledge of Thy greatness; but as they see it revealed to one so wicked and base as I am, I look upon it as a great thing if there should be any found to believe me. Blessed be Thy name, and blessed be Thy compassion; for I can trace, at least in my own soul, a visible improvement. Afterwards I wished I had continued in that trance for ever, and that I had not returned to consciousness, because of an abiding sense of contempt for everything here below; all seemed to be filth; and I see how meanly we employ ourselves who are detained on earth.

5. When I was staying with that lady of whom I have been speaking,[456] it happened to me once when I was suffering from my heart,—for, as I have said,[457] I suffered greatly at one time, though not so much now,—that she, being a person of great charity, brought out her jewels set in gold, and precious stones of great price, and particularly a diamond, which she valued very much. She thought this might amuse me; but I laughed to myself, and was very sorry to see what men made much of; for I thought of what our Lord had laid up for us, and considered how impossible it was for me, even if I made the effort, to have any appreciation whatever of such things, provided our Lord did not permit me to forget what He was keeping for us.

6. A soul in this state attains to a certain freedom, which is so complete that none can understand it who does not possess it. It is a real and true detachment, independent of our efforts; God effects it all Himself; for His Majesty reveals the truth in such a way, that it remains so deeply impressed on our souls as to make it clear that we of ourselves could not thus acquire it in so short a time.

7. The fear of death, also, was now very slight in me, who had always been in great dread of it; now it seems to me that death is a very light thing for one who serves God, because the soul is in a moment delivered thereby out of its prison, and at rest. This elevation of the spirit, and the vision of things so high, in these trances seem to me to have a great likeness to the flight of the soul from the body, in that it finds itself in a moment in the possession of these good things. We put aside the agonies of its dissolution, of which no great account is to be made; for they who love God in truth, and are utterly detached from the things of this life, must die with the greater sweetness.

8. It seems to me, also, that the rapture was a great help to recognize our true home, and to see that we are pilgrims here;[458] it is a great thing to see what is going on there and to know where we have to live; for if a person has to go and settle in another country, it is a great help to him, in undergoing the fatigues of his journey, that he has discovered it to be a country where he may live

---

[456] Ch. xxxiv. Doña Luisa de la Cerda, at Toledo.

[457] Ch. iv. § 6.

[458] 1 St. Peter ii. 11: "Advenas et peregrinos."

in the most perfect peace. Moreover, it makes it easy for us to think of the things of heaven, and to have our conversation there.[459] It is a great gain, because the mere looking up to heaven makes the soul recollected; for as our Lord has been pleased to reveal heaven in some degree, my soul dwells upon it in thought; and it happens occasionally that they who are about me, and with whom I find consolation, are those whom I know to be living in heaven, and that I look upon them only as really alive; while those who are on earth are so dead, that the whole world seems unable to furnish me with companions, particularly when these impetuosities of love are upon me. Everything seems a dream, and what I see with the bodily eyes an illusion. What I have seen with the eyes of the soul is that which my soul desires; and as it finds itself far away from those things, that is death.

9. In a word, it is a very great mercy which our Lord gives to that soul to which He grants the like visions, for they help it in much, and also in carrying a heavy cross, since nothing satisfies it, and everything is against it; and if our Lord did not now and then suffer these visions to be forgotten, though they recur again and again to the memory, I know not how life could be borne. May He be blessed and praised for ever and ever! I implore His Majesty by that Blood which His Son shed for me, now that, of His good pleasure, I know something of these great blessings, and begin to have the fruition of them, that it may not be with me as it was with Lucifer, who by his own fault forfeited it all. I beseech Thee, for Thine own sake, not to suffer this; for I am at times in great fear, though at others, and most frequently, the mercy of God reassures me, for He who has delivered me from so many sins will not withdraw His hand from under me, and let me be lost. I pray you, my father, to beg this grace for me always.

10. The mercies, then, hitherto described, are not, in my opinion, so great as those which I am now going to speak of, on many accounts, because of the great blessings they have brought with them, and because of the great fortitude which my soul derived from them; and yet every one separately considered is so great, that there is nothing to be compared with them.

11. One day—it was the eve of Pentecost—I went after Mass to a very lonely spot, where I used to pray very often, and began to read about the feast in the book of a Carthusian;[460] and reading of the marks by which beginners, proficients, and the perfect may know that they have the Holy Ghost, it seemed to me, when I had read of these three states, that by the goodness of God, so far as I could understand, the Holy Ghost was with me. I praised God for it; and calling to mind how on another occasion, when I read this, I was very deficient,—for I saw most distinctly at that time how deficient I was then from what I saw I was now,—I recognized herein the great mercy of our Lord to me, and so began to consider the place which my sins had earned for me in hell, and praised God exceedingly, because it seemed as if I did not know my own soul again, so great a change had come over it.

12. While thinking of these things, my soul was carried away with extreme violence, and I knew not why. It seemed as if it would have gone forth out of the body, for it could not contain itself, nor was it able to hope for so great a good. The impetuosity was so excessive that I had no power left, and, as I think, different from what I had been used to. I knew not what ailed my soul, nor what it desired, for it was so changed. I leaned for support, for I could not sit, because my natural strength had utterly failed.

13. Then I saw over my head a dove, very different from those we usually see, for it had not the same plumage, but wings formed of small shells shining brightly. It was larger than an ordinary dove; I thought I heard the rustling of its wings. It hovered above me during the space of an *Ave Maria*. But such was the state of my soul, that in losing itself it lost also the sight of the dove. My spirit grew calm with such a guest; and yet, as I think, a grace so wonderful might have disturbed and frightened it; and as it began to rejoice in the vision, it was delivered from all fear, and with the joy came peace, my soul continuing entranced. The joy of this rapture was exceedingly great; and for the rest of that festal time I was so amazed and bewildered that I did not know what I was doing, nor how I could have received so great a grace. I neither heard nor saw anything, so to speak, because of my great inward joy. From that day forth I perceived in myself a very great progress in the highest love of God, together with a great increase in the strength of my virtues. May He be blessed and praised for ever! Amen.

---

[459] Philipp. iii. 20: "Nostra autem conversatio in coelis est."
[460] The *Life of Christ*, by Ludolf of Saxony.

14. On another occasion I saw that very dove above the head of one of the Dominican fathers; but it seemed to me that the rays and brightness of the wings were far greater. I understood by this that he was to draw souls unto God.

15. At another time I saw our Lady putting a cope of exceeding whiteness on that Licentiate of the same Order, of whom I have made mention more than once.[461] She told me that she gave him that cope in consideration of the service he had rendered her by helping to found this house,[462] that it was a sign that she would preserve his soul pure for the future, and that he should not fall into mortal sin. I hold it for certain that so it came to pass, for he died within a few years; his death and the rest of his life were so penitential, his whole life and death so holy, that, so far as anything can be known, there cannot be a doubt on the subject. One of the friars present at his death told me that, before he breathed his last, he said to him that St. Thomas was with him.[463] He died in great joy, longing to depart out of this land of exile.

16. Since then he has appeared to me more than once in exceedingly great glory, and told me certain things. He was so given to prayer, that when he was dying, and would have interrupted it if he could because of his great weakness, he was not able to do so; for he was often in a trance. He wrote to me not long before he died, and asked me what he was to do; for as soon as he had said Mass he fell into a trance which lasted a long time, and which he could not hinder. At last God gave him the reward of the many services of his whole life.

17. I had certain visions, too, of the great graces which our Lord bestowed upon that rector of the Society of Jesus, of whom I have spoken already more than once;[464] but I will not say anything of them now, lest I should be too tedious. It was his lot once to be in great trouble, to suffer great persecution and distress. One day, when I was hearing Mass, I saw Christ on the Cross at the elevation of the Host. He spoke certain words to me, which I was to repeat to that father for his comfort, together with others, which were to warn him beforehand of what was coming, and to remind him of what He had suffered on his behalf, and that he must prepare for suffering. This gave him great consolation and courage; and everything came to pass afterwards as our Lord had told me.

18. I have seen great things of members of the Order to which this father belongs, which is the Society of Jesus, and of the whole Order itself; I have occasionally seen them in heaven with white banners in their hands, and I have had other most wonderful visions, as I am saying, about them, and therefore have a great veneration for this Order; for I have had a great deal to do with those who are of it, and I see that their lives are conformed to that which our Lord gave me to understand about them.

19. One night, when I was in prayer, our Lord spoke to me certain words, whereby He made me remember the great wickedness of my past life. They filled me with shame and distress; for though they were not spoken with severity, they caused a feeling and a painfulness which were too much for me: and we feel that we make greater progress in the knowledge of ourselves when we hear one of these words, than we can make by a meditation of many days on our own misery, because these words impress the truth upon us at the same time in such a way that we cannot resist it. He set before me the former inclinations of my will to vanities, and told me to make much of the desire I now had that my will, which had been so ill employed, should be fixed on Him, and that He would accept it.

20. On other occasions He told me to remember how I used to think it an honorable thing to go against His honor; and, again, to remember my debt to Him, for when I was most rebellious He was bestowing His graces upon me. If I am doing anything wrong—and my wrong-doings are many—His Majesty makes me see it in such a way that I am utterly confounded; and as I do so

---

[461] F. Pedro Ibañez. See ch. xxxiii. § 5, ch. xxxvi. § 23. "This father died Prior of Trianos," is written on the margin of the MS. by F. Bañes (*De la Fuente*).

[462] St. Joseph, Avila, where St. Teresa was living at this time.

[463] See below, § 41.

[464] F. Gaspar de Salazar: see ch. xxxiii. § 9, ch. xxxiv. § 2. It appears from the 179th letter of the Saint (lett. 20, vol. i. of the Doblado edition) that F. Salazar was reported to his Provincial, F. Juan Suarez, as having desire to quit the Society for the Carmelite Order.

often, that happens often also. I have been found fault with by my confessors occasionally; and on betaking myself to prayer for consolation, have received a real reprimand.

21. To return to what I was speaking of. When our Lord made me remember my wicked life, I wept; for as I considered that I had then never done any good, I thought He might be about to bestow upon me some special grace; because most frequently, when I receive any particular mercy from our Lord, it is when I have been previously greatly humiliated, in order that I may the more clearly see how far I am from deserving it. I think our Lord must do it for that end.

22. Almost immediately after this I was so raised up in spirit that I thought myself to be, as it were, out of the body; at least, I did not know that I was living in it.[465] I had a vision of the most Sacred Humanity in exceeding glory, greater than I had ever seen It in before. I beheld It in a wonderful and clear way in the bosom of the Father. I cannot tell how it was, for I saw myself, without seeing, as it seemed to me, in the presence of God. My amazement was such that I remained, as I believe, some days before I could recover myself. I had continually before me, as present, the Majesty of the Son of God, though not so distinctly as in the vision. I understood this well enough; but the vision remained so impressed on my imagination, that I could not get rid of it for some time, though it had lasted but a moment; it is a great comfort to me, and also a great blessing.

23. I have had this vision on three other occasions, and it is, I think, the highest vision of all the visions which our Lord in His mercy showed me. The fruits of it are the very greatest, for it seems to purify the soul in a wonderful way, and destroy, as it were utterly, altogether the strength of our sensual nature. It is a grand flame of fire, which seems to burn up and annihilate all the desires of this life. For though now—glory be to God!—I had no desire after vanities, I saw clearly in the vision how all things are vanity, and how hollow are all the dignities of earth; it was a great lesson, teaching me to raise up my desires to the Truth alone. It impresses on the soul a sense of the presence of God such as I cannot in any way describe, only it is very different from that which it is in our own power to acquire on earth. It fills the soul with profound astonishment at its own daring, and at any one else being able to dare to offend His most awful Majesty.

24. I must have spoken now and then of the effects of visions,[466] and of other matters of the same kind, and I have already said that the blessings they bring with them are of various degrees; but those of this vision are the highest of all. When I went to Communion once I called to mind the exceeding great majesty of Him I had seen, and considered that it was He who is present in the most Holy Sacrament, and very often our Lord was pleased to show Himself to me in the Host; the very hairs on my head stood,[467] and I thought I should come to nothing.

25. O my Lord! ah, if Thou did not throw a veil over Thy greatness, who would dare, being so foul and miserable, to come in contact with Thy great Majesty? Blessed be Thou, O Lord; may the angels and all creation praise Thee, who orders all things according to the measure of our weakness, so that, when we have the fruition of Thy sovereign mercies, Thy great power may not terrify us, so that we dare not, being a frail and miserable race, persevere in that fruition!

26. It might happen to us as it did to the laborer—I know it to be a certain fact—who found a treasure beyond his expectations, which were mean. When he saw himself in possession of it, he was seized with melancholy, which by degrees brought him to his grave through simple distress and anxiety of mind, because he did not know what to do with his treasure. If he had not found it all at once, and if others had given him portions of it by degrees, maintaining him thereby, he might have been more happy than he had been in his poverty, nor would it have cost him his life.

27. O Thou Treasure of the poor! how marvelously Thou sustains souls, showing to them, not all at once, but by little and little, the abundance of Thy riches! When I behold Thy great Majesty hidden beneath that which is so slight as the Host is, I am filled with wonder, ever since that vision, at Thy great wisdom; and I know not how it is that our Lord gives me the strength and courage necessary to draw near to him, were it not that He who has had such compassion on me, and still has, gives me strength, nor would it be possible for me to be silent, or refrain from making known marvels so great.

---

[465] 2 Cor. xii. 2: "Sive in corpore nescio, sive extra corpus nescio."
[466] See ch. xxviii.
[467] Job iv. 15: "Inhorruerunt pili carnis meæ."

28. What must be the thoughts of a wretched person such as I am, full of abominations, and who has spent her life with so little fear of God, when she draws near to our Lord's great Majesty, at the moment He is pleased to show Himself to my soul? How can I open my mouth, that has uttered so many words against Him, to receive that most glorious Body, purity and compassion itself? The love that is visible in His most beautiful Face, sweet and tender, pains and distresses the soul, because it has not served Him, more than all the terrors of His Majesty. What should have been my thoughts, then, on those two occasions when I saw what I have described? Truly, O my Lord and my joy, I am going to say that in some way, in these great afflictions of my soul, I have done something in Thy service. Ah! I know not what I am saying, for I am writing this as if the words were not mine,[468] because I am troubled, and in some measure beside myself, when I call these things to remembrance. If these thoughts were really mine, I might well say that I had done something for Thee, O my Lord; but as I can have no good thought if Thou gives it not, no thanks are due to me; I am the debtor, O Lord, and it is Thou who art the offended One.

29. Once, when I was going to Communion, I saw with the eyes of the soul, more distinctly than with those of the body, two devils of most hideous shape; their horns seemed to encompass the throat of the poor priest; and I beheld my Lord, in that great majesty of which I have spoken,[469] held in the hands of that priest, in the Host he was about to give me. It was plain that those hands were those of a sinner, and I felt that the soul of that priest was in mortal sin. What must it be, O my Lord, to look upon Thy beauty amid shapes so hideous! The two devils were so frightened and cowed in Thy presence, that they seemed as if they would have willingly run away, has Thou but given them leave. So troubled was I by the vision, that I knew not how I could go to Communion. I was also in great fear, for I thought, if the vision was from God, that His Majesty would not have allowed me to see the evil state of that soul.[470]

30. Our Lord Himself told me to pray for that priest; that He had allowed this in order that I might understand the power of the words of consecration, and how God failed not to be present, however wicked the priest might be who uttered them; and that I might see His great goodness in that He left Himself in the very hands of His enemy, for my good and for the good of all. I understood clearly how the priests are under greater obligations to be holy than other persons; and what a horrible thing it is to receive this most Holy Sacrament unworthily, and how great is the devil's dominion over a soul in mortal sin. It did me a great service, and made me fully understand what I owe to God. May He be blessed for evermore!

31. At another time I had a vision of a different kind, which frightened me very much. I was in a place where a certain person died, who as I understood had led a very bad life, and that for many years. But he had been ill for two years, and in some respects seemed to have reformed. He died without confession; nevertheless, I did not think he would be damned. When the body had been wrapped in the winding-sheet, I saw it laid hold of by a multitude of devils, who seemed to toss it to and fro, and also to treat it with great cruelty. I was terrified at the sight, for they dragged it about with great hooks. But when I saw it carried to the grave with all the respect and ceremoniousness common to all, I began to think of the goodness of God, who would not allow that person to be dishonored, but would have the fact of his being His enemy concealed.

32. I was almost out of my senses at the sight. During the whole of the funeral service, I did not see one of the evil spirits. Afterwards, when the body was about to be laid in the grave, so great a multitude of them was therein waiting to receive it, that I was beside myself at the sight, and it required no slight courage on my part not to betray my distress. I thought of the treatment which that soul would receive, when the devils had such power over the wretched body. Would to God that all who live in mortal sin might see what I then saw,—it was a fearful sight; it would go, I believe, a great way towards making them lead better lives.

33. All this made me know more of what I owe to God, and of the evils from which He has delivered me. I was in great terror. I spoke of it to my confessor, and I thought it might be an illusion of Satan, in order to take away my good opinion of that person, who yet was not accounted a very

---

[468] The biographers of the Saint say that she often found, on returning from an ecstasy, certain passages written, but not by herself; this seems to be alluded to here (*De la Fuente*).

[469] § 22.

[470] St. John of the Cross, *Ascent of Mount Carmel*, bk. ii. ch. xxvi. vol. i. p. 183.

good Christian. The truth is, that, whether it was an illusion or not, it makes me afraid whenever I think of it.

34. Now that I have begun to speak of the visions I had concerning the dead, I will mention some matters which our Lord was pleased to reveal to me in relation to certain souls. I will confine myself to a few for the sake of brevity, and because they are not necessary; I mean that they are not for our profit. They told me that one who had been our Provincial—he was then of another province—was dead. He was a man of great virtue, with whom I had had a great deal to do, and to whom I was under many obligations for certain kindnesses shown me. When I heard that he was dead, I was exceedingly troubled, because I trembled for his salvation, seeing that he had been superior for twenty years. That is what I dread very much; for the cure of souls seems to me to be full of danger. I went to an oratory in great distress, and gave up to him all the good I had ever done in my whole life,—it was little enough,—and prayed our Lord that His merits might fill up what was wanting, in order that this soul might be delivered up from purgatory.

35. While I was thus praying to our Lord as well as I could, he seemed to me to rise up from the depths of the earth on my right hand, and I saw him ascend to heaven in exceeding great joy. He was a very old man then, but I saw him as if he were only thirty years old, and I thought even younger, and there was a brightness in his face. This vision passed away very quickly; but I was so exceedingly comforted by it, that I could never again mourn his death, although many persons were distressed at it, for he was very much beloved. So greatly comforted was my soul, that nothing disturbed it, neither could I doubt the truth of the vision; I mean that it was no illusion.

36. I had this vision about a fortnight after he was dead; nevertheless, I did not omit to obtain prayers for him and I prayed myself, only I could not pray with the same earnestness that I should have done if I had not seen that vision. For when our Lord showed him thus to me, it seemed to me afterwards, when I prayed for him to His Majesty,—and I could not help it,—that I was like one who gave alms to a rich man. Later on I heard an account of the death he died in our Lord—he was far away from here; it was one of such great edification, that he left all wondering to see how recollected, how penitent, and how humble he was when he died.

37. A nun, who was a great servant of God, died in this house. On the next day one of the sisters was reciting the lesson in the Office of the Dead, which was said in choir for that nun's soul, and I was standing myself to assist her in singing the versicle, when, in the middle of the lesson, I saw the departed nun as I believe, in a vision; her soul seemed to rise on my right hand like the soul of the Provincial, and ascend to heaven. This vision was not imaginary, like the preceding, but like those others of which I have spoken before;[471] it is not less certain, however, than the other visions I had.

38. Another nun died in this same house of mine, she was about eighteen or twenty years of age, and had always been sickly. She was a great servant of God, attentive in choir, and a person of great virtue. I certainly thought that she would not go to purgatory, on account of her exceeding merits, because the infirmities under which she had labored were many. While I was saying the Office, before she was buried,—she had been dead about four hours,—I saw her rise in the same place and ascend to heaven.

39. I was once in one of the colleges of the Society of Jesus, and in one of those great sufferings which, as I have said,[472] I occasionally had, and still have, both in soul and body, and then so grievously that I was not able, as it seemed to me, to have even one good thought. The night before, one of the brothers of that house had died in it; and I, as well as I could, was commending his soul to God, and hearing the Mass which another father of that Society was saying for him when I became recollected at once, and saw him go up to heaven in great glory, and our Lord with him. I understood that His Majesty went with him by way of special grace.

40. Another brother of our Order, a good friar, was very ill; and when I was at Mass, I became recollected and saw him dead, entering into heaven without going through purgatory. He died, as I afterwards learned, at the very time of my vision. I was amazed that he had not gone to purgatory. I understood that, having become a friar and carefully kept the rule, the Bulls of the Order had been of use to him, so that he did not pass into purgatory. I do not know why I came to have this revealed

---

471 See ch. xxvii.
472 Ch. xxx. § 9.

to me; I think it must be because I was to learn that it is not enough for a man to be a friar in his habit—I mean, to wear the habit—to attain to that state of high perfection which that of a friar is.

41. I will speak no more of these things, because as I have just said,[473] there is no necessity for it, though our Lord has been so gracious to me as to show me much. But in all the visions I had, I saw no souls escape purgatory except this Carmelite father, the holy friar Peter of Alcantara, and that Dominican father of whom I spoke before.[474] It pleased our Lord to let me see the degree of glory to which some souls have been raised, showing them to me in the places they occupy. There is a great difference between one place and another.

Chapter XXXIX.

Other Graces Bestowed on the Saint. The Promises of Our Lord to Her. Divine Locutions and Visions.

1. I was once importuning our Lord exceedingly to restore the sight of a person who had claims upon me, and who was almost wholly blind. I was very sorry for him, and afraid our Lord would not hear me because of my sins. He appeared to me as at other times, and began to show the wound in His left hand; with the other He drew out the great nail that was in it, and it seemed to me that, in drawing the nail, He tore the flesh. The greatness of the pain was manifest, and I was very much distressed thereat. He said to me, that He who had borne that for my sake would still more readily grant what I asked Him, and that I was not to have any doubts about it. He promised me there was nothing I should ask that He would not grant; that He knew I should ask nothing that was not for His glory, and that He would grant me what I was now praying for. Even during the time when I did not serve Him, I should find, if I considered it, I had asked nothing that He had not granted in an ampler manner than I had known how to ask; how much more amply still would He grant what I asked for, now that He knew I loved Him! I was not to doubt. I do not think that eight days passed before our Lord restored that person to sight. My confessor knew it forthwith. It might be that it was not owing to my prayer; but, as I had had the vision, I have a certain conviction that it was a grace accorded to me. I gave thanks to His Majesty.

2. Again, a person was exceedingly ill of a most painful disease; but, as I do not know what it was, I do not describe it by its name here. What he had gone through for two months was beyond all endurance; and his pain was so great that he tore his own flesh. My confessor, the rector of whom I have spoken,[475] went to see him; he was very sorry for him, and told me that I must anyhow go myself and visit him; he was one whom I might visit, for he was my kinsman. I went, and was moved to such a tender compassion for him that I began, with the utmost importunity, to ask our Lord to restore him to health. Herein I saw clearly how gracious our Lord was to me, so far as I could judge; for immediately, the next day, he was completely rid of that pain.

3. I was once in the deepest distress, because I knew that a person to whom I was under great obligations was about to commit an act highly offensive to God and dishonorable to himself. He was determined upon it. I was so much harassed by this that I did not know what to do in order to change his purpose; and it seemed to me as if nothing could be done. I implored God, from the bottom of my heart, to find a way to hinder it; but till I found it I could find no relief for the pain I felt. In my distress, I went to a very lonely hermitage,—one of those belonging to this monastery,—in which there is a picture of Christ bound to the pillar; and there, as I was imploring our Lord to grant me this grace, I heard a voice of exceeding gentleness, speaking, as it were, in a whisper.[476] My whole body trembled, for it made me afraid. I wished to understand what was said, but I could not, for it all passed away in a moment.

4. When my fears had subsided, and that was immediately, I became conscious of an inward calmness, a joy and delight, which made me marvel how the mere hearing a voice,—I heard it with

---

[473] § 34.
[474] § 15. Fr. Pedro Ibañez.
[475] Ch. xxxiii. § 10. F. Gaspar de Salazar.
[476] 3 Kings xix. 12: "Sibilus auræ tenuis."

my bodily ears,—without understanding a word, could have such an effect on the soul. I saw by this that my prayer was granted; and so it was; and I was freed from my anxieties about a matter not yet accomplished, as it afterwards was, as completely as if I saw it done. I told my confessors of it, for I had two at this time, both of them learned men, and great servants of God.

5. I knew of a person who had resolved to serve God in all earnestness, and had for some days given himself to prayer, in which he had received many graces from our Lord, but who had abandoned his good resolutions because of certain occasions of sin in which he was involved, and which he would not avoid; they were extremely perilous. This caused me the utmost distress, because the person was one for whom I had a great affection, and one to whom I owed much. For more than a month I believe I did nothing else but pray to God for his conversion. One day, when I was in prayer, I saw a devil close by in a great rage, tearing to pieces some paper which he had in his hands. That sight consoled me greatly, because it seemed that my prayer had been heard. So it was, as I learnt afterwards; for that person had made his confession with great contrition, and returned to God so sincerely, that I trust in His Majesty he will always advance further and further. May He be blessed for ever! Amen.

6. In answer to my prayers, our Lord has very often rescued souls from mortal sins and led others on to greater perfection. But as to the delivering of souls out of purgatory, and other remarkable acts, so many are the mercies of our Lord herein, that were I to speak of them I should only weary myself and my reader. But He has done more by me for the salvation of souls than for the health of the body. This is very well known, and there are many to bear witness to it.

7. At first it made me scrupulous, because I could not help thinking that our Lord did these things in answer to my prayer; I say nothing of the chief reason of all—His pure compassion. But now these graces are so many, and so well known to others, that it gives me no pain to think so. I bless His Majesty, and abase myself, because I am still more deeply in His debt; and I believe that He makes my desire to serve Him grow, and my love revive.

8. But what amazes me most is this: however much I may wish to pray for those graces which our Lord sees not to be expedient, I cannot do it; and if I try, I do so with little earnestness, force, and spirit: it is impossible to do more, even if I would. But it is not so as to those which His Majesty intends to grant. These I can pray for constantly, and with great importunity; though I do not carry them in my memory, they seem to present themselves to me at once.[477]

9. There is a great difference between these two ways of praying, and I know not how to explain it. As to the first, when I pray for those graces which our Lord does not mean to grant,—even though they concern me very nearly,—I am like one whose tongue is tied; who, though he would speak, yet cannot; or, if he speaks, sees that people do not listen to him. And yet I do not fail to force myself to pray, though not conscious of that fervor which I have when praying for those graces which our Lord intends to give. In the second case, I am like one who speaks clearly and intelligibly to another, whom he sees to be a willing listener.

10. The prayer that is not to be heard is, so to speak, like vocal prayer; the other is a prayer of contemplation so high that our Lord shows Himself in such a way as to make us feel He hears us, and that He delights in our prayer, and that He is about to grant our petition. Blessed be He for ever who gives me so much and to whom I give so little! For what is he worth, O my Lord, who does not utterly abase himself to nothing for Thee? How much, how much, how much,—I might say so a thousand times,—I fall short of this! It is on this account that I do not wish to live,—though there be other reasons also,—because I do not live according to the obligations which bind me to Thee. What imperfections I trace in myself! what remissness in Thy service! Certainly, I could wish occasionally I had no sense, that I might be unconscious of the great evil that is in me. May He who can do all things help me!

11. When I was staying in the house of that lady of whom I have spoken before,[478] it was necessary for me to be very watchful over myself, and keep continually in mind the intrinsic vanity of all the things of this life, because of the great esteem I was held in, and of the praises bestowed on me. There was much there to which I might have become attached, if I had looked only to myself; but I looked to Him who sees things as they really are, not to let me go out of His hand. Now that I

---

[477] See St. John of the Cross, *Ascent of Mount Carmel*, bk. iii. ch. i, p. 210).

[478] Ch. xxxiv. § 1.

speak of seeing things as they really are, I remember how great a trial it is for those to whom God has granted a true insight into the things of earth to have to discuss them with others. They wear so many disguises, as our Lord once told me,—and much of what I am saying of them is not from myself, but rather what my Heavenly Master has taught me; and therefore, in speaking of them, when I say distinctly I understood this, or our Lord told me this, I am very scrupulous neither to add nor to take away one single syllable; so, when I do not clearly remember everything exactly, that must be taken as coming from myself, and some things, perhaps, are so altogether. I do not call mine that which is good, for I know there is no other good in me but only that which our Lord gave me when I was so far from deserving it: I call that mine which I speak without having had it made known to me by revelation.

12. But, O my God, how is it that we too often judge even spiritual things, as we do those of the world, by our own understanding, wresting them grievously from their true meaning? We think we may measure our progress by the years which we have given to the exercise of prayer; we even think we can prescribe limits to Him who bestows His gifts not by measure[479] when He wills, and who in six months can give to one more than to another in many years. This is a fact which I have so frequently observed in many persons, that I am surprised how any of us can deny it.

13. I am certainly convinced that he will not remain under this delusion who possesses the gift of discerning spirits, and to whom our Lord has given real humility; for such a one will judge of them by the fruits, by the good resolutions and love,—and our Lord gives him light to understand the matter; and herein He regards the progress and advancement of souls, not the years they may have spent in prayer; for one person may make greater progress in six months than another in twenty years, because, as I said before, our Lord gives to whom He will, particularly to him who is best disposed.

14. I see this in certain persons of tender years who have come to this monastery,—God touches their hearts, and gives them a little light and love. I speak of that brief interval in which He gives them sweetness in prayer, and then they wait for nothing further, and make light of every difficulty, forgetting the necessity even of food; for they shut themselves up for ever in a house that is unendowed, as persons who make no account of their life, for His sake, who, they know, loves them. They give up everything, even their own will; and it never enters into their mind that they might be discontented in so small a house, and where enclosure is so strictly observed. They offer themselves wholly in sacrifice to God.

15. Oh, how willingly do I admit that they are better than I am! and how I ought to be ashamed of myself before God! What His Majesty has not been able to accomplish in me in so many years,—it is long ago since I began to pray, and He to bestow His graces upon me,—He accomplished in them in three months, and in some of them even in three days, though he gives them much fewer graces than He gave to me: and yet His Majesty rewards them well; most assuredly they are not sorry for what they have done for Him.

16. I wish, therefore, we reminded ourselves of those long years which have gone by since we made our religious profession. I say this to those persons, also, who have given themselves long ago to prayer, but not for the purpose of distressing those who in a short time have made greater progress than we have made, by making them retrace their steps, so that they may proceed only as we do ourselves. We must not desire those who, because of the graces God has given them, are flying like eagles, to become like chickens whose feet are tied. Let us rather look to His Majesty, and give these souls the reins, if we see that they are humble; for our Lord, who has had such compassion upon them, will not let them fall into the abyss.

17. These souls trust themselves in the hands of God, for the truth, which they learn by faith, helps them to do it; and shall not we also trust them to Him, without seeking to measure them by our measure which is that of our meanness of spirit? We must not do it; for if we cannot ascend to the heights of their great love and courage,—without experience none can comprehend them—let us humble ourselves, and not condemn them; for, by this seeming regard to their progress, we hinder our own, and miss the opportunity our Lord gives us to humble ourselves, to ascertain our own shortcomings, and learn how much more detached and more near to God these souls must be than we are, seeing that His Majesty draws so near to them Himself.

---

[479] St. John iii. 34: "Non enim ad mensuram dat Deus spiritum."

18. I have no other intention here, and I wish to have no other, than to express my preference for the prayer that in a short time results in these great effects, which show themselves at once; for it is impossible they should enable us to leave all things only to please God, if they were not accompanied with a vehement love. I would rather have that prayer than that which lasted many years, but which at the end of the time, as well as at the beginning, never issued in a resolution to do anything for God, with the exception of some trifling services, like a grain of salt, without weight or bulk, and which a bird might carry away in its mouth. Is it not a serious and mortifying thought that we are making much of certain services which we render our Lord, but which are too pitiable to be considered, even if they were many in number? This is my case, and I am forgetting every moment the mercies of our Lord. I do not mean that His Majesty will not make much of them Himself, for He is good; but I wish I made no account of them myself, or even perceived that I did them, for they are nothing worth.

19. But, O my Lord, do Thou forgive me, and blame me not, if I try to console myself a little with the little I do, seeing that I do not serve Thee at all; for if I rendered Thee any great services, I should not think of these trifles. Blessed are they who serve Thee in great deeds; if envying these, and desiring to do what they do, were of any help to me, I should not be so far behind them as I am in pleasing Thee; but I am nothing worth, O my Lord; do Thou make me of some worth, Thou who loves me so much.

20. During one of those days, when this monastery, which seems to have cost me some labor, was fully founded by the arrival of the Brief from Rome, which empowered us to live without an endowment;[480] and I was comforting myself at seeing the whole affair concluded, and thinking of all the trouble I had had, and giving thanks to our Lord for having been pleased to make some use of me,—it happened that I began to consider all that we had gone through. Well, so it was; in every one of my actions, which I thought were of some service, I traced so many faults and imperfections, now and then but little courage, very frequently a want of faith; for until this moment, when I see everything accomplished, I never absolutely believed; neither, however, on the other hand, could I doubt what our Lord said to me about the foundation of this house. I cannot tell how it was; very often the matter seemed to me, on the one hand, impossible; and, on the other hand, I could not be in doubt; I mean, I could not believe that it would not be accomplished. In short, I find that our Lord Himself, on His part, did all the good that was done, while I did all the evil. I therefore ceased to think of the matter, and wished never to be reminded of it again, lest I should do myself some harm by dwelling on my many faults. Blessed be He who, when He pleases, draws good out of all my failings! Amen.

21. I say, then, there is danger in counting the years we have given to prayer; for, granting that there is nothing in it against humility, it seems to me to imply something like an appearance of thinking that we have merited, in some degree, by the service rendered. I do not mean that there is no merit in it at all, nor that it will not be well rewarded; yet if any spiritual person thinks, because he has given himself to prayer for many years, that he deserves any spiritual consolations, I am sure he will never attain to spiritual perfection. Is it not enough that a man has merited the protection of God, which keeps him from committing those sins into which he fell before he began to pray, but he must also, as they say, sue God for His own money?

22. This does not seem to me to be deep humility, and yet it may be that it is; however, I look on it as great boldness, for I, who have very little humility, have never ventured upon it. It may be that I never asked for it, because I had never served Him; perhaps, if I had served Him, I should have been more importunate than all others with our Lord for my reward.

23. I do not mean that the soul makes no progress in time, or that God will not reward it, if its prayer has been humble; but I do mean that we should forget the number of years we have been praying, because all that we can do is utterly worthless in comparison with one drop of blood out of those which our Lord shed for us. And if the more we serve Him, the more we become His debtors, what is it, then, we are asking for? for, if we pay one farthing of the debt, He gives us back a thousand ducats. For the love of God, let us leave these questions alone, for they belong to Him. Comparisons are always bad, even in earthly things; what, then, must they be in that, the knowledge

---

[480] See ch. xxxiii. § 15.

of which God has reserved to Himself? His Majesty showed this clearly enough, when those who came late and those who came early to His vineyard received the same wages.[481]

24. I have sat down so often to write, and have been so many days writing these three leaves,—for, as I have said,[482] I had, and have still, but few opportunities,—that I forgot what I had begun with, namely, the following vision.[483]

25. I was in prayer, and saw myself on a wide plain all alone. Round about me stood a great multitude of all kinds of people, who hemmed me in on every side; all of them seemed to have weapons of war in their hands, to hurt me; some had spears, others swords; some had daggers, and others very long rapiers. In short, I could not move away in any direction without exposing myself to the hazard of death, and I was alone, without any one to take my part. In this my distress of mind, not knowing what to do, I lifted up my eyes to heaven, and saw Christ, not in heaven, but high above me in the air, holding out His hand to me, and there protecting me in such a way that I was no longer afraid of all that multitude, neither could they, though they wished it, do me any harm.

26. At first the vision seemed to have no results; but it has been of the greatest help to me, since I understood what it meant. Not long afterwards, I saw myself, as it were, exposed to the like assault, and I saw that the vision represented the world, because everything in it takes up arms against the poor soul. We need not speak of those who are not great servants of our Lord, nor of honors, possessions, and pleasures, with other things of the same nature; for it is clear that the soul, if it be not watchful, will find itself caught in a net,—at least, all these things labor to ensnare it; more than this, so also do friends and relatives, and—what frightens me most—even good people. I found myself afterwards so beset on all sides, good people thinking they were doing good, and I knowing not how to defend myself, nor what to do.

27. O my God, if I were to say in what way, and in how many ways, I was tried at that time, even after that trial of which I have just spoken, what a warning I should be giving to men to hate the whole world utterly! It was the greatest of all the persecutions I had to undergo. I saw myself occasionally so hemmed in on every side, that I could do nothing else but lift up my eyes to heaven, and cry unto God.[484] I recollected well what I had seen in the vision, and it helped me greatly not to trust much in any one, for there is no one that can be relied on except God. In all my great trials, our Lord—He showed it to me—sent always some one on His part to hold out his hand to help me, as it was shown to me in the vision, so that I might attach myself to nothing, but only please our Lord; and this has been enough to sustain the little virtue I have in desiring to serve Thee: be Thou blessed for evermore!

28. On one occasion I was exceedingly disquieted and troubled, unable to recollect myself, fighting and struggling with my thoughts, running upon matters which did not relate to perfection; and, moreover, I did not think I was so detached from all things as I used to be. When I found myself in this wretched state, I was afraid that the graces I had received from our Lord were illusions, and the end was that a great darkness covered my soul. In this my distress our Lord began to speak to me: He bade me not to harass myself, but learn, from the consideration of my misery, what it would be if He withdrew Himself from me, and that we were never safe while living in the flesh. It was given me to understand how this fighting and struggling are profitable to us, because of the reward, and it seemed to me as if our Lord were sorry for us who live in the world. Moreover, He bade me not to suppose that He had forgotten me; He would never abandon me, but it was necessary I should do all that I could myself.

29. Our Lord said all this with great tenderness and sweetness; He also spoke other most gracious words, which I need not repeat. His Majesty, further showing His great love for me, said to me very often: "Thou art Mine, and I am thine." I am in the habit of saying myself, and I believe in all sincerity: "What do I care for myself?—I care only for Thee, O my Lord."

---

[481] St. Matt. xx. 9-14: "Volo autem et huic novissimo dare sicut et tibi."

[482] Ch. xiv. § 12.

[483] The Saint had this vision when she was in the house of Doña Luisa de la Cerda in Toledo, and it was fulfilled in the opposition she met with in the foundation of St. Joseph of Avila. See ch. xxxvi. § 18.

[484] 2 Paralip. xx. 12: "Hoc solum habemus residui, ut oculos nostros dirigamus ad Te."

30. These words of our Lord, and the consolation He gives me, fill me with the utmost shame, when I remember what I am. I have said it before, I think,[485] and I still say now and then to my confessor, that it requires greater courage to receive these graces than to endure the heaviest trials. When they come, I forget, as it were, all I have done, and there is nothing before me but a picture of my wretchedness, and my understanding can make no reflections; this, also, seems to me at times to be supernatural.

31. Sometimes I have such a vehement longing for Communion; I do not think it can be expressed. One morning it happened to rain so much as to make it seem impossible to leave the house. When I had gone out, I was so beside myself with that longing, that if spears had been pointed at my heart, I should have rushed upon them; the rain was nothing. When I entered the church I fell into a deep trance, and saw heaven open—not a door only, as I used to see at other times. I beheld the throne which, as I have told you, my father, I saw at other times, with another throne above it, whereon, though I saw not, I understood by a certain inexplicable knowledge that the Godhead dwelt.

32. The throne seemed to me to be supported by certain animals; I believe I saw the form of them: I thought they might be the Evangelists. But how the throne was arrayed, and Him who sat on it I did not see, but only an exceedingly great multitude of angels, who seemed to me more beautiful, beyond all comparison, than those I had seen in heaven. I thought they were, perhaps, the seraphim or cherubim, for they were very different in their glory, and seemingly all on fire. The difference is great, as I said before;[486] and the joy I then felt cannot be described, either in writing or by word of mouth; it is inconceivable to any one what has not had experience of it. I felt that everything man can desire was all there together, and I saw nothing; they told me, but I know not who, that all I could do there was to understand that I could understand nothing, and see how everything was nothing in comparison with that. So it was; my soul afterwards was vexed to see that it could rest on any created thing: how much more, then, if it had any affection thereto; for everything seemed to me but an ant-hill. I communicated, and remained during Mass. I know not how it was: I thought I had been but a few minutes, and was amazed when the clock struck; I had been two hours in that trance and joy.

33. I was afterwards amazed at this fire, which seems to spring forth out of the true love of God; for though I might long for it, labor for it, and annihilate myself in the effort to obtain it, I can do nothing towards procuring a single spark of it myself, because it all comes of the good pleasure of His Majesty, as I said on another occasion.[487] It seems to burn up the old man, with his faults, his lukewarmness, and misery; so that it is like the phoenix, of which I have read that it comes forth, after being burnt, out of its own ashes into a new life. Thus it is with the soul: it is changed into another, whose desires are different, and whose strength is great. It seems to be no longer what it was before, and begins to walk renewed in purity in the ways of our Lord. When I was praying to Him that thus it might be with me, and that I might begin His service anew, He said to me: "The comparison thou has made is good; take care never to forget it, that thou mayest always labor to advance."

34. Once, when I was doubting, as I said just now,[488] whether these visions came from God or not, our Lord appeared, and, with some severity, said to me: "O children of men, how long will you remain hard of heart!" I was to examine myself carefully on one subject,—whether I had given myself up wholly to Him, or not. If I had,—and it was so,—I was to believe that He would not suffer me to perish. I was very much afflicted when He spoke thus, but He turned to me with great tenderness and sweetness, and bade me not to distress myself, for He knew already that, so far as it lay in my power, I would not fail in anything that was for His service; that He Himself would do what I wished,—and so He did grant what I was then praying for; that I was to consider my love for Him, which was daily growing in me, for I should see by this that these visions did not come from Satan; that I must not imagine that God would ever allow the devil to have so much power

---

[485] Ch. xx. § 4.
[486] Ch. xxix. § 16.
[487] Ch. xxix. § 13.
[488] § 28.

over the souls of His servants as to give them such clearness of understanding and such peace as I had.

35. He gave me also to understand that, when such and so many persons had told me the visions were from God, I should do wrong if I did not believe them.[489]

36. Once, when I was reciting the psalm *Quicumque vult*,[490] I was given to understand the mystery of One God and Three Persons with so much clearness, that I was greatly astonished and consoled at the same time. This was of the greatest help to me, for it enabled me to know more of the greatness and marvels of God; and when I think of the most Holy Trinity, or hear It spoken of, I seem to understand the mystery, and a great joy it is.

37. One day—it was the Feast of the Assumption of the Queen of the Angels, and our Lady—our Lord was pleased to grant me this grace. In a trance He made me behold her going up to heaven, the joy and solemnity of her reception there, as well as the place where she now is. To describe it is more than I can do; the joy that filled my soul at the sight of such great glory was excessive. The effects of the vision were great; it made me long to endure still greater trials: and I had a vehement desire to serve our Lady, because of her great merits.

38. Once, in one of the colleges of the Society of Jesus, when the brothers of the house were communicating, I saw an exceedingly rich canopy above their heads. I saw this twice; but I never saw it when others were receiving Communion.

Chapter XL.
Visions, Revelations, and Locutions.

1. One day, in prayer, the sweetness of which was so great that, knowing how unworthy I was of so great a blessing, I began to think how much I had deserved to be in that place which I had seen prepared for me in hell,—for, as I said before,[491] I never forget the way I saw myself there,—as I was thinking of this, my soul began to be more and more on fire, and I was carried away in spirit in a way I cannot describe. It seemed to me as if I had been absorbed in, and filled with, that grandeur of God which, on another occasion, I had felt.[492] In that majesty it was given me to understand one truth, which is the fulness of all truth, but I cannot tell how, for I saw nothing. It was said to me, I saw not by whom, but I knew well enough it was the Truth Itself: "This I am doing to thee is not a slight matter; it is one of those things for which thou owes Me much; for all the evil in the world comes from ignorance of the truths of the holy writings in their clear simplicity, of which not one iota shall pass away."[493] I thought that I had always believed this, and that all the faithful also believed it. Then he said, "Ah, My daughter, there are few who love Me in truth; for if men loved Me, I should not hide My secrets from them. Knows thou what it is to love Me in truth? It is to admit everything to be a lie which is not pleasing unto Me. Now thou does not understand it, but thou shalt understand it clearly hereafter, in the profit it will be to thy soul."

2. Our Lord be praised, so I found it; for after this vision I look upon everything which does not tend to the service of God as vanity and lies. I cannot tell how much I am convinced of this, nor how sorry I am for those whom I see living in darkness, not knowing the truth. I derived other great blessings also from this, some of which I will here speak of, others I cannot describe.

3. Our Lord at the same time uttered a special word of most exceeding graciousness. I know not how it was done, for I saw nothing; but I was filled, in a way which also I cannot describe, with exceeding strength and earnestness of purpose to observe with all my might everything contained in the divine writings. I thought that I could rise above every possible hindrance put in my way.

4. Of this divine truth, which was put before me I know not how, there remains imprinted within me a truth—I cannot give it a name—which fills me with a new reverence for God; it gives

---

[489] See ch. xxviii. §§ 19, 20.

[490] Commonly called the Creed of St. Athanasius.

[491] Ch. xxxii. § 1.

[492] Ch. xxviii. § 14.

[493] St. Matt. v. 18: "Iota unum aut unus apex non præteribit a lege."

me a notion of His Majesty and power in a way which I cannot explain. I can understand that it is something very high. I had a very great desire never to speak of anything but of those deep truths which far surpass all that is spoken of here in the world,—and so the living in it began to be painful to me.

5. The vision left me in great tenderness, joy, and humility. It seemed to me, though I knew not how, that our Lord now gave me great things; and I had no suspicion whatever of any illusion. I saw nothing; but I understood how great a blessing it is to make no account of anything which does not lead us nearer unto God. I also understood what it is for a soul to be walking in the truth, in the presence of the Truth itself. What I understood is this: that our Lord gave me to understand that He is Himself the very Truth.

6. All this I am speaking of I learnt at times by means of words uttered; at other times I learnt some things without the help of words, and that more clearly than those other things which were told me in words. I understood exceedingly deep truths concerning the Truth, more than I could have done through the teaching of many learned men. It seems to me that learned men never could have thus impressed upon me, nor so clearly explained to me, the vanity of this world.

7. The Truth of which I am speaking, and which I was given to see, is Truth Itself, in Itself. It has neither beginning nor end. All other truths depend on this Truth, as all other loves depend on this love, and all other grandeurs on this grandeur. I understood it all, notwithstanding that my words are obscure in comparison with that distinctness with which it pleased our Lord to show it to me. What think you must be the power of His Majesty, seeing that in so short a time it leaves so great a blessing and such an impression on the soul? O Grandeur! Majesty of mine! what is it Thou art doing, O my Lord Almighty! Consider who it is to whom Thou gives blessings so great! Does Thou not remember that this my soul has been an abyss of lies and a sea of vanities, and all my fault? Though Thou has given me a natural hatred of lying yet I did involve myself in many lying ways. How is this, O my God? how can it be that mercies and graces so great should fall to the lot of one who has so ill deserved them at Thy hands?

8. Once, when I was with the whole community reciting the Office, my soul became suddenly recollected, and seemed to me all bright as a mirror, clear behind, sideways, upwards, and downwards; and in the center of it I saw Christ our Lord, as I usually see Him. It seemed to me that I saw Him distinctly in every part of my soul, as in a mirror, and at the same time the mirror was all sculptured—I cannot explain it—in our Lord Himself by a most loving communication which I can never describe. I know that this vision was a great blessing to me, and is still whenever I remember it, particularly after Communion.

9. I understood by it, that, when a soul is in mortal sin, this mirror becomes clouded with a thick vapor, and utterly obscured, so that our Lord is neither visible nor present, though He is always present in the conservation of its being. In heretics, the mirror is, as it were, broken in pieces, and that is worse than being dimmed. There is a very great difference between seeing this and describing it, for it can hardly be explained. But it has done me great good; it has also made me very sorry on account of those times when I dimmed the luster of my soul by my sins, so that I could not see our Lord.

10. This vision seems to me very profitable to recollected persons, to teach them to look upon our Lord as being in the innermost part of their soul. It is a method of looking upon Him which penetrates us more thoroughly, and is much more fruitful, than that of looking upon Him as external to us, as I have said elsewhere,[494] and as it is laid down in books on prayer, where they speak of where we are to seek God. The glorious St. Augustin,[495] in particular, says so, when he says that neither in the streets of the city, nor in pleasures, nor in any place whatever where he sought Him, did he find Him as he found Him within himself. This is clearly the best way; we need not go up to heaven, nor any further than our own selves, for that would only distress the spirit and distract the soul, and bring but little fruit.

---

[494] Ch. iv. § 10.

[495] "Ecce quantum spatiatus sum in memoria mea quærens Te, Domine; et non Te inveni extra eam… Ex quo didici Te, manes in memoria mea, et illic Te invenio cum reminiscor Tui et delector in Te" (*Confess.* x. 24). See *Interior Castle*, Sixth Mansion, ch. iv.

11. I should like to point out one result of a deep trance; it may be that some are aware of it. When the time is over during which the soul was in union, wherein all its powers were wholly absorbed,—it lasts, as I have said,[496] but a moment,—the soul continues still to be recollected, unable to recover itself even in outward things; for the two powers—the memory and the understanding—are, as it were, in a frenzy, extremely disordered. This, I say, happens occasionally, particularly in the beginnings. I am thinking whether it does not result from this: that our natural weakness cannot endure the vehemence of the spirit, which is so great, and that the imagination is enfeebled. I know it to be so with some. I think it best for these to force themselves to give up prayer at that time, and resume it afterwards, when they may recover what they have lost, and not do everything at once, for in that case much harm might come of it. I know this by experience, as well as the necessity of considering what our health can bear.

12. Experience is necessary throughout, so also is a spiritual director; for when the soul has reached this point, there are many matters which must be referred to the director. If, after seeking such a one, the soul cannot find him, our Lord will not fail that soul, seeing that He has not failed me, who am what I am: They are not many, I believe, who know by experience so many things, and without experience it is useless to treat a soul at all, for nothing will come of it, save only trouble and distress. But our Lord will take this also into account, and for that reason it is always best to refer the matter to the director. I have already more than once said this,[497] and even all I am saying now, only I do not distinctly remember it; but I do see that it is of great importance, particularly to women, that they should go to their confessor, and that he should be a man of experience herein. There are many more women than men to whom our Lord gives these graces; I have heard the holy friar Peter of Alcantara say so, and, indeed, I know it myself. He used to say that women made greater progress in this way than men did; and he gave excellent reasons for his opinion, all in favor of women; but there is no necessity for repeating them here.

13. Once, when in prayer, I had a vision, for a moment,—I saw nothing distinctly, but the vision was most clear,—how all things are seen in God and how all things are comprehended in Him. I cannot in any way explain it, but the vision remains most deeply impressed on my soul, and is one of those grand graces which our Lord wrought in me, and one of those which put me to the greatest shame and confusion whenever I call my sins to remembrance. I believe, if it had pleased our Lord that I had seen this at an earlier time, or if they saw it who sin against Him, we should have neither the heart nor the daring to do so. I had the vision, I repeat it, but I cannot say that I saw anything; however, I must have seen something, seeing that I explain it by an illustration, only it must have been in a way so subtle and delicate that the understanding is unable to reach it, or I am so ignorant in all that relates to these visions, which seem to be not imaginary. In some of these visions there must be something imaginary, only, as the powers of the soul are then in a trance, they are not able afterwards to retain the forms, as our Lord showed them to it then, and as He would have it rejoice in them.

14. Let us suppose the Godhead to be a most brilliant diamond, much larger than the whole world, or a mirror like that to which I compared the soul in a former vision,[498] only in a way so high that I cannot possibly describe it; and that all our actions are seen in that diamond, which is of such dimensions as to include everything, because nothing can be beyond it. It was a fearful thing for me to see, in so short a time, so many things together in that brilliant diamond, and a most piteous thing too, whenever I think of it, to see such foul things as my sins present in the pure brilliancy of that light.

15. So it is, whenever I remember it, I do not know how to bear it, and I was then so ashamed of myself that I knew not where to hide myself. Oh, that some one could make this plain to those who commit most foul and filthy sins, that they may remember their sins are not secret, and that God most justly resents them, seeing that they are wrought in the very presence of His Majesty, and that we are demeaning ourselves so irreverently before Him! I saw, too, how completely hell is deserved for only one mortal sin, and how impossible it is to understand the exceeding great wickedness of committing it in the sight of majesty so great, and how abhorrent to His nature such

---

[496] Ch. xx. § 26.
[497] Ch. xxv. § 18, ch. xxvi. § 4. See St. John of the Cross, *Mount Carmel*, bk. ii. ch. xxii.
[498] § 8.

actions are. In this we see more and more of His mercifulness, who, though we all know His hatred of sin, yet suffers us to live.

16. The vision made me also reflect, that if one such vision as this fills the souls with such awe, what will it be in the day of judgment, when His Majesty will appear distinctly, and when we too shall look on the sins we have committed! O my God, I have been, oh, how blind! I have often been amazed at what I have written; and you, my father, be you not amazed at anything, but that I am still living,—I, who see such things, and know myself to be what I am. Blessed for ever be He who has borne with me so long!

17. Once, in prayer, with much recollection, sweetness, and repose, I saw myself, as it seemed to me, surrounded by angels, and was close unto God. I began to intercede with His Majesty on behalf of the church. I was given to understand the great services which a particular Order would render in the latter days, and the courage with which its members would maintain the faith.

18. I was praying before the most Holy Sacrament one day; I had a vision of a Saint, whose Order was in some degree fallen. In his hands he held a large book, which he opened, and then told me to read certain words, written in large and very legible letters; they were to this effect: "In times to come this Order will flourish; it will have many martyrs."[499]

19. On another occasion, when I was at Matins in choir, six or seven persons, who seemed to me to be of this Order, appeared and stood before me with swords in their hands. The meaning of that, as I think, is that they are to be defenders of the faith; for at another time, when I was in prayer, I fell into a trance, and stood in spirit on a wide plain, where many persons were fighting; and the members of this Order were fighting with great zeal. Their faces were beautiful, and as it were on fire. Many they laid low on the ground defeated, others they killed. It seemed to me to be a battle with heretics.

20. I have seen this glorious Saint occasionally, and he has told me certain things, and thanked me for praying for his Order, and he has promised to pray for me to our Lord. I do not say which Orders these are,—our Lord, if it so pleased Him, could make them known,—lest the others should be aggrieved. Let every Order, or every member of them by himself, labor, that by his means our Lord would so bless his own Order that it may serve Him in the present grave necessities of His Church. Blessed are they whose lives are so spent.

21. I was once asked by a person to pray God to let him know whether his acceptance of a bishopric would be for the service of God. After Communion our Lord said to me: "When he shall have clearly and really understood that true dominion consists in possessing nothing, he may then accept it." I understood by this that he who is to be in dignity must be very far from wishing or desiring it, or at least he must not seek it.

22. These and many other graces our Lord has given, and is giving continually, to me a sinner. I do not think it is necessary to speak of them, because the state of my soul can be ascertained from what I have written; so also can the spirit which our Lord has given me. May He be blessed for ever, who has been so mindful of me!

23. Our Lord said to me once, consoling me, that I was not to distress myself,—this He said most lovingly,—because in this life we could not continue in the same state.[500] At one time I should be fervent, at another not; now disquieted, and again at peace, and tempted; but I must hope in Him, and fear not.

---

[499] Yepez says that the Order here spoken of is the Carmelite, and Ribera understands the Saint to refer to that of St. Dominic. The Bollandists, n. 1638-1646, on the whole, prefer the authority of Ribera to that of Yepez and give good reasons for their preference, setting aside as insufficient the testimony of Fray Luis of the Assumption, who says he heard himself from the Venerable Anne of St. Bartholomew that the Order in question is the Order of our Lady of Mount Carmel. Don Vicente, the Spanish editor, rejects the opinion of Ribera, on the ground that it could not have been truly said of the Dominicans in the sixteenth century that the Order was in "some degree fallen," for it was in a most flourishing state. He therefore was inclined to believe that the Saint referred to the Augustinians or to the Franciscans. But, after he had printed this part of his book, he discovered among the MSS. in the public library of Madrid a letter of Anne of St. Bartholomew, addressed to Fray Luis of the Assumption, in which the saintly companion of St. Teresa says that the "Order was ours." Don Vicente has published the letter in the Appendix, p. 566.

[500] Job xiv. 2: "Nunquam in eodem statu permanet."

24. I was one day thinking whether it was a want of detachment in me to take pleasure in the company of those who had the care of my soul, and to have an affection for them, and to comfort myself with those whom I see to be very great servants of God.[501] Our Lord said to me: "It is not a virtue in a sick man to abstain from thanking and loving the physician who seems to restore him to health when he is in danger of death. What should I have done without these persons? The conversation of good people was never hurtful; my words should always be weighed, and holy; and I was not to cease my relations with them, for they would do me good rather than harm."

25. This was a great comfort to me, because, now and then, I wished to abstain from converse with all people; for it seemed to me that I was attached to them. Always, in all things, did our Lord console me, even to the showing me how I was to treat those who were weak, and some other people also. Never did He cease to take care of me. I am sometimes distressed to see how little I do in His service, and how I am forced to spend time in taking care of a body so weak and worthless as mine is, more than I wish.

26. I was in prayer one night, when it was time to go to sleep. I was in very great pain, and my usual sickness was coming on.[502] I saw myself so great a slave to myself, and, on the other hand, the spirit asked for time for itself. I was so much distressed that I began to weep exceedingly, and to be very sorry. This has happened to me not once only, but, as I am saying, very often; and it seems to make me weary of myself, so that at the time I hold myself literally in abhorrence. Habitually, however, I know that I do not hate myself, and I never fail to take that which I see to be necessary for me. May our Lord grant that I do not take more than is necessary!—I am afraid I do.

27. When I was thus distressed, our Lord appeared unto me. He comforted me greatly, and told me I must do this for His love, and bear it; my life was necessary now. And so, I believe, I have never known real pain since I resolved to serve my Lord and my Consoler with all my strength; for though he would leave me to suffer a little, yet He would console me in such a way that I am doing nothing when I long for troubles. And it seems to me there is nothing worth living for but this, and suffering is what I most heartily pray to God for. I say to Him sometimes, with my whole heart: "O Lord, either to die or to suffer! I ask of Thee nothing else for myself." It is a comfort to me to hear the clock strike, because I seem to have come a little nearer to the vision of God, in that another hour of my life has passed away.

28. At other times I am in such a state that I do not feel that I am living, nor yet do I desire to die but I am lukewarm, and darkness surrounds me on every side, as I said before;[503] for I am very often in great trouble. It pleased our Lord that the graces He wrought in me should be published abroad,[504] as He told me some years ago they should be. It was a great pain to me, and I have borne much on that account even to this day, as you, my father, know, because every man explains them in his own sense. But my comfort herein is that it is not my fault that they are become known, for I was extremely cautious never to speak of them but to my confessors, or to persons who I knew had heard of them from them. I was silent, however, not out of humility, but because, as I said before,[505] it gave me great pain to speak of them even to my confessors.

29. Now, however,—to God be the glory!—though many speak against me, but out of a zeal for goodness, and though some are afraid to speak to me, and even to hear my confession, and though others have much to say about me, because I see that our Lord willed by this means to provide help for many souls,—and also because I see clearly and keep in mind how much He would suffer, if only for the gaining of one,—I do not care about it at all.

30. I know not why it is so, but perhaps the reason may in some measure be that His Majesty has placed me in this corner out of the way, where the enclosure is so strict, and where I am as one that is dead. I thought that no one would remember me, but I am not so much forgotten as I wish I was, for I am forced to speak to some people. But as I am in a house where none may see me, it seems as if our Lord had been pleased to bring me to a haven, which I trust in His Majesty will be secure. Now that I am out of the world, with companions holy and few in number, I look down on

---

[501] See ch. xxxvii. §§ 4, 6.

[502] See ch. vii. § 18.

[503] Ch. xxx. § 10.

[504] Ch. xxxi. §§ 16, 17.

[505] Ch. xxviii. § 6.

the world as from a great height, and care very little what people say or know about me. I think much more of one soul's advancement, even if it were but slight, than of all that people may say of me; and since I am settled here it has pleased our Lord that all my desires tend to this.

31. He has made my life to me now a kind of sleep; for almost always what I see seems to me to be seen as in a dream, nor have I any great sense either of pleasure or of pain. If matters occur which may occasion either, the sense of it passes away so quickly that it astonishes me, and leaves an impression as if I had been dreaming,—and this is the simple truth; for if I wished afterwards to delight in that pleasure, or be sorry over that pain, it is not in my power to do so: just as a sensible person feels neither pain nor pleasure in the memory of a dream that is past; for now our Lord has roused my soul out of that state which, because I was not mortified nor dead to the things of this world, made me feel as I did, and His Majesty does not wish me to become blind again.

32. This is the way I live now, my lord and father; do you, my father, pray to God that He would take me to Himself, or enable me to serve Him. May it please His Majesty that what I have written may be of some use to you, my father! I have so little time,[506] and therefore my trouble has been great in writing; but it will be a blessed trouble if I have succeeded in saying anything that will cause one single act of praise to our Lord. If that were the case, I should look upon myself as sufficiently rewarded, even if you, my father, burnt at once what I have written. I would rather it were not burnt before those three saw it, whom you, my father, know of, because they are, and have been, my confessors; for if it be bad, it is right they should lose the good opinion they have of me; and if it be good, they are good and learned men, and I know they will recognize its source, and give praise to Him who hath spoken through me.

33. May His Majesty ever be your protector, and make you so great a saint that your spirit and light may show the way to me a miserable creature, so wanting in humility and so bold as to have ventured to write on subjects so high! May our Lord grant I have not fallen into any errors in the matter, for I had the intention and the desire to be accurate and obedient, and also that through me He might, in some measure, have glory,—because that is what I have been praying for these many years; and as my good works are inefficient for that end, I have ventured to put in order this my disordered life. Still, I have not wasted more time, nor given it more attention, than was necessary for writing it; yet I have put down all that has happened to me with all the simplicity and sincerity possible.

34. May our Lord, who is all-powerful, grant—and He can if He will—that I may attain to the doing of His will in all things! May He never suffer this soul to be lost, which He so often, in so many ways, and by so many means, has rescued from hell and drawn unto Himself! Amen.

Epilogue
I.H.S.

The Holy Spirit be ever with you, my father.[507] Amen. It would not be anything improper if I were to magnify my labor in writing this, to oblige you to be very careful to recommend me to our Lord; for indeed I may well do so, considering what I have gone through in giving this account of myself, and in retracing my manifold wretchedness. But, still, I can say with truth that I felt it more difficult to speak of the graces which I have received from our Lord than to speak of my offences against His Majesty. You, my father, commanded me to write at length; that is what I have done, on condition that you will do what you promised, namely, destroy everything in it that has the appearance of being wrong. I had not yet read it through after I had written it, when your reverence sent for it. Some things in it may not be very clearly explained, and there may be some repetitions; for the time I could give to it was so short, that I could not stop to see what I was writing. I entreat

---

506 See ch. xiv. § 12.

507 This letter, which seems to have accompanied the "Life," is printed among the other letters of the Saint, and is addressed to her confessor, the Dominican friar, Pedro Ibañez. It is the fifteenth letter in the first volume of the edition of Madrid; but it is not dated there.

your reverence to correct it and have it copied, if it is to be sent on to the Father-Master, Avila,[508] for perhaps some one may recognize the handwriting. I wish very much you would order it so that he might see it, for I began to write it with a view to that I shall be greatly comforted if he shall think that I am on a safe road, now that, so far as it concerns me, there is nothing more to be done.

Your reverence will do in all things that which to you shall seem good, and you will look upon yourself as under an obligation to take care of one who trusts her soul to your keeping. I will pray for the soul of your reverence to our Lord, so long as I live. You will, therefore, be diligent in His service, in order that you may be able to help me; for your reverence will see by what I have written how profitable it is to give oneself, as your reverence has begun to do, wholly unto Him who gives Himself to us so utterly without measure.

Blessed be His Majesty for ever! I hope of His mercy we shall see one another one day, when we, your reverence and myself, shall see more clearly the great mercies He has shown us, and when we shall praise Him for ever and ever. Amen. This book was finished in June, 1562.

---

[508] Juan de Avila, commonly called the Apostle of Andalusia.

www.ingramcontent.com/pod-product-compliance
Lightning Source LLC
Chambersburg PA
CBHW031124090426
42738CB00008B/966